Lecture Notes in Computer Science 3014

Commenced Publication in 1973
Founding and Former Series Editors:
Gerhard Goos, Juris Hartmanis, and Jan van Leeuwen

Springer
Berlin
Heidelberg
New York
Hong Kong
London
Milan
Paris
Tokyo

Frank van der Linden (Ed.)

Software Product-Family Engineering

5th International Workshop, PFE 2003
Siena, Italy, November 4-6, 2003
Revised Papers

 Springer

Volume Editor

Frank van der Linden
Philips Medical Systems N.V., BL Medical IT
QV-1, Veenpluis 4-6, PO Box 10000, 5680 DA Best
The Netherlands
E-mail: Frank.van.der.linden@philips.com

Library of Congress Control Number: 2004105721

CR Subject Classification (1998): D.2.11, K.6, D.2

ISSN 0302-9743
ISBN 3-540-21941-2 Springer-Verlag Berlin Heidelberg New York

Springer-Verlag is a part of Springer Science+Business Media

springeronline.com

© Springer-Verlag Berlin Heidelberg 2004
Printed in Germany

Typesetting: Camera-ready by author, data conversion by Olgun Computergrafik
Printed on acid-free paper   SPIN: 10999257   06/3142   5 4 3 2 1 0

Preface

This book contains the proceedings of the 5th International Workshop on Product Family Engineering, PFE-5. This workshop was held in Siena, Italy, November 4–6, 2003. This workshop was the fifth in the series, with the same subject, software product family engineering. These workshops have been held initially irregularly about every 18 months since 1996. Since 1999 the workshop has been held every second year in the fall. The proceedings of the second, third and fourth workshops were published as Springer LNCS volumes 1429, 1951 and 2290.

The workshops were organized within co-operation projects of European industry. The first two were organized by ARES (Esprit IV 20.477) 1995–1999; this project had 3 industrial and 3 academic partners, and studied software architectures for product families. Some of the partners continued in the ITEA project if99005 ESAPS (1999–2001). ITEA is the software development programme (Σ! 2023) within the European Eureka initiative. ITEA projects last for 2 years, and ESAPS was succeeded by CAFÉ (ITEA if00004) for 2001–2003 and FAMILIES (ITEA if02009). This fifth workshop was initially prepared within CAFÉ and the preparation continued in FAMILIES.

As usual Henk Obbink was the workshop chair, and Linda Northrop and Sergio Bandinelli were the co-chairs.

The programme committee was recruited from a collection of people who have shown interest in the workshop on earlier occasions:

Felix Bachmann	André van den Hoek	Rob van Ommering
Sergio Bandinelli	Kari Känsälä	Dewayne Perry
Len Bass	Peter Knauber	Serge Salicki
Joe Bauman	Philippe Kruchten	Juha Savolainen
Günter Böckle	Frank van der Linden	Klaus Schmid
Jan Bosch	Alessandro Maccari	Steffen Thiel
Paul Clements	Nenad Medvidovic	David Weiss
Jean-Marc DeBaud	Robert Nord	
Stefania Gnesi	Henk Obbink	

This workshop attracted many more papers than the previous ones. This is an indication that product family engineering has spread across the world, and has become an accepted way of doing software engineering. Many of those ahs to be rejected, and even now there were more papers accepted than what is good for a 3-day workshop. Even though we had enough discussions. Only authors of accepted papers were invited to the workshop. This time we had about 55 participants. However, we have to think about the format, and we may change it for the next occasion, planned for the fall of 2005.

The meeting place was again excellent. The weather was fine for that time of the year. The medieval city of Siena has a nice atmosphere and the famous Chianti wine is produced in the neighboring countryside. During the week of the workshop the first local wine of 2003 was opened in Siena. Alessandro Fantechi of the University of Florence, and Alessandro Maccari of Nokia acted as local hosts. It was done perfectly.

February 2004   Frank van der Linden

Table of Contents

Product Derivation

Transition to Family Development

Industrial Experience

Evolution

Decisions and Derivation

Research Topics and Future Trends

Jan Bosch[1], Henk Obbink[2], and Alessandro Maccari[3]

[1] University of Groningen, Department of Computing Science
PO Box 800, NL 9700 AV Groningen, The Netherlands
jan.bosch@cs.rug.nl
[2] Philips Research, Eindhoven
henk.obbink@philips.com
[3] Nokia Mobile Software, Web Service Technologies
PO Box 100, FIN 00045 Nokia Group, Finland
alessandro.maccari@nokia.com

1 Introduction

The PFE conference ended with a plenary debate revolving around research topics and future trends in the area of product family engineering. The organizers of the panel asked the conference participants to write down what they thought were the most interesting areas to research on. We took some of them for discussion during the plenary, and came out with a number of relevant trends. This paper summarizes the main findings, outlining the main research and development issues, and proposing, where appropriate, some hints for solutions.

2 Future Trends

The session started by summarizing the relevant future trends, as forecast by companies nowadays. The discussion highlighted a number of facts, listed below.

The *size* of software systems is on the continuous increase, both in the number of functional elements and in the amount of work that is necessary to develop a single product. An internal study by Philips indicates that the workload for development of an average product increases by a factor of 10 every 7-8 years. Moreover, the trend shows an increase in the number of errors that need to be corrected during the testing phase. This can be quantified in an order of magnitude every 10 years approximately. Studies like this also show that the trend is posed to continue in the future, as software is the core of innovation, and often constitutes the competitive edge, especially for companies that make mass-market products. The increase in size and errors is an obvious result of an increase in overall complexity.

The amount of *variability* in software product families is also visibly increasing, for two main reasons: i) there is a tendency to move variability from hardware to software, thus increasing the flexibility of the system configuration and decreasing the cost of variance; ii) design decisions are usually delayed as much as possible during the software development process. Often, variability is totally resolved only at the moment of installation of the software system. Both these trends imply that binding time is also continuously pushed as closer to runtime as possible. There is speculation that in the future all binding will be done at runtime, and a considerable amount of research has focused on this topic in recent times.

F. van der Linden (Ed.): PFE 2003, LNCS 3014, pp. 1–5, 2004.

3 General Trends, New Technologies, Methods and Processes

During the discussion, several new technologies were mentioned as being "hot". Dynamic software architectures, multi-dimensional separation of concerns, model-driven architecture (MDA), grid computing and server farms are the object of an increasing number of research papers, as well as the centre of many development projects. The recent standardization effort that several IT companies have carried out has put web services in the centre of attention. Many define web services as *the* new paradigm in distributed computing, and all major companies are trying to agree on a successful business model that would ramp up the adoption of the technology.

As concerns new methods and processes, software variability management is definitely a key part of the development and maintenance activities for product families. Also, agile software development and evolution methods seem to be among the most debated topics, at least in the research world, and their application to organizations that develop product families must be investigated (for instance, by means of experience reports and case studies). Finally, to reflect the importance of web services, the concept of web service centric software engineering is gaining popularity, and a vast take-up can be forecast if web services really turn out to be a major development in computer science and business alike.

These new methods, however, are refinements (at different levels of detail) of the "traditional" software engineering methods that are already used by organizations that develop software product family. The general agreement was that the community hasn't recently witnessed any radical technological innovation of a substantial importance. In contrast, it was remarked that the need for innovation, at least on the European front, seems to be pressing. Software development companies have a tendency to outsource most of their development (and therefore most of their knowledge) to countries where programmers' wages are low. The general trend for companies based in the European Union is to buy infrastructure (e.g. operating systems) from the United States, and develop the software applications that run on top of it outside the Union. This generates a lack of innovation and drive that is threatening Europe's position as one of the world's leading countries for software development. The participants to the conference remarked that the research and development community should tackle this problem, and find solutions that keep competitiveness in the continent.

The discussion then switched to a number of technical topics that were deemed important for future research. The following sections briefly analyze the main ones.

3.1 Variability Management

The conference participants felt that the topic of variability management, though extensively treated in research and even dedicated workshops, still left some important research questions unanswered. Dependencies between variation points and variants, for instance, have not yet been understood. A parallel problem is feature interaction, which looks at the same issues, but centered on requirements. This brings up research questions on the relationship among variability points across abstraction levels, and along the product lifecycle.

Another topic that deserves attention is unsystematic variability. Do the same methods apply when the variability factors cannot be assumed to behave in the same way across time?

In general, there was a general feeling that the phenomenon of variability needs to be better understood, perhaps by means of practical or empirical research. People remarked that variation is still not (easily enough) manageable, and that a definition and implementation of appropriate variation mechanisms is needed before the topic is fully understood and companies can apply the corresponding methodologies.

3.2 Product Family Lifecycle (Requirements, Architecture, Implementation)

The discussion covered the interesting topic lifecycle management for product family. We know that managing the development and evolution of a product family requires somewhat different approaches and methodologies than those used with a self-standing software system. In particular, the conference delegates underlined the importance of architectural assessment before evolutionary maintenance activities take place. People also advocated a unified approach and technology for all the activities in a product family lifecycle (requirements, architecture, design, code, documentation, test cases, and so forth in a product family).

In general, there was a common agreement on the need to narrow the gap between research on new features and applications and the actual implementation of these features and applications in real products. The community should get closer to the "real" world, and continuously test the methods, processes and features that are object of research against the needs of companies and non-profit organizations that operate in the sector.

3.3 Product Derivation and Tool Support

In this line of discussion, it was remarked that some sort of "expert-system" derivation of product family instances would help the maintenance and evolution process. Certainly, in many cases tools can effectively support the management complexity (especially for architectural model generation and reverse engineering).

During the discussing it was emphasized that, in order to be effective and widely adopted, tools must be simple and must not require more work than what they are supposed to save.

3.4 Evolution

The conference participants spent some time discussing the topic of product family evolution. It was remarked that, especially in the requirements and architecture areas, evolution patterns haven't been studied well enough, and mechanisms that help companies evolve a product line are still relatively unexplored. More research is advocated on this topic.

3.5 Validation of Product Family Benefits

Validation was felt to be an essential issue. A relevant slice of the software product family methodologies that this community has researched in the past years still lack experimental validation. This holds for qualitative aspects, as the impact of product family engineering approaches on software quality has not yet been estimated. However, we also miss an extensive quantitative estimation of the (mostly economical) trade-off between the costs that the introduction of a product family approach bears and the benefits it brings. It was remarked that economic models should focus on cost, but not limit to it.

Finally, some people observed that most of the techniques and methods that the community has investigated in the last few years have not been experimentally validated in the large scale. With the exception of a few large companies, most of the case studies that are usually presented in research conferences concern small and medium organizations. The scalability of the approach is not automatically guaranteed, as the increase in the company size brings additional complexity and dependencies. This should be further investigated.

Nevertheless, remarks were heard about the absence of a fully established practice for product family engineering for small/medium enterprises. In such companies, the

3.6 Organization and Management

The presence of several people with experience in industrial software product family development may have been the reason behind the large amount of discussion concerning organization and management.

One of the most compelling issues was felt to be the management of product populations, or multi-level product lines, where the variation points are hierarchically distributed. Also, the debate dwelled on methods that enable to make product families a success in a cross-organizational setting. One possible solution, which hasn't been looked into to a sufficient extent, is incremental introduction of product family engineering. Especially for large organizations, it was felt that it could help the companies realize the importance of the approach, and measure the benefits in a gradual way.

Interesting subjects of debate were the social issues related to product family management. In practice, a large part of the management work, especially in large company, involves contacts with other people. Social sciences have helped understand the constraints and relationships that rule the daily life of organizations, so they could be of help in this specific case.

Finally, it was remarked that we should focus some research effort on defining funding and business models to support strategic reuse across products in a family.

4 Conclusion

We conclude by listing some of the research topics that, according to the general opinion of the community, need urgent attention. One of the keynote speakers enumerated model-driven architecture, generative programming, and aspect-oriented programming as three key techniques that need development. Concerning aspect-oriented modeling, some people remarked that it had already been listed as a topic during the ESAPS project, but no satisfying results were achieved. In fact, the partners couldn't even agree on a common definition. We should make a new start with a fresh approach in this research thread.

The conference ended with a discussion on what the future may bring. A number of basic laws have governed the evolution of computing technology, proving to be true until now despite large skepticism: Moore's law (transistor density doubles every 18 months), Gilder's law (communication bandwidth doubles every 12 months) and the storage law (storage capacity doubles every 9 months).

Assuming these laws continue to be valid, in 100 years computers will be billions of times faster. Humans will not be able to fully exploit the features of such systems, nor to write programs that master their complexity. Now, the mathematical foundations of our techniques and the techniques themselves are not progressing at the same speed as the machines that they are supposed to help us program and manage. We can conservatively forecast that already in 10 or 15 years we will not be able to handle such complexity. This leaves us with a lot of unused computational power.

One way to exploit this gap in computational power will be by using it in favour of easier programming paradigms. We will use the new power to simplify programming languages and the general user interface of these new machines. One possible outcome is the integration of the methodologies we have debated here into programming languages, thus getting them closer to our way of thinking.

For sure, performance optimization techniques are likely to disappear in the long term. However, what is to be of this new programming environment still remains the biggest open issue in the field.

Testing Variabilities in Use Case Models[*]

Erik Kamsties, Klaus Pohl, Sacha Reis, and Andreas Reuys

Software Systems Engineering, University of Duisburg-Essen
Schützenbahn 70, 45117 Essen, Germany
{kamsties,pohl,reis,reuys}@sse.uni-essen.de

Abstract. The derivation of system test cases for product families is difficult
due to variability in the requirements, since each variation point multiplies the
number of possible behaviors to be tested. This paper proposes an approach to
develop domain test cases from use cases that contain variabilities and to derive
application test cases from them. The basic idea to avoid combinatorial explo-
sion is to preserve the variability in domain test cases. New strategies to capture
variability in test cases are suggested, which in combination help dealing
with all basic types of variability in a use case and in its relationships (e.g.,
<<include>>).

1 Introduction

System testing in the context of a product family has the same goal as in the context
of a single system, checking the quality of software systems. Product family testing
can be separated into *domain testing*, i.e., testing the core assets of a product family,
and *application testing*, i.e., testing the artifacts of a particular customer-specific
product. Domain system testing mainly comprises the production of reusable test
artifacts. Application system testing comprises the reuse and adaptation of those artifacts and the development of additional ones due to customer-specific requirements.
These test artifacts are used to carry out system testing on a customer-specific product.

In domain testing, variability prevents from directly applying test techniques
known from single system engineering, because the variation points introduce another
magnitude of complexity to the possible behaviors to be tested. The most obvious
solution to this problem is to bypass domain testing and focus on application testing.
However, it cannot be afforded to develop test cases from scratch for each application. But products of a family differ to some extent thus the problem arises how test
artifacts developed for one product can be reused to ensure *systematic* testing of the
following product.

The goal of the approach proposed in this paper is to derive system test cases for
domain and application testing from use cases that contain variabilities. Efficient
derivation of application test cases is accomplished by preserving the variabilities that

---

[*] This work was partially funded by the CAFÉ project "From Concept to Application in System Family
Engineering"; Eureka Σ! 2023 Programme, ITEA Project ip00004 (BMBF, Förderkennzeichen 01 IS
002 C) and the state Nord-Rhein-Westfalia.

F. van der Linden (Ed.): PFE 2003, LNCS 3014, pp. 6–18, 2004.

can be found in use cases in the domain test cases. The focus of this paper is on the introduction of variability into domain test cases.

We aim at supporting existing representations for test cases rather than proposing extensions to deal with variability. In this paper, we use the UML [10] for representation of test artifacts, because the UML is frequently used in industry.

There is some related work along these lines, e.g., [8], [9]. Our contribution is a set of new strategies to deal with variability in test cases. Because current and new strategies all have some weaknesses, we suggest a combination of strategies to be able to deal in an effective way with all kinds of variabilities that can be found in use cases.

The remainder of this paper is structured as follows. Section 2 discusses the related work. Section 3 explains the strategies behind our approach. Section 4 describes test case derivation in domain and application testing. Section 5 illustrates our approach using a simplified example of booking a flight, and Section 6 summarizes the contribution of this paper and provides an outlook on future work.

2 Related Work

Use cases have been introduced by Jacobson to describe the interaction between a user and a system to achieve a goal. We subsume under the term *use case model* a UML use case diagram [10] and a set of accompanying textual descriptions that follow a specific use case description template. A use case diagram consists of actors, use cases, and relationships (include, extend, generalization). A textual use case description mainly comprises a goal, a main scenario, alternative scenarios, exceptional scenarios, a pre-, and a post-condition [2].

All parts of a use case model as mentioned above are subject to variability. An exception seems to be the goal of a use case. The goal is assumed to be invariant, because a use case is derived from a goal and a change in a goal would result in a completely new use case. Halmans and Pohl distinguish essential and technical variability [4]. Essential variability describes the variability of a product family from a customer/user point of view. Use cases are well suited to express essential variability, in particular, variability in constraints on functions (can be expressed by pre- and post-conditions), in behavior and functions (by main, alternative, and exceptional scenarios), and in users (by actors).

Moreover, a variation point has several characteristics as discussed in [3], [4], [5], [12]. Important characteristics include *existence* (selection of variants is optional or mandatory, number of variants that can be chosen, e.g., 1-of-*n*), *alternative* (whether the set of variants is open, i.e., more variants can be added, or closed), *constraints* between the variants (e.g., requires, excludes), and *binding time*. Several extensions to the use case notation were suggested to incorporate the characteristics of a variation point into a use case model, e.g. [1], [4].

We found two approaches for product family testing, which specifically address the questions how to deal with variability in requirements during domain testing and how to derive application test cases from domain test cases. We subsume their basic strategies under the terms abstraction and parameterization.

Following the *abstraction* strategy, general domain test cases are developed through abstraction from differences among possible variants. Application test cases are specialized from these test cases, i.e., the general test statements are refined with respect to the chosen variants. McGregor follows this strategy and provides examples based on textually described test cases [8].

Following the *parameterization* strategy, parameterized domain test cases are developed and application test cases are derived from binding the parameters. The approach by Nebut et al. supports the derivation of domain test cases and the *automated* derivation of application test cases for system testing [9]. The approach consists of two steps. In the first step, parameterized domain test cases ("test patterns") based on UML sequence diagrams are developed. In the second step, test cases for application testing are synthesized from the test patterns.

3   New Strategies for Test Case Derivation

In single system testing, use cases are tested by deriving test cases that reach a particular coverage. Usually, some type of branch coverage is applied on the control flow graph that is underlying the different flows of events ("use case graph"). Several approaches to use case based testing (UCBT) including our ScenTED approach (scenario-based test derivation; [6], [7]) argue to make this control flow explicit in order to systematize and to automate the derivation of test cases. For this purpose, these approaches utilize, e.g., UML activity diagrams as depicted in Fig. 1.

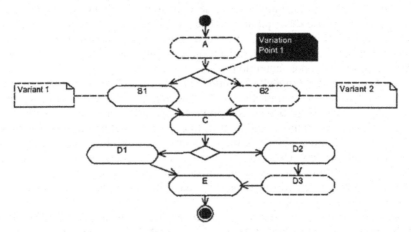

Fig. 1. Use Case Scenarios Represented as an Activity Diagram.

In product family engineering, variability in a use case usually manifests in additional decisions and branches as shown in Fig. 1 (i.e., Variant 1 of the variation point is realized by branch B1 and Variant 2 by B2). The branches that reflect variants of a variation point cannot be treated using simple branch coverage, because this would result in incomplete application testing (i.e., not all branches would be tested for each application). In the example, two test cases would result {A, B1, C, D1, E} and {A, B2, C, D2, D3, E}. If Variant 1 is chosen for a customer-specific product, then the branch {D2, D3} is not tested and vice versa. Rather, branch coverage should be reached for each application, which leads to four test cases in the above example.

That is, variabilities in the flow of events let exponentially grow the number of test cases required to reach some type of (use case) branch coverage for each possible application.

The basic idea is to introduce variability into domain test cases. In the above example, two test cases would result (i.e., {A, {{B1}$_{v1}$, {B2}$_{v2}$}$_{vpl}$, C, D1, E} and {A, {{B1}$_{v1}$, {B2}$_{v2}$}$_{vpl}$, C, D2, D3, E}); the subscript refers to the variants and respective variation points. The number of resulting test cases remains manageable and traceability between use cases and test cases is improved by the same concepts of variability in the two artifacts.

Different strategies are needed to deal with variability in product family testing. The reason is that *one* variation point in a use case can be reflected in *several* variation points in different test cases. In the above example, the variation point vp1 of Fig. 1 affects two test cases. Consequently, a highly effective representation for variation points is needed. However, the effectiveness depends on the nature of the variation point. Large variations, e.g., caused by variability in <<include>> relationships, must be tackled differently than small variations, e.g., in a single parameter.

We suggest two new strategies, segmentation and fragmentation, in addition to the previously mentioned strategies. An overview of all strategies is shown in Fig. 2. The figure shows what kinds of reusable domain test cases are developed during domain engineering (DE) based on use cases that contain variability. Moreover, it shows the activities necessary to derive application test cases from those reusable domain test cases during application engineering (AE).

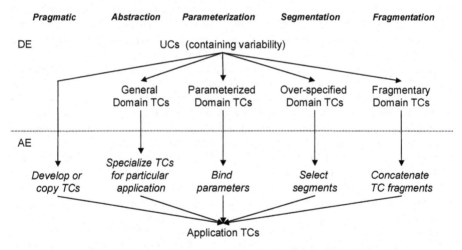

Fig. 2. Test Case Derivation Strategies for Product Families.

The pragmatic strategy, mentioned already in the introduction, is to apply single system testing to a product family. That is, to bypass the development of reusable domain test cases. Instead, only application test cases are developed when concrete applications are known or can be estimated. The obvious drawback of the pragmatic strategy is that reuse is limited to copying those test cases of one application that fit to the next application. That is, test cases can be directly reused only if the related use case is implemented by a new application with the same variants. Maintenance problems with application test cases may arise if changes to core assets are made.

Abstraction and parameterization were identified in the related work. The drawback of the abstraction strategy is that information about the differences among the variants is abstracted away in a test case. When the chosen variants are known, application test cases can be specialized, i.e., test steps for the particular variants are derived and added to the general domain test cases. If the same variants are chosen in different applications, the same work could be done several times.

The drawback of the parameterization strategy is that it is limited to the parameterization mechanisms offered by the chosen representation. For example, most kinds of variability in the flow of events (i.e., in main, alternative, or exceptional scenarios, or in the relation among use cases) cannot be expressed well in a UML sequence diagram using the available parameterization mechanism, because parameters are supported only within single messages.

Because of these drawbacks, we suggest two new strategies, segmentation and fragmentation. Each of the new strategies is explained and justified in the following.

The idea of the *segmentation* strategy is to derive "over-specified" domain test cases. Instead of an abstraction or parameterization, a variation point is reflected in a test case by a set of test case segments, whereas each test case segment reflects a variant of the variation point. The test case is "over-specified" as it covers all contingencies. Application test cases are derived by selecting the segments that test the chosen variants.

The rationale for the segmentation strategy is its capability to capture variants in a test case, which is not possible using the abstraction strategy, and to deal with those types of variability that cannot be efficiently captured by parameterization. The drawback of this strategy is that the segments are *contained* in the over-specified test case. That is, if two test cases share a variation point then redundant segments would result.

Following the *fragmentation* strategy, separate, fragmentary domain test cases are derived for variant and common parts of a test case, which are later combined to arrive at complete test cases. As previously discussed, the scenarios of a use case can be represented as an activity diagram. The idea is to derive a fragmentary test case so that the whole use case graph is covered and fragments can be shared with other domain test cases. If used in an extreme way, a test case fragment is derived for each branch of the use case graph including those branches that represent variants. Application test cases are derived by concatenation of these fragmentary test cases.

The rationale for the fragmentation strategy is to avoid redundancy that occurs for example if the same variation points are contained in different test cases, as discussed earlier in this section. The drawback of this strategy is that its application results in a number of resulting test case fragments may cause considerable maintenance effort.

Of course, more strategies can be envisioned that the two discussed above. However, we found them sufficient, as they help to cover all types of variability in a use case model.

This discussion shows that there is no single good strategy to derive test cases for product families. Each strategy has its strengths and weaknesses. Therefore, a combinational approach for test case derivation is needed. Such a combination, utilizing UML sequence diagrams as test case representation, is presented in the following section.

4   New UCBT Approach Based on Integration of Strategies

The goal of our new UCBT approach is to derive system test cases for domain and application testing from use cases that contain variabilities. In order to facilitate reuse of domain test cases in application testing, variability is introduced to domain test cases. Our aim is to allow for variability in all parts of a use case model (including variability in use case relationships) and to support all characteristics of a variation point (e.g., existence) as far as they are relevant for testing.

We outline in the following a comprehensive UCBT approach that realizes the above goal. We use UML sequence diagrams to represent test cases, because they are easy to understand. Messages *to* the system represent the input of the test case and messages *from* the system represent the expected output. However, other representations can be supported as well, but may require a different treatment of variabilities.

4.1   Developing Reusable System Test Cases

We discuss in the following how different types of variability in a use case affect the derivation of test cases and how to capture the variabilities using sequence diagrams using the strategies for making domain test cases reusable outlined in the previous section. We assume in the following that the reader has a UCBT approach, such as ScenTED, in place and we provide information only on how to deal with variability in test case derivation. The characteristics of the variation points in a use case model (e.g., binding time) can be ignored while deriving domain test cases. They come into play when deriving application test cases. The subsection is organized along the different types of variability that may appear in a use case.

Variability in Flow of Events (Main, Alternative, and Exceptional). Variability in the flow of events (main, alternative, and exceptional) may affect only a single scenario step, i.e., the difference between two or more variants is just one step.

Parameterization recommends itself if a variation point manifests in a single message. In the scheme shown in Fig. 3, parameterization is used to capture a variation point concerning data sent in a message.

The possible variants are described in the attached note. There is no need to repeat the variability information of a variation point in a test case. Rather, the black notes are used as pointers to that information in the use case model.

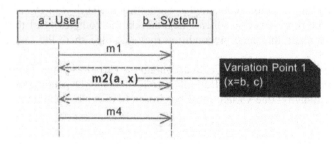

Fig. 3. Variability in a single message using parameterization strategy.

Segmentation can be applied as well, but would result in two messages. Parameterization allows for a minimal documentation overhead.

The segmentation strategy is best suited, if the variability in the control flow affects different actors in a sequence diagram and/or affects more than the data sent in one message. The scheme illustrated in Fig. 4 is useful in this case. In order to distinguish the segments, the respective messages are annotated with an identifier of the variant they belong to (e.g., "(v1)" means Variant 1). A note embraces the segments, i.e., the variants of a variation point in the test case. In the example, m1 and m6 are common to all variants. The variation point has two variants, "v1" and "v2", and comprises the messages m2 to m5.

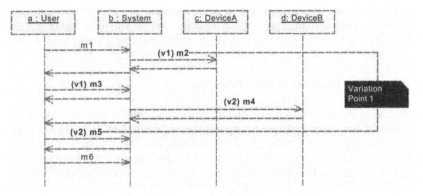

Fig. 4. Variability in control flow using segmentation strategy.

Parameterization cannot be applied in this case, because parameters can be used in UML sequence diagrams only within single messages. Fragmentation can be applied as well, but several fragments would result, which require more creation, maintenance, and reuse effort than a single test case.

We found the abstraction strategy in all cases not suitable, because the different variants cannot be captured. The only case where abstraction makes sense is an open variation point that has no specific variants that are determined in domain engineering. Then, abstraction can be nicely used to sketch envisioned variants.

Variability in Precondition. A precondition is ensured in UCBT by a prefix scenario that drives the system under test into the start state. If variability appears in the precondition this can be therefore handled as variability in the flow of events. That is, the selection of the representation scheme depends on the complexity of the variants. If two use cases share the same precondition they can also share the same prefix scenario.

Fig. 5 depicts a prefix scenario that contains a variation point. Parameterization was used, because the variants differ only in one message. Depending on the selected product functionality, one variant must be chosen to execute the main part of the test case.

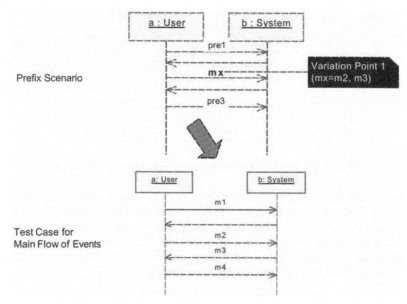

Fig. 5. Variability in precondition using parameterization strategy.

Variability in Postcondition. A postcondition summarizes the state reached by the main or alternative flow of events. If there is variability in the postcondition, this should be reflected in the main or alternative flow of events and, thus, no additional actions are required for the postcondition.

Variability in Actors. Variability in the actors involved in a use case does not necessarily affect test case derivation. If the variability concerns only human actors no special action is required, because test engineers usually simulate the different human actors. If different external systems are concerned, then each test case might be affected that is derived from those use cases in which the variable actor is involved.

Variability in the actor is captured with the segmentation strategy. Fig. 4 shows different external systems that are involved in a test case ("DeviceA", "DeviceB"). Fragmentation can be applied as well, but several fragments would result, which require more creation, maintenance, and reuse effort than a single test case.

Variability in Relationships (<<include>>). It is relatively easy to deal with relationships between use cases without variability. The flows of events of the base use case and the included use cases are viewed as one big use case graph. Branch coverage can then be applied to derive test cases. Fig. 6 shows a base use case A that includes a use case C. The included use case C has two alternative flows of events, thus two test cases T1 and T2 result. The use case A has one path, in which C is not included, so test case T3 results. Test case T4 results from use case B.

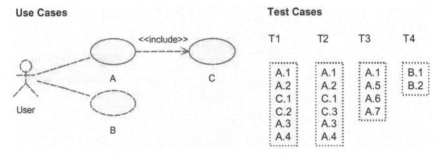

Fig. 6. Test cases for <<include>> relationship between use cases.

Variation points concerning relationships require more effort to deal with. The simple, but perhaps rare, case is that the included use cases contain no alternative or exceptional cases. Then, the included use cases can be simply seen as variants in the flow of events and the segmentation strategy is applied. In Fig. 7, the Steps m1 and m6 are the steps of the base use case. Variant 1 (Steps m2, m3) reflects one included use case and Variant 2 (Steps m4, m5) reflects the other included use case.

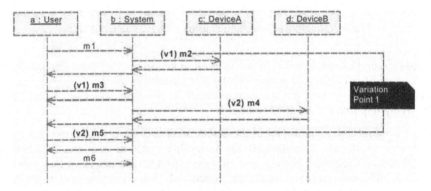

Fig. 7. Variability in <<include>> relationship using segmentation strategy.

Otherwise, the fragmentation strategy is applied using the following procedure:

1. Derive test cases for the included use cases as defined by the applied UCBT. That is, several test cases are derived, which are of course fragmentary, because the context of the base use case is missing.
2. Derive test cases for the base use case as defined by the applied UCBT and thereby ignore the <<include>> relationship.
3. Analyze test cases derived for the base use case if they are affected by the <<include>> relationship. Usually, the affected test cases are at least those that test the success scenarios. Each affected test case is split in two fragments, so that they can be concatenated in application testing with one of the test cases of the included use case.

Fig. 8 shows the result of the fragmentation strategy given a base use case that has a variable <<include>> relationship to the use cases B and C. The two fragmentary test cases on the left side resulted from splitting the test case of the base use case. The included use case B is simple and can be covered by one test case. The included use case C is more complicated and needs several test cases. Of course, the resulting test case fragments need some kind of annotation that indicates which fragments can be concatenated to construct a complete test case.

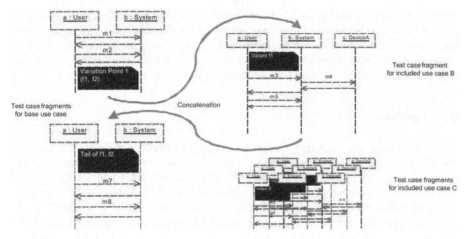

Fig. 8. Variability in <<include>> relationship using fragmentation strategy.

Combination of Several Variation Points in a Use Case. We have discussed so far the treatment of different types of variation points in a use case in isolation. If several variation points appear in a use case the above schemes can be easily used in combination. One exception is variability in relationships. If an included use case again includes other variant use cases then the fragmentation strategy may lead to a number of relatively small fragments (e.g., just a single interaction) and the maintenance effort may become too large. In this case, the pragmatic strategy remains as last solution. That is, test cases are derived for the known or most likely applications.

The result of test case derivation is a set of reusable domain test case fragments. One ends up with (1) prefix test fragments, which establish the preamble for the main part of a test case and (2) test case fragments for the main part, i.e., the various flows of events, possibly further fragmentized when <<include>> relationships are involved. The combination of these fragments into complete test cases is subject of application testing.

4.2 Derivation of System Tests for Application Testing

Because the focus of this paper is on the introduction of variability in domain test cases, we only sketch the derivation of application test cases. In application engineering, most variants are bound to variation points. This fact implies that (1) we can bind the variants in our test case fragments and (2) we can combine them into application test cases. Binding the variants in the test case fragments is easy: for parameterization parameters are bound, for abstraction concrete messages are inserted, and for segmentation the messages that concern the unwanted variants are removed. In case of fragmentation, test fragments of the base use case are concatenated with the fragments of the selected included use cases.

The characteristics of a variation point affect the assembly of test cases. If more than one variant of a variation point is chosen then the respective test case fragment is duplicated for each of those variants. The variants in these test case fragments are bound accordingly, so that each variant is covered at least once (consider constraints among variants). Run-time variability can be handled in the same way. If variants have been added in application engineering, because a variation point was open then respective test case fragments are developed. Finally, the different types of test case fragments, i.e., prefix and main part, are combined into full test cases.

5 Example

We illustrate our approach using a simple example of booking a flight. The use case "booking via internet" is shown in Fig. 9. The use case contains two variation points. Variation point VP1 concerns the flow of events (Variants V1.1 and V1.2), and VP2 concerns the data exchanged in one interaction (Variants V2.1 and V2.2). The corresponding domain test case is shown in Fig. 10. Variation point VP1 is realized in the test case using the segmentation strategy, and VP2 is realized using the parameterization strategy. The derivation of application test cases is straight forward if the additional characteristics of the variation points, such as binding time, are available. The messages annotated V1.1 or V1.2 are removed, and the parameter *customer data* is replaced by *name, address* or *forename, surname, city*.

Attribute		Actor	Step
Name			Booking a flight via internet
Precondition			The customer has chosen a flight
Main	1.	Customer	starts the booking process[VP1]
Scenario	2.	System	displays the customer data
	3.	Customer	confirms the data
	4.	System	asks for flight data
	5.	Customer	selects flight data
	6.	System	shows the data of the chosen flight and asks for confirmation
	7.	Customer	confirms the booked flight
Variation Points **VP1**			
V1.1	1.	System	asks for customer data [VP2]
	2.	Customer	enters his data
V1.2	1.	System	asks for login and password
VP2	2.	Customer	enters login and password
V2.1			name, address
V2.2			forename, surname, city

Fig. 9. Use Case with two Variation Points.

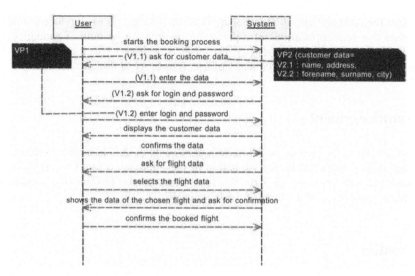

Fig. 10. Test Case of the Use Case with two Variation Points

6 Conclusion and Future Work

This paper provides an approach for deriving reusable system test cases for domain and application testing based on use case models. We emphasized the derivation of domain test cases and only sketched the derivation of application test cases. The focus of this paper was on dealing with variability in use case models. The new idea presented in this paper is a combination of existing and new strategies to introduce variability into test cases so that our approach is capable of dealing with all kinds of variabilities that occur in use case models. Also, simple combinations of several variation points as shown in the example in previous section can be easily handled within a test case. We used UML sequence diagrams to represent reusable domain test cases, and we are convinced that our way of introducing variability into domain test cases well extends to other representations.

The presented approach helps to save effort in test case generation. However, since the domain test cases cover all variants, higher upfront investments are necessary and savings materialize only in the long term. Short-term savings can be realized if only those test cases are executed that are related to the distinguishing features between different products of a product family.

Further methodological issues arise from the variability in use cases. One open question is when a set of domain test cases can be considered as complete in the sense that it ensures sufficient coverage of the variabilities in a use case model. Initial ideas on coverage criteria for product family testing can be found in [11]. Another open issue is the treatment of variabilities in <<extend>> relationships.

Next steps of our future work include the utilization of current test tools for dealing with variability in test cases. Moreover, we aim at supporting early system testing through test applications, i.e., applications that are built only to test the core assets in a system test. Early testing is needed in cases where there is no initial customer who sponsors the development of an initial application. The goal is to convince a *potential* customer that real applications of a particular quality can be built. To identify such test applications, a prioritization of the use cases is necessary based on factors such as value to potential customers, frequency of use, feasibility of use, and criticality.

Acknowledgement

We would like to acknowledge the helpful comments of the anonymous referees, the inspiration and opportunities for validation of our approach offered by employees of Siemens Medical Solutions, in particular Josef Weingärtner, Helmut Götz, and Jürgen Neumann, and the general support from Thomas Rinke.

References

1. Bertolino, A.; Fantechi, A.; Gnesi, S.; Lami, G.; Maccari, A.; "Use Case Description of Requirements for Product Lines"; Proceedings of the International Workshop on Requirements Engineering for Product Lines 2002 (REPL'02), Technical Report: ALR-2002-033, AVAYA labs, 2002
2. Cockburn, Alistair; "Writing Effective Use Cases"; Addison Wesley 2001.
3. Coriat, M.; Jourdan, J.; Boisbourin, F., "The SPLIT Method – Building Product Lines for Software-Intensive Systems", Donohoe, P. ed. Software Product Lines: Experience and Research Directions. Denver, Colorado, August 28-31, 2000. Boston, MA: Kluver Academic Publishers, 147-166, 2000.
4. Halmans, G.; Pohl, K.; "Communicating the variability of a software-product family to customers", *Journal of Software and Systems Modeling*, Springer-Verlag, 2003.
5. Jacobson, Ivar; Griss, Martin; Jonsson, Patrik; "Software Reuse, Architecture, Process and Organization for Business Success"; Addison Wesley, 1997.
6. Kamsties, Erik; Pohl, Klaus; Reuys, Andreas; Reis, Sacha; "Use Case- and Architecture-based Derivation of Generic Test Cases for System and Integration Tests for Software Product Families", CAFÉ Deliverable SSE-WP4-20020930-01, University of Essen, October 2002.
7. Kamsties, Erik; Pohl, Klaus; Reuys, Andreas; "Supporting Test Case Derivation In Domain Engineering", accepted for publication at the Seventh World Conference on Integrated Design and Process Technology (IDPT-2003), Austin, USA, December 2003.
8. McGregor, John D.: "Testing a Software Product Line". Technical Report CMU/SEI-2001-TR-022, 2001.
9. Nebut, Clementine; Pickin, Simon; Le Traon, Yves; Jezequel, Jean-Marc; "Reusable Test Requirements for UML-Modeled Product Lines". In Proceedings of the International Workshop on Requirements Engineering for Product Lines (REPL'02), pages 51–56, September 2002.
10. OMG Unified Modeling Language Specification, Object Management Group, Version 1.4, 2001.
11. Reuys, Andreas; Kamsties, Erik; Reis, Sacha; Pohl, Klaus; "Derivation of Domain Test Scenarios from Activity Diagrams", International Workshop on Product Line Engineering the Early Steps: Planning, Modeling, Managing (PLEES03), Erfurt, Germany, September 2003.
12. Svahnberg, M.; Gurp, J. van; Bosch, J.; "On the Notion of Variability in Software Product Lines", Proceedings of Working IEEE/ IFIP Conference on Software Architecture, 2001.

Exploring the Context of Product Line Adoption

Stan Bühne[1], Gary Chastek[2], Timo Käkölä[3], Peter Knauber[4],
Linda Northrop[5], and Steffen Thiel[6]

[1] University of Duisburg-Essen
Institute for Computer Science & Business Information Systems (ICB)
Schützenbahn 70, 45117 Essen, Germany
buehne@sse.uni-essen.de
[2] Software Engineering Institute, Carnegie Mellon University
Pittsburgh, PA 15213-3890, USA
gjc@sei.cmu.edu
[3] University of Jyväskylä, Dept. Computer Science & Information Systems
P.O. Box 35, FIN-40 351 Jyväskylä, Finland
timokk@cc.jyu.fi
[4] Mannheim University of Applied Sciences, Department of Computer Science
Windeckstrasse 110, D-68163 Mannheim, Germany
p.knauber@fh-mannheim.de
[5] Software Engineering Institute, Carnegie Mellon University
Pittsburgh, PA 15213-3890, USA
lmn@sei.cmu.edu
[6] Robert Bosch Corporation, Corporate Research and Development
Software Technology (FV/SLD)
Eschborner Landstr. 130-132, D-60489 Frankfurt am Main, Germany
steffen.thiel@de.bosch.com

Abstract. To successfully adopt a product line approach an organization needs to define its adoption goals, conceive a strategy, and implement a plan to achieve those goals. This process is repeated for each business unit and individual affected by the product line adoption. This paper describes how the characteristics of the market, organization, business unit, and individual influence product line adoption goals, strategies, and plans.

1 Introduction

The tremendous benefits of taking a product line approach for similar software-intensive systems are well documented [1]. What's not as clear, however, is how to effectively achieve an operational software product line, often called product line adoption. The "Launching and Institutionalizing" practice area of the Framework for Software Product Line Practice[SM] lays out what must occur in organizational adoption, as well as useful specific practices [2]. Related work has involved: Böckle and associates, who further studied software product line adoption and institutionalization needs from an organizational standpoint [3]; Bosch, who examined the maturity and evaluation of product line artifacts [4]; and Schmidt and Verlage, who describe the economic impact of product line adoption [5].

[SM] Framework for Software Product Line Practice is a service mark of Carnegie Mellon University.

F. van der Linden (Ed.): PFE 2003, LNCS 3014, pp. 19–31, 2004.

The road to product line success is really organization specific, and yet none of the above research has carefully considered the context in which product line adoption takes place, or the influence that context can and should have on the adoption strategy, and, consequently, on the success or failure of the adoption effort.

Our main objective in this paper is to explore the context for product line adoption at multiple levels and then to demonstrate the usefulness of that context characterization by means of an example. After discussing what product line adoption entails, we divide the context landscape into multiple levels, discuss the influencing factors at each one, and investigate the potential relationships between the levels. Choosing core asset development as a specific adoption objective, we show how understanding and characterizing the adoption context can help you choose an appropriate strategy. We summarize our results and then conclude with projections about how this reasoning can be further applied for greater advantage.

2 Product Line Adoption

Product line adoption involves moving from some form of developing software-intensive systems via a single-system mentality to developing a family of software-intensive systems that form a product line. A *product line* is defined as a set of software-intensive systems sharing a common, managed set of features that satisfy the specific needs of a particular market segment from a common set of core assets in a prescribed way. The adoption endgame is to have a core asset base, to build products from it, and to have supportive processes and organizational structures in place.

An organization usually decides to adopt a product line approach with specific business goals in mind. Those goals will, at least to some extent, be unique to the organization and depend on the line of business and the market position. To achieve its goals, the organization selects one or more adoption strategies that specify how it will embrace product line practice. The chosen strategies must help achieve the goals, be appropriate for the organization's size and talent pool, and exploit any successful legacy assets or processes. An adoption plan then shows in detail what activities or tasks must be accomplished to implement those strategies. Figure 1 shows the tightly knit connection between the adoption goals, strategies, and plans.

In any given organization, a hierarchical set of goals, strategies, and plans reflecting the different levels of the organization might exist. For example, an adoption task associated with a business unit could be the goal for a specific individual.

In this vein, the whole concept of product line adoption becomes very personal to the organization; the exact context seems to play a significant role in shaping the adoption.

3 The Context of Product Line Adoption

This context consists of multiple layers with the outermost one being the market of the products being produced. In any market, each specific organization plays a distinguishable role. Typically inside each organization, discrete business units exist, and within them, there are individuals who perform the work. Figure 2 depicts adoption context as these layers of influence, which can be peeled away one by one to gain visibility into the underlying rings – a sort of onion-skin model.

Fig. 1. Adoption Goals, Strategies, and Plans.

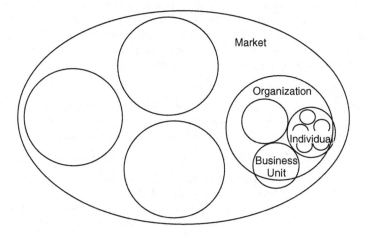

Fig. 2. The Circles of Adoption Influence.

More importantly, relationships exist among the circles. The outer circles provide resources for and put constraints on the inner circles. Goals of the inner circles depend on a characterization (and the resulting plans) of the outer circles. Market conditions affect organizations – that is, organizations in a certain market cannot make context-free decisions. In turn, organizational goals, strategies, and plans affect the business units within, and individuals take their lead from unit-wide decisions and plans. It is also possible that some business units have their own market relationships and community efforts. The ability to alter the state and inclinations of the entities represented by the concentric circles becomes more difficult as you move from the inside out; it is much more difficult to influence the market than to influence a particular individual. The next four sections examine the four circles of influence with their respective influencing factors.

3.1 Market

Although the market itself is not goal driven, it defines the intercompany playing field. The following market characterizations directly influence any product line effort within an organization belonging to that market:

- *How large is the market volume (the number of products potentially needed)?*

Whereas a large market is no guarantee for the successful adoption of a product line strategy, a small market leaves almost no chance to successfully exploit the potential product line benefits.

- *How mature is the market?*

The better a market (i.e., the products, and the targeted market segments and its needs) is understood, the easier it is to predict the evolution of the products in it and, consequently, to increase the likelihood that investing in product line core assets will pay over time. In very immature markets, such predictions are difficult, therefore increasing the investment risk. On the other hand, the market cannot be too homogeneous. It must be "similar enough" so that a set of features can be shared across product variants. But there must also be differentiating characteristics so that individual features can be developed to meet the specific needs of each market segment. For example, in developing countries, the markets might be large enough but too homogeneous to warrant product lines.

- *Do open standards exist for this market?*

Open standards are a good basis for establishing a reference architecture. That architecture, in turn, enables buying and selling components from/to competitors in the market, which supports the infrastructure build-up of product lines.

- *How safety-critical is the software in the products that constitute this market?*

For example, server and client products pose very different safety and reliability requirements. Server products need to be reliable because they typically provide the infrastructure for many clients. Often, client applications, like typical desktop products, are less safety-critical because their failure does not cause severe damage or injury. Typically when a product is built from a set of high-quality product line assets, it will also be of high quality. Such a product obviously fits better into a market that requests a high level of reliability.

- *Are there clear market leaders?*

To some extent, the market leader can define the direction in which a market will evolve, and establish or influence emerging standards [6]. The leader is well positioned to invest in the right product line assets to protect or even improve its market position in the future. Often, competitors in the same market must follow defacto standards set by the market leader's products, making predictions about the return of investment (ROI) from core asset development difficult.

The individual organizations within the market largely determine these characterizations, with the exception of market size and maturity. Conversely, these characterizations influence what any of those organizations can do. If we assume that the market conditions are favorable for product line development, we can move to the next circle of influence, namely the organization.

3.2 Organization

The organizational context is roughly defined by the market conditions. Organizational goals therefore have to fit in this context. Additionally, the following organizational characteristics influence an organization's goals and, consequently, both its product line adoption process and its business unit (the next layer in the circles of adoption influence).

- *What is the organization's current position in the market? How high is the probability that the organization will become a market leader?*

Depending on the market's form (monopoly, oligopoly, or polypoly), the current market share (leader, stable position, or newcomer), and the organizational goals, the organization can follow different strategies to maintain or improve its market position. Examples are sumo (i.e., buying competitors or crushing them with superior force), classical (i.e., being an early mover in new technologies, leveraging the installed base, and locking in customers by creating switching costs), and judo (i.e., moving rapidly to uncontested grounds and giving way when attacked by a superior force) [7]. When it adopts a product line approach successfully, an organization can expand its total market penetration by addressing the needs of new market segments related to its existing segments with relatively limited costs. But that organization would also face some jeopardies. For example, in the face of fierce competition, it might need to move to new markets before it has enough resources or the appropriate domain knowledge. Thus, a good and stable market position can help build a reasonable asset base for the market.

- *How closely is the organization connected with its customers?*

If the organization has a close connection to its customers, it usually has a better understanding of their needs. This understanding enables the organization to both develop the right core assets and appropriately adapt existing assets. Both activities are a prerequisite for achieving an effective product line. A close connection to the customer is a key factor for optimizing the asset base. If the organization is just loosely connected to the customers, it needs a strong market position to "dictate" product standards.

- *How much control does the organization have over the product specification?*

Having control over the product specification is another important factor for an organization. The more the organization can control how features, user interfaces, and other aspects are implemented, the more it can gain from core asset development and the better it can plan for evolution of the product line. However, in some market segments, full control over product specification is not easy to achieve. For example, customer needs in the automotive supplier market often include individual design constraints such as the use of specific commercial off-the-shelf (COTS) components or the support of customer-specific interfaces. These constraints might limit the optimization of core assets and need to be negotiated carefully. Typically, good control over product specification can be achieved when the organization is in a leading market position and offers new products that the market has not been anticipated or when the customers are the end users of the products (i.e., they don't impose hard constraints on the organization's development).

- *How likely is it that the organization will sell the asset base as well as products built from it?*

In addition to selling products in the product line, an organization can generate revenue by selling platform standards, that is, the asset base itself. If the market is mature and demands a product line for a specific domain (e.g., telecommunications), the organization can sell the asset base to competitors as a kind of "open platform" or "framework."

- *How high is the motivation to use a product line approach?*

The readiness to adopt a product line approach (from the organization's point of view) basically depends on two factors: (1) is the organization forced to use a product line approach to remain competitive, and (2) can some other organizational strategy be leveraged to maintain or even extend its market position? If the organization firmly believes that a product line approach is essential to achieving its goals, both its motivation for adopting the approach and its commitment to stay the product line course would likely be high. If, on the other hand, a product line approach is not critical to its success or was chosen arbitrarily, the probability of a successful product line adoption will likely be low.

- *How stable is the funding source for development and evolution of the core asset base?*

The funding source for an asset base might be key customers, other product lines or business units, corporate development funds, or project business (i.e., selling tailored solutions and services). Key customers are a viable option because they can provide a comprehensive view of essential assets in the corresponding domain. Typically, key customers are or evolve into trusted long-term partners who can tolerate higher risks with respect to defects and unexpected development problems than normal customers. They often provide more stability for asset development than internal champions (e.g., top managers) because all too frequently champions change positions and leave the product line effort without the needed financial backing. On the other hand, the organization has to be sure that the paying customers are the right ones – that is, that they truly represent the needs of the targeted market segments. The organization needs a backup plan or migration strategy to avoid unnecessary risks with "wrong" customers. To ensure stability, a balanced mix of funding sources is best.

- *How strong is the high-level management commitment for a product line approach?*

The decision to adopt a product line approach for the organization requires commitment from high-level management. That commitment is needed to ensure adequate resources of manpower, time, and funding, and to provide the necessary direction and orchestration, organizational structure, training, and proper incentives for business units and individuals to move to the product line approach.

The organization-wide strategies to achieve product line goals can involve a top-down dictum or policy; for example, "All business units will use a product line approach for the families of software-intensive products within its sphere of influence." Alternatively, the organization can proceed bottom-up: pilot product line efforts are begun in one or more business units and tracked carefully, and then product line practices are systematically rolled out to the entire organization. Many organizations choose some combination of top-down and bottom-up strategies. Independent of the direction the strategies take, a plan should exist for enacting them. Such a plan defines goals for individual business units as depicted in Figure 3.

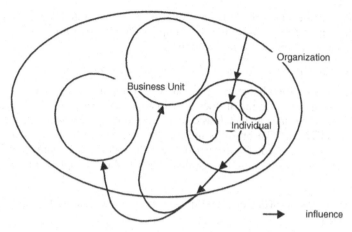

Fig. 3. Interdependencies of Organizational Adoption Strategy and Business Unit Goals.

3.3 Business Unit

Typically, an organization is composed of multiple business units. Each unit accepts the goals that are imposed on it by the organization and might define some of its own goals as well as the strategies to achieve them. For example, an organization might impose cost-reduction goals over its business units. However, different business units might choose different ways to achieve those goals. For example, one business unit might apply a strategy to improve its production capabilities to achieve better yield rates, while another unit might decide to merge two product lines to reduce its development and maintenance effort.

The following business unit characteristics directly influence product line adoption:

- *How much experience has the business unit had with products in the targeted product line?*

  When a business unit has developed plenty of "successful" products for the relevant domain, it understands that domain and can find the essential assets relatively easily. In contrast, if the business unit is going to develop an asset base for a new (and unknown) market, the probability of successful adoption declines.

- *How many high-quality legacy assets does the business unit have for this product line?*

  Business units that already have high-quality assets from single-system development (i.e., essential artifacts that are highly reusable among several products) are in a better position to build up a stable and valuable asset base than those who don't. Despite the high quality, however, the adaptability of these legacy assets can still thwart adoption success.

- *What is the current degree of process discipline within the business unit?*

  If the business unit has already embraced standardized engineering procedures for developing its products, the discipline required to smoothly adopt a product line approach will be much more natural than in an organization with chaotic procedures. Existing process discipline will simplify the adoption process and accelerate the development time of the core asset base.

- *How much domain-specific talent already exists in the business unit?*

Domain-specific knowledge is essential in developing a reasonably stable asset base. If domain-specific talent does not already exist from single-system development, it might be unclear which assets are the same among different products and which are different. The business unit in this case has to be aware that additional time and/or cost is needed to further develop this talent. If domain-specific knowledge is unavailable, it must be acquired, thus making adoption more lengthy or costly.

- *How keen is the software engineering expertise, in particular the software architecture skills?*

Software engineering expertise (not just programming experience) – in particular, software architecture skills are essential for product line adoption and success. The business unit should be evaluated with respect to its software engineering capability, especially in software architecture practices. Business units with well-honed architecture skills are more likely to develop successful product lines.

- *How deeply engrained is the single-system mentality within the business unit? How intrinsically adverse to a product line approach is the workforce?*

If the organizational structure and culture are fixed to single-system development, there is no visible need to change processes, or there is no strong leadership to carry the tide, the adoption is likely to fail. Cultural resistance to any technology change is a steep barrier that takes years to overcome.

- *How dependent is the business unit on proprietary tools built and used to support a single-system approach?*

If the business unit is heavily vested in "legacy" tools constructed specifically for single-system development, adoption of a product line approach would require that the tools be reengineered, or that new ones be acquired and taught to individuals. This would involve a significant investment that might hamper product line adoption.

- *How clear are the current business and product strategies? Is there a willingness (or an ability) to communicate the business strategy throughout the business unit?*

Communicating the motivation for product lines (or at least the reason why things should change) is a key factor when dealing with organizational change. If the proposed strategy is unclear or ineffectively communicated, there is little chance that the organizational goals will be met.

- *How equipped is the business unit to perform activities situated within each of the 29 practice areas described in the Framework for Software Product Line Practice [2]? What availability of talent will be needed to compensate for any expertise shortages?*

To address the 29 essential practice areas, appropriate talent is required. A business unit has to determine if that talent is available in the unit, or in other business or cross-sectional units of the organization. If existing personnel are not able to satisfy the demands, external domain specialists, architecture specialists, or other experts are needed to educate, coach, and support the business unit personnel. The more knowledge and expertise already on hand, the easier the adoption process will be.

Typically in very small organizations, there is no need for business units, and so there is little distinction between the organizational and business unit contexts. For those organizations, their contextual factors and the business unit levels of the adoption influence circles apply together.

3.4 Individual

Individuals, of course, make up business units, and it is individuals who ultimately determine whether new processes, methods, and tools are adopted in their everyday organizational practice. The following characteristics of individuals influence product line adoption strategies:

- *Do the individuals have the necessary (additional) capacity to "learn" product line engineering?*

  Personnel often have only the time to fulfill their routine job responsibilities and no more. The move to a new approach demands additional time to learn new processes and possibly acquire new skills. If the business unit is not willing to offer enough time, training, compensation, and other necessary support, the individuals' investment will not be adequate for successful adoption.

- *Do the individuals have the necessary expertise? And if not, how will they get it?*

  Without appropriate expertise, individuals cannot understand, contribute to, and execute the new processes. Additional training and/or knowledge-transfer is necessary to create and use a stable, high-quality asset base.

- *How motivated are the individuals? Are they willing to learn and apply product line engineering methods?*

  Change is difficult for most people, and so like business units, individuals need motivation to embrace a product line approach. The reason for the shift to a product line approach should be transparent to all individuals in the business unit.

- *Will the individuals gain or lose from product line engineering?*

  In most cases, individuals are willing to exert the additional effort to change only if they benefit from it. Often when new processes and tools are implemented, some people benefit, while others just get more work. Thus, the organizational goals and business unit strategies should be designed to benefit as many individuals as possible. Moreover, the anticipated benefits should be communicated broadly and well.

Different from the previous layers (market, organization, and business unit), the individual factors are more psychological. Individuals' views change based on their comfort level and their perceptions as to whether the change will adversely affect them. The individuals in any organization need to be carefully enlisted in the adoption process; the adoption of a product line approach must be carefully orchestrated to empower the workforce instead of making it feel uncomfortable or exploited.

4   Using Context Characterizations in Choosing an Adoption Strategy for Core Asset Development

As described in Section 2, a product line approach involves three essential activities: (1) development[1] of core assets, (2) development of products, and (3) management of the product line operation at both technical and enterprise levels [1]. For a business unit moving to a product line approach, the development of a core asset base is part of the adoption process. In fact, having the core asset base may well be a product line goal of the business unit or at least an objective that is tied to a goal. However, the order in which core asset and product development occur is not fixed, and hence, a business unit can choose from different strategies. It can choose a strictly proactive strategy that focuses first on developing the core assets [8]. In so doing, the unit would first define the product line scope (which provides a kind of mission statement for the other core assets) and then design the product line architecture, components, and other assets accordingly with the right built-in variation points to cover the scope [9]. The business unit could also select a reactive strategy, which suggests that it begins with one or more existing products and uses them to generate the product line core assets. The products might actually have been built before product line adoption was considered.

An incremental strategy, which is yet a third option, is a proactive/reactive hybrid [10]. Following it, a business unit develops the core assets gradually and develops products during the process. For example, it would develop part of the core asset base, presumably the product line architecture and some components; develop one or more products, and then evolve part of the rest of the asset base; develop another set of products; evolve more of the asset base; and so on. An incremental strategy assumes the ambition to build a product line from the outset.

The proactive approach has obvious advantages – once the core asset base has been developed, products come to market extremely quickly with a minimum of code writing. However, developing the product line architecture, components, and other core assets is a significant up-front investment that requires considerable up-front predictive knowledge. The reactive approach has the advantage of a much lower cost of entry to product lines, but requires that the quality of the architecture and the product components used as the basis for the asset base must be robust, extensible, and appropriate for future product line needs. The incremental approach seems to offer the best of both worlds, but in many respects has the same disadvantages of both its reactive and proactive siblings – just in weaker doses.

If the contextual characterizations described in Section 3 influence product line adoption as we suggested, the organizational factors mentioned in Section 3.2 constitute the context for the business unit. Therefore, there should be some context-dependent heuristics to help a business unit choose which strategy to follow for core asset development. Table 1 presents such guidance in terms of dependencies between the context characterizations and core asset development strategies.

---

[1] The term *develop* is meant generically and might actually involve building individual assets anew, buying them off the shelf, or mining them from existing assets. This use of the word *develop* as it pertains to core assets and products is consistent with its usage by the Software Engineering Institute (SEI) [1].

Table 1. Dependencies Between Organizational Context Characteristics and Core Asset Development Strategies.

	H/M/L=Needs to be at least high/medium/low	Adoption Strategies for Core Asset Development							
		Proactive		Incremental		Reactive			
Organizational Factors	Market Leader (H, M, L)	H		M	M or L				
	Degree of Connection with Customers (H, M, L)				H or M		L		
	Control of Product Specification (H, M, L)	H		M	L		L		
	Sell Asset Base (H, M, L)		H			L			
	Strength of Motivation to use Product Lines (H, M, L)	H	H	H or M	H or M		L		
	Stable Funding for Core Asset Base (H, M, L)	H		M	M			L	
	High-level Management Commitment (H, M, L)	H	H	H	H				L

The first column of Table 1 lists the factors that influence the choice of an organizational adoption strategy as described in Section 3.2. The remaining columns list the mentioned categories of adoption strategies: proactive, incremental, and reactive. The body of the table depicts the dependencies between the organizational factors and adoption strategies whereas every column represents necessary factors for the corresponding adoption strategy. The cells of the table are marked with "H" for "needs to be high," "M" for "needs to be at least medium," "L" for "needs to be at least low," or left empty meaning that the respective factor does not influence the choice to be made. The columns should be read as an AND condition: the respective adoption strategy is applicable only if all conditions in the corresponding column are met.

For example, to choose a proactive or incremental strategy, there must be high-level management commitment; if high-level management commitment is medium or even low, only a reactive strategy is applicable. One possible precondition set for choosing an incremental strategy is: a medium likelihood to become market leader, high or medium motivation to use product lines, medium control of product specification, a medium stable funding source for core asset development, and high-level management commitment. A good connection to customers can compensate for not being in control of product specification (customers will communicate their requirements for future products early) and even outweigh a less desirable position in the market.

Once the business unit chooses an appropriate strategy, it should baseline its current state according to the dimensions of the business, architecture, process, and organization (BAPO) framework [11] [12], the 29 practice areas of the Framework for Software Product Line Practice [2], the PuLSE™ customization factors [13], or some other comprehensive software product line yardstick, and then perform a gap analysis. Using the results of that analysis, the business unit can then follow a planning process such as the one proposed by Jones and Northrop to develop an adoption plan [14].

5 Conclusion

Adopting a software product line potentially affects all levels of an organization. To do so successfully, each affected organizational level must set its adoption goals, conceive a strategy, and implement a plan to attain those goals. The adoption goals, strategies, and plans are influenced by the characteristics of market, organization, business unit, and individual.

Future research is needed to validate whether the levels and characteristics identified in this paper are minimal but sufficient to predict successful adoption. It should also refine and empirically validate the model of the interdependencies between organizational characteristics and adoption strategies. Furthermore, models of the interdependencies between the business unit, individual characteristics, and the adoption strategies need to be developed.

There is also an interorganizational context level possibly distinguishable from the market that we did not discuss. More and more companies are organizing into relatively complex value networks that utilize layered product architectures. Each layer serves as a platform (asset base) for the next layer and utilizes the services of the underlying layer. Companies that want to become major players in their market should develop and control their platforms so that the maximum number of high-quality products and services are built on top. In such an interorganizational context, the product lines become virtual and recursive – that is, each platform represents productized core assets and the layers built on top of it are platforms as well. Companies can choose to focus only on the development of productized core assets for one layer or vertically integrate across layers. It would be interesting to investigate how this context affects the characteristics in the four lower levels identified in this paper.

References

1. P. Clements, L. Northrop. Software Product Lines: Practices and Patterns. Boston, MA: Addison-Wesley, 2002.
2. P. Clements, L. Northrop. A Framework for Software Product Line Practice, Version 4.1. Pittsburgh, PA: Software Engineering Institute, Carnegie Mellon University, 2002. http://www.sei.cmu.edu/plp /framework.html.
3. G. Böckle, J. Munoz, P. Knauber, C. W. Krueger, J. C. Sampaio do Prado Leite, F. van der Linden, L. Northrop, M. Stark, D. M. Weiss. Adopting and Institutionalizing a Product Line Culture, 49-59. Proceedings of Software Product Lines Second International Conference. San Diego, California, August 19-22, 2002. New York, NY: Springer-Verlag, 2002.
4. J. Bosch. Maturity and Evolution in Software Product Lines: Approaches, Artefacts and Organization, 257-271. Proceedings of Software Product Lines Second International Conference. San Diego, California, August 19-22, 2002. New York, NY: Springer-Verlag, 2002.

5. K. Schmidt, M. Verlage. The Economic Impact of Product Line Adoption and Evolution. IEEE Software, Vol. 19, No. 4, July/August 2002, 50-57.
6. M. A. Cusumano, R. W. Selby. Microsoft Secrets: How the World's Most Powerful Software Company Creates Technology, Shapes Markets, and Manages People. New York, New York: The Free Press, 1995.
7. C. W. Cusumano, D. B. Yoffie. Competing on Internet Time: Lessons from Netscape and Its Battle with Microsoft. New York, NY: The Free Press, 1998.
8. C. W. Krueger. Easing the Transition to Software Mass Customization, 282-293. Proceedings of the 4th International Workshop on Software Product Family Engineering. Bilbao, Spain, October 3-5, 2001. Berlin, Germany: Springer-Verlag, 2002.
9. S. Thiel, A. Hein. Modeling and Using Product Line Variability in Automotive Systems. IEEE Software, Vol. 19, No. 4, July/August 2002, 66-72.
10. D. Muthig. A Light-Weight Approach Facilitating an Evolutionary Transition Towards Software Product Lines. Stuttgart, Germany: Frauenhofer IRB Verlag, 2002.
11. P. America, H. Obbink, R. van Ommering, F. van der Linden,. CoPAM: A Component-Oriented Platform Architecting Method Family for Product family Engineering, 167-180. Proceedings of Software Product Lines First International Conference. Denver, Colorado, August 28-31, 2000. Boston, MA: Kluwer Academic Press, 2000.
12. J. G. Wijnstra. Critical Factors for a Successful Platform-Based Product Family Approach, 68-89. Proceedings of Software Product Lines Second International Conference. San Diego, California, August 19-22, 2002. New York, NY: Springer-Verlag.
13. K. Schmid, T. Widen. Customizing the PuLSE™ Product Line Approach to the Demands of an Organization, 221-238. Proceedings of the 7th European Workshop on Software Process Technology, (EWSPT'2000) (LNCS 1780). Kaprun, Austria, February 21-25, 2000. New York, NY: Springer-Verlag, 2000.
14. L. Jones, L. Northrop. Software Process Improvement Planning. 1-24. Proceedings of the European Software Engineering Process Group Conference. Amsterdam, Netherlands, June 7-10, 1999. Milton Keynes, UK: European Software Process Improvement Foundation, 1999.

A Quantitative Model of the Value of Architecture in Product Line Adoption*

Klaus Schmid

Fraunhofer Einrichtung für Experimentelles Software Engineering,
Sauerwiesen 6, D-67661 Kaiserslautern, Germany
schmid@iese.fhg.de
+49 (0) 6301 707 - 158

Abstract. Product line adoption is a key issue in product line development, as the right adoption approach is central to the overall success of product line de velopment. Thus, this is a strongly discussed area of product line engineering. While so far, guidelines and experiences on the best approach to product line adoption have been presented, no detailed quantitative model was provided.

In this paper we present a quantitative model of the product line adoption prob-lem. From this model we deduce general guidelines for product line adoption, particularly highlighting the role of the architecture in the cost-effective adop-tion of a product line.

1 Introduction

While product line development is well recognized as a systematic approach to gain the benefits of large-scale reuse, the specific approach of migrating to a product line is still under discussion. The major opposing views in this context are the approaches of *proactive* and *reactive* product line adoption, as introduced in [2]. A simlar distinction is made in the *incremental vs. big-bang* development distinction [9] or the *heavy-weight* vs. *lightweight* distinction of product line development [5].

While in general arguments have been exchanged that are in favor for both of the positions, so far no agreement on the respective benefits and no detailed analysis exist. Some exceptions are an experimental comparison of the two approaches [6] and some qualitative guidelines [9].

These shortcomings lead us to search for a quantitative model of product line tran-sition. This model aims at the analysis of the respective benefits of the proactive and reactive approach and the constraints under which they can be accrued. While the overall costs of product line development are determined by a large number of factors [3], in this model, we focus specifically on the impact of modularity in a product line architecture on product line adoption as it plays a key role in the discussions.

In the following section, we will discuss in more detail the problem of product line adoption and how we will model this in this paper. In Section 3, we will briefly illus-trate an example situation, that highlights our main concerns and describes the origi-

---

* This work has been partially funded by Eureka Σ! 2023 Programme, ITEA project ip00004, Café.

F. van der Linden (Ed.): PFE 2003, LNCS 3014, pp. 32–43, 2004.

nal context in which this model was developed. The core part of our contribution is given in Section 4, where we describe our valuation model for the product line adoption case. In the following section we will discuss the implications of our model for guidelines on product line adoption. Finally, in Section 6 we will conclude.

2 The ADOPTION MODEL

While commonly the potential product line approaches are discussed in terms of their extremes (e.g., the proactive vs. reactive dichotomy), these are simply a short-hand for a continuum of different approaches. This variation dimension can be characterized as the degree to which up-front development investments are made. While this is a continuum, there is one medium position, which considerably differs if compared to the other approaches. This position is proactive architecting (i.e., structuring of the software), combined with a reactive implementation approach.

Thus, we see three main approaches for dealing with variabilities, that must be distinguished in this paper:

1. If a variability is not immediately needed for any product, it is not taken into account as part of the product line infrastructure. This corresponds to the traditional reactive approach.
2. The medium position corresponds to a light-weight, architecture-centric approach. If a variability is not needed right away, the architecture should be developed in a way that takes this variation into account (see below), even if no implementation is yet provided for the variability.
3. The proactive extreme is a full analysis of the potential variabilities that are known and providing architectural measures in order to accommodate these variabilities as well as implementing the variabilities that are identified by product line scoping as part of development [8].

While the various positions are just points in a continuum, they provide pronounced key positions which we will use as the basis for our analysis. Moreover, each of these decisions must be performed for each of the potential variability points, providing us with an enormous decision space. However, as the same analysis apply for all of these individual decisions, we will focus here on deciding on the realization of a single variability.

At this point we need to describe in more detail what we mean with taking a variation into account during architecting. The development of an architecture and the availability of an architecture provide many different value contributions to a product line project. Here, we will focus on the value of *modularity* [10]. In particular for variabilities we will assume that taking into account a variability in the architecture will reduce the number of points in the software, where a variation mechanism is needed for representing this variability as opposed to an ad-hoc approach.

We define the following terms in order to describe the impact of variability:

Variation point (VP) – a variation point corresponds to a consistent change in a software product due to a variability. This is independent of the number of positions in the implementation that are affected.

Variation impact point (VIP) – a variation impact point denotes a position in the realization (independent of the binding time) where a variation point takes effect.

Consequently, there is a 1:n relationship between VPs and VIPs. An example would be a variability where web-interfaces as well as window-interfaces could be relevant to a product line. This would correspond to a single VP, but surely a large number of VIPs in the documentation, different parts of the code, etc.

Hence, we can describe our fundamental assumption as:

Taking a VP into account during architecting will lead to a smaller number of VIPs than if it would not have been taken into account[1].

As a basis for our model we will distinguish between the implementation of a capability *cap* and of the variability mechanism(s) *vm*. The capability in the example above could be a window-interface. This can be regarded as a single implementation, independent of the number of VIPs relevant to integrating it into the system. On the other hand, we will need one *vm*-implementation per VIP. Thus, we will regard the effort for capability implementation as independent of the software architecture, while the effort for *vm*-implementation will be proportional to the number of VIPs.

In the following section, we will discuss the cost implications of this assumption.

3   The Example

The initial motivation for this analysis came from a specific industrial project aimed at setting up a new product line in an organization. The actual parameters we are using in our discussion are derived from this example.

In this project we faced the major issue that a certain capability of the system (in our case: distribution) could not be excluded from the variabilities (meaning: while all foreseeable products would be localized, it could be possible that some future product would require to be distributed). Of course such a capability would have a strong impact on the architecture and would require a lot of added implementation effort (both for implementing the basic capabilities as well as for the variability mechanisms). The key questions we were facing were:

- Should we fully develop the necessary variability (proactive)
- Should we ignore it until a product that requires it must be built?

These and other options were evaluated. Finally, we decided to spend significant effort to ensure that the product line architecture would support the requirement of distribution (as a variant), but we delayed the implementation until such a functionality would actually be required.

The value model we describe below formalizes this situation as a basis for supporting this decision.

4   The Value Model

The key criterion we use in order to determine the optimal product line transition approach is the value a specific alternative generates or, in case this can not be resolved without uncertainty, its expected value. In this section, we will describe the

---

[1] There are typically a large number of VPs in a product line. It will usually not be possible to minimize the number of VIPs simultaneously for all VP.

basic formulas and assumptions we used for developing our value model. As our key value driver, we will use in this context a model of the overall development effort. Along the way we will discuss some conclusions that can be drawn from this model.

The key questions that the model is supposed to answer are:

- As we expect thorough architecting to reduce on average the number of VIPs for each variability, we need to ask: how does the overall cost vary as a function of the number of VIPs?
- How do costs vary depending on the probability that the capability is needed at all?

In order to answer these questions we need to introduce the following parameters.

4.1 Model Parameters

Implicit in these questions is the notion of time. Whenever we ask whether something will eventually pay off, we need to take into account the time we are looking ahead. Additionally, we need to take into account how often systems will be build during this time and a discounting rate in order to describe to what degree money is depreciated over time (this is called discounted cash-flow analysis [7]). This leads us to the following definitions:

- Number of years taken into account: y.
- Number of systems developed during this time: N.
  (we will use n to denote the number of systems that have been developed up to a certain time).
- Discount rate r.

In addition we will use the following parameters in order to describe the costs associated with the development of a variability implementation:

- Effort for an implementation of the capability (this is needed only once per product line): EC.
- Number of variation impact points for the variability in the overall infrastructure: vip.
- Effort for the design and implementation of the variability mechanis[2]: $Evm = Evmd + vip * Evmi$.
- In order to take into account that a specific variability might be needed not in the first system, but in a later one, we denote the probability that it is needed in a system by p.

Besides the basic costs of implementing the variability we also need to take into account that the maintenance of more complex code will usually lead to higher effort [4]. This complexity is increased if we add a lot of variabilities early on:

- We will use the factor cc (complexity cost) to denote this cost contribution that stems from the addition of variability. We will use the formula $Scc = cc * vip$ to denote the cost from added complexity in developing a system.

---

[2] While design costs can be expected can be expected to be independent of the number of occurrences, this will not hold for the implementation costs.

If a variability is implemented at a later point in time (in the reactive mode), initial costs are saved, however, a different type of costs will come up at a later point in time:

- Changes that are performed at a later point in time, typically require a higher amount of effort (as this involves design changes, removing code, etc.) [1]. We call this the cost overhead *co*. *co* gives the added cost over the implementation of the variability mechanisms as part of initial development.
- If variability is added at a later point in time, the already developed systems require specific handling (e.g., adapting them to the existing infrastructure). This added cost is defined per VIP and per already existing system. We call it cost retro-fit: *cr*.

With the above definitions we are able to compare the implications of the different costs for the various product line entry scenarios.

4.2 The Cost of Variability

In order to determine the cost of introducing the variability (*EVI*) into the product line there are two main cases: either we introduce it in the beginning (at *n=0*), or we introduce it a later point in time (*n>0*):

1. (n = 0) $EVI(n) = EC + Evm$
2. (n > 0) $EVI(n) = EC + Evm * co + cr * n * vip$

The last term in the formula above captures the amount of effort required for retrofitting the existing infrastructure to reflect the updated variability handling mechanisms. As this is also a process over time, we also need to take the discounted cash flow approach into account. This is denoted as *EVI'(n)*:

3. $EVI'(n) = EVI(n) * (1-r)^{\wedge}(n/N*y)$

(We assume the systems are evenly distributed over time)

Using these formulas, we can now analyze how the cost of variability introduction will vary depending on the specific time of variability introduction and on other parameters, like the number of *vips* that are required for this variability.

This is shown in Figure 1. Here, we used a scenario with the following parameters (y =5, r =10%, EC = 10 PW, Evm = 2PW + vip*0.2PW, cr= 0.2, co=0.4, N=10) [PW = person-week]. The numbers in this scenario have been taken from estimates from a real project, which provided the initial motivation for this model.

From Figure 1 we can see that the number *vip* has a strong impact on the overall costs of variability. In particular, we can see that the difference in costs for different *vip*-numbers is even increasing with larger numbers of systems that are built. We can easily understand the underlying functions qualitatively and how they lead to this effect:

The functions state that the number of VIPs has not a large impact if the variability mechanisms are implemented right away (cf. eq. 1 and 2). The gap that occurs to the second value for each of the graphs is motivated by the second term in equation 2. Finally, the third term leads to the fact that the maximum occurs at a large number of systems for larger values of *vip*. The fact that the values are actually going down for larger numbers of systems is motivated by the discounted cash-flow effect, which is introduced by equation 3.

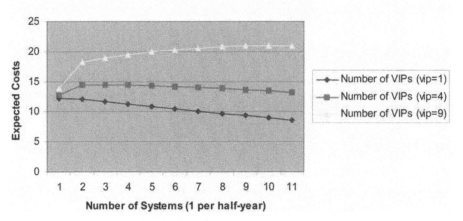

Fig. 1. Variability Introduction Costs.

While we captured in the above equations the costs from a late introduction of variability, the savings are not adequately represented as we neglected the costs of handling the more complex infrastructure that is created if we introduce the variabilities earlier.

Using *Scc,* as defined above, we can describe the costs that are incurred during the development of system *n* by an earlier introduction of variability as follows:

4. Scc'(n) = Scc * (1-r)^(n/N*y)

However, we need to take into account the cost for all systems after the introduction of the variability. This is given below:

$$5.\ \text{Tcc(n)} = \sum_{i=n}^{N} \text{Scc'(i)}$$

Consequently, if we introduce the variability with system *n*, then the total costs incurred by introducing the variability are given by:

6. *CV(n) = EVI'(n) + Tcc(n).*

The correction provided by *Tcc(n)* is very small for realistic values of *cc* (e.g., 0.05). The effect of this is shown in Figure 2. The main difference to Figure 1 is that also for a variability introduction for an earlier system the number *vip* has a stronger influence on the total costs.

From the arguments put forward so far, we can see that the number of changes (*vip*) that need to be made is a key driver for the overall costs and thus the preferability of a specific adoption approach. However, even if we know that the costs for a late introduction of a variability are very high, we will usually not implement it if it is very unlikely that we will need it. We will now turn to the impact of the probability of the need of the functionality on our total costs.

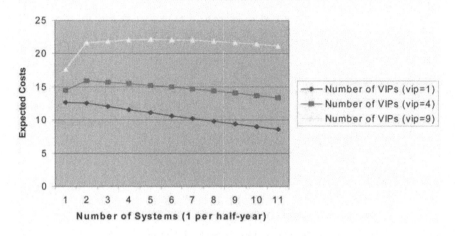

Fig. 2. Total Variability Costs.

4.3 Modeling the Stochastic Process

While so far we focused purely on what happens if the variability is introduced at a certain point in time, we can now turn to the question, when will it actually be introduced?

If we assume that the variability is introduced as soon as it is needed, but not earlier, we can focus on the question: when will we need this variability?

As this is usually not known exactly for later products, it must be modelled as a stochastic process, i.e., for each new product in the product line, there is a certain probability p, that this product will need the additional capability introduced by the variability[3].

In mathematical terms we are now asking for the expected value of the total variability costs $E(CV)$. This is given by the following formula:

$$7.\ \ E(CV) = \sum_{i=1}^{N} CV(i) \times (1-p)^{i-1} \times p$$

We can now determine our expected total costs based on the varying parameter *p*.

An analysis of this dependency is given in Figure 3. There we related the expected costs with the probability that we will need the added capability. In this figure, we used *vip = 4*, but for other values of *vip*, we will get on a qualitative level the same results: the costs rise sharply, as the introduction of the functionality becomes more probable; beyond a certain threshold the costs are slightly reducing as now the probability is very high that the variability is introduced very early and the "low-cost" upfront development solution takes a stronger effect.

---

[3] Note, that different functionalities in the product line may have strongly different values of *p*.

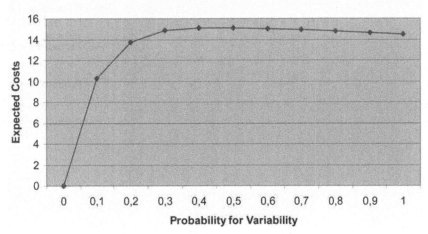

Fig. 3. Cost / Probability Relationship.

Thus, we can conclude that a delayed variability implementation is only beneficial from a total cost perspective if the probability of the introduction of the variability is very low (0.2 or smaller in our example).

Based on this model, we our now able to compare the situation of introducing a new variability at need with the up-front introduction of the variability and relate it with the two parameters we found particularly influential in our model: the probability p and the number of VIPs vip.

This is shown in Figure 4. This graph compares the cost figures for different numbers of modules based on different probabilities of introduction with immediate introduction. (Note, that immediate introduction corresponds in our model with a probability of 100% that we will need this capability and the variability in the first product.)

We see here that the number of modules has a much stronger impact if we introduce the variability on a per-need basis than if it is introduced right away. Moreover, we see that even for low probabilities (e.g., 0.2) the cost for a per-need introduction can become larger than for immediate introduction, if a large number of VIPs is impacted[4].

5   Product Line Introduction Strategy

While, of course, the specific numbers that are given in our diagrams relate to the specific base numbers we choose, the qualitative view of the diagrams is independent of these concerns. For example, the specific point of intersection in Figure 4 between the immediate implementation and the expected value for *p=0,2*, which is a *vip* of

---

[4] Note, that *vip* denotes the total number of positions in the implementation (including documentation) impacted by a variability, so our upper bound of 10 in the diagram is actually rather small.

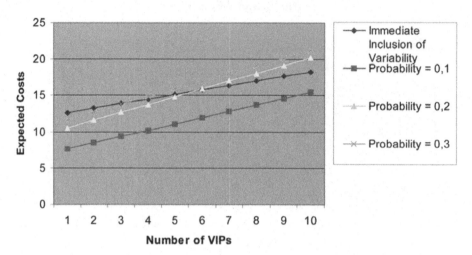

Fig. 4. Immediate vs. Delayed Variability Introduction.

approximately 5, will vary depending on the specific values we select. But, the fact that there will be an intersection will always remain. This is why we focused in this paper purely on qualitative interpretations.

Based on the model we defined in the preceding section, we are now able to return to the core question of this paper:

Which approach to building the product line infrastructure should be used (proactive, reactive, anything in between) and which criteria determine the selection?

As we saw in Section 4, the two parameters:

- Number of places impacted by the implementation of a variability (*vip*)
- The probability that the variability is actually needed (*p*)

have a major impact on the total cost of the product line introduction approach. Thus, they play a key role when deciding which approach to choose in a specific situation.

In general, we identify from Figure 4, that if the probability that the variability is actually needed is rather low, it is of course preferable to be reactive, i.e., implement the variability only on a per need basis. For higher probabilities of need of the feature, the balance usually shifts very soon. This shift is mostly driven by three parameters: *co*, *cr*, and *cc*. The higher the ratio *cr/cc* the more preferable it is to develop the variability initially. On the other hand *co* has a strong impact on the gap that occurs directly from the immediate implementation to any later implementation of the variability mechanisms. Here, we choose a value of 0.4 (implying there is a 40% overhead for late implementation) which is probably at the upper range of the spectrum. Choosing smaller values will result in a higher preference for a reactive approach.

At this point it is time to revisit our key assumption: a good product line architecture leads to an improved encapsulation of the variability. (This is of course no far-fetched assumption, as we will expect a good software architecture to encapsulate all concerns of central relevancy.) In Figure 5 we provide a zoomed version of Figure 4,

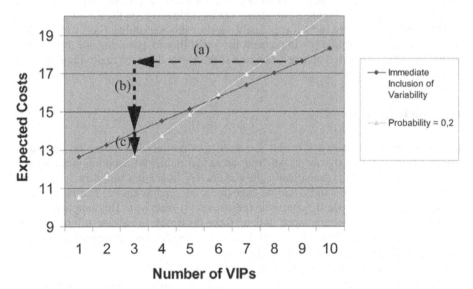

Fig. 5. The Impact of Modularization in a Product Line Architecture.

where we focus on the intersection of the curve for immediate variability implementation and the curve for probability $p = 0.2$.

If we assume that a straightforward implementation which would take a specific variability – let's call it v – not into account would lead to a *vip* of 9, then the optimal approach would be the up-front implementation of the variability (even if the probability that it is actually needed is rather low, as with $p = 0.2$). It is important to note that we made the assumption that in purely reactive development no *up-front* restructuring for a specific variability is made, which is in line with the general interpretation [2].

On the other hand, if we take this specific variability into account during architecture development, this will lead to a reduction of *vip*. In Figure 5 we assume a reduction to a vip of 3 (cf. arrow *(a)*). This restructuring would have a strong impact on the (variability) costs. In our example it would relate to a reduction of approximately 3 PW *(b)*, which corresponds to a saving of about 15% of the total cost. A saving that could be completely spent on architecting without shifting the balance. This architecting would have an interesting side-effect. For a *vip* of 3, the reactive implementation is actually more beneficial *(c)*. It would lead to the additional saving of about one personweek.

So, in this case the optimal strategy would actually be what we described as the intermediate or evolutionary strategy: perform a strong modularization through the development of a product line architecture that takes the variability into account, but perform the actual implementation with all the associated overhead costs only in case the variability is actually needed.

In our example situation (cf. Section 3), we estimated p to be somewhere between 0.1 and 0.2. At the same time the capability implementation would be rather expensive and all initial architecture sketches lead to a high value of *vip* for this variability. In accordance with this analysis we decided in our example (cf. Section 3) to use the strategy exemplified in Figure 5: we spent considerable effort on the development of a product line architecture, which can easily support this variability (i.e., with a small number of *vip*), but we did not implement the variability mechanisms nor the capability so far. This will only be done when and if the variability is actually required by a product.

6 Conclusions

In this paper we discussed a model forselecting a product line transition approach. The model development was driven from an actual industrial adoption situation and enabled us to discuss systematically the parameters impacting this decision. As we found in our discussion (and could be expected), no general answer can be given on the preference for a specific approach (proactive vs. reactive). This emphasizes the need for any product line manager, making these decisions, to have an informed opinion on the parameters that apply in his setting. Using this model a detailed analysis can be provided in a straight-forward manner.

Nevertheless, some general guidelines could be identified:

- Late implementation of a variability seems to pay off (over a large product line) only if the probability that the variability is required is very low.
- In general an up-front implementation of a variability seems to be the least costly approach if the probability that the variability is actually required by a product is not too low.
- The development of a product line architecture that modularizes the variabilities seems to play a key role in lowering overall development costs.

Of course, there are usually other aspects, like the availability of resources, that will have an impact on the decision whether to use a proactive, a reactive, or an intermediate approach.

According to our analysis, if the probability for a variability is low, it is a key strategy to proactively consider the variability in the architecture, while performing the actual implementation purely reactively, a mixed approach that – to our knowledge – has not been described so far. This strongly links architecting to scoping, as it implies that in general it seems to be the most effective approach to proactively scope the product line, perform the development of the architecture on the complete scope, but then adequately select those variabilities that are needed with a certain minimum probability for implementation.

References

1. Barry W. Boehm, Chris Abts, Winsor A. Brown, Sunita Chulani, Bradford Kendall Clark, Ellis Horowitz, Ray Madachy, Donald J. Reifer, and Bert Steece. *Software Cost Estimation with COCOMO II*. Prentice Hall PTR, 2000.
2. Paul Clements and Charles Krueger. Point – counterpoint: Being proactive pays off – eliminating the adoption barrier. *IEEE Software*, July/August 2002.
3. Paul Clements and Linda Northrop. *Software Product Lines*. Addison-Wesley, 2001.

4. Stephen G. Eick, Todd L. Graves, Alan F. Karr, J.S. Marron, and Audris Mockus. Does code decay? assessing the evidence from change management data. *IEEE Transactions on Software Engineering*, 27(1):1–12, 2001.
5. John D. McGregor, Linda M. Northrop, Salah Jarrad, and Klaus Pohl. Initiating software product lines. *IEEE Software*, 19(4):24–27, 2002.
6. Dirk Muthig. *A Light-Weight Approach Facilitating an Evolutionary Transition Towards Software Product Lines*. PhD thesis, University of Kaiserslautern, IRB Verlag, 2002.
7. Klaus Schmid. An initial model of product line economics. In Frank van der Linden, editor, *Proceedings of the Fourth International Workshop on Product Family Engineering (PFE-4), 2001*, volume 2290 of *Lecture Notes in Computer Science*, pages 38–50. Springer, 2001.
8. Klaus Schmid. A comprehensive product line scoping approach and its validation. In *Proceedings of the 24th International Conference on Software Engineering*, pages 593–603, 2002.
9. Klaus Schmid and Martin Verlage. The economic impact of product line adoption and evolution. *IEEE Software*, 19(6):50–57, July/August 2002.
10. Kevin J. Sullivan, William G. Grisworld, Yuanfang Cai, and Ben Hallen. The structure and value of modularity in software design. In *Proceedings of the Joint International Conference on Software Engineering and ACM SIGSOFT Symposium on the Foundations of Software Engineering, September 2001, Vienna*, 2001.

Multi-view Variation Modeling for Scenario Analysis

Pierre America, Eelco Rommes, and Henk Obbink

Philips Research
Prof. Holstlaan 4, 5656 AA,Eindhoven
The Netherlands
{pierre.america,eelco.rommes,henk.obbink}@philips.com

Abstract. We propose an approach using scenarios to describe a spectrum of possible futures and analyze them to assess and improve the ease of accommodating new requirements by a system architecture. Variation modeling forms an important part of the analysis. This paper focuses on an approach to variation modeling across multiple architectural views. The models do not only display the variability in these views, but also the relationships between them. In particular, they can show how choices in one view influence choices in the other views.

1 Introduction

The system architecture of a successful product family typically enjoys a long life (ten years or more). During this long life, the architecture will invariably have to deal with new requirements. We are currently developing a method to assess and improve the ease of accommodating such new requirements by a system architecture. This paper reports on the results so far, focusing on our approach to multi-view variation modeling.

Since it is impossible to predict the future exactly, we consider various scenarios of different kinds to describe a spectrum of possible futures of interest to the system under development. The scenarios are further analyzed across multiple architectural views. Part of this analysis is to capture the differences and commonalities among the scenarios, and possible architectural responses to these differences. We have found that variation models covering multiple views are a useful tool to do this. Such models explicitly express the relationships between variation points across and within views, e.g. allowing architectural reasoning from customer needs to implementation issues, and vice versa.

We have applied the approach in a practical case study about medical equipment for the cardiac catheterization lab. This case study is introduced in Section 2 and used as a running example throughout the paper. Section 3 introduces the main views that we use to describe architectures and the artifacts that fill them. This shows the basic context of our approach to variation modeling. Then Section 4 describes more extensively how we model the variation points within and across views. We present (simplified) models from our case study as examples. Finally Section 5 presents some conclusions.

F. van der Linden (Ed.): PFE 2003, LNCS 3014, pp. 44–65, 2004.
© Springer-Verlag Berlin Heidelberg 2004

2   Case Study: 3D Catheterization Laboratory

As a running example, we will use a case study to illustrate the techniques and methods used in this paper. The system we consider is the cardiac catheterization laboratory – cathlab for short. (see Figure 1) This is a room in a hospital where a cardiologist diagnoses or treats certain heart problems. The kind of problems that are of interest to our case study, have to do with arteries being narrowed (or even completely blocked) by plaque. Such narrowings diminish the flow of blood and thus the delivery of oxygen to certain parts of the heart, which could result in among other things a heart attack or stroke. To gain insight into the problem, the cardiologist needs to visualize the patient's blood vessels. He or she does so using specialized X-ray equipment that is available in the cathlab. Because blood vessels do not scatter X-rays very well, a contrast fluid is inserted in the vessels. This fluid is harmful to the patient, and it is therefore delivered only locally and in small amounts. This is done by means of a catheter, which is inserted into a major vessel and then navigated to the spot that the cardiologist wants to visualize. Thus, an important function of the cathlab is the visualization of arteries and the flow of blood inside them. Often, treatment is also possible by catheterization during the same procedure.

In our case study, we examined the possibilities to extend the cathlab with 3D capabilities, in particular 3D rotational angiography (3DRA); a technique to construct a 3D model of the arteries from a large number of X-ray images taken from different angles [1]. Such a model can help the cardiologist during diagnosis and treatment of heart problems.

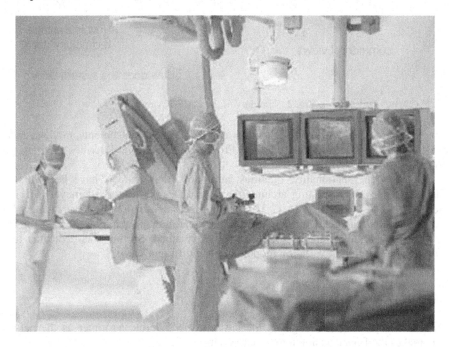

Fig. 1. The catheterization laboratory (cathlab)

3 The CAFCR Views

In the architecting method that we are developing, the purpose of architecture is to bridge the gap between the needs, objectives, and wishes of the customer and their realization by available technology. In order to achieve this, we follow the COPA approach [2,3]. In this approach the overall structure of the architecture description consists of five views that span this gap between customer and technology. These views are summarized in Figure 2.

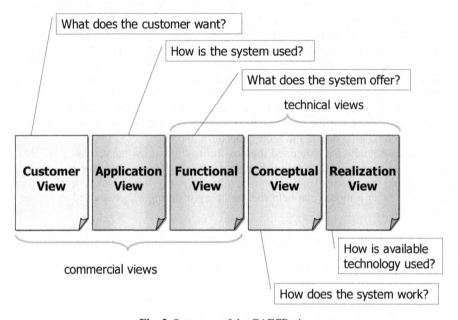

Fig. 2. Summary of the CAFCR views

The views are filled with artifacts (this is a generic term for documents, models, code, etc., used among others in the Unified Process [4]). Table 1 describes the way we propose to do that.

The rows on functionality, qualities, and supporting artifacts have been largely adapted from various existing architecting approaches, such as Bredemeyer [5], Siemens [6], RUP [7], and COPA [2,3]. The approach to variation, however, is new for our scenario-based architecting approach. In the following paragraphs, each of the CAFCR views and its artifacts are concisely explained. Section 4 is dedicated to a thorough description of variation modeling in the different views.

3.1 The Customer View

This view captures knowledge on the customer. We define customer as the person who makes the final decision to buy our system.

Table 1. Artifacts in the CAFCR views

	Customer	**Application**	**Functional**	**Conceptual**	**Realization**
Variation	Variation model	Variation model	Variation model	Variation model	Variation model
Functionality	Value proposition	User scenarios	Feature dictionary	System decomposition	Technology mapping
Qualities	Customer drivers	Quality requirements	Quality properties	Principles Mechanisms	Mechanisms Conventions
Supporting artifacts	Context diagram Trend analysis PESTLE analysis Competitor / complementer analysis	System context Workflow context Domain model	Feature / value matrix	Collaborations Information models	Collaboration estimations Supplier roadmaps

Major questions addressed in the customer view are:

- Who is our customer? Who are the major stakeholders who influence the customer's decision? What are their objectives, needs, and wishes?
- What is the customer's context? Who are his competitors, complementers? What external forces influence the customer? Who are our own competitors and complementers? (All of them are possible suppliers to our customers.)
- What is the essential value that our product offers to the customer?

A *value proposition* is a concise statement explaining the added value of the system to a specific stakeholder or set of stakeholders. Preferably, such value proposition should indicate clearly how the stakeholder's key drivers are addressed, while avoiding the pitfall of overly generic statements.

In this context, a *customer driver* is a motivating factor for a particular stakeholder, or in other words, it is something that the stakeholder wants or does not want. Typically, there are many drivers that play a role, and among each other they are often causally related. In the end, we are mainly interested in the drivers of our own customer, but often these are related to the drivers of our customer's customers (sometimes across several stages in a value chain), and other stakeholders. All these relationships can be expressed using influence diagrams [8,9]. Figure 3 shows an example from our case study.

Once we have analyzed these relationships, we can identify the *key* drivers: These are the things that directly make the stakeholders happy. The COPA approach [2,3] uses a kind of diagram with several columns, listing key drivers, derived drivers, and application drivers. In that kind of diagram there is a clear distinction of key drivers, but it is difficult to express the relationships among the various stakeholders.

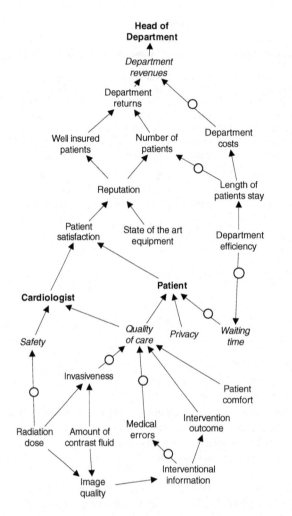

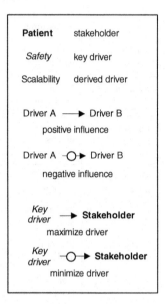

Fig. 3. Influence diagram of stakeholders and drivers

Analyzing drivers and their relationships is not an easy task, because stakeholders rarely make explicit what really motivates them. The general tendency among system architects is to make an analysis that is far too shallow: There are few people that get directly happy by having metallic paint on their car or a better MPEG encoder. It is more likely that they want to impress the neighbors with their beautiful car or to be entertained by a movie without being disturbed by artifacts in the images. Finding the deeper motivators of your customer may lead to better and sometimes even easier ways to satisfy his needs.

One of the stakeholders of the cathlab is the cardiologist. One of the cardiologist's key drivers is *safety*: performing numerous procedures per day means he or she spends a lot of time near X-ray equipment. It is therefore important to make sure that as little harmful radiation as possible is received by the cardiologist.

We investigate the customer context in three artifacts. A *context diagram* is a model, visually displaying the customer and his relationships with influential entities surrounding him. We typically use an informal boxes-and-arrows notation. Examples of such influential entities in the context of the cardiology department are patients, health management organizations and the hospital administration. A *trend analysis* is a summary of the major trends in the customer domain, the forces causing them, and their effects over time. A *PESTLE analysis* is a well-known categorization of external influences in marketing and business analysis (see, for example [10]). By looking at Political, Economical, Social-cultural, Technological, Legal, and Environmental issues surrounding a business or product, we gather input on its macro context in a structured way.

A *competitor/complementer analysis* is made of the entities that are active in the same market as our customer:

- *Competitors* provide the same kind of service or product. Competitors of a cardiology department are other hospitals or private clinics.
- *Complementers* provide a different kind of service or product that is useful or even necessary in combination with our product. Family doctors typically are complementers.

The competitor/complementer analysis gives information about the market we are developing for. This knowledge is essential to make the right product. We include our own competitors and complementers in the same description as our customer's.

A good analysis of competitors and complementers not only identifies who the competitors and complementers are and what services or products they provide, but also lists their strengths and weaknesses.

3.2 The Application View

In this view we study how the systems that we are architecting can be used to fulfill the customer's needs.

Major questions addressed in the application view are:

- How do our stakeholders apply the systems we provide to achieve their objectives?
- Which stakeholders will use the system? In what ways? How does this usage fit their way of working?
- In what context must our system operate? What other systems are in use?

In our approach, the *user scenarios* form the main ingredient of the application view. User scenarios are short stories describing an actor using an envisioned system to accomplish some goal. A sentence from such a scenario could be:

"Dr. Hart prepares for the intervention using a workstation. He has access to all information concerning the patient and selects the diagnostic images that should be available during the procedure."

Such scenarios describe the envisioned system in a way that all stakeholders can understand. This makes them well suited for making architectural decisions as well as describing the consequences of such decisions.

In order to cover sufficiently many possibilities, we use a significant number of scenarios (in our relatively simple case study, we used five user scenarios.) Fortunately, these scenarios do not have to differ from top to bottom, but they can have a lot in common. Therefore we propose a structure as illustrated in Figure 4 using UML.

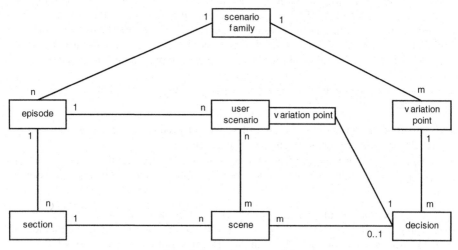

Fig. 4. Scenario metamodel

We consider a family of scenarios, which together cover a number of episodes. An episode is a contiguous period of time during which a task is performed. For example, in our case study the cathlab intervention itself is a single episode, but one could also consider other episodes, e.g. planning before or reporting after the intervention. An episode again consists of a number of sections, each of which describes a more or less atomic action. On the other hand, a scenario family also deals with a number of variation points, where each variation point allows a number of different decisions. An example from our case study is the degree to which two systems in a cathlab collaborate: only at the level of exchanging data, or do they recognize and support each other's workflow? Now a user scenario is a concrete description of an episode, where for each variation point exactly one decision is taken. Such a scenario can consist of a number of scenes, where each scene covers one section of the episode, and where for each scene at most one decision on a variation point applies. This means that each section corresponds with at most a single variation point, although one variation point can be handled by many sections.

User scenarios are related to use cases [11] in some ways, but significantly different in others. Figure 5 shows the relationship between the various concepts. User scenarios are roughly equivalent to *usage narratives* (in the terminology of [11]). A usage narrative is a story envisioning a system in use, revealing the motivations and intentions of the actors. An important difference with our user scenarios is that usage narratives only include *behavioral* information, whereas user scenarios may address *architectural qualities* as well. A *use case* is an abstract concept of a single, roughly atomic task in which user and system cooperate, and as such it corresponds to a section in an episode. Such a task can be carried in a number of ways, described in *use*

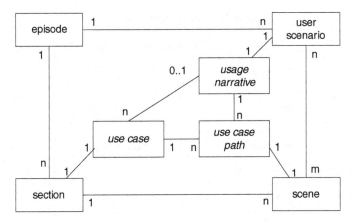

Fig. 5. Relation between user scenarios and use cases (in italics)

case paths. A use case path is a sequence of actions and interactions that occurs under certain conditions, expressed without *ifs* or branching. Therefore this corresponds to a scene.

User scenarios and use cases are complementary: user scenarios will typically be written earlier in the project lifecycle, when options for the envisioned system's architecture are explored. The resulting scenarios can be used as usage narratives to guide use case writing for requirements gathering.

As we will see in Section 4.4, there is a lot of variation in the application view. It is not necessary to cover all the possibilities in separate user scenarios. Rather, we limit ourselves to the most important ones. The resulting structure can be represented in a table of the form shown by Table 2, as long as the number of variation points is not too large. Here column spanning means that the scene to its left is also used for the current scenario. For example, Scenario 1b starts with Scene 1.1a and Scenario 2c ends with Scene 2.4b. Scenes are reused across scenarios when the same decision is taken on that particular variation point. Several ways can be used to indicate the variation points and decisions in the table, such as the use of color codes and scenario names.

Quality requirements give precise definitions of the various quality attributes that play a role in the systems under development. We mainly concentrate on what a particular attribute means, rather than on the exact values that the system should satisfy. A quality requirement for the cathlab could center around the clinician's safety. An attribute could then be the total time in a procedure during which the system generates radiation while the clinician is at the patient table.

The *system context* gives an overview of the other systems that interact with the system under development and their mutual roles. For this purpose a UML deployment diagram, perhaps combined with a component diagram, is often a suitable notation. Examples of systems in the context of the cathlab are other imaging systems, or administrative workstations used for scheduling the cathlab.

Table 2. Example scenario structure

Episode 1	Scenario 1a	Scenario 1b	Scenario 1c	Scenario 1d
Navigate catheter	Scene 1.1a		Scene 1.1c	
Perform 3DRA	Scene 1.2a	Scene 1.2b		Scene 1.2d
Place stent	Scene 1.3a		Scene 1.3c	Scene 1.3d
Episode 2	**Scenario 2a**	**Scenario 2b**		**Scenario 2c**
Collect images	Scene 2.1a			Scene 2.1c
Collect data	Scene 2.2a	Scene 2.2b		
Clinical report	Scene 2.3a	Scene 2.3b		Scene 2.3c
Billing report	Scene 2.4a	Scene 2.4b		

The *workflow context* describes the flow of activities that typically goes on around the system under development. While the usage of the system under development is described in detail in the user scenarios, the workflow gives an overview that includes activities where the system under development is not directly involved. Often this overview can be kept so generic that the differences between the various user scenarios do not matter here. UML activity diagrams often form an adequate notation to express such a workflow context.

A *domain model* describes the most important concepts that play a role when talking about the system under development and its usage. Indicating the relationships between these concepts as well can provide a more thorough understanding of the concepts themselves [12]. Such a domain model can typically be expressed very well in one or more UML class diagrams.

3.3   The Functional View

This view intends to describe the externally perceivable properties of the system under development, in a concise way. Where such a property indicates the presence of a certain piece of functionality, we typically call it a feature. Where such a property is not solely about the functionality, we typically call it a quality.

The *description* (not the content) of the functional view tries to be as independent as reasonably possible from the way the system is used or the way it is implemented. In this respect, the functional view can be seen as an interface between the customer and application views on the one hand and the conceptual and realization views on the other hand.

Major questions addressed in the functional view are:

- What is the system's behavior?
- What features and what qualities does it offer?

In answering these questions, commercial considerations play an important role.

A *feature dictionary* describes the features that are of importance to the architecture in a few sentences. This enables us to use short names for them in other artifacts, like the variation model, without losing accuracy. For example, the feature 'local 3DRA' means that 3DRA functionality is integrated into the X-ray modality without the need for a separate workstation.

Quality properties give the values for the various quality attributes that the systems under development should satisfy. For example, the mean total radiation time per procedure could be set to no more than ten minutes.

A *feature/value matrix* can guide the decisions on which features should go into which system. It associates a value with each feature. It is most convenient if this value is an amount of money, and whenever this is reasonably possible this is the preferred content of the matrix. It may still be necessary to distinguish various market segments, various strategic scenarios, or other important influencing factors. In this way, the matrix looks like Table 3.

Table 3. Feature/value matrix

Scenario:	Strategic Scenario 1			Strategic Scenario 2		
Segment:	Low End	Midrange	High End	Low End	Midrange	High End
Feature 1	€ ...	€ ...	€ ...	€ ...	€ ...	€ ...
Feature 2	€ ...	€ ...	€ ...	€ ...	€ ...	€ ...
Feature 3	€ ...	€ ...	€ ...	€ ...	€ ...	€ ...
Feature 4	€ ...	€ ...	€ ...	€ ...	€ ...	€ ...

Often, however, it is not reasonably possible to give a simple number for the value of a feature. In such cases it may help to show the relationship between the features and the key customer drivers. Table 4 shows an example of this. Note that it may be useful to construct a corresponding feature/cost matrix as well. This would fit here in the functional view, even though the cost itself would be largely determined by the conceptual and realization views.

Table 4. Features/key drivers matrix

	Key driver 1	Key driver 2	Key driver 3	Key driver 4	Key driver 5	Key driver 6
Feature 1	++	+		+/-	+	-
Feature 2	+			+	+	
Feature 3	- -		+		+	
Feature 4	+	+		+/-	+	-

3.4 The Conceptual View

The goal of this view is to describe the essential concepts that govern how the system works.

Major questions addressed in the conceptual view are:

- What are the parts that comprise the system? How do these parts cooperate?
- What principles and patterns are used in the system design?

The *system decomposition* describes how a system works by showing its components and how they fit together. This can be done in a UML diagram, but a free-format boxes and lines diagram can be more expressive.

Architectural *principles* help designing an architecture by guiding the many decisions to be taken. We like the Bredemeyer approach [13], which suggests the following template for principles:

Table 5. Template for describing principles

Principle Name	*Give the principle a catchy name*
Description	*Statement of the principle*
Rationale/Benefits	*Describe the reasoning behind the principle. Where applicable, provide traceability to business or architectural objectives.*
Implications	*Identify implications such as actions that need to be undertaken, and constraints implied by the principle.*
Counterargument	*Describe a reasonable counter to this principle.*

The most surprising element is the inclusion of a counterargument. This mainly serves to exclude trivial principles. In turn, the counter itself can be represented as an architectural principle.

Mechanisms are pervasive properties of the architecture that serve to achieve certain quality properties (for example, the consistent usage of a certain design pattern). One such mechanism could be to make use a 3D graphics card for rendering in the cathlab.

A *collaboration* is a description of how a certain architecture could realize a particular use case. Because of this, collaborations form a useful tool to come from a set of scenarios to an architecture: You can start with an existing architecture or an initial best guess and then develop collaborations for the most important use cases, modifying the architecture whenever that is necessary.

Collaborations can be described using UML collaboration diagrams. Compared to their companions, the sequence diagrams, these collaboration diagrams have the advantage that they can show the underlying architecture in the same view. To emphasize this, one can also use free-format diagrams. This is especially advisable if the components do not work together in single-shot interactions, but for example by exchanging continuous data streams.

An *information model* defines the structure and meaning of information that is stored in the system and exchanged between its components. This information may be exchanged via interfaces that are specific for the particular information model (comparable to static typing in programming languages) or via generic interfaces. Especially in the latter case the information model is an essential part of the architecture description, since it cannot be derived from the interface definition. Complex systems can have more than one information model, describing the information stored or exchanged by different components in the system.

An information model should have a clear relationship to a corresponding domain model, so that the information stored and exchanged in the system has a clear relationship with the concepts that are important in the application area.

UML class diagrams are a good way to express an information model.

3.5 The Realization View

The realization view describes how the system is realized using available technologies.

Major questions addressed in the realization view are:

- What technology is used to implement the system?
- Which parts do we make ourselves and which do we buy from third parties?

The main task of the realization view is to show which parts of the conceptual architecture are realized using which technologies. This we call the *technology mapping*. A convenient way of describing this technology mapping is showing a system decomposition diagram and annotating that with the relevant technology choices. An example is the use of a Gigabit Ethernet network to connect the cathlab with external workstations.

The meaning and purpose of *mechanisms* here is the same as in the conceptual view. They are mentioned here again because often a specific choice for a technology makes it useful to describe new or more detailed mechanisms. An example of a mechanism is to use a DirectX 9.0 compliant 3D graphics card for rendering.

Conventions are rules to be followed during the implementation of the system. They serve to streamline the development process. They may or may not be observable in the end product. An example of a performance related convention is not to use malloc() statements in inner loops.

Collaboration estimations are used to find out whether a collaboration that implements a certain use case is likely to satisfy all the applicable quality requirements. Given specific technology choices, one can perform a rough estimation. For example, when in the collaboration two components exchange data using a particular interconnect, then one can estimate how long that data exchange will take on the basis of the bandwidth of the interconnect and the amount of data and compare that to the quality requirements for performance. Such estimations are never a guarantee, since there may still be bottlenecks that are not considered, but they can help to find some problems at an early stage.

Predicting the developments of technologies in the computing area is always difficult. Up to now we have been able to rely on Moore's Law, which states that computing power doubles roughly every eighteen months. Less well known are Gilder's Law [14], which says that networking bandwidth doubles every nine months, and a comparable observation saying that mass storage doubles every twelve months. However, these laws do not give precise predictions about which specific technology will be available or even prevalent in a number of years.

Developments on a short term (a few years) are often indicated in official [15] or unofficial [16] *roadmaps*. Of course, these roadmaps cannot be trusted completely. Nevertheless extracting the relevant parts of these roadmaps provides a good basis for taking technology decisions.

3.6 Cross-View Relationships

Together, the views and their artifacts sketch a more or less complete picture of the problem and solution domains. Each artifact shows the system under development from a slightly different viewpoint. The artifacts do not stand alone, but form a whole, strongly connected both across and within views. This connection is best visible in the repeating elements across artifacts of the same and different views. Examples of such repeating elements are:

- The customer drivers are reused in the quality requirements, quality properties and feature/key drivers matrix.
- The application variation model serves as a basis for the user scenario episodes.
- The user scenarios are a source of features of the functional variation model.

These are but a few examples of different artifacts explicitly reinforcing each other. A more precise description of all relationships is beyond the scope of this paper.

4 Variation Modeling

When considering various possible scenarios it is important to get an overview of the commonalities and differences not only among these scenarios, but also among the various architectural responses to the scenarios. Here the construction of a model can be of help in several ways:

1. *To structurally explore the variation space in the various views, and the relationships between them.*
   By modeling the variation space, we quickly get a feeling of the complexity and main issues in the domain. It is relatively easy to spot gaps in a model, ensuring that the variation space will be explored more thoroughly. The flipside of the coin is that models tend to get very large. It is essential to be practical in this respect and not to try to include everything in the domain.
   By using recurring elements in the models across the views, it is possible to show relationships between choices in one view and the other.
2. *To guide and document the choices that were made, as well as the options that were disregarded.*
   The resulting models can be used to guide decisions. Which features will the system have? What kinds of application will it support? These choices can be made visible in the models, e.g. by using color/grayscales or by restructuring the models, and thus serve as documentation for the decisions taken. Because the (original)

models contain the full range of possibilities considered, they also show the options that were not chosen. This can help to avoid endless reconsidering of the same options. The models do not include every detail necessary to make a decision. They are a useful tool to explore options and document decisions, but the final decision should not be based on the models alone.

3. *To enhance communication and raise awareness about these choices between the architecture's stakeholders.*
   The notations chosen for these variation models are simple enough to be understood by anyone, regardless of their professional background. This allows stakeholders other than the architect to review or even co-create the models. For the customer view, for example, marketers or sales people could cooperate.

Techniques for modeling variation have been under development in the field of product families or product lines [17,18]. However, the diversity that our approach deals with is larger, in two ways:

1. Product family development takes into account only the products that are intended to be developed. By contrast, our approach takes into account various alternatives from which only one or a few will be chosen, depending on future circumstances.
2. Most existing product family development approaches concentrate on the explicit modeling of diversity in the *features* of the products, corresponding to the functional view in CAFCR. In our approach, we propose to construct variation models for the other views as well, to get a good overview of the diversity in those views and the relationships between them. Since such an overview is useful for product families as well, we propose to follow a similar multi-view variation modeling approach for product families even without considering multiple scenarios.

We will now look at ways to model variation in each of the five CAFCR views. For explanatory purposes, we use a different order of views than is usual. The models presented here were simplified for the purpose of this publication.

4.1 Functional View

The functional variation model gives an overview of all relevant features. In designing a system or system family, this model is typically used to make and document the final decision on which features should be included by the system or systems. The features that are excluded in this decision can be disregarded and possibly even removed from the model. However, in our scenario approach, which aims at assessing and improving the future-proofness of architectures, we can only remove features that are not necessary for any of the scenarios that we consider likely.

As a starting point for this model, we chose to take one of the best approaches developed for describing feature variation in product families, which is described by Ferber et al. [19]. This approach makes use of two models in conjunction: A tree model, giving the main structure of the feature variation, and a dependency model, which can express additional constraints that cut across the tree model.

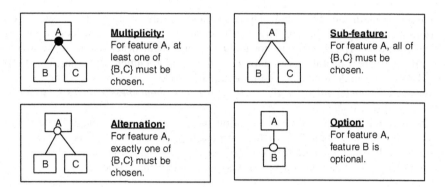

Fig. 6. Variation model notation for tree models [19]

In our own approach, we can use this notation largely unchanged for the variation model of the functional view, since that is what it was developed for originally. Figure 6 gives an explanation of the notation for the tree model. We generalized the tree to a directed acyclic graph, so that different parents can share a subgraph. In our case study there was no need for a separate dependency model once we did this.

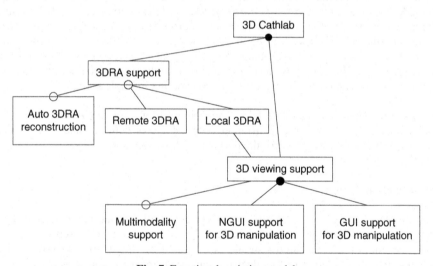

Fig. 7. Functional variation model

The variation model for the functional view is shown in Figure 7. This is an acyclic graph, directed top-down. It shows the possible features of the 3D cathlab and how we can choose between them. The remainder of this section explains the nodes of this graph and their relationships.

The 3D cathlab should either support generating 3D images, viewing them or both. Generating 3D images is done through 3DRA support. Optionally, the cathlab could have an 'auto 3DRA reconstruction' feature, which is a workflow enhancement.

The 3DRA functionality can be offered by a separate workstation (remote 3DRA) or it can be built into the X-ray equipment (local 3DRA). If a separate 3DRA workstation is used, the viewing of 3DRA images can be performed on this workstation. If 3DRA is available locally, the cathlab must have 3D viewing support.

3D viewing support is also obligatory if there is no support for 3DRA. Multimodality support means that the cathlab can handle 3D images from modalities other than X-ray (e.g. magnetic resonance imaging). It is optional, and without it only 3D images are supported, possibly generated by other 3D cathlabs. Either or both of the features 'NGUI support' or 'GUI support for 3D viewing' must be implemented. NGUI support means that the cathlab has some sort of non-graphical user interface to support 3D viewing.

4.2 Conceptual View

For the conceptual view, the same notation can be used, but the concept of "feature" must be interpreted more broadly. The conceptual variation model consists largely of "internal features". Such an internal feature is a property of the system that cannot be observed from the system's behavior alone, but refers to the way the system is designed. Typically such an internal feature concerns the incorporation of a design concept in the system. Some "real" features, which occur in the functional view variation model, can also turn up here, typically at the top of a subtree that describes the possible implementations of such a feature in terms of internal features.

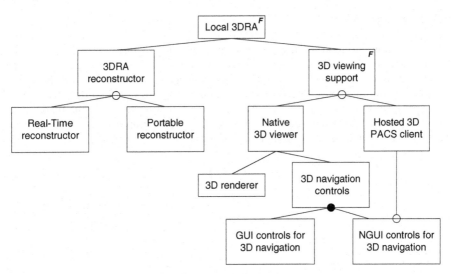

Fig. 8. Conceptual variation model

The relationship between different views is typically expressed by a feature in a preceding view becoming the root of a subgraph in a subsequent view, which explores possible ways of implementing this feature. The variation model for the conceptual view, shown in Figure 8, indicates how the features from the functional view could be implemented by architectural concepts. Such "functional features" are marked with an 'F'. This model has a treeform with nodes located above their subtrees. We will traverse the nodes of this tree depth-first, from left to right, explaining the relationships.

To implement the feature 'local 3DRA', we need both a 3DRA reconstructor and 3D viewing support. The latter relationship is also part of the functional variation model.

A reconstructor has the task to use many parts of two-dimensional X-ray data to calculate a three-dimensional model. This can be done by a real-time reconstructor, specialized for this type of X-ray equipment, or a slower, but portable reconstructor can be used. This indicates a trade-off between performance and reusability.

The '3D viewing support' feature is taken from the functional variation model. It can be implemented in two ways: by a native 3D viewer or by a hosted 3D PACS client.

A native viewer is dedicated to the cathlab environment. It needs a 3D renderer to visualize the 3D images, as well as some sort of 3D navigation controls to enable the user to manipulate the models. In turn, these controls could be implemented as software (GUI controls for 3D navigation) or in hardware (NGUI controls for 3D navigation). The latter also appears as a feature in the functional variation model.

A Picture Archiving and Communication System (PACS) supports the long time storing and viewing of medical images. Typically, such a system has client software for viewing all kinds of medical data, including three-dimensional models. The 3D viewing feature could be implemented by hosting such a PACS client on the X-ray equipment. As such a client would have its own GUI controls, providing a non-graphical interface is optional.

4.3 Realization View

The realization variation model again contains "internal features". The same notation can be used for the realization view. Again, a realization feature is a possible choice in the realization view. Internal features at the conceptual level are indicated by a 'C'.

In the variation model (Figure 9) we see different ways to map the architectural concepts from the conceptual view onto available technology. Again, the model has a tree-form, although it could become an a-cyclic directed graph should the need arise. We will traverse the tree and explain the nodes and their relationships.

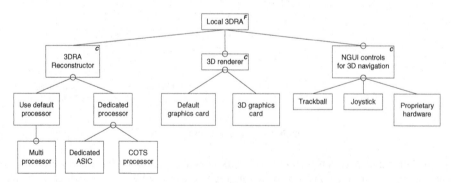

Fig. 9. Realization variation model

As the letters 'F' and 'C' indicate, some features were taken from the functional and conceptual variation models. We abbreviated the relationships between these features in this model for clarity and simplicity.

In this model, we concentrate on the 'local 3DRA' feature, which was introduced in the functional variation model. It has three sub-features, each coming from the conceptual view: 3DRA reconstructor, 3D renderer and NGUI controls for 3D navigation.

There are two main choices for the 3DRA reconstructor in this view. It could run on a processor already present in the cathlab system, or it could have a dedicated processor, for which we have the choice between an ASIC and a commercially available (COTS) processor. Optionally, the cathlab could be equipped with a multiprocessor to enhance the 3D reconstruction. We stop detailing here to prevent the model from growing too much. A realistic model could include details such as specific types of processors.

To implement the 3D renderer, we have two options: either to use a default graphics already present in the system, or to use a specialized 3D graphics card.

To support local 3DA, non-graphical controls could be used (NGUI controls for 3D navigation). Such controls could have the form of a trackball, or a joystick, or some other form of proprietary hardware could be used.

4.4 Application View

Building an application variation model is difficult. A moderately complex, but well-engineered system can typically be used in a large number of different ways. If we also want to model the variation allowed by a number of architectural variants of such a system, the resulting variation is extremely large. This variation stems from a number of different sources:

- Variation in properties (features) among the architectural variants.
- Variation in the (technical) context of the system.
- Variation in the business goals and practical purposes of using the system.
- Variation in personal preferences among users.

Capturing all these variations in a single model is impossible in most cases. Therefore it can be a good idea to build smaller models around the issues that are most difficult to decide on. Often it is useful to build mixed models, where variation points in the application view are related to variation points in the other views (usually customer and functional view).

The application variation model contains actions, not features. Therefore we use rounded rectangles, corresponding to the UML notation for activities [20]. We also do not limit ourselves to a tree but use a directed acyclic graph. Arrowheads are omitted, as all relations are directed top-down. Note that this model is not a workflow model: It does not express the order of activities, but only whether a particular activity is or is not performed.

The variety of procedures performed in a cathlab is very large. Even our full case study model does not cover all possible variation. Here, in Figure 10, we show a small model with possible subactivities of a particular medical procedure.

Angioplasty is a procedure where a tiny balloon is placed at the tip of a catheter. It is navigated to a blocked artery and then inflated to widen the blockage and restore local blood flow. To prevent the artery from closing again, a wire mesh tube called a *stent* may be left behind in the artery. It is necessary to perform some measurements on the blockage, to determine the correct width and length of the stent.

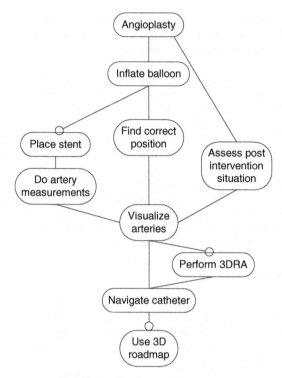

Fig. 10. Application variation model

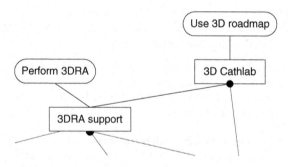

Fig. 11. Adding application elements (actions) to the functional variation model

To find the correct position of such a balloon or stent, it is necessary to visualize the surrounding arteries and assess their situation. This is done using X-ray equipment and a catheter, as described in Section 2. Navigation of the catheter can optionally be done using a 3D roadmap. Such a roadmap could result from an earlier diagnostic procedure, or constructed during this procedure using 3DRA. Note that, in order to perform 3DRA, it is also necessary to navigate the catheter.

After the ballooning, the new situation is assessed by visualizing the arteries again.

Having explained application view variation modeling, we are able to make the relationship with the functional variation model explicit. Figure 11 shows a small part of that model, together with the activities that especially concern the 3D support in the cathlab. The use of a 3D roadmap is supported by the 3D cathlab. To be able to perform 3DRA, the cathlab must have support for it.

It is not necessary to use letters to distinguish activities from features, because of the different forms of the nodes.

4.5 Customer View

At the very least, a customer variation model should express the basic market segmentation that underlies the design of the product portfolio. Other differences among the customers are also useful, especially if they might have consequences for the system under development.

For this model, we are confronted with new phenomena: On the one hand, we encounter unbounded variation, for example in the number of cathlabs an organization may own, or in the languages that are used. On the other hand, we see that certain choices for a variation point are actually special cases of more general choices, for example, specialized cardiac care as a special case of cardiac care. Adapting the notation of [19] to deal with these phenomena would inevitably make the notation of more complex, endangering our goal of enhanced communication. Instead, we propose to express the customer variation model in a UML class diagram, a notation that enables us to express everything we need. Although the UML itself is complex in its size, class diagrams form a relatively small part of the language and we limit ourselves to the main concepts of those. Such use of class diagrams does stretch the meaning of the UML a little.

The variation model for the Customer view is shown in Figure 12. We have identified the cardiology department as our customer. The cardiologist, although an important user and stakeholder, does not make the decision to buy a cathlab. That decision is (usually) made on departmental level. The influence that the cardiologist has on this decision should be expressed in the customer drivers diagram.

This model places the cardiology department in the center, with the variation points around it. UML stereotypes are used to indicate the customer and the variation points. In this model, there are three ways of specifying the choices that can be made at a variation point: by cardinality, by instantiation, or both.

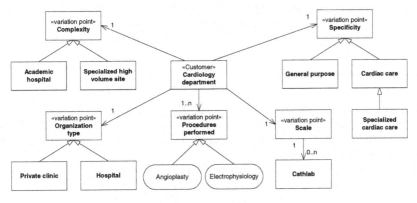

Fig. 12. Customer variation model

Complexity, organization type, specificity, and procedures performed belong to the group of variation points that use instantiation. A choice is made by choosing a specific subclass of the variation point. As can be seen at 'specificity', this instantiation can be nested. A cardiology department could be either general purpose, or provide cardiac care only. In the latter case, it could be specialized.

Cardinality is used by 'scale', and 'procedures performed'. In this context, scale means the number of cathlabs that a cardiology department owns. Procedures performed means the number of different procedures, as well as which procedures. Note that the possible choices for this variation point have a different shape: They are activities that also occur in the application variation model.

5   Conclusions

During the long life of a system architecture, invariably new requirements will come up. Since it is not possible to predict these requirements upfront, we use scenarios to describe a spectrum of possible futures that affect the architecture. The paper shows our approach to analyze the consequences of such alternative scenarios, using multi-view variation modeling. However, the approach to multi-view variation modeling is also useful for product family development without considering multiple scenarios.

Not only can these variation models express the variation in the various views, but they can also show the relationships between the views. In particular, they can show how choices in one view influence choices in the other view. The importance of keeping track of the relationships between multiple architecture views has been explained in [21].

The mutual relationships between these models can be indicated by common elements (e.g., features from the functional model that also occur in the conceptual variation model). While constructing a variation model for our customer view we encountered new phenomena, not covered by existing techniques to model variation.

When constructing these models for realistic architectures, they tend to become very large. More research is needed to find ways to deal with the size and complexity of such large models.

Armed with a technique for modeling variation across multiple views, we can now tackle various scenarios and analyze their impact on the architecture of our product family. We hope to publish more about this soon.

Acknowledgements

We thank our colleagues Cristian Huiban and Eugene Ivanov of the Scenario-Based Architecting project, Jürgen Müller, Nico Schellingerhout and Peter van den Hamer who reviewed an early version of this paper, and many other people at Philips Research and Philips Medical Systems.

This work was carried out in the European ITEA project Café.

References

1. Save Time and Lives with a Faster, Smarter 3D-RA. *WWW*, Philips Medical Systems, November 2002. http://www.medical.philips.com/main/news/theme/3dra/3dra.pdf
2. Pierre America, Henk Obbink, Rob van Ommering, and Frank van der Linden: CoPAM: A Component-Oriented Platform Architecting Method Family for Product Family Engineering. In: Patrick Donohoe, ed.: *Software Product Lines: Experience and Research Directions, Proceedings of the First Software Product Lines Conference (SPLC1)*, Denver, Colorado, August 28-31, 2000, Kluwer, p. 167-180.
3. Henk Obbink, Jürgen K. Müller, Pierre America, Rob van Ommering, Gerrit Muller, William van der Sterren, and Jan Gerben Wijnstra: COPA: A Component-Oriented Platform Architecting Method for Families of Software-Intensive Electronic Products. Tutorial for SPLC1, the First Software Product Line Conference, Denver, Colorado, August 2000. http://www.extra.research.philips.com/SAE/COPA/COPA_Tutorial.pdf
4. Ivar Jacobson, Grady Booch, and James Rumbaugh: *The Unified Software Development Process*. Addison-Wesley, 1998.
5. Ruth Malan and Dana Bredemeyer: The Visual Architecting Process. *White paper*, February 2002. http://www.bredemeyer.com/pdf_files/VisualArchitectingProcess.PDF
6. Christine Hofmeister, Robert Nord, and Dilip Soni: *Applied Software Architecture*. Addison-Wesley, 1999.
7. Philippe Kruchten: *The Rational Unified Process, an Introduction*. Addison-Wesley, 1999.
8. Kent Beck: *Test-Driven Development: By Example*. Addison-Wesley, The Addison-Wesley Signature Series 2003.
9. Gerald Weinberg: *Systems Thinking*. Dorset House, Quality Software Management New York, 1992.
10. Philip Kotler: *Marketing Management*. Prentice Hall, 11th edition, 2002.
11. Alistair Cockburn: *Writing Effective Use Cases*. Addison-Wesley, The Crystal Collection for Software Professionals 2001.
12. Pierre America and Jan van Wijgerden: Requirements Modeling for Families of Complex Systems. In: Frank van der Linden, ed.: *IW-SAPF 3: Third International Workshop on Software Architecture for Product Families*, Las Palmas de Gran Canaria, Spain, March 15-17, 2000, Springer, LNCS Vol. 1951, p. 199-209.
13. Dana Bredemeyer: Software Architecture Workshop. 2002. www.bredemeyer.com
14. George Gilder: *Telecosm: The World After Bandwidth Abundance*. Touchstone, 2002.
15. Intel Processor Roadmap. *WWW*, 2003. http://www.intel.com/products/roadmap/
16. Endian.net roadmap. *WWW*, 2003. http://endian.net/roadmap.asp
17. Frank van der Linden, ed.: *Software Product-Family Engineering. 4th International Workshop PFE 2001*, Bilbao, Spain, October 3-5, 2001, Springer, LNCS Vol. 2290.
18. Gary J. Chastek, ed.: *Software Product Lines: Second International Conference (SPLC2)*, San Diego, California, August 19-22, 2002, Springer, LNCS Vol. 2379.
19. Stefan Ferber, Jürgen Haag, and Juha Savolainen: Feature Interaction an Dependencies: Modeling Features for Reengineering a Legacy Product Line. In: Gary J. Chastek, ed.: *Software Product Lines: Second International Conference (SPLC2)*, San Diego, California, August 19-22, 2002, Springer, LNCS Vol. 2379, p. 235-256.
20. Grady Booch, James Rumbaugh, and Ivar Jacobson: *The Unified Modeling Language User Guide*. Addison-Wesley, 1998.
21. Gerrit Muller, Jürgen K. Müller, and Jan Gerben Wijnstra: Multi-View Architecting. White paper, Philips Research, March 2003. http://www.extra.research.philips.com/natlab/sysarch/IntegratingCAFCRPaper.pdf

A Meta-model for Representing Variability in Product Family Development

Felix Bachmann[1], Michael Goedicke[2], Julio Leite[3], Robert Nord[1],
Klaus Pohl [2], Balasubramaniam Ramesh[4], and Alexander Vilbig[5]

[1] Software Engineering Institute
{fb,rn}@sei.cmu.edu
[2] University of Duisburg-Essen
goedicke@informatik.uniessen.de
[3] University of Toronto
jcl@cs.toronto.edu
[4] Georgia StateUniversity
bramesh@gsu.edu
[5] Technical University of Munich
vilbig@in.tum.de

Introduction

Effective product family based development depends on exploiting the commonality and variability in customer requirements. The desirability of variability in products is driven by the (manifest and hidden) needs of the various target market segments identified by various organizational units like sales and marketing. These are informed by other critical components of the context in which product families are developed including the technological capabilities, people/human resources available with the organization, the policies and procedures of the organization, and the strategic objective of the organization. Variability Management is seen as the key aspect that differentiates conventional software engineering and software product line engineering [Kruger 02]. Variability in a product family is defined as a measure of how members of a family may differ from each other [WeissLai 99]. Variability is made explicit using variation points. Variation points are places in design artifacts where a specific decision has been narrowed to several options but the option to be chosen for a particular system has been left open [Atkinson 01]. Identification of the points of variability is crucial in proliferating variety from a single product platform. A central component of product family approach is the management of variability. The product family development process involves managing variations among different members of the family by identifying common and variable aspects in the domain under consideration.

The need to explicitly represent variability to facilitate their identification and exploitation has been recognized by recent research. Various extensions to UML (Unified Modeling Language) have been proposed to tailor it to represent variability [Clauss 01]. This work suggests a first-class representation of variability with its own properties and interfaces. Svahnberg and Bosch [Svahnberg 00] discuss several issues related to implementation of variability, viz., the level of abstraction in which variability has to be introduced and the different possible states of variation points. Feature-based recognition of variability, proposed by Lee et al [Lee 12], suggests that

F. van der Linden (Ed.): PFE 2003, LNCS 3014, pp. 66–80, 2004.
© Springer-Verlag Berlin Heidelberg 2004

variability should be analyzed in terms of product features. The explicit representation of variability in various phases of the product development process including requirements engineering, architecture description, implementation, as well as mechanisms needed to facilitate the systematic exploitation of variability during product derivation have been suggested by such recent literature. However, there been have no attempts to provide a uniform representation of variability across various phases of the process. Our research proposes to fulfill this void.

In contrast to prior research (discussed in detail in Section 4), which has developed representations of variability within the context of specific product development activities such as architecture specifications, we argue for a uniform representation of variation across various activities where variability is introduced and exercised. This approach will also help understand and model the dependencies between variability introduced at different phases. A major goal of this approach is to separate out the representation of variability from the representation of various assets developed in the product development lifecycle while maintaining the traceability between them.

A Conceptual Model of Variation

It is widely recognized that the complexity of current software development justifies the simultaneous use of several models to specify and communicate characteristic views or aspects of a software system with regard to the involved stakeholders of the development process. For example, a requirements model based on features or use cases describes a high-level, user-oriented view on system functionality, while architecture and component models focus on system structure and interaction from a more technical, design-oriented point of view. Consequently, in the development of a product family which comprises a number of related software systems according to carefully managed variations and choices, it is necessary to introduce a dedicated model of variation which captures these important engineering decisions, their effects on other development assets, as well as the dependencies between them.

Figure 1 presents our initial proposal for such a model of variation in product line development as an UML class diagram, focusing on the fundamental concepts and their relations on a fairly high level of abstraction. In this model, a **Variation Point** represents an explicit engineering decision to allow for several alternative **Variants** with regard to selected **Assets** of system development. Depending on the nature of these assets as constituents of other development views (see below), a variation point describes the choice between a number of functional features available to the user, different structures and interaction patterns in the product line architecture, or alternative software components in product implementation, for example. Although this choice is not necessarily exclusive, i.e. it is well possible to choose several of the available variants at once, each unique selection will ultimately lead to a distinguished product of the overall product family. Moreover, a given variation point or variant may depend on other, possibly previous decisions which enable or restrict the available alternatives. Given a proper semantics for interpretation of the model, it is conceivable to refine the general **depends-on** relation to a number of more specific relations like **requires**, **ensures**, or **excludes**.

In addition to these fundamental relations between variation points, variants, and assets, the proposed model introduces a number of concepts and associations which

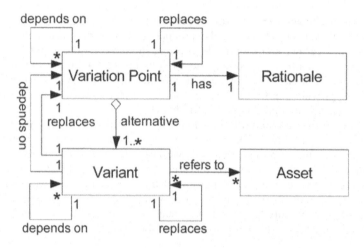

Fig. 1. Variation Model

appear useful in the methodical application of variation engineering in product line development: Rationale captures the original intent and motivation to define a variation point, providing valuable background information to the application engineer who actually selects particular variants for the product in question. In effect, this concept may be regarded as an extension point of the model which allows including further information like time of variation point introduction, responsible actor, or visibility to other roles in the development process. A similar motivation to include process-related information in the model is exemplified by the relation replaces in Figure 1. It represents the fact that variation points and variants are subject to a development process of their own, with constant elaboration and modification of intermediate results. The mentioned relation represents this particular development history, recording relations to earlier versions of variation points which are no longer relevant due to later refinement in this part of the model. This approach is somewhat similar to configuration management, albeit on a more specific, model-related level.

Because of the importance of variations in product line development, we propose to consider the contents of a variation model as a separate, dedicated view on a system which interacts with all other well-known views like requirements, architecture, or implementation. Figure 2 illustrates this approach of multiple views in system development, emphasizing the fact that a given variation point may influence a number of different views according to the nature of the assets to which its variants refer. Consequently, it is only natural to gather this information in a separate view of the system, thereby reducing the overall complexity of each individual view. By this, we avoid the introduction of non-standard extensions to existing description techniques. It is also the case that, as such, we motivate variation as a first-class subject. With more experience in explicit treatment of variation, better description techniques for this particular development view are to be expected in the future, leading to further refinements, clarifications, and improvements to the conceptual model presented in this section. From the complexity of the description techniques hinted at in Figure 2, it is also obvious that proper tool support is essential to cope with systems of realistic size in industry.

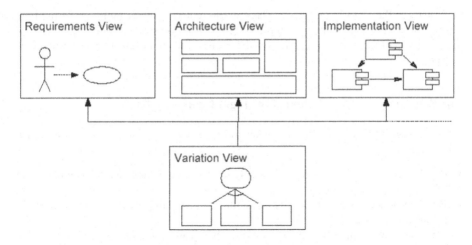

Fig. 2. Multiple Views in Product Line Development

To further clarify the proposed approach, it is helpful to consider the relation between the notion of an asset and an artifact. We understand assets (cf. Figure 1) as a package of relevant artifacts that provide a solution to a given problem. Assets can be of different granularity, may allow different degrees of customization (or variability), and can be applied (or targeted) at different phases of software development. On the other hand, an asset constitutes a reusable software artifact in itself, and as such it may be employed in different stages of software development and their respective views. Of course, in an actual application of this concept, it is necessary to provide a rigorously controlled mapping between assets linked to a variant and their related artifacts in different system views.

In order to motivate and illustrate our proposal, we proceed to apply the abstract model of variation to a concise application example in Section 3.

The Sample System: A Version of the Light Control System

We illustrate the explicit representation of variation points and variants as first class objects using a simplified example of a home automation domain (light control). Starting with the variability of the light control system defined during the requirements engineering phase, we discuss and illustrate the changes (evolution) of the variability of the light system based on architectural and implementation decisions.

Note, that the aim of the example is to show the explicit representation of the variation points and their variants across the different development phases, i.e. on the introduction of a phase-spanning variability viewpoint. Moreover, the focus is on the illustration of the capabilities of the variability viewpoint in terms of selective retrieval of affected development assets in each development phases. The focus of the example is not on the development process itself.

In our example, we assume a light control system with a single light source controlled either via a local control panel locally and/or a remote control system. The local control panel does need not be in the same room as the light source, but it must be at least in the vicinity (e.g. somewhere in the rented space or building) of the light source. In contrast, the remote control system can be outside the building, i.e. some kind of network is assumed to transmit the desired information between the involved components.

The Requirements Specification of the Light Control System

The light control system is defined by several requirements. The ones relevant for our example are:

- R1: The light control system has a single light source, which can be switched on or off
- R2: The actual status of the light system (light on; light off) is displayed at the controlling device
- R3: The system can have either a local control panel for switching the light on/off and for displaying the actual status, or a remote control panel or both
- R4: The system should be available in a dependable and non-dependable version. The non-dependable version should report the actual status of the light based on the light on/off function, the dependable version should include a mechanism, which ensures that the reported status reflects "reality" – i.e. the dependable version should be more reliable wrt. the light system's feedback of the actual light status.

Note, that there are many variants to make the report of the actual light status more dependable. Since those variants are heavily influenced by the overall chosen architecture, we assume that those variants are discussed during the architectural phase (of course with all stakeholders, including the users).

As indicated by the requirements above, there are two variation points:

- V1: local and/or remote control.
- V2: dependable or non-dependable light status indicator

Figure 3 depicts these variation points (triangle) and their variants (oval).

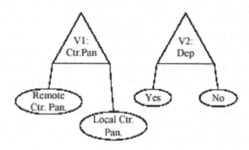

Fig. 3. The two variation points and their variants defined during the Requirements stage

Towards Realisation: The System Architecture

Let us assume that for the light control system, a coarse grained architecture was derived as depicted in Figure 4. The blocks depicted denote software components with export and import interfaces, the arrows denote actual use relationships between components. The architecture consists of a central component "control" with its used components "Light source" and "access". The component "Light source" offers operations to switch the light on and off. The "access" component facilitates the access of the user to the system and maintains the light status (similar to an on/off button). It further controls the light indicator, which displays the light status (on/off) to the user.

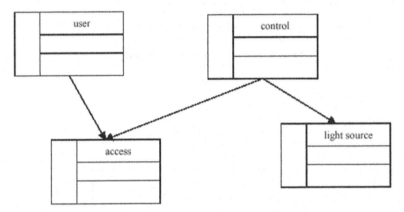

Fig. 4. The coarse grained Architecture of the Light Control System

During the design of the system various possibilities where discussed (also with the end users) and – among others – the following design decisions have been made:

- Remote Access: The remote access to the system should be realized via a WEB-Interface
- Dependability: Four decisions about the dependability of the system have been made
  o Redundant light sensors should be included by the system, which allow a dependable feedback if the light is actually on. Those sensors should be placed close to the light source. This facilitates that the system does not report a "light on"-status if the light source is malfunctioning for some reason (e.g. broken or missing light bulb).
  o The remote access to the system should be secure.
  o The system should be available with secure remote access and/or redundant light sensors.
  o Other aspects of dependability like broken light sensor wires or systematic sensor failure should not be considered.

Given the above decisions the variation points and the variants model has to be adapted. The resulting changes are depicted in Figure 5: a) the variant "remote control panel" was refined into a variant "remote control via Web-Interface and b) the variants "dependable light sensors" and "dependable Web" for the variation point "Dependability" have been introduced. Besides these changes in the variation viewpoint (see Figure 3) the design decision, of course, leads to a refinement of the architecture. This refinement is depicted in Figure 6.

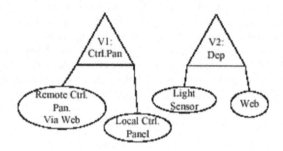

Fig. 5. The "refined" variability model

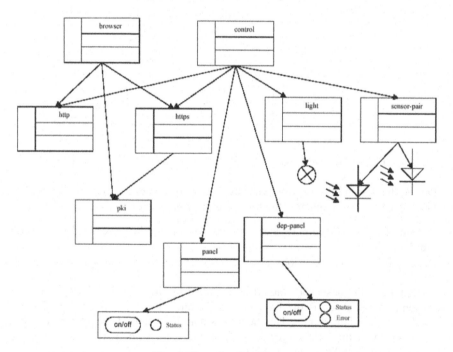

Fig. 6. The refined architecture

On the left hand side of Figure 6, the remote control access via Web is depicted. For the non-dependable Web-Interface, the component "browser" uses the "http" component. For the dependable Web-Interface, the components "https" and "pki" have been introduced to ensure the secure information transfer via the "un-secure" web. Moreover, the architecture now differentiates between a control panel for the non-dependable system and a control panel for the dependable system. The main difference between the two control panels is the indication of an error in the system, indicated via an error control light. Finally, the component light source has been refined into a component "light" (which controls the light source) and a component "sensors-pair" which controls the light sensor pair.

Based on the interrelations between the variation viewpoint and the development assets (see Section 2) we are now able to use the variability model to highlight the architectural components affected by a chosen variation. For example, in Figure 7, the choice of "remote control via Web" and the "dependable Web" have been made in the variability viewpoint. As a consequence, the effected architectural components "pki" and "https" and their connections are highlighted.

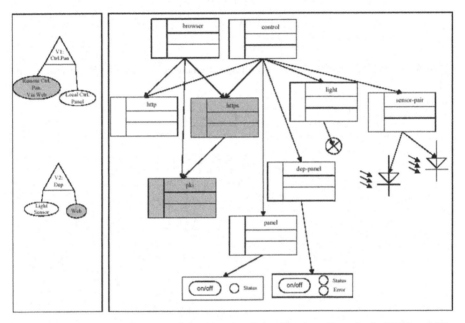

Fig. 7. Architectural components effected by the choice "Remote Control via Web" and "Dependable Web"

Similarly, we would be able to highlight the requirements influenced by a particular "binding" of the variation points. Moreover, we could highlight the variation points and the variants which effect a given design component. For example, for the sensor-pair component, the variation point V2 and V3 and the variants Light sensor would be highlighted.

Implementation Stage: More Variants

At the implementation stage an additional choice is made available to the user of the system. Here the set of products covered contains a choice to use a "fat" pc with a normal browser and a small device like a PDA, which has only a limited set of resources available to realize the remote access via http or https. This is shown in an additional variation point structure in the figure below:

The variation point RAC relates to AC in the remote variant of AC and LAC relates to the local variant of the AC variant, which remains the same as above.

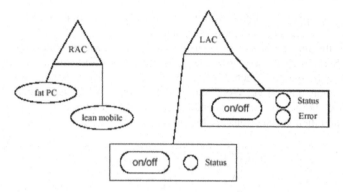

Fig. 8. Additional implementation variants allowing remote access via a fat PC or lean mobile device

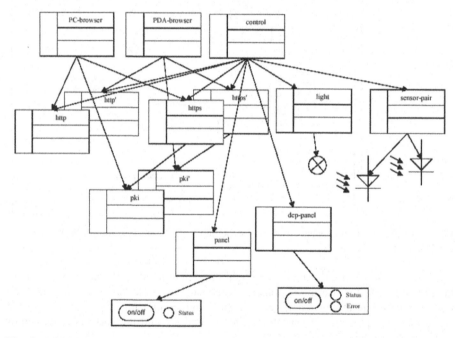

Fig. 9. Additional components (http', https', pki') are introduced at implementation level to accommodate a fat pc and lean mobile

In Figure 9 the aforementioned variation regarding the remote access device (pc or mobile) is covered by introducing additional components. The primed components (http', https', etc.) are introduced to accommodate the additional variation by using a lean platform.

One can see easily that the overall architectural picture gets quite complicated and the additional information contained in the variation point structure facilitates the distinction of the variants. Thus in a similar way as we saw in Figure 13 the various choices can be expressed in high lighting components and related connections be-

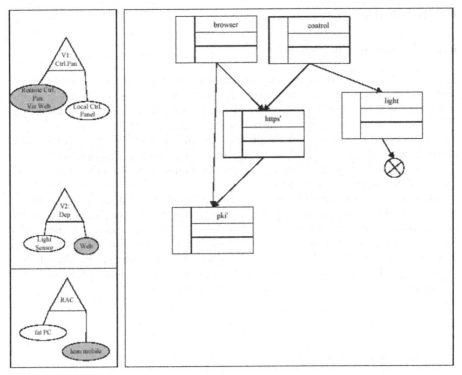

Fig. 10. Introducing additional choices at the implementation level in addition to fig. 7

tween them. In Figure 10 we depicted the additional choice – in addition to the choices high lighted in Figure 7 – that a lean mobile device is used to implement the remote secure access as the only means to control the light system.

In order to show the benefit gained by the proposed approach we removed here all components from the system, which are not needed according to the choices made by selecting certain variants from the variation point structure. Here we control the system by lean mobile and we have secure access via the web.

This limited example shall suffice to show the benefits to maintain the variation point structure as an additional view for the structures describing the desired system at the various development stages. The variation point structure is also instrumental in showing the dependencies and space of variants in the discussions with the stakeholders and potential users of the systems.

In addition the notation sketched here can easily be extended to cover more aspects. In particular choices, which exclude or necessitate each other, can be made explicit. Also cardinalities can be added in the style known from class or ER-diagrams.

Related Work

Reusable Asset Specification (RAS)

The RAS Consortium is an industry association with the objective of enabling the supply, management and consumption of reusable software assets. The business objective of the RAS consortium is to define an industry standard for the identification, management and consumption of reusable software assets [RAS].

RAS defines assets as a package of relevant artifacts that provide a solution to a problem. Besides the artifacts, an asset also includes further descriptions, such as overview, classification, solution, and usage (see Figure 11). This description is provided to make an asset more reusable.

Assets can be of different granularity, may allow different degrees of customization (or variability), and can be applied (or targeted) at different phases of software development. In this context an artifact is defined as: "…any item that is input to or output from the software development process, or tools, etc." [RAS]. Artifacts can contain variability points (Figure 12), which are locations that may be altered, customized, modified, or supplied by an artifact consumer. A variability point can define the artifact's variability at design time, code time, and run time.

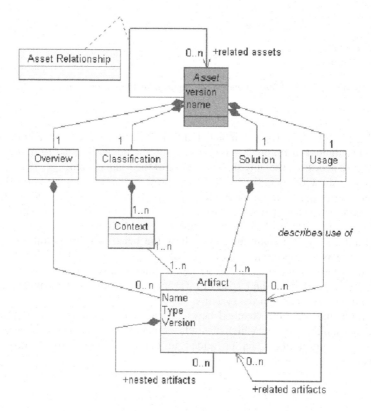

Fig. 11. Meta-model of Asset

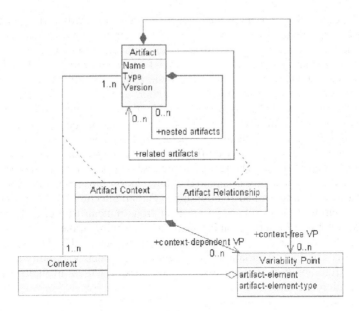

Fig. 12. Meta-model of Artifact

Compared with our model, the RAS model describes how a variant can be created from an asset by changing locations in artifacts specified by variability points. This feature is not included in our model. In RAS, there is no concept of variation points to group assets, belonging to the same decision, together as it is presented in our model. RAS assumes that this relationship is described by a relationship between either artifacts (see related artifacts relation) or assets (see related assets relation).

Product Line Variability

Steffen Thiel and Andreas Hein at the Robert Bosch Corporation present a model for product line variability [Thiel 02a,b]. They extend the ANSI/IEEE 1471 [IEEE 00] recommended practice for architectural description to address the needs for documenting product lines by introducing extensions to model variability in features and in the architecture. Features are organized into a feature model. The feature model describes functional and nonfunctional requirements of the members or the product line. The feature model structures the requirements into a tree that shows common and variable features for the product line variants and a network that places constraints on what combinations are possible. The details are not part of the model but the reader is referred to models such as FORM [Kang 98] where common and variable features are identified and classified. These models describe variability through optional, alternative, and "or" features.

The architectural variability model is described by architectural variation points. Architectural variability represents alternative design options that are not bound during the modeling of the product line architecture. Variation points are explicitly modeled in the architecture description and related to architectural design elements. Architectural variation points show the architecture solution to variable features. Variation points are specified by a variation point specification that records variability information such as dependency (among variation points), binding time (when the decision has to be made), resolution rules (to resolve a variation), and rationale.

Compared to our model, the Bosch model focuses on variation of architecture. Well understood models of features are recognized and the relationship between requirements and architecture is shown. The authors recognize the need to relate the model to other work products required for product line development and acknowledge that variation does exist in other assets. However models for code assets and the relationship of these assets to architecture are not explicitly shown.

The Bosch model introduces two different models to represent variation in features and variation in architecture. The feature model uses one kind of node to represent the asset (i.e., feature). Variability is captured in the relationships among the nodes and in the properties of the nodes and relationships. The architecture model introduces the notion of a variation point related to an asset (requirement/feature, architecture design). It does not make a separation between the description of the variation (variation point), the choices (variants), and asset as we do in our model. The Bosch model places other constraints on variation not present in our model. Variability is defined in terms of configurability (variation in space) and doesn't address evolution or modifiability (variation over time).

Variability in Product Families

Martin Becker presents a general model of variability in a product family [Becker 03]. A distinction is made between variability at the specification level and the realization level. At the specification level the main modeling concept is the variable feature. This includes information about dependencies and binding time. The notion of a profile is introduced to specify a member of the product family. It tracks the variability-related decisions that were taken to configure a member of the product family. At the realization level, a variation point designates where the variability is realized, at least partially.

Like the Bosch work, this model focuses on variation at the architecture level and the relationships between variability at the specification level and the realization level. Two different models are used to represent variability at the specification and realization levels. Variability and variants appear at the specification level. The notions of variation point, mechanism, and associated assets are restricted to the realization level.

Abstraction Levels

Jilles van Gurp, Jan Bosch, and Mikael Svahnberg posit that variability can be associated with different "abstraction levels" a system undergoes in development (from requirement specification to running code) [van Gurp 01]. They introduce a terminology for describing variability in terms of variation points and variants. Variation points can be characterized as being in one of three states: implicit, designed, or bound. Furthermore a distinction is made between the set of variants associated with a variation point as being open to extension or closed. Variants occur in one of three patterns: single variant, optional variant, and multiple parallel variants.

The authors then focus on features as a useful abstraction for describing variability. This takes the form of a tree structure that makes distinctions among mandatory features, optional features, variant features, and external features. This feature graph is used to express variability that is then mapped to software artifacts in other levels of abstraction in the development process.

Frame of Reference for Variability

Michel Jahring and Jan Bosch suggest a representation and normalization of variability as a step towards creating a frame of reference [Jahring 02]. Variability mechanisms are classified and represented according to the introduction and the binding of variation points. The need for tool support to manage the great number of variation points, the associated variants with their dependencies is emphasized. Variability is discussed for the typical software artifacts created during the traditional software development lifecycle, such as requirements, architecture, design, implementation, etc. A case study of a mobile communication system based on the TETRA standard is included to discuss various aspects of variability.

Jahring and Bosch follow the notion of variation points and variants as represented by our model. However, the need for keeping binding time flexible requires explicit introduction of classes of variability mechanisms that binds variation points to artifacts, which is not represented in our model.

A Variation Point Model

Diana L Webber and Hassan Gomaa suggest a variation point model that: a) visualizes variation points, b) adds a variation point view to requirements and reference architecture, and c) uses UML with extension to model variation points in design. Three types of variation points, used in a design, are presented: inheritance, parameterization, and call back. An example, were a variation point is introduced by requirements and bound by using architectural mechanisms, is presented.

Compared with our model where variation points can be bound to any artifact, this is a very limited view because a variation point can only be bound in the architecture. Using an extension of UML to represent variation points is not explicitly discussed in our model.

Conclusions

We have proposed a uniform representation of variation across various activities where variability is introduced and exercised in the product line development process. This approach explicitly represents the dependencies between variability introduced at different phases. The key issue is the separation of the representation of variability from the representation of the various assets developed in the product development lifecycle.

Factoring out the variability makes it possible to focus just on the variation issue, providing a simple and clean representation to support the management of the product lines. Of course, for this strategy to work properly there should be a solid platform for handling configuration management issues, which we believe will be exacerbated by the factoring out of variability. Managing the traces to and from the artifacts to the variation point is a complex task, which needs a solid configuration management support.

We believe that the benefits of factoring out variability outweigh the problems it may bring in terms of handling complexity. With the proper infrastructure, our approach seeks to facilitate the maintenance of traceability between various assets.

References

[IEEE 00] IEEE Product No.: SH94869-TBR: Recommended Practice for Architectural Description of Software-Intensive Systems. IEEE Standard No. 1471-2000.

[RAS] Reusable Asset Specification, Rational website,
http://www.rational.com/rda/consortium.jsp

[Becker 03] M. Becker. Towards a General Model of Variability in Product Families. In: Proceedings of the Software Variability Management Workshop. 2003. University of Groningen, Groningen, The Netherlands.

[Jahring 02] M. Jaring and J. Bosch, Representing Variability in Software Product Lines: A Case Study, Proceedings of the Second Software Product Line Conference (SPLC2), pp. 15-36, August 2002.

[Kang 98] Kang, K.C., et al., FORM: A feature-oriented reuse method with domain-specific reference architectures. Annals of Software Engineering, 1998. 5(1-4): p. 26.

[Jacobson 97] Jacobson, I., Griss, M., Jonsson, P., Software Reuse-Architecture, Process and Organization for Business Success. ACM Press, New York, NY, 1997

[Thiel 02a] Modeling and Using Product Line Variability in Automotive Systems, Steffen Thiel and Andreas Hein, IEEE Software July/August 2002, p. 66ff

[Thiel 02b] Thiel, S. and A. Hein, Systematic Integration of Variability into Product Line Architecture Design. Lecture notes in computer science, 2002(2379): p. 130-153.

[van Gurp 01] J. van Gurp, J. Bosch, and M. Svahnberg. On the Notion of Variability in Software Product Lines. In: Proceedings of the Working IEEE/IFIP Conference on Software Architecture (WICSA 2001). 2001.

[Webber 02] Modeling Variability with the Variability model Diana L. Webber and Hassan Gomaa LNCS 2319, p. 109 ff Springer-Verlag 2002

[Kruger 02] Krueger, Charles W. (2002). "Variation Management for Software Product Lines". The Second Product Line Conference (SPLC 2), San Diego, CA, USA.

[WeissLai 99] Weiss, David M. and Chi Tau Robert Lai (1999). "Software Product-Line Engineering: A Family-based Software Development Process". Reading, MA, Addison-Wesley.

[Atkinson 01] Atkinson, Colin, Joachim Bayer, Christian Bunse, Erik Kamsties, Oliver Laitenberger, Roland Laqua, Dirk Muthig, Barbara Paech, Jurgen Wust and Jorg Zettel (2001). "Component-Based Product Line Engineering with UML", Addison-Wesley Pub Co.

[Clauss 01] Clauss, Matthias (2001). "Generic Modeling using UML Extensions for Variability". Workshop on Domain Specific Visual Languages: An OOPSLA 2001 Workshop, Tampa Bay, Florida.

[Svahnberg 00] Svahnberg, Mikael and Jan Bosch (2000). "Issues Concerning Variability in Software Product Lines". Proceedings of the Third International Workshop on Software Architectures for Product Families, Berlin, Germany, Springer Verlag.

[Lee 12] Kwanwoo Lee, Kyo C. Kang, and Jaejoon Lee (2002), Concepts and Guidelines of Feature Modeling for Product Line Software Engineering, In Proceedings of the Second International Conference, SPLC 2, San Diego, CA, USA, August 19-22, 2002.

Variability Dependencies
in Product Family Engineering

Michel Jaring and Jan Bosch

University of Groningen
Department of Mathematics and Computing Science
PO Box 800, 9700 AV Groningen, The Netherlands
{Jaring,Bosch}@cs.rug.nl
http://www.cs.rug.nl/Research/SE

Abstract. In a product family context, software architects anticipate product diversification and design architectures that support variants in both space (multiple contexts) and time (changing contexts). Product diversification is based on the concept of variability: a single architecture and a set of components support a family of products. Software product families need to support increasing amounts of variability, leading to a situation where variability dependencies become of primary concern. This paper discusses (1) a taxonomy of variability dependencies and (2) a case study in designing a program monitor and exception handler for a legacy system. The study shows that the types of variability dependencies in a system depend on how the system is designed and architected.

1 Introduction

Composing software products from software components is not a recent concept. Early work on software components already appeared three and a half decades ago [1], followed by the idea to develop so-called program families [2]. This has evolved into practical software engineering approaches that share the ability to promote software reuse across many products. An example of software reuse in practice is the successful adoption of software product families in industry. The goal of the software product family approach is the systematic reuse of core artifacts for building related software products. A software product family typically consists of a product family architecture, a set of components and a set of products. Each product derives its architecture from the product family architecture, instantiates and configures a subset of the product family components and usually contains some product specific code [3].

When developing a software product family, software architects try to prepare the family architecture for different product contexts, i.e., they prepare the architecture to support product diversification. Product diversification is based on the concept of variability and appears in all family artifacts where the behavior of an artifact can be changed, adapted or extended. Examples of variability are a configuration wizard to select the language or a license key entered by the customer to enable (or disable) particular functionality. Variability is implemented by delaying design decisions to a specific moment in the software development process, i.e., variant selection is delayed until a particular development or deployment phase such as implementation or run-time

F. van der Linden (Ed.): PFE 2003, LNCS 3014, pp. 81–97, 2004.
© Springer-Verlag Berlin Heidelberg 2004

is reached. A typical example of a delayed design decision is a software system that
dynamically adapts its run-time behavior relevant to its environment by either selecting
embedded alternatives or by binding modules. The software architecture of such a system
is dynamic, i.e., it is neither static during development nor at run-time. Dynamic software
architectures [4] are an extreme form of variability, i.e., it is not possible to delay design
decisions beyond run-time. Even a conditional expression is sometimes considered as
a form of variability, meaning that virtually all software architectures exhibit a certain
amount of dynamic behavior.

1.1   Variation Points

So-called variation points have been introduced in [5] and are often used to express
variability. A variation point refers to one or more delayed design decisions, has as an
associated set of variants and indicates a specific moment in the development process. A
typical example of a variation point is the preprocessor directive shown in Fig. 1. In this
example, the variation point provides a choice in software operation mode, the available
variants are embedded and simulation mode and the actual selection of a variant is
delayed until the source code is compiled. In other words, the design decision 'operation
mode' is not taken prior to compilation, meaning that the consequences of this decision
should not affect the development phases prior to compilation.

```
#define EMBEDDED /* SIMULATION */

#ifdef SIMULATION
        #include <stdio.h>
#endif

#ifdef EMBEDDED
        #include <drivers.h>
#endif
```

Fig. 1. Variation point for selecting either embedded or simulation mode during compile-time:
simulation mode does not require hardware drivers, but standard I/O instead

Starting system development from scratch means that any system can be built. As
also discussed in [6] and [7], all design decisions are still open, but they are not left
open deliberately. In other words, they do not refer to a particular variation point and
are therefore implicit. Design decisions become explicit in the development process
when the corresponding variation point (or points) is identified, i.e., when it is taken
into account that different variants may occur. Once a variation point is identified, it
is an unbound state, meaning that a specific variant for this variation point has not yet
been selected from the set of variants associated with this point. The variation point is
bound as soon as a variant is selected and incorporated into the system. This means that
a variation point is in one of the following states:

- Implicit: the design decision is not deliberately left open.
- Explicit: the design is decision is deliberately left open:

- Unbound: no variant has been selected from the set of variants associated with the variation point, i.e., the design decision is open until it binds a variant.
- Bound: a particular variant is selected from the set of variants associated with the variation point and incorporated into the system, i.e., the design decision is final.

The set of variants associated with a given variation point defines the type of this variation point:

- Open variation point: the set of variants can be extended.
- Closed variation point: the set of variants can not be extended.

1.2   Lifecycle

A software system is the result of a number of development and deployment phases. Each phase relates to its own representation, e.g., requirement collection relates to requirement specification, whereas implementation relates to source code. As shown in Fig. 2, software development consists of transformations of these representations and each phase is considered as a different abstraction level of the system. Design decisions are taken during each transformation, but some of these decisions are deliberately left open (delayed) to support variability. A variation point is made explicit (introduced) at a particular phase and bound at this phase or after this phase in the software lifecycle. The arrows are unidirectional in Fig. 2, but traversing back and forth through the phases is common in case of iterative software development.

In relation to Fig. 1, the choice for embedded or simulation mode is taken during compile-time (binding the variation point), but was already taken into account before compilation during, e.g., the architectural process (introduction of an unbound variation point). This implies that both modes have to be taken into account between the moment of introducing and binding this variation point, meaning that a variation point is often not related to one particular lifecycle phase such as architecture or design, but to a combination of phases instead.

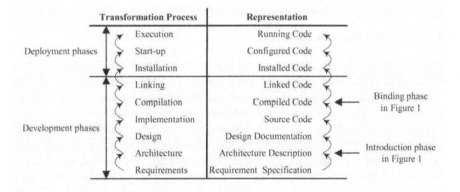

Fig. 2. Transformation processes and their representation in the software lifecycle

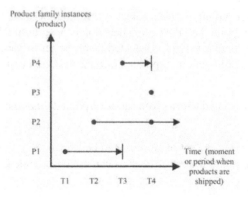

Fig. 3. Software product family: product diversification in space and time

1.3 Product Diversification

There are two relatively independent development cycles in software product family engineering, viz. domain and application engineering. Domain engineering is responsible for the design, development and evolution of the reusable artifacts, i.e., the product family architecture and shared components. Application engineering, on the other hand, is about adapting the product family architecture to the architecture of the required product. In other words, domain engineering *prepares* for product diversification and application engineering is the *act* of product diversification itself.

In a successful product family, the family architecture typically provides a firm basis for product diversification in two dimensions, viz. space and time. Being able to derive products in both space and time is one of the main goals, if not the main goal in product family engineering. The space dimension is concerned with software artifacts in multiple contexts at a given moment in time, whereas the time dimension is concerned with software artifacts in a given context over a period of time. For example, in Fig. 3, product P1 is instantiated at time T1 and exists during T1, T2 and T3, whereas P2 is re-instantiated at T4 to, e.g., replace a component with an improved version of this component.

1.4 Variability Dependencies

Modern software needs to support increasing amounts of variability. The reason for this is threefold. Firstly, variability is transferred from mechanics and hardware to software. For example, a dedicated feedback control unit implemented in hardware is replaced with a real-time software component that is selected from a set of components implementing different types of feedback controllers. Secondly, software introduces functionality that was not available before. For example, small-sized mobile phones are only possible with software, i.e., software provides new and more functionality 'per cubic centimeter' than other techniques such as dedicated hardware. Thirdly, there is a trend to delay design decisions to the latest moment in the lifecycle that is still economically feasible. For example, software systems adapt themselves to a changing environment using expert systems for selecting the appropriate components at run-time, i.e., variation points are bound just before certain functionality is required. The increasing amount of variability leads to a situation where variability engineering becomes of primary concern in software development. The number of variation points for industrial product families may range in the thousands, which is already a challenging number to manage, but the number of variability dependencies typically has an exponential relationship to the number of variation points, meaning that it is impossible to manage variability without systematic approaches. Implicit dependencies erode the architecture, making it harder to modify the system, but it also complicates the product derivation process, i.e., how to determine whether a particular product configuration is possible if the variability dependencies are not known?

1.5   Outline

This paper presents our research in progress. The next section discusses a taxonomy of variability dependencies. The taxonomy is used in a case study in designing a program monitor and exception handler for a legacy system in section 3. The study shows that the types of variability dependencies in a system depend on how the system is designed and architected. Future and related work is surveyed in section 4 and 5, respectively. The paper is concluded in section 6.

2   A Taxonomy of Variability Dependencies

We detail a case study of a large-scale product family of Magnetic Resonance Imaging (MRI) scanners developed by Philips Medical Systems in [8]. The study illustrates how variability can be made an integral part of system development at different levels of abstraction and identifies several research questions. This section focuses on one of these questions: *what types of variability dependencies exist?*

2.1   System Variability

Software product family engineering is characterized by two main types of development, i.e., development with an embedded and development with a non-embedded perspective. Embedded software is used to control electronic products not normally identified as computers, meaning that it usually executes on an internal microcontroller or a Digital Signal Processor (DSP) to control other product components. Typically, such software must be extremely reliable, very efficient, compact, and precise in its handling of the rapid and unpredictable timing of inputs and outputs. Non-embedded software, on the other hand, is intended to run on a separate computer, often a personal computer or work station, and may be used to enhance the operation of another device or devices. One of the main differences between embedded and non-embedded software is the hardware, i.e., as opposed to non-embedded software, embedded software is typically (very) hardware dependent.

It is sometimes argued that there is no actual distinction between embedded and non-embedded software. From a theoretical viewpoint, two alternative programs and the hardware they run on can easily be equivalent, even if one appears to be embedded and the other does not. This may be true in theory, but it generally does not hold in practice.

For example, the display size of mobile phones in pixels depends on the manufacturer and sometimes even varies within a particular product family. The different display sizes are hardware variants and each variants requires a specific display driver. In other words, the software is either dedicated to a specific display size or incorporates a variation point that supports different display sizes in the form of variants, i.e., these two alternatives are not equivalent.

Product families are often embedded systems that strongly depend on hardware, but this is hardly addressed in presentations of ideal applications. Due to dependencies between soft- and hardware, the concept of software reuse in an embedded system typically overestimates the flexibility of software. Supporting the differences in hardware is called the hardware challenge in [9].

In academia, system development is often considered as being independent from the hardware, i.e., the software does not have to take the hardware into account. However, organizations that develop complex systems tend to use a more generalized approach, i.e., system development comprises both soft- and hardware aspects. The reuse infrastructure in a product family may consist of only software or a combination of soft- and hardware. This is also the approach taken by the CAFÉ project (from Concept to Application in system-Family Engineering), i.e., the focus is on software, but in a soft- and hardware context. The main goal of the CAFÉ project is the development of procedures and methods for introducing product families into the development of software-intensive systems with a focus on organization and business concerns. See [10] for more information on the CAFÉ project.

As detailed in [8], we have identified (at least) two types of *software* variability in relation to the *hardware* configuration of a system:

- Hardware neutral variability: software variability independent from the hardware configuration, e.g., multiple language support in a mobile phone.
- Hardware enforced variability:
  - Software variability that depends on the hardware configuration, e.g., text output formatting depending on the display size.
  - Software variability that is required to enable the hardware configuration, e.g., display drivers.

Literature on variability most often refers to hardware neutral variability, i.e., it generally assumes that variability originates from software and not from the combination of soft- and hardware. We refer to variability as the *combination of hardware neutral and hardware enforced variability*, i.e., system variability.

2.2 Describing Variability

Binding a variation point involves establishing a relationship between the variation point and the selected variant. This relationship may imply certain dependencies (constraints), e.g., a system generally requires that specific variation points are bound to have a working, minimal system. There can be many different types of dependencies and pinpointing them requires a more formal way to describe variability. We use a notation that has many characteristics of a constraint specification language. Constraint specification languages have been developed outside the immediate software engineering research community such as the Configuration Management (CM) community and have been used in practice for several decades now. Please note that we are trying to pinpoint the different types of variability dependencies and that we use a constraint specification language as a tool to prevent ambiguities. In other words, it is a means and not a goal in itself. The following nomenclature aims for describing variability in system-independent terms, i.e., independent from a particular system, method or organization:

- The set of all variation points: $VP = \{vp_a, vp_b, vp_c, \ldots\}$
- The set of variants for vp_x: $vp_x = \{v_{x1}, v_{x2}, v_{x3}, \ldots\}$
- The power set (the set of subsets) of all variants:
  $V = \{\{v_{a1}, v_{a2}, v_{a3}, \ldots\}, \{v_{b1}, v_{b2}, v_{b3}, \ldots\}, \{v_{c1}, v_{c2}, v_{c3}, \ldots\}, \ldots\}$
- A relationship between vp_x and v_{xn}, i.e., vp_x binds v_{xn}: (vp_x, v_{xn})

The dependencies between variation points and variants can be expressed in the form of conditional expressions:

- if vp_x is bound then vp_y should be bound: **if** vp_x **then** vp_y
- if vp_x is bound then vp_y should bind v_{yn}: **if** vp_x **then** (vp_y, v_{yn})
- if vp_x binds v_{xn} then vp_y should be bound: **if** (vp_x, v_{xn}) **then** vp_y
- if vp_x binds v_{xn} then vp_y should bind v_{ym}: **if** (vp_x, v_{xn}) **then** (vp_y, v_{ym})

Dependencies may involve negation, meaning that the condition and expression of the **if-then** statement can exclude variation points or variants from binding. For example, if vp_x binds v_{xn} then vp_y should <u>not</u> bind $v_y m$ is expressed as **if** (vp_x, v_{xn}) **then** $\neg(vp_y, v_{ym})$. A relationship between a variation point and a variant may impose dependencies on other variation points and variants. For example, if vp_x is bound then <u>both</u> vp_y <u>and</u> vp_z should also be bound is expressed as **if** vp_x **then** $(vp_y \wedge vp_z)$. Similarly, if vp_x is bound then <u>or</u> vp_y <u>or</u> vp_z should be bound is expressed as **if** vp_x **then** $(vp_y \vee vp_z)$, i.e., it is an XOR operation[1].

2.3 Taxonomy

Binding (or not binding) a variation point generally imposes dependencies on other variation points and variants. As listed in Table 1, we have identified four main types of variability dependencies, each of which consisting of four subtypes. Each type has specific characteristics, i.e., a dependency between variation points has consequences that are different from a dependency between variants. In accordance with the concept of system variability, the taxonomy relates to both hardware neutral and hardware enforced variability, e.g., binding a *hardware* variant may impose dependencies on a *software* variation point. Please note that binding a variation point is not a dependency, but a relationship that may impose or is subject to dependencies instead.

The taxonomy shows sixteen different subtypes of variability. These subtypes may explain why dependencies often exhibit different kinds of behavior while appearing similar in the first instance. An important 'source' of implicit dependencies is underestimating the complexity of dependencies associated with apparently simple variation. As we argued in [11], this is often due to a lacking representation of variability dependencies.

---

[1] It can be argued that the OR operation should also be part of the nomenclature.

Table 1. Taxonomy of variability dependencies

Type	Description	Subtypes
I	Dependencies between variation points vp_x and vp_y	**if** vp_x **then** vp_y **if** vp_x **then** $\neg vp_y$ **if** $\neg vp_x$ **then** vp_y **if** $\neg vp_x$ **then** $\neg vp_y$
II	Dependencies between variation point vp_x and variant v_{yn}	**if** vp_x **then** (vp_y, v_{yn}) **if** vp_x **then** $\neg(vp_y, v_{yn})$ **if** $\neg vp_x$ **then** (vp_y, v_{yn}) **if** $\neg vp_x$ **then** $\neg(vp_y, v_{yn})$
III	Dependencies between variant v_{xn} and variation point vp_y	**if** (vp_x, v_{xn}) **then** vp_y **if** (vp_x, v_{xn}) **then** $\neg vp_y$ **if** $\neg(vp_x, v_{xn})$ **then** vp_y **if** $\neg(vp_x, v_{xn})$ **then** $\neg vp_y$
IV	Dependencies between variants v_{xn} and v_{ym}	**if** (vp_x, v_{xn}) **then** (vp_y, v_{ym}) **if** (vp_x, v_{xn}) **then** $\neg(vp_y, v_{ym})$ **if** $\neg(vp_x, v_{xn})$ **then** (vp_y, v_{ym}) **if** $\neg(vp_x, v_{xn})$ **then** $\neg(vp_y, v_{ym})$

We conducted a case study in designing a component for a legacy system. The study shows that the types of variability dependencies in a system depend on how the system is designed and architected. We describe the variability in constraint specification language style and use the taxonomy to pinpoint the type of dependency that characterizes the reuse infrastructure of this component.

3 Case Study: Sophalgo Data Systems

We outlined a generic program monitor and exception handler for (very) resource critical applications in cooperation with Sophalgo Data Systems. Examples of such applications are a dedicated component that synchronizes the processes that run in a real-time environment on a multitude of PowerPCs and on-the-fly data monitoring of data streams to trace anomalies such as a control unit that suddenly operates outside its bounds. The requirements were available in casual format, which we have adapted slightly to aid the reader's understanding. Interestingly, we have underestimated the complexity of this problem in the first instance, particularly the number of implied requirements and dependencies.

3.1 Requirements

The Program Monitor and Exception Handler (PMEH) consists of two parts, viz. the monitor and the handler. The program monitor traces program flow (procedure call tree) and resource usage, i.e., space (memory) and time (CPU ticks). The exception handler takes control of system program flow in case of unexpected situations or erroneous conditions. If an exception is raised, control is given to the handler, which then can undertake (recovery) actions. When the handler is finished, the program continues at a predetermined location or terminates. Programming languages like C do not have exception handling mechanisms, meaning that exceptions are handled through special error codes or by calling library routines. As shown in Fig. 4, the PMEH is to be integrated into a legacy software system written in C or C++ without changing existing functionality.

```
void legacy(int y)
{
    PMEH(..., func_id, nr_ticks, mem_size, ...);
    PMEH(..., y, ...); /* pre-condition check */
    /* legacy */
    PMEH(..., y, ...); /* post-condition check */
    PMEH(..., func_id, nr_ticks, mem_size, ...);
}
```

Fig. 4. Exception handling with the PMEH in a C legacy system

Program Monitor. The PMEH traces program flow by logging the following program monitor data in an output file PMEH_output.txt at the beginning and end of every procedure:

- Procedure name;
- Number of CPU ticks since program invocation;
- Size of allocated program memory;
- Descriptor to indicate entering or leaving the procedure.

Exception Handler. The PMEH is also used to check the pre- and post-conditions of the procedure arguments. The following exception handler data is logged in PMEH_output.txt at the beginning and end of every procedure:

- Variable name;
- Variable value;
- Non-critical system variables are checked against a minimum and maximum values that are passed with the PMEH call;
- System critical variables are checked against a list available to the PMEH for minimum and maximum values. This list also includes preferred value ranges for normal operation.

In case of a false pre- or post-condition, the PMEH decides on the progress of the program to handle the unexpected situation. Exception information is written in PMEH_output.txt. The PMEH may take one or more of the following actions:

- Cancel current input vector;
- Skip all input vectors;
- Clear memory data space, backtrack to one step before the exception and copy preferred values into the data space;
- Terminate program (emergency exit).

Additional Information. The exception handler detects erroneous input and is essential for preventing system failure. System failure includes both soft- and hardware aspects, e.g., mechanical damage of physical machine components that operate in the micrometer range due to faulty software parameters. The program monitor, on the other hand, is used for debugging purposes, but can not prevent system failure. Disabling (parts of) the PMEH is necessary for research and testing purposes. The exception handler is mandatory and the program monitor is strongly preferred for normal operation. The PMEH itself is resource intensive and constrains the operating range of the system.

3.2 Variability Analysis

As shown in Fig. 5, two variation points have been identified by analyzing the requirements, viz. the Program Monitor (PM) and the Exception Handler (EH). Each point has one variant, the actual program monitor and exception handler, respectively. This first analysis resulted in the following definition for the PMEH:

- $PMEH \equiv VP = \{PM, EH\}$
- $PM = \{PM\}$
- $EH = \{EH\}$

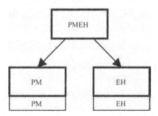

Fig. 5. First analysis: Program Monitor and Exception Handler (PMEH). PM: Program Monitor. EH: Exception Handler

As obvious as this first analysis may seem, it does not meet the requirements. For example, during normal operation the exception handler has to be available, but this is not addressed in the analysis. To complicate matters, this condition does not concur with the requirement that the PMEH can be (partly) turned on or off for research and testing purposes. Such conflicting requirements are common in variability engineering, but simple solutions like Fig. 5 are often used as a basis for implementation. Needless to say, if the PMEH would have been implemented according to this first analysis, the result would be several implicit variability dependencies at best. Summarizing, research and testing mode is without additional conditions, but normal operation also requires:

- The program monitor is strongly preferred: $PM = $ **true**
- The exception handler is mandatory: $EH = $ **true**

Another requirement for the exception handler reads clear memory data space, backtrack to one step before the exception and copy preferred values into the data space. This is core functionality of the exception handler, but it implies that backtrack information is available. After consulting the main architect it became clear that the program monitor provides this information, meaning that if the exception handler is mandatory, then so is the program monitor. This would result in one single variation point that has the entire PMEH as the only possible option. However, this was considered unacceptable by the architect, because such 'dominant' variation points that do not allow for selecting particular pieces of functionality undermine system flexibility. A solution was found by not identifying program monitor and exception handler variants, but feedback and feedforward variants instead. The feedback variant does not affect system program flow, as opposed to the feedforward variant. In other words, by looking at the PMEH *from the perspective of the system it has to interact with*, feedback and feedforward are the main actions. Consulting the architect also revealed an additional requirement. To increase system reliability, a valid product configuration should bind all variation points. This means that all points have to be considered during the configuration process, i.e., the product derivation process becomes more deliberate. This (new) requirement is met by adding the empty variant to each variant set in the PMEH. As shown in Fig. 6, the analysis now identifies a system (PMEH) and a subsystem level (FB and FF), meaning that the PMEH can be a system level variation point without taking the specifics of the program monitor and exception handler into account.

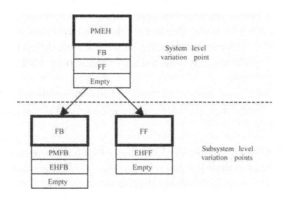

Fig. 6. Second analysis: Program Monitor and Exception Handler (PMEH). FB: Feedback. FF: Feedforward. PMFB: Program Monitor Feedback. EHFB: Exception Handler Feedback. EHFF: Exception Handler Feedforward

Additional dependencies for <u>normal mode</u> are:

- The PMEH has to be bound with a non-empty variant:
$(PMEH, Empty) = $ **false**
- The program monitor is strongly preferred:
if $\neg(PMEH, Empty)$ **then** $(FB, PMFB)$
- The exception handler is mandatory:
if $\neg(PMEH, Empty)$ **then** $((FB, EHFB) \wedge (FF, EHFF))$

The notation shows that variation point PMEH has two variants (FB and FF) that both have to be bound in case of normal mode. Variation point FB is subject to a similar condition. Such discrepancies are easy to find with the proper tools and although tooling is not necessary at the moment, for large-scale software systems computerized analysis of the dependencies is an absolute must. The results of the final analysis is shown in Fig. 7 and abstract the feedback and feedforward variants:

- $VP = \{PMEH, PMFB, EHFB, EHFF\}$
- $PMEH = \{FB, FF, Empty\}$
- $PMFB = \{PMFB, Empty\}$
- $EHFB = \{EHFB, Empty\}$
- $EHFF = \{EHFF, Empty\}$

Dependencies for <u>normal mode</u>:

- $(PMEH, FF) = \textbf{true}$
- **if** $(PMEH, FF)$ **then** $((PMFB, PMFB) \wedge (EHFB, EHFB)$
  $\wedge (EHFF, EHFF))$

Dependencies for <u>research and testing mode</u>:

- **if** $(PMEH, FF)$ **then** $((PMFB, PMFB) \wedge (EHFB, EHFB)$
  $\wedge (EHFF, EHFF))$

The feedforward option requires both the program monitor and exception handler, which concurs with normal mode. Please note that the dependencies are virtually the same for both normal and research and testing mode. The only difference is the condition that the feedforward option has to be selected for variation point PMEH in normal mode, i.e., $(PMEH, FF) = \textbf{true}$.

As said, a valid product configuration should bind all variation points to ensure all points will be considered during the configuration process. This results in the following additional dependencies:

- **if** $\neg(PMEH, FB) \wedge \neg(PMEH, FF)$ **then** $(PMEH, Empty)$
- **if** $(PMEH, Empty)$ **then** $((PMFB, Empty) \wedge (EHFB, Empty)$
  $\wedge (EHFF, Empty))$

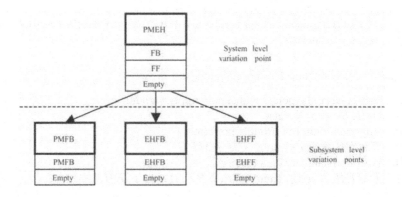

Fig. 7. Third analysis: Program Monitor and Exception Handler (PMEH). FB: Feedback. FF: Feedforward. PMFB: Program Monitor Feedback. EHFF: Exception Handler Feedforward

3.3 Dependency Types

Although relatively small, the case study is a good example of the complexity that comes with variation. Solutions often appear as 'obvious', but may have hidden aspects that are important for preventing implicit dependencies. Taking Table 1 into account, the type of variability dependency found in the PMEH is of type IV (first subtype), i.e., **if** (vp_x, v_{xn}) **then** (vp_y, v_{ym}). In other words, the PMEH is characterized by dependencies between variants, i.e., dependencies are not at the more abstracted level of variation points, but at the level of specific variants. This means that introducing a new variant does not just require re-analyzing the consequences for just one variation point, it requires re-analyzing the consequences for *all* variants in the PMEH. Having dependencies at the variant level is the result of dividing the PMEH into a system and subsystem level, i.e., dependencies have been moved away from the (legacy) system into the PMEH. The PMEH architecture, design and implementation are the *result* of identifying the variation points and variants together with their relationships and dependencies. The PMEH is in the process of being implemented according to our analysis and documented for internal use.

In conclusion, this case study shows that the types of variability dependencies in a system depend on how the system is designed and architected.

4 Future Work

When conducting our case studies [8][11], we found that variability is often addressed in a consistent and reproducible way in industry. However, we also observed that systems are sometimes architected for the consequences of variability at a specific development phase, but not always for the concept itself throughout the system lifecycle. This is perhaps due to the various areas of expertise such as electronics, physics, computing science, management etc. of the people involved in variability engineering. It seems that each area of expertise has a focus on one or several lifecycle phases, but not on the lifecycle as a whole. Interestingly, the variability questions that arise in industry tend to be independent of the areas of expertise. Examples of such questions are:

- What are the technical and business consequences of having dependencies?
- How to document variability, particularly in legacy systems?
- What is considered good practice in product family engineering, to focus on product derivation or product diversification? Is there a real difference?
- What types of variability dependencies exist?
- Except for the number of dependencies in a system, is it also important to limit the number of dependency types?
- What can we learn from the configuration management community?

The following research questions require further work if we assume that a constraint specification language is used to define and describe variability dependencies:

- Following Parnas' arguments for tabular notations [12], is a constraint specification language in a tabular notation a good way to express variability?
- Taking the different moments of introducing and binding a variant into account, are there concerns that require the use of temporal logic operators?

– How to check the consistency of the dependency expressions?
– Is a constraint specification language scaleable?
– How to enforce the expressions of a constraint specification language in everyday software engineering?

We are currently applying the taxonomy of variability dependencies to the Enterprise Resource Planning (ERP) software of Baan Company. ERP stands for any integrated multi-module application software that helps performing business transactions. The size of the ERP code base is over 5000 kilo lines of code. Once we have pinpointed the different types of variability dependencies in the ERP system and assuming the taxonomy suffices, we want to investigate if different types of variability have a different impact on the system in terms of product configuration and verification abilities. Product configuration is about composing a product, whereas verification is about determining if a particular product configuration is possible.

5   Related Work

Software reuse has been a long standing ambition in the software engineering community, dating back to the late 1960s [1] and 1970s [2]. Particularly the object-oriented paradigm became popular during the 1980s and led to object-oriented frameworks. These frameworks evolved in several directions, one of which software product families. The notion of software product families has received considerable attention in both research and industry since the 1990s. European projects such as ARES, PRAISE, ESAPS and CAFÉ, the software product line initiative at the Software Engineering Institute (SEI) [13] and the first conferences in the field such as [14] have paved the way for accepting the software product family concept in main stream software engineering. For example, methods with a focus on software product family engineering such as the Family-oriented Abstraction, Specification and Translation (FAST) process presented in [15] have found their way to industry.

Product family engineering is based on product diversification, i.e., it is based on the concept of variability: a single architecture and a set of components support a family of products. Variability is often expressed in terms of variation points, which notion has been introduced in [5] as part of the reuse process. Several variability mechanisms are discussed in [16]. This book also discusses how design decisions remove variability from an architecture. Patterns are used to model variability in software product families in [17], but it has a distinct focus on the design phase and not on the software lifecycle as a whole. Design patterns are elements of reusable software and discussed in detail in [18]. A domain-independent model of software system design and construction is presented in [19]. The model is based on interchangeable software components (variants) and aims for large-scale reuse.

Features have been suggested in [5] as a useful abstraction to describe variability. Features apply to both the space and time dimension and are defined as follows. A feature is a logical unit of behavior that is specified by a set of functional and quality requirements [3]. The underlying idea is that a feature groups related requirements, meaning that features abstract from requirements. Features can be seen as incremental units of development [20], meaning that they do not relate to a single development phase, but to a number of transformation processes instead. A feature that depends on other features is a so-called crosscutting feature. Crosscutting features make it difficult to properly implement variability and once more illustrate the need for a systematic and reproducible approach to software system design. A categorization of features, among which variant features, is suggested in [21]. A variant feature is an abstraction for a set of related features and is either optional or mandatory, e.g., in Figure 1, the variant features are embedded and simulation mode.

The number of variation points in industrial product families may range in the thousands and the number of variability dependencies typically has an exponential relationship to the number of variation points, meaning that it is virtually impossible to manage variability without systematic approaches. As pointed out in [22], higher level abstraction and parameterization techniques are not well-suited for dealing with ah hoc variation of features found in different members of a product family. Managing variability requires a scalable approach with the ability to represent the reuse infrastructure. Examples of such approaches are Koala [23] and the Building Block Method [24], which both have been developed in industry with scalability in mind.

An interesting approach towards product line engineering is the Software Product Line Integrated Technology (SPLIT) method [25]. It is a global framework that helps defining and building software product lines and uses a decision model for selecting variation points. It is focused on domain engineering and developed in cooperation with industry. A systematic approach to integrating variability with product line architecture design is presented in [26]. This approach, as in accordance with our own findings, assumes that variability is the basis of architecting a system family.

The notion of variability is also explored in the Configuration Management (CM) community. CM is a discipline that oversees the entire lifecycle of a product family. As discussed in, e.g., [27], CM requires identification of the components to be controlled and the structure of the product, control over changes to the components, accurate and complete record keeping and a mechanism to audit or verify any actions. As argued in [28], the definition should be broadened to include manufacturing issues, process management and team work. Another definition is given in [29]: CM is a discipline whose goal is to control changes to large software system families through the functions of component identification, change tracking, version selection and baselining, software manufacture and managing simultaneous updates.

6   Conclusions

This paper discusses (1) a taxonomy of variability dependencies and (2) a case study in designing a program monitor and exception handler for a legacy system.

6.1   Taxonomy

System variability is a generalization of hardware neutral and hardware enforced variability, i.e., variation points and variants appear in both soft- and hardware and may depend on each other regardless of their origin. Binding a variation point means establishing a *relationship* between the variation point and a variant. This relationship may impose *dependencies* (constraints) on other variation points and variants. Trying to answer the question what types of variability dependencies exist?, this paper discusses a taxonomy of variability dependencies. The taxonomy identifies four main types of variability dependencies, each of which consisting of four subtypes. These sixteen subtypes may explain why dependencies often exhibit different kinds of behavior while appearing similar in the first instance. The constraints imposed by each type have been explored in various areas of research, e.g., the configuration management community, but are sometimes implicit in product family development.

6.2   Case Study

The case study outlines a generic program monitor and exception handler in a resource critical legacy environment. The study shows that the types of variability dependencies in a system depend on how the system is designed and architected. It also shows that apparently simple system requirements can entail complicated, in the first instance unforeseen variability relationships and dependencies. The variability relationships and dependencies have been derived from the requirements using a formal approach to ensure all dependencies are found. The PMEH dependencies are between variants, i.e., introducing a new variant does not just require re-analyzing the consequences for a single variation point, it requires re-analyzing the consequences for *all* variants. The PMEH architecture, design and implementation are the *result* of identifying the variation points and variants together with their relationships and dependencies.

References

1. McIlroy, M.D.: Mass Produced Software Components. NATO Software Engineering Conference, Garmisch, Germany (1968) 138-155
2. Parnas, D.L.: On the Design and Development of Product Families. IEEE Transactions on Software Engineering, Vol. 2, No. 1 (1976) 1-9
3. Bosch, J.: Design & Use of Software Architectures: Adopting and Evolving a Product-Line Approach, Addison-Wesley (2000)
4. Oreizy, P., Gorlick, M.M., Taylor, R.N., Heimbigner, D., Johnson, G., Medvidovic, N., Quilici, A., Rosenblum, D.S., Wolf, A.L.: An Architecture-based Approach to Self-Adaptive Software, IEEE Intelligent Systems, Vol. 14, No. 3 (1999) 54-62
5. Jacobson, I., Griss, M., Jonsson, P.: Software Reuse: Architecture, Process and Organization for Business Success. Addison-Wesley (1997)
6. Gurp, J. van, Bosch, J., Svahnberg, M.: On the Notion of Variability in Software Product Lines. Proceedings of the Working IEEE/IFIP Conference on Software Architecture, Amsterdam, The Netherlands (2001) 45-54
7. Bosch, J.: Organizing for Software Product Lines. Proceedings of the Third International Workshop on Software Architectures for Product Families, Las Palmas de Gran Canaria, Spain (2000) 117-134
8. Jaring, M., Krikhaar, R.L., Bosch, J.: Representing Variability in a Family of MRI Scanners. Accepted for publication in Software Practice and Experience (2003)
9. Maccari, A., Heie, A.: Managing Infinite Variability. Workshop on Software Variability Management, Groningen, The Netherlands (2003)

10. CAFÉ: From Concept to Application in System-Family Engineering. http://sse.informatik.uni-essen.de/CAFE/

11. Jaring, M., Bosch, J.: Representing Variability in Software Product Lines: A Case Study. Proceedings of the Second Software Product Line Conference, San Diego, USA (2002) 15-36

12. Parnas, D.L., Madey, J., Iglewski, M.: Precise Documentation of Well-Structured Programs. Transactions on Software Engineering, Vol. 20, No. 12 (1994) 948-976

13. Clements, P., Northrop, L.: Software Product Lines: Practices and Patterns. Addison-Wesley (2001)

14. Donohoe, P. (ed.): Software Product Lines: Experience and Research Directions (Proceedings of the First Software Product Line Conference, Denver, USA). Kluwer Academic Publishers (2000)

15. Weiss, D.M., Lai, C.T.R.: Software Product-Line Engineering: A Family-Based Software Development Process. Addison-Wesley (1999)

16. Jazayeri, M., Ran, A., Linden, F. van der: Software Architecture For Product Families: Putting Research into Practice. Addison-Wesley (2000)

17. Keepence, B., Mannion, M.: Using Patterns to Model Variability in Product Families. IEEE Software, Vol. 16, No. 4 (1999) 102-108

18. Gamma, E., Helm, R., Johnson, R., Vlissides, J.: Design Patterns: Elements of Reusable Object-Oriented Software. Addison-Wesley, (1995)

19. Batory, D., O'Malley, S.: The Design and Implementation of Hierarchical Software Systems with Reusable Components. ACM Transactions on Software Engineering and Methodology, Vol. 1, No. 4 (1992) 355-398

20. Gibson, J.P.: Feature Requirements Models: Understanding Interactions. Feature Interactions in Telecommunication Networks IV, Canada, Montreal (1997) 46-60

21. Griss, M.L., Favaro, J., d'Allesandro, M.: Integrating Feature Modeling with the RSEB. Fifth International Conference on Software Reuse, Victoria, Canada (1998) 76-85

22. Karhinen, A., Ran, A., Tallgren, T.: Configuring Designs for Reuse. Symposium on Software Reusability, Boston, USA (1997) 199-208

23. Ommering, R. van, Linden, F. van der, Kramer, J., Magee, J.: The Koala Component Model for Consumer Electronics Software. IEEE Computer, Vol. 33, No. 3 (2000) 78-85

24. Linden, F.J. van der, Müller, J.K.: Creating Architectures with Building Blocks. IEEE Software, Vol. 12, No. 6 (1995) 51-60

25. Coriat, M., Jourdan, J., BoisBourdin, F.: The SPLIT Method: Building Product Lines for Software Intensive Systems. Proceedings of the First Software Product Line Conference, Denver, USA (2000) 147-166

26. Thiel, S., Hein, A.: Systematic Integration of Variability into Product Line Architecture Design. Proceedings of the Second Software Product Line Conference, San Diego, USA (2002) 130-153

27. Buckley, F.J.: Implementing Configuration Management: Hardware, Software and Firmware. IEEE Press (1996)

28. Dart, S.A.: The Past, Present and Future of Configuration Management. Carnegie Mellon University, Software Engineering Institute, Technical Report CMU/SEI-92-TR-8 ESC-TR-92-8, http://www.sei.cmu.edu/legacy/scm/abstracts/absPastPresentFuture.html (1992)

29. Tichy, W.F.: Tools for Software Configuration Management. Proceedings of the International Workshop on Software Version and Configuration Control, Grassau, Germany (1988) 1-20

Managing Component Variability
within Embedded Software Product Lines
via Transformational Code Generation

Ian McRitchie, T. John Brown, and Ivor T.A. Spence

School of Computer Science, The Queen's University of Belfast
Belfast, N.I., UK
{i.mcritchie,tj.brown,i.spence}@qub.ac.uk

Abstract. This paper presents a transformative code generation technique for the static optimization and customization of embedded software. The approach supports the development of product families by separating core functionality from variable facets. The implementation technique utilizes generative programming techniques in order to minimize runtime memory requirements and maximize performance within an embedded environment.

1 Introduction

The application of product-line engineering practices has demonstrated the potential for increased productivity and improved software quality when applied to families of related software systems [1] [2]. Productivity improvements are achieved by exploiting the commonality across the software family, to achieve high levels of reuse[1]. A major issue, however, is the management of variability. The ability to implement highly adaptable software components is one way to capitalize on the commonality within software families, and at the same time manage variability. The techniques developed by Brown et al. [3] support the implementation of structurally and functionally adaptable software components. Such components encapsulate the common functionality required by all members of the family and manage the variant facets by parameterization. However, these techniques have features that make them suboptimal in the context of embedded systems. Conversely, it is within the embedded software domain that many opportunities exist for the use of product-line methods.

This paper presents an approach for managing software component variability targeted towards embedded environments. Although there are several implementation techniques for supporting component adaptation, this work utilizes the adaptable component model [3] optimized for application within embedded systems. The transformative mechanism is applicable to several implementation strategies. Therefore, the focus of this work is on the transformational approach rather than a detailed examination of the underlying component model.

The transformational approach enables the auto-generation of highly optimized components from work products that contain the core functionality and structured

---

[1] This work is part of a joint research initiative with Nortel Networks aimed at evolving techniques facilitating software reuse within embedded distributed real-time telecommunication systems.

F. van der Linden (Ed.): PFE 2003, LNCS 3014, pp. 98–110, 2004.
© Springer-Verlag Berlin Heidelberg 2004

argument lists encoded in XML (extensible Markup Language) [4] that supply the variant facets. The approach applies generative programming techniques to minimize runtime memory requirements and maximize performance.

The paper is organized as follows: Section 2 reviews the basic component model utilized for implementation; Section 3 outlines the constraints of the embedded environment; Section 4 describes the component generation schema; Section 5 discusses issues arising from the developed approach; Section 6 summarizes our contribution.

2   Managing Variability from Design to Implementation

Variability is an inevitable characteristic of software families. Any engineering methodology for software families must therefore provide mechanisms for managing variability through the design and implementation stages. The literature describes a variety of strategies for managing variation across software families or between successive versions of the same product [5] [6]. These approaches generally follow a product line design flow by defining a relatively fixed architecture with individual products created by customizing the software components that populate the architecture. The challenge in adapting such predefined software components for a specific product is the recognition that certain concerns of complex software systems cannot be constrained within singular units. The implementation of such properties tends to cut across the decomposition hierarchy of the system. The result of these *crosscutting concerns* is an increased coupling between modular units. This crosscutting results in reduced reusability and adaptability.

Design strategies based upon modular decomposition mechanisms such as collaborations, [7] dimensions [8] and aspects [9] have emerged for managing concerns which crosscut a number of software modules. A collaboration supporting the implementation of crosscutting features may be viewed as a set of objects and a set of roles which enable the objects to interact to provide a specific capability. Software may be constructed as a collection of collaborations each of which provides a specific capability. Figure 1 shows three objects with corresponding collaborations within an abstract application. *Collaboration 1* adds software extensions to all three objects. *Collaboration 3* only requires extensions to objects *A* and *C*.

	Object A	Object B	Object C
Collaboration 1	Role A1	Role B1	Role C1
Collaboration 2	Role A2	Role B2	Role C2
Collaboration 3	Role A3		Role C3

Fig. 1. The intersection of collaborations and objects represent roles

Design techniques for the development of such customizable software components are often targeted towards specific implementation mechanisms. For example, collaboration-based design is closely associated with mixin layers [10] as the implementation mechanism. Mixin layers supports the inclusion of variant facets or roles, which are an optional extension to a number of modular components. Therefore, mixin layers provide a convenient implementation framework for collaborations, and have been proposed as a mechanism for handling variability in software product lines. These approaches complement further implementation level mechanisms such as *traits classes* and *traits templates* [11] which provide a facility for the management of meta-information.

This work focuses on the implementation phase, and the strategies proposed can be considered to complement the design strategy provided by the ADLARS relational architecture description language introduced in a related paper [12]. The strategy is intended to support the management of variability at the architecture design stage. ADLARS provides the concept of a component template, which is a single entity, embracing a variety of possible derivatives. Each derivative is characterized by a specific internal architecture and related external interface. Component derivatives are related back to product feature combinations. Component template designs emerge at the domain engineering stage. At the application engineering stage, actual product feature sets may then be used to select the required component derivative.

The developed approach provides implementation support for collaborations if optional component roles are supported by optional internal components, rather than mixins. Thus in the ADLARS design methodology the previous design may be expressed as indicated in figure 2.

	Cmp A	Cmp B	Cmp C
Collaboration 1	SubCmp A1	SubCmp B1	SubCmp C1
Collaboration 2	SubCmp A2	SubCmp B2	SubCmp C2
Collaboration 3	SubCmp A3		SubCmp C3

Fig. 2. Collaboration based design implemented using the adaptable component model

The described approach utilizes an extended adaptable component model [3] to support the implementation of variant functionality by code parameterization. The model relies upon parameterization and class composition to achieve functional and structural adaptability. It allows large adaptable components to be defined with nested adaptable components, which remain unbound until instantiation of the outer component. This may lead to large numbers of parameters being defined by outer components.

A key aspect of the model is the use of recursively structured argument lists, as a means of marshalling and organizing arguments. The *feature set* of the intended product can be used to derive the subcomponent architecture of each component instance. The subcomponent architecture determines the parameter requirements and therefore the content of the recursive argument list which each component requires. A *crosscutting* feature will be related to a number of components, and its inclusion will therefore be reflected in the argument lists of those components. The content of the argument list will typically include functions and values. The argument list captures the configuration knowledge needed to fix the internal structure and functionality needed for a particular product.

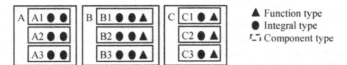

Fig. 3. Three adaptable components with corresponding recursive argument lists

Figure 3 illustrates 3 adaptable components, each with nested subcomponents for performing different roles. Each component defines a set of variation points as parameters. For example, the argument list for *A* accepts 3 argument lists – 1 for each subcomponent. The argument list defines 2 integral types. Figure 2 shows components *A* and *C* collaborating within *SubCmp A1* and *SubCmp C1* to provide specific functionality. Therefore, by customizing each individual component, the collaboration may also be modified or extended to provide specific features.

This mechanism supports the management of variability across product-lines at two levels. The plug-in arguments implement fine grained *diversity* with the component providing *commonality*. Optional and alternative subcomponents support coarser grained variability. The actual capability of an adaptable component is undetermined until configured by the arguments passed via the recursive argument list. A consequence of using class parameterization for nested classes is a declarative style of configuration and potentially *unbounded* adaptability. The configuration complexity is transferred to the management of the parameter list rather than the class, which represents the fixed functionality.

These benefits are balanced by a number of disadvantages that make the direct use of the adaptable component model problematic in some situations. For example, the use of this approach within the development of embedded systems presents a challenge as the recursive list and component parameterization must be managed without incurring a runtime overhead within a constrained embedded system.

3   Constraints within an Embedded Environment

Embedded software is subject to a different set of constraints than those applied within the domain of general purpose computing. The utilization of memory is often a critical issue, as memory is a direct cost within embedded products. The use of dynamic memory allocation poses a number of difficulties. Dynamic memory allocation (DMA) requires dedicated memory in the form of a runtime heap manager module and header information for each allocated block. The problem of external fragmentation preventing allocation is a significant danger within systems that may execute for months or even years between reboots. DMA may also violate real-time constraints if the time required for the memory manager to search the free-list for a block of the right size is not bounded. Some real-time operating systems (RTOS) provide a heap with deterministic performance and subsequent overhead. For these and other reasons, the challenge is to optimize the use of *static* and *automatic* memory allocation within the target domain.

The adaptable component implementation techniques described in [3] utilize DMA in the implementation of the recursive argument list. The utilization of memory is also sub-optimal in some situations. For example, where an optional subcomponent is omitted from its parent outer, the outer component methods that depend on functionality provided by the inner component are unavailable. The implementation methods in [3] could still result in the inclusion of object code for such methods. The exact behavior is dependent upon the optimizing capabilities of the individual compiler. For these reasons the original set of implementation methods [3] must be considered suboptimal in the context of embedded systems.

The extended approach introduced in this paper retains the use of C++, and makes use of some of the more advanced capabilities of the language. The approach utilizes a subset of the language that avoids features such as virtual functions, RTTI (Run Time Type Information), and operator overloading which incur a runtime performance overhead [13]. The necessary metaprogram and adaptable component code is realized by auto-generation.

4   Generating Product Specific Software Components

Product variation within current development processes is often managed within the build process. Embedded systems development often makes use of complex build processes to integrate systems written using multiple languages supporting several technologies. For example, modular variability within an embedded product line is often managed in procedural languages such as C and assembly by the use of pre-processing directives embedded in the source code. Therefore, conditional compilation is utilized to manage static component variability. The dynamic adaptation of components can be achieved at runtime using low-level techniques based on pointer manipulation.

Object-oriented (OO) languages provide several mechanisms supporting both static and dynamic polymorphism. However, support for dynamic configuration such as the RTTI and virtual functions mechanisms found in C++ impose a runtime overhead that violate the previously outlined constraints. Subtype polymorphism permits variables of a given type to hold objects of its subtypes. However, when creating a product family this may lead to a large number of subtypes. The management of this degree of variability is possible using inheritance-based approaches. However, the large number of derived classes introduces problems of code duplication and an increased maintenance requirement. C++ provides generic parameters in the form of function templates and class templates. Type parameters provide a mechanism for the compile time manipulation of the underlying type information.

Metaprogramming techniques operate using the syntax and semantics of the source code, whereas, preprocessing directives operate on the string representation of the source. The developed approach uses a combination of transformative generation and metaprogramming to manage component variability. A generator is used to manipulate the basic artifacts for assembly as C++ adaptable components.

In this approach, the automatic generation of product specific components requires the completion of several prerequisite activities. Firstly, a Pareto-optimal architecture [14] with corresponding artifacts must be defined for the product family during the domain engineering cycle. The architecture conforms to multiple objectives for all possible product variations within the family. The common and variant artifacts may be considered as building blocks for the implementation of the final system. Secondly, a component specification encoded in XML must be created as part of the application-engineering phase. The engineering tasks for creating such artifacts utilizing an appropriate architecture are beyond the scope of this paper. However, a generative approach to the construction of software components presumes that the manual assembly of reusable artifacts can be automated using a generator.

4.1 A Transformational Generator

The *transformational* generator [15] used in this approach, is a static metaprogram that manages the customization of components. The generator produces code which executes at compile time or runtime for the customization, optimization and assembly of components. The generator accepts two inputs for each required component.

Fig. 4. Product generation

The first input is a representation of the argument list encoded in an XML based specification language [4]. This notation is designed to simplify and capture complex domain concepts within suitable language constructs. The second input is a *work product* that holds both XML encoded meta-information used within the generation process and the C++ source code for the component. The generator supports an efficient implementation by bringing forward the binding time and enabling generation-time analysis. For example, the inclusion of a particular optional subcomponent may be managed at generation-time rather than incurring a compile-time or runtime overhead. For each component required to build the product, the generator outputs the C++ meta-program code needed to produce the custom configuration and optimized C++ source code for the component. The product generation process has three main phases - analysis, weaving and generation.

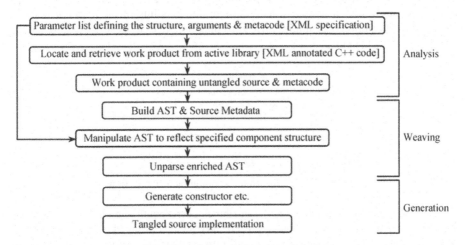

Fig. 5. Outline of the product generation process

4.2 Analysis

The XML specification identifies the specified set of work products. The required work products representing the domain knowledge are selected from a repository. The C++ code is extracted from each individual work product and parsed to produce an abstract syntax tree (AST). The constraints of the target environment result in the work products retaining a C-like syntax. The AST is traversed to gather information on the static dependencies of the work product in relation to external components and optional parameters. This creates a chain of dependencies linking optional parameters and components. If a feature is implemented within an individual work product or by a collaboration of work products then it is possible to define the static dependencies and relationships between work products. Tables detailing these dependencies are then stored. The meta-information from the work product including the abstract syntax tree and the dependency tables is passed forward to the weaving stage.

4.3 Weaving

The concept of weaving is generally defined as the transformation of untangled source code and another program into a final tangled source code. The weaving process makes use of the XML specification of the argument list and the XML meta-information from the work product. The AST is decorated with information according to the specified composition and dependencies identified within the composition. The decorated tree reflects the component specification. The composition of the work products can be highly complex depending upon the relationships identified within the feature diagram.

    As a running example that illustrates important points of our discussion it is useful to consider a configurable application. Figure 6 is a feature diagram of an application for recording customer details. The recording of the first and last names of a customer is a *required* feature. The recording of the email and phone details are *optional* features. A configuration for a particular application consists of the first and last name of the customer, with possibly phone and/or email details. In order to illustrate the approach the discussion is restricted to examining the handling of the *optional* features indicated in the following simplified feature diagram such as the recording of phone and email contact details.

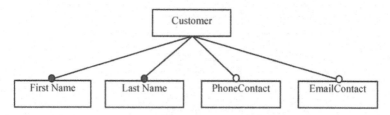

Fig. 6. Feature diagram for a configurable application

If the XML specification excludes the attributes corresponding to a specific feature, the dependencies of those attributes are checked to determine the relationship with other modules. This dependency check will return either an empty list indicating that no external work products are dependent upon the excluded parameters or a list containing the work product dependencies.

For example, suppose that the *EmailContact* feature is implemented within a single independent work product. The work product itself is implemented as a single class. The following code snippet describes part of the *EmailContact* work product containing the C++ source and XML *metacode* for weaving the specified component.

```
<class name="EmailContact" aspects="ExceptionHandler">>

<parameter name="name_" matches="fname" </parameter>

<classbase>

        boolean   addEmail(){...} ;

        ...// remaining function members

</classbase>

</class>
```

The component derived from the work product implements the feature independently of any other components. If the attributes associated with a particular feature are not passed to the work product, code is not generated for the component. Additional modules are not affected by the removal of the component and the final optimized product no longer contains the component.

However, usually the dependency check will return a list of dependencies since significant features are generally implemented within collaborations. For example, suppose an alternative implementation of the *EmailContact* feature is defined within a collaboration as shown in figure 7. The feature is implemented by the interaction of adaptable components *A*, *B* and *C*. The static dependency chains identified in the analysis stage define three components which interact to provide the optional feature. The feature is excluded by not including the attributes corresponding to the *subcomponent* supporting the feature. Additional runtime or compile-time program logic must be inserted to cope with the optional feature.

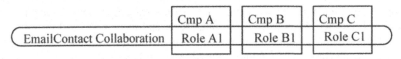

Fig. 7. An optional feature implemented within a collaboration

Any calls to function members which utilize subcomponents *A1*, *B1* or *C1* will first have to check for the inclusion of the supporting attributes supplied by the argument list of the component. The methods cannot simply be removed since they may be used within other roles provided by the component. Therefore the check within the function alters the behavior according to the configuration. In the adaptable component model this is performed by inserting a runtime check in the source code. The check is inserted by manipulating the AST defined within the previous analysis stage as outlined in figure 8.

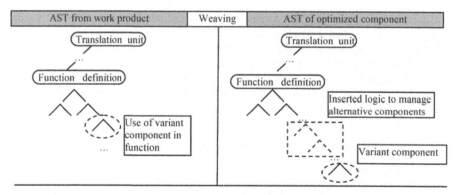

Fig. 8. The abstract syntax tree is manipulated to reflect the specified component structure

The AST may also be manipulated to include additional generated constructs defined during the domain engineering cycle. For example, the *aspects* attribute within the class tag in the previous code snippet indicates that the generator should construct suitable exception handling code for function members of the *EmailContact* class. The decorated AST produced at this stage reflects only the minimal program logic supplied by the final component. The final decorated syntax tree is unparsed to create the C++ code for the optimized component, with the exception of the component's constructor. This is produced at the next and final stage.

4.4   Generation

The generation process creates the C++ metaprogram code needed to create the argument list for the component. This is mainly derived from the XML specification of the argument list. The class constructor is also created at this stage as the generator has already identified the required subcomponents. There is no unnecessary runtime logic placed in the constructor for selecting or omitting subcomponents. Therefore, the generated program code is the minimum required for the specified components.

The final step is to generate an interface to the component. The conventional approach to component based implementation is to encapsulate the component services behind well-defined interfaces. These interfaces tend to be restricted in order to conform to a particular component framework. However, the transformational approach produces an interface only for the required set of roles for a particular product. The interface is *undefined* up to the point of generation. Therefore, the specification of the component interface is defined by the *roles* performed by the component.

5   Discussion

This paper has presented a generative approach for managing component variability within an embedded software product line. The use of a generator permits the rapid revision of design considerations such as the component variability arising within a specific product line architecture. The capability to rapidly configure and assemble a collection of components within the architecture directly reduces the development time and subsequent time to market. The outlined approach utilizes a single generator for a particular domain. The generator itself is targeted towards a particular implementation mechanism corresponding closely to the selected design strategy. The previous example exploited the adaptable component model. However, an alternative implementation mechanism such as mixin layers could be utilized by the same generator.

Furthermore, the generator supports the explicit association of high-level system properties with implementation level constructs defined within a general purpose programming language. The code generated for each product only supports the particular product rather than all members of the product family. This produces readable source code and avoids any reliance upon an optimizing compiler for the exclusion of unnecessary object code. The encapsulation of the meta-information of the product line within the generator may also be exploited for additional development tasks such as documentation and testing.

The configuration of the generator depends only on the mechanisms to be used for managing adaptability in the chosen target language. If the target language changes or the mechanisms for component adaptation change, then some parts of the generator will need modification. Otherwise the generator is fixed and is independent of any aspect of the architecture or the application domain.

A significant advantage of the outlined approach is that it exploits the current widespread availability of XML-based document transformation tools and robust public domain parser generators. This application of public domain technologies greatly reduces the effort in constructing a bespoke generator. The capability to readily construct suitable robust generators increases the range of suitable domains. The use of XML-based schema offsets the problem of creating numerous non-interoperable domain specific languages. The complexity of the generator is generally defined by the degree of automation determined during the domain engineering phase. A greater degree of automation generally involves extending the generator actions. However, the overhead in constructing the generator may be controlled by constraining the extent of the automation. The predefined components are the natural output of the domain engineering phase.

As with any supporting implementation mechanism for a product-line development strategy, the significant advantages of using a transformational approach must be balanced against the initial overhead and associated risks. Although there is growing tool support for generator components, the construction of bespoke generators for a particular domain remains an effort-intensive engineering task. The domain must be mature and well-understood to justify automating the process of component assembly. The concepts which are defined within the input specification and corresponding actions of the generator must be clearly defined during the domain engineering phase. The generated code is constrained by the intended implementation model/language and the associated supporting technology. For example, the adaptable component model does incur a runtime overhead when constructing multiple alternative components. Similarly the use of the mixin layers as the target model may result in object code duplication if the same layer is used multiple times in a composition [10]. It is notable that these overheads may also indicate a flaw in the intended system design.

Furthermore, the use of any mechanism which may modify the design intentions expressed within the source code raises issues of ownership and transparency of the development process. Practical concerns such as requirements modeling, traceability, testability, performance and cost effectiveness of applied generative techniques remain areas of active investigation.

The issues arising by the use of mechanisms which may modify the intentions of the designer are by no means specific to the outlined technique. Emerging software engineering paradigms are usually supported by mechanisms which manipulate source code to include additional functionality. For example, the aspect-oriented programming paradigm [9] supports the decomposition of a problem into a number of functional components and aspects that crosscut the components. A number of tools and techniques have been developed for supporting such modular crosscutting based on source code manipulation. AspectJ is a tool which accepts Java and aspect source files and generates Java code containing the crosscutting aspects [16]. The outlined approach is a step towards exploiting techniques for the separation of concerns for the development of software product families.

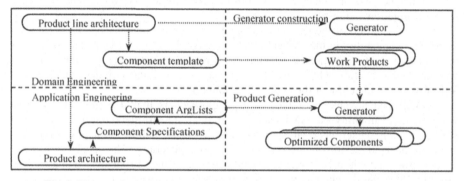

Fig. 9. The transformational approach within a product line development process

Concerns about the automated transformation of source code may be addressed in part by integrating the transformative approach within an overall design flow. Assuming a mature domain and appropriate supporting technology there are no fundamental implementation drawbacks in the use of transformative generation of specific products. Work is currently progressing on the integration of the developed approach within a broader product line design flow as shown in figure 9. A detailed examination of this approach is beyond the scope of this paper. However, following the approach proposed using the ADLARS architecture description language, it is possible to map architectural concepts to generator constructs. For example, the ADLARS notion of a component template is similar to that of a work product used by the generator. Therefore, there is a developing relationship between design level constructs and the use of transformational code generation without constraining the approach to a particular design flow.

6   Conclusion

The transformational approach provides a flexible implementation framework for both fixing the common functionality and managing the natural variation within any product family. In this work an implementation mechanism for a specific design technique and component model is automated for application within embedded systems. The first step in this process was the identification of the constraints of the embedded environment and subsequent development of the suitable representation for the recursive argument list. The next step was the provision of an auto-generation facility capable of generating the optimized component code and the metaprogram code to create the recursive argument list. The revised component model and implementation technique permits the construction of low overhead adaptable components suitable for embedded environments.

In the developed approach the reusable artifact is separate from the mechanism utilized to implement application variability. It is notable that the component model and strategy of collaboration-based design approach could be exchanged for another design strategy and/or implementation model. Therefore, the same form of transformational code generation strategy could be adapted to support further implementation mechanisms for variability management such as mixin-programming methods. In terms of language and supporting technology the transformative approach is essentially language independent. The developed transformational generator can be adapted to operate with any target language by replacing a small number of generator modules.

Current applications have been confined to small-scale systems such as simple device drivers. Indications from these studies suggest that the auto-generated component code is comparable to hand crafted C code in terms of memory usage. Future work will focus on gaining experience with more extensive case studies. These applications will also address issues such as traceability, debugging and integration with existing software. Work is currently progressing on the application of the transformational approach to the development of a small customizable embedded application with a variable feature set. The rigorous profiling of a significant case study will further clarify the overhead of the transformative code generation technique in relation to current development practices.

References

1. "A Framework for Software Product-Line Practice – Version 4.1", Software Engineering Institute, Carnegie Mellon University, URL: http://www.sei.cmu.edu/plp/framework.html.
2. L. Brownsword and P. Clements, "A Case Study in Successful Product Line Development", Technical Report CMU/SEI-96-TR-016, SEI, Carnegie Mellon University.
3. T. J. Brown, I. Spence and P. Kilpatrick, "Adaptable Components for Software Product-Line Engineering", Proc. of the Second International Conference on Product Lines (SPLC2), August 2002, ed. Gary Chastek, Springer-Verlag LNCS 2379, 2002.
4. C. Cleveland, "Program Generators with XML and Java", Prentice Hall, XML Book Series, ISBN 0-7923-7311-1, 2000.
5. M. Jarring and J. Bosch, "Representing Variability in Software Product-Lines: a Case Study", Proc. of the Second International Conference on Product Lines (SPLC2), August 2002, ed. Gary Chastek, Springer-Verlag LNCS 2379, 2002.
6. R. van Ommering and J. Bosch, "Widening the Scope of Software Product Lines – From Variation to Composition", Proc. of the Second International Conference on Product Lines (SPLC2), August 2002, ed. Gary Chastek, Springer-Verlag LNCS 2379, 2002.
7. T. Reenskaug, E. Anderson, A. Berre, A. Hurlen, A. Landmark, O. Lehne, E. Nord-Hagen, E. Ness-Ulseth, G. Oftedal, A. Skaar and P. Stenslet, "OORASS: Seamless support for the creation and maintenance of object-oriented systems", Journal of Object-Oriented Programming 5, 6 (Oct.), pp.27-41, 1992.

8. P. Tarr, H. Ossher, W. Harrison and S. M. Sutton Jr. "N degrees of separation: Multidimensional separation of concerns," Proceedings of the 21st International Conference on Software Engineering (ICSE'99), May, pp.107–119, 1999.
9. G. Kiczales, J. Lamping, A. Mendhekar, C. Maeda, C.V. Lopes, J. M. Loingtier, and J. Irwin, "Aspect-Oriented Programming", Proc. 11th European Conference – Object-Oriented Programming (ECOOP'97), Jyväskylä, Finland, June 1997, Askit, M. and Matsuoka, S. (eds.) , Springer-Verlag, LNCS 1241, pp.220-242.
10. Y. Smaragdakis and D. Batory, "Mixin Layers: An Object-Oriented Implementation technique for Refinements and Collaboration-Based Designs", ACM Transactions on Software Engineering and Methodology, Vol. 11, No. 2, April 2002, pp. 215-255.
11. N. C. Myers, "Traits: a new and useful template technique," C++ Report, June 1995. URL: www.cantrip.org/traits.html
12. T.J. Brown, I. Spence "A Relational Architecture Description Language for Software Families", Proc. of the Product Family Engineering Workshop (PFE), November 2003, ed. F. van der Linden, Springer-Verlag, 2003 (to appear).
13. P. L. Plauger, "Embedded C++: An Overview", Embedded Systems Programming, 10, 13, December 1997.
14. M. Eisenring, L. Thiele and E. Zitzler, "Conflicting Criteria in Embedded System Design," IEEE Design and Test, 17, 2, pp.51-59, 2000.
15. I. McRitchie, I. Spence and T.J. Brown, "A Java Framework For The Static Reflection, Composition And Synthesis Of Software Components", Proc. of ACM Principles and Practice of Programming in Java 2003.
16. G. Kiczales, E. Hilsdale, , J. Hugunin, M. Kersten, J. Palm, W. G. Griswold, "An Overview of AspectJ", Proc. 15th European Conference – Object-Oriented Programming (ECOOP'01), ed. Knudsen, J. L., Springer-Verlag, LNCS 2072, pp. 327-353, 2001.

Evolving a Product Family in a Changing Context

Jan Gerben Wijnstra

Philips Research Laboratories
Prof. Holstlaan 4
5656 AA, Eindhoven, The Netherlands
JanGerben.Wijnstra@philips.com

Abstract. The notion of software product families is becoming more and more popular, both in research and in industry. There is no single best product family approach that is suitable for all, since each product family has its unique context. Such a context comprises elements such as scope, organization, and business strategy. As these elements can change over time, the product family approach may have to evolve with them. In this paper we describe our ideas for a method to assess the variability approach of an existing product family, and to improve that approach to match the changing context. This is illustrated in a case study from the medical imaging domain. This product family in question started out with only a few family members, but over time, the growth in the number of different applications and new application domains have put higher variability demands on the family. These changes also require an evolution in the product family approach. We will describe the current product family approach and the changing requirements on this approach. We also performed a partially automated analysis of the variation to give us a good overview of the way variation is currently handled in the system. Based on that, a direction for evolving the product family approach is proposed.

Keywords: product family, evolution, variation mechanisms, architecture

1 Introduction

Product families have already been introduced in various parts of the software industry. An important decision when introducing a product family is how the variability will be handled. No uniform approach exists because of different business and architecture requirements and constraints from process and organization. The decision on the product family approach is not a once-in-a-lifetime decision. The changing context of a product family may require the approach to be adjusted. The requirements for the variation may initially be quite modest, but will most probably grow over time. It is important to take into account such changes during the lifetime of a product family. If this is not done it will become more and more difficult for the family to serve its purpose, e.g. it might become difficult to bring the right products to the market at the right time.

In this paper we will discuss how to assess a product family approach for the way it deals with variation, and how this approach can be improved to meet future demands. We have applied these ideas for a specific product family from the medical domain. This product family is a so-called modality, which can be used for acquiring and viewing images for medical purposes. Examples of medical modalities are conven-

F. van der Linden (Ed.): PFE 2003, LNCS 3014, pp. 111–128, 2004.
© Springer-Verlag Berlin Heidelberg 2004

tional X-ray, Computed Tomography, Magnetic Resonance Imaging, and Ultra Sound equipment. The development of the modality we studied started about two decades ago.

In this paper we want to discuss our ideas for a method to assess and improve the way variability is dealt with within a product family, based on the changing context in which the product family approach is applied. This approach consists of a number of steps. These steps are (see also Fig. 1):

- We first need to know what the current situation is and what changes are expected towards the future, e.g. the scope of the product family will be increased. For this we used the BAPO/CAFCR reasoning framework as explained in section 2.1, to which we added specific questions that relate to the handling of variation. This step mainly involves interviews with experts and input from documentation.
- Although the previous step already partly deals with the handling of variation, usually more detailed information on the handling of variation at system realization level is needed. In this second step, depending on the situation, the source code, documentation and experts can be consulted. In our case we applied automated extraction of variability information from the source code, which we used as input when consulting experts.
- Based on the information obtained in the previous two steps, we make an analysis of the variation. To structure this analysis, we use three areas of attention, namely the overall handling of variation, the selection of variation points, and the mechanisms to realize variation. This analysis leads to improvement suggestions. These improvement suggestions have to match with the future direction as identified in the first step. They again affect the evolution steps of the product family.

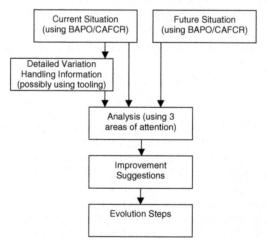

Fig. 1. Variability Improvement Steps

The paper is structured along the steps described above. In section 2, we discuss the current situation for the product family, followed by the product family's changing context. In section 3 we discuss how automated extraction will give more insight into the realization of the variation. Based on that, we will present in section 4 some elements from the assessment and improvement suggestions for the product family. We briefly discuss related work in section 5, followed by conclusions in section 6.

2 Current Status and Future Changes

In this section, we briefly describe which kind information was gathered on the current status of the product family (section 2.2) and the expected changes in the future (section 2.3), with a focus on the handling of variation. We used a particular reasoning framework for structuring the information as described in section 2.1.

2.1 Reasoning Framework

The BAPO (Business, Architecture, Process, and Organization) reasoning framework [11] places architecture in the context of business, organization and process. It defines logical relations between them (the arrows in Fig. 3). For example, the business provides the rationale for the definition of the architecture: why is it needed, what should it achieve? Conversely, the architecture supports the business. Five architectural views are distinguished within the architecture. These views range from the world of the customer to the realization of the product, as follows:

- **C**ustomer view (the customer's world)
- **A**pplication view (applications important to the customer)
- **F**unctional view (requirements for a system used in a customer application)
- **C**onceptual view (architectural concepts of the system)
- **R**ealization view (realization technologies for building the system)

The customer and application views explain why a product is needed. The functional view expresses what the product should do. The conceptual and realization views express how the product is built.

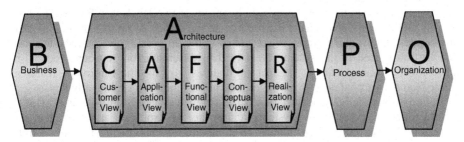

Fig. 2. BAPO/CAFCR Reasoning Framework

Each of the elements of BAPO/CAFCR deal with a number of topics, of which some can have an impact on the way how the variation should be supported in the future. By asking the question how these specific topics will evolve in the future, it becomes clearer how the handling of variation must evolve in order to match with the changing context. Of course, the current status of relevant items within BAPO/CAFCR must also be known. Some examples of questions that we used for the various elements of BAPO/CAFCR are:

- business: 'Does the product family have to cover a larger application domain?' or 'Will other existing products be merged into the product family?'
- architecture, conceptual view: 'Which architectural concepts will be introduced in the future?'
- process: 'What should be improved for the development processes in the future?'
- organization: 'Will there be one or several development sites in the future?' .

In the remainder of this paper we largely focus on how variation can be handled in the conceptual and realization views of the product family architecture. These views are affected by their context. Even though the rationale in BAPO runs from left to right, in practice the process and organization impact the conceptual view and realization view as well as the other way round. This is because it is rarely possible to set up a process or organization from scratch. For making the right decisions on the handling of variation, a good understanding of the context as described in the BAPO framework and its changes is mandatory. More information on how variation can be modeled in the five CAFCR views can be found in [2].

2.2 Current Status

We considered variation in our product family from various viewpoints using the BAPO reasoning framework. We used several of the diagrams and techniques as described in the BAPO/CAFCR framework focusing on the variability. In addition we have used some additional questions to get the focus on variation for the current status and also the future changes, e.g. what are currently bottlenecks in the product family approach, or what are the main architecture concepts envisaged for the coming years? In this section we have limited ourselves to the functional, conceptual, and realization view within the architecture.

The customer can tailor the system to his needs at two levels, see Fig. 5. The first level is that the customer selects the product he/she wants. A number of products are predefined. The available products are related to the different types of image acquisition hardware used in the system. Next to that, differentiation between products is made for the various markets via specific features, e.g. specific cardiology features. These features are contained in packages that the customer can additionally buy.

Before discussing how the variation is handled inside the system, it is important to have a rough overview of the system architecture. The software architecture of the system is decomposed into a number of components. Each member of the family contains the same components. This makes the architecture *variant free* [12]; the variation is not visible at the architectural level, it is dealt with inside the various software components.

When considering the realization of the variation in our product family, we make a distinction between configuration items and software options. A *configuration item* deals with a variable piece of hardware and the corresponding software. Usually, one of several variants must be selected for a configuration item; only one of them may be present in the system. An example of such a configuration item is the table on which the patient is lying; each variant may support different movements of the table. However, there are also optional configuration items; they may or may not be present in the system, for example an ECG module. A *software option* is a variable piece of functionality that is realized entirely in software. An example is an improved

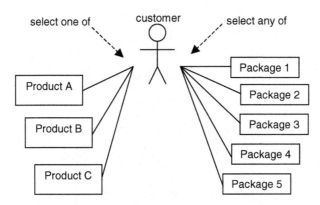

Fig. 3. Product External Handling of Variation

algorithm for processing the acquired images. If a certain option becomes common-place, a software option may become a standard part of all products. This family contains over thirty configuration items and over fifty software options. Fig. 7 shows a schematic representation of the variant free architecture. The specific functionality for configuration items and software options is realized within the components. There is usually no one-to-one mapping between configuration items/software options and components.

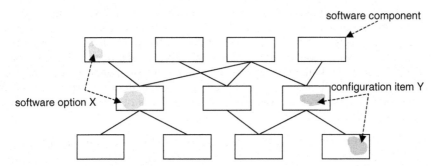

Fig. 4. Variant Free Architecture with Configuration Items and Software Options

Each configuration item or software option provides the end user with one or more features, see Fig. 9. Some configuration items can be used without enabling software options; other configurations are only useful if one or more related software options are enabled too. Some software options can also be used without configuration items.

Both the checks for the configuration items and the software options are performed during or after initialization-time, enabling the installation of the same software on each product; the configuration of configuration items and software options determines which code will be used. The total code base contains more than 3.5 million lines of code, mainly written in C and C++.

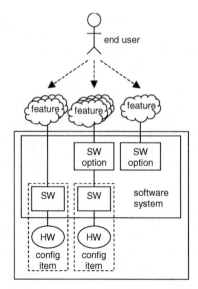

Fig. 5. Configuration Items and Software Options

2.3 Future Changes

Product families usually have a long lifetime, during which various changes will occur in the context in which it is applied. It is very important to consider these changes and determine whether and how they will influence the product family, because "If you don't know where you are going, any road will take you there"[1]. If no action is taken, the product family may turn out to be much more restraining than it is enabling.

In this paper we will not go into too much detail about all of the expected changes that can have an impact on the variation. Some examples of possible future changes related to the elements of BAPO/CAFCR could be:

- The market to be covered will expand, e.g. to include cardio vascular applications (*business*)
- The customers want the system to be more closely integrated with the rest of the hospital (*customer view*)
- The system must be tunable to the hospital's workflow (*application view*)
- Various new features will have to be integrated into the system (*functional view*)
- At an architectural level the interfaces will be handled more explicitly, see [15] for more details (*conceptual view*)
- The code will evolve from C and C++ towards C# (*realization view*)
- A shorter time-to-market cycle is desirable for certain features (*process*)
- The product family will be worked on at several development sites (*organization*)

---

[1] George Harrison from 'Any Road'.

3 Variation Extraction

In this section, we first deal with the question what variation we will take into account. After that, it is described how we extracted the relevant variation information from the system. This information forms an extension of the information on the current status as presented in section 2.2.

3.1 What Variation to Take into Account?

A lot of variation can exist in a 3.5 million LOC system, so we have to restrict ourselves on the variation that we want to analyze. One classification of variation is based on the user groups of the variable functionality.

- One group is the functionality that is needed by the developers, manufacturers, and field-service engineers of the system. This variation is not relevant to the end-user, but very important to deliver a good product. This variable functionality includes for example test code (different test modes), or tracing functionality that can be switched on or off.
- The other group is formed by the functionality that is seen by the end-users of the system. Most options and configuration items of the modality fall into this second category.

We focus on this second group of variable functionality that deals with the end-user.

At certain points in the code it is checked what the configuration of the system is. These checks involve configuration parameters that indicate the actual configuration of the system. We identify two ways in which the different configurations can be handled in the system:

- *generic*
  An example here is configuration information that represents a list of printers connected to the system. Such a list is handled by one piece of code that is flexible enough to handle different kinds of printers. As a consequence, no specific code is needed for specific values.
- *specific*
  An example here is the type of table on which the patient is laying, and which motorized movements this table supports. This has impact on the driver that has to be loaded, and on the applications that are possible. This really influences which pieces of code are executed. Specific pieces of code are needed here.

In this paper the focus will be on the second category. In this category the variation is usually realized with specific pieces of code for each value of the configuration parameter. So, we are looking for pieces of functionality that are enabled and disabled in a particular family member, depending on its configuration.

3.2 Extracting the Variation from the System

A brief description of the currently applied variation approach was given in section 2.2. However, we need more detailed information on the realization of the variation in the system to be able to assess how the variability approach should evolve, encompassing the various variation mechanisms, how many checks are performed on configuration parameters, where the variable code can be found, etc. Such information is usually not instantly available. Since the system is very large, we applied an automated process to extract variation information out of the system's code. Various approaches exist for extracting information from a system, e.g. as described in [14]. For our case, we use a lightweight dedicated approach using Perl-scripts. This will give us sufficient information.

The system's source code contains two types of functions to check the configuration items and software options (check_configuration_item(...), check_soft-ware_option(...)). We used these functions as an entry-point to the variation in the system. We extracted these variation points using a number of Perl scripts. The initial result of these scripts is a file containing one line for each combination of filename together with configuration item or software option, where one or more checks are performed on the configuration item or software option. We used this basic information to generate three different views, by 'lifting' (see [14]) the information from file to component, subsystem and system level. Table 1 gives an overview of the found variation points, where the number of checks performed on software options and configuration items are indicated per subsystem. From this table it can be concluded that the configuration items are only checked in subsystems A through C. The options are mainly checked in the subsystem B.

Table 1. Software Options and Configuration Items in the Subsystems

	software options	configuration items
subsystem A	19	219
subsystem B	193	184
subsystem C	16	187
subsystem D	8	
subsystem E	9	
subsystem F	7	

The output of the scripts was used for further analysis. The checks on software options and configuration items were usually performed in an *'if'* or *'switch'* statement, followed by a few lines of specific code. These lines are usually not the only ones that are specific to a certain variation; there are several ways in which other parts of the source code are involved as well, including:

- *function calls in the statement*
  In the 'if' or 'switch' statement, another function may be invoked. This invoked function can be configuration specific.
- *configuration specific return value*
  The function in which the configuration check is performed returns a value that is used by the caller to make a configuration specific decision.
- *global variables*
  The function in which the configuration check is performed translates the configuration parameter into a global variable value that is used by other parts of the software (e.g. certain UI fields may be enabled during initialization).

A consequence of this is that not all variable code can be found immediately via our tooling. In theory it should be possible to find all variable code in an automated way. For example, program slicing [17] can be used to create views on the code related to configuration parameters. It is however not our aim to make a complete analysis of the code; the most important techniques for realizing variation should become clear. As a consequence we decided to involve domain experts, using a representative subset of the found variation points as a starting point. These domain experts have sufficient knowledge to relate an automatically found variation point to other variable function-ality in the system. This second step is illustrated in Fig. 11 as the manual step, as opposed to the automated extraction step using Perl scripts.

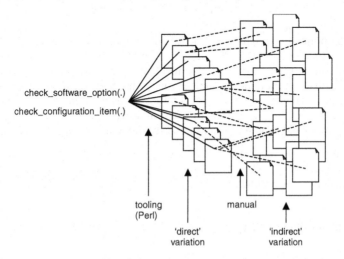

Fig. 6. Identifying Variable Pieces of Code

4 Variation Assessment and Improvement

In this section we provide a brief overview of the assessment and improvements of the variability in the product family. This will be done based on three areas of atten-tion, as described in section 4.1. In sections 4.2 through 4.4 we will discuss our results for these areas of attention. For the improvements, it is important to indicate how they will help in dealing with the future context, which was described in section 2.3. For example, by improving the clustering of functionality per configuration item, it be-comes easier to develop the functionality of one configuration item on a single site (organizational issue), and it supports the releasing of individual features (process issues). In section 4.5 the evolution based on the improvement suggestions is dis-cussed.

4.1 Areas of Attention

When considering variation in a system, different aspects play a role to come to a successful deployment of the variation. The three main aspects are listed below:

- *Overall handling* of variable items in the architecture and development
  For a successful handling of the variation in the system it is important to have an overall approach, dealing with the steps to introduce new variation in the system, how the variation should be documented, etc.. This approach should give the context in which the variation has to be realized. This means that it should be expressed what the expectations are for now and the coming years.
- The selection of the actual *variation points* in the system
  It is important to identify what the variable items are in the system, and how their variable behavior is related to the system. This determines which variation points are needed throughout the system. For a large system it is recommended to base these decisions on an explicit system wide variation model.
- The *mechanisms* used to realize the variation
  When the points of variation are identified, they have to be realized in the code. Several mechanisms exist to do that. One important criterion is to not have unnecessary variation in the set of variation mechanisms that are used. It should be easy to work with the variation mechanisms; they should not add to the complexity of the system. Another criterion is the need for extensibility and how the mechanisms support that; e.g. how easy is it to add a new variant to a variation point? The mechanisms should enable product family development and not restrain it.

So, in summary, it is important to have an overview of the variation points in the system, mechanisms to realize this variation, and a process to structure the work on variation, including its documentation.

4.2 Overall Handling of Variation

This section deals with the process of handling variation. An overall approach is essential to successfully handle the variation in the system, because a certain variation can impact several components throughout the system, and these components can be developed by different people at different sites. Such an approach should give the context in which the variation has to be realized, including issue such as development process and documentation. This also supports conceptual integrity, which according to Brooks [7] is the most important consideration in system design.

When dealing with variation, the developers should have a clear view on how the various configuration items and software options are related to the software components in the system, i.e. traceability. It depends on several factors how this traceability information can be handled best. If the development crew is relatively small and the degree of variation is low this information can be handled different than when a large crew is involved that is distributed over various development sites and a lot of variation has to be supported. In the latter case, more attention must be paid to documenting the traceability information. In our case, the experience and knowledge of the developers are an important factor, but the growing scope and size of the development crew means also that more attention will have to be paid to traceability. For example, when adding a new variant of a configuration item, all variation points must first be found in the code. This will take more and more time. The documentation should help when answering questions like 'which parts of the system are affected when an existing configuration item is changed, or similar one is added?'.

4.3 Selection of Variation Points

It is important to determine what variable items must be realized in the system, and how their variable behavior is related to the elements of the architecture. This will determine which variation points are needed throughout the system. For a large and complex system, such decisions should be based on a model that captures the variable items, in our case the configuration items and software options, and their commonalities and differences, e.g. for the different variants of a configuration item. The UML notation can for example be used for this. Such a model must then be related to the architectural elements of the system, e.g. the components. As an example, in [1] the requirements model, which also models the variation, is used as the basis for the design. In that case the relation between the variation and how it was realized in the system was explicit. The relation between a variation model and the software architecture is graphically shown in Fig. 13. We should note here that there is not usually a one-to-one mapping of configuration items or software options to variation points in the system; one configuration item or software item will usually lead to several variation points.

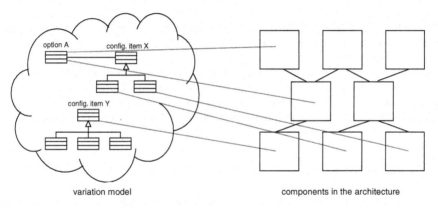

Fig. 7. Variation Model and Architecture

For the product family in our case a model of the configuration items in the system is present. Not only does this model contain the different variants for each configuration item, it also makes abstractions in the form of properties/capabilities of a configuration item. This kind of abstractions are important because without them, all variation points would be related to specific configuration items or software options. Introducing a new variant of a configuration item would then imply a lot of updates. This can be avoided if the more abstract properties are used. As an example, different tables exist on which the patients are lying during image acquisition, each supporting a different set of motorized movements. By using these movements as capabilities, the application software can simply ask for the presence of a movement (capability) instead of checking the presence of a specific configuration item representing a table. Within a variation model, the various capabilities that are useful can also be made explicit. This is illustrated in Fig. 15. In this example, Table Y supports all three movements, while the other two table support only two movements.

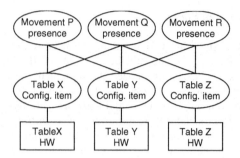

Fig. 8. Layers of Variation

The model of the variation in our case study is related to the source code by the fact that most names of the elements in the model are equal to names of the software components in the realization of the system. However, not all variation in the realization is directly related to this model. It is important for at least the architects and senior designers to have an overview of where the variation is realized in the system. How this overview is documented depends on the situation; if several development sites are involved, more detailed documentation is usually needed. If the variation is documented well, the less experienced developers will be able to solve variability issues themselves more often.

Having such an explicit model is also beneficial when defining the interfaces of the components, which will become a more prominent role in the architecture. It is much easier to identify the variable and stable parts when using such a configuration model. The properties of the configuration items can also be used in the interfaces to shield the specific configuration items.

4.4 Variation Mechanisms

When the points of variation have been identified, they need to be realized in the code. In this section we consider how the variation points are implemented in the system via various mechanisms. We distinguish between the concepts of the mechanisms and how the mechanisms are realized in software.

Our focus here is on the mechanisms that are related to function calls that check the configuration items and software options. When considering these variation mechanisms, we noticed that most of these mechanisms are used during system's initialization-time. Consider the following examples:

- *configuration based GUI*
  During initialization, the GUI (Graphical User Interface) is built based on the configuration settings. This means that specific menus and buttons are added, which are connected to specific piece of software. Such a piece of software is activated when the users selects it during run-time, see Fig. 17.
- *configuration specific parameters*
  Specific configuration items are translated into values for parameters (a kind of capabilities). The parameters are read out of so-called resource files, see Fig. 19. These parameters are used at various places in the software. In this way, no references to specific configuration items are needed.

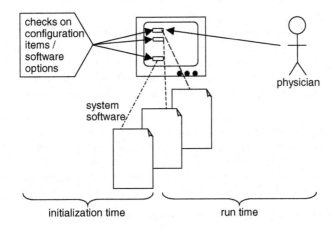

Fig. 9. Setting up the GUI

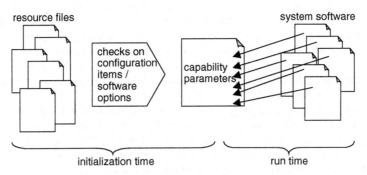

Fig. 10. Setting up the Capability Parameters

Although these concepts are useful for dealing with variation, if they are implemented in such a way that it becomes difficult to extend and evolve the system, their value rapidly decreases. This is why we not only considered concepts, but also studied their realization. Some points of attention include:

- hard-coded checks on specific configuration item instances
  Some functions may contain a lot of hard-coded checks on various specific instances. This is usually a result of the growing variation over time, where each new specific instance is added without considering the overall variability design. This means that when a new variant of a certain configuration is introduced, these functions need to be updated. An alternative is to use the properties in the checks instead of the specific instances.
- various specific function calls in a generic function
  The maintenance can become complicated when a function that contains generic functionality performs function calls to specific configuration items. Such a generic function needs to be updated when changes are made in the set of supported configuration items or software options. It would be better to reverse the dependency here; the specific code should refer to the generic code, and not the other way around.

- hard-coded characteristics in several files
  The characteristics of some configuration items may be hard-coded in various files throughout the system. This may be a result of the fact that in a growing system, these characteristics are needed at more places than initially anticipated, or something that seemed fixed in the start turned out to be variable. Several components are affected when these characteristics change. It should be tried to group these characteristics per variable item.

We have based our improvement proposals on the items like the ones discussed above. These improvements are aimed at increasing the maintainability in the changing context of the modality. For example, it should be relatively easy to add new features in an independent way (reducing the time-to-market), or to divide the development between various groups. The two main issues we have identified are:

- separation between generic and specific functionality
  We identified that there is not always a clear separation between the generic and specific code. One reason for this is the evolutionary growth of the system. More and more features have been added over time. Where previously only one type of hardware was used, there are now an increasing number of alternatives, which has resulted in more and more specific code. The specific code was simply added to the generic code. This is not desirable from a maintenance point-of-view. The generic code should be separate from the specific code. Ideally the generic code will not include any references to the specific code. Unfortunately, some generic pieces of functionality have a reference to specific functionality. In some cases it is possible to remove this dependency, i.e. the generic functionality does not have to know the specific files. Instead, the specific files have to make known their functionality to a kind of broker service, using a suitable abstraction. Such a design provides more flexibility, since the specific files can be updated or new ones can be added without changing the generic functionality, see Fig. 11.

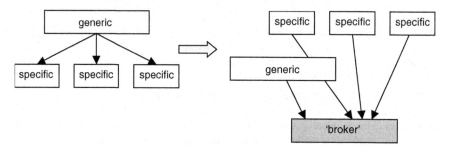

Fig. 11. Removal of Generic-to-Specific Dependencies

When looking at the Design Patterns book by the Gang of Four [8], a number of patterns are based on abstraction and the separation of generic and specific functionality. Examples of such patterns that can be used in this context are: abstract factory, bridge and factory method.

- grouping specific functionality
  The specific code and data of some of the configuration items is distributed over a number of components. This makes it difficult to see where changes are needed when such a configuration item is updated. It is best to localize the variability func-

tionality related to a configuration item or software option in one or a few components. The localization helps to deal with some of the changes as listed in section 2.3. For example, it becomes easier to add new configuration items and software options, reducing the time-to-market for new features. Furthermore, in a multi-development organization, it becomes easier to divide the work over the various development groups. To support grouping, some kind of packaging of the specific code could be introduced.

These general suggestions can be used to improve the variation realization techniques in the code. We will illustrate this using an example. In various functions, checks are performed on specific instances, and based on that function a call is performed. Such a function may also be necessary for a new variant of a configuration item, which will require adding a check on the new variant. To support the adding of new variation, updates of the existing files should be avoided. In such a situation it is useful to use a property of the configuration item or software option.

On the left hand side of Fig. 23 below, we see a function performing function calls based on the presence of two specific configuration items. If a third similar configuration item were added, the code would have to be adapted. In this example we already assume that polymorphism is used to define the interfaces of the configuration items. The right hand side of Fig. 23 shows how this can be improved. Instead of checking for specific configuration items, a kind of property is used in the form of the name of an interface. If this interface is present in the system, functionX can be performed. A reference to this interface is requested via a kind of broker [6]. If this interface is returned, functionX can be invoked.

Design A

```
void applicationFunction ()
{
    ...
    if (configItemAPresent()) {
        configItemA.functionX ();
    } elsif (configItemBPresent()) {
        configItemB.functionX ();
    }
    ...
}
```

Design B

```
void applicationFunction ()
{
    ...
    broker.getInterface('IFoo');
    IFoo.functionX ();
    ...
}
```

Fig. 12. Using a Capability and a Broker

4.5 Evolution

In [19] two main introduction scenarios for product families are described. One scenario is the situation where a start is made with one product to which more and more variation is added, requiring redesigns. This scenario seems comparable to the case that we studied in this paper. This product family started out as a product into which more and more configuration parameters have been added. The next step is to focus on separate components (generic and specific) and the definition of clear interfaces between these components. From this point-of-view it becomes also clear that in the beginning it suffices to use the experts as a source of information on variation, because the variation was still limited. But in a context were the number of developers increases and also the variation, it becomes important to handle the variation more explicitly.

The evolution of a product family is a continuous process where changes can only be made in relatively small steps. As a consequence, the proposed changes cannot be realized instantaneous. Instead, the changes will have to be introduced gradually. For example, when a subsystem has to be redesigned because it becomes too difficult to integrate new functionality, this is an excellent opportunity to apply the proposed ideas for handling variation.

5 Related Work

The work presented in this paper relates to the assessment of product family architectures and their evolution. In the area of architecture assessment, usually a broad scope is considered for the assessment. It is however possible to assess an architecture for a limited set of architecture concerns. For example, in SARA (Software Architecture Review and Assessment, [9]) several architecture concerns are identified. For each of these architecture concerns assessment methods need to be filled in. Part of the work presented in this paper can be seen as a way of assessing the variability against the future requirements. In [10] scenarios are used to assess the product family architecture for its support for evolution.

In the area of improving an architecture with respect to various quality attributes, more information can be found in [4]. There it is described how an architecture can iteratively be assessed and transformed to improve it support of qualities like performance, maintainability or reliability. Also other product development methodologies have elements that deal with evolution, like for example the PuLSE methodology [3]. PuLSE consists of a number of components, and one of them deals with the evolution process. In our paper we illustrated that during the lifetime of a product family architecture decisions must be revisited from time to time. Our focus is on one quality attribute, namely the handling of variability. The methods mentioned above are broader in scope but also less detailed on the evolution in the handling of variation.

In [5] and [16] various classifications are presented for the evolution of product families. Different sources for evolution are identified, e.g. the introduction of a new product, new features, new infrastructure, improvement of a quality attribute. In our paper we focused on the evolution that has to do with the handling of variation. Of course, not all evolution has to do with variation; other quality attributes may also change, or parts may be added to the system that provide new functionality.

6 Conclusions

In this paper we have discussed a method for the analysis of the variability of a product family. In our experience, a product family is exposed to constant changes in the outside world. These changes can be related to business, architecture, process, or organizational issues. It is therefore essential that we review earlier decisions to see whether improvements are needed with respect to the variability approach.

We used the BAPO/CAFCR reasoning framework as a starting point for our analysis, to describe the current situation and the expected future situation. We focused on the variability; how is it dealt with now, and what changes will have an impact on that method? We used automated extraction of the variation inside the system to provide us with a good basis for the analysis. We then consulted experts to complete our overall picture.

We used the gathered information as input for our analysis, paying particular attention to the following areas: the overall handling of variability, the identification of variation points, and the way the variation is realized in the system. We analyzed each of these areas and proposed improvements in the light of the changing context. For our particular case study, the main suggestions for improvement are to make an explicit model of the variation, to separate the generic from the specific functionality, to increase the clustering of the specific functionality, and to apply a more uniform approach. It is of course important that these suggestions fit in with the overall architectural approach and its future direction.

Acknowledgements

We thank our colleagues René Krikhaar and Eelco Rommes who reviewed an early version of this paper, and many other people at Philips Research and Philips Medical Systems.

This work was carried out in the European ITEA project Café.

References

1. Pierre America, Jan van Wijgerden, *Requirements Modeling for Families of Complex Systems*, Proceedings of the 3rd International Workshop on Software Architectures for Product Families, Springer Verlag LNCS 1951, pp. 199-209, 2000.
2. Pierre America, Eelco Rommes, Henk Obbink, *Multi-View Variation Modeling for Scenario Analysis*, Proceedings of the PFE-5 (this volume), Siena, November 2003.
3. Joachim Bayer, Oliver Flege, Peter Knauber, Roland Laqua, Dirk Muthig, Klaus Schmid, Tanya Widen, and Jean-Marc DeBaud, *PuLSE: A Methodology to Develop Software Product Lines*, Proceedings of the 5th Symposium on Software Reusability, pp. 122-131, Los Angeles, May 1999.
4. Jan Bosch, *Design & Use of Software Architectures*, Addison-Wesley, 2000.
5. Jan Bosch, Alexander Ran, *Evolution of Software Product Families*, Proceedings of the 3rd International Workshop on Software Architectures for Product Families, Springer Verlag LNCS 1951, pp. 168-183, 2000.
6. Frank Buschman, Regine Meunier, Hans Rohnert, Peter Sommerlad, Michael Stal, *A System of Patterns*, Wiley, 1996.
7. Frederick P. Brooks, *The Mythical Man-Month – Essays on Software Engineering*, Addison-Wesley, 1975.
8. Erich Gamma, Richard Helm, Ralph Johnson, John, Vlissides, *Design Patterns*, Addison-Wesley, 1995.
9. Philippe Kruchten et al., *Software Architecture Review and Assessment (SARA) Report*, http://www.rational.com/media/products/rup/sara_report.pdf, 2002.
10. Alessandro Maccari, *Experiences in Assessing Product Family Software Architecture for Evolution*, Proceedings of the 23rd IEEE International Conference on Software Engineering, Orlando, May 2002.

11. Henk Obbink, Jürgen Müller, Pierre America, Rob van Ommering, Gerrit Muller, William van der Sterren, Jan Gerben Wijnstra, *COPA: A Component-Oriented Platform Architecting Method for Families of Software-Intensive Electronic Products*, Tutorial at the SPLC1, Denver, August 2000.
(http://www.extra.research.philips.com/SAE/COPA/COPA_Tutorial.pdf)
12. Dewayne E. Perry, *Generic Architecture Descriptions for Product Lines*, Proceedings of the Second International Workshop on the Development and Evolution of Software Architectures for Product Families, Springer Verlag LNCS 1429, pp. 51-56, 1998.
13. Martin Pinzger, Harald Gall, Jean-Francois Girard, Jens Knodel, Claudio Riva, Wim Pasman, Jan Gerben Wijnstra, *Architecture Recovery for Product Families*, Proceedings of the PFE-5 (this volume), Siena, November 2003.
14. André Postma, *A Method for Module Architecture Verification and its Application on a Large Component-Based System,* Journal paper in Information and Software Technology, Vol. 45, No. 4, pp.171-194, March 2003.
15. Tobias Rötschke, René Krikhaar, *Architecture Analysis Tools to Support Evolution of Large Industrial Systems*, Proceedings of the International Conference on Software Maintenance, Montréal, October 2002.
16. Mikael Svahnberg, Jan Bosch, *Evolution in Software Product Lines: Two Cases*, Journal of Software Maintenance, Vol. 11, No. 6, pp. 391-422, 1999.
17. Frank Tip, *A Survey of Program Slicing Techniques*, Journal of Programming Languages, 3(3), September 1995.
18. Jan Gerben Wijnstra, *Critical Factors for a Successful Platform-based Product Family Approach*, Proceedings of the 2nd Software Product Line Conference, San Diego, Springer Verlag LNCS 2379, pp. 68-89, August 2002.
19. Jan Gerben Wijnstra, *Classifying Product Family Approaches using Platform Coverage and Variation*, submitted for publication to 'Software: Practice and Experience'.

Towards a UML Profile for Software Product Lines[*]

Tewfik Ziadi[1], Loïc Hélouët[1], and Jean-Marc Jézéquel[2]

. IRISA-INRIA, Campus de Beaulieu 35042 Rennes Cedex, France
{tziadi,lhelouet}@irisa.fr
. IRISA-Rennes1 University, Campus de Beaulieu 35042 Rennes Cedex, France
jezequel@irisa.fr

Abstract. This paper proposes a UML profile for software product lines. This profile includes stereotypes, tagged values, and structural constraints and it makes possible to define PL models with variabilities. Product derivation consists in generating product models from PL models. The derivation should preserve and ensure a set of constraints which are specified using the OCL.

1 Introduction

The Unified Modeling Language (UML) [5] is a standard for object-oriented analysis and design. It defines a set of notations (gathered in diagrams) to describe different aspects of a system: use cases, sequence diagrams, class diagrams, component diagrams and statecharts are examples of these notations. A UML *Profile* contains stereotypes, tagged values and constraints that can be used to extend the UML metamodel.

Software Product Line engineering aims at improving productivity and decrease realization times by gathering the analysis, design and implementation activities of a family of systems. Variabilities are characteristics that may vary from a product to another. The main challenge in the context of software Product Lines (PL) approach is to model and implement these variabilities. Even if the product line approach is a new paradigm, managing variability in software systems is not a new problem and some design and programming techniques allows to handle variability; however outside the Product Line context, variability concerns a single product, i.e variability is inherent part of a single software and is resolved after the product is delivered to customers and loaded into its final execution environment. In the product line context, variability should explicitly be specified and is a part of the product line. Contrarily to the single product variability, PL variability is resolved before the software product is delivered to customers. [1] calls the variability included in a single product "the run time variability", and the PL variability is called "the development time variability". UML includes some techniques such as inheritance, cardinality range, and class template that allow the description of variability in a single product i.e variablity is specified in the product models and resolved at run time. Furthermore, it is interesting to use UML to specify and to model not only one product but a set of products. In this case the UML models should be considered as reference models from which product models can be derived and created. This variability corresponds to the product line variability. In this paper we consider this type of

---

[*] This work has been partially supported by the FAMILIES European project. Eureka Σ! 2023 Program, ITEA project ip 02009.

F. van der Linden (Ed.): PFE 2003, LNCS 3014, pp. 129–139, 2004.

variability and we use UML extension mechanisms to specify product line variability in UML class diagrams and sequence diagrams. A set of *stereotypes*, *tagged values* and structural *constraints* are defined and gathered in a UML profile for PL.

The paper is organized as follows: Section 2 presents the profile for PL in terms of stereotypes, tagged values and constraints, Section 3 presents the use of this profile to derive product models from the PL, Section 4 presents related work, and Section 5 concludes this work.

2   A UML Profile for Product Lines

The extensions proposed here for PL are defined on the UML 2.0 [5] and they only concern the UML class diagrams and sequence diagrams. We use an ad - hoc example to illustrate our extensions. The example concerns a digital camera PL. A digital camera comports an interface, a memory, a sensor, a display and may comport a compressor. The main variability in this example concerns the presence of the compressor, the format of images supported by the memory, which can be parameterized and the interface supported. We distinguish three types of interfaces: Interface 1, Interface 2, and Interface 3.

2.1   Extensions for Class Diagrams

UML class diagrams are used to describe the structure of the system in terms of classes and their relationships. In the context of Product Lines, two types of variability are introduced and modeled using stereotypes.

Stereotypes

- **Optionality.** Optionality in PLs means that some features are optional for the PL members. i.e: they can be omitted in some products. The stereotype <<optional>> is used to specify optionality in UML class diagrams. The optionality can concern classes, packages, attributes or operations. So The <<optional>> stereotype is applied to *Classifier*, *Package* and *Feature* metaclasses.
- **Variation.** We model variation point using UML inheritance and stereotypes: each variation point will be defined by an abstract class and a set of subclasses. The abstract class will be defined with the stereotype <<variation>> and each subclass will be stereotyped <<variant>>. A specific product can choose one or more variants. These two stereotypes extend the metaclass *Classifier*. The alternative variability especially defined in feature driven approaches is a particular case of our variation variability type where each product should choose one and only one variant. This can be modeled using OCL (Object Constraint Language) [10] as a mutual exclusion constraint between variants. The mutual exclusion constraint will be presented in Section 3.

Constraints. A UML profile also includes constraints that can be used to define structural rules for all models specified by the defined stereotypes. An example of such profile constraint concerns the stereotype <<variant>>. It specifies that all classes stereo-typed <<variant>>, should have one and only one ancestor among all its ancestors stereotyped <<variation>>. This can be formalized using the OCL as follows:

context <<variant>>
inv: self.supertype → select(oclIsKindOf(Variation))→size()=1

Example. Figure 1 shows the class diagram of the camera PL example, the Com-pressor class is defined with the stereotype <<optional>> to indicate that some camera products do not support the compression feature. The camera interface is de-fined as an abstract class with three concrete subclasses: Interface 1, Interface 2, and Interface 3. A specific product can support one or more interfaces, so the stereotype <<variation>> is added to the abstract class Interface. All subclasses of the interface abstract class are defined with the stereotype <<variant>>. Notice that the class diagram of the camera PL includes a class template Memory with a parameter that indicates the supported format of images. This type of variability is resolved at run time and all camera products include it.

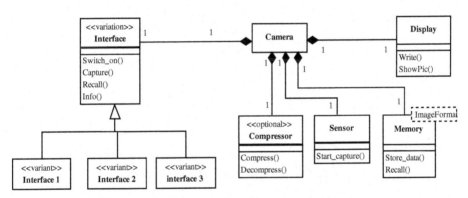

Fig. 1. The class diagram of the Camera PL

2.2   UML Extensions for Sequence Diagrams

In addition to class diagrams, UML includes other diagrams that describe other aspects of systems. Sequence diagrams model the possible interactions in a system. They are generally used to capture the requirements, but can then be used to document a system, or to produce tests. The UML 2.0 [5] makes sequences diagrams very similar to the ITU standard MSC (Message Sequence Chart)[7]. It introduces new mechanisms, especially interaction operators such as alternative, sequence, and loop to design respectively a choice, a sequencing, and a repetition of interactions. [11] proposes three constructs to introduce variability in MSC. In this subsection we formalize this proposition in terms of extensions on the UML 2.0 metamodel for sequence diagrams. Before describing these extensions, we briefly present sequence diagrams as defined in UML 2.0 metamodel.

Sequence Diagrams in UML 2.0. Figure 2 summarizes the UML 2.0 metamodel part that concerns sequence diagrams (interested readers can consult [5] for a complete description of the metamodel). The *Interaction* metaclass refers to the unit of behavior that focuses on the observable exchanges of information between a set of objects in the sequence diagram. The *Lifeline* metaclass refers to the object in the interaction. *InteractionFragment* is a piece of an interaction. The aggregation between the *Interaction* and the *InteractionFragment* specifies composite interaction, in the sense that an interaction can enclose other sub-interactions. The *CombinedFragment* defines a set of interaction operators that can be used to combine a set of *InteractionOperand*. All possible operators are defined in the enumeration *InteractionOperator*. The *EventOccurence* metaclass refers to events that occur on a specific lifeline, these events can be either sending, receiving messages or other kinds. The notation of an interaction in a sequence diagram is a solid-outline rectangle (see Figure 3 for example). The keyword **sd** followed by the name of the interaction in a pentagon in the upper left corner of the rectangle.

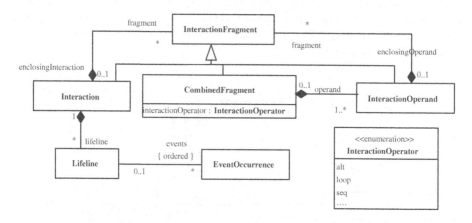

Fig. 2. UML 2.0 metamodel: Interaction part [5]

Stereotypes and Tagged Values. Variability for sequence diagrams is introduced in terms of three constructs: Optionality, Variation and Virtuality, in what follows we formalize these constructs using stereotypes and tagged values on the UML 2.0 metamodel.

- **Optionality.** Optionality proposed for sequence diagrams comports two main aspects: optionality for objects in the interaction, and optionality for interactions themselves. Optionality for object is specified using the stereotype <<optionalLifeline>> that extends the *Lifeline* metaclass. Optional interactions are specified by the stereotype <<optionalInteraction>> that extends the *Interaction* metaclass.
- **Variation.** A variation point in a PL sequence diagram means that for a given product, only one interaction variant defined by the variation point will be present in the derived sequence diagram. The *Interaction* encloses a set of sub-interactions, the variation mechanism can be specified by two stereotypes: <<variation>> and <<variant>>; the both stereotypes extend the *Interaction* metaclass. To

distinguish different variants in the same sequence diagram, we associate to the interaction stereotyped with <<variant>> a tagged value: {variation = Variation} to indicates its enclosing variation point(the enclosing interaction stereotyped with <<variation>>).

- **Virtuality.** A virtual part in a sequence diagram means that this part can be redefined for each product by another sequence diagram. The virtual part is defined using a stereotype <<virtual>> that extends the *Interaction* metaclass.

An interaction can be a variation point and a variant for another variation point in the same time. This means that it is enclosed in the interaction stereotyped <<variation>> and in the same time it encloses a set of interaction variants. In this situation, the interaction is defined with the two stereotypes: <<variation>> and <<variant>>.

Constraints. Structural constraints can be associated to the stereotypes and the tagged value defined above. For example, the constraint that concerns the <<variant>> stereotype and that specifies that each interaction stereotyped <<variant>> should be enclosed in one and only one interaction stereotyped <<variation>> can be formalized using OCL as an invariant to the <<variant>> stereotype:

context<<variant>>
inv: self.enclosingInteraction → select(oclIsKindOf(Variation)→ size()=1

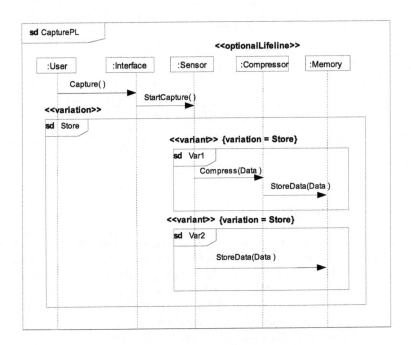

Fig. 3. The Sequence Diagram Capture

Example. Figure 2 shows the `CapturePL` sequence diagram that concerns the camera PL example. It illustrates the interaction to capture and to store data into the memory. This sequence diagram includes two types of variability: the presence of the `Compressor` object and the variation in the interaction `Store`. The `Compressor` lifeline is defined as optional, and the interaction `Store` (stereotyped `<<variation>>`) defines two variants interaction `Var1` and `Var2` (stereotyped `<<variant>>`) to store data into the memory. The first stores data after its compression and the second one stores them without compression. The tagged value {`variation = Store`} is added to the two interactions variants.

Table 1. Stereotypes and tagged values in the UML profile for PL

Stereotype/Tagged values	Applies to	Description
<<optional>>	Classifier, Package, Feature	Indicates that the element (classifier, package, or feature) is optional.
<< variation>>	Classifier	Indicates that the abstract class represents a variation point with a set of variants.
<<variant>>	Classifier	Indicates that a class is a variant of a variation point.
<<optionalLifeline>>	Lifeline	Indicates that the lifeline in the sequence diagram is optional.
<<optionalInteraction>>	Interaction	Indicates that the behavior described by the interaction is optional.
<<variation>>	Interaction	Indicates that the interaction is a variation point with two or more interaction variants.
<<variant>>	Interaction	Indicates that the interaction is a variant behavior in the context of a variation interaction.
<<virtual>>	Interaction	Indicates that the interaction is a virtual part.
{variation = Variation}	<<variant>>	Indicates the variation point related to this variant.

2.3   The Profile Structure

Table 1 summarizes the defined stereotypes and tagged values in the UML profile for PL. Figure 4 illustrates the structure of the proposed profile for PL (we follow notations for profiles as defined in [5]). Stereotypes are defined as class stereotyped with `<<stereotype>>`. UML metaclasses are defined as classes stereotyped with `<<metaclass>>`. Tagged values are defined as attributes for the defined stereotypes. The extensions proposed for class diagrams are defined in the `staticAspect` package, and thus for sequence diagrams are gathered in the `dynamicAspect` package. The `<<variant>>` stereotype in the `staticAspect` (respectively in the package

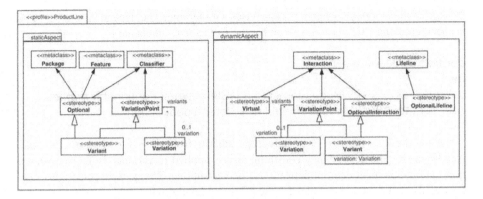

Fig. 4. UML profile for PL

dynamicAspect) inherits from the <<optional>> stereotype (respectively from the <<optionalInteraction>> stereotype). This means that each variant is optional too.

3   From PL Models to Product Models

A UML profile includes not only stereotypes, tagged values and constraints but also a set of operational rules that define how the profile can be used. These rules concern for example code generation from models that conform to this profile or model transformations. For the PL profile, this part can be used to define the product derivations as model transformations. A product derivation consists in generating from PL models the UML models of each product. The product line architecture is defined as a standard architecture with a set of constraints [2]. PL constraints guide the derivation process. In what follows we present two types of PL constraints: the generic constraints that apply to all PL, and specific constraints that concern a specific PL. We show how these constraints should be considered for the derivation process.

3.1   Generic Constraints

The introduction of variability, and more especially optionality in the UML class diagrams (specified by the <<optional>> stereotype), improves genericity but can generate some incoherences. For example, if a non-optional element depends on an optional one, the derivation can produce an incomplete product model. So the derivation process should *preserve* the coherence of the derived products. [12] proposes to formalize coherence constraints using OCL. Constraints that concern any PL model are called *Generic Constraints*. An example of such constraint is the dependency constraint that forces non optional elements to depend only on non optional elements. A dependency in the UML specifies a require relationship between two or more elements. It is represented in the UML meta-model [5] by the meta-class *Dependency*; it represents the relationship between a set of suppliers and clients. An example of the UML Dependency is the

"Usage", which appears when a package uses another one. The dependency constraints is specified using OCL as an invariant for the *Dependency* metaclass[1]:

context Dependency
inv:
self.supplier exists(S:ModelElement | S.isStereotyped ('optional')) **implies**
self.client **forAll**(C:ModelElement | C.isStereotyped('optional'))

While the <<variant>> stereotype inherits from the <<optional>> one (see Figure 4), the dependency constraint also is applied to variants. In the sens that a non-optional element can not depends on the variant one. The generic constraints may be seen as well-formedness rules for the UML modeled product line.

3.2   Specific Constraints

A fundamental characteristic of product lines is that all elements are not compatible. That is, the selection of one element may disable (or enable) the selection of others. For example in the sequence diagram CapturePL in Figure 4 the choice of the variant Var1 in the specific product needs the presence of the compressor object. Dependencies between PL model elements are called *Specific Constraints*. They are associated to a specific product line and will be evaluated on all products derived from this PL. So another challenge for the product derivation is to *ensure* specific constraints in the derived products. These constraints can be formalized as OCL meta-level constrains [12]. The following constraint specifies the presence dependency in the sequence diagram CapturePL between the interaction variant Var1, and the Compressor lifeline. i.e: the presence of the interaction variant Var1 requires the presence of the Compressor lifeline. It is added as an invariant to the *Interaction* metaclass:

context Interaction
inv: self.fragments → **exists** (I: IntercationFragment | I.name ='Var1') **implies**
self.lifeline → **exists** (L:Lifeline | L.name='Compressor')

In addition to the presence constraint, specific constraints include the mutual exclusion constraint. It expresses in a specific PL model that two optional classes cannot be present in the same product. This can be formalized using OCL, for example the mutual exclusion constraint between two optional classes called C1 and C2 in a specific PL is expressed using OCL as an invariant to the Model meta-class[2]:

context Model
inv:
self.presenceClass('C1') **implies not** self.presenceClass('C2'))
and (self.presenceClass('C2') **implies not** self.presenceClass('C1'))

---

[1] isStereotyped(S) : boolean is an auxiliary OCL operation indicates if an element is stereotyped by a string *S*.

[2] presenceClass(C) : boolean is an auxiliary OCL operation indicates if a class named C is present in a specific UML Model.

3.3   Product Models Derivation

The products derivation consists in generating from the PL models (UML class diagrams and sequence diagrams) models for each product. Product line models should satisfy generic constraints *before* the derivation while the derived product model should satisfy specific constraints. This means that generic constraints represent the pre-conditions of the derivation process and specific constraints represent the post - conditions for the derivation process:

DeriveProduct(PLModel : **Model**):**Model**
pre: –check generic constrains on PLModel
post: – check specific constraints on the derived product model.

Figure 5 shows the derived class diagram for a camera product. This product does not support the compression feature and only supports Interface 1 and Interface 2. It is obtained from the PL class diagram by removing the class Compressor and the class Interface 3. Figure 6 shows the derived Capture sequence diagram for this camera product. It is obtained by removing the Compressor lifeline and the choice of the Var2 interaction (the Var1 interaction is removed).

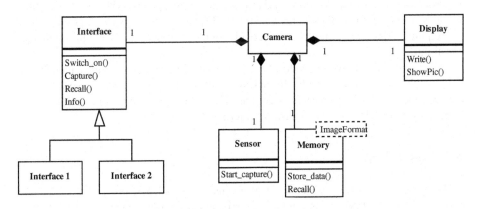

Fig. 5. The derived class diagram for a specific camera product

4   Related Work

Many work have studied modeling of PL variability using UML. [4] uses UML extensions mechanisms to specify variability in UML diagrams. However, despite the <<optional>> stereotype for UML statecharts and sequence diagrams, these extensions mainly focuses on the static aspects of the PL architecture. To model dynamic aspects of PLs, we have proposed three constructs to specify variability in sequence diagrams.

KobrA [1] is a method that combines product line engineering and component-based software development. It uses the UML to specify component. Variability is introduced

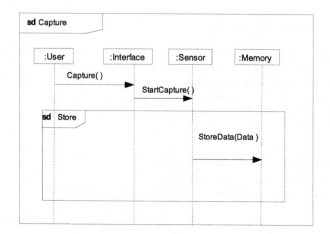

Fig. 6. The derived Sequence Diagram for a specific camera product

in the KobrA components using the <<variant>> stereotype. This stereotype is used to model any feature that are not common to all product. [3] proposes a set of UML extensions to describe product line variability. They only concern UML class diagrams. While we use OCL to model specific constraints, [3] models them using two stereotypes: <<require>> and <<mutex>> respectively for the presence and the exclusion mutuel constraint.

[9] proposes notations for product lines. They are gathered in the profile called UML-F. In fact this profile is defined for frameworks and it only concerns static aspects of the product line. [8] proposes a metamodel based on UML for product line architectures. Variability is introduced only in terms of alternatives.

5   Conclusion

In this paper, we have proposed a set of extensions as a UML profile for PL. These extensions concern UML class diagrams, and sequence diagrams. They are defined on the UML 2.0 metamodel. This profile is not yet implemented. We have only proposed some constraints, the definition of the defined profile should be refined with more constraints.

We intend to implement this profile with the UMLAUT. UMLAUT [6] is a framework for building tools dedicated to the manipulation of models described using the UML. A new version of the UMLAUT framework is currently under construction in the Triskell[3] team based on the MTL (Model Transformation Language), which is an extension of OCL with the MOF (Meta-Object Facility) architecture and side effect features, so it permits us to describe the process at the meta-level and to check OCL constraints. The MTL language can be used to define the derivation process.

---

[3] www.irisa.fr/triskell

References

1. Colin Atkinson, Joachim Bayer, Christian Bunse, Erik Kamsties, Oliver Laitenberger, Roland Laqua, Dirk Muthig, Barbara Paech, Jürgen Wüst, and Jörg Zettel. *Component-based Product Line Engineering with UML*. Component Software Series. Addison-Wesley, 2001.
2. Clements.P Bass.L and Kazman.R. *Software Architecture in Practices*. Addison-Wesley, 1998.
3. Matthias Clauß. Modeling variability with uml. In *GCSE 2001 Young Researchers Workshop*, 2001.
4. J.C Duenas, W. El Kaim, and Gacek C. Style, structure and views for handling commonalities and varibilities - esaps deliverable (wg 2.2.3). Technical report, ESAPS Project, 2001.
5. Object Management Group. Uinified modeling language specification version 2.0: Superstructure. Technical Report pct/03-08-02, OMG, 2003.
6. Wai-Ming Ho, Jean-Marc Jézéquel, Alain Le Guennec, and François Pennaneac'h. UMLAUT: an extendible UML transformation framework. In *Proc. Automated Software Engineering, ASE'99, Florida*, October 1999.
7. ITU-T. Z.120 : Message sequence charts (MSC), november 1999.
8. Dirk Muthig and Colin Atkinson. Model-driven product line architectures. In Gary J. Chastek, editor, *Software Product Lines, Second International Conference, SPLC 2, San Diego, CA, USA, August 19-22, 2002, Proceedings*, volume 2379 of *Lecture Notes in Computer Science*. Springer, 2002.
9. Wolfgang Pree, Marcus Fontoura, and Bernhard Rumpe. Product line annotations with uml-f. In Gary J. Chastek, editor, *Software Product Lines, Second International Conference, SPLC 2, San Diego, CA, USA, August 19-22, 2002, Proceedings*, volume 2379 of *Lecture Notes in Computer Science*. Springer, 2002.
10. J. Warmer and A. Kleppe. *The Object Constraint Language-Precise Modeling with UML*. Object Technology Series. Addison-Wesley, 1998.
11. Tewfik Ziadi, Loïc Hélouët, and Jean-Marc Jézéquel. Modeling behaviors in Product Lines. In *Proceedings of Requirement Engineering for Product Lines Workshop (REPL02)*, pages 33–38, September 2002.
12. Tewfik Ziadi, Jean-Marc Jézéquel, and Frédéric Fondement. Product line derivation with uml. In Jilles van Gurp and Jan Bosh, editors, *Proceedings Software Variability Management Workshop*, pages 94–102. University of Groningen Departement of Mathematics and Computing Science, 2003.

Applying System Families Concepts to Requirements Engineering Process Definition*

Amador Durán[1], David Benavides[1], and Jesus Bermejo[2]

· Department of Computer Languages and Systems
University of Seville, Reina Mercedes S/N, 41012 Seville, Spain
amador@lsi.us.es,benavides@us.es
· Telvent
Tamarguillo, 29, 41006 Seville, Spain
jesus.bermejo@telvent.abengoa.com

Abstract. In this paper, some experiences gained during the definition of a unified, common software development process for several companies in Telvent are presented. Last year, Telvent made the decision of developing a unique software development process which was flexible enough to be adapted to specific practices and needs of the different companies. In this paper we focus mainly on the experiences gained during the definition of the requirements engineering process, al-though many of them are also applicable to other software development processes. One of the most interesting experiences from our point of view is that, al-though the definition process was started using a top-down approach and well-know techniques like data flow diagrams, we eventually end up applying requirements engineering techniques like glossaries, scenarios or conflict resolution for the definition of the requirements engineering process itself. On the other hand, the need of having adaptable processes for the different companies in Telvent made us adopt a *process family* approach, i.e. adopting an approach similar to the system families development, thus defining a core process that could be adapted to specific needs of specific companies in a predefined, controlled manner. The experiences gained in the definition of the process family were applied to the definition of requirements engineering process for product line development, which is briefly presented in this paper.

Keywords: Requirements Engineering Process, Systems Families

1 Introduction

Definition and adoption of requirements engineering (RE) processes in software development companies is a complex task not easy to accomplish [10,13]. This task is even harder in a company like Telvent, composed of several companies developing a wide spectrum of systems like information systems, real–time control systems or satellite communication systems.

Each company has its own specific needs for developing software, depending on the type of software, the customer characteristics, the standards to be applied, if they are project-oriented or product-oriented, etc.

* This work is partially supported by the Eureka Σ! 2023 programme, ITEA ip00004 project CAFÉ and by the Spanish CICYT project TIC 2000–1106–C02–01 (GEOZOCO).

F. van der Linden (Ed.): PFE 2003, LNCS 3014, pp. 140–151, 2004.

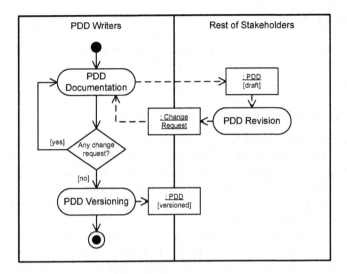

Fig. 1. PDD Iterative Workflow

In 2002, Telvent decided to adopt an ISO–12207–based [9], common software development process that should fit the needs of all its companies thus avoiding the maintenance of several internal standards and saving training costs when some employees had to move from one company to another within Telvent. For that purpose, some research staff from the Department of Computer Languages and Systems of the University of Seville were hired by Telvent as consultants. In this context a process family approach was used where a commin core process was defined. This process serve as base for specific processes in different companies therefore it includes *process variability*

For the definition of the common processes, at least one person from each company, including quality assurance people and consultants from the University of Seville, was selected. Depending on the specific process, i.e. requirements engineering, software design, software testing, etc., one or two persons were selected as responsible for writing a draft version of the corresponding process description document (PDD). Then, the draft version of the PDD was reviewed during meetings in which all stakeholders took part. The people responsible for the PDD registered the proposed changes and then presented an updated version of the PDD in the next meeting. This iterative process ended when no more change proposals were submitted and the PDD was baselined, as shown in the UML activity diagram in figure 1.

In this paper, we focus on the problems we found, the solutions we applied and the experience we gained during the definition of the RE process. The rest of the paper is organized as follows. In section 2, some initial problems are described. In section 3 we present how we addressed the variability in the core RE process so it could be adapted to different needs of the companies in Telvent. In section 4 we briefly described the RE process for product line developed applying some of the experiences described in previous sections. Finally in section 5 we present some conclusions.

2   Initial Problems

In this section we present some of the initial problems we identified at the beginning of the definition process and how they were, totally or partially, solved applying RE techniques.

2.1   Lack of a Common Vocabulary

One of the first detected problems was the lack of a common vocabulary among all stakeholders. Depending on their backgrounds, the type of software they were used to developing or the standards they had had to apply in previous developments, the vocabularies of the involved people were quite different from each other. This problem provoked that many hours in the initial meetings were wasted discussing subtle semantic aspects about some words or phrases.

In order to solve this problem, and after some disappointing meetings, we decided to follow Leite's approach [11] of building a glossary (also know as *lexicon*) at the beginning of the process in order to understand the language of the problem before the problem itself. Items in the glossary should defined not only their corresponding concepts (*notions* in Leite's terminology) but also their interactions (*behavioral responses* in Leite's terminology) with other concepts, as shown in figure 2, where references to other glossary items are underlined[1]. As a matter of fact, the glossary was the first official document in which we started to work.

...

Change request: Request for the modification of any item previously baselined. The author of the change request can be any member of the Software Development Group or any other person working in the corresponding product line. The motivation for the change request can be an error detection in the corresponding product or an enhance suggestion. Change requests must be processed by the Change Control Board.

...

Change Control Board: Group composed of senior programmers from the Software Development Group, the Product Test Manager, the Configuration Control Manager, and the Documentation Manager. The mission of this board is to manage all change requests, perform the corresponding impact analysis and allocate the responsibilities for the change process.

...

Fig. 2. Glossary excerpt

If some stakeholders did not agree about the meaning of a specific concept even after consulting standards glossaries like [8], we voted what we considered the meaning of the concept and the glossary was updated democratically. In this way, we saved time and avoid personal confrontation apart of developing a comprehensive and useful glossary of software development terms.

---

[1] In the HTML version of the glossary, references to other items were actually hyperlinks.

Fig. 3. Adopted notation for complex activities and use of tagged values

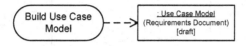

Fig. 4. Adopted notation for *whole/part* object flows

2.2   Lack of Common Process Notation

Another initial problem was the selection of a diagrammatic process notation that was accepted by all stakeholders and helped them have a way of visualizing processes' sequence of tasks and a general overview of process interactions.

Data flow diagrams (DFD) [15] were rapidly discarded because of the impossibility of representing neither sequence of activities nor conditional flows. After discarding DFDs, UML activity diagrams [12] were considered as a tentative notation and eventually adopted with some adaptations from the original notation. These adaptations were the following:

1. In order to know what PDD described the corresponding activity in an activity diagram, we added a *tagged value*[2] in every activity which was described in a PDD, as shown in figure 3. The tagged value was named *PDD* and its value was the corresponding code of the PDD in which the activity was described in more detail.
2. Although in the last version of UML (UML 1.4 [12]), complex activities are depicted by adding a small activity diagram in the lower left corner of the activity icon, the lack of a CASE tool supporting this and other changes introduced in UML 1.4 made us adopt an easier-to-draw notation. In the adopted notation, a complex activity is drawn using a dash line, as show in figure 3.
3. More often than not, output object flows of activities were parts of documents to be generated during some process. In order to show this in the activity diagrams, we adopted the notation for object flows that can be seen in figure 4, in which for *part* objects, the corresponding *whole* object name is also included in the object flow icon right under the name of the *part* object inside parentheses. In the example depicted in figure 4, the Use Case Model object flow is part of the Requirements Document object flow.
4. Those object flows that were shared by two or more processes, i.e. *interface object flows*, were depicted adding a shadow on the lower left corner of the object flow icon, as shown in figure 5.

---

[2] *Tagged values* are one of the extensibility mechanisms of UML. Tagged values are pairs {*name=value*} used to add extra information to model elements.

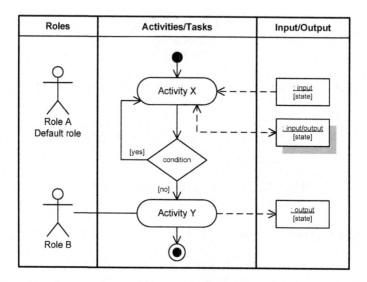

Fig. 5. Adopted notation for swimlanes

5. When many actors participated in an activity diagram, the use of more than three or four different swimlanes made the diagrams very complex to be drawn and difficult to read. On the other hand, a high number of object flows in a diagram resulted in too much crossing lines. In order to avoid these two problems, a different use of swimlanes was adopted.

We decided to use only three swimlanes. The first swimlane was used for including *roles*, i.e. actors performing or participating in some activity in the diagram. The second swimlane was used for activities and tasks. The third one was used for input/output object flows. In this way, the resulting diagrams were much more easier to be created and read (see figure 5). If a role participated in an activity, an association between the role and the activity was added to the diagram.

In the case a role participated in all activities in a diagram, the role was considered as a *default role* and associations between the default role and all the activities were not drawn, making the diagram easier to read.

For example, in figure 5 role *A* participates in activities *X* and *Y*, while role *B* participates only in activity *Y*.

2.3   Describing Process Interactions

Although the use of enhanced UML activity diagrams increased communication and agreement among all stakeholders, having a *big picture*, i.e. an overview of all processes and their interactions, was still a problem. For that purpose, one of the stakeholders took the responsibility of developing a *process map*.

The process map should show all ISO–12207 high–level processes and their interactions, i.e. the products they interchanged with each other, usually documents or software.

After some weeks of work, the final result was an A0 size sheet with dozens of icons and crossing lines which was difficult to understand. In order to make the process map more usable, different views of it were developed. Each view was focused on only one of the processes and their interactions, thus simplifying the initial process map.

Anyway, since the processes in the process map were the ISO–12207 high level processes, i.e. development, operation, maintenance, management, configuration management, etc. (see [9] for more details), it was still very difficult to know what was the interaction between processes in specific situations.

In other words, if a new employee were hired, performing a specific task taking into account all process interactions would make necessary to read several documents carefully and deduced the implied interactions. Something that would probably take too much time.

In order to avoid these problems, we consider the use of *scenarios* [11], i.e. descriptions of interactions in a given situation. For example, *what happens when a customer applies for a change and the requirements document is not baselined yet?*, *what if the requirement document is already baselined?*, *what are the roles implied?*.

After considering different scenario description techniques (including different approaches for use case descriptions like [2] or [6]), we eventually chose Leite's scenarios because of their simplicity and expressiveness (see [11] for a detailed description).

We introduced some adaptations to the original notation. For example, we dropped the *exceptions* section after some initial descriptions because it seemed unnecessary for our purposes. We added a *variations* section in the scenario description in order to describe possible alternatives to process enactment. We also introduced substeps into conditional blocks in order to ease reading. As proposed by Leite, glossary items in the scenario text are underlined and references to other scenarios appear in upper case. See figure 6 for an example.

3   Introducing Variability in the Common RE Process

A high–level model of the RE process was developed and agreed among all stakeholders (see figures 7 and 8). In this RE process, three main subprocesses were identified, namely requirements development, requirements negotiation and requirements management. The responsibilities of each process the following:

- Requirements Development: this is the most important subprocess and it is responsible for the elicitation, analysis, verification and validation of requirements. It is composed of four activities forming what we call the *requirements pipeline* whose responsibilities are:
  - Requirements Elicitation: this activity is responsible of eliciting requirements from customers and users and producing a draft version of requirements. It is the most complex one due to the needed human interaction. The usual techniques are interviews, meetings, observation, documentation analysis, etc.
  - Requirements Analysis: this activity is responsible for analyzing elicited requirements in order to identify conflicts. If conflicts are identified, they must be solved by the Requirements Negotiation subprocess. The usual technique is requirements modelling.

Title: Register a new Customer Request before requirements are baselined.
Goal: Make requirements according to customers needs.
Context: The project has started and the Requirements Document is not baselined yet.
Resources: Requirements Document, Requirements Management Tool, Configuration Management Tool.
Roles: Customer, Requirements Engineer, Project Manager, Configuration Management Manager, Software Quality Assurance Group.

Steps:

1. A Customer informs of a new Customer Request.
2. The Requirements Engineer registers the new request using a Requirements Management Tool.
3. The Requirements Engineer performs an Impact Analysis of the Customer Request.
4. The Requirements Engineer informs the Project Manager of the results of the Impact Analysis of the Customer Request.
5. Depending on the Impact Analysis, the Project Manager makes the decision of accepting the Customer Request, rejecting the Customer Request or Organizing a Meeting of the Change Control Board.
6. If the Customer Request is eventually accepted, then
    6.1 The Customer Request is incorporated into the Requirements Document as a new Requirement.
    6.2 The Configuration Management Manager manages the new version of the Requirements Document.
    6.3 The Software Quality Assurance Group performs Requirements Verification on the new Requirement.
7. If the Customer Request is eventually rejected, then
    7.1 The Customer Request is incorporated into the Requirements Document as a Rejected Change Request.
    7.2 The Configuration Management Manager manages the new version of the Requirements Document.

Variations:

1. A Customer may inform of a new request by phone (to a previously specified contact person in our company), by fax, by email (to a contact person) or personally.

2. Depending on the maturity of the Requirements Engineering process at the company developing the project, the Requirements Management Tool can be a spreadsheet tool like Excel or an actual Requirements Management Tool like DOORS or Requisite Pro.

3. Depending on the facilities provided by the Requirements Management Tool, the Requirements Engineer can perform the Impact Analysis manually or using the Requirements Management Tool. In both cases, a previous Traceability policy has to be considered in the Software Development Plan.

4. Depending on the company policy (or the project policy), if the impact of the Customer Request is considered to be non significant by the Requirements Engineer, steps 4 and 5 can be skipped, so the Project Manager is not directly informed of the Customer Request.

6.2/7.2 Depending on the Configuration Management Plan of the project, these steps can be performed automatically without the intervention of the Configuration Management Manager.

Fig. 6. Scenario Example

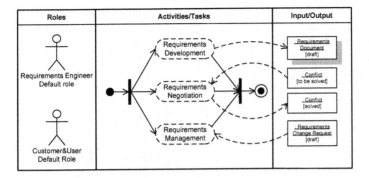

Fig. 7. High–level Requirements Engineering Process

- Requirements Verification: this activity is responsible for verifying analyzed requirements in order to detect defects. If defects are found, they must be solved by the requirements writers in the Requirements Elicitation activity. The usual techniques are checklists, formal reviews, inspections, etc.
- Requirements Validation: this activity is responsible for validating verified requirements, thus confirming that they are consistent with the intentions of customer and users. As in the Requirements Verification activity, if conflicts are found, they must be solved by the Requirements Negotiation subprocess. The usual technique is user interface prototyping.

– Requirements Negotiation: this subprocess is responsible for solving all conflicts identified during the Requirements Development subprocess. The solved conflicts are fed back into the Requirements Elicitation activity, the head of the requirements pipeline.
– Requirements Management: this subprocess is responsible for the management of the Requirements Engineering process. Their main responsibilities are requirements change request management and traceability.

Apart from the variations section of process scenarios like the one in figure 6, which allows the introduction of a certain amount of variability in the RE process, once a high–level model of the RE process was developed and agreed among all stakeholders (see figures 7 and 8), it was needed to include different needs from different companies in Telvent. Following a product line approach [1], we identified different *features* which could be necessary in order to tailor the core RE processes for the different companies in Telvent.

3.1   Elicitation Techniques Variability

One of the first features identified as variants were elicitation techniques, requirements documents templates and (single) requirements templates. Some companies were used to apply interviews as the only elicitation technique while others used questionnaires, group meetings or even video–conference for widely distributed projects.

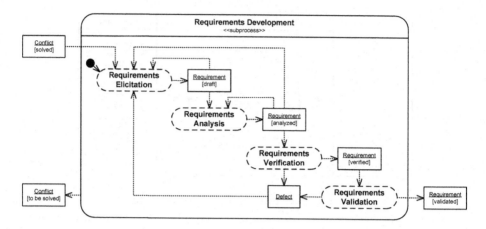

Fig. 8. Requirements Development Subprocess

For requirements analysis, some companies preferred structured techniques like entity-relationship diagrams and data flow diagrams while other preferred object-oriented techniques.

In order to express these possible variants we adopted stereotyped UML class diagrams similar to the notation proposed in [14]. For example, the hierarchy of elicitation techniques in figure 9 is presented as a feature of the requirements elicitation activity. When a company has to tailor the requirements elicitation activity, some of the elicitation techniques must be chosen. In this case, an important issue about feature selection was the selection criteria. Some heuristics were also developed in order to help project managers chose the right feature, i.e. the right elicitation technique. Those heuristics were based on the previous work by Davis and Hickey [4].

3.2   Roles Variability

Another configurable *feature* of the RE process was the roles of the different Telvent personnel performing the RE process. Role names and responsibilities had to be adapted to the different backgrounds of the Telvent companies[3].

There was also the possibility of determining for every project if a role was played simultaneously by another person playing another role or by a specific person playing one role only.

For example, in figure 10 the Requirements Verifier role can be played by the person playing the Requirements Engineer role, by the person playing the SQA role o by a person playing the Requirements Verifier role specifically.

3.3   Documentation Variability

Another important aspect of the RE process variability was the documentation to be delivered. Depending on the customer, sometimes the requirements document should be

---

[3] Actually, role names are in the way to be universally adopted in all Telvent companies, although there is an adaptative period of 2 years. Role names were one of the concepts which generated more discussion when building the glossary of software development terms (see section 2.1).

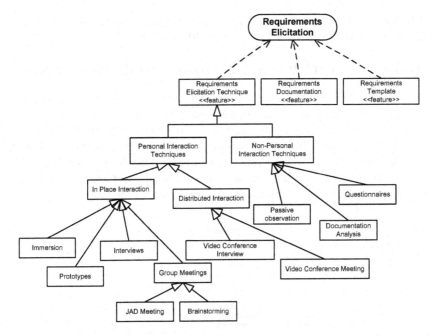

Fig. 9. Requirements Elicitation Techniques Feature Hierarchy

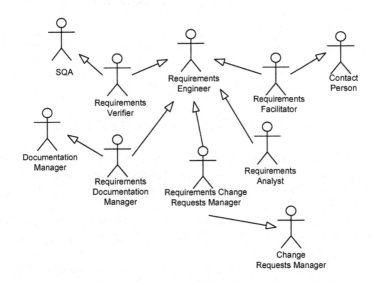

Fig. 10. Requirements Engineering Role Hierarchy

written using IEEE–830 [7], MÉTRICA [3] (Spanish Government Methodology, similar to SSADM) or other official standards. Keeping the same core RE process, concrete products were tailored in order to be compliant with standards like those previously mentioned.

The way how requirements were written, i.e. a requirements template [5], was also considered as a possible variable feature of the RE process.

4   Definition of a RE Process for Systems Families Development

One of the most important middle–term goals of Telvent at the beginning of the definition of common software development processes was to adopt a product line approach [1] in some of their companies. From the experience gained in the definition of the "process family" for RE, some results were extrapolated into an RE process family for product line development. An overview of the new RE core process for product line development is shown in figure 11, where key activities are highlighted and the Requirements Development subprocess has been flattened for the sake of simplicity.

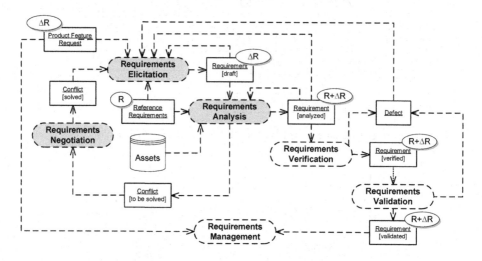

Fig. 11. RE Process for Systems Families Development

The main difference between the single–product RE process and the product line oriented RE process is the introduction of the Reference Requirements and the set of reusable assets as inputs of the Requirements Elicitation, Analysis and Negotiation activities.

In this new RE process, Requirements Elicitation is responsible for identifying new product features, but taking into account reference requirements, so the degree of freedom is substantially reduced.

Requirements Analysis is responsible not only for the identification of conflicts in new requirements (delta requirements), but also for the identification of conflicts between new requirements and reference requirements, which can be a much harder work than for a project–oriented RE process. What is more, in order to identify conflicts, assets in the product line must be taken into account, making the activity more complex.

On the other hand, solving conflicts, i.e. Requirements Negotiation, is now a critical activity. Conflicts must be solved not only from a logical point of view, but also taking into consideration economical and market issues.

5   Conclusions

The main lesson we have learned after our experience is that defining a common process (software development process, RE process or other kind of process) for different organizations with different needs is a complex task that can be seen as a RE problem where RE techniques can be successfully applied. From an abstract point of view, our task was to develop a product – a RE process embedded in a system/software development process – that must satisfy different, sometimes contradictory, stakeholders' needs. If we had taken the reflexive RE approach from the beginning, instead of trying to impose a common RE process in a top–down fashion, we would have saved time and effort.

Applying the same solutions for the definition of an RE process family, we have started the definition of a RE process family for product line development, part of which has been briefly presented in this paper.

Another interesting lesson is that, sometimes, a product families approach can help in requirements negotiation. If an agreement is not possible, maybe we can develop a small product family satisfying incompatible stakeholders' needs.

References

1. P. Clements and L. Northrop. *Software Product Lines: Practices and Patterns*. Addison–Wesley, 2002.
2. A. Cockburn. *Writing Effective Use Cases*. Addison–Wesley, 2001.
3. CSJ. Metodología de Planificación, Desarrollo y Mantenimiento de Sistemas de Información. MÉTRICA Versión 3 (Borrador). Borrador, Consejo Superior de Informática, 2000. Disponible en http://www.map.es/csi/pg5m42.htm.
4. A. Davis and A. Hickey. Learn how to select the "right" requirements elicitation technique. In *Tutorial at RE'02*, 2002.
5. A. Durán, B. Bernárdez, A. Ruiz, and M. Toro. A Requirements Elicitation Approach Based in Templates and Patterns. In *WER'99 Proceedings*, Buenos Aires, 1999.
6. A. Durán, A. Ruiz, R. Corchuelo, and M. Toro. Supporting Requirements Verification Using XSLT. In *Proceedings of the IEEE Joint International Requirements Engineering Conference*. IEEE CS Press, 2002.
7. IEEE. Recommended Practice for Software Requirements Specifications. IEEE/ANSI Standard 830–1998.
8. IEEE. IEEE Standard Glossary of Software Engineering Terminology. IEEE Standard 610.12–1990, Institute of Electrical and Electronics Engineers, 1990.
9. ISO/IEC. Information Technology–Software Life Cycle Processes. International Standard 12207 : 1995, International Organization for Standarazition, 1995.
10. G. Kontoya and I. Sommerville. *Requirements Engineering: Processes and Techniques*. Wiley, 1997.
11. J. C. S. P. Leite, H. Hadad, J. Doorn, and G. Kaplan. A Scenario Construction Process. *Requirements Engineering Journal*, 5(1), 2000.
12. OMG. Unified Modeling Language, v1.4. Technical report, September 2001.
13. I. Sommerville and P. Sawyer. *Requirements Engineering: A Good Practice Guide*. Wiley, 1997.
14. Jilles van Gurp, Jan Bosch, and Mikael Svahnberg. On the notion of variability in software product lines. In *Proceedings of the Working IEEE/IFIP Conference on Software Architecture (WICSA'01)*, 2001.
15. E. Yourdon. *Modern Structured Analysis*. Prentice–Hall, 1989.

Elicitation of Use Cases for Product Lines

Alessandro Fantechi[1], Stefania Gnesi[2], Isabel John[3], Giuseppe Lami[2], and Jörg Dörr[3]

[1] Dip. di Sistemi e Informatica, Università di Firenze, Italy
[2] CNR - Istituto di Scienza e Tecnologie dell'Informazione "A. Faedo", Pisa, Italy
[3] Fraunhofer Institute for Experimental Software Engineering (IESE)
Kaiserslautern, Germany

Abstract. Use Cases can be employed in system requirements engineering to capture requirements from an external point of view. In product line modeling, commonalities and variabilities of a family of systems have to be described. In order to support variability modeling for product lines with Use Cases, extensions and modifications of Use Cases have to be provided. Capturing the variations characterizing the different products is a key issue for product line requirements engineering. This paper describes an approach to derive product line requirements in the form of Use Cases, starting from the analysis of user documentations of existing systems. We provide a disciplined approach to integrate legacy information found in existing documentation into product line Use Cases and illustrate this with an example.

1 Introduction

The development of industrial software systems may often benefits from the adoption of a development cycle based on the so-called system-families or product lines approach [18] [7]. This approach aims at lowering production costs by sharing an overall reference architecture and concepts of the products, but allows them to differ with respect to particular product characteristics in order to e.g. serve different markets. The production process in product lines is therefore organized with the purpose of maximizing the commonalities of the product family and minimizing the cost of variations [13].

In the first stage of a software project, usually called requirements elicitation [12], the information and knowledge of the system under construction is acquired. When eliciting and modeling requirements on a product line two different problems have to be addressed. On one side there is the problem of capturing requirements common to all members of the product line and requirements valid only for parts of the line members. On the other side there is the problem of specializing and instantiating the generic product line requirements into application requirements for a single product.

To deal with these problems, the relations between line and product requirements have to be represented in the modeling approach, and the concepts of parameterization, specialization and generalization need to be supported by the modeling concepts.

When building a new product line, the approach to do so can either be independent (a company starts a product line without any predecessor products), project-integrating (existing systems under development will be integrated into the product line), reengineering driven (legacy systems have to be reengineered into the product line) or

F. van der Linden (Ed.): PFE 2003, LNCS 3014, pp. 152–167, 2004.

leveraged (the company sets up a product line based on a product line that is already in place) [23]. User documentation that is useful as input for product line modeling can be found in the cases of project-integrating, reengineering-driven and leveraged product line engineering. Therefore, user documentation is the first choice to start the elicitation process for the information needed in product line modeling.

As developing a product line is a complex task, in depth knowledge of the problem domain often is a prerequisite for a successful product line. So, when a company starts to do product line engineering often systems already exist that can be used as a knowledge base for the new product line. Figure 1 describes this situation.

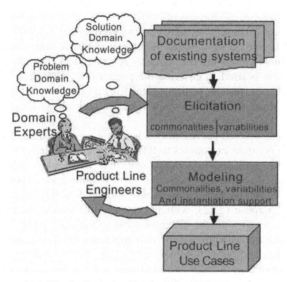

Fig. 1. Capturing Product Line Use Cases

Domain experts with knowledge in the problem or application domain, together with product line engineers with knowledge in the solution domain (the processes and products in product line engineering) have to elicit and model commonalities and variabilities in a highly interactive and time consuming process.

In this paper we describe an approach for elicitation and modeling Use Cases of product lines from existing user documentation. Use Cases are a powerful tool to capture functional requirements for software systems. They allow structuring requirements documents with use goals and provide a means to specify the interaction between a certain software system and its environment [8]. A Use Case defines a goal-oriented set of interactions between external actors and the system under consideration.

With the proposed approach commonalities and variabilities can be expressed and managed within Use Cases. Use Cases are able to describe both the common characteristics of all the products belonging to a product line and the variations that differentiate products among them. Use Cases describing only one line member are then obtained by an instantiation process. The primary information source used for elicitation is the user documentation of systems coming from the same application domain as the product line under development.

The paper is structured as follows: in Section 2 we describe textual Use Case, in Section 3 we describe how the notation for Use Cases can be extended in order to represent all types of variability needed to model a product line (and to support instantiation). In Section 4 we describe the elicitation of information needed for the Use Cases. We illustrate elicitation and modeling on a practical example in Section 5 and conclude the paper in section 6.

2 Use Cases

A Use Case [8] describes the interaction (triggered by an external actor in order to achieve a goal) between a system and its environment. A Use Case defines a goal-oriented set of interactions between external actors and the system under consideration. The term actor is used to describe the person or system that has a goal against the system under discussion. A primary actor triggers the system behavior in order to achieve a certain goal. A secondary actor interacts with the system but does not trigger the Use Case.

A Use Case is completed successfully when its goal is satisfied. Use Case descriptions also include possible extensions to this sequence, e.g., alternative sequences that may also satisfy the goal, as well as sequences that may lead to failure in completing the service in case of exceptional behavior, error handling, etc. The system is treated as a "black box"; thus, Use Cases capture who (actor) does what (interaction) with the system, for what purpose (goal), without dealing with system internals. A complete set of Use Cases specifies all the different ways to use the system, and therefore defines the whole required behavior of the system. Generally, Use Case steps are written in an easy-to-understand, structured narrative using the vocabulary of the domain. A scenario is an instance of a Use Case, and represents a single path through the Use Case. Thus, there exists a scenario for the main flow through the Use Case, and as many other scenarios as the possible variations of flow through the Use Case (e.g., triggered by options, error conditions, security breaches, etc.). Scenarios may also be depicted in a graphical form using UML Sequence Diagrams.

Figure 2 shows the template of the Cockburn's Use Case taken from [8]. In this textual notation, the main flow is expressed, in the "Description" section, by an indexed sequence of natural language sentences, describing a sequence of actions of the system. Variations are expressed (in the "Extensions" section) as alternatives to the main flow, linked by their index to the point of the main flow from which they branch as a variation. This natural language form of Use Cases has been widely used in industrial practice to specify use cases , e.g at Nokia [11].

3 Product Lines Use Cases (PLUCs)

Following the Product Line Engineering Process Reference Model defined in the CAFÉ project [18], and shown in Figure 3, product line development is characterized by two processes: domain engineering and application engineering. Domain engineering is the process aiming at developing the general concept of a product line together with all the assets which are common to the whole product line, whereas application engineering is the process aiming at designing a specific product.

USE CASE #	< the name is the goal as a short active verb phrase>	
Goal in Context	<a longer statement of the goal in context if needed>	
Scope & Level	<what system is being considered black box under design> <one of: Summary, Primary Task, Sub-function>	
Preconditions	<what we expect is already the state of the world>	
Success End Condition	<the state of the world upon successful completion>	
Failed End Condition	<the state of the world if goal abandoned>	
Primary, Secondary Actors	<a role name or description for the primary actor>. <other systems relied upon to accomplish Use Case>	
Trigger	<the action upon the system that starts the Use Case>	
Description	Step	Action
	1	<put here the steps of the scenario from trigger to goal delivery, and any cleanup after>
	2	<...>
	3	
Extensions	Step	Branching Action
	1a	<condition causing branching> : <action or name of sub-Use Case>
Sub-Variations		Branching Action
	1	<list of variations>

Fig. 2. Use Cases template

During application engineering a customer specific application will be defined. However, differently from the usual single product development, the definition process of the customer specific application is not only influenced by the requirements of the customer but also by the capabilities of the product line.

This diagram shows that it is possible to move from the product line level (by means of the system line engineering activity) to the product level and vice versa (by means of the system line reverse engineering activity).

Going upwards, applications are developed considering the capabilities of the product line specializing, extending and adding line requirements. Consequently, software product lines need more sophisticated requirement processing and requirements should deal with variability.

In particular, product line requirements can be considered in general as composed of a constant and a variable part. The constant part includes all those requirements dealing with features or functionalities common to all the products belonging to the line and that, for this reason, do not need to be modified. The variable part represents those functionalities that can be changed to differentiate a product from another.

Variability can be seen from two different perspectives: the first is the product perspective where each variability has to be considered as an aspect to be instantiated. From the product line perspective a variability can be seen as a goal to be reached by abstracting all the instances related to the existing products belonging to a product line.

It is possible to move from the product line level to the product level by an instantiation process and on the contrary from the product level to the product line level by an abstraction process. In these two different processes the main objects to pay attention on are variations. A possible extension of Use Cases to express variability during

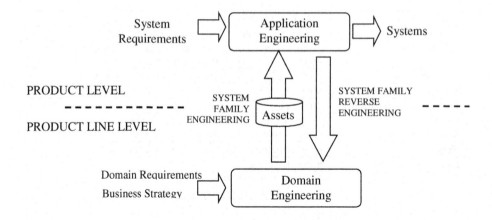

Fig. 3. The CAFÉ-Product Line reference framework

requirements engineering of product lines is an extension based on structuring the Use Cases as having two levels: the product line level and the product level [5]. In this way product-related Use Cases should be derived from the product line-related Use Cases by an instantiation process.

This approach considers the variations implicitly enclosed into the components of the Use Cases. The variations are then represented by tags that indicate those parts of the product line requirements needing to be instantiated for a specific product in a product-related document. For doing that, tags are included into the Use Case scenarios (both main scenario and extensions) in order to identify and specify variations. The tags represent three kinds of variability: Alternative, Parametric, and Optional.

1. Alternative components: they express the possibility to instantiate the requirement by selecting an instance among a predefined set of possible choices, each of them depending on the occurrence of a condition;
2. Parametric components: their instantiation is connected to the actual value of a parameter in the requirements for the specific product;
3. Optional components: their instantiation can be done by selecting indifferently among a set of values, which are optional features for a derived product.

The instantiation of these types of variabilities will lead to a set of different product-related Use Cases. As an example, a Use Case in the PLUC notation is presented in Figure 4.

This Use Case describes the activities related to the submission of a project document. Let's suppose that it can be possible to submit different two types of documents: either slides (in the .ppt format) or papers (in .doc, pdf. or .ps format). Curly brackets are introduced into the Use Case elements, variables (here V1 and V2) describe the variation points within the use case. The possible instantiations and the type of the variations is given within the use case and the possible values are described with logical expressions.

Use Case Name: Submission of a document

Primary Actor: the author

Goal: Preparation and submission of a project document

Secondary Actor: Project's web server

Main Success Scenario:

1. The author writes a document {[**V1**] of a certain class} according to the {[**V2**] appropriate} format within the submission deadline

2. Author puts the document on the project document repository

Extensions:

1a. The author misses the submission given deadline:

A remind is sent to the author from the web server manager

Variabilities:

V1: 1. Slides   V1 alternative

    2. Paper

V2: if V1=1 then file .ppt   V2 parametric/ optional

else if V1=2 then file.doc or file.pdf or file.ps1.

Fig. 4. Example of a Use Case in the PLUC notation

4   Elicitation of Information for Product Line Use Cases

Product Line Engineering includes the construction of a reusable set of assets. Constructing such a reusable asset base for specific products in a domain is a more sophisticated task than the development of assets for a single system because several products with their commonalities and variabilities have to be considered. This implies the planning, elicitation, analysis, modeling and realization of the commonalities and variabilities between the planned products.

Usually, the development of a product line is not a green field task. Legacy systems exist that shall be integrated into a product line. The information from those systems is a valuable source for building the reusable assets. This information from existing systems can be found in the code, in architecture descriptions and in requirements specifications [14]. All this information can be found in documents produced during the lifecycle of the existing systems.

4.1   Benefits of Using Legacy Information

Until now, the information needed to build a product line model is elicited interactively with high expert involvement. As domain experts have a high workload and are often unavailable, high expert involvement is a risk for the successful introduction of a product line engineering approach in an organization.

There is a lack of guidance on how to integrate textual information found in legacy documents into product line models.

Single system elicitation methods cannot be taken as they are, because multiple documentations have to be compared, commonalities and variabilities have to be elicited and additional concepts (e.g. abstractions, decisions) are needed. Systematically integrating legacy documentation into product lines models supports:

- Integration and reuse of textual information.
- Feasibility of product line modeling by decreasing the effort the domain experts have to spend with interviews and meetings.
- Increased acceptance of the product line in the development organization because there is confidence in the legacy products and reusing the legacy information instead of developing everything from scratch reduces the effort to build the product line. Better traceability from the product line to the existing system.

There are different kinds of legacy documentation (requirements specs, user manuals, design documents...). As Use Cases are more and more used in domain modeling (e.g. [6], [13], [15]), it is important to have a closer look on how to elicit information for product line Use Cases. Use Cases describe the system from a users point of view. Therefore, user manuals are the most important source of information as input for Use Cases. In this paper, we adopt an approach for controlled elicitation, which guides product line engineers and domain stakeholders in how to elicit knowledge from existing documents and how to transform documentation into product line models. This approach is called the PuLSE[1] - CaVE-approach (Commonality and Variability Elicitation) that is integrated into the PuLSE-Framework for product line engineering [4] that is a customizable and flexible framework for all phases of product line engineering. CaVE is an approach for structured and controlled integration of user documentation of existing systems into the product line [16].

With the elicitation approach common and variable features [17], Use Case elements, tasks [21] and requirements can be elicited. We focus on the elicitation of Use Case elements here. As existing systems are the basis for this approach, it can be seen as a reengineering method for documents transferring user documentation into basic elements of information for product line Use Cases. The approach was validated in two case studies [16], further case studies, as a deeper empirical validation will follow. The approach consists of the following phases (see Figure 5):

- Preparation
- Search
- Selection, change and modification

The first two steps of the approach can be performed by persons who just have a slight domain understanding, they do not have to be domain experts. The third step requires involvement of domain experts as there the valid documentation entities have to be selected. We will now describe the three steps in more detail.

4.2 Preparation

Preparation consists of the four sub steps collection, selection, division and browsing. During collection, user documentation for the systems that should be integrated into the product line and of systems that are related should be collected to have all needed information available. In the case of a project-integrating product line adoption (c.f.

---

[1] PuLSE is a registered trademark of Fraunhofer IESE.

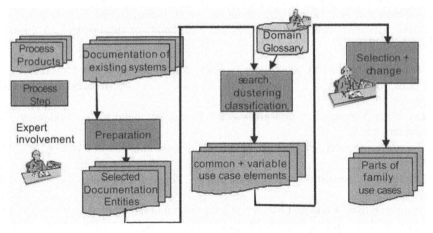

Fig. 5. An outline of the elicitation approach

section 1) these are all user-documentations of the systems currently under development (as far as they already exist), in the case of a reengineering-driven or leveraged product line adoption all user documentations of existing systems in the domain have to be considered. As parallel reading of more than one document requires divided and increased attention and leads to lower performance [28], the number of documents to be read in parallel should be reduced to a minimum. So, if there are more than 3 systems, select two or three documents that cover the variety of systems (e.g., one documentation of a low-end system, one of a high end system and one typical system) to compare for a first search in the documents. The other documents can be used to complete the elicited information after completing the search phase.

After selecting the three typical documentations, divide them into manageable and comparable parts of 3 to 10 pages (e.g., comparable subchapters). In browsing, for each of those manageable parts (or for a subset of those parts that includes typical sub domains) browse through them in order to decide the amount of variability in them. There are two alternatives:

For those document parts that differ in less than 30% of the text compare the documents in parallel in the following phases.

For those document parts that differ in more than 30% of the text, process them one after another in the following phases. Start the analysis with the biggest document.

4.3 Search

In the search step the identified document parts are analyzed and Use Case elements are searched. The elements to be identified in the documents, which should be sized from one word to at most 5-6 lines, are marked and tagged in the source documents. Common and variable Use Case elements that can be identified are (see. Figure) names, actors, goals, preconditions, steps of descriptions, success conditions, extensions.

Common and variable use case elements can be identified and marked in the text with the following heuristics (specific rules-of-thumb or arguments derived from experience[27]):

- Headings of sections or subsections typically contain names of Use Cases.
- Phrases like "only by", "by using", "in the case of" can be markers for Use Case preconditions.
- Use Case preconditions and goals can typically be found in the beginning of a chapter.
- Use Case preconditions can be found before or within the description of a Use Case.
- Phrases like "normally" "with the exception", "except" can mark Use Case extensions.
- Numbered lists or bulleted lists are markers for an ordered processing of sequential steps and describe Use Case descriptions.
- Sentences that describe interactions with the system in the form of "to do this…do that…" are Use Case descriptions.
- Passive voice is typically a marker for system activity (e.g. "The volume of the radio is muted" = the system mutes the volume of the radio). These sentences can be used in the Use Case description.

Commonalities and variabilities in those elements can be found with the following heuristics:

- Arbitrary elements occurring only in one user manual probably are optional elements.
- Headings or subheadings that only occur in one of the documentations can be Use Cases that are optional as a whole.
- Headings or subheadings that have slightly different names or headings or subheadings that have different names but are at the same place in the table of contents can be hints for alternative Use Cases.
- Phrases that differ in only one or a few words can be evidence for alternatives.
- If numerical values in the document differ they can be parametrical variabilities.
- Menu items that are described only in some of the documents can be hints for optional or alternative functionality (Use Cases or parts of them).

With the support of these heuristics, which help in finding a relevant part of the Use Case elements and variabilities, the user documents should be marked (e.g. with different colors for different Use Case elements and for variabilities) and integrated into an intermediate document. The list of heuristics is expected to grow as further case studies are performed. Further Use Case elements that are identified without the help of the heuristics are added. The identified elements should be extracted from the document and tagged with attributes containing the information needed for selecting appropriate elements for modeling the product lines requirements in terms of PLUCs. Table 1 shows the elements of such a notation.

Table 1. Attributes for the elicited text items

Attribute	Values	Description
ID	e.g. 1...n or doc.number	A unique identifier for the element
Value	text	The text of the element that was found in the document
Document	Identifiers	The identifiers of the documents this element was found in
Use Case Type	Use Case elements	The elements of Use Cases (description, precondition..) the text matches to
Var Type	Comm., opt, alt, param.	The hypothesis for the variability type of the element (default is commonality)
Parent	ID	The element, this element is part of
Use Case relations	Use Case Name	A possible Use Case this element is related to
Var relations	List of IDs	The IDs of other elements that contain alternatives or different parameters for this element

4.4 Selection

In the last step, selection, the extracted and tagged elements have to be checked and possibly adjusted by a domain expert. The domain expert will change the elements regarding the following aspects:

- Is a text element that was marked as a possible Use Case element, a Use Case element in the new product line?
- Is an element marked as optional/alternative really an optional/alternative element in the new product line?
- Are the Use Cases to be built out of the elements the right Use Cases to describe the systems of the product line?

The relations (see last lines of Table 1) are used to make comparisons between the documents easier, to establish traceability to the source documents and, with tool based selection, to support navigation in the elements and between the sets of documents. With these elements the domain expert and the requirements engineer can built use cases using the information about the elements collected in the tags. With the help of the tags and by putting together the elements from the document and adding parts of the use cases that are not mentioned in the document use cases in the notation described in Section 3 can be easily built.

5   Application on a Case Study

In this section the approach described in Section 4 to derive Use Cases using the PLUC notation is applied on an industrial case study to show its applicability:

existing user manuals of two mobile phones from the same product line that, from here in after, we indicate as P1 and P2, have been considered.

When the elicitation process is applied to a single product, the effort can be concentrated on the identification of the correspondences between the parts of the manual and the Use Case elements. Starting from a fragment of a user manual of a mobile phone, represented in Figure 6, a possible correspondence with standard Use Case elements can be shown.

When product families requirements have to be derived, starting from several documents, each related to a particular product of the product line, the process shown before is not in general sufficient. In this case all the commonalities and variabilities should be derived as the outcome of the elicitation phase. With reference to the approach described in Section 4, after the collection, selection and division phases the function descriptions of the user manuals have been identified as being the basic documentation entities for the elicitation process. In this case study the description of the GAMES functionality of the two phones P1 and P2 has been taken as example.

The browsing phase determines the amount of commonalities and variabilities between the two entities under analysis. It is then evident that the two products differ at least for the set of games provided to the user and for the presence of the WAP connection. Figure 7 shows how the parts of the user manuals of the mobile phones P1 and P2 related to the GAMES functionality can be put in relation after the preparation phase.

In the search phase the identified parts are analysed and the Use Case elements are searched. The found commonalities and variabilities are extracted and tagged and then integrated into an intermediate document represented in Table 2 in a tabular format. Where each row of this table represents an elicited text item according to the scheme of Table 1.

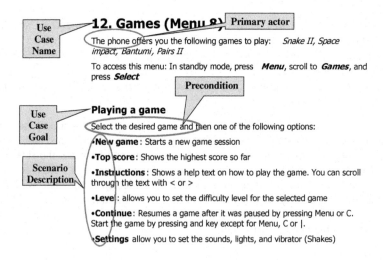

Fig. 6. Correspondences between user manual parts and Use Case elements

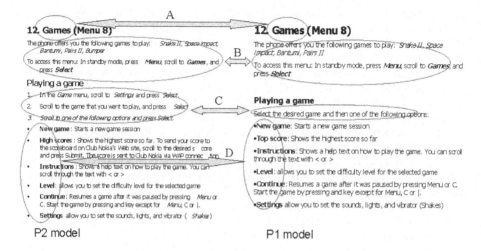

P2 model   P1 model

Fig. 7. Correspondences between P1 and P2

Table 2. Text items elicited in the case study

ID	Value	Doc.	Use Case Type	Parent	Var Type	Use Case relations	Var Relations
P1.1	The phone	P1	Actor	-	Comm.	UC Games	P2.1
P1.2	Games to play: SnakeII, Space impact, Bantumi, PairsII,	P1	Scenario Description	-	Comm	UC Games	P2.2
P1.4	Bumper	P1	Scenario Description	P1.2	Opt	UC Games	
P1.5	To access this menu: press menu, scroll to games, select	P1	Precondition	-	Comm	UC Games	P2.3
P1.6	In the game menu, scroll to settings and press select	P2	Scenario Description	-	Opt	UC Games	-
P2.1	The phone	P2	Actor		Comm.	UC Games	P1.1
P2.2	Games to play: SnakeII, Space impact, Bantumi, PairsII,	P2	Scenario Description	-	Comm	UC Games	P1.2
P2.3	To access this menu: press menu, scroll to games, select		Precondition	-	Comm	UC Games	1.3

The outcome of this phase is an intermediate document, which is obtained from both the previous ones by tagging the common parts and the detected variabilities. The final outcome of the selection phase could be a first version of a Use Case expressed in the PLUC formalism.

Realistically, we do not have to expect that the variable parts to be tagged could be identified simply by a "difference" operation between the two docs. For example, the text elements put in correspondence by the C double arrow in Figure 7 have the same meaning, but, in the case of the P1 model they seem suitable for being put in the Precondition element of the resulting Use Case, while for the P2 model they seem more suitable for being considered as belonging to the Scenario.

The resulting Use Case will depend on the decision on how to mark these text elements. Such a decision cannot be made in general but should be left to a domain expert in the selection phase of the approach. This can be made either as a case-by-case decision for each element or as a general parameter to select before applying the process. In Figure 8 a possible outcome in the PLUC format of the product line requirements related to the GAME functionality is shown.

Primary Actor: the user, the {[*V0*]} mobile phone (the system)
Goal: play a game on a {[*V0*]} mobile phone and record score
Preconditions: the function GAMES has been selected from the main MENU
Main Success Scenario:
- The system displays the list of the available games: SnakeII, Space impact, Bantumi, PairsII and {[**V1**] additional}
- The user select a game
- The system displays the logo of the selected game
- The user selects the difficulty level by following the {[*V2*] appropriate} procedure and press YES
- The system starts the game and plays it until it goes over
- The user records the score achieved and {[*V3*] possibly} send the score to Game Club via WAP
- The system displays the list of the {[*V1*] available} games
- The user presses NO

| *V0*: alternative | 1. | P1 model |
| | 2. | P2 model |

| *V1*: optional | if *V0*=2 then Bumper | |

V2: parametric	if *V0*=1 then procedure-A:	- press Select
		- scroll to Settings and press YES
		- scroll to Difficulty Level and press YES
		- select the desired difficulty level, press YES
	else if *V0*=2 then procedure-B:	- press Select
		- scroll to Level and press YES
		- select the desired difficulty level, press YES

| *V3*: parametric | if *V0*=1 then function not available | |
| | else if *V0*=2 then function available | |

Fig. 8. The resulting PLUC

6 Conclusions

In this paper we described an approach for elicitation and specification of Use Cases for product lines based on existing user documentation. Use Cases, which are quite common in single system requirements engineering are also often used in product line engineering to model requirements on a line of systems. The approach we describe here supports capturing of the information found in user documentation of legacy systems and the specification of this information in Use Cases that are extended with a mechanism to express variabilities. Up to now, there only small case studies exist with the approach, additional case studies and applications are described in [5] and [16]. It still has to be shown that the approach scales to large product families, but as the elicitation, analysis and modeling of the use cases can be performed subdomain by subdomain in larger systems we hope that the approach will scale.

There are several approaches for domain analysis and product line modeling. An overview on domain analysis methods like FODA [17], ODM [24] or Commonality Analysis within FAST [26] can be found in several surveys like [9] or [2]. But in most of these approaches, the integration of legacy systems into the domain analysis phase is not described in depth. In ODM [24], the primary goal is the systematic transformations of artifacts (e.g., requirements, design, code, tests, and processes) from multiple existing systems into assets that can be used in multiple systems. ODM stresses the use of legacy artifacts and knowledge as a source of domain knowledge and potential resources for reengineering/reuse. MRAM [20] is a method that describes how to analyze and select appropriate textual requirements for a product line but their focus is on the transition from domain engineering rather than on the transition between existing systems and domain engineering. There are some methods from single system requirements elicitation that describe how to elicit information from existing documents. Alexander and Kiedaisch [1], Biddle [4] and the REVERE Project [22] focus on reusing natural language requirements in different forms. The QuARS approach [10], the KARAT approach [25] and Maarek [19] apply natural language processing or information retrieval techniques to requirements specifications in order to improve their quality. The approach that we describe here overcomes the shortcomings of other approaches by explicitly considering variability and integrating user documentation into product line modeling and modeling of use cases.

With the help of an automatic tool, the selection of the text elements and the tagging with the attributes could be performed semi-automatically. The process of analyzing a user manual using information retrieval methods [3] in a semi-automated process opens up the possibility to capitalize on the wealth of domain knowledge in existing systems considered for migration to next-generation systems. Converting these existing requirements into domain models can reduce cost and risk while reducing time-to-market. Tool support can increase efficiency of processing and correctness of the results significantly for the techniques proposed and can relieve experts and product line engineers. It is planned to develop an elicitation tool which integrates document-analysis and information retrieval techniques like indexing or morphology to support document-based modeling of the commonalities and variabilities of planned products in the domain of a product. This tool can then support stakeholders in the domain in identifying, eliciting and analyzing commonalities and variabilities in the domain, which are retrieved from the existing documents. Such a tool could integrate existing tools that, by means of natural language processing techniques, are able to analyze documents and to point out particular sentences or special wordings, to give support for the search phase.

Acknowledgements

This work was partially supported by the Eureka Σ!2023 Programme., ITEA (ip00004, Project CAFÉ). We wish to thank Alessandro Maccari from NOKIA for interesting discussions on the topics of this paper.

References

1. I. Alexander and F. Kiedaisch. Towards recyclable system requirements. In ECBS'02, 9th IEEE Conference and Workshops on Engineering of Computer-Based Systems, April 2002, Lund, Sweden, 2002.
2. G. Arango. Domain analysis methods. In W. Shaefer, R. Prieto-Diaz, and M. Matsumoto, editors, Software Reusability. Ellis Horwood, 1993.
3. R. Baeza-Yates and B. Ribeiro-Neto. Modern information retrieval. Addison-Wesley, 1999.
4. J. Bayer, O. Flege, P. Knauber, R. Laqua, D. Muthig, K. Schmid, T. Widen, and J.-M. De-Baud. PuLSE: A Methodology to Develop Software Product Lines. In Proceedings of the Symposium on Software Reusability (SSR'99), Los Angeles, CA, USA, May 1999. ACM.
5. A. Bertolino, A. Fantechi, S. Gnesi, G. Lami, A. Maccari, Use Case Description of Requirements for Product Lines, REPL'02, Essen, Germany, September 2002.
6. Robert Biddle, James Noble, and Ewan Tempero. Supporting Reusable Use Cases. In Proceedings of the Seventh International Conference on Software Reuse, April 2002.
7. P. C. Clements and L. Northrop. Software Product Lines: Practices and Patterns. SEI Series in Software Engineering. Addison-Wesley, August 2001
8. A. Cockburn. Writing Effective Use Cases. Addison Wesley, 2001.
9. J.-M. DeBaud and K. Schmid. A Practical Comparison of Major Domain Analysis Approaches - Towards a Customizable Domain Analysis Framework. In Proceedings of SEKE'98,San Francisco, USA June 1998.
10. F. Fabbrini, M. Fusani, S. Gnesi, and G. Lami. The linguistic approach to the natural language requirements quality; benefit o the use of an automatic tool. In Proceedings of the 26th Annual IEEE Computer Society Nasa Goddard Space Flight Center Software Engineering Workshop, 2001.
11. A. Fantechi, S. Gnesi, G. Lami, and A. Maccari, Application of Linguistic Techniques for Use Case Analysis, RE'02, Essen, Germany, September 2002
12. J. A. Goguen, Charlotte Linde, Techniques for Requirements Elicitation, Proceedings of the 1st International Symposium on Requirements Engineering, p.152-163, 1993
13. G. Halmans, K. Pohl   Communicating the Variability of a Software-Product Family to Customers Journal of Software and Systems Modeling, Springer, 2003 to appear
14. I. John. Integrating Legacy Documentation Assets into a Product Line. In: Proceedings of the Fourth International Workshop on Product Family Engineering (PFE-4), Bilbao, Spain, October 2001.
15. I. John, D. Muthig, Tailoring Use Cases for Product Line Modeling, REPL'02, Essen, Germany, September 2002
16. I. John, J. Dörr. Extracting Product Line Model Elements from User Documentation. Technical Report, Fraunhofer IESE, 2003
17. K. Kang, S. Cohen, J. Hess, W. Novak, and S. Peterson. Feature-Oriented Domain Analysis (FODA) Feasibility Study. Technical Report CMU/SEI-90-TR-21, Software Engineering Institute, Carnegie Mellon University, November 1990.
18. F. van der Linden. Software Product Families in Europe: The Esaps and Café Projects. IEEE Software, 19(4):41--49, JulyAugust 2002.
19. Y. S. Maarek, D. M. Berry, and G. E. Kaiser. GURU: Information retrieval for reuse. In P.Hall, editor, Landmark Contributions in Software Reuse and Reverse Engineering. Unicom Seminars Ltd, 1994.
20. M. Mannion, B. Keepence, H. Kaindl, and J. Wheadon. Reusing Single System Requirements for Application Family Requirements. In Proceedings of the 21st International Conference on Software Engineering (ICSE'99), May 1999.
21. B. Paech and K. Kohler. Task–driven Requirements in Object-oriented Development. In Leite, J., Doorn, J., (eds) Perspectives on Requirements Engineering, Kluver Academic Publishers, 2003, to appear

22. P. Rayson, L. Emmet, R. Garside, and P. Sawyer. The REVERE project: experiments with the application of probabilistic nlp to systems engineering. In Pro-ceedings of 5th International Conference on Applications of Natural Language to Information Systems (NLDB'2000). Versailles, France, June, LNCS 1959, 2000.
23. K. Schmid and M. Verlage. The Economic Impact of Product Line Adoption and Evolution. IEEE Software, 19(4):50--57, JulyAugust 2002.
24. Software Technology for Adaptable, Reliable Systems (STARS). Organization Domain Modeling (ODM) Guidebook, Version 2.0, June 1996.
25. B. Tschaitschian, C. Wenzel, and I. John. Tuning the quality of informal software require-ments with KARAT. In Proceedings of the Third International Workshop on Requirements Engineering: Foundations of Software Quality (REFSQ'97), 1997.
26. D. M. Weiss and C.T.R. Lai. Software Product Line Engineering: A Family Based Soft-ware Development Process. Addison-Wesley, 1999.
27. http://www.whatis.com
28. C.D. Wickens. Processing resources in attention. In R. Parasuraman & R. Davies (eds.), Varieties of attention (pp.63-101). New York, 1984, Academic Press

RequiLine: A Requirements Engineering Tool for Software Product Lines

Thomas von der Maßen and Horst Lichter

Research Group Software Construction
RWTH Aachen
Ahornstr. 55, 52074 Aachen
{vdmass,lichter}@cs.rwth-aachen.de

Abstract. Software Product Lines are characterized through common and variable parts. Modeling variability is one of the most important tasks during the analysis phase. Domain analysis and requirements elicitation will bring up a huge amount of requirements and dependencies between product characteristics. Feature modeling is one approach to deal with complexity in expressing several requirements in features and structure them hierarchically in feature diagrams. Unfortunately the requirements and feature models become very complex as well. An adequate tool support is needed to manage the feature models and to support the linkage to requirements. Our research group has developed a prototype of a requirements engineering tool that supports the requirements engineering process for software product lines.

1 Background and Motivation

The development of software-intensive systems shift more and more from single product development to the establishment of software product lines. The benefits that can be achieved reach from shorter release cycles and broader product palettes, over reducing the development and maintenance costs to standardization procedures in usage and distribution. The advantages of performing a product line development are obvious, but will be purchased with high initial establishing costs and a serious and demanding development process. *Building a software product line and bringing it to market requires a blend of skillful engineering as well as both technical and organizational management* [1]. The development must be carefully planned because decisions will not only affect one, but several products and will drive on or limit the whole product line. Initial problems arise in the domain analysis and during the requirements engineering phase. The task of the domain analysis is to capture the domain or domains, which the product line will address. Therefore the scope of the product line has to be fixed to define which parts of the domain lay within and which lay outside the product line. The requirements engineering has to elicit the requirements: requirements that are shared by all members of the product line and requirements which are specific for one or several special products. The requirements engineering has to manage a huge amount of requirements, mandatory or variable, and the interactions and dependencies between them. Therefore during requirements elicita-

F. van der Linden (Ed.): PFE 2003, LNCS 3014, pp. 168–180, 2004.

tion, analysis and verification we have to deal with very complex structures and interweavements.

Reuse is the main driver to achieve the benefits, mentioned above. While typically code and code fragments are reusable assets, product line development aims in reusing any artifact that will be created during the whole domain engineering, like high level architectures, documentation, use cases and requirements [2]. That means coarse granular reuse. Coarse granular reuse needs high level artifacts and deals with the huge amount of requirements. Hence, it is necessary to abstract from fine granular requirements and to pay attention to high level characteristics of domains and products.

One approach to describe high level reusable characteristics is the Feature-Oriented Domain Analysis method described in [3]. A feature is defined as a prominent user-visible aspect, quality, or characteristic of a software system or systems. Since its introduction in 1990, feature modeling has been more and more appreciated by requirements engineers and domain analysts. There are several approaches [4], [5], [6], [7], [8] for modeling features that are all based on the initial approach presented by Kang et al [3]. Goals and purposes of feature modeling shifted from domain modeling to product line modeling and feature models are used to define and to verify product configurations. Additional modeling elements, groupings and views have been introduced to fulfill the requirements that were put on feature modeling.

Unfortunately feature models and the corresponding diagrams become very complex and difficult to survey and maintain, very quickly. Therefore an adequate tool support is needed to manage features, their relationships and dependencies and to link them to requirements. The strong demands for a tool support for developing software product lines have been described in detail in [9].

In this paper we present the functionality of a requirements engineering tool for software product lines. The tool named *RequiLine* is able to handle the requirements and feature models of software products. It manages features, relationships and dependencies, providing consistency checks and a query interface.

We have organized this paper as follows: in section two, a meta-model for feature modeling is presented. Section three describes the requirements that we put on the development of *RequiLine*. Section four describes the functionalities provided by *RequiLine*, its architecture and design rationales. Though *RequiLine* provides the core functionality that is required it is still a prototype and under development. Therefore we give in section five an outlook on our future work to enhance the capabilities of our tool.

2 Feature Modeling

As mentioned above, feature modeling becomes more and more popular. It is well suited to support the development of software product lines. There has been a lot of research in developing feature modeling approaches. Lichter et al compare some of those approaches and draw conclusions from the analysis [10]. Though the approaches diverge in the purpose of features, all agree about the core of required modeling elements. Based on the approaches analyzed in [10] the meta-model depicted in Figure 1 defines the modeling elements and their relationships:

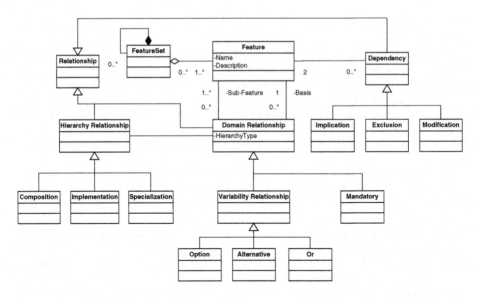

Fig. 1. Meta-Model for Feature Modeling

We have chosen to model variability as first class relationship modeling elements instead of modeling them as special features. For example, in literature [3], [5], [6], options are mostly modeled as optional features. With respect to reusing features, a feature might be optional in one domain and mandatory in another, so that variability might change in different domains. To meet these concerns we have modeled variability and commonality as relationships. Though the focus on modeling relationships lies on the characteristic variability of the domain, expressed through the domain relationships, the type of the hierarchy connection between a father and a child feature needs to be expressed, too. To avoid modeling two relationships between two features, the hierarchy type is expressed through a tagged value at the domain relationship. This solution provides major flexibility in combining variability and structural information. The modeling elements and their semantics have been summarized in Table 1. The meta-model described above shows the essence of modeling elements, mostly all feature modeling approaches agree with. A classic example of a feature model is depicted in Figure 2. It shows the feature graph of an automobile. An automobile, as the overall concept, consists of a motor, a transmission and optionally, it might have air conditioning. Therefore an automobile is a composition of a transmission, a motor and it may have an air conditioning system [15].

The alternative-child-features are connected by a specialization relationship with their father feature, because they do represent special father features. The dependencies show that a 4-cylinder motor and an automatic transmission are mutual exclusive, so that they cannot be part of the same product, whereas an 8-cylinder motor always requires the automatic transmission.

Even this very simple example shows the complexity of feature models. Therefore a suitable tool is needed to manage the collection of features, their relationships and their dependencies. In the next section we want to analyze the requirements on a requirements engineering tool for software product lines.

Table 1. Semantic of feature modeling relationships

Element	Type	Semantic	Characteristic
Domain Relationship	Mandatory	If the father feature is selected, the child feature must be selected as well	
	Option	If the father feature is selected, the child feature can but has not to be selected	
	Alternative	If the father feature is selected, exactly one feature of the set of alternative-child-features must be selected	Implicit mutually exclusion between alternative-child-features
	Or	If the father feature is selected, at least one feature of the set of or-child-features must be selected	
Hierarchy Relationship	Composition	Indicates, that the child feature is part of the father feature	
	Implementation	Indicates, that the child feature is an implementation of the father feature	
	Specialization	Indicates, that the child feature is a special father feature	
Dependency	Implication	If one feature is selected the implied feature has to be selected as well, ignoring their position in the feature tree or graph	Transitive
	Exclusion	Indicates that both features cannot be selected at the same time and are therefore mutually exclusive	Symmetric
	Modification	Expresses that the selection of one feature implies that an attribute of another feature is modified in some way. A modification relationship does not imply, that the modified feature must be selected as well, but just states, if the related feature is selected than its attribute is modified, specified by the modification-relationship	
Feature Set		Allows any logical or functional grouping of features	

3   Tool Support for Software Product Line Development

As we stated in the last section, feature modeling is a suitable approach as it provides a flexible formalism to express domain and product characteristics. Because of complexity and usability reasons, it is recommended and surely required to have an adequate tool support while modeling software product lines providing an integrated solution for the domain and application engineering processes. Existing, professional commercial requirements engineering tools provide excellent support in managing software requirements, but do not support any feature modeling concepts. As variabil-

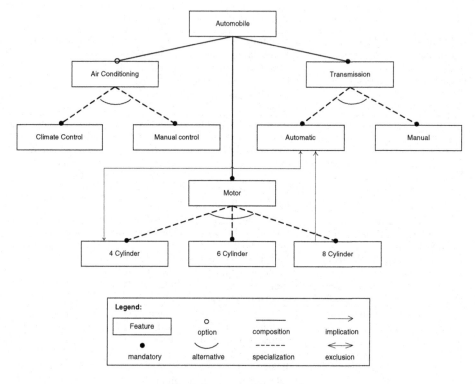

Fig. 2. Feature graph example

ity is one of the important characteristics of software product lines it must be explicitly modeled and managed from an abstract point of view, so that it can be communicated to domain experts and clients. Hence, a requirements engineering tool for software product lines should therefore support feature modeling, including the concepts
and notational elements, stated in section 2. Furthermore, tool support is needed that
goes beyond graphical editors for drawing feature diagrams. Features must be captured together with descriptive information, creation and update dates, status, priority
and other information that has to be included in any requirements shell. Semantic
information that is needed for an automated consistency check and queries on feature
repositories must be managed as well.

3.1 Requirements

In the following subsection we list the requirements that have to be addressed by a
requirements engineering tool for software product lines:

1. Support for Feature Modeling

Features, characterized by name and a unique identifier, description and rational must
be managed. Further, additional information about the status, source, priority, customer satisfaction, maturity and history information must be handled. We follow the

recommendation of the Volere Requirements Shell [11] that proposes these kinds of attributes for requirements. Besides these attributes, the relationships defined in the meta-model must be supported by a potential tool. Any supporting material, like text documents, table sheets, diagrams, pictures or other types of needed documentation should be attached as well, that helps to explain the features any further.

2. Support for Requirements Modeling
Requirements have to be managed as well, concerning the same attributes, assisting information and implication and exclusion dependencies that have been stated for features. The possibility of linking features on a very abstract level to requirements that substantiate these features have to be provided, too, to gain information about which feature is addressed by which requirements and vice versa.

3. Managing Product Lines and Their Members
Features and requirements must be attached to the product lines platform or to a product, characterizing whether the feature or requirement is shared by all members of the product line or is a special product feature or requirement. Hence, information on product lines and products has to be managed by a tool.

4. Product Configurator
Especially a product configurator must offer support in instantiating products. This can be done by provide assistance in resolving variation points and in avoiding building inconsistent configurations by regarding dependencies between features and requirements.

5. Providing a Query Interface
A query interface is needed to express queries on the feature or requirements models. Information about feature or requirement dependencies, variation points, platform or special product features or requirements helps the requirements engineers to gain a quick overview and supports the product configuring process.

6. Providing a Consistency Checker
A consistency checker has to analyze the feature models with respect to their integrity. Inconsistent models have to be detected. Product configurations have to be analyzed, as well: checking if dependencies have been taken into account or if variation points have been resolved properly, for example.

7. View Support
The tool should provide different views on the feature and requirements models. Product managers for example are only interested in the product they are responsible for. Therefore the tool must allow hiding all features and requirements that do not address their product.

8. User Management
The tool should provide an adequate user management by roles to allow authentication and rights management on product lines and products.

9. Data Import and Export
To support data exchange with other tools a flexible data exchange interface is necessary to provide data import and export.

10. Quality Requirements
High usability is a prerequisite to gain acceptance of the tool users. Performance and scalability are important issues as well, concerning the huge amount of features and requirements that have to be considered while modeling a product line.

These major requirements have to be fulfilled by a requirements engineering tool for software product lines.

3.2 Existing Tools

Existing, commercial requirements engineering tools provide excellent support in managing software requirements, but do not support any feature modeling concepts. As feature modeling provides modeling variability from an abstract point of view, a requirements engineering tool for software product lines should support feature modeling, including the formalism concepts and notational elements, stated in section 2.

DECIMAL a requirements engineering tool for product lines [12] has been developed at the Department of Computer Science at the Iowa State University. DECIMAL allows managing domain and product specific characteristics and it provides a consistency check on user-defined rules for deriving new products. Unfortunately it is not based on feature modeling concepts and does not provide any querying interface, view support or user management.

Ami Eddi 1.3 [13], a tool developed at the University of Applied Sciences Kaiserslautern (Germany), allows creating feature models and provides an editor for drawing feature diagrams. As the feature models are used to assist the generative programming concepts described in [5] it does not correspond to the needed modeling elements mentioned above and does not support the management of software product lines. The evaluated prototype unfortunately lacks of stability, scalability and usability.

In the next section we present the tool *RequiLine* that we have developed to meet all the requirements listed above.

4   RequiLine

The development of *RequiLine* has been mainly driven by the claimed requirements, listed in section 3 and therefore to overcome the deficiencies existing requirements engineering tools have in managing variability and dependencies. Our experience shows, that requirements engineering tools are used together with graphical editors to draw feature models. Unfortunately the created drawings do lack of any semantic and could not be used for queries or consistency checks. *RequiLine* is a first study to close this gap.

4.1 Architecture and Interfaces

Our approach implements a repository-based tool box, where dedicated requirements engineering tools share the same data repository, storing features and requirements. Figure 3 shows the overall architecture of *RequiLine*. Beside the flexibility in the tool box architecture that is open for integrating future tools providing more functionality, non-functional requirements have to be considered, while designing and implementing *RequiLine*. The most important non-functional requirements that have to be addressed are performance and scalability, because a huge amount of requirements and features, together with their relationships have to be managed. Therefore we have decided to implement the central repository based on a relational database system. The prototype of *RequiLine* works on the Oracle 8i database and has been successfully tested under Oracle 9i, as well.

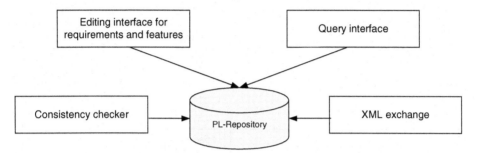

Fig. 3. Overall architecture of *RequiLine*

RequiLine stores the data in the database und it just keeps the actual feature or requirement that's under work in memory. Therefore performance and scalability is mostly determined by the underlying database.

RequiLine needs an Oracle client that communicates with the Oracle server. Network access is provided therefore as well. A client machine just needs *RequiLine* and an Oracle Net Client. The database connectivity is established either by an ODBC or OLEDB provider.

In order to guarantee great flexibility the database connection is not limited to Oracle. A SQL-command file stores the statements needed by *RequiLine* and gives a translation to the database SQL dialect. Therefore any relational database can be used together with *RequiLine* without changing any lines of code - the adaptation of the SQL-command file is sufficient. *RequiLine* supports the export and import of whole product line projects, members of the product line and single features and requirements to XML-files, too. A DTD-file specifies the structure of the XML-file and instructs *RequiLine*, which information has to be processed. This allows the import of entities from other projects or repositories and provides the connectivity to other tools.

RequiLine has been developed under the Microsoft .NET Framework [14]. The chosen programming language is C#. The embedding of *RequiLine* is depicted in Figure 4.

4.2 Main Capabilities

In this subsection we want to present the main capabilities of *RequiLine* that have been implemented yet.

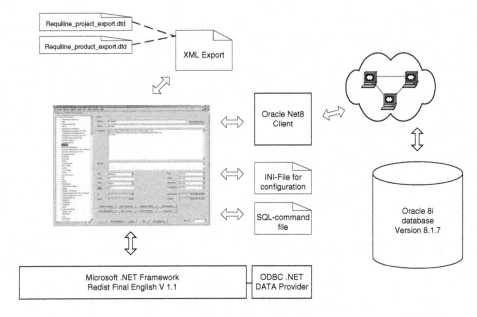

Fig. 4. Embedding of *RequiLine*

4.2.1 Entering Features and Requirements

Figure 5 shows the graphical user interface of *RequiLine* after the user has authorized himself successfully and has opened a product line project. The main window consists out of three tabbed panes: one for managing the products of the product line, one for managing the features and one for managing requirements. The presented feature tab, shows on the left side all modeled features – alphabetically ordered and ordered by membership to platform and products. The right pane includes all information about the actual selected feature and can be edited here.

The buttons at the bottom let the user define domain relationships, dependencies, feature attributes and feature sets and allow adding any kind of supporting material that is helpful for describing the feature. All tools like user management, import / export, consistency checker and query interface can be reached from the menu bar.

4.2.2 Consistency Check

The consistency checker analyzes, whether the feature and requirements models are consistent and completely specified and it categorizes its findings into errors (severe problems) and warnings (light problems). Completeness is analyzed in the way that the checker verifies, if all requirements or feature properties like state, version, priority etc. have been set. If not, a warning message is generated that informs the user about the specific attribute. Consistency means, that the following aspects are considered:

- Correctness of domain relationships: no two different domain relationships between two features or requirements; no insulated feature or requirements
- Correctness of dependencies: no contradicting dependencies and consideration of transitive dependencies

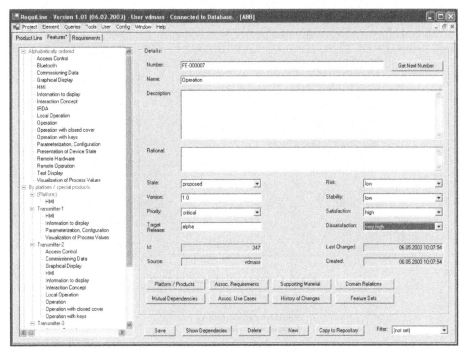

Fig. 5. *RequiLine's* main window

- Resolving of variation points: Are variations points resolved correctly by a configured product?
- Partitioning of features and requirements: Is the affiliation of features and requirements to platform and products accurate?

All checks can be performed simultaneously or can be individually selected by the user referring to features and / or requirements. Figure 6 depicts the window of the consistency checker, where the user can define which checks should be performed and whether errors and/or warning should be reported. The consistency checks provide helpful information to the user and assist him in building stable and correct feature and requirements models.

4.2.3   Query Interface

The query interface provides numerous predefined queries that have been found to be most helpful for the users. The queries can be performed on the feature and the requirements model. The predefined queries include information about all the modeled dependencies and variation points that need most attention to the domain engineers. Furthermore the user can get information about the models of the whole product line or can put the focus on a selected product. Additionally all features and requirements can be retrieved that have been modeled as platform or special product features or requirements.

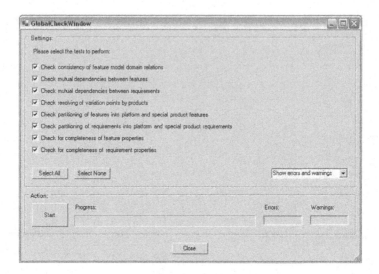

Fig. 6. Consistency checker window

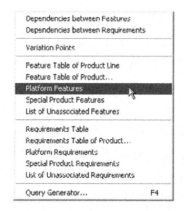

Fig. 7. Selectable predefined queries

If the user is interested in information that is not covered by the predefined queries a query generator gives the user the power to define his own queries. This can be done by selecting the entities that should be retrieved and by defining filters to constrain the queries. For example it is possible to retrieve "all variation points that provide an alternative-selection" or "which features belong to product No. 1 and product No. 2 but are not part of the platform model". The predefined queries and the query generator are depicted in figures 7 and 8.

All queries generate a report and display the results in a formatted output. The reports can additionally be printed out.

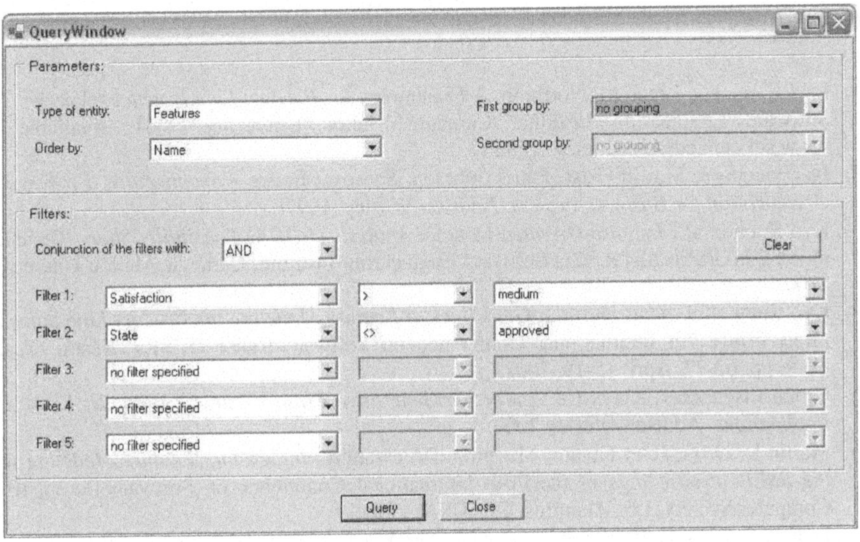

Fig. 8. Query generator

5 Evaluation and Future Work

RequiLine is still under development and has currently not exceeded the prototype status. It aims to support the requirements engineering activities of software product line development. The core system provides a rich amount of functionality and provides much flexibility and space for enhancements and future capabilities. Nevertheless, the core system runs stable.

The implemented user interface offers the functionalities of the underlying core system to the user; it needs to be improved in design and layout. The disadvantage of *RequiLine* lies of course in the lack of usability. The prototype does not come with a graphical editor, that lets the user draw feature diagrams, but just forces the user to define features and their relationships through table based selections. Integrating the graphical editor is one of the main tasks that is under development right now. Furthermore the assistance in product configuration is another required feature. Whereas *RequiLine* currently gives no support in configuring products, a future version will include a wizard that guides the user during the configuration process, by disabling inconsistent configurations or including platform features and requirements automatically into any product. Model enhancements that have not been addressed by *Requi-Line* so far, like attributing relationships and version control are interesting and required features, as well.

RequiLine has been initially evaluated in a large student project [14] to get a first impression of the tool usage. At this point I would like to thank Michael Matzutt, for implementing the initial version of *RequiLine* and providing a stable core system. This evaluation shows that the tool fulfills the demanded requirements. Right now, *RequiLine* is being evaluated in cooperation with a partner from the automotive industry. Nevertheless, we need further evaluation through real-life software projects to complete our studies.

References

1. Paul Clements, Linda M. Northrop, *A Framework for Product Line Practice - Version 4.1*, Software Engineering Institute, Carnegie Mellon University, 2001. Available at: www.sei.cmu.edu/plp/framework.html.
2. Ivar Jacobson, Martin Griss, Patrik Jonsson, *Software Reuse – Architecture, Process and Organization for Business success*, Addison-Wesley, 1997.
3. Kyo Kang et al., *Feature-Oriented Domain Analysis (FODA) Feasibility Study*, Technical report CMU/SEI-90-TR-021, Software Engineering Institute, Carnegie Mellon University, 2000.
4. Kyo Kang et al., *Concepts and Guidelines of Feature Modeling for Product Line Software Engineering*, 7th International Conference on Software Reuse (ICSR), Austin, Texas, USA, pp. 62-77, April 15-19, 2002.
5. Ulrich Eisenecker, Krzysztof Czarnecki, *Generative Programming – Methods, Tools, and Applications*, Addison-Wesley 2000.
6. Martin L. Griss, John Favaro, Massimo d'Alessandro, *Integrating Feature Modeling with the RSEB*, Proceedings of the Fifth International Conference on Software Reuse, IEEE Computer Society, Los Alamitos, CA, USA, 1998.
7. D. Fey, R Fajta, A. Boros, *Feature modeling: A meta-model to enhance usability and Usefulness*, in SPLC2, LNCS 2379, pages 198–216. Springer, 2002.
8. J. Savolainen et al., *Feature analysis*, Technical report, ESAPS, June 2001.
9. Len. Bass, Paul. Clements, Patrick. Donohoe, John. McGregor, Linda. Northrop, *Fourth Product Line Practice Workshop Report*, CMU/SEI-2000-TR-002, Software Engineering Institute, Carnegie Mellon University, 2000.
10. Horst Lichter, Alexander Nyßen, Thomas von der Maßen, Thomas Weiler, *Vergleich von Ansätzen zur Feature Modellierung bei der Softwareproduktlinienentwicklung*, Aachener Informatik Berichte, Aachen 2003.
11. Suzanne Robertson, James Robertson, *Mastering the Requirements Process*, Addison-Wesley, 1999.
12. Prasanna Padmanabhan, Robyn R. Lutz, *DECIMAL: A Requirements Engineering Tool for Product Families*, Proceedings of the International Workshop on Requirements Engineering for Product Lines, Avaya Labs, Technical Report ALR-2002-033, 2002.
13. Mario Selbig, Frank Blinn, *Ami Eddi 1.3*, University of Applied Sciences Kaiserslautern, 2002, Available at: www.generative-programming.org
14. Michael Matzutt, *Entwicklung eines Werkzeugs zur Anforderungsmodellierung bei Software-Produktlinien*, Diploma thesis, Software Construction Group – RWTH Aachen, Aachen, 2003.
15. John MacGregor, *Requirements Engineering in Industrial Product Lines*, Proceedings of the International Workshop on Requirements Engineering for Product Lines, Avaya Labs, Technical Report ALR-2002-033, 2002.

PLUTO: A Test Methodology for Product Families

Antonia Bertolino and Stefania Gnesi

Istituto di Scienza e Tecnologie della Informazione, CNR
Area della Ricerca di Pisa
56100 Pisa, Italy
{a.bertolino,s.gnesi}@isti.cnr.it

Abstract. The testing stage for a product belonging to a family is a crucial and expensive part of development. Yet the derivation of test cases for product families has so far received little attention. We focus here on test planning, that is the most critical part of testing. We outline a simple methodology we are developing for this purpose, called PLUTO, relying on the early requirements specification expressed as Use Cases. We also overview the related literature.

1 Introduction

Although reuse of software artifacts has long been advocated and pursued, it is only in the last few years that software producers have started to introduce a systematic and pervasive reuse strategy throughout the development process. Reuse is put in place between applications sharing similar functionality and user requirements, but at the same time possessing each specific features that make them different from one another. These "kin" applications form what is called a *product family* or a *product line* [10], whereby [14] the first term originated within a series of European industrial-cooperation projects, while the second was introduced by the US community. We will use here the two terms interchangeably.

When building a new product line different approaches can be followed [20]: a product line can be defined from scratch, without starting from any predecessor products; several systems contemporaneously under development are integrated into the product line; or, legacy systems are reengineered into the product line.

In any case, following the Process Reference Model defined in the CAFÉ project [3], [14], product line development is characterized by two correlated processes: Domain engineering and Application engineering, as shown in Figure 1. Domain engineering is the process aiming at developing the general concept of a product line together with all the assets that are common to the whole product line, whereas Application engineering is the process aiming at designing a specific product of the family and eventually produces a customer specific application as in a traditional process.

It is possible to move from the family level to the product level by an instantiation process and on the contrary from the product level to the family level by an abstraction process.

F. van der Linden (Ed.): PFE 2003, LNCS 3014, pp. 181–197, 2004.
© Springer-Verlag Berlin Heidelberg 2004

Differently from the usual single product development, the definition process of a customer specific application that is an instance of a family is influenced not only by the requirements of the customer, but also by the capabilities of the product line. Consequently, software product families need more sophisticated requirement analysis and processing methods.

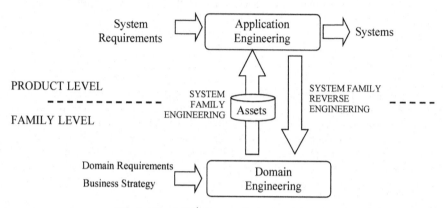

Fig. 1. The CAFÉ-Process Reference Model.

The most evident and perhaps most urging question is how to handle and represent *variability* [9]. Behind the many commonalities, product family instances in fact necessarily yield variable features, because these constitute precisely what allows for achieving different variants and customized applications. Seen from another perspective, variation points are a way to defer some crucial design decisions [7] until the point where these must be eventually drawn. Indeed, variability and flexibility are the top most desirable characteristics of a product family specification. But variability in a sense amounts to *ambiguity*: where we have been preached for years that a system specification should be made as precise and rigorous as possible, here we must find ways for specifying a product family by leaving some features undecided, i.e., ambiguous.

Specification of product family requirements has drawn large attention in the recent software engineering literature, e.g., [1],[8],[11],[16]. However requirement engineering is only one task of product line engineering. Little attention has been devoted instead to a closely related problem that is *how to test product families*. It is now well recognized that testing takes a predominant amount of the development resources and schedule. Therefore, also reuse of test assets is a crucial issue in production processes. And, in the same manner that a product family specification and design must tackle variability, this need applies for testing as well.

As identified in [9], considering the Application engineering process, the phase in which the majority of variation points are introduced is the requirement specification phase. Accordingly, we believe that planning ahead for testing within the Application engineering process must start from the requirements. In this view, our research addresses the testing of product lines, based on the requirements expressed in the well-known formalism of Use Cases [5].

In Section 2, we discuss some general issues of testing for product families. In Section 3 we present the PLUTO methodology to derive specific test cases for product families. An application example is presented in Section 4. An extension of the PLUTO methodology to cover functional dependencies between requirements is given in Section 5. We briefly overview related work in Section 6 and we draw some conclusions in Section 7.

2   Testing Product Lines Starting from the Requirements

Speaking in general product line requirements can be considered as composed of a fixed and a variable part. The fixed part includes all those requirements dealing with features or functionalities common to all the products belonging to the line and that, for this reason, do not need to be modified when an application is instantiated. The variable part represents instead those functionalities that differentiate a product from another.

We can hence say that the requirements specification of a PL comprises a common part **R**, specifying the common (mandatory) requirements of all the products belonging to the PL, plus a variable part $\mathbf{R}_{var}$, which defines the variations points distinguishing the different products of the PL, i.e.:

PL Reqs = R + R$_{var}$

Considering again the CAFÉ Process Reference Model (Figure 1), the **PL Reqs** constitute a family asset that is built incrementally along the Domain engineering process.

When a specific product Pr belonging to this family is instantiated in the Application engineering process, its requirements are of course not re-derived from scratch, but are obtained in principle by instantiating the variable part in the PL requirements that will lead to a set of different product-related requirements, i.e.:

Pr Reqs = R + R$_{ist}$

As previously discussed, the need to put in place a policy of asset reuse for the definition of application requirements is widely recognized, and several approaches have been proposed to tackle variability at this stage. The motivations are clearly enhancing productivity and reducing the costs of requirements specification. Our claim is that these same motivations call for applying an *asset reuse policy to the activities of test planning and management* as well, which may be even more expensive and effort-prone than requirements definition.

Intuitively, a methodology for testing PLs should work at both levels of Domain and Application engineering (Figure 1): at the Domain level it should allow a tester to describe a generic frame of test cases pertaining to the whole PL domain. In other terms, the family test plan should include a list of *mandatory test cases* **T**, i.e., those tests that apply to the whole domain and correspond roughly to the mandatory requirements **R**, and a variable part $\mathbf{T}_{var}$, which refers to test cases significant at the application level, and that *need to be instantiated from* $\mathbf{R}_{var}$ *for each specific product*, i.e.:

PL Tests = T + T$_{var}$

At the Application level, the methodology should then allow testers to directly instantiate the frame of test cases relative to a specific product, inclusive of generic and specific test features, i.e.:

Pr Tests = T + T$_{ist}$

In practice, the **PL Tests** are not saved once and for all, but more plausibly are incrementally obtained as the result of an iterative process from family to product and backward from product to family. Moreover, as we will also see below in our examples, this list serves only as a conceptual reference: nobody will ever use it to test the family, which is again an abstract reference concept. It is the specific list of **Pr Tests** that is of real interest for a tester, because eventually the test cases are to be executed on a product, not on a PL.

3 PLUTO: A Simple Test Methodology for Product Families

Our proposal to address the testing of Product Lines starting from requirements is PLUTO[1] (Product Lines Use case Test Optimization), a simple and intuitive methodology for the early derivation of test cases[2] from PF requirements described as Product Lines Use Cases (PLUCs). PLUCS have been introduced in [1]. To make this paper self-contained, before introducing PLUTO, we provide below a short overview of PLUCs.

3.1 Use Cases for Product Families

Use Cases are a powerful tool to capture functional requirements. They provide a means to specify the interaction between a system and its environment and allow for structuring the requirements according to the user goals.

Graphical object modeling languages have become very popular in recent years. Among those, UML [9] introduces a set of graphical notation elements for Use Case modeling. UML Use Case diagrams are easy to understand and constitute a good vehicle of communication. However, they mainly serve as a sort of table of content for Use Cases, just presenting the connections between actors and Use Cases, and the dependencies between Use Cases.

The requirements regarding the system behavior cannot be specified in detail with UML Use Case diagrams, therefore several authors have proposed to augment the UML Use Case diagrams with textual and tabular descriptions. In particular, an effective and widely used technique for specifying Use Cases was presented by Alistair

---

[1] PLUTO has been also introduced in an extended abstract appeared in [2].

[2] A remark is noteworthy: although we generically speak in terms of "test cases", this is not compliant with the common meaning of a test case as the precise specification of a test input, a sequence of events and the expected output. We deal rather with *abstract descriptions of test scenarios*: our test cases are actually scenarios of use that need to be tested for validating that the user requirements are satisfied. A refinement process from these abstract descriptions to more concrete ones is needed for obtaining executable test cases.

Cockburn in [4]. The technique is based on natural language specification for scenarios and extensions, which are thus simply expressed by phrases in plain English language. This makes requirements documents easy to understand and communicate, even to non-technical people. We also adopt Cockburn's Use Cases, but extend them with specific annotations to handle PL variability.

A Use Case [4] describes the interaction (triggered by an external actor in order to achieve a goal) between a system and its environment. Every Use Case constitutes a goal-oriented set of interactions between external actors and the system under consideration. The term *actor* is used to describe any person or system that has a goal against the system under discussion or interacts with the system to achieve some other actor's goal.

A primary actor triggers the system behaviour in order to achieve a certain goal. A secondary actor interacts with the system, but does not trigger the Use Case. A Use Case is completed successfully when the goal associated to it is reached. Use Case descriptions also include possible extensions to this sequence, e.g., alternative sequences that may also satisfy the goal, as well as sequences that may lead to failure in completing the service in case of exceptional behaviour, error handling procedures, etc. The system is treated as a "black box": Use Cases capture *who* (actor) does *what* (interaction) with the system, for what *purpose* (goal), without dealing with system internals.

A complete set of Use Cases specifies all the different ways actors can use the system, and therefore defines the whole required behaviour of the system.

Generally, Use Case steps are written in an easy-to-understand, structured narrative using the vocabulary of the domain. The language used for the description is usually English. Any other natural language can be used as well. A scenario is an execution path of a Use Case. The main flow is expressed, in the "Description" section, by an indexed sequence of natural language sentences, describing a sequence of actions of the system, called also "Main success scenario". This represents a single path through the Use Case that leads to success in achieving the goal. Scenarios may also be depicted in a graphical form using UML sequence diagrams.

Alternatives to the main flow are expressed in the "Extensions" section, and are linked by their index to the point of the main flow from which they branch out.

PLUCs [1] extend Cockburn's Use Cases [5], allowing variations to be easily described. Variations are explicitly enclosed into the sections of the Use Cases by means of **tags** that indicate those parts of the PL requirements to be instantiated for customizing a specific product of the line.

More specifically, the tags can represent three kinds of variability:

- **Alternative tags:** they express the possibility to instantiate the requirement by selecting an instance among a predefined set of possible choices. The selection is independent from other variation points;
- **Parametric tags:** their instantiation is connected to the actual values of a parameter in the requirements for the specific product, each of them depending on the occurrence of a condition;
- **Optional tags:** their instantiation can be done by selecting indifferently among a set of values, which are optional features for a derived product.

3.2 The Test Methodology

Commonalities and variabilities also affect test planning in product lines: starting from this consideration we have defined the PLUTO methodology, that is inspired by the well-known Category Partition (CP) method [19], but expands it with the capability to handle PL variabilities and to instantiate test cases for a specific customer product.

In the original CP method, for each functional unit (here a PLUC), the tester identifies the environment conditions (the required system properties for a certain functional unit) and the parameters (the explicit inputs for the unit) that are relevant for testing purposes: these are called the *categories*. For each category the significant (from the tester's viewpoint) values that it can take are then selected, called the *choices*. A suite of test cases is obtained by taking all the possible combinations of choices for all the categories.

To prevent the construction of redundant, not meaningful, or even contradictory combinations of choices, in CP the choices can be annotated with *constraints*, which can be of two types: *i*) either properties or *ii*) special conditions. In the first case, some properties are set for certain choices, and *selector* expressions related with them (in the form of simple IF conditions) are associated with other choices: a choice marked with an IF selector can then be combined only with those choices from other categories that fulfill the related property. The second type of constraints is useful to reduce the number of test cases: some markings, namely "error" and "single", are coupled to some choices. The choices marked with "error" and "single" refer to erroneous or special conditions, respectively, that we intend to test, but that need not to be combined with all possible choices.

The list of all the choices identified for each category, with the possible addition of the constraints, forms a **Test Specification**. It is not yet a list of test cases, but contains all the necessary information for instantiating them by unfolding the constraints.

The CP method described above had to be adapted for dealing with the possible presence of the tags defined above, identifying the PL variation points. However, this can be done quite easily: we use the tags similarly to the original concept of CP constraints, i.e., in the Test Specification we associate the variability tags to the corresponding choices; then, in the process of test derivation we match the tag values in such a way to establish the combinations that are relevant with respect to a specific application. In particular, in case of:

– an Optional tag: the corresponding feature is taken into account or not depending on whether it is present in the application;
– an Alternative tag: the relevant feature is selected;
– a Parametric tag: the feature corresponding to the pertinent value is taken.

Note that actually Parametric tags do not directly contribute to the task of identifying the test scenarios: in fact, they do not identify possible selections, but rather assign the appropriate features once some other related tags are fixed.

Another specific characteristic of test cases derived from Use Cases is the presence of several scenarios, i.e., the main success scenario and in addition the possible extensions. Of course all of them must be exercised during testing. Therefore the Test

Specification of PLUCs will normally include a category "Scenarios", in which all the specified scenarios are listed.

As our approach is based on structured, natural language requirements, the test derivation has to be done partially manually. In particular, the identification of relevant Categories and of the Choices to be tested is left to the tester's judgment, and this is natural. However, lexical and syntactical analyzers for natural language requirements could be used to extract useful information to identify the relevant Categories.

When considering the repository of all Use Cases specified for a PL, it will often be the case that some scenarios in a Use Case depend on other scenarios in another Use Case, because of the presence of *cross-cutting features*. To handle them, we annotate the PLUC with a specific note such as "See another PLUC". In general, whenever a test specification includes such a directive, the derivation of test cases is made by combining the relevant choices from the two related PLUCs. Note that the annotation is made in the PLUC that triggers the test cases.

With reference to the requirements conceptual framework in Section 2, we will have that the set **T** of mandatory test cases for a PL is given by those test cases that do not include variability tags, i.e., by those combinations of choices that are common throughout the family. On the other hand, all the possible combinations of choices involving tags form the set $\mathbf{T_{var}}$ of variable test cases. The complete set **PL Tests** of mandatory and variables test cases, which would be obtained in this way, form the family asset of test cases. As said, we do not derive actually the list of **PL Tests**, rather we derive the PL Test Specification and leave it unfolded.

The test cases are derived when a specific product is being developed after having instantiated the tags in each PLUC to the appropriate values. More precisely, for each Test Specification relative to each PLUC a different set of test cases will correspond to each specific product of the PL, depending on the tag values. We observe that this intermediate step of tag instantiation between the definition of the Test Specification and the derivation of the test sets is the means by which in PLUTO we tackle variability. For readers familiar with the traditional CP test method, this is also what makes PLUTO basically different from the traditional CP, in which we depict only one set of test cases corresponds directly to each Test Specification.

We point up this conceptual difference with the help of a scheme. In Figure 2 we depict: in part a) the process of test derivation in the traditional CP method, where the test cases are directly unfolded from the test specifications; in part b) the more articulated process of PLUTO. As shown, there are two stages: the derivation of test specifications, belonging to the family; then, a family of different sets of test scenarios can be derived from each PLUC, depending on the instantiation of tags.

4 An Example

An example of a PLUC is presented in Figure 3. We propose the description of the GamePlay Use Case applicable to different mobile phones belonging to a same PL. We assume that the products differ at least for the set of games made available to the user and for the provision or not of WAP connectivity.

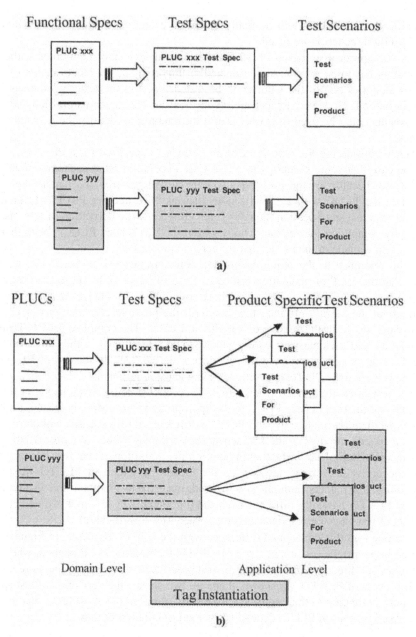

Fig. 2. A Scheme of the PLUTO Methodology.

Curly brackets are introduced into the Use Case elements, and tags (here **[Vo]**, **[V1]**, and **[V2]**) indicate the variation points within the Use Case. Moreover, the possible instantiations of the variable parts and the type of the variations are defined within the Variations section within the PLUC.

PL USE CASE GamePlay

Goal: Play a game on a **[Vo]** Mobile Phone and record score
Scope: The **[Vo]** Mobile Phone
Level: Summary
Precondition: The **[Vo]** Mobile Phone is on
   Trigger: Function GAMES has been selected from the main menu
Primary actor : The Mobile Phone user
Secondary actors: The {**[V0]** Mobile Phone} (the system)
                The Mobile Phone Company
Main success scenario
   1. The system displays the list of the {**[V1]** available} games
   2. The user selects a game
   3. The user selects the difficulty level
   4. The user starts the game and plays it until completion
   5: The user records the score achieved {**[V2]** and sends the score to Club XXX via WAP}

Extensions
   1a. No game is available:
      1a1. return to main menu
   3a. The user starts the game and plays it until an incoming call arrives. See CallAnswer.

Variations
V0: Alternative:
            0. Model0
            1. Model1
            2. Model2

V1: Parametric
if V0=0 then display msg "No game available"
   else if V0=1 then Snakell or Space Impact
   else if V0=2 then Snakell or Space Impact or Bumper.

V2: Optional
   when V0=2

Fig. 3. Example of a Use Case in the PLUC notation.

For illustration purposes, we now apply the Pluto approach to the GamePlay PLUC in Figure 3. As a first step, from an analysis of it we identify the following Categories: "Mobile Phone Model", "Games", "Difficulty Level", "Scenarios", "Club". These identify the relevant characteristics to be varied when testing the Mobile Phone system for validating the user requirements with respect to the functionality of playing games.

Now we proceed with partitioning these categories into the relevant choices, i.e., we single out for each of the categories the values that are the relevant cases to be considered in specific tests.

When applying the CP method to PLs, in general we will have that some of the choices will be available for all the products of the family. On the other hand, some of the categories are specialized into choices that depend on the specific product considered. For instance, the category "Club", which relates to the capability to exchange the achieved game score with other Club affiliates, is relevant only for those models that support WAP connection. Hence it cannot be tested for any potential applications of the family, but only for those supporting this feature. This is specified in the GamePlay PLUC by means of the **V2** optional tag. Hence, when the test cases are being derived, we make use of this tag similarly to the constraints formalism of the CP method. As shown in Figure 4, we derive the possible choices pertaining to the "Club" category, but we annotate them with the appropriate selector, which is a simple IF condition stating that these choices are of interest only when property P2 is satisfied (which happens for Model2).

The complete Test Specification is shown below in Figure 4.

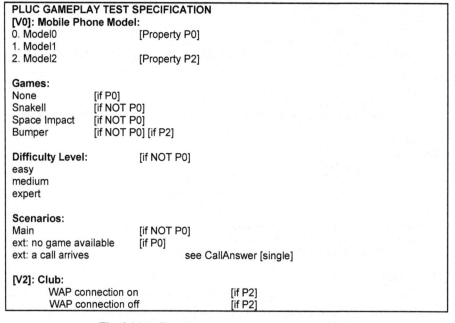

Fig. 4. Main Test Categories for the GamePlay PLUC.

If we now apply to this test specification a generator that takes out all the possible combinations of choices, we would obtain a list of test cases, which correspond to the **PL Tests** list. This list would include all the potential test cases for all the products of the family relative to the PLUC under consideration. However, what is more interesting in our opinion, is that we can instead derive directly the **Pr Tests** list for a specific product of interest. This is obtained very easily by just instantiating the relative tags. So, for instance, if we are interested to test the Model2 product of this family, we set property P2 to true and derive all and only the combinations that remain valid.

As an example, we list below in Figure 5 some of the test cases that would be so obtained for different products, i.e., for different tag assignments. We show these as abstract descriptions and leave to the reader the task to figure out the obvious transformation of these into the corresponding functional test scenarios.

In Figure 5 the test cases **Ti, Tj1, Tj2** all refer to a simpler situation in which the features in a PLUC do not depend on the features of another PLUC. Test **Tk** instead needs further consideration. It considers the choice "a call arrives" of the Scenarios category, which has a specific "see CallAnswer" annotation. This is an example of a cross-cutting feature, whose notion we have introduced in Sect. 3.2. We now see below how this can be handled in the Pluto methodology.

```
Tag V0=0
    Ti:
    Mobile Phone Model: Model 0
    Games:  None
    Scenarios:          ext: no game available


........


Tag V0=2
    Tj1:
    Mobile Phone Model: Model 2
    Games:  Snakell
    Difficulty Level:   easy
    Scenarios:          main
    Club:   WAP connection on


    Tj2:
    Mobile Phone Model: Model 2
    Games:  Bumper
    Difficulty Level:   expert
    Scenarios:          main
    Club:   WAP connection on


........


    Tk:
    Mobile Phone Model: Model 1
    Games:  Space Impact
    Difficulty Level:   medium
    Scenarios:          ext: a call arrives - see CallAnswer
```

Fig. 5. Some Test Scenarios.

5   Extending the Methodology

When considering the repository of all Use Cases specified for a PL, it will often be the case that some scenarios in a Use Case depend on other scenarios in another Use Case, because of the presence of cross-cutting features. Referring to the example used so far, let us suppose that the Mobile Phone PL under consideration provides for some applications the capability to save the current status of a game being played in the case that an incoming call arrives. The user may answer or refuse the call. Then, after the communication is closed, the game can be resumed from the status in which it was interrupted.

PL USE CASE CallAnswer
Goal: Answer an incoming call on a **[V0]** Mobile Phone
Scope: The **[V0]** Mobile Phone
Precondition: Signal is available; Mobile Phone is switched on
Trigger: Incoming call
Primary actor : The user
Secondary actors: The { **[V0]** Mobile Phone} (the system)
⠀⠀⠀⠀⠀⠀⠀⠀⠀⠀⠀⠀⠀⠀The Mobile Phone Company
Main success scenario
⠀⠀1.The user accepts the call by pressing the Accept button
⠀⠀2. The system establishes the connection by following the { **[V1]** appropriate } procedure.
Extensions
⠀⠀1a. The call is not accepted:
⠀⠀⠀⠀⠀⠀⠀⠀⠀⠀1a.1. the user presses the Reject button
⠀⠀⠀⠀⠀⠀⠀⠀⠀⠀1a.2. scenario terminates
PL Variability Features
⠀⠀**V0**: Alternative:
⠀⠀⠀⠀⠀0. Model0
⠀⠀⠀⠀⠀1. Model1 **[V2]**
⠀⠀⠀⠀⠀2. Model2 **[V2]**

⠀⠀**V1**: Parametric:
⠀⠀case V0 of
⠀⠀0: Procedure A:
⠀⠀⠀⠀2.1 Connect Caller and callee
⠀⠀1 or 2: if V2= a then Procedure B
⠀⠀⠀⠀2.1 Interrupt the game
⠀⠀⠀⠀2.2 Connect Caller and callee
⠀⠀else if V2= b then Procedure C:
⠀⠀⠀⠀2.1 Save current game status
⠀⠀⠀⠀2.2 Interrupt the game
⠀⠀⠀⠀2.3 Connect Caller and callee

⠀⠀**V2**: Alternative:
⠀⠀a. games available, but if interrupted status is not saved
⠀⠀b. games available, and if interrupted status is saved

Fig. 6. Another PLUC example.

This case depicts a cross-cutting feature arising from a functional dependency between the GamePlay PLUC and another Use Case, the CallAnswer PLUC, that describes the handling of incoming calls and that we have already referred in Figure 3. The description of the CallAnswer PLUC is reported in Figure 6.

Considering the CallAnswer PLUC (independently from the GamePlay PLUC), we assume we have already derived a Test Specification by applying to it the PLUTO methodology, as shown in Figure 7.

Similarly to what we have done for GamePlay, if we take all the potential combinations of choices in the CallAnswer Test Specification, in respect of the associated constraints, we would obtain the list of test scenarios relative to this Use Case.

It is clear however that the PLUCs GamePlay and CallAnswer are related with respect to the possibility to interrupt and then retrieve a game play because a call arrives. To identify that a dependency exists, as said, when we elicited the Use Cases we have annotated the related scenario in the GamePlay PLUC with the note "See CallAnswer".

PLUC CALLANSWER TEST SPECIFICATION
[V0]: Mobile Phone Model:
0. Model0   Property P0
1. Model1   Property P1
2. Model2   Property P1

Saving:
a. game status is not saved   [if P1]
b. game status is saved   [if P1]

Scenarios:
Main: Call is accepted
ext: Call is refused

Fig. 7. Main Test Categories for the CallAnswer PLUC.

Correspondingly, in the process of deriving the test cases from the GamePlay Test Specification (see Figure 4) the case that a call arrives is contemplated in all those tests in which for the "Scenarios" category the choice "ext: a call arrives" is taken. In Figure 5 the test case **Tk** for instance selects this choice (we report it again below):

Tk:
Mobile Phone Model: Model 1
Games: Space Impact
Difficulty Level: medium
Scenarios: ext: a call arrives

However, as described in the CallAnswer PLUC, when a call arrives several behaviors are possible. This test hence is not complete: it must be further refined into several related test cases, considering each of the possible combinations of choices offered in its turn by the CallAnswer Test Specification.

Hence for example from the above **Tk**, considering the Test Specification relative to the CallAnswer PLUC (Figure 7), we get at least four refined test cases as follows:

Tk-1:
Mobile Phone Model: Model 1
Games: Space Impact
Difficulty Level: medium
Scenarios: ext: a call arrives
                Saving: game status is not saved
                Scenarios : Call is accepted

Tk-2:
Mobile Phone Model: Model 1
Games: Space Impact
Difficulty Level: medium
Scenarios: ext: a call arrives
                Saving: game status is saved
                Scenarios : Call is accepted

Tk-3:
Mobile Phone Model: Model 1
Games: Space Impact
Difficulty Level: medium
Scenarios: ext: a call arrives
                Saving: game status is not saved
                Scenarios : Call is refused

Tk-4:
Mobile Phone Model: Model 1
Games: Space Impact
Difficulty Level: medium
Scenarios: ext: a call arrives
                    Saving: game status is saved
                    Scenarios : Call is refused

More in general, whenever a test specification includes a directive "See another PLUC", the derivation of test cases is made by combining the relevant choices from the two related PLUCs. Note that the annotation is made in the PLUC that triggers the test cases, in our example the GamePlay PLUC.

Note also that in the GamePLay Test Specification we have marked the choice "ext: a call arrives" with the [single] constraint, described in Section 3.2. In fact, to reduce the number of test scenarios, we have decided not to test separately the arrival of a call together with all possible combinations of GamePlay choices (that are being tested already along the main scenario). Instead we select one representative combination (as the **Tk** example above) on the side of GamePlay, and from this we then derive as many tests as are the possible refinements when considering the CallAnswer Test Specification.

6   Related Work

The field of Product Lines testing is very young. We quickly overview related work, for the purpose of identifying relevant differences and commonalities with our ongoing research.

In [15] test-related activities in a product line organization are described. Test-related activities are organized into a test process that is purposely designed to take advantage of the economies of scope and scale that are present in a product line organization. These activities are sequenced and scheduled so that a test activity expands on the testing practice area described by Clements and Northrop [4]. Here we present a test case derivation strategy for PLs described starting from a very general description like the Use Cases are. We can say therefore that the main difference between [15] and [4], and our work, stays in the focus, which is there on the process while here is on the methodology. A mutual influence between these two directions of work would certainly be desirable and beneficial.

In [12] the authors propose that variability is introduced in the domain-level test cases, correspondingly to the variabilities present in the Use Cases, and that application specific test cases are then derived from them. The derivation strategy depends on how the variability is expressed, and different approaches, including Abstraction, Parameterization, Segmentation, Fragmentation, and Instantiation are overviewed. It is envisaged that a combination of these approach needs to be used. The approach is still preliminary and details are missing, in particular it is not clear to what extent it can be automatized. However, the idea of combining several derivation approaches is interesting and our approach could probably be incorporated in this general framework as one of the derivation strategies (in particular the Parameterization one).

In [18] an approach to expressing test requirements and to formally validate them in a UML-based development process which takes into account product lines (PL) specificities is presented. Behavioral test patterns (i.e., the test requirements) are built as combinations of use-case scenarios, these scenarios being product-independent and therefore constituting reusable PL assets. The difference between this approach and ours is that from a methodological point of view they propose a whole process from early modeling of requirements to test cases starting from UML specifications, whereas we instead exploit the description of a PL given in natural language and work at the analysis early stages. Perhaps the two approaches could be considered in combination, as addressing different concerns of PL life cycle.

Product line testing is also addressed in RITA [13], an environment under development at the University of Helsinki. RITA is orthogonal to our work, in that it is specifically designed for framework and framelet-based PLs, and does not assist the generation of test cases from requirements. Instead, assuming that the test cases are supplied in input, the environment is conceived for supporting test scripting, execution, result evaluation, and more in general for helping with all the test process management activities.

Different from ours finally are some recent approaches that attack the testing problem based on the product line software architectures. Indeed, the increased use of product line architectures in today's software development poses several challenges for existing testing techniques. In [17] those challenges are discussed as well as the opportunities for addressing them. The Component+ architecture [6] defines instead standardized test interfaces that minimize the effort needed to verify the components by extending software components with configurations.

7   Conclusions

We have discussed the important issue of test planning for product families starting from the PL requirements, expressed as PLUCs, which are an extension of Cockburn's Use Cases.

After analyzing the need for handling variability and reusing Test Specifications across products of a same family, we have proposed the PLUTO methodology, that is inspired by the Category Partition method, but expands it with the capability to handle PL variabilities and to instantiate test cases for a specific customer product.

As our approach is based on structured, natural language requirements, the test derivation has to be done partially manually. In particular, the identification of relevant Categories and of the Choices to be tested is left to the tester's judgment, and this is natural. However, lexical and syntactical analyzers for natural language requirements could be used to extract useful information to identify the relevant Categories.

With regard to the derivation of the test cases from the Test Specification, instead, this task can be easily automated, and we are currently working at a PLUTO tool implementation. We plan also to investigate the integration of some of the available lexical/syntactical analyzers in the PLUTO tool to further automate the test generation process.

Our objective here was to propose a simple and intuitive methodology to manage the testing process of product lines, based on the Use Case requirements. The proposed methodology helps derive a set of Test Specifications, each relative to a PL Use Case, as an asset of the family, and a suite of application specific test cases, when a customized application is defined within the product line.

This work is clearly a first step towards a more comprehensive testing strategy for families. Further refinement of the approach is ongoing, as well as the development of automated support tools. On the other hand, as we have seen, the topic of product families testing is relatively new, and therefore this paper is also intended as a contribution to trigger further research.

Acknowledgments

This work was partially supported by the Eureka Σ!2023 Programme, ITEA (ip00004, Project CAFÉ).

References

1. Bertolino, A., Fantechi, A., Gnesi, S., Lami, G., Maccari, A. Use Case Description of Requirements for Product Lines, REPL'02, Essen, Germany, Avaya Labs Tech. Rep. ALR-2002-033, September 2002.
2. Bertolino, A., Gnesi, S., Use Case-based Testing of Product Lines, Proc. ESEC/FSE 2003, p. 355-358, ACM Press.
3. Café project homepage, at: http://www.extra.research.philips.com/euprojects/cafe/.
4. Clements, P.C., Northrop, L. Software Product Lines: Practices and Patterns. SEI Series in Software Engineering. Addison-Wesley, August 2001.
5. Cockburn, A. Writing Effective Use Cases. Addison Wesley, 2001.
6. Component+, "D4 – BIT Case studies", *www.componentplus.org*, October 2002
7. van Gurp, J., Bosch, J., and Svahnberg, M. On the Notion of Variability in Software Product Lines, Proc. of the Working IEEE/IFIP Conference on Software Architecture (WICSA 2001), p. 45-54.
8. Halmans, G., Pohl K., Communicating the Variability of a Software-Product Family to Customers, Journal of Software and Systems Modeling, Vol. 2, p.15-36 Springer, March 2003.
9. Jaring, M., and Bosch, J. Representing Variability in Software Product Lines: A Case Study. In Chastek G. J. (Ed.): Proc. Software Product Lines, 2nd Int. Conf, SPLC 2, San Diego, CA, USA, August 19-22, 2002, LNCS 2379, p.15-36.
10. Jazayeri, M., Ran, A., van der Linden, F. Software Architecture for Product Families: Principles and Practice, Publishers: Addison-Wesley, Reading, Mass. and London, 1998.
11. John, I., Muthig, D. Tailoring Use Cases for Product Line Modeling, International workshop on requirements Engineering for Product Line (REPL'02), 2, Avaya Labs Technical Report ALR-2002-033, September 2002.

12. Kamsties, E., Pohl, K., Reis, S., and Reuys, A., "Testing Variabilities in Use Case Model", *5th International Workshop on Product Family Engineering*, Siena, November 2003.
13. Kauppinen, R., Taina J., RITA Environment for Testing Framework-based Software Product Lines. *Proceedings of the Eighth Symposium on Programming Languages and Software Tools (SPLST'2003)*, Kuopio, Finland, June 2003, 58-69, University of Kuopio, 2003.
14. van der Linden, F. Software Product Families in Europe: The ESAPS & Café Projects, IEEE Software July/August 2002.
15. MacGregor, J. D. Testing a Software Product Line, *Technical Report,* CMU/SEI-2001-TR-022.
16. von der Massen, S., Lichter H. Modeling Variability by UML Use Case Diagram, International workshop on requirements Engineering for Product Line (REPL'02), Avaya Labs Technical Report ALR-2002-033, September 2002
17. Muccini H., van der Hoek A., Towards Testing Product Line Architectures, Electronic Notes in Theoretical Computer Science 82 No. 6, 2003.
18. Nebut C., Pickin S., Le Traon Y. and Jézéquel,, J-M. Reusable Test Requirements for UML-Modeled Product line, REPL'02, Essen, Germany, Avaya Labs Technical Report ALR-2002-033, September 2002.
19. Ostrand, T.J., and Balcer, M.J. The Category Partition Method For Specifying and Generating Functional Tests. ACM Comm. 31 (6), June 1988, pp. 676-686.
20. Schmid K., Verlage, M. The Economic Impact of Product Line Adoption and Evolution. IEEE Software, 19(4): 50--57, July-August 2002.

A Requirement-Based Approach
to Test Product Families

Clémentine Nebut, Franck Fleurey, Yves Le Traon, and Jean-Marc Jézéquel

IRISA,
Campus Universitaire de Beaulieu,
35042 Rennes Cedex, France
{Clementine.Nebut,Franck.Fleurey,Yves.Le_Traon,
Jean-Marc.Jezequel}@irisa.fr

Abstract. Use-cases have been identified as good inputs to generate test cases and oracles at requirement level. To have an automated generation, information is missing from use cases, such as the exact inputs of the system, and the sequential constraints between the use cases. The contribution of this paper is then two-fold. First we propose a contract language for PF functional requirements expressed as parameterized use cases; this language supports the specification of variant parts in the requirements. Then we provide a method, a formal model and a prototype tool to automatically generate both functional and robustness test cases specific to a product from the PF requirements. We study the efficiency of the generated test cases on a case study[1].

1 Introduction

Product families (PF) are currently undergoing a resurgence of interest, some factors being the relentless pace of hardware development, the growing complexity of software systems, and the need to respond promptly to more rapidly-changing consumers habits. PF conception and design brings up a large number of novel issues, among them, PF testing methods. As underlined in [8], PF requirements assist design evaluation, and consequently play a crucial role in driving the functional testing task. However, there is a real difficulty in ensuring that the requirements of a PF are satisfied on all the products. In other words, *requirements-based testing* of a product family is an arduous task, which is in serious need of automation. In this paper, we propose a method implemented in a prototype tool, which allow product-specific test objectives to be generated from the PF requirements (expressed in the UML with use cases). Our approach aims at using the sequential dependencies existing between the use cases to generate relevant test objectives. We propose to associate contracts to the use cases of the PF, to express those dependencies. Those contracts are then interpreted, an execution model is built for each product, and thanks to adequate test criteria, test objectives are automatically generated by our prototype.

The rest of the paper is organized as follows. Section 2 presents a contract language for PF functional requirements and illustrates it on a case study. Section 3 details the

---

[1] This work has been partially supported by the FAMILIES European project. Eureka Σ! 2023 Program, ITEA project ip 02009.

F. van der Linden (Ed.): PFE 2003, LNCS 3014, pp. 198–210, 2004.
© Springer-Verlag Berlin Heidelberg 2004

generation of functional and robustness test objectives from requirements enhanced with contracts. This generation is based on a use case labeled transition system, and we propose test coverage criteria to extract test objectives from this model. Section 4 is an experimental part aiming at studying on a case study both the relevance of the generated test objectives and their effectiveness. The key question addressed is to determine if test cases generated at very high level of a PF are still relevant at product-specific code-level. Section 5 and 6 respectively briefly states the related work and gives our conclusions and future work.

2   A Contract Language for Functional PF Requirements

In this section, we present a way to express the sequential constraints existing between the use cases of a PF, remaining within the UML. In general, the partial order existing between the uses cases is given in their textual description, or just left implicit. We here propose to make it explicit in a declarative way, associating contracts (i.e. pre and post conditions) to the use cases. Using contracts is a good way to express easily and quickly the mutual obligations and benefits among functional requirements, expressed with use-cases. Pre and post conditions are attached as UML notes to each use case, and are first-order logical expressions. In the following, we present our case study and then use it to illustrate the contracts.

2.1   A Case Study: A Virtual Meeting Server PF

Our case study is a virtual meeting server PF offering simplified web conference services. It is used in the advanced courses of the Univ. of Rennes. The whole system contains more than 80 classes but a simplified version is presented here with few variants for the sake of readability (only functional variants appear since we address functional testing). Our case study is thus a simplistic example of PF, but is sufficient to illustrate our method.

The virtual meeting server PF (VMPF) permits several different kinds of work meetings to be organized on a distributed platform. When connected to the server, a user can enter or exit a meeting, speak, or plan new meetings. Each meeting has a manager. The manager is the participant who has planned the meeting and set its main parameters (such as its name, its agenda, ...). Each meeting may also have a moderator, designated by the meeting manager. The moderator gives the floor to a participant who has asked to speak. Before opening a meeting it, he or she may decide that it is to be recorded in a log file. The log file will be sent to the moderator after the closing of the meeting. The corresponding use case diagram is given on Figure 1.

Three types of meetings exist:

— *standard meetings* where the current speaker is designated by a moderator (nominated by the organizer of the meeting). In order to speak, a participant has to ask for the floor, then be designated as the current speaker by the moderator. The speaker can speak as long as he or she wants; he or she can decide to stop speaking by sending a particular message, on reception of which the moderator can designate another speaker.

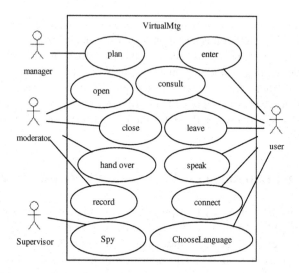

Fig. 1. Use case diagram.

- *democratic meetings* which are like standard meetings except that the moderator is a FIFO robot (the first client to ask for permission to speak is the first to speak)
- *private meetings* which are standard meetings with access limited to a certain set of users.

We define our PF describing the variation points and products (the commonalities corresponding to the basic functionalities of a virtual meeting server, as described above).

Variation Points. In this article, for the sake of simplicity, we only present 5 variation points in our VMPF:

- the limitation or lack of it, of the number of participants to 3.
- the type of meetings available; possible instantiations correspond to a selection of 1, 2, or all of the 3 types of possible meetings.
- the presence or absence of a facility enabling the moderator to ask for the meeting to be recorded.
- the languages supported by the server (possible languages being English, Spanish, French).
- the presence or absence of a supervisor of the whole system, able to spy and log it.

The other variation points which are not described here concern the presence of a translator, OS on which the software must run, various interfaces - from textual to graphical, network interface etc... Testing all the possible products independently is inescapable. In our case, this would mean testing (2*7*2*7*2*3*3)=2352 products (considering 3 OS and 2 GUIs). In order to simplify the presentation, in this paper we only consider 3 products (a demonstration edition, a personal edition, and an enterprise edition). However, this does not in any way reflect a restriction on the method. The characteristics of the 3 products are given in table 1.

Table 1. Variation points and products.

edition	demonstration	personal	enterprise
meeting limitation	true	true	false
meeting types	{std}	{std, democ, priv}	{std, democ, priv}
recording	false	false	true
language	{En}	{En}	{En, Fr, Sp}
supervisor	false	false	true

The *demonstration edition* manages standard meetings only, limited to 3 participants. Only English is supported, and no supervisor is present.

The *personal edition* provides the three kinds of meetings but still limits the number of participants. Only English is supported, and no supervisor is present.

The *enterprise edition* limits neither the type of meeting nor the number of participants. It is possible for the moderator to record the meeting. English, Spanish and French re supported: each participant chooses his or her preferred language, the default being English. A supervisor is present.

2.2 Use Cases Parameters and Contracts

We here present our contract language for requirements. The declarative definition of such contracts expressions is simple to achieve and forces the requirement analyst to be precise and rigorous in the semantics given to each use case, being in the same time flexible and easy to maintain and to modify: writing contracts is quite an easy task as soon as the use cases are well defined.

Use Cases Parameters. We consider parameterized use cases ; parameters allow us to determine the inputs of the use case (denoted UC in the following). Actors involved in the use case are particular parameters. For example, the *enter* use case is parameterized by the entering participant, and the entered meeting. It is expressed as follows:

```
UC enter (u:participant, m:meeting).
```

Parameters can be either actors (like the participant *u* in the UC enter) or main concepts of the application (like the meeting *m* in our example). Those main concepts will probably be reified in the design process, and are pointed out as business concepts in the requirements analysis. All types are enumerated types, they are only needed when the use case orderings are deduced (from the execution model presented below). For example, each participant and each meeting are declared by a specific label.

Contracts: Logical Expressions on Predicates. The UC contracts are first-order logical expressions on predicates, that are declared as follows:

```
UC plan (u:participant, m:meeting).
pre logical-expression
post logical-expression
```

A predicate has a name, and a set of typed formal parameters potentially empty (those parameters are a subset of the use cases parameters). The predicates are used to describe facts (on actors state, on main concepts states, or on roles) in the system. In this way, the predicate's names may generally be either semantical derivatives of a use case names (as *opened*), or role names (as *moderator*) or a combination of both. The predicates names are semantically rich: in this way, the predicates are easy to write and to understand. In order for the contracts to be fully understandable, the semantics of each predicate has to be made explicit, the most precisely possible so as to avoid any ambiguity in the predicate's sense. As an illustration, here are two examples of predicates, with their semantics:

- *created(m)* is a predicate which is true when the meeting *m* is created and false otherwise;
- *manager(u,m)* is a predicate which is true when the participant *u* is the manager of the meeting *m* and false otherwise.

Since classical boolean logic is used, a predicate is either true or false, but never undefined.

The precondition expression is the guard of the use case execution, and the postcondition expresses the new values of the predicates after the execution of the use case. The operators are the classical ones of boolean logic: the conjunction (*and*), the disjunction (*or*) and the negation (*not*). The implication (*implies*) is used to condition a new assertion with an expression. It allows the specification of results depending on the preconditions of a use case. Quantifiers (*forall* and *exists*) are also used in order to increase the expressive power of the contracts.

Contracts in the PF Context. In a PF, some requirements are common to all the products and some of them are only present in certain products, depending on variation points. That is why our contract language allows to specify which parts of the requirements depend on a certain variant. We thus propose to add tags (in fact UML tagged values) on contracts or on use cases, specifying which variants they depend on. If a tag is attached to an element e, then e is valid only for the product selected by this tag, i.e. the product owning one of the variant specified in the tag. By default, an element e with no tag is valid for all the products. The format of those tags is: *VP{variant_list}*, where *VP* is a variation point name, and *variant_list* is a list of instantiations of the variation point. For example, in our VMPF, the tag *recording{true}* selects the product owning a recording facility, i.e. the enterprise edition, and the tag *language{En}* selects the products handling the English language, i.e. all the products. Several contracts of the same type can thus be added to the same element, if they are tagged differently. When several preconditions (resp. postconditions) are selected for a same product, they are conjuncted.

An example of contracts is given on figure 2: the use case *enter* requires the entering participant u to be connected, and the entered meeting m to be opened. For a private meeting, u must be authorized in m, and for limited meetings, there must be strictly less than 3 participants already entered in m.

From a set of use cases with contracts of a product family, and using the characteristics of each product given in terms of variants, a set of use cases with contracts can be automatically built for each product, following Algorithm 1.

UC enter(u:participant; m:mtg)
pre connected(u) **and** opened(m)
pre priv(m)}**implies** authorized(u,m) {*VPMeetingType(priv)*}
pre not exists (u,v,w:participant) {entered(u,m) **and** entered(v,m) **and** entered(w,m)
 and u/=v **and** v/=w **and** w/=u} {*VPLimitation(true)*}
post entered(u,m)

Fig. 2. Contracts of the use case *enter.*

Algorithm 1 Algorithm to extract a product requirements from the product family requirements.

```
algorithm extractRequirementsForAProduct
param p: the product
result : requirements R(p) for p
for each use case uc in the PF requirements
  if no tag is present or p.satisfies(tag)
  then
    add uc to R(p)
  end
end
for each use case uc in R(p)
  for each precondition in uc
    if a tag is present and not p.satisfies(tag)
    then
      remove precondition
    end
  end
  for each postcondition in uc
    if a tag is present and not p.satisfies(tag)
    then
      remove postcondition
    end
  end
end
return R(p)
```

---

3   Automatic Test Generation
from Use Cases Enhanced with Contracts

In this section, we explain how we exploit the enhanced use cases to generate test objectives. We first build a use case transition system per product and then exploit it with several criteria to generate relevant test objectives.

3.1   The Use Case Transition System

From a requirement analysis leading to a set of use cases enhanced with pre and post conditions, we propose to build a representation of the valid sequences of use cases.

Since pre and post conditions contain parameters, this representation also deals with those parameters. In fact, the idea is to "instantiate" the use cases with a set of values replacing its parameters. As an example, in the virtual meeting, we want to obtain the ordering of use cases with 2 participants *p1* and *p2*, and a meeting named *m1*. The instantiated use cases of *plan(p:participant,m:meeting)* are *plan(p1,m1)* and *plan(p2,m1)*. In the following, we call *instantiated use cases* (resp. *predicates*) the set of use cases (resp. predicates) obtained by replacing its set of parameters by all the possible combinations of their possible specific values.

A Transition System to Represent Valid Sequences of Use Cases. The valid sequences of use cases are represented by a transition system M defined by $M = (Q, q_0, A, \hookrightarrow)$ where:

- Q is a finite non-empty set of states, each state being defined as a set of instantiated predicates,
- q_0 is the initial state,
- A is the alphabet of actions, an action being an instantiated use case,
- $\hookrightarrow \subseteq Q \times A \times Q$ is the transition function.

We call such a transition system a Use Case Transition System (UCTS). States of the UCTS represent the state of the system (in terms of value of predicates) at different stages of execution. Transitions, labeled with an instantiated use case, represent the execution of an instantiated use case. A path in the UCTS is thus a valid sequence of use cases. A partial UCTS obtained for the demonstration edition is given on figure 3.

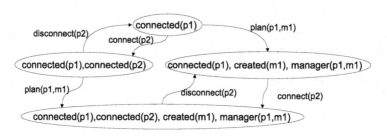

Fig. 3. UCTS extract.

Due to its finite set of states (itself due to the finite number of combinations of predicates), the UCTS is itself finite. Its maximal size in the worst case is $2^{n_p} \prod_{i=1}^{n_v} v_i$ states, where n_v is the number of types used, v_i is the number of possible values for each type i, and n_p is the number of predicates. This maximal size is reached when all the predicates use all the types, and when all the possible states are reachable from the initial state. In practice, this maximal size is never reached. For the demonstration edition with 3 participants and one meeting, the UCTS has 11600 states. The size of the UCTS grows up with the number of use cases, and thus with the complexity of the system to test. Thus for large system, building the UCTS is very expensive in memory and in time. To tackle this problem, work in underway to use an abstraction on certain parameters, in order to reduce the UCTS size.

Building Algorithm. The first step to build a UCTS for each specific product is to extract the requirements for each product from the PF requirements. This is simply done parsing the variation notes in the requirements, and using a table such as Table 1. Then, for each product-specific requirements, Algorithm 2 is applied to build the UCTS. Upon initialization, the initial state is deduced from the initial true predicates. Then the algorithm tries successively to apply each use case with all the combinations of effective parameters, as a puzzle game. Applying a use case is possible when its precondition is true w.r.t the set of true predicates contained in the current state's label, and leads to create an edge from the current state to the state representing the system after the postcondition is applied. The algorithm stops when all the reachable states are explored.

To obtain instantiated use cases from the formal description of use cases, the instances of each type are given, it corresponds to the enumeration of all the types of the system. In practice, we give to the building algorithm all the instances it has to deal with, under the form of a declaration. As an example, to deal with 3 participants and 1 meeting, we declared:

```
user1, user2, user3 : PARTICIPANT
m1 : MEETING
```

Algorithm 2 Algorithm producing the UCTS.

```
algorithm buildUCTS
param initState: STATE ; useCases : SET[ACTION]
var
  result : UCTS
  to_visit : STACK[STATE]
  currentState : STATE
  newState : STATE
init
  result.initialState←initState
  to_visit.push(initState)
body
  while (to_visit≠∅)
  do
    currentState←to_visit.pop
    ∀ uc ∈useCases | currentState ⇒uc.pre
      do
        newState ← apply(currentState, uc)
        if newState ∉result
        then
          result.Q ←result.Q ∪ {newState}
          to_visit.push(newState)
        fi
        result.↪ ←result.↪ ∪ {(currentState,uc,newState)}
      done
  done
end
```

3.2   Test Case Generation w.r.t Coverage Criteria

A UCTS is a representation of all the possible orderings of use cases. Thus from a UCTS, we aim at generating test objectives w.r.t a given UCTS covering criterion. We define in this sub-section one **structural criterion** to cover a UCTS and one **semantical criterion**, which is not based on the UCTS itself but on the contracts system.

Test Objective: A test objective (TO) is defined here as a sequence of instantiated use cases. Note that generally, a test objective cannot be directly used on an implementation: a test case generator is needed to obtain test cases from TOs.

Test Objectives Set Consistency with an UCTS: A test objectives set is said to be consistent with an UCTS iff each TO exercises a path of the UCTS. A path in the UCTS is here defined as the classical notion of path in a graph, the first vertex corresponding to the initial state.

All Instantiated Use Cases Criterion: (AIUC) A test objective set *TOs* satisfies the *all instantiated use cases* coverage criterion for a use case transition system *ucts* iff each instantiated use case of the system is exercised by at least one TO from *TOs*.

All Precondition Terms Criterion: (APT) A test objective set *TOs* satisfies the *All Precondition terms* criterion for a contracts system iff each use case is exercised in as many different ways as there are predicates combinations to make its precondition true.

We defined other criteria such as covering all vertices or all edges of the UCTS but they were leading to inefficient tests (*all vertices*) or to a too large number of tests (*all edges*). Intuitively, the criterion *All Precondition Terms* (APT) guarantees that all the possible ways to apply a use case are exercised: a use case can be applied when its precondition is true ; this precondition being a logical expression on predicates, there are several valuations of the predicates which makes it true (as an example, if a precondition is $a\ or\ b$, 3 valuations makes it true: (a, b); $(a, not\ b)$; $(not\ a, b)$). The criterion *APT* will find sequences of use cases such that each use case is applied with all the possible valuations of the expression : $(precondition = true)$. To implement this criterion, all those valuations are computed, and then paths in the UCTS are found to reach states that verify those constraints. The two criteria are implemented with a breadth first search of the UCTS from the initial state. Such a technique ensures that the obtained TOs sets are consistent with the considered UCTS. The choice of a breadth-first visit is made in order to obtain smaller TOs: small tests are more meaningful and humanely understandable than larger ones.

3.3   Robustness Testing

The tests generated as described above ensure that the application under test fits the requirements, but do not verify that violating contracts causes errors. To generate robustness tests from enhanced UCs, the contracts must be detailed enough so that all the unspecified behaviors are incorrect. If so, the UCTS built from the enhanced use cases will be used as an oracle for the robustness. To improve the contracts, we propose to use a requirement simulator, which allows the requirement analyst to see step by step which use cases are applicable, and then to determine if his or her requirements are sufficient. This simulator interactively computes valid sequences of instantiated use cases: all the choices are made by the simulator's user, by selecting an instantiated use case in a list of all the applicable instantiated use cases.

As soon as the requirements are precise enough, the generated UCTS can be used as an oracle for robustness tests. The principle is to generate paths that lead to an invalid application of a use case. The idea is thus to exercise correctly the system and then make a non specified action. The execution of such a robustness test must lead to a failure (in our example, the receipt of an error message). If not, a robustness weakness has been detected. The goal is thus to test the robustness/defensive code of the system. The difficulty is to propose an adequate criterion and the UCTS plus the contracts provide all the information we need for that purpose. The criterion we use to generate robustness paths with the UCTS is quite similar to the *All Precondition Terms* one: for each use case, it looks for all the shortest paths leading to each of the possible valuations that violate its precondition.

Robustness Criterion: A test objective set *TOs* satisfies the robustness criterion for a contracts system iff each use case is exercised in as many different ways as there are predicates combinations to make its precondition false.

The robustness tests test the defensive code of the application, which is not tested with the functional tests previously generated. Joining the two sets of tests, not only will we test that the application does what it should (according to the requirements) but also that it does not what it should not.

4   Experimental Validation: Test Cases Generation and Efficiency Measures

This section offers an experimental validation of the proposed approach. As explained in Section 3, our test generation from requirements provides the tester with test objectives, i.e. sequences of instantiated use cases. To produce concrete test cases from TOs, a mapping has to be performed. For our study, we used an ad hoc test case generator, since a UC exactly corresponds to a command of the system in our example. We obtained the test cases using a template associated to each use case giving the syntactic requirements of the implementation. In this section, we give an overview of the test objectives synthesized for the 3 products, then we study the efficiency of the tests generated for the demonstration edition.

4.1   Test Generated for the 3 Products

From the PF use cases enhanced with contracts, we derived one specific UCTS per product, and then we generated the test cases (TC). Statistics are given in table 2 (demonstration, personal and enterprise edition are respectively denoted DE, PE, and EE). A study of those TCs reveals that common tests have been generated (corresponding to commonalities of the PF), and specific tests have been generated for each product, due to the different combinations of variants in the products.

Table 2. Statistics on generated tests.

Edition	DE	PE	EE
# generated TC with AIUC	50	65	78
# generated TC with APT	15	18	21
# generated TC for robustness	65	110	128
average size of the tests	5	4	4

4.2 Study of the Generated Test Efficiency for Demonstration Edition

For the experimental validation, we used a Java implementation of the virtual meeting. Around 9% of the code is dead code. Nevertheless, this code is relevant: it consists of pertinent but unused accessors, which could be used in future evolutions of the system. Functional testing cannot deal with this code: it has to be tested during the unit test step. For the following study, we removed those 9% of dead code to focus on the efficiency of our tests on reachable code. Around 26% of the code is robustness code: robustness w.r.t. the specification which asserts that only the required functions are present, and robustness w.r.t. the environment which asserts that the inputs coming from the environment are correct.

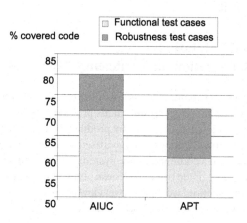

Fig. 4. Code coverage of the tests.

The results of the code coverage measures are given in figure 4. The APT (resp. AIUC) criterion covers 71% (resp. 60%) of the functional code. Note that since the AIUC criterion generates much more TC than the APT one, the APT criterion is more efficient in terms of covered statement per TC. Since our robustness tests stem from functional requirements, they cannot cover all the robustness code but they cover 100% of the robustness code w.r.t. requirements. The uncovered code concerns syntactic verification of the inputs treatment of network exceptions, these aspects are specific to the distributed platform. Globally, the robustness tests add a 10% code coverage to the functional tests.

This study shows that tests generated from the requirements expressed at the PF level are relevant at the product code level, with the use of adequate criteria.

5   Related Work

While OO testing is becoming an important research domain [9, 3] and while the PF approach is increasingly being used in industry [4, 5], among the numerous test case generation techniques that can be found in the literature, few of them have been adapted to the PF context. The survey of [9] shows that until now, most test case generation has been done manually, the only test automation being in the generation of test scripts or test harnesses. It insists on the difficulty and the cost of writing test-case generators for PFs. If some PL testing process are proposed in the literature, few of them are automated: for example, in [1], a three-phase, methodological, and code-based testing approach is proposed and in [2], a testing process is detailed to perform functional, structural and state-based testing of a PL.

Independently from the PL context, the main contribution for system testing from use cases can be found in [6], where the authors propose to express the sequential constraints of the use cases with an extended activity diagram. If activity diagrams can seem suitable to this purpose, we soon discovered that they quickly become far too complicated and unreadable. On the opposite, contracts on the use cases remain a simple way to express the dependencies.

6   Conclusion and Future Work

This paper presents a requirement-based testing technique for PF, that utilizes the PF use-cases to generate product-specific functional test objectives. This technique is associated with a light formalism to express at the PF level, in a declarative way, but unambiguously, the mutual dependencies between requirements, in terms of pre/post conditions (kind of "contracts"). From these enhanced requirements, a labeled transition system per product is built that captures all possible valid use-case sequences from an initial configuration, and coverage criteria are used to extract relevant correct sequences which cover a large part of the product code. Though our approach certainly not replace integration or unit testing stages, that allow specific aspects (that are not described at very high level) to be covered, for the strict coverage of functional and robustness code, results are good since all the code that could be covered has been covered. All our method is supported by a prototype tool, which is integrated in the Objecteering CASE tool.

Future work concerns the building of a generic mapper from test objectives to test cases, using scenarios, as well as a validation of our approach with another case study. We will to adapt it to requirements classification methods such as the one of [7].

References

1. Mark Ardis, Nidel Daley, Daniel Hoffman, and David Weiss. Software product lines: a case study. *Software - Practice and Experience*, 30(7), 2000.

2. Colin Atkinson, Joachim Bayer, Christian Bunse, Erik Kamsties, Oliver Laitenberger, Roland Laqua, Dirk Muthig, Barabara Paech, Jürgen Wüst, and Jörg Zettel. *Component-based product line engineering with UML*. 2002.
3. Robert V. Binder. *Testing object-oriented systems*. Addison-Wesley, 2000.
4. Jan Bosch. Product-line architectures in industry: a case sudy. In *Proc. of the 1999 International Conference on Software Engineering (ICSE 99*, pages 544–554, New York (USA), 1999.
5. L.G. Bratthal, R. Van Der Geest, H. Hofmann, E. Jellum, Z. Korendo, R. Martinez, M. Orkisz, C. Zeidler, and J.S. Andersson. Integrating hundred's of products through one architecture - the industrial IT architecture. In *Proc. of the 24th International Conference on Software Engineering (ICSE 2002)*, pages 604–614, New York (USA), 2001.
6. L. Briand and Y. Labiche. A uml-based approach to system testing. *Journal of Software and Systems Modeling*, pages 10–42, 2002.
7. J. Kuusela and J. Savolainen. requirements engineering for product families. In *Proc. of the 2000 International Conference on Software Engineering*, pages 61–69, 2000.
8. R.R. Lutz. Extending the product family approach to support safe reuse. *journal of systems ans software*, 53:207–217, 2000.
9. J.D. McGregor and D.A. Sykes. *A practical Guide to Testing Object-Oriented Software*. Addison Wesley, 2001.

Theorem Proving
for Product Line Model Verification

Mike Mannion and Javier Camara

School of Computing and Mathematical Sciences
Glasgow Caledonian University
70 Cowcaddens Road, Glasgow, G4 0BA
United Kingdom
M.A.G.Mannion@gcal.ac.uk
Tel: +44 (0)141-331-3285

Abstract. Product line models of requirements can be used to drive the selection of requirements of new systems in the product line. Validating any selected single system is difficult because product line models are large and complex. However by modelling variability and dependency between requirements using propositional connectives a logical expression can be developed for the model and then selection validation can be achieved by satisfying the logical expression. This approach can be used to validate the model as a whole. A case study with nearly 800 requirements is presented and the computational aspects of the approach are discussed.

1   Introduction

Software Product Line Engineering is the discipline of engineering a set of software-intensive systems sharing a common, managed set of features that satisfy the specific needs of a particular market segment or mission and that are developed from a common set of core assets in a prescribed way [1]. To achieve large-scale software reuse within an product line, many software product line methods [2-6] advocate deriving implemented reusable components from early lifecycle work-products including requirements. *Single* systems are then built from a selection of reusable components. In building single systems the first task is to select desired requirements from the set of product line requirements.

A product line model consists of a pool of numbered, atomic, natural language requirements, a domain dictionary and a set of discriminants. It contains all requirements in all the existing systems in the product line, can be constructed as a lattice of parent-child relationships and is typically large. The requirements in the model are all related to each other in parent-child relationships. Some parents will have children that vary across systems in the product line. These variants are called discriminants. Requirements belonging to each variant appear in the tree beneath the variant. FODA [2] and FORM [5] take a similar approach to modelling, but use features not requirements.

F. van der Linden (Ed.): PFE 2003, LNCS 3014, pp. 211–224, 2004.
© Springer-Verlag Berlin Heidelberg 2004

The value of a product line model lies in the cleanness and efficiency with which it can be used to generate a valid set of single system requirements that satisfy the constraints in the product line model. Ensuring product line models are valid is difficult because they are larger and more complex than single system requirement models. However assuming a product line model is valid, a verifiable product line model is one from which it is possible to select at least one set of single requirements from the model that satisfy the relationships between the requirements in the model.

In [7, 8] we assumed that the product line model had been constructed and validated and we identified 2 methods of selection of requirements from the product line model. *Free selection* allows a requirements engineer to browse a product line model and simply copy and paste a single requirement from anywhere in the model to the new instance. It does not use the constraints built into the lattice structure to guide model traversal and can lead to selection combinations being made that are invalid e.g. 2 mutually exclusive requirements can be selected or requirements that must be included can be omitted. In addition there can be an untenable number of choices making single system specifications time-consuming to generate and check that they are free of errors. However, because different engineers will each have a different understanding of a product line, inherently different problem-solving styles and a healthy scepticism that a given product line model will neither be accurate nor contain all the relationships between requirements, the flexibility afforded by free selection is a characteristic many engineers are reluctant to give up.

Discriminant-based selection is grounded in using the lattice structure to drive selection and permits choices to be made only at discriminant points. This ensures that the choices produce a valid set of single system requirements and reduces the time spent on specification but flexibility for the single system requirements engineer is reduced.

In [9] we began to address these issues by sketching how a product line model can be represented using propositional logic and offered a mobile phone worked example to illustrate. By considering each requirement as an atom and each relationship between requirements as a logical expression, a logical expression for the product line model can be developed. A selected combination of requirements drawn from the product line model can then be tested using this expression. This verification approach is independent of the selection method. In this paper we have refined the mobile phone worked example and also present a case study using data for a spacecraft control operating system.

Section 2 presents the mobile phone worked example and some issues that concern product line model verification. Section 3 shows how a product line model can be represented using propositional connectives and how selections from the model can be verified using propositional calculus. Section 4 describes the results of the method applied to spacecraft control data. Finally we discuss some computational and other issues.

Table 1. Mobile Phone Product Line Requirements.

No.	Requirement
R1	There shall be an address book facility.
R1.1	There shall be the facility to add a telephone number.
R1.2	There shall be the facility to search for a telephone number.
R1.3	There shall be the facility to delete a telephone number.
R2	The mobile phone shall be able to store $X telephone numbers.
R3	The mobile phone shall have a memory capacity of @MEMORY_SIZE.
R3.1	The built-in memory shall be extendible using additional memory within @MEMORY_RANGE.
R4	The status of the mobile phone shall at any given time be @PHONE_STATUS.
R4.1	The mobile phone shall respond @COMMAND_NUM commands simultaneously within $COMMAND_RESPONSE seconds.
R5	The mobile phone shall require the network services of one telecommunications carrier at a time.
R5.1	The telecommunications carrier shall be Vodafone.
R5.2	The telecommunications carrier shall be Deutsche_Telecom.
R6	There shall be the facility to make a telephone call.
R6.1	A telephone call shall be made by pressing the numeric digits that form a telephone number.
R6.2	A telephone call shall be made by storing the telephone number in built-in memory and then pressing a memory recall button.
R6.3	A telephone call shall be made by pressing a ringback facility to dial the number of the last incoming call.
R6.4	A telephone call shall be made by using speech recognition technology to say the telephone numbers aloud.
R6.4.1	The speech recognition facility shall only recognise single digit numbers.
R7	The mobile phone shall have an email facility.
R8	There shall be the facility to use one or more email protocols.
R8.1	There shall be the facility to use the Post Office Protocol.
R8.2	There shall be the facility to use the Internet Message Access Protocol.
R8.3	There shall be the facility to use the Simple Mail Transfer Protocol.

2 Product Line Models

Table 1 shows a product line model of mobile phone requirements. Product line requirements can be categorised as directly reusable requirements and variable requirements. Directly reusable requirements are common to each product in a product line. R1-R1.3 illustrate some directly reusable requirements for a mobile phone. A variable requirement is a parameterised requirement, a discriminant, or a parameterised discriminant. In Table 1 requirements R2 and R3 are parameterised requirements where $ means the parameter is local to that requirement and @ means the parameter is applicable to all the requirements. Discriminants can take three forms:

- mutual exclusion (*single adaptor*): a set of mutually exclusive requirements from which only one can be chosen in any system in the application family. R5-R5.2 show that a mobile phone user can switch from carrier A to carrier B without having to buy a new phone i.e. the phone can deal with either, but it is possible to use the services of only one of these carriers.

- a list of alternatives (*multiple adaptor*), which are not mutually exclusive, but at least one must be chosen. R6-R6.4.1 show there can be several ways of making a mobile phone call but there must be at least one.

- option: a single optional requirement that may or may not be chosen. R7 shows a mobile phone may or may not have an email facility.

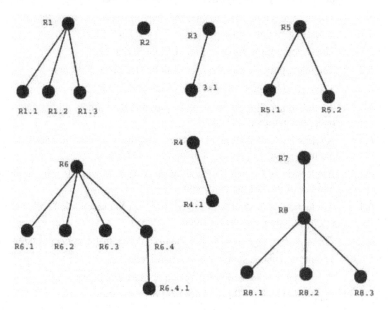

Fig. 1. Mobile Phone Product Line Model.

Figure 1 is the product line model for the requirements in Table 1. In a product line model the links between requirements are parent-child links so that requirements can be modelled hierarchically in a lattice. This is a reasonable assumption and is a reflection of common requirements document structures. A requirement can have zero to many children. Dependencies between discriminants can also be represented in the hierarchy. R7-R8.3 shows that while email maybe an option, the list of email protocols it supports will be a list of alternatives from which at least one will be chosen.

3 Product Line Model Verification

Once a product line model has been constructed its usefulness can be established by addressing the following questions.

Q1. *Does there exist any single system that satisfies the relationships in the product line model?* A valid product line model is one in which it is possible to select at least one set of single requirements from the model that satisfy the relationships between the requirements in the model. An invalid product line model is one from which it is not possible to make such a selection.

Q2. *Given a subset of product line requirements, can we know if it forms a valid single system?* The motivation for building a product line model is often to seek efficiency gains in the specification, design and production of a set of products that already exist and/or a set of products that are visualised for the future. Typically validation activities will focus specifically on ensuring these product sets can be specified from the model.

Q3. *How many valid single systems can be built using this product line model?* Product line models contain many points of variation. The number of single systems that can be generated is proportional to the number of variation points. The number returned as a response to this query may be a useful product line model design guide. A small number may mean that there may not be sufficient flexibility in the system for future markets. A large number may mean that there is unnecessary flexibility and that the model should be further constrained. Such interpretations will depend on the product type, the organisation's market share and its marketing strategy.

Q4. *What requirements do the valid single systems contain?* As a product line model becomes larger it becomes difficult to see by inspection all the possible products that can be built from the product line model. New product ideas may be spawned from valid requirement selection combinations not previously considered.

We can express the relationships between requirements in a product line model using propositional connectives and propositional calculus. We assume that parameterised requirements and parameterised discriminants have had their parameter values instantiated before we apply the propositional calculus.

3.1 Sub-graphs

The logical expression of a product line lattice is the conjunction of the logical expressions for each of the sub-graphs and is achieved using logical AND. If G_i and G_j are the logical expressions for 2 different sub-graphs of a lattice then the logical expression for the lattice is:

$$G_i \wedge G_j \tag{1}$$

3.2 Parent-Child Relations

The logical expression for a single adaptor discriminant is logical AND. If a_i is a parent requirement and a_j is a child requirement such that the selection of a_j is dependent on a_i then $a_i \wedge a_j$. If a_i also has other children a_k ... a_z then:

$$a_i \wedge (a_k \wedge \dots \wedge a_z) \tag{2}$$

3.3 Single Adaptor Discriminant

The logical expression for a single adaptor discriminant is exclusive OR. If a_i and a_j are requirements such that a_i is mutually exclusive to a_j then $a_i \oplus a_j$.

3.4 Multiple Adaptor Discriminant

The logical expression for a multiple adaptor discriminant is logical OR. If a_i and a_j are requirements such that at least one requirement must be chosen then $a_i \vee a_j$.

3.5 Option Discriminant

The logical expression for an option discriminant is a bi-conditional[1]. If a_i is the parent of another requirement a_j then the relationship between the 2 requirements is $a_i \leftrightarrow a_j$.

Table 2 summarises the relationships and logical definitions of the model.

The general expression for a product line model is $G_1 \wedge G_2 \wedge \dots \wedge G_n$ where G_i is a_i Я a_j Я a_k Я ... Я a_n and Я is one of $\wedge$, $\vee$, $\oplus$, or $\leftrightarrow$.

Table 2. Product Line Model Relations and Formal Definitions.

Product Line Relation	Formal Definition
Sub-graph	$G_i \wedge G_j$
Dependency	$a_i \wedge a_j$
Single Adaptor Discriminant	$a_i \oplus a_j$
Multiple Adaptor Discriminant	$a_i \vee a_j$
Option Discriminant	$a_i \leftrightarrow a_j$

The logical expression for the mobile phone product requirements shown in Figure 1 are:

---

[1] $a_i \leftrightarrow a_j$ is TRUE when a_i and a_j have the same values.

$$((R1 \wedge (R1.1 \wedge R1.2 \wedge R1.3)) \wedge \dots\dots\dots\dots\dots\dots (G_1)$$
$$(R2) \wedge \dots\dots\dots\dots\dots\dots\dots\dots\dots\dots\dots\dots\dots\dots\dots\dots\dots (G_2)$$
$$(R3 \wedge R3.1) \wedge \dots\dots\dots\dots\dots\dots\dots\dots\dots\dots\dots\dots\dots (G_3)$$
$$(R4 \wedge R4.1) \wedge \dots\dots\dots\dots\dots\dots\dots\dots\dots\dots\dots\dots\dots (G_4)$$
$$(R5 \wedge (R5.1 \oplus R5.2)) \wedge \dots\dots\dots\dots\dots\dots\dots\dots (G_5)$$
$$(R6 \wedge (R6.1 \vee R6.2 \vee R6.3 \vee (R6.4 \wedge R6.4.1))) \wedge \dots (G_6)$$
$$(R7 \leftrightarrow (R8 \wedge (R8.1 \vee R8.2 \vee R8.3))) \dots\dots\dots\dots (G_7)$$

We can instantiate the requirements in the logical expression to TRUE or FALSE depending on whether they appear in the single system or not. A verifiable single system is one for which the product line logical expression evaluates to TRUE. Otherwise the single system is unverifiable.

4   Computational Considerations

We constructed a C programme that took as input a product line model and output the product line model as a logical expression. Additional C functions were written to find answers to questions 1-3. We used a depth first search algorithm to traverse the search space. Each node in the lattice structure contains the following fields:

- *selection value*: this identifies whether the node has been selected by the user and can be TRUE or FALSE;
- *evaluation*: this is the result of the evaluation of the expression assigned to the node and can be TRUE or FALSE;
- *requirement id*: the identifier of the node;
- *type*: this can be DR directly reusable requirement, SA single adaptor, MA multiple adaptor, O option;
- *child#*: the number of child requirements;
- *child1... childN*: These are pointers to the children of the requirement within the subgraph.

Question 1. Does there exist any single system that satisfies the relationships in the product line model?: We need to show that there is at least one combination in each graph in the system that evaluates to TRUE. One effective method of testing this is to assign TRUE to all directly reusable requirements and then systematically evaluate each possible system, graph by graph, by alternatively allocating TRUE or FALSE to discriminant requirements. When any combination of selections in one of the graphs causes the graph to evaluate to FALSE, the logical expression for the entire system is FALSE and hence that system does not satisfy the relationships in the product line model.

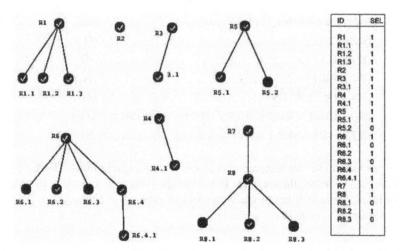

ID	SEL
R1	1
R1.1	1
R1.2	1
R1.3	1
R2	1
R3	1
R3.1	1
R4	1
R4.1	1
R5	1
R5.1	1
R5.2	0
R6	1
R6.1	0
R6.2	1
R6.3	0
R6.4	1
R6.4.1	1
R7	1
R8	1
R8.1	0
R8.2	1
R8.3	0

Fig. 2. Requirement Selection And Equivalent Boolean Vector Representation.

Question 2. *Given a subset of product line requirements, can we know if it forms a valid single system?*: During the construction of a single system, TRUE is assigned to those requirements that are selected and FALSE is assigned to those not selected. There are a number of different methods for traversing the product line model lattice structure and making selections from it. Regardless of the selection method, the same set of selected requirements should generate the same result. Debugging becomes a matter of isolating the graph in which the wrong selection combinations have been made. We will consider 2 methods: free selection and discriminant-based selection.

Example 1. Suppose some requirements are freely selected (indicated by ✓ in Figure 2) from the mobile phone product line model: The product line logical expression becomes:

$$((T \wedge (T \wedge T \wedge T \wedge T)) \wedge \dots\dots\dots\dots\dots\dots(G_1)$$
$$(T) \dots\dots\dots\dots\dots\dots\dots\dots\dots\dots\dots\dots\dots(G_2)$$
$$(T \wedge (T \wedge T)) \dots\dots\dots\dots\dots\dots\dots\dots\dots\dots(G_3)$$
$$(T \wedge T)\dots\dots\dots\dots\dots\dots\dots\dots\dots\dots\dots\dots(G_4)$$
$$(T \wedge (T \oplus F)) \wedge \dots\dots\dots\dots\dots\dots\dots\dots\dots(G_5)$$
$$(T \wedge (F \vee T \vee T \vee (T \wedge T))) \wedge \dots\dots\dots\dots\dots(G_6)$$
$$(T \leftrightarrow (T \wedge (F \vee T \vee F)))\dots\dots\dots\dots\dots\dots\dots\dots(G_7)$$

(G_1), (G_2), (G_3), (G_4), (G_5), (G_6) and (G_7) each evaluate to TRUE. Hence $G_1 \wedge G_2 \wedge G_3 \wedge G_4 \wedge G_5 \wedge G_6 \wedge G_7$ evaluates to TRUE.

Example 2. Suppose the selected requirements are the same as in Example 1 except that the directly reusable requirement R1.3 in G_1 is *not* selected. The product line logical expression becomes:

$$((T \wedge (T \wedge T \wedge F \wedge T)) \wedge \ldots\ldots\ldots\ldots\ldots\ldots (G_1)$$

$$(T) \ldots\ldots\ldots\ldots\ldots\ldots\ldots\ldots\ldots\ldots\ldots\ldots\ldots\ldots (G_2)$$

$$(T \wedge (T \wedge T)) \ldots\ldots\ldots\ldots\ldots\ldots\ldots\ldots\ldots (G_3)$$

$$(T \wedge T) \ldots\ldots\ldots\ldots\ldots\ldots\ldots\ldots\ldots\ldots\ldots (G_4)$$

$$(T \wedge (T \oplus F)) \wedge \ldots\ldots\ldots\ldots\ldots\ldots\ldots (G_5)$$

$$(T \wedge (F \vee T \vee T \vee (T \wedge T))) \wedge \ldots\ldots\ldots\ldots (G_6)$$

$$(T \leftrightarrow (T \wedge (F \vee T \vee F))) \ldots\ldots\ldots\ldots\ldots\ldots\ldots (G_7)$$

(G_1) now evaluates to FALSE. (G_2), (G_3), (G_4), (G_5), (G_6) and (G_7) each evaluate to TRUE. Hence $G_1 \wedge G_2 \wedge G_3 \wedge G_4 \wedge G_5 \wedge G_6 \wedge G_7$ evaluates to FALSE.

If a discriminant-based selection method is used, then *prior* to selection, TRUE is assigned to all directly reusable requirements. The selection algorithm permits decisions to be made only at discriminant points. During selection TRUE is assigned to those discriminants selected and FALSE to those not selected. These values are substituted into the product line logical expression. Using this approach Example 2 can not occur because the value of R1.3 will always be TRUE.

We implemented the discriminant-based selection method using a depth-first algorithm that started at a root node that is artificially added to the structure to provide a link between all the graphs in the hierarchy. Figure 3 shows the steps of the evaluation algorithm.

Question 3. *How many valid single systems can be built using this product line model?*: The answer to question 3 is the number of combination selections for which the logical expression will evaluate to TRUE. For a product line model with N requirements, since each requirement can assume possible values of TRUE or FALSE, this can mean computing 2^N different possible values of the product line logical expression. In Figure 1 N=24 i.e. 2^{24}=16777216 possible single systems can be generated from the mobile phone product line model. This is a small number that is computationally tractable on the modern desktop PCs available to engineers. Much larger product line models will yield greater search spaces which may be computationally intractable. However the search space can be pruned by using 2 different methods. The first method is to exploit the parent-child links. If a parent is FALSE there is no need to consider the values of its children. For example in Figure 1 when R1 is FALSE there is no need to consider the various combinations of values of R1.1-R1.4, hence there is a reduction in possible systems of 2^4. A similar approach to requirements R3, R4, R5, R6, R7, R8 yields additional reductions of 2^0, 2^0, 2^2, 2^4, 2^0, 2^3 i.e. 2^9. Hence the total number of systems 2^{24-13} i.e. 2^{11}.

Alternatively, as with Question 1, we can prune the search space by assigning the value TRUE to the directly reusable requirements and permit variations in value only for discriminants. In Figure 1 R1, R1.1, R1.2, R1.3, R1.4, R2, R3, R3.1, R4, R4.1, R5, R6, R6.4.1, R8 can be set to TRUE leaving the possible variations at R5, R6, R7, R8 to be 2^2, 2^4, 2^1, 2^3 i.e. 2^{10}. Combining both methods means the possible variations are 2^1 at R5, 2^4 at R6, and 2^3 at R7/R8, a total of 2^8 i.e. 256 possible systems. A re-

After all selections have been made such that each *selection* value at requirement node N is set to TRUE or FALSE, and each *evaluation* value at
each requirement node is set to UNKNOWN then for each requirement node
N:

1. If N is a leaf node ("L") and its type is "O" then set N's *evaluation*
    to TRUE.
2. If N is a leaf node ("L") and its *selection* is TRUE then set N's
    evaluation to TRUE otherwise set *evaluation* to FALSE.
3. If N is a parent and all of N's children have their *evaluation* type set
    to TRUE or FALSE then goto step 4 else for each child belonging
    to N with evaluation type set to UNKNOWN goto step 1.
4. If N's *type* is "DR" and all its children have their *evaluation* set to
    TRUE, set N's *evaluation* to TRUE otherwise set evaluation to
    FALSE.
5. If N's *type* is "O", its *selection* is TRUE and its children that are
    DR, SA or MA have their evaluation set to TRUE then set N's
    evaluation to TRUE otherwise set it to FALSE.
6. If N's *type* is "O", its *selection* is FALSE and any of its children
    have their *evaluation* set to TRUE *then* set N's *evaluation* to
    FALSE otherwise set it to TRUE.
7. If N is of *type* "SA", and only one of its children has its *selection* to
    TRUE, set N's *evaluation* to TRUE otherwise set it to FALSE.
8. If N is of *type* "MA", and at least one child has its *selection* to
    TRUE, set N's *evaluation* to TRUE otherwise set it to FALSE.
9. Find the next node to evaluate in the graph; return to step 1.

Fig. 3. Product Line Model Selection Validation Algorithm.

refinement on this method is not to count known invalid combinations e.g. $(T \wedge T)$ or
$(F \wedge F)$ at single adaptors and $(F \wedge F.. \wedge F)$ at multiple adaptors. Table 3 shows the
number of variations in each graph of the mobile phone product line model. Multiply-
ing these values gives 210.

Question 4. *What requirements do the valid single systems contain?* The answer to
this question is an information presentation issue for each of the answers found for
question 3.

5 Case Study

To evaluate the product line verification technique we had access to data used for the
generation of a spacecraft control operating system, SCOS-2000, provided by the
Operations Centre of the European Space Agency Operations Centre (ESOC). Spacecraft control operating systems are increasing in complexity placing greater demands
upon mission control centres. Increased budgetary constraints mean that these sys-

Table 3. Variation Points in Mobile Phone Product Line Model.

Graph	Possible Variations
G1	1
G2	1
G3	1
G4	1
G5	2
G6	15
G7	1
G8	7

tems must be developed and operated with greater efficiency. The trend is to move towards systems that are easily customised across a range of missions with a high level of reuse across systems. The aim of SCOS-2000 was to define a configurable spacecraft control operating system infrastructure from which it is possible to define instances of SCOS-2000, called Mission Control Systems. The SCOS-2000 User Requirements Definition [10] document describes the requirements for the entire generic system from a user's perspective. In ESOC, requirements definitions consist of numbered atomic natural language requirements and software systems. SCOS-2000 has several generic sub-systems e.g. Commanding, Procedure Execution, On-Board Software Maintenance, Telemonitoring and Display. Differences between Mission Control Systems are caused by variations to these sub-systems. Each sub-system has its own Software Requirements Document (SRD), a software requirements specification primarily written in natural language. In [9] we described how we built a product line model of the Commanding sub-system, based on its SRD [10]. Commanding is concerned with the transmission and receipt of commands to control the spacecraft.

Table 4 shows that there were 778 product line commanding requirements most of which were directly reusable requirements. The lattice structure of the model contained 27 graphs of varying sizes the largest having 152 nodes and the smallest having 1 node. Underlying our approach is the assumption that the lattice structure can be constructed as a set of logically independent ANDed graphs in which no requirement has multiple parents. In the original data there were between 10-20 requirements that had multiple parents. We examined each of these requirements closely and felt able to eliminate one of the parents in each case without changing the intent of the model.

The product line model was held as a simple table in a text file. We instantiated the values of the parameterised requirements and parameterised discriminants in the text file. The text file was used as the input file to a C program that generated a logical expression and was able to answer Questions 1-3 (Table 5). The tests were run on a PentiumIV 1.7Ghz with 256 Mb DDR memory. The instruction set with which the tool was compiled was Pentium-optimized. Typically the time taken to find an answer to Questions 1-3 was less than 1 second of elapsed time.

Table 4. Spacecraft Control Product Line Model.

Number of directly reusable requirements (DR)	689
Number of single adaptor discriminants (SA)	9
Number of multiple adaptor discriminants(MA)	52
Number of Optional requirements (O)	15
Parameterised Requirements	13
Number of graphs	27
Maximum graph size	152
Minimum graph size	1
Maximum tree depth	10

Table 5. Spacecraft Control Product Line Model Validation.

Q1: Does there exist any single system that satisfies the relationships in the product line model?	Yes
Q2: Given a subset of product line requirements, can we know if it forms a valid single system?	Yes
Q3: How many valid single systems can be built using this product line model?	3,458,764,513,820,540,928

6 Discussion

The size and complexity of the spacecraft control product line model makes it very difficult and time-consuming to know whether the model is valid through inspection. This technique verifies for a product line engineer whether any valid single system can be selected and how many can be selected, giving confidence that the constructed product line model can be used to help generate new systems in the product line. It is readily understandable, easy to automate and by assigning TRUE to directly reusable requirements runs quickly. The technique does not prevent model constructions that may be unusual but may help draw attention to them and encourage revisiting their design.

In answering Question 2 for the user of any debugging tool it is not enough to know if the input data is valid or not but when and where it is not valid. A product line engineer does not just want to understand if a product line model is invalid, but what might be added, removed or changed to make the set valid. By partitioning the model into graphs and evaluating sub-branches of the graph using a depth-first approach we can identify which part of the graph is causing failure.

The product line of commanding requirements is medium size and the variability within it small. Nevertheless there are in principle 2^{778} possible systems. It is computationally intractable using today's serial processors to step though each of these possibilities and identify which is TRUE and which is FALSE. However by exploiting the parent-child links and assigning the value TRUE to the directly reusable requirements the number of computations is reduced to the order of $3 * 2^{18}$. Whilst such a large number may at least give cause for concern that at the highest level there is more variability than is actually required for commanding systems, the number is too large and hence not helpful for identifying easily the differences that will cause significantly different product designs. (Arguably even the 210 variations in the mobile phone product line model is a too large number.) Further work is needed to refine the validation process so that we can identify those variation points in requirements that are likely to cause significant design variations. In [11] we have started some work to use features to map requirements on to high-level design components.

A future line of investigation is to consider extending the propositional logic framework to predicate logic to provide a cleaner representation of parameterised requirements and parameterised discriminants, particularly when the value of the parameter has a bearing on the choice of other requirements and discriminants.

7 Conclusion

We have developed a technique for product line model validation that uses propositional logic connectives and calculus. We have explained how a product line model can be represented as a logical expression. This expression can be instantiated by the requirements selected for a single system and used to establish whether the selected set is valid or not. Techniques for product line model validation are important because such models are large, complex and prone to error during construction. We have demonstrated the technique by generating a set of requirements for a detailed worked example of a mobile phone and a case study in spacecraft control systems.

References

1. Clements, P., Northrop, L., Software Product Line: Practices and Patterns, Addison-Wesley, 2002.
2. Cohen, S., Hess, J., Kang, K., Novak, W., and Peterson, A.: Requirement-Oriented Domain Analysis (FODA) Feasibility Study, Special Report CMU/SEI-90-TR-21, Carnegie Mellon University (1990).
3. Jacobson, I., Griss, M., and Jonsson, P.: Software Reuse: Architecture, Process and Organisation for Business Success, Addison-Wesley, ISBN 0-201-92476-5 (1997).
4. Organisation Domain Modelling (ODM) Guidebook Version 2.0, STARS-VC-A025/001/00, June 14 (1996), Electronic Systems Center, Air Force Systems Command, USAF, MA 01731-2816.

5. Bayer, J., Gacek, C., Muthig, D., Widen T., PuLSE-I: Deriving Instances From A Product Line Infrastructure, 7th IEEE International Conference on Engineering Conference on Computer-Based Systems, 3-7 April 2000, Edinburgh, ISBN 0-7695-0604-6.
6. Kang, K., Feature Oriented Reuse Method, IEEE Software, July-August 2002.
7. Mannion, M., Keepence, B., Kaindl, H., Wheadon, J.: Reusing Single System Requirements From Application Family Requirements, in Proc. of the 21st IEEE International Conference on Software Engineering (ICSE99), May (1999) 453Œ462.
8. Mannion, M., Lewis, O., Kaindl, H., Montroni, G., Wheadon, J., Representing Requirements of Generic Software in an Application Family Model, Lecture Notes in Computer Science (LNCS 1844), Software Reuse: Advances in Software Reusability, ed W Frakes, 6th Int'l Conference, ICSR-6, Vienna, Austria, 27-29 June 2000, ISSN 0302-9743, pp. 153-169.
9. Mannion, M., Product Line Model Validation, Proceedings of 3nd Software Product Line Conference, San Diego, August 2002.
10. SCOS-2000 Commanding Software Requirements Document, S2K-MCS-SRD-0002-TOS-GCI, Issue 2.0, 21st May 1999.
11. Savolainen, J., Vehkomäki, T., Mannion M., An Integrated Model for Requirements Structuring and Architecture Design, 7th Australian Workshop on Requirements Engineering, Deakin University, Melbourne, Australia, 2-3 December 2002.

A Koala-Based Approach for Modelling and Deploying Configurable Software Product Families

Timo Asikainen, Timo Soininen, and Tomi Männistö

Helsinki University of Technology, Software Business and Engineering Institute,
P.O. Box 9600, FIN-02015 HUT, Finland
{timo.asikainen,timo.soininen,tomi.mannisto}@hut.fi
http://www.soberit.hut.fi/

Abstract. An approach for modelling configurable software product families (CSPFs) and for automated configuring of product individuals using the models is presented. It is based on a similar approach for configuring physical products. The conceptual foundation and syntax of the Koalish modelling language used for this purpose are defined. The language extends Koala, a component model and architecture description language, with explicit variation modelling mechanisms. Koalish is further provided a formal semantics by defining a translation from it to Weight Constraint Rule Language (WCRL), a form of logic programs. This allows using an existing inference tool for WCRL, *smodels,* to implement the reasoning needed in the configurator. The configurator is able to construct all valid product individuals, with respect to a Koalish model of a CSPF, that satisfy a given set of requirements. The implemented functionality of the configurator has been tested using small-scale toy examples, for which it performs adequately.

1 Introduction

During the last couple of years, software product families (SPFs) have gained increasing popularity as a reuse method [1, 2]. The most systematic class of software product families can be called *configurable product bases* [3]: a company with a configurable software product base does not deploy different products for each customer by designing and implementing the system from re-usable assets and product specific code, but instead the configurable product base is configured to the requirements of a customer by, e.g., selecting components and setting run-time parameters and compiler flags.

However, configuring can be a complex task: it has been pointed out in [1] that configuration is both error-prone and time-consuming; the authors consider tool support to be a solution to this problem. Of course, tools supporting the configuration cannot produce correct configurations without knowledge of what these are: i.e., there must exist some kind of model describing what are the legal individuals of the configurable product base.

F. van der Linden (Ed.): PFE 2003, LNCS 3014, pp. 225–249, 2004.
© Springer-Verlag Berlin Heidelberg 2004

In this paper, we present an approach to solve the above-described problems, i.e., modelling configurable product bases, and efficiently deploying individuals from these. We concentrate on *configurable software product families (CSPFs)*, a subclass of software product families similar to configurable product bases. A configurable software product family has the property that individuals of the family can be deployed in a systematic manner; there is no need for coding within components, and not much need for adding glue code between them.

Our approach is based on applying techniques developed in the *product configuration* domain [4, 5], a subfield of artificial intelligence, to modelling and deploying individual systems from CSPFs. In the approach, CSPFs are described using *explicit* and *declarative* knowledge representation techniques: explicitness means that knowledge is described in a direct and unambiguous way; further, declarativeness means that the (formal) meaning of the representation can be specified without reference to how the knowledge is applied procedurally [6].

The knowledge representation technique in our approach is *Koalish*, a modelling language the conceptual basis of which we have introduced in [7]. Koalish is built on the basis of Koala [8], an architecture description language (ADL) developed and in industrial use at Philips Consumer Electronics: Koalish adds new variation mechanisms to Koala, namely the possibility of selecting the number and type of parts of components, and writing constraints that must hold for the individuals of the CSPF. We believe that the practical success of Koala gives Koalish a solid foundation.

The deployment support in our approach is based on treating Koalish descriptions of CSPFs as formal entities, and applying inference tools to these. In more detail, Koalish is given formal semantics by translating it to *Weight Constraint Rule Language* (WCRL), a general-purpose knowledge representation language [9]. The use of WCRL is motivated by the fact that it has been shown to be suitable for representing knowledge about configurable non-software products [10, 11]. An inference tool, *smodels* [9] operating on WCRL is used to carry out reasoning tasks necessary for configuration. These tasks include supporting the customer in finding a description of an individual that is correct with respect to the Koalish model of the family and satisfies the specific requirements of a customer. It should be noticed that such descriptions are *abstract* in the sense that they are not dependent on any specific realisation tool, such as make or some compiler. Still, the descriptions are intended to be detailed enough to be easily translated into inputs of any realisation tool. Hence, our approach is generally applicable in that it is independent from any specific set of realisation tools.

Certain parts of our approach have already been implemented: we have specified a syntax and conceptual basis for Koalish, and implemented the translation from Koalish to WCRL. The *smodels* inference tool can be used to enumerate all the correct individuals of a CSPF, and to find a specific individual matching the requirements of a customer. We have tested the implemented parts using small-scale toy examples.

The rest of this paper is structured as follows. Next, in Section 2, we give an overview of product configuration as a domain of research. Thereafter, we introduce Koalish, our language for modelling CSPFs (Section 3). Section 4 discusses WCRL and describes the translation from Koalish to WCRL. Thereafter, Section 5 outlines the tool support planned for our approach, and the current status of the support. Discussion and comparison to previous work follow in Section 6. Finally, conclusions and an outlook for future work round up the paper in Section 7.

2 Product Configuration

In this section, we provide an overview of *product configuration* research, a subfield of artificial intelligence [4] that has inspired the approach presented in this paper. At the end of this section, be briefly motivate our endeavour of transferring results between the product configuration and product family engineering domains by drawing parallels between concepts in the domains.

Research on product configuration domain is based on the notion of *configurable product*: a configurable product is such a product that each product individual is adapted to the requirements of a particular customer order. Historically, the configurable products studied in the domain have been non-software products, typically mechanical and electronics products. A fundamental characteristic of a configurable product is that it has a modular structure: product individuals consist of pre-designed components, and different product variant can be produced by selecting different components. [12]

The possibilities for adapting the configurable product are predefined in a *configuration model* that explicitly and declaratively describes the set of legal product individuals. A specification of a product individual, *configuration*, is produced in the *configuration task* based on the configuration model and a set of customer requirements.

Efficient knowledge-based information systems, *product configurators*, have become an important and successful application of artificial intelligence techniques for companies selling products adapted to customer needs [4]. The basic functionality of a configurator is to support a user in finding a configuration of a given configuration model matching his specific needs. Examples of the kinds of support provided are: A configurator represents the available choices in a way that enables the user to easily enter his requirements. Further, the configurator makes deductions based on the requirements the user has entered so far, and prevents the user from making incompatible choices; finally, the user can at any point ask the configurator to automatically return a configuration that is valid with respect to the configuration model and satisfies the requirements entered so far. The above-described functionality is based on using declarative configuration models, and efficient, sound, and complete inference tools operating on these.

Product configurators have been reportedly applied to a number of different kinds of products; perhaps the most challenging kinds of products have been telephone switching systems at Siemens [13], and other kind of telecommunication products at AT&T [14]. At Siemens, the problem instances have been considerably large: typically, a configuration has included tens of thousands of components with hundreds of thousands of attributes, and over 100,000 connection points. Finally, product configurators have become parts of ERP (Enterprise Resource Planning) systems, such as

SAP [15], and Baan [16], and are also available as embeddable products (see, e.g., http://www.ilog.fr/products/configurator).

It is easy to see that the notion of CSPF is very similar to that of a configurable product: both a CSPF and a configurable product describe a set of systems (software or physical products), and these systems can be produced without any creative work, such as coding the case of software, or designing new components in the case of physical products. Therefore, the idea of transferring results between the domains seems to be worth investigating.

3   Koalish – A Language for Modelling CSPFs

In this section, we give an overview of Koalish[1], our language for describing the variability of CSPFs. We briefly recap the basic concepts of Kola and then explicate the modelling concepts of Koalish, concentrating on the ones added to the concepts of Koala. A brief discussion on the concepts of Koala missing from Koalish ends the section.

3.1   Koala

Koala [8, 17] is a component model (in the sense of Microsoft COM) and an architecture description language (ADL) that has been developed at Philips Consumer Electronics to be used in developing embedded software for consumer electronic devices. Between 100 and 200 developers distributed over ten sites are involved with Koala, and a number of products developed with Koala are in the market [17].

The main modelling elements of Koala are *components* that have *interfaces* as their explicit connection points. A component is defined as "an encapsulated piece of software with an explicit interface to its environment"; an interface is a "small set of semantically related functions". *Functions* correspond to function signatures e.g. in the C programming language. Each interface is either a *requires* or a *provides* interface: a requires interface signals that the component having the interface requires some service from its environment. Similarly, a provides interface signals that the component provides such a service to its environment.

Besides interfaces, components can have other components as their *parts*, or in other words, *contain* other components. The semantics of parts are those of encapsulation: a component that is a part of another component can only be accessed from within the containing component. A *configuration* is a component that is not a part of any other component and has no interfaces.

Both interfaces and components are typed. Both component and interface types specify the properties of their instances: component types specify the interfaces and parts, and interface type the functions of their instances. Interface types are organised into *subtype* relation based on the following criteria: the pair (a, b) of interface types

---

[1] The name 'Koalish' simply stands for 'Koala-like'.

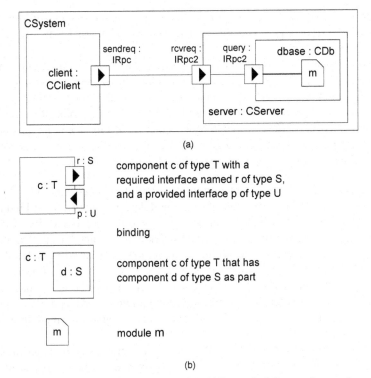

Fig. 1. (a) A sample Koala model. (b) Legend of the notation used.

is in the subtype relation, read as *a* is a subtype of *b*, if (and only if) every function in *b* is also a function of *a*.

There can exist *bindings* between interfaces. The semantics of a binding are as follows: when a function in a requires interface of a component is called, the call is delegated to the interface in another component to which the required interface is bound. In other words, the bindings denote the flow of function calls in a network of component connected through bindings between their interfaces. It is important to notice that bindings are antisymmetric: *a* being bound to *b* implies that *b* is not bound to *a*. Further, it is said that *a* is bound by its *tip* to the *base* of *b*. The terms base and tip can be understood by the visual syntax of Koala, they refer to the base and tip of the triangular symbols used for interfaces.

Example. Throughout the paper, we will use a client-server system as a running example. At this stage, we use a simplified version of the example to illustrate the concepts of Koala.

The example system is illustrated in Fig. 1 (a). Fig. 1 (b) contains a legend of the notation used; the notation is the same notation that is used in Koala papers, see, e.g., [8]. Component *CSystem* is a configuration: it is not a part of another component and it has no interfaces. The intuition is that a *CSystem* represents the entire software. The parts of *CSystem* are *client* and *server* of types *CClient* and *CServer* representing the client and the server in the system, respectively. The server *component* in turn has a part named *dbase* of type *CDb*; this part represents an internal data storage of the server.

The above-mentioned components have interfaces: *client* has a requires interface named *sendreq* of type *IRpc*, and server a provides interface named *rcvreq* of type *IRpc2*. The intuition is that the client sends its requests through *sendreq*, and the server receives these through *rcvreq*. In addition, the *dbase* component has a provides interface *query* of type *IRpc2*; the intuition is that the database can be queried usign this interface. Finally, there are bindings between the interfaces: *sendreq* is bound (by its tip) to (the base of) *rcvreq*, which is, in turn, bound to *query*. ∎

Modules are units of implementation in Koala: all the implementation code is contained in modules. Components encapsulate modules, and there can be bindings between both requires and provides interfaces, and modules: a provides interface being bound to a module implies that the module implements the functions in that interface; on the other hand, a module being bound to a requires interface signals that the module uses the functions in the requires interface. Therefore, modules form the start and end points of functions calls: at the conceptual level, each function call has its origin in a module, and thereafter the call flows through a number of requires and provides interfaces, until it reaches a provides interface that is bound to a module where the function is implemented.

Based on the above description of the flow of function calls, it should be evident that in order for the function calls to work properly, the bindings between interfaces must conform to some well-formedness criteria: e.g., a binding between two provides interfaces are allowed only when one of the components containing one of the interfaces is a part of the component containing the other interface. Further, each interface must be bound by its tip to exactly one interface: no binding at all would imply that there is no implementation for its function; on the other hand, two or more bindings would result in unambiguity, as there would be no way to decide which implementation for the functions should be selected. The rules concerning the allowed and necessary bindings between interfaces in Koala are termed *binding rules*. We will not give a detailed definition of the binding rules in this paper; the interested reader should refer to the Koala papers, or to [7].

Components can include *attributes*, or *properties* or *parameters*, as they are also called, which parameterise the component in different ways. Components obtain values for their attributes through their requires interfaces. In addition, there can be dependencies between different attribute values: an attribute having certain value can imply that some other attributes have specific values. *Diversity spreadsheets* are used to specify the dependencies between attributes.

In addition to their role as loci of implementation, modules serve other purposes. A *switch* is a special case of a module. The purpose of a switch is to allow an interface to be bound into alternative interfaces based on some parameter value. Further, a module can be used to bind an interface by its tip to the base of multiple interfaces: the interface is bound by its tip to the module, and the code in the module serialises the calls to the interfaces.

3.2 Koalish

In this section, we present Koalish, a language for modelling CSPFs. The syntax of Koalish is given in an appendix. The language is based on a conceptualisation obtained by combining the basic modelling elements of Koala with a number of variability mechanisms stemming from the product configuration domain, see, e.g., [18]. More specifically, the variability mechanisms introduced are the possibility of selecting the number and type of parts of components, and writing constraints.

A *Koalish model* is a description of a CSPF written in Koalish. Such a model consists of a set of *component types, interfaces types, attribute value types*, and *constraints*. Further, *configurations* consist of sets of *component* and *interface instances*, and of relations describing which component instances are parts of other component instances, which interface instances are interfaces of which component instances, which bindings exist between interfaces, and which values attributes have. The relation of the above-introduced concepts to those in Koala is the following: component and interface instances correspond to component and interfaces, respectively, and a configuration (as defined here) is equivalent to the concept of configuration in Koala.

As stated in the introduction, configurations are purported to serve as descriptions of individual systems in CSPFs. Obviously, not all configurations represent such a system: e.g., it is possible that two components are mutually parts of each other, which is certainly not possible in, e.g., Koala. Therefore, we introduce the concept of a *valid configuration* with the intuition that a configuration can serve as a description of a system in the CSPF described by a specific Koalish model if and only if it is a valid configuration. In the following, we will describe what is required from a valid configuration.

Components and Compositional Structure. A component type is a description of an encapsulated piece of software with an explicit interface. The instances of component types correspond to components in Koala.

The compositional structure of component instances is specified through *part definitions* in component types. A part definition consists of a *part name*, a *set of possible part types*, and a *cardinality definition*. In the following, the component type containing the part definition is referred to as the *whole type*.

The semantics of a part definition is as follows. The part name distinguishes the role in which different component instances are parts of instances of the whole type. The set of possible part types contains the component types the instances of which may occur as parts of instances of the whole type with the associated part name. The cardinality is an integer range that specifies the number of component instances that must occur as parts (of an instance of the whole type) with the given name. A part definition is reflected in a valid configuration as follows: An instance of the whole type has the number of components instances specified by the cardinality as its parts by the part name. Each part must be an instance of one of the possible part types. The fact that a component instance has a component instance as a part with a given name is conceptualised as the two instances being in the *has-part* relation with the name.

Example. Fig. 2 contains the Koalish description of a CSPF involving clients and servers. The component type representing an entire client-server systems, *CSystem*, has a part definition according to which valid instances of *CSystem* must have at least one and at most three clients, both of which either of type *CBasicClient* or *CExtendedClient*. Further, the second part definition of *CSystem* states that valid instances of the types must have an instance of either of type *CServer* or *CServer2*. ∎

In each Koalish model, exactly one component type must be declared to be the *root component type*. A valid configuration must include exactly one instance of the root component type; this instance corresponds to a Koala configuration. Further, every component instance, except for root, must be a part of some component instance.

Koala excludes self-containment from the composition hierarchy, i.e., the composition hierarchy must indeed by a hierarchy. Therefore, we require that no component includes, even transitively, a part definition where the component type is one of the possible part types. Notice that this implies that there is no self-containment for instances.

Connection Points. An interface type is a description of a set of *functions*. In Koalish, functions are represented as scalar values, i.e., functions do not include a description of return values or parameter names and types. The instances of interface types correspond to interfaces in Koala. Finally, Koalish includes the subtype relation between interfaces. The relation is defined similarly as in Koala.

The connection points of component instances are defined in a manner similar to how their compositional structure was defined through part definitions above. In more detail, the vehicle for achieving this is *interface definitions*. An interface definition consists of an *interface name*, an *interface type*, a *direction definition*, an *optionality definition*, and a *groundedness definition*. The semantics of the interface name is similar to that of part name. Further, the interface type has the same function as the set of possible part types in the context of part definitions, with the exception that only one possible type can be specified. The direction definition has two possible values, *requires* and *provides*, with the obvious semantics. The optionality definition can take two values: *optional* and *mandatory*. The semantics of the optional-value is that the instances of the component type may have an interface conforming to the definition, whereas for the value mandatory the instances must have one.

The notion of groundedness is not as such present in Koala. It is included in Koalish as a kind of abstraction from the concept of module in Koala missing from Koalish. However, information about modules is essential when reasoning about valid configurations: unless an interface is bound to a module, it must be bound to another interface. Therefore, the notion of groundedness is included in Koalish, with the semantics that all the interface instance that are not grounded must be bound to an interface according to the binding rules of Koala.

An interface definition is reflected in a valid configuration as follows: If the interface is mandatory (optional), an instance has (may have) an interface instance of the interface type as its interface. The instance is either a provides or requires instance,

```
model client-server root type CSystem

interface IRpc {
    f;
}

interface IRpc2 {
    f; g;
}

component CBasicClient {
    requires
        interface IRpc caller;
}

component CExtendedClient {
    requires
        interface IRpc2 caller;
}

component CDb {
    provides
        interface IRpc2 query grounded;
}

component CServer {
    provides
        interface IRpc callee;
    contains
        component CDb dbase;
    connects
        callee = dbase.query;
}

component CServer2 {
    provides
        interface IRpc2 callee;
    contains
        component CDb dbase;
    connects
        callee = dbase.query;
}

component CSystem {
    contains
        component (CExtendedClient, CBasicClient) client[1-3];
        component (CServer,CServer2) server;
    constraints
        client part cardinality >= 2 => server instance of CServer2
}
```

Fig. 2. A client-server CSPF represented in Koalish.

and grounded or not grounded according to the direction and groundedness definitions, respectively. The fact that a component instance has an interface instance as an
interface with a given name is conceptualised as the two instances being in the *has-
interface* relation with the interface name.

Example. The example in Fig. 2 includes two interface types, namely *IRpc*, *IRpc2*.
As the type *IRpc* contains only the single function *f*, and type *IRpc2* contains a function with the same name, *IRpc2* is a subtype of *IRpc*. In addition, each interface type
is trivially a subtype of itself.

Of the client types, *CBasicClient* defines a mandatory interface named *caller* of type *IRpc*, and *CExtendedClient* of type *IRpc2*. On the server side, both *CServer* and *CServer2* define mandatory interfaces named *caller*; in *CServer*, the type of the interface is *IRpc*, and in *CServer2 IRpc2*. Finally, component type *CDatabase* defines a mandatory provides interface named *query* of type *IRpc2*. ■

Attributes. In addition to part and interface definitions, components can include *attribute definitions*. The attribute definitions specify the *attributes* the instances of the component types must have; the attributes of component instances contain relevant information about the instances.

Each attribute definition consists of an *attribute name*, and an *attribute value type*. The attribute name specifies the name of the attribute, and the attribute value type the set of values the attribute may have.

An attribute definition is reflected in a valid configuration as follows: each instance of the component type has an attribute with the attribute name, and the value of the attribute is one of the possible values enumerated in the attribute type. The fact that a component instance has an attribute with a given value is conceptualised as the component instance, the attribute name, and the attribute value being in the *attr-value* relation.

Constraints. Component and interface types form the basic machinery of Koalish: using them, it is possible to specify a range of CSPFs. However, it is not hard to see that the modelling concepts discussed so far are not expressive enough to capture all relevant aspects of Koala: e.g., the dependencies between attribute values would be hard to express using part and interface definition; similarly, it would be hard to capture the knowledge embedded in switches. In order to overcome this lack in expressiveness, we introduce *constraints* into Koalish; constraints are also present in many conceptualisations of configuration knowledge, see, e.g., [18].

Constraints are logical conditions that must hold for a valid individual of the CSPF. They expressed in a *constraint language*, an integral part of Koalish. In short, constraints can refer to the parts and interfaces of component instances and bindings between interfaces and functions, and such references can be combined using Boolean connectives.

Example. There is only one constraint in the example: it is specified that if there are two or more clients in the system, then the server must be of type *CServer2*. ■

3.3 Omitted Concepts

Not all concepts of Koala have a counterpart in Koalish. More specifically, the omitted concepts include module, switch, and diversity spreadsheet. In general, concepts were omitted in order to keep the conceptual basis of Koalish as simple as possible while retaining the characteristics necessary for modelling variability. In the following, be will briefly discuss the most important omitted concepts.

The reason for not including module as a locus of implementation is that from the viewpoint of our approach, the information captured in the groundedness definition is sufficient: interface instances that are not grounded must be bound to other interfaces, whereas grounded interfaces must may not be bound; the exact module to which a grounded interface is bound seems to have no implications on variability.

Module as method for connecting an interface by its tip to multiple interfaces seems to be a solution to an implementation level problem: how to specify the order of function calls when an interface is bound by its tip into multiple interfaces. Koalish, on the other hand, is not concerned with implementation level issues, and therefore connecting an interface by its tip to multiple interfaces would not incur any problems.

It would seem to be an easy and straightforward task to translate switches into constraints having the form of an implication; consequently, there seems to be no need for a separate switch construct.

Diversity spreadsheets can be easily modelled as a set of constraints having the form of an implication.

Finally, it should be noticed that the omitted concepts discussed above could easily be introduced to the syntax of Koalish: we assume that extending the syntax with constructs for modelling, e.g., switches, would be a minor issue, and translating these constructs into the fundamental concepts of Koalish, e.g., constraints, would be straightforward.

4 Formalisation of Koalish

In this section, we provide Koalish with formal semantics. We start by giving a brief overview of Weight Constraint Rule Language (WCRL) [9]. Thereafter, we show how Koalish models can be translated into WCRL.

4.1 Weight Constraint Rule Language

WCRL [9] is a general-purpose knowledge representation formalism similar to logic programs. Although general-purpose, WCRL has been designed to allow the easy representation of configuration knowledge about non-software products. Furthermore, it has been shown to be suitable for representing configuration modelling concepts, see [10]. This suggests that WCRL is a reasonable choice for the knowledge representation formalism of our approach as well. Further, an inference system *smodels* (see http://www.tcs.hut.fi/Software/smodels) operating on WCRL has been shown to have a very competitive performance compared to other problem solvers, especially in the case of problems including structure [9].

Weight constraint rules are of the form:

$$C_0 \leftarrow C_1, ..., C_n,$$

where each Ci is a *weight constraint*. Each weight constraint is a of the form:

$$L \leq \{a_1 = w_{a_1}, ..., a_n = w_{a_n}, not\ b_1 = w_{b_1}, ..., not\ b_1 = w_{b_m}\} \leq U.$$

Above, the a_i and b_j are *atoms*, and the a_i and *not* b_i are *literals*. Each literal is associated with a weight: e.g., w_{a_1} is the weight of a_1.

A set of atoms S is defined to satisfy a weight constraint if (and only if):

$$L \leq \sum_{a_i \in S} w_{a_i} + \sum_{b_i \notin S} w_{b_i} \leq U .$$

A weight constraint rule is satisfied by a set of atoms S if and only if the head C_0 is satisfied whenever each constraint C_i in its body is satisfied. A *program* P is defined as a set of weight constraints. P is satisfied by S if and only if every weight constraint rule in P is satisfied by S.

A set of atoms S is a *stable model* of program P if (i) S satisfies P and (ii) S is *justified* by P. We will use an example to illustrate what is meant by S being justified by P; the exact definition is out of the scope of this paper, and can be found in, e.g., [9]. Consider the program

$$0 \leq \{ a = 1, b = 1 \} \leq 1 \leftarrow c$$

The set of atoms $\{a\}$ satisfies the only rule in program, and thus the program itself. However, $\{a\}$ is not justified by the program, as the body of the rule is not satisfied. In fact, the only stable model of this program is the empty set. If the rule $c \leftarrow$ was added to the program, then the program would have three stable models: $\{a, c\}$, $\{b, c\}$, and $\{c\}$.

Above, we have discussed some core features of weight constraints rules. However, for practical purposes we will use some additional syntactical constructs that enhance the knowledge representation capabilities of weight constraints rules, but do not affect their fundamental semantics. In the following, we will use an example illustrating the structure of a company board to illustrate the discussion.

First, rules of the form $1 \leq \{ l = 1 \}$ are written simply as l. Further, rules where every weight has value one, i.e., rules of the form

$$l \leq \{ a_1 = 1, \ldots, a_n = 1, \textit{not } b_1 = 1, \ldots, \textit{not } b_n = 1 \} \leq u$$

are termed *cardinality constraints* and written as

$$l \{ a_1, \ldots, a_n, \textit{not } b_1, \ldots, \textit{not } b_n \} u.$$

A missing lower bound is interpreted as $-\infty$, and a missing upper bound as ∞. Further, the shorthand

$$\leftarrow C_1, \ldots, C_n$$

is used for rules where the head C_0 is an unsatisfiable constraints, such as $1 \leq \{\}$. This kind of rules are termed *integrity constraints*. Finally, rules with an empty body, that is, of the form

$$C_0 \leftarrow$$

are termed *facts*.

In order to write rules that apply to sets of atoms, we use rules involving *variables*. The idea of variables is that when occurring in a rule, each variable refers to a certain set of *object constants*; the set of object constants to which each variable refers is defined by a set of *domain predicates* occurring on the left side of the rule. As an example, consider a rule stating that the chairman of the board is also a member of the board:

$$member(X) \leftarrow chair(X)$$

Here, the possible values of variable X are those object constants x for which domain predicate $chair(x)$ holds; the set of these object constants is termed the *range* of the domain predicate. In common terms, the intuitive semantics of rules with variables is that the rule is written out with each possible combination of variables. Notice also the notation used: the names of variables begin with an uppercase, and those of object constants and predicates are written in lowercase.

The range of domain predicates is defined by using facts, such as

$$female(alice) \leftarrow \quad male(bob) \leftarrow \quad female(carol) \leftarrow ,$$

or in terms of other domain predicates. As an example, the following two rules have the effect that the range of *person* is the union of the range of *female* and *male*:

$$person(X) \leftarrow female(X)$$
$$person(X) \leftarrow male(X)$$

The following cardinality constraint specifies that there must be at least five and at most seven members in a board:

$$5 \{ member(X) : person(X) \} 7 \leftarrow$$

The shorthand involving colon in the head is equivalent to writing *member(x)* for all the x for which *person(x)* is true inside the braces. Finally,

$$\leftarrow chair(X), vice(X), person(X)$$

is an example of an integrity constraint. The semantics is that the chair and the vice-chair must be different persons.

4.2   Translation from Koalish to WCRL

The goal of the translation is to provide a function that takes a Koalish model as input, and produces as output a WCRL program. In the following, we will only outline the general structure and some parts of the translation; for more details, see [7].

The following definition describes the connection between the original model and the WCRL program resulting from the translation.

Definition. Given a Koalish model M, the valid configurations of M are the stable models of the WCRL program $t(M)$, where t is the translation to be described below.■

When giving the translation, we assume that the Koalish model serving as input is syntactically correct and obeys the semantic constraints stated in Section 3.2. This assumption releases us from the task of explicitly specifying all the properties that must hold for a WCRL program representing some Koalish model. As an example, it holds that every interface instance must be either a provides or a requires instance. We could use the following rules to rule out the converse:

$$\leftarrow \{ prov(I), req(I) \} 0, int(I)$$
$$\leftarrow 2 \{ prov(I), req(I) \}, int(I)$$

Above, the domain predicate $prov(i)$ $(req(i))$ denotes the fact that i is a provides (requires interface), and $int(i)$ the fact that i is an interface instance.

However, the syntax of Koalish together with the properties of the translation guarantee that each interface instance is indeed either a provides or requires instance. Therefore, there is no need to include the above rules in the WCRL programs.

The rules in the translated model $t(M)$ fall into two categories: there are *ontological definitions* common to all translated models, and *model dependent rules* that depend to the Koalish model M being translated.

Ontological Definitions. Ontological definitions encode properties that must hold for any valid configuration of a Koalish model. In the following, we will present some ontological definitions and the reasons for introducing them.

The fact that each configuration must contain exactly one instance of the root component type is captured with the following rule:

$$1 \ \{ \ in(C) : root(C) \ \} \ 1 \leftarrow$$

Above, the predicate $in(c)$ is true if component c is in a configuration, and the domain predicate $root(c)$ holds exactly when c is an instance of the root component type.

Further, all the other component instances must be part of some other component instance in order to be in a valid configuration:

$$in(C_2) \leftarrow hp(C_1, C_2, N), ppa(C_1, C_2, N), pan(N)$$

The predicate $hp(c_1, c_2, n)$ has the semantics that component instance c_1 has component instance c_2 as a part with part name n. Finally, the domain predicate $hp(c_1, c_2, n)$ tells that c_2 may occur as a part of c_1 with part name n, and $pan(n)$ implies that n is a part name.

Model Dependent Rules. The non-constant part of the program, i.e., the part depending on the particular Koalish model, is produced by considering each interface and component type in turn. As an example of interface types, consider the interface type *IRpc* from our running example (recall Fig. 1). First, we introduce the domain predicate $rpc(i)$ with the semantics that the constant symbol i is an instance of *IRpc*. Further, we need to say that all instances of *IRpc* are interfaces:

$$int(I) \leftarrow rpc(I)$$

Finally, we introduce the rule

$$cf(I, f) \leftarrow rpc(I)$$

to capture the fact the *IRpc* contains function f; here, the domain predicate $cf(i, f)$ has the semantics that interface instance i contains function f.

Similarly as for interface types and instances above, we use domain predicates to represent component types, and object constants to represent their instances. As an example of translating other information related to component types, let us consider interface definitions: the interface definition of *CBasicClient* of a requires interface named *caller* with interface type *IRpc* is translated into the following set of rules:

1 { *hi(C, I, caller)* : *client(C), rpc(I), req(I)* } 1 ← *in*(C), *client*(C)

In the above rule, *hi* is the interface analogue for *hp* (see above).

The translation of constraints is somewhat more complicated than the translation of the other parts of Koalish. In common terms, simple constraints can be mapped into integrity constraints involving the predicates introduced above, e.g., *in* and *hp*. More complex constraints can be formed by combining simple constraints.

As an example, the constraint introduced in the running example is captured by the following rule:

← 2 { *pa(R, C, client)* : *ppa(R, C, client)* }, *pa(R, C_1, server), server(C_1), root(R)*

Finally, it should be noticed that while translating part and interface definitions, it is necessary to ascertain that a sufficient amount of object constants corresponding to component and interfaces instances is created. That is, we must introduce constant symbols and facts that give these symbols the semantics that they represent instances. As an example, when translating the interface definition of *CBasicClient* discussed above, we would need to introduce a new constant symbol i_n, and the following rules to give the interface the correct type and direction:

$$rpc(i_n) \leftarrow \qquad req(i_n) \leftarrow$$

5   Tool Support

In this section, we first describe the architecture of the tool support of our approach. Thereafter, we discuss the current implementation status and preliminary experiences, and finally briefly discuss the complexity of the computational tasks that must be solved in order to provide the tool support described.

5.1   Architecture

Fig. 3 depicts the general architecture of the planned supporting tools. The supporting tools are split into two subsystems: modelling support and deployment support. In the following, we will discuss the functionality of each of these parts in turn.

Modelling Support. The purpose of the tools supporting the modelling process is to enable the easy creation and management of a Koalish model, and translating the model into a form in which it can be utilised in the deployment process. The first of these tasks, creating a Koalish model, is similar to the task of writing a description of a software system using some ADL or other similar notion.

In the second task, the Koalish model is translated to WCRL, as is outlined above in Section 4.2. Once a Koalish model has been mapped into a WCRL model, the WCRL representation can be repeatedly used as the basis of the deployment process.

Deployment Support. The goal of the deployment process is that a customer finds a valid configuration of the CSPF satisfying his unique *requirements*. The customer uses an interface designated to the specific CSPF at hand to enter his requirements for the configuration. The inference engine supports the customer in the following ways.

First, given a set of customer requirements, the inference engine can be used to calculate a *partial stable model*. A partial stable model describes what must be true, what must not be true, and what is still unknown in a stable model of the CSPF that satisfies the set of customer requirements. The partial stable model can be used, e.g., to prevent a customer from making incompatible choices by disabling alternatives that are ruled out by the partial model. Second, at any point, the inference engine can be used to find a stable model that satisfies the customer requirements entered so far; this is also possible even when no customer requirements have been entered.

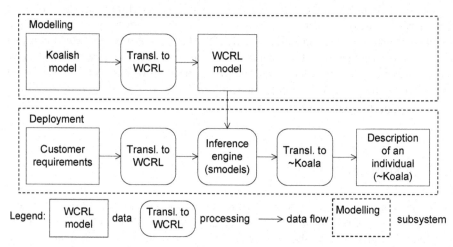

Fig. 3. The architecture of the suggested tool support system.

Once a valid configuration has been found, it can be translated into an input of a realisation tool, such as make. Another possibility is to translate the output into a language allowing it to be inspected and analysed by engineers. This language cannot be Koala or Koalish: Koalish can only represent types, and Koala uses references to component types to specify the compositional structure of components; a stable model can, however, contain multiple instances of the same type that are different in what parts and interfaces they have. Therefore, it is necessary to describe the compositional structure of component instances by embedding the entire description of all their parts in their description; in Fig. 3, we have denoted this undefined language with ~Koala.

5.2 Implementation Status

So far, we have implemented a program that takes as an input a Koalish model conforming to the syntax given in the appendix and maps the model into WCRL. The WCRL model can be used to generate all the valid configurations of the CSPF described by the Koalish model; alternatively, it is possible to compute the descriptions of individuals that fulfil requirements given in WCRL. Further, we have implemented a program that maps the configurations output by the inference engine into system descriptions that resemble Koala models of software systems, i.e., to the language denoted with ~Koala in Fig. 3.

We have tried out the functionality described above using small-scale examples of fictitious CSPFs. The examples are similar to the one presented in Fig. 2: the number of component and interface instances in the configurations has been less than ten, and the number of stable models (valid configurations) has ranged from zero to few dozens. So far, the results obtained have met our expectations: the stable models computed have corresponded to what we have expected to be the valid configurations. Further, there have been no performance problems: in a typical case, configurations have been generated at a rate of dozens of configurations per second.

5.3 Complexity Issues

The computational tasks related to generating configurations satisfying specific requirements are potentially very complex for WCRL [9]. To alleviate this, *smodels* system provides a tool to pre-compile a WCRL rule set to sets of simpler rules, so called *basic constraint rules* without variables. This pre-compilation can be done off-line and the resulting (potentially much larger) rule set then used repeatedly to configure the product. However, even for such simpler rules, the computational task corresponding to configuration remains NP-complete [10], i.e. in the worst case exponential in the size of the configuration model. Hence, the efficiency of the tool support must be carefully tested. Based on some preliminary experiences from the mechanical product domain with a few dozen components and/or attributes [20] and initial experience with configuring Linux a distribution with hundreds of packages [21], the worst-case does not appear to occur with such products.

6 Discussion and Comparison with Previous Work

In this section, we first briefly evaluate the work presented in this paper, and thereafter compare it to related previous work.

6.1 Evaluation

Above, we have outlined an approach for supporting the modelling and deployment of CSPFs. Although the approach has not so far been properly empirically validated by trying it out with real software product families, there are some points that speak in favour of the feasibility of our approach.

The approach is based on Koala, an ADL that is in industrial use at Philips Consumer Electronics. Hence, it can be assumed that the conceptualisation underlying our approach has at least some relevance. On the other hand, committing to Koala limits the applicability of our approach to CSPFs that can be described using the concepts of Koala. However, although there are significant differences between different ADLs, Koala shares many of its core modelling concepts with other ADLs [22].

Feasibility of the overall approach is supported by the fact that a similar approach has been successfully implemented for non-software products in the prototype tool WeCoTin [11], although the conceptualisations differ, as will be discussed below.

Our approach supports the easy creation and maintenance of models of CSPFs in two ways. First, there is no need for programming, as the models are represented in Koalish, an explicit and declarative language. Second, the syntax of Koalish is close to that of Koala and many other languages (e.g., IDL, Interface Definition Language) commonly used by software engineers. Therefore, assuming Koalish should not require excessive effort.

Finally, our approach is generally applicable. This is a consequence of the fact that we do not aim at producing concrete software systems. Instead, we produce descriptions of software systems that are *abstract* in the sense that they are not dependent on any specific realisation tool, such as make or some compiler. Still, the descriptions are intended to be detailed enough to be easily translated into inputs of any realisation tool.

6.2 Comparison with Previous Work

This paper is strongly based on earlier work done in the product configuration domain. Both the overall approach and the specific variability mechanisms presented in this paper have earlier been implemented for non-software products [11, 18, 23]. However, the application of techniques developed in the product configuration domain to software products families is a relatively new idea. In the following, we will discuss some existing configurators and conceptualisations of configuration knowledge and compare them with the work presented in this paper.

Let us first compare the concepts of Koalish with the most widely sited conceptualisations of configuration knowledge, namely [18] and [23]. The most important concepts in these are: *components*, *ports*, *resources*, and *functions*. To begin with, the concept of component is similar on both sides: components represent the constituent parts of systems being modelled, they can be defined a compositional structure, and they have explicit connection points: ports and interfaces play this role in the configuration modelling conceptualisations and Koalish, respectively. However, ports are different from Koalish interfaces in that unlike interfaces, ports have no internal structure. Of the remaining concepts, resources are used to model the production and use of certain quantities in components, and the flow of these entities across components. Example of this kind of entities are disk space in computers, and electric power in electronics devices. Functions, on the other hand, describe a product from non-technical or customer point of view; the ability of a computer to play music from CDs could be modelled as a function. Neither resources nor functions have a counterpart in Koalish.

Further, there exists academic prototype [11] and commercial configurators, see, e.g., http://www.ilog.fr/products/configurator. These configurators provide their users with a wide range of support, similar to the kind of support described in Section 5.1. Therefore, using existing configurators to support the deployment task in our approach would be a reasonable first choice. However, differences in the underlying conceptualisations of the configurators and Koalish may hinder the application of existing configurators to configuring Koalish: e.g., the components in WeCoTin cannot be defined any connection points, a fundamental ingredient of Koala and Koalish.

There exists some earlier work on applying configuration techniques to software. In [24], Geyer and Becker consider this idea, but reject it as inapplicable: They argue that a configuration technique must support aggregation in order to be usable for configuring software. They further claim that knowledge-based configuration-techniques fail to support aggregation and concentrate on modelling inheritance structure. However, e.g., the conceptualisation presented in [18] supports the representation of aggregate structures of both components and functions.

On the other hand, Hotz and Krebs in [25], and Hein and MacGregor in [26] represent approaches to managing the variability of software product families based on using knowledge-based configuration techniques. Both of these approaches agree with ours in what would the role of configuration be in product family engineering. However, what differentiates our work from their is that our work is based on explicitly modelling the architectural structure of a CSPF and operating on this structural model, whereas neither Hotz and Krebs nor Hein and MacGregor commit to any specific conceptualisation. Further, Hotz and Krebs use procedural knowledge to guide the inferences; therefore, albeit the procedural knowledge is specified declaratively, the results from the inferences may be affected by the procedural knowledge. This is in contrast to our approach, where the results from the inferences depend solely on the Koalish model at hand, and the requirements entered by the customer.

Generative programming is a software engineering paradigm with goals similar to configuration: according to Czarnecki and Eisenecker [27] generative programming pertains to modelling software system families such that based on a particular requirements specification, a highly customised and optimised system can be automatically manufactured from elementary implementation components. However, in spite of the similarity of goals, there are fundamental differences between our approach and generative programming. First, unlike generative programming, we do not aim at producing concrete code, but descriptions that unambiguously specify systems as combinations of components, interfaces, relations between these, and attribute values. Second, the main focus of our approach is in managing the complexity in finding a valid configuration conforming to the requirements of the customer, whereas generative programming techniques typically concentrate on code-level issues, such as code size and performance.

There is a body of research concentrated on modelling the variability of software product lines [28-30]. Certainly, our approach is likewise aiming at modelling the variability of CSPFs. What seems to differentiate our work from other research in the area is that our work is based on using architectural models, whereas most of the related work aims at modelling features, see, e.g., [31]. The difference between architectural and feature models is significant: architectural models could be characterised as providing a technical view, while features describe look at the systems mainly from the customer's or user's viewpoint.

Besides Koala, a large number of ADLs have been reported [22]. Most of the ADLs resemble Koala in that they describe the architecture of software systems in terms of components and their connection points. However, what differentiates Koala from the majority of other ADLs is that most other ADLs include the notion of *connectors* as entities mediating the interactions between components.

As Koala is an ADL, or at least very similar to many ADLs, and Koalish in turn shares its major modelling concepts with Koala, it is obvious that Koalish is closely related to ADLs. However, a differentiating factor is that unlike Koalish, the majority of ADLs are focused on describing single systems. Of course, there are exceptions: one of them is Acme [32], an ADL originally designed to serve as an interchange language between ADLs. Acme includes the concepts of *type* and *style*. Types can be used to describe the common properties of component, connector, and connection point instances, and styles those of systems. Therefore, types and styles can be considered to be variability mechanisms, with component and interface types and Koalish models as their counterparts in Koalish.

The difference between Acme and Koalish is that the types and styles in Acme merely state requirements that must hold for the instances or systems, whereas Koalish models and types intentionally describe all the properties of valid configurations and instances of these. In other words, the Koalish model must justify everything that is in its configuration; no similar condition holds for Acme.

However, another exception among the ADLs is the approach to describing software product families proposed by André van der Hoek et al. [33]. In their work, architectural models can be annotated with *evolution, optionality*, and *variability*. Out of these, there, evolution is the only concept for which there is no counterpart in our approach. In van der Hoek's terminology, variability pertains to multiple possible components or *connections*, as they call connectors, implementing the same functionality; it is required that all the components have the same interface. Further, optionality refers to components, connectors, and interfaces that may or may not be present in a system. It is easy to see that Koalish includes both optionality and variability, with the limitation that there is no concept in Koalish corresponding to connections. Optionality is achieved through cardinalities in part definitions and optional interfaces. The form of variability present in van der Hoek's approach is equivalent to multiple possible part types in a part definition with the additional limitation that all the possible part types must have exactly the same set of interfaces.

However, our approach and that of van der Hoek et al. differ in that in van der Hoek's approach, each variant and optional entity is guarded by a Boolean expression involving attributes: the entity is selected if and only if the expression evaluates to true. Our approach does not include similar or any other kind of guards as mandatory elements, although such guards could easily be simulated using constraints. Further, our approach provides declarative and formal semantics, and complete and sound inference algorithms for these. In addition, our approach especially addresses the problem of generating valid configurations satisfying a set of customer requirements, whereas van der Hoek et al. seem to provide no tool support for this.

Finally, there are approaches independent from both featural and architectural descriptions for modelling the variability of software product families. A prime example of such an approach is that proposed by Schmid and John [34]. In their approach, a *decision model* is used to represent the decisions needed to come up with an unambiguous individual of the family, and the interdependencies between the decisions. In addition, the approach includes a mapping from the outcomes of the decisions into artefacts constituting the product family. Examples of such artefacts requirements documentation and source code, and different variants based on the decisions can be realised, e.g., by including and excluding parts of the source code by using ifdefs.

Although our approach and that of Schmid and John attack similar sets of problems, there are significant differentiating factors between the approaches. First, unlike the approach of Schmid and John, our approach makes a commitment to a conceptualisation of CSPFs, and includes a language (Koalish) concretizing the conceptualisation. Consequently, the approach of Schmid and John is more general than that of ours, but provides less support for modelling and deployment. Second, similarly as van der Hoek et al. and unlike we, Schmid and John seem not to provide tool support for finding configurations matching specific customer requirements.

7 Conclusions and Further Work

We have presented an approach for modelling configurable software product families and for automated configuring of product individuals using the models. We defined the conceptual foundation and syntax of a modelling language, Koalish, used for this purpose. The language extends Koala, a component model and architecture description language, with explicit variation modelling mechanisms for capturing alternative and optional components and constraints on how components, their attributes and interfaces can be used to build a working product individual. Koala is used in real industrial context and hence provides a good foundation for the modelling method. We further provided Koalish a formal semantics by defining a translation from it to Weight Constraint Rule Language (WCRL), a form of logic programs. This allows using an existing inference tool for WCRL, *smodels,* to implement the reasoning needed in a configurator. We have implemented a configurator that is able to construct all valid product individuals, with respect to a Koalish model of a CSPF, that satisfy a given set of requirements. The implemented functionality of the configurator has been tested using small-scale toy examples, for which it performs adequately.

Further research is needed in order to bring the approach closer to practice. The configuration tool support should be extended to enable more efficient creation and maintenance of configuration models by developing a graphical syntax for Koalish and a modelling tool supporting it. Further, a graphical user interface for configuring a product individual should be developed. Given these, the expressive power and usability of the modelling method and configuration support should be evaluated in real software development contexts with real software product families. Such case studies should investigate whether the modelling method is usable by software engineers and suitable for modelling the variability in a sufficiently wide range of different kinds of configurable software product families. At least two potentially necessary extensions can be identified in this respect: modelling the features [28] [29] and evolution [21, 33] of the product family. Furthermore, as the computational cost of configuration tasks based on our approach is in the worst case rather high, the scalability and efficiency of the configurator should be tested using larger and more complex products.

Acknowledgements

We gratefully acknowledge the financial support from the Academy of Finland (project number 51394) and National Technology Agency of Finland (Tekes).

References

1. Clements, P. C. and Northrop, L.: Software Product Lines - Practices and Patterns. Addison-Wesley, Boston (MA) (2001)
2. Bosch, J.: Design and Use of Software Architectures: Adapting and Evolving a Product-Line Approach. Addison-Wesley, Boston (MA) (2000)
3. Bosch, J.: Maturity and Evolution in Software Product Families: Approaches, Artefacts and Organization. In: Chastek, Gary J.: Proceedings of the Second Software Product Line Conference (SPLC 2) (2002) 257-271
4. Faltings, B., Freuder, E. C.: Special Issue on Configuration. IEEE Intelligent Systems 14(4) (1998) 29-85
5. Darr, T., Klein, M., McGuinness, D. L.: Special Issue on Configuration Design. Artificial Intelligence for Engineering Design, Analysis and Manufacturing 12(4) (1998) 293-397
6. Lakemeyer, G., Nebel, B. Foundations of Knowledge Representation and Reasoning - A Guide to This Volume. In: Lakemeyer, G., Nebel, B. (eds.): Foundations of Knowledge Representation and Reasoning, Lecture Notes in Artificial Intelligence 810. Springer, Berlin-Heidelberg. (1994) 1-12
7. Asikainen, T., Soininen, T., Männistö, T.: A Koala-Based Ontology for Configurable Software Product Families. In: Configuration Workshop of 18th International Conference on Artificial Intelligence (IJCAI) (2003)
8. van Ommering, R., van der Linden, F., Kramer, J., Magee, J.: The Koala Component Model for Consumer Electronics Software. IEEE Computer 33(3) (2000) 78-85
9. Simons, P., Niemelä, I., Soininen, T.: Extending and Implementing the Stable Model Semantics. Artificial Intelligence 138(1-2) (2002) 181-234
10. Soininen, T., Niemelä, I., Tiihonen, J., Sulonen, R.: Representing Configuration Knowledge with Weight Constraint Rules. In: Proceedings of the AAAI Spring 2001 Symposium on Answer Set Programming: Towards Efficient and Scalable Knowledge Representation and Reasoning (2001)
11. Tiihonen, J., Soininen, T., Niemelä, I., Sulonen, R.: A Practical Tool for Mass-Customising Configurable Products. In: Proceedings of the International Conference on Engineering Design (ICED'03), Stockholm, Sweden (2003)

12. Soininen, T., Stumptner, M.: Introduction to Special Issue on Configuration. Artificial Intelligence for Engineering Design, Analysis and Manufacturing 17(1-2) (2003) 1-2
13. Fleischanderl, G., Friedrich, G., Haselböck, A., Schreiner, H., Stumptner, M.: Configuring Large Systems Using Generative Constraint Satisfaction. IEEE Intelligent Systems 13(4) (1998) 59-68
14. McGuinness, D. L., Wright, J. R.: An Industrial-Strength Description Logic-Based Configurator Platform. IEEE Intelligent Systems 14(4) (1998) 69-77
15. Haag, A.: Sales Configuration in Business Processes. IEEE Intelligent Systems 13(4) (1998) 78-85
16. Yu, B., Skovgaard, J.: A Configuration Tool to Increase Product Competitiveness. IEEE Intelligent Systems 13(4) (1998) 34-41
17. van Ommering, R.: Building Product Populations with Software Components. In: Proceedings of the 24th International Conference on Software Engineering (ICSE 2002) (2002) 255-265
18. Soininen, T., Tiihonen, J., Männistö, T., Sulonen, R.: Towards a General Ontology of Configuration. Artificial Intelligence for Engineering Design, Analysis and Manufacturing 12(4) (1998) 357-372
19. Tiihonen, J., Soininen, T., Niemelä, I., Sulonen, R.: Empirical Testing of a Weight Constraint Rule Based Configurator. In: Configuration workshop of the 15th European Conference on Artificial Intelligence (ECAI 2002), Lyon, France (2002) 17-22
20. Kojo, T., Männistö, T., Soininen, T.: Towards Intelligent Support for Managing Evolution of Configurable Software Product Families. In: Proceedings of 11th International Workshop on Software Configuration Management (SCM-11), Lecture Notes in Computer Science 2649. Springer, Berlin Heidelberg (2003) 86-101
21. Tiihonen, J., Soininen, T., Niemelä, I., Sulonen, R.: A Practical Tool for Mass-Customising Configurable Products. In: Proceedings of the International Conference on Engineering Design (ICED'03), Stockholm, Sweden (2003)
22. Medvidovic, N., Taylor, R. M.: A Classification and Comparison Framework for Software Architecture Description Languages. IEEE Transactions on Software Engineering 26(1) (2000) 70-93
23. Felfernig, A., Friedrich, G., Jannach, D.: Conceptual Modeling for Configuration of Mass-Customizable Products. Artificial Intelligence in Engineering 15(2) (2001) 165-176
24. Geyer, L., Becker, M.: On the Influence of Variabilities on the Application-Engineering Process of a Product Family. In: Chastek, Gary J.: Proceedings of the Second International Conference on Software Product Lines (SPLC2). Lecture Notes in Computer Science 2379. Springer, Berlin - Heidelberg (2002) 1-14
25. Hotz, L., Krebs, T.: Supporting the Product Derivation Process with a Knowledge-Based Approach. In: Software Variability Management Workshop of ICSE'03 (2003)
26. Hein, A., MacGregor, J.: Managing Variability with Configuration Techniques. In: Software Variability Management Workshop of ICSE'03 (2003)
27. Czarnecki, K. and Eisenecker, U. W.: Generative Programming. Addison-Wesley, Boston (MA) (2000)
28. Kang, K., Cohen, S. G., Hess, J. A., Novak, W. E., Peterson, S. A.: Feature-Oriented Domain Analysis (FODA) - Feasibility Study. CMU/SEI-90-TR-21, Software Engineering Institute, Carnegie Mellon University (1990)
29. Thiel, S., Hein, A.: Modeling and Using Product Line Variability in Automotive Systems. IEEE Software 19(4) (2002) 66-72

30. van Gurp, J., Bosch, J., Svahnberg, M.: On the Notion of Variability in Software Product Lines. In: Proceedings of the Working IEEE/IFIP Conference on Software Architecture (WICSA 2001) (2001) 45-54
31. Kang, K., Lee, J., Donohoe, P.: Feature-oriented Product Line Engineering. IEEE Software 19(4) (2002) 58-65
32. Garlan, D., Monroe, R. T., Wile, D.: Acme: An Architecture Description Interchange Language. In: Proceedings of CASCON'97 (1997)
33. van der Hoek, A., Heimbigner, D., Wolf, A. L.: Capturing Architectural Configurability: Variants, Options, and Evolution. Technical report CU-CS-895-99, University of Colorado (1999)
34. Schmid, K., John, I.: A Practical Approach to Full-Life Cycle Variability Management. In: Workshop on Software Variability Management (SVM) of 25th International Conference on Software Engineering (2003) 41-46

Appendix: Koalish Syntax

⟨*koalish model*⟩ ::= 'model' ⟨*identifier*⟩ 'root type' ⟨*identifier*⟩ ⟨*type definitions*⟩

⟨*type definitions*⟩ ::= {⟨*component type definition*⟩ |
  ⟨*interface type definition*⟩ |
  ⟨*attribute type definition*⟩}*

⟨*component type definition*⟩ ::= 'component type' ⟨*identifier*⟩ '{' {⟨*provides section*⟩
  ⟨*requires section*⟩ ⟨*contains section*⟩ ⟨*connects section*⟩ ⟨*attribute section*⟩
  ⟨*constraint section*⟩}* '}'

⟨*interface type definition*⟩ ::= 'interface type' ⟨*identifier*⟩ '{'{⟨*identifier*⟩ ';'}* '}'

⟨*provides section*⟩ ::= 'provides' ⟨*interfaces*⟩

⟨*requires section*⟩ ::= 'requires' ⟨*interfaces*⟩

⟨*interfaces*⟩ ::= ⟨*identifier*⟩ ⟨*interface specification*⟩ {',' ⟨*interface specification*⟩}* ';'

⟨*interface specification*⟩ ::= ⟨*identifier*⟩ { 'optional' | 'grounded' }*

⟨*contains section*⟩ ::= 'contains' ⟨*components*⟩

⟨*components*⟩ ::= 'component' ⟨*possible types*⟩ ⟨*identifier*⟩ [⟨*cardinality*⟩] ;

⟨*possible types*⟩ ::= ⟨*identifier*⟩ | '(' ⟨*identifier*⟩ {',' ⟨*identifier*⟩}*

⟨*cardinality*⟩ ::= ⟨*integer*⟩ ['-'⟨*integer*⟩]

⟨*connects section*⟩ ::= 'connects' ⟨*binding*⟩*

⟨*binding*⟩ ::= [⟨*identifier*⟩'.'] ⟨*identifier*⟩ '=' [⟨*identifier*⟩'.'] ⟨*identifier*⟩

⟨*attribute type definition*⟩ ::= ⟨*identifier*⟩ '=' '{' ⟨*enumerated value*⟩ '}' ';'

⟨*enumerated value*⟩ ::= ⟨*constant*⟩ | ⟨*identifier*⟩

⟨*attribute section*⟩ ::= 'attributes' ⟨*attribute definition*⟩

⟨*attribute definition*⟩ ::= ⟨*identifier*⟩ ⟨*identifier*⟩ {',' ⟨*identifier*⟩}* ';'

⟨*constraint section*⟩ ::= 'constraints' ⟨*constraint expression*⟩

⟨*constraint expression*⟩ ::= ⟨*boolean primitive*⟩ |
  ⟨*boolean primitive*⟩ {'and' ⟨*boolean primitive*⟩}* |

⟨*boolean primitive*⟩ {'or' ⟨*boolean primitive*⟩}* |
⟨*boolean primitive*⟩ '=>' ⟨*boolean primitive*⟩
⟨*boolean primitive*⟩ ::= ['not'] {⟨*configuration predicate*⟩ |
    '(' ⟨*constraint expression*⟩ ')' | ⟨*comparison*⟩}
⟨*configuration predicate*⟩ ::= 'present' '(' ⟨*object reference*⟩ ')' |
    ⟨*object reference*⟩ 'instance of' ⟨*identifier*⟩ |
    'bound' '(' ⟨*interface reference*⟩ ')' |
    'has instances' '(' ⟨*identifier*⟩ ')'
⟨*comparison*⟩ ::= ⟨*arithmetic expression*⟩ ⟨*comparison op*⟩ ⟨*arithmetic expression*⟩
⟨*comparison op*⟩ ::= '=' | '!=' | '<' | '>' | '<=' | '>='
⟨*arithmetic expression*⟩ ::= ['+' | '-'] ⟨*term*⟩ { {'+' | '-' | '*' | '/' | mod} ⟨*term*⟩}*
⟨*term*⟩ ::= ⟨*constant*⟩ | '(' ⟨*arithmetic expression*⟩ ')' | ⟨*configuration value*⟩
⟨*configuration value*⟩ ::= 'number of instances' '(' ⟨identifier⟩ ')' |
    'part cardinality' '(' ⟨*part reference*⟩ ')' |
    'value' '(' ⟨*interface reference*⟩ ',' ⟨*identifier*⟩ ')'
⟨*object reference*⟩ ::= ⟨*object reference*⟩ | ⟨*interface reference*⟩
⟨*part reference*⟩ ::= [⟨*part reference*⟩'.'] ⟨*identifier*⟩ | 'root' |
    'owner' '(' ⟨*object reference*⟩ ')'
⟨*interface reference*⟩ ::= [⟨*part reference*⟩'.'] ⟨*identifier*⟩ |
    'bound interface' '(' ⟨*interface reference*⟩ ')'

Feature Binding Analysis
for Product Line Component Development

Jaejoon Lee and Kyo C. Kang

Department of Computer Science and Engineering
Pohang University of Science and Technology (POSTECH), PIRL
31 San, Hyoja-Dong, Pohang, Kyoung-buk, Republic of Korea
{gibman,kck}@postech.ac.kr
http://selab.postech.ac.kr

Abstract. Feature analysis, which provides commonality and variability information of a product line, is essential for product line asset development. Moreover, feature binding information (i.e., when and how product features are included to products and delivered to customers) also drives product line component design. Feature binding can be examined from three perspectives: what
features are bound (feature binding unit), when features are bound (feature
binding time), and how features are bound (feature binding techniques), and
this information must be made available to component design so that composition of components for feature binding becomes feasible. In this paper, we introduce an approach to analyzing feature binding from the three perspectives
(i.e., what, when, and how) and illustrate how the analysis results can be used
for component development of a product line.

1 Introduction

Feature analysis, which provides commonality and variability information of a product line, is essential for product line asset development [1], [2], [3], [4]. This information is not, however, sufficient for product line component development. Feature
binding information (i.e., when and how features are included to products and delivered to customers) also drives product line component design. For instance, a set of
features may be built into product line assets at product line asset development time,
some of which may be made available for customers to select at installation time of a
product. Therefore, when and how features will be bound to products should be analyzed thoroughly, and this information must be made available to component design.

Feature binding can be examined from three perspectives: what features are bound
(feature binding units), when features are bound (feature binding time), and how
features are bound (feature binding techniques). When a feature is bound to a product, there exists a set of features that need to be together for correct operation of the
product. These sets (i.e., 'binding units') are the units of commonality and variability,
and they should be used to identify variation points so that composition of components for feature binding becomes feasible.

F. van der Linden (Ed.): PFE 2003, LNCS 3014, pp. 250–260, 2004.

The decision of when feature binding should occur (i.e., 'binding time') also affects component design. For instance, when features need to be selected at the installation time, load table technique may be used for component design. Therefore, components must be designed to allow binding of features at the time they are required.

Selection of 'binding techniques' should be made with consideration of required binding time and quality requirements (e.g., flexibility, performance, development cost, etc.). When the available memory space is limited, for instance, dynamic binding techniques may be used to load and execute only the required features in the memory.

In this paper, we introduce an approach to analyzing feature binding from the three perspectives and illustrate how the analysis result can be used to develop components for a product line. A home integration system (HIS) product line, which controls and manages a collection of devices to maintain security and safety of a building or a house, is used to demonstrate the concept. HIS generally includes the features in the table below. More advanced products may include features, such as climate control and lighting, that optimize living conditions.

Table 1. Product Features of a HIS product line.

Product Feature	Explanation
fire detection & control	Fire events are detected by monitoring smoke detectors and heat sensors installed in the house. When a fire event is detected, HIS turns the alarm and all sprinklers on and unlocks all HIS-controlled doors. HIS also sends a pre-recorded voice message to the fire station and the owner over the telephone line to inform them of the incident. Once the fire is under control, the alarm and all sprinklers will be turned off but doors will remain unlocked for the duration of time preset by the owner.
intrusion detection & control	Intrusion events are detected by monitoring motion sensors. When an intrusion event is detected, HIS turns the alarm on and locks all HIS-controlled doors. Also, HIS sends a voice message to the police station and the owner.
flood detection & control	Flood events are detected by monitoring moisture sensors. When a flood event is detected, HIS shuts off the water main of the house. When moisture is detected on the basement floor, the sump pump will be activated.
security	The entrance and exit of all personnel are verified and recorded with identification information (e.g., name, time, ID number, etc.). There are various devices for the verification such as fingerprint recognition, voice recognition, etc. Also, the access to every room inside a building can be controlled by each person's job function.

The following section introduces an approach to feature binding analysis, and product line component development based on the analysis results is demonstrated in section 3. Section 4 concludes this paper with discussions.

2 Feature Binding Analysis

The primary input to feature binding analysis is a feature model, which captures commonality and variability of a product line in terms of features. Fig. 1 shows a feature model of the HIS product line. Capability features of HIS consist of service features (e.g., *Intrusion, Fire, Flood*, etc.) and operational features (e.g., *Alarm, Pumping,* etc.). Operating environment features of HIS include *Moisture Sensor* and *Sump*

Sump Pump, and domain technology features include technical features (e.g., *Monitoring & Detecting*) for implementing service and operational features. Compared with domain technology features, implementation technique features are more generic and might be applicable to other product lines (e.g., the *TCP* and *UDP* features are used to provide an Internet connection in the HIS product line, but they can also be used in an electronic bulletin board product line.). Details of feature analysis and guidelines can be found in [5].

In the following sections, each of the perspectives on feature binding is discussed.

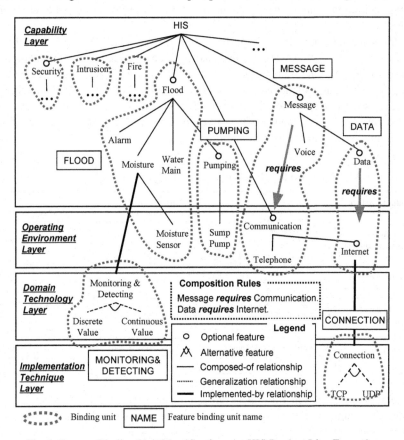

Fig. 1. Feature Binding Unit Identification: An HIS Product Line Example.

2.1 Feature Binding Unit Analysis

We define a feature binding unit as a set of features that are related to each other via composed-of, generalization/specialization, and implemented-by relationships and composition rules (i.e., require and mutually exclude) in a feature model. Features that belong to a same binding unit work for a common service and, therefore, they have to exist together for correct operation of the service.

Feature binding unit identification starts with identification of independently configurable service features. (For short, we will call these features as service features in the remainder of this paper.) A service feature represents a major functionality of a system and may be added or removed as a service unit. In HIS, *Flood*, *Fire*, and *Intrusion* features are examples of service features.

A service feature uses other features (e.g., operational, environmental, and implementation features) to function properly and the constituents of a binding unit can be found by traversing the feature model along the feature relationships and composition rules. For example, as we start from the *Flood* service feature, *Alarm, Moisture, Water Main, Pumping, Moisture Sensor, Sump Pump*, and *Monitoring & Detecting* features can be identified. All these feature are needed to provide the flood service.

Within a feature binding unit, there may exist optional or alternative features that should be selected based on customer's needs. These features impose variations on the component design and, therefore, they have to be identified as separate feature binding units. For example, only one of the sub-features of *Monitoring & Detecting* can be selected based on the device type that a customer may choose. (See the *Monitoring & Detecting* feature at the domain technology layer in Fig. 1.)

Note that the *Communication* feature is included in the *MESSAGE* feature binding unit, although the feature type is optional. This is because the *Message* feature requires the *Communication* feature according to the composition rule, and they have to be together to provide the message service properly. (See the arrows for the 'require' composition rule in Fig. 1.) After all feature binding units are identified, a name is assigned to each feature binding unit; the feature name that represents a binding unit was given to the corresponding feature binding unit but the name was written in upper case letters to distinguish it from the name of the feature. (See the dotted circles and the names of binding units in Fig. 1.) Once features are grouped into feature binding units, a binding time analysis is performed for the feature binding units.

2.2 Feature Binding Time Analysis

Generally, feature binding time has been looked at from the software development lifecycle viewpoint ('product lifecycle view') [3], [6], in which the focus has been given to at which phase of the lifecycle a feature is incorporated into a product. In product line engineering, however, there exists another dimension that is based on the *binding state* of a feature binding unit. That is, some feature binding units may be developed and included in product line assets at asset development time, but their availability can be determined at installation time by enabling or disabling the feature binding units. Furthermore, activation of the available feature binding units may be controlled to avoid a feature interaction problem[1]. Thus, feature binding time analysis with additional view on *feature binding state* (which includes *inclusion* and *availability* states and *activation rules*) provides a more precise framework for feature binding analysis.

---

[1] The problem of unexpected side effects when a feature is added to a set of features is generally known as the feature interaction problem.

The 'product lifecycle view' consists of four phases: asset development, product development, pre-operation, and operation. After product line assets are developed, a product is developed with product specific features and the assets. Then, the product is delivered, installed, and configured for a customer during the pre-operation phase.

Each phase of the product lifecycle shows the binding states of feature binding units. For example, if the inclusion and availability states of a feature binding unit are determined during product line asset development, the feature binding unit is allocated to both the inclusion and availability columns of the asset development phase. (See the *FIRE* and *INTRUSION* feature binding units in the bottom row in Fig. 2.) If the inclusion state of a feature binding unit is determined during product development and the availability state of the feature binding unit is determined during installation, the feature binding unit is allocated to the inclusion column of the product development phase and also to the availability column of the pre-operation phase. (*FLOOD* and *MESSAGE* are examples of such feature binding units.)

In the 'feature binding state view,' the inclusion feature binding state indicates when, in the product lifecycle phases, a feature binding unit is physically included in a product, and the availability binding state indicates when, in the product lifecycle phases, those included feature binding units become available to users (i.e., the feature binding unit is ready for use with all its implementation techniques are bound). Once the feature binding unit becomes available, it is now ready to be activated, as long as it abides by the activation rules among feature binding units. (See the horizontal axis in Fig. 2.)

Product Lifecycle View

	Inclusion	Availability	Activation rule
Operation	PUMPING	PUMPING	
Pre-operation (Installation)		FLOOD, MESSAGE, DATA, CONNECTION, MONITORING& DETECTING	• MESSAGE *requires* INTRUSION, FIRE, or FLOOD activated.
Product development	FLOOD, MESSAGE, DATA, SECURITY, CONNECTION	SECURITY	• FIRE *has higher priority than* FLOOD. • FIRE *has higher priority than* INTRUSION.
Asset development	FIRE, INTRUSION, MONITORING& DETECTING	FIRE, INTRUSION	

Inclusion   *Availability*   *Activation rule*   **Feature Binding State View**

Fig. 2. Feature Binding Time Analysis.

The activation rules provide information on concurrency of feature binding unit activation and they are defined in terms of mutual exclusion, dependency, and priority schemes. As an intuitive example, room temperature can be kept stable by turning on both an air-conditioner and a heater at the same time, but this is not a desirable behavior. Their activation rule should be 'mutual exclusion' to avoid such situation.

One of the major drivers for binding time decision is the feature delivery method determined during market analysis [4]. Some features may be pre-packaged in all products as 'standard features,' while others may be selected from a list at pre-operation time. For example, *FIRE* would be pre-packaged in all products and, therefore, it should be included and made available at the asset development phase. On the other hand, *MESSAGE* has high cost implications and its type was determined to be optional. Though the feature is included in a product at the product development phase, its availability is determined at the pre-operation phase after a salesman negotiates with customers over the product price (See the second column at Fig. 2.).

Next section illustrates how the feature binding analysis results can be used for product line component development.

3 Product Line Component Development

The primary inputs to component development include a feature model, feature binding unit and binding time analysis results, and a design object model[2]. Design objects are embodiment of functionalities required for the product line. Once a design object model is defined, these objects in the model are allocated to concrete components for implementation. In this section, identification of variation points in the design object model, exploration of binding techniques, and specification of product line components are illustrated with examples.

3.1 Variation Point Identification

For feature binding to be feasible, variation points for optional and alternative binding units should be identified in the design object model. Since features within a binding unit should exist together, their binding to a product should be explicitly identified in the design object model. We also need to be sure that all objects that implement the features of a binding unit are bound together with appropriate implementation techniques. For example, when the *FLOOD* binding unit is incorporated into a product and becomes available, the objects that implement each of its constituting features (i.e., *Moisture, Moisture Sensor*, and *Alarm*) should also be bound in the product for correct operation of *FLOOD*.

To manage variation points for a binding unit consistently, explicit mapping between binding units and variation points should be established. If there is difficulty establishing this relationship, the related objects should be examined for further decomposition, refinement, or restructuring. If a binding unit is optional and its parent binding unit is also optional, its binding requires the parent binding unit be bound beforehand, and this dependency should also be preserved among variation points in

---

[2] A feature-based approach to object-oriented development can be found in [7].

the object model. For example, *FLOOD* should be bound in advance for the binding of *PUMPING*. This dependency is preserved in the object model, as the variation point of *FloodResponder* object is located at the lower level than the variation point of *EventResponder* object in the aggregation hierarchy. (See Fig. 3.)

In Fig. 3, each bubble represents an optional or alternative binding unit and arrows show the corresponding variation points (denoted by ■) identified in the object model. For example, the variation point for *FLOOD* is identified at the end of the line connecting *EventResponder* and *FloodResponder* objects for an aggregation relationship. That is, if *FLOOD* is determined not to be available in a product at pre-operation time (See Fig. 2.), then the aggregation relation between the two objects is removed, and the objects that implement the *FLOOD* binding unit are not accessible by users. After the variation points are identified, implementation techniques for feature binding should be explored.

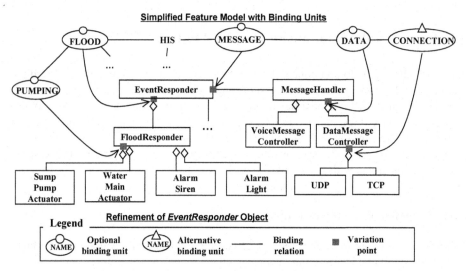

Fig. 3. Mapping between Binding Units and Variation Points in the Design Object Model.

3.2   Feature Binding Technique Exploration

Selection of binding techniques depends both on binding time and quality attributes (e.g., flexibility) required for products. Delaying binding time to a later phase of the lifecycle may provide more flexibility, but applicable implementation techniques are limited and they usually require more performance overheads. Therefore, guidelines for the selection of feature binding techniques are required to help asset developers make decisions properly.

For that purpose, we propose a classification of feature binding techniques based on the feature binding states: binding techniques for the feature 'inclusion' and for the feature 'availability.' Techniques belonging to the former class should be able to control feature inclusion by including or excluding code segments or components from products. Code generation, pre-processing, macro processing [8], ICD (Internet Component Download) [9] are some examples of this class. These techniques allow products to include multiple features physically but their availability can be determined at a later phase. (See the left two columns in Fig. 2.).

The second class of techniques provides mechanisms for enabling or disabling accesses to features. Load tables and authentication based access control [10] are techniques belong to this class. In the HIS product line, for instance, the load table technique is used to determine the availability of *FLOOD*, *DATA*, etc. at the pre-operation phase. When the system starts to execute, it refers to the load table to determine which features should be made available to the user.

In addition to those techniques belonging to the two classes, we should also explore techniques for dynamic or static binding of features. While some features may be bound statically, other features may require dynamic binding for flexibility or memory space efficiency. Dynamic binding of objects, menus, and plug-ins [11] are techniques belong to this class. For example, *PUMPING* is bound at the operation time, as its device drivers for sump pumps may vary.

In the following section, an implementation of the HIS example is illustrated.

3.3   Component Specification

Next, we refine the design object model into concrete components with the selected feature binding techniques. Product line component design consists of specifications of components and relationships among them. (See Fig. 4 for the specifications of the *EventResponder* and *FloodResponder* components.)

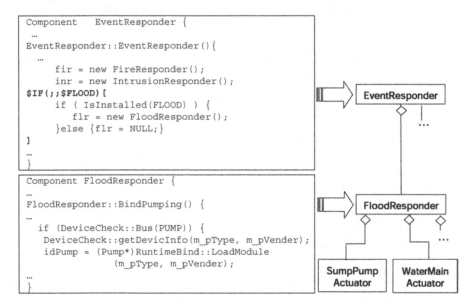

Fig. 4. Component Specifications of *EventResponder* and *FloodResponder* for Feature Binding.

For the product development time inclusion of *FLOOD*, the macro language (i.e., IF(;;$FLOOD) [...]) is used, and for the pre-operation time availability, the load table is used. Instantiation of the *FloodResponder* depends on the return value of IsInstalled(FLOOD), which confirms whether or not *FLOOD* is allowed to be made available. (See the left upper part of Fig. 4.)

Once a customer is authorized to use *PUMPING* at operation time (See the operation time row at Fig. 2.), the FloodResponder::BindPumping method of the *FloodResponder* is invoked. Then, it searches for an appropriate device driver for the installed sump pump type and binds it to provide the pumping service. (See the left lower part of Fig. 4.)

One of the ways the feature activation rules can be handled is to define a policy or policies (e.g., event priority) for preventing incorrect behaviors from occurring, and there could be many design alternatives for enforcing these policies. One design approach could be to have a policy-hiding component that manages priorities among features.

For example, the policies for handling feature activation rules among the *FIRE*, *INTRUSION*, and *FLOOD* are specified using Statechart. We specified two different Statecharts (i.e., one for the priority specification with FLOOD and the other for the priority specification without FLOOD) and from which program codes are generated after verification, and then the generated codes are allocated to *EventDNMDriver-WithFlood* and *EventDNMDriverWithoutFlood*, respectively. Depending upon the availability of *FLOOD*, one of them is instantiated as shown in Fig. 5. We also adapted the Observer pattern [11] to maintain the global state information consistently among event detecting components. The global state information is maintained by the *EventDNMDriver* component and, whenever the global state is changed, the updated state is informed to all local components (i.e., detectors). (See the association between *EventDNMDriver* and *Detector* in Fig. 5.)

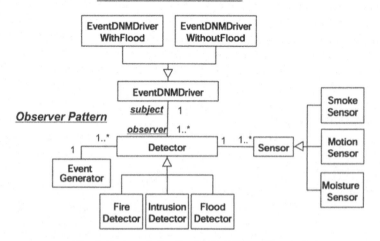

Fig. 5. Feature Activation Policy Hiding Component.

4 Conclusions

Engineering product line components to accommodate decisions of what, when, and how features are included to products and delivered to customers is one of the challenges that are different from those in single application development. A product line may be targeted for more than one market segment and each market segment may require a unique set of features, and/or a certain feature binding time and feature binding techniques that are different from others. Therefore, product line components must be designed with consideration of not only the commonalities and variabilities of a product line, but also the feature binding requirements.

In this paper, we introduce an approach to feature binding analysis and illustrate how the analysis results can be used for product line component development. During feature binding analysis, feature binding units are identified and feature binding time is determined with consideration of feature activation rules and market needs. With the analysis results, variation points are identified in a design object model and binding techniques are explored based on feature binding time.

We found that explicit identification of feature binding units, and binding time decisions with views on product line lifecycle and feature binding states clarified requirements for feature binding. It should be noted that binding time itself might also change. Changeability of binding time needs to be explored and be incorporated into product line development. The explicit identification of feature binding unit and time was essential for identifying and managing consistency among variation points, and selecting appropriate binding techniques.

Our future work includes a technical evaluation of binding techniques from quality perspectives, and we hope that this research will lead us to develop guidelines for selecting feature binding techniques.

References

1. Bosch, J.: Design & Use of Software Architectures. Addison-Wesley and ACM Press (2000).
2. Coplien, J., Hoffman, Daniel, Weiss, D.: Commonality and Variability in Software Engineering. IEEE Software, 15(6), November/December (1998) 37-45.
3. Czarnecki, K, Eisenecker, U.: Generative Programming: Methods, Tools, and Applications, Reading, MA: Addison Wesley Longman, Inc. (2000).
4. Kang, K., Lee, J., Donohoe, P.: Feature-Oriented Product Line Engineering. IEEE Software, 19(4), July/August (2002) 58-65.
5. Lee, K., Kang, K., Lee, J.: Concepts and Guidelines of Feature Modeling for Product Line Software Engineering. In: Gacek, C. (eds.): Software Reuse: Methods, Techniques, and Tools. Lecture Notes in Computer Science, Vol. 2319. Springer-Verlag, Berlin Heidelberg (2002) 62-77.
6. Bosch, J., Florijn, G., Greefhorst, D., Kuusela, J., Obbink, J. H., Pohl, K.: Variability Issues in Software Product Lines. In: van der Linden, F. (eds.): Software Product Family Engineering. Lecture Notes in Computer Science, Vol. 2290. Springer-Verlag, Berlin Heidelberg (2002) 13-21.

7. Lee, K., Kang, K., Chae, W., Choi, B.: Feature-Based Approach to Object-Oriented Engineering of Applications for Reuse. Software Practice and Experience, **30**(9) (2000) 1025-1046.

8. Basset, P. G.: Framing Software Reuse: Lessons From The Real World. Prentice Hall, Yourdon Press (1997).

9. Microsoft Developers Network (MSDN), Introduction to Internet Component Download (ICD), http://msdn.microsoft.com/workshop/delivery/download/overview/entry.asp.

10. Sun Microsystems, Inc., Java Authentication and Authorization Service (JAAS), http://java.sun.com/security/jaas/doc/api.html.

11. Gamma, E., Helm, R., Johnson, R., Vlissides, J.: Design Patterns: Elements of Reusable Object-Oriented Software. MA: Addison Wesley Longman, Inc. (1995).

Patterns in Product Family Architecture Design

Svein Hallsteinsen, Tor Erlend Fægri, and Magne Syrstad

SINTEF Telecom and informatics, N-7465 Trondheim, Norway
{svein.hallsteinsen,tor.e.fegri,magne.syrstad}@sintef.no

Abstract. The common architecture is a central asset of a product family. But in many cases variations in quality requirements between family members make it difficult to standardise architectural solutions across the family. Therefore the common architecture has to support variation. In this paper we propose an approach to product family architecture design, modelling and use based on architecture patterns and their relationship to quality attributes that supports the representation of an open architecture and the specialisation of this architecture to meet product specific quality requirements.

1 Introduction

The common software architecture is a central asset of any software product family [2,6]. Primarily it is the quality requirements and the anticipated execution environment that dictate the design of the architecture. In very homogeneous product families the idea of a common architecture is unproblematic. Although the functionality may vary considerably between member applications, the applications have very similar quality requirements and common architectural solutions are viable.

However, in our work with introducing product family engineering in software companies developing and delivering information systems of various sorts packaged as standard products, we often see the need for more heterogeneous product families. Here, the quality requirements and the anticipated execution environment vary considerably between member applications and the common architecture has to allow for different architectural choices in different applications.

One way to cope with this is to simply leave the architecture open (i.e. underspecified) on the points where the variation in requirements makes it impossible to standardise architectural decisions. This approach has the drawback that it becomes more difficult to identify and build common components reusable across all family members while it also complicates the derivation of member products by transferring difficult architectural decisions to the product derivation process.

In this paper we propose an approach to representing open architectures that seek to alleviate these drawbacks by encoding more explicitly foreseen variations in quality requirements and decision support for specialising the architecture for a given set of specific quality requirements. The approach is based on the following three main elements:

- use of patterns as architectural building blocks;
- use of variation points to make explicit the allowed variation in the composition of patterns for a given architecture;

F. van der Linden (Ed.): PFE 2003, LNCS 3014, pp. 261–268, 2004.

- guidelines for the resolution of variation points based on knowledge of the effect of using a pattern in an architecture on quality properties of applications built according to this architecture.

The paper is organised as follows: Section 2 introduces patterns, quality models and decision models as tools for modelling product family architectures. Section 3 explains how concrete product architectures can be derived. Section 4 gives a summary of how our approach has been validated in industry, section 5 contains a discussion of related work and section 6 presents initial conclusions and suggestions for future work.

2   Modelling Open Product Family Architectures

The architecture of a product family has both a prescriptive and a descriptive purpose. Here we focus on the prescriptive aspect, which is to constrain and alleviate the task of the application designers by providing a template for application design. It does this by standardising solutions to design problems recurring across the members of the product family.

Patterns as building blocks. Defining solutions to recurring problems is exactly what patterns are about, so therefore patterns form natural building blocks for architectures[1]. Moreover, established patterns often have known effects on quality attributes [7] making it possible to reason about the effect of choosing one pattern over another. Thus the backbone of our architecture model is a pattern language encompassing the recommended patterns and relevant relations between them. These are uses (one pattern uses another pattern in its solution), specialises (one pattern is a specialisation of another) and conflicts (two patterns cannot be used together).

We are using the tem pattern in a rather broad sense, meaning any problem solution pair recommended by the architecture either generally or to meet particular quality requirements. This means that the pattern language may contain both established patterns widely known an used throughout the software community, and "local" pattern particular to the product family. In the latter case some may argue that this is not a proper use of the term pattern, since we are talking about a local invention. However, as long as we are talking about a recurring problem within the product family and a solution prescribed by the architecture, and the architect has an idea about how it influences the quality properties of the derived products, we prefer to call it a pattern.

Encoding architectural variation. We divide the pattern language into two parts, the base part and the varying part. The base part contains the enforced patterns, the ones that all applications must use. The varying part contains patterns that an application may choose to use or not.

The varying part is organised into variation points. There are two kinds of variation points: optional patterns and alternative patterns. An optional pattern is one that may be included in an application architecture or not. Alternative patterns is a group of

---

[1] In this paper we do not distinguish patterns and styles. Styles we understand as high level patterns with a strong overall organising effect on a system.

patterns basically solving the same problem (often they are alternative specialisations of a more abstract pattern), but in different ways and with different effects on achievable quality attributes, and where the application programmer can choose the one that best fits the requirements of the application.

Decision support. The specialisation of the architecture for a given set of quality attributes is supported by a set of design guidelines. We have adopted the ISO 9126 standard as the basis for modelling quality but with the possibility to break down the quality attributes defined in the standard into more detailed ones. Scenarios are used to link quality attributes and patterns in the design guidelines. A scenario describes a typical requirement related to one or more quality attributes and is also related to one or more patterns in the pattern language promising to achieve that requirement. Constructed as stimulus-response pairs, scenarios are effective instruments for reasoning about the effect of patterns on quality attributes. A pattern may contribute to satisfy multiple quality attributes, and the same quality attribute may be affected by multiple patterns. More importantly, quality attributes influence each other through the choice of patterns used in the architecture. For example, a pattern may have a positive impact on performance but may affect maintainability negatively.

The design guidelines are organised into variation points in a similar way to the variable part of the pattern language, with optional scenarios and alternative scenarios. Table 1 below illustrates a decision guideline dealing with variation in the handling of changes in the quality in the client-server connection: If the user of the application requires continued service in the case of communication failures of the client server connection, the architecture should be based upon the self reliant client pattern. However, if continuous service is not required, the rich or thin client pattern may be used.

Table 1. Example decision guideline.

Variation in client-server connection availability		Pattern	Affects quality attributes
Stimulus	Responses		
Communication failure between client and server	Denial of service	Thin client	Fault tolerance Recoverability
	Partial service	Rich client	
	Continued service	Self reliant client	

Components. Patterns define roles and collaboration between roles. In a system designed and implemented according to a set of patterns these roles are filled by component implementations. Normally a component plays a role in more than one pattern.

In the architecture we also include component specifications which are defined by the synthesis of a set of roles from different patterns and possibly also collaboration models related to the functionality of the system. Consider for instance a business component in a layered architecture with stateless serverside business components. The patterns involved are layering with a business component layer, and stateless components. The business component has a role in the layering pattern, in the stateless component pattern and in one or more use case related scenarios defining the business services provided by the component.

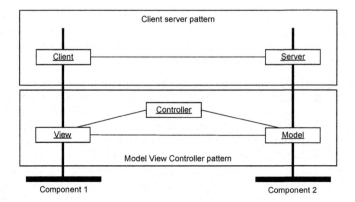

Fig. 1. Components playing different roles.

Figure 1 above illustrates how components may play different roles in a given instantiation of the architecture. One component plays the role of a *client* in one pattern and the role of a *view* in another etc. The *controller* role in the figure may be played by either component 1 or component 2.

In summary, Figure 2 below illustrates our open architecture reference model. The use and applicability of the model will be discussed in the following sections.

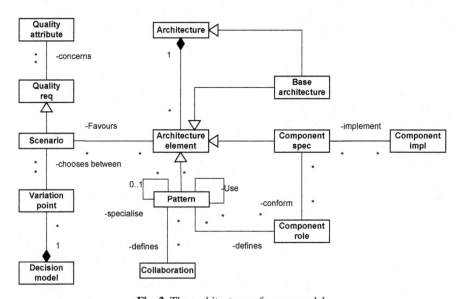

Fig. 2. The architecture reference model.

3 Deriving Family Member Architectures

Using the open architecture to support application architecture design involves the following steps:

- First specialise the quality model by resolving the variation points in light of the particular quality requirements of the application. For each optional scenarios decide whether it is relevant or not. For each group of alternative scenarios select the one that best fits the needs of the application.
- Then use the decision model to select patterns from the family pattern language that fits the specialised quality model. The scenarios specified by the quality model match scenarios labelling design rules in the decision model which point to patterns promising to contribute to satisfying the scenario. Together with the base part of the family architecture the selected patterns form the pattern language of the application.
- Finally select component specifications that matches the specialised pattern language.

Since patterns normally affect more than one quality attribute there may be tradeoff situations. The priorities of the scenarios may help to resolve such situations.

4 Validation

The method to modelling product family architectures that we have described in the preceding sections is being validated and refined through our long-term collaboration with Norwegian software companies. Most of them are SMEs, developing products within the distributed information systems category. The pressure to deliver more products, at lower costs and within shorter time-frames enforces them maximise the value of their investments in developing software assets. All of the companies we have worked with show a strong overall commitment to adopt product family engineering practices in order to accomplish this. However, the maturity of the adoption vary.

We have developed a reference architecture for the construction of product family for information systems with particular requirements in the area of client device adaptivity. We validated the reference architecture on real-world product family efforts by performing numerous architecture evaluations at the companies (in form inspired by the ATAM[SM] and ARID[SM] methods [3]). In summary, we have gained confidence that our approach is both useful and effective. The obtained results have been used to refine and validate our quality models, the pattern language and the decision model. Most importantly, these architecture evaluations have shown that the different companies' product families can be captured and modelled by our reference architecture.

The experience for these architecture evaluation exercises has convinced us that using patterns or pattern like constructs as building blocks of architectures is a good idea. During the evaluations we have identified patterns used in the architectures and related them to quality properties of the product family. This form of architectural documentation, which normally did not exist on beforehand was generally very well received both by the architects and the developers.

As an example we consider variation in terms of client device adaptivity. A recurring variation point observed among the companies is variability in deployment models. On one hand, the benefits of low-cost client deployment as exemplified by web-based clients, promote server-centric products architectures. On the other hand, rich user interfaces that exploit the resources on powerful PCs, are popular among users that use the software for longer periods of time or are periodically disconnected from the network. Thus, software architectures that can support this variability are needed.

These requirements have been incorporated into the quality model, the pattern language and the decision model (please refer to section 2 for descriptions). The quality model included with our reference architecture covers these aspects of variability. The underlying decision model associates these quality attributes with a set of patterns. Figure 3 below is an example from our pattern language that includes patterns that are mainly concerned with variability in deployment models. The dotted arrows denote specialisation relationships. When a pattern specialises multiple other patterns, we refer to patterns that include and specialise aspects from multiple other patterns.

Presumably, most of these patterns are well-known to the reader [4,5]. The patterns that have been identified and added to our pattern language are *anyside component* and *adapting client*. As the name implies, the first pattern denotes components that are deployable on either the client or the server machine.

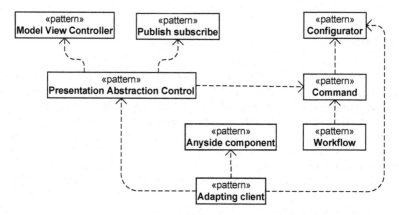

Fig. 3. Pattern language example (adaptivity qualities).

The latter denotes a client device that is able to dynamically adapt to context changes through configuration changes (see e.g. [9] for scenario descriptions). Both patterns are documented in [1]. The anyside component pattern, likely to be stateless for scalability at the server side, appear to be a viable solution to some of these requirements and is already being investigated. The adapting client pattern is more involved, but promise to address additional adaptivity qualities.

5   Related Work

Philips, as one of the early adopters of product family engineering practices in Europe, has gathered a large amount of knowledge and experience within the area of platform based software development. Of particular relevance to our work are efforts related to product populations [12]. Product populations seeks to address the problem of increasing levels of complexity and scale in software product development by advocating and controlling reuse of assets between product families. The approach to architecture design presented in this paper can be used to address variability management in product populations.

Work done at SEI on ABASs [11] and later within the ADD method [7], is based on similar assumptions to ours. For example, that certain quality properties can be associated with architectural patterns. Additionally, we have drawn upon existing validation techniques from SEI, such as ATAM[SM] and ARID[SM] [3].

The OOram method, developed by T. Reenskaug et.al. [10], advocates the use of role models and derivation of object specifications by role synthesis. This has inspired our ideas on component roles and the derivation of component specifications based on role synthesis.

6 Conclusions and Future Work

We have argued that in product families significant variation in quality requirements is often the case, and that this requires variation also in the family architecture. Just leaving the architecture unspecified on the points where applications must be allowed to make own architectural decisions is not a satisfactory solution as it leaves too much to application programming. Using patterns as architectural building blocks, and encoding the relationship between quality attributes and optional or alternative patterns in the architecture, we have proposed a way to represent family architectures that allows for variability while retaining strong design support for application development.

So far our approach has been used to represent a reference architecture for information systems intended to provide services over the internet and having to cope with variations in user context and the capabilities of network connections and client devices. This exercise has provided promising experience with the quality models, decision models and patterns as a vehicle to encode architecture design support. During the development of the reference architecture we evaluated several real life family architectures to collect requirements and validate our results. The findings of these evaluations also supported our assumption that family architectures in this domain must embed variation.

Now we are about to embark on validating the proposed approach on the modelling of product family architectures where we will also need to model the implementation framework supporting the architecture. This will give us the opportunity to test also the derivation of component specifications and their relation to implemented framework components in the context of a family architecture embedding variation.

Acknowledgements

The work reported here has been carried out in the context of the Café[2] and DAIM[3] projects. The collaboration with both academic and industrial partners in these projects has provided valuable inspiration and feedback to our work.

---

[2] ITEA project ip00004, Café.
[3] Norwegian technology development project led by ICT-Norway and partially funded by the Norwegian research council.

References

1. DAIM Software Engineering Handbook. Available through ICT-Norway 2003 (www.ikt-norge.no).
2. Jan Bosch. Design and Use of Software Architectures - Adopting and Evolving a Product-Line Approach. Addison-Wesley, 2000.
3. Paul Clements, Rick Kazman, Mark Klein. Evaluating Software Architectures: Methods and case studies, Addison Wesley, 2002.
4. Frank Buschmann, Regine Meunier, Hans Rohnert, Peter Sommerland, and Michael Stal. Pattern-Oriented Software Architecture - A system of Patterns, Wiley, 1996.
5. Douglas Schmidt, Michael Stal, Hans Rohnert, and Frank Buschmann. Pattern-Oriented Software Architecture Volume 2 – Patterns for Concurrent and Networked Objects, Wiley, 2001.
6. Mehdi Jazayeri, Alexander Ran, Frank Van Der Linden. Software Architecture for Product Families: Principles and Practice. Addison Wesley, 2000.
7. Len Bass, Mark Klein, and Felix Bachmann. Quality Attribute Design Primitives and the Attribute Driven Design Method. 4th Intl. Workshop on Product Family Engineering, Bilbao, Spain, 2001.
8. Svein Hallsteinsen, Eric Swane. Handling the diversity of networked devices by means of a product family approach. 4th Intl. Workshop on Product Family Engineering, Bilbao, Spain, 2001.
9. Mehul Mehta, Nigel Drew, Chrostoph Nierdermeier. Reconfigurable terminals: An overview of Architectural Solutions. IEEE Communications Magazine, August 2001.
10. Trygve Reenskaug with Per Wold and Odd Arild Lehne. Working with objects – The Ooram software engineering method. Manning Publications, 1996.Rob van Ommering. Building product populations with software components. International Conference on Software Engineering 2002, Orlando 2002.
11. Mark Klein and Rick Kazman. Attribute-based architectural styles. SEI Technical report CMU/SEI-99-TR-022, 1999.
12. Rob van Ommering. Building product populations with software components. International Conference on Software Engineering 2002, Orlando 2002.

Differencing and Merging within an Evolving Product Line Architecture

Ping Chen, Matt Critchlow, Akash Garg, Chris Van der Westhuizen,
and André van der Hoek

Department of Information and Computer Science
University of California, Irvine
Irvine, CA 92697-3425 USA
{pchen,critchlm,agarg,cvanderw,andre}@ics.uci.edu

Abstract. Propagating changes from one place in a product line architecture to another is a difficult problem that occurs in a variety of settings. Currently, no automated tools exist that help an architect in doing so, and performing the task by hand in the face of a large product line architecture can be error-prone and difficult. To address this problem, we have built a set of tools for automating the process. Our approach breaks down into a two-step solution: (1) automatically determining the difference between two selected (versions of) a product architecture, and (2) automatically merging the difference back into a different location in the original product line architecture. In this paper, we detail each of these two steps and evaluate our solution on an example word processor product line architecture.

1 Introduction

Consider the following three scenarios that may occur in architecting a product line architecture:

1. A series of changes have been made to one particular variant of a subsystem. After the changes have been made, it turns out they are useful in some of the other variants as well. The architect now wishes to take the changes and apply them to those other variants [2].
2. In order to experiment with a new piece of functionality without interfering with the main line of development, the architect creates a new branch and implements the functionality on this branch first. It turns out that the functionality can be incorporated, and the architect now wishes to move the new functionality back into the main line of development [1].
3. To ensure accurate and responsive customer service, company policy requires a product architecture to be maintained independently from the main product line architecture after it has been deployed to a customer. During maintenance, however, the architect makes some changes to the individual product architecture that would benefit the overall product line architecture if they could be incorporated. The architect now wishes to move those changed back into the product line architecture [4].

F. van der Linden (Ed.): PFE 2003, LNCS 3014, pp. 269–281, 2004.
© Springer-Verlag Berlin Heidelberg 2004

A common concern throughout these scenarios is the need for the architect to be able to propagate a set of changes within the realm of a single product line architecture, e.g., from one place in the product line architecture to another. Although it is possible to do this by hand, it may not always be feasible (or desirable) when considering a product line architecture consisting of many inter-related products that each comprise a large set of components. In such cases, manually propagating changes is highly error-prone and labor-intensive.

In this paper, we describe our solution to this problem. Our approach centers on the use of differencing and merging techniques that are specific to product line architectures. In particular, we have designed and implemented two automated algorithms: (1) a differencing algorithm for determining the set of changes between two (versions of) a product architecture selected out of an overall product line architecture, and (2) a merging algorithm with which such changes are merged back into a different location in the product line architecture. The algorithms complement Ménage, our design environment for managing the evolution of product line architectures [8], and enhance it with automated support for propagating changes throughout an evolving product line architecture.

The remainder of this paper is organized as follows. Section 2 discusses our overall approach. Section 3 defines our representation for capturing an architectural difference and presents our differencing algorithm in detail. Section 4 describes the merging algorithm, and illustrates how it can be used to propagate changes throughout a product line architecture. Section 5 discusses our experience in using the algorithms. We conclude by briefly discussing related work in Section 6 and discussing future in Section 7.

2 Approach

Figure 1 illustrates our overall approach based on the third scenario discussed in the introduction. First, a product line architecture is precisely defined (for instance, by using Ménage [8]). This results in a product line architecture specification from which individual product architectures can then be selected for delivery to customers (PA

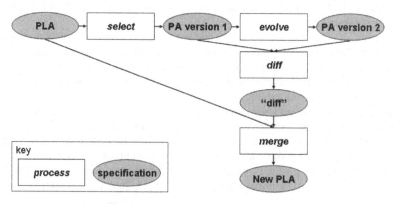

Fig. 1. Overall Process for Scenario 3.

version 1). Based on customer feedback, PA version 1 is changed and evolves into version 2, which is, once again delivered to the customer. The changes turn out to be useful to some parts of the original product line architecture as well, and now must be propagated into its specification. To do so, the architect first uses the differencing algorithm to precisely determine the changes that were made between PA versions 1 and 2. This results in an architectural "diff" file, which can then be merged back into the product line in a specified location, resulting in a new PLA that contains the new functionality.

We must make two observations regarding the process presented in Figure 1. First, similar processes can be defined for the other scenarios discussed in the introduction. Although the top line of process steps and specifications will be different, the same differencing and merging algorithms will be used in exactly the same way to propagate desired changes within the original product line architecture. The second observation regards the generality of the process: the algorithms are not limited to differencing and merging individual product architectures in which all variation points have been resolved. Instead, they fully support operation over specifications that still may contain "open" variation points.

In our previous work, we developed differencing and merging algorithms that operate on single software architectures [11]. These algorithms lay the basis for the algorithms we discuss here, but they also exhibit a number of shortcomings that make them unsuited for the context of product line architectures. In particular, they rely on identifiers to determine commonality; they do not handle type differences; they do not address hierarchical substructures; and they only operate at the level of components and connectors. In contrast, the algorithms we define in this paper adhere to the following objectives:

- *The algorithms do not rely on identifiers to establish commonality.* Different versions of a product line architecture will have parts that can be comprised of the same elements, but those elements must have different identifiers since they can evolve separately. As a result, our algorithms must based similarity on both the type and structure of elements.
- *The algorithms integrally address hierarchical substructure.* Virtually every product line architecture is composed in a hierarchical fashion; our algorithms should be able to handle differences at each level.
- *The algorithms are fine-grained.* In particular, the algorithms do not operate at the level of components as a whole, but are able to express subtle differences in component interfaces, differences in the way links connect components and connectors, and differences in mappings from high-level interfaces to interfaces in a substructure.

Overall, then, we take a highly semantic approach. Rather than applying semantically-neural differencing and merging algorithms [10], we wish to be able to operate and view changes in terms of architectural elements. Only then can an architect easily understand the context of the changes and apply the algorithms without having to make complex mental translations from changed lines of text to the actual architectural elements that they describe.

3 Differencing Product Line Architectures

The first step in our approach is to determine exactly which changes must be propagated. For this purpose, we constructed a representation for capturing the changes and implemented an algorithm for helping architects in automatically calculating the changes as a difference between two particular selections out of a product line architecture. Below, we discuss each in detail.

3.1 Difference Representation

Our existing work relies on the xADL 2.0 framework and infrastructure for representing and accessing product line architectures [5]. We have chosen to design our representation for differences as an extension of the framework. In particular, we have extended the set of XML schemas that define the xADL 2.0 language with a new schema for capturing architectural differences. Figure 2 presents the structure of this schema. The schema is defined as a recursive hierarchy of DIFFPART elements. Each DIFFPART corresponds to a level in the architecture and describes the set of changes to

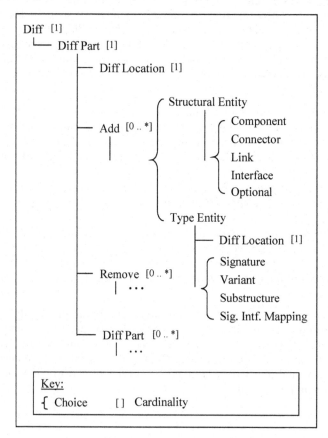

Fig. 2. Difference Representation.

that level as a set of additions of new elements, a set of removals of existing elements, and (as a series of lower-level DIFFPART elements) a set of changed elements.

Most of the representation is fairly straightforward, but we make the following observations regarding the schema. First, we note that additions are either structural in nature or type based. Structural changes represent changes to the structure of a component or connector type and determine the hierarchical composition of the type. For instance, the difference in the structure of a component type could state that it now includes an additional component and connector instance, as hooked up to the remainder of the internal elements of the original component type. Type-based differences concern the definition of a component or connector type, and include changes in its signatures (definitions of which functionality it provides), changes in its variation points (addition of new and removal of old variants), and changes in the mapping from its signatures to its internal component and connector instances. By separating structural changes from type-based changes, and capturing those changes in terms of detailed modifications, our representation achieves a fine-grained level of expressiveness that is semantically in sync with the remaining family of xADL 2.0 schemas to which it belongs.

The second observation pertains to the fact that each DIFFPART includes a DIFFLO-CATION to precisely identify the component or connector (type) to which the associated differences belong. This allows the representation to capture hierarchical changes, since each DIFFLOCATION identifies exactly which hierarchical part of a product line architecture it addresses. Note that a DIFFLOCATION is relative to the DIFFPART in which it is contained: this avoids having to use globally unique identifiers when differencing and merging product line architectures.

Finally, we observe that our representation supports the specification of changes in variation points. For instance, the "optional" that can be added or removed represents an optional element (with associated guard) in the product line architecture. Similarly, a "variant" represents a changing alternative in the product line architecture (again, with associated guard) [8].

3.2 Differencing Algorithm

A significantly simplified version of part of our differencing algorithm is presented in Figure 3. The algorithm takes as input the xADL 2.0 specifications of two product architectures that each may or may not have any variation points left (in essence, thus, the algorithm is able to difference complete product line architectures, although that is typically not a very useful operation). In addition, it takes as input a starting point for each specification. The starting point is necessary since it should be possible to generate the difference between parts of a product architecture, since one does not always want to have the complete difference. For instance, the feature that has to be propagated back into the product line architecture may be at a lower level in the architecture and some unwanted changes may have been made at a higher level in that same architecture. The starting point allows an architect to hone in on just the feature they want to propagate and ignore any of the other changes.

```
boolean diffComponents(Component[] origComps,
  Component[] newComps, DiffPart diffPart)
{
  boolean changed, tempChanged;
  for(i = 0;i < origComps.length; i++)
  {
    origDesc = getDescription(origComps[i]);
    for(j = 0;j < newComps.length;j++)
    {
      newDesc = getDescription(newComps[j]);
      // If there is a component with the same
      // name in both architectures
      if(origDesc == newDesc)
      {
        tempChange = diffInterfaces(
          getAllInterfaces(origComps[i]),
          getAllInterfaces(newComps[j]),
          diffPart );
        changed = tempChange || changed;

        // perform diff on the optionality guard
        tempChange = diffOptional(
          getOptional(origComps[i]),
          getOptional(newComps[j]), diffPart );
        changed = tempChange || changed;

        tempChanged = diffType(getType(origComps[i]),
          getType(newComps[j]), diffPart);
        changed = tempChange || changed;|
        break;
      }
    }
    // didn't find the original component in the new
    // architecture so it must have been removed
    if(j == newComps.length)
      removeComponent(origDesc, diffPart);
  }
  // Add any remaining elements that belong in the new
  // architecture but not in the original architecture
  AddNewElements( diffPart );
  return changed;
}
```

Fig. 3. Parts of Differencing Algorithm.

Note that a starting point is needed for both the original product architecture and the new product architecture. As part of the evolution of the product architecture, certain components may have been moved up or down to a different level. To be able to directly compare those elements a starting point is needed in each of the product architectures.

The difference algorithm operates by recursively iterating through all elements in the original architecture that are reachable from the starting point and comparing them with their corresponding elements in the new architecture. If an element does not exist in the new architecture, the element was removed and the diff will contain a remove instruction. Conversely, if an element exists in the new architecture that does not exist in the old architecture, an addition is entered into the diff. When an element exists in both the old and the new architecture, the algorithm compares the details of the elements to achieve a fine-grained diff. For example, when a component instance exists in both the old and new document, the difference algorithm verifies whether its interfaces are the same, whether or not its optionality is the same (and, if optional, whether it has the same Boolean guards governing its optionality), and whether it is of the same type. Only when all of these are exactly the same, the algorithm concludes that the component instance has not changed; otherwise, instructions are placed in the diff to account for the difference. The algorithm performs similar comparisons for all other elements.

3.3 Differencing Example

Figure 4 introduces a simple example word processor product line architecture that contains an optional component PRINT, a variant component SPELL CHECKER, and an optional variant component GRAMMAR CHECKER. The component USER INTERFACE also has a substructure that includes the components TOOLBAR AND DISPLAY. For simplicity and space reasons, the example ignores many details, such as, among others, connectors, interfaces, signatures, and various mappings of interfaces. It is noted, however, that the overall approach remains exactly the same.

In staying with scenario 3 as introduced in Section 1, imagine that the French product architecture is selected as shown in Figure 5. The product architecture includes the optional COMPONENT PRINT, but does not include a GRAMMAR CHECKER. Based upon customer request, the product architecture is modified to include functionality for viewing pictures; this required the addition of two new components: PICTURE DECODER and PICTURE DISPLAY (Figure 5). It is determined that it is useful to include this functionality in the other variants of the product architecture, necessitating a need to propagate the changes to the product line architecture shown in Figure 4. As a first step in this process, the architect uses our implementation of the differenc-

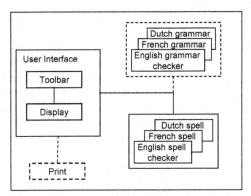

Fig. 4. Example PLA.

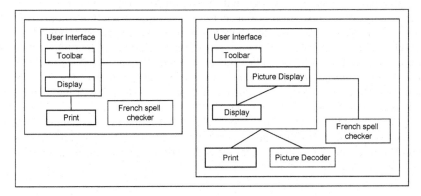

Fig. 5. Original and Evolved French Word Processor.

ing algorithm, resulting in a diff file. The diff file contains a root DIFFPART that contains two parts: the addition of the component PICTURE DECODER and another DIFF-PART, which contains the addition of the component PICTURE DISPLAY to the component USER INTERFACE.

4 Merging

Complementing the differencing algorithm is our merging algorithm. The merging algorithm propagates a set of changes as captured in a diff file into a particular part of a target product line architecture. As such, it takes the series of individual changes contained in the diff file and applies each instruction in turn. The result, assuming the merge is successful, is a new product line architecture in which the new functionality is now available.

Similar to the differencing algorithm, the merging algorithm takes as input a starting point that describes where in the target product line architecture the differences must be applied. Again, this allows selective merging into specific parts of the product line, as to not disturb other parts.

Parts of the merging algorithm are shown in Figure 6. It operates by iterating through the hierarchal instructions of a diff document and, at each step, adding all elements that need to be added and removing all elements that need to be removed. The algorithm does so by alternating over structural changes and type-level changes. This is inherent to the underlying xADL 2.0 representation for product line architectures. Since each structural element is typed, the algorithm ensures that it updates all necessary types when changes to a structural layer have been completed.

Clearly, due to the fine-grained nature of our algorithm, it is possible for conflicts to occur during the merging of changes. Among many others, it is possible that the algorithm attempts to remove a non-existing element, add an element that already exists, and add to a substructure that no longer exists. In such cases, the algorithm issues a warning message but continues the merging process. Our decision was to make a best-effort attempt rather than simply abandoning merging altogether; often, an architect will be able to correct merge problems relatively easily after the merging algorithm has completed its actions (but see our future work plans in Section 7).

To exemplify the operation of our merge algorithm, we apply it to the example of Figures 4 and 5. After determining the set of necessary changes using our differencing algorithm and merging those changes back into the original product line architecture, Figure 7 shows the resulting product line architecture. We note that the two new components (shown in bold) are available in each of the language variants of the product line architecture; any product architecture that is now selected will include the components PICTURE DISPLAY and PICTURE DECODER.

Again, we note that the example omits many of the fine-grained details concerning the operation of the algorithm. Space constraints prohibit us to show and discuss all of them. We refer the interested reader to the algorithms themselves, which are publicly available.

```
void mergeStructure(Structure structure, DiffPart diffPart)
{
    for(int i = 0; i < diffPart.getNumRemoves(); i++)
    {
        Remove remove = diffPart.getRemove(i);
        /* Check for all structural entities to remove such as
        Components, Connectors, Links, Interfaces, Signatures,
        SubArchitectures, Variants and Signature Interface
        Mappings */
        removeElements(structure, remove);
    }
    for(int i = 0; i < diffPart.getNumAdds(); i++)
    {
        Add add = diffPart.getAdd(i);
        /* Check for all structural entities to add such as
        Components, Connectors, Links, Interfaces, Signatures,
        SubArchitectures, Variants and
        SignatureInterfaceMappings */
        addElements(structure, add);
    }
    // For each DiffPart in diffPart merge into the correct
    // substructure or variant
    for(int i = 0; i < diffPart.getNumDiffParts(); i++)
    {
        Object ref =
        getTypeToMergeInto(diffPart.getDiffPartAt(i));
        Structure subArch = ref.getSubStructure();
        if(subArch == null)
            mergeType(ref.getType(), diffPart.getDiffPartAt(i));
        else
            mergeStructure(subArch, diffPart.getDiffPartAt(i));
    }
}

// this also deals with merging into variants
void mergeType(Type type, DiffPart diffPart)
{
    for(int i = 0; i < diffPart.getNumRemoves(); i++)
    {
        Remove remove = diffPart.getRemove(i);
        /* Check for all type entities to remove, such as:
        Signatures, SubArchitectures, Variants and
        SignatureInterfaceMappings */
        removeTypeElements(type, remove);
    }
    for(int i = 0; i < diffPart.getNumAdds(); i++)
    {
        Add add = diffPart.getAdd(i);
        /* Check for all type entities to add, such as:Signatures,
        SubArchitectures, Variants and SignatureInterfaceMappings
        */
        addTypeElements(type, add);
    }
    // For each DiffPart in diffPart merge into the correct
    // substructure or variant
    for(int i = 0; i < diffPart.getNumDiffParts(); i++)
    {
        Object ref =
        getTypeToMergeInto(diffPart.getDiffPartAt(i));
        Structure subArch = ref.getSubStructure();
        if(subArch == null)
            mergeType(ref.getType(), diffPart.getDiffPartAt(i));
        else
            mergeStructure(subArch, diffPart.getDiffPartAt(i));
    }
}
```

Fig. 6. Parts of Merge Algorithm.

5   Evaluation

We tested the functionality of our algorithms by running them on a product line architecture for a hypothetical entertainment system. The architecture contains 4 versions
of the entertainment system, each consisting of roughly 30 components and connectors with a maximum hierarchical depth of four levels; the architectural layout for the
entertainment system is shown as it appears in Ménage in Figure 8.

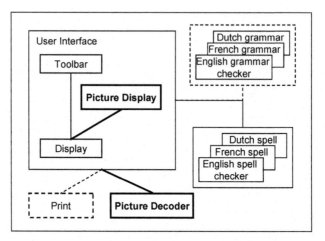

Fig. 7. Resulting PLA.

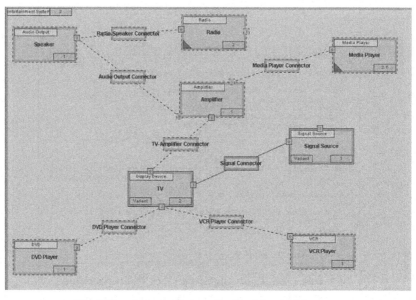

Fig. 8. Entertainment System Product Line Architecture.

The following example is based on the first scenario introduced in Section 1. Suppose an architect is working on the entertainment system product line architecture and decides to make enhancements to one of the DISPLAY DEVICE variants: the FLAT SCREEN DISPLAY. After making sufficient changes he realizes that these changes can be leveraged and used in the other type of display device: namely, the PLASMA DISPLAY.

Figure 9 illustrates the internal structure of the two DISPLAY DEVICE variants; it can be seen that the PLASMA DISPLAY component has no substructure whereas the FLAT SCREEN DISPLAY component contains an internal structure. He can then run the

Differencing tool on the two DISPLAY DEVICE variants and then propagate the set of changes to the PLASMA DISPLAY by means of the Merge tool. Figure 10 shows the resulting PLASMA DISPLAY after the merge process.

In this example the internal structure was propagated to only one other variant and the changes were seemingly small. This was done to illustrate the usefulness of the tools while keeping the example fairly small and understandable. However, one can imagine the convenience offered by these tools when the architectural change consists of hundreds of components to be propagated to many different product architectures.

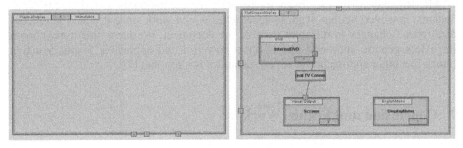

Fig. 9. Plasma Display (left) and Flat Screen Display (right).

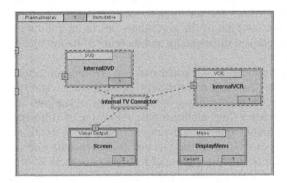

Fig. 10. Resulting Plasma Display.

Our tests lead to two critical observations. First, we note that our algorithms are efficient: both the differencing and merging algorithm run in polynomial time and scale up to large product line architectures. Second, we observed an interesting effect of the merging algorithm: it is possible for a merge to have hidden side-effects, namely when other parts of the product line architecture use the same elements that are being changed. While this problem may occur during "traditional" merging of code, it is far more likely to occur in product line architectures because of the high levels of reuse and sharing of types. We intend to upgrade our algorithms to issue a warning when this occurs, and intend to update our design environment (Ménage) with a process that will check out relevant elements such that side effects are avoided and impact is limited to individual branches only.

6 Related Work

Our approach differs from other methods of differencing and merging [3,6,9,10] in that it is semantic in nature. Our difference representation and algorithms are specifically designed to deal with product line architectures, and as such give us the distinct benefit of being able to difference and merge hierarchical structures at a fine-grained level. Other approaches are syntactic in nature and typically operate on text files [10]. At best, some semantics is built in, such as the differencing and merging tools for HTML [6] and XML [9]. Even though our representation is a xADL 2.0 XML Schema, however, neither of those approaches would work since it would not recognize related changes in different parts of the document. We have, therefore, chosen for a less generic approach that is more powerful and applicable to our situation (much like other approaches in which semantics is important [7]).

7 Conclusion and Future Work

The differencing and merging algorithms presented in this paper can accurately capture changes between different product architectures and propagate them back into the originating product line architecture. This provides automated support for deriving new product architectures that incorporate these changes – a property not present in previous work. The strength of the algorithms lies in their ability to handle, at a semantic level, fine-grained differencing and merging of hierarchically composed product line architectures.

The approach presented in this paper makes a positive contribution to the management of evolving product line architectures; however, it is clear that further research is necessary to explore related areas. While our approach allows for differencing and merging within product line architectures, the issue of differencing and merging across different product line architectures remains to be addressed. Moreover, we wish to create tools to visualize the process of differencing and merging to provide architects with support for detecting and resolving conflicts swiftly. Finally, we observe that our algorithms provide a particular form of architectural refactoring support. We intend to further explore this area in hopes of devising other, more advanced algorithms for this purpose.

Availability

Implementations of our algorithms can be downloaded from http://www.isr.uci.edu/-projects/archstudio/.

Acknowledgements

The authors thank Eric Dashofy for his valuable contributions to the development of this project. Effort funded by the National Science Foundation under grant numbers CCR-0093489 and IIS-0205724.

References

1. T. Asikainen, T. Soininen, and T. Männistö. *Towards Intelligent Support for Managing Evolution of Configurable Software Product Families.* Proceedings of the ICSE Workshops SCM 2001 and SCM 2003 Selected Papers, 2003: p. 86-101.
2. J. Bosch, *Design and Use of Software Architectures: Adopting and Evolving a Product-Line Approach.* Addison Wesley, 2000.
3. J. Buffenbarger. *Syntactic Software Merging.* Proceedings of the Software Configuration Management: ICSE SCM-4 and SCM-5 Workshops Selected Papers, 1995: p. 153-172.
4. P. Clements and L.M. Northrop, *Software Product Lines: Practices and Patterns.* Addison-Wesley, New York, New York, 2002.
5. E.M. Dashofy, A. van der Hoek, and R.N. Taylor. *An Infrastructure for the Rapid Development of XML-Based Architecture Description Languages.* Proceedings of the 24th International Conference on Software Engineering, 2002: p. 266-276.
6. F. Douglis, et al., *The AT&T Internet Difference Engine: Tracking and Viewing Changes on the Web.* World Wide Web Journal, 1998. 1(1): p. 27-44.
7. J. Estublier. *Defining and Supporting Concurrent Engineering Policies in SCM.* Proceedings of the Tenth International Workshop on Software Configuration Management, 2001.
8. A. Garg, et al. *An Environment for Managing Evolving Product Line Architectures.* Proceedings of the International Conference on Software Maintenance, 2003.
9. IBM, *XML Diff and Merge Tool,* http://www.alphaworks.ibm.com/tech/xmldiffmerge, 2002.
10. T. Mens, *A State-of-the-Art Survey on Software Merging.* IEEE Transactions on Software Engineering, 2002. 28(5): p. 449-462.
11. C. Van der Westhuizen and A. van der Hoek. *Understanding and Propagating Architectural Changes.* Proceedings of the Working IFIP Conference on Software Architecture, 2002: p. 95-109.

A Relational Architecture Description Language for Software Families

T. John Brown, Ivor T.A. Spence, and Peter Kilpatrick

School of Computer Science, The Queen's University of Belfast, Belfast BT71NN
N. Ireland, U.K.
{tj.brown,i.spence,p.kilpatrick}@qub.ac.uk

Abstract. Software Product-Line Engineering has emerged in recent years, as an important strategy for maximising reuse within the context of a family of related products. In current approaches to software product-lines, there is general agreement that the definition of a reference-architecture for the product-line is an important step in the software engineering process. In this paper we introduce ADLARS, a new form of architecture Description language that places emphasis on the capture of architectural relationships. ADLARS is designed for use within a product-line engineering process. The language supports both the definition of architectural structure, and of important architectural relationships. In particular it supports capture of the relationships between product features, component and task architectures, interfaces and parameter requirements.

1 Introduction

In the process of engineering a software family, it is widely recognized that the definition of a reference architecture for the family is an important step. This may be a fixed architecture, which every product within the family shares, but in many instances the diversity between products will make it necessary to allow some flexibility at the architectural level. In practice, before one embarks on the definition of a reference architecture for a family of products, it is necessary to identify and catalogue the common and variant features and functionality across the intended product family. Among researchers and practitioners of software product-line engineering, this form of commonality-variability analysis is frequently performed in terms of feature-oriented domain analysis methods. Feature oriented domain analysis (FODA) methods emerged from work at the SEI [1][2]. Although the basic methodology continues to be extended and developed [3][4][5], feature based analysis methods are now a near-standard technique in the early phase of software family engineering.

This paper describes ongoing work on the design of an architecture description language, called ADLARS, for use in the definition of product-line reference architectures. ADLARS is oriented towards embedded, real-time software, but its use is not limited to this field. It has both a textual and a visual syntax, which is still under development. ADLARS is at an early stage of development, and the long-term aim is to evolve a language with a number of novel characteristics, which we view as important in the context of software product-lines. In the first instance, the language is intended for use within a product-line engineering process in which feature-oriented domain

F. van der Linden (Ed.): PFE 2003, LNCS 3014, pp. 282–295, 2004.
© Springer-Verlag Berlin Heidelberg 2004

modeling is also used. ADLARS architecture descriptions reference features from the feature model and build feature dependent task and component templates which capture the relationships between product features and architectural structure. Feature modeling techniques are still evolving [3][4][5], but there are core aspects that are common to all approaches. ADLARS assumes that features will be categorized as mandatory, optional or alternative.

ADLARS also provides design support for the use of some advanced implementation methods for defining adaptable software, which have emerged from other aspects of our research. A basic framework for implementing adaptable software components was described in [6]. Recent work includes the development of transformational code generation techniques, which are described in a companion paper [8]. In the longer term, we envisage a product-line engineering process incorporating the use of AD-LARS at the architecture design stage, along with implementation techniques similar to those described in [8].

2 Background Issues

The basic concept of an architecture description language, as a notation for describing the structure and interconnections within a software system, is not new and quite a number of ADLs have been designed. Although they all share the aims of abstracting away from implementation detail and capturing the higher level architecture of software systems, there is some diversity in terms of what they provide. A useful survey may be found in [9]. Many have emerged from research related to software architecture in the general sense. Few ADLs have been designed specifically for use in the context of engineering software Product-lines, although some, such as *Koala* [7] are in regular industrial use.

Historically, our work on the development of ADLARS was stimulated by a collaborative research project with Nortel Networks. ADLARS design has been influenced by the style of event-driven embedded software found within telecommunications network products, although it is not exclusively directed towards that domain. Its design reflects the aim of describing architecture at a level of abstraction which practical users in industry will find appropriate. In some respects it is therefore less abstract than other ADLs, some of which do not, for example, distinguish passive software components which communicate synchronously, from active components (tasks / processes) which execute concurrently and communicate asynchronously.

3 ADLARS Rationale

The central distinguishing feature about ADLARS is its emphasis on capturing architectural relationships. The most important relationships targeted are those between product features and software architecture. The assumption is made that a feature model for the application domain will be available as a precursor to the architecture design process. Implicit also is the assumption that all products within a family will not have strictly identical software architectures. ADLARS is intended to allow the architect to describe the manner in which the software structure and interfaces change in response to variations in the product feature set. An ADLARS architecture description therefore acts as a bridge between the requirements space and the solution space. In the former, different products within a family provide different feature combinations. In the latter, components are combined and customized in differing ways, to provide the feature combinations that characterize individual products. Our effort to develop ADLARS springs from the belief that a notation that can capture the relationships between these two worlds can make an important contribution to a streamlined, tool-supported product-line engineering process.

The following description does not attempt to cover every detail of the language, but concentrates instead on illustrating the notational features that support the capture of architectural relationships, which is the principal novelty in the language at its present state of development.

4   ADLARS Fundamentals

ADLARS describes the structural aspects of architectures in terms of a three-level view, which is illustrated in figure 1. This is augmented by a behavioral partitioning into what are called *interaction themes*. Within an interaction theme, all interaction, communication and behaviour is related to one particular theme or purpose. Commonly occurring themes may include, for example, system configuration or system management. There will typically be multiple interaction themes in an ADLARS definition, and individual component or task instances may participate in several themes.

At the top level, architectures are viewed as a collection of *task instances* that execute concurrently and communicate asynchronously. Task instances are created from

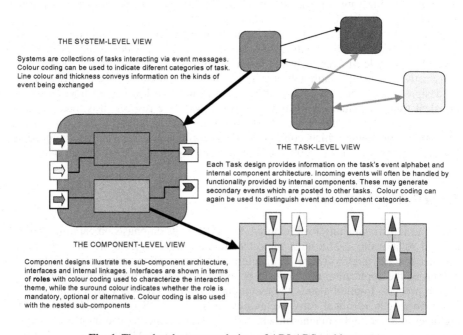

THE SYSTEM-LEVEL VIEW

Systems are collections of tasks interacting via event messages. Colour coding can be used to indicate diferent categories of task. Line colour and thickness conveys information on the kinds of event being exchanged

THE TASK-LEVEL VIEW

Each Task design provides information on the task's event alphabet and internal component architecture. Incoming events will often be handled by functionality provided by internal components. These may generate secondary events which are posted to other tasks. Colour coding can again be used to distinguish event and component categories.

THE COMPONENT-LEVEL VIEW

Component designs illustrate the sub-component architecture, interfaces and internal linkages. Interfaces are shown in terms of **roles** with colour coding used to characterize the interaction theme, while the suround colour indicates whether the role is mandatory, optional or alternative. Colour coding is also used with the nested sub-components

Fig. 1. Three-level conceptual view of ADLARS architectures.

task templates, which are defined in terms of their event alphabets and internal component architectures. Within the definition of a task template, we enumerate the associated mandatory, optional and alternative features, and their relationships to contained components and supported events. Creating a *task instance* from a task template requires provision of the actual feature sub-set that the instance is required to support. The relationships captured within the task template definition enable the internal structure and event alphabet of the instance to be readily derived.

The *component* level view represents the lowest level within an ADLARS description. Components are passive software units, characterized by the interfaces that they provide and require. They can be of any size and may contain nested sub-components, to any level of nesting. Once again we define component templates and enumerate the mandatory, optional and alternative features with which they are associated. Component instances, like task instances, are created by providing actual feature sub-sets.

To complement the descriptions of tasks and components, ADLARS provides a system dictionary, which is a structured dictionary of names and terms with supporting textual explanations.

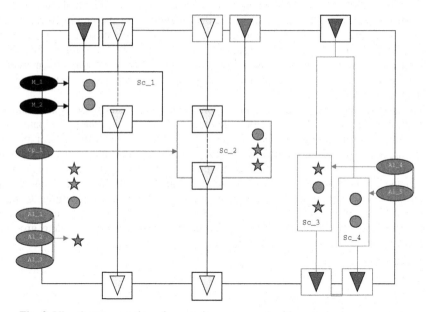

Fig. 2. Visual representation of a complex component with nested sub-components.

5 Component Templates

A component template definition embodies a collection of possible component configurations and directly relates these to features occurring in the feature model. Visually, a component template with nested sub-components may appear as in fig. 2.

Features associated with the component are represented as colour-coded ellipses with different colours for mandatory, optional and alternative features, respectively. Features can be linked to related sub-components. For example optional feature *Op_1* is linked to *Sc_2*. *Sc_2's* surround colour indicates that it is an optional sub-component, only included in instances of the component which are required to support the optional feature. Alternative feature groups are shown with a linking bar, and may be related to alternative sub-components (e.g. *Al_4~5*) or possibly component parameters (e.g. *Al_1~3*). Component parameters are shown using either circular spots, which indicate a normal parameter such as a numeric value, or stars, which indicate a parameter that conveys functionality. (This could be implemented as a pointer to function in C/C++, see [6].) Interfaces are illustrated using an enclosed triangle, in a style borrowed from *Koala* [7]. Triangle colour indicates the interaction theme with which the interface element is associated; surround colour indicates whether the interface element is always supported by component instances, sometimes supported, or is one of a number of alternative interface features. Interface elements are not necessarily simple methods, but may be *roles* i.e. collections of related method calls. Roles are discussed in more detail later.

ADLARS has a textual syntax that combines both formal elements and informal elements consisting of free text descriptions (a form of structured commenting). These informal elements are targeted at the needs of non-technical stakeholders, but could also be extracted to form part of the documentation of the architecture, for example during review-based assessment processes. The first informal element to appear in the textual definition of a component template is labeled responsibilities and is intended to contain a general description of the component's main responsibilities within the architecture. Other informal elements are described below in the context in which they appear.

The first formal element within a component template description is an enumeration of the *interaction themes* within which the component template participates. The next element is a sub-section listing the features associated with the component. These are a sub-set of the features within the complete feature model for the domain. Only the names of features are included, and these are the same names as are used within the domain feature model. Mandatory, optional and alternative features are listed separately. Note that there may be multiple sets of alternative features. Component instances can be expected to support only one feature from each set of alternatives. The term *characteristic feature set* is used to describe the complete group of features associated with a component template.

```
features supported:

{

    mandatory: {Mand_1, Mand_2} ;

    optional: { Opt_1 } ;

    alternatives: { (Alt_1,Alt_2,Alt_3), (Alt_4,Alt_5) } ;

} ;
```

Also present will be a parameter definition section, and a sub-component definition section listing the component's contained sub-components and expressing their relationships with supported features. This is one of the key areas of novelty in the language, and serves to establish the relationship between supported features and sub-component architecture. Two forms of conditional statement are provided. The first of these is the *when* statement, which is principally used to link optional features with sub-component instances that support them. Its generic form is:

```
when (boolean_expression)

{

    details of component(s) to be included ;

};
```

The boolean expression will normally be an expression involving optional features. It may be a simple expression or a complex expression constructed using the standard logical operators. The second form of statement used is the *alt* statement. It is used principally to relate alternative features to alternative sub-components that support them, and its generic form is:

```
alt

{

   (boolean_expression1)

      details of sub-component(s) to be included if

      boolean_expression1 is true ;

   (boolean_expression2)

      details of sub-component(s) to be included if

      boolean_expression1 is false and

      boolean_expression 2 is true ;

   (boolean_expressionN)

      details of sub-component(s) to be included if

      boolean_expressionN is true and preceding

      boolean expressions are false

  etc.

  } ;
```

An *alt* statement may have any number of limbs. Its boolean expressions are evaluated in order and the sub-components chosen for inclusion are those corresponding to the first boolean expression that evaluates to true.

Referring back to figure 2, the textual description of the sub-component architecture for this component would read as follows:

```
sub-components:

{

contents:

  {

    inst: Sc_1(paramSc1) : componentTemplate1 ;

    when (supporting (Opt_1))

      {
```

```
    inst: Sc_2(paramSc2)  : componentTemplate2 ;
  } ;
  alt:
  {
     (supporting (Alt_4) )
        inst: Sc_3(paramSc3)  : componentTemplate3 ;
     (supporting (Alt_5) )
        inst: Sc_4(paramSc4)  : componentTemplate4 ;
  } ;
  etc.
} ;
```

Note that sub-component *Sc_1* is present in all circumstances. The *when* statement tells us that Component *Sc_2* is only included if the optional feature *Opt_1* is to be supported. Likewise the *alt* statement tells us, for example, that sub-component *Sc_4* is only included if alternative feature *Alt_5* is to be supported. Thus the *when* and *alt* constructs allow expression of the conditionality relationships between supported features and the sub-component architecture.

5.1   Component Template Interface Descriptions

A component template's interface is described in terms of *roles*. A role is just a group of associated interface elements. A large component may provide a number of roles and these may fall within different interaction themes. Moreover, support for a particular role may depend on the inclusion of specific sub-components. For example, an optional sub-component may be present or absent within any component instance. If it is absent from a particular component instance, then some interface elements may not be provided by that instance. This dependence is expressed within component template interface definitions by pre-qualifying the role name with the name of the required sub component(s).

```
  interactionTheme1:
  {
    RoleNameA ;
    {Sc_2} :: RoleNameB ;
    {Sc_1, Sc_3} :: RoleNameC ;
        etc.
  } ;
```

In this code fragment, *RoleNameA* is always provided, but *RoleNameB* is only provided if the component instance contains the sub-component *Sc_2*, and *RoleNameC* requires both sub-components *Sc_1* and *Sc_3* to be present. A Component template's complete interface description consists of an enumeration of role names, grouped under appropriate interaction themes and pre-qualified, where appropriate, by required sub-components. This notation serves to capture the key relationships between the sub-components contained in a component instance, and the interface that that component instance provides.

Roles are then described in detail *outside* the component template definition. The following example illustrates part of a typical role definition.

```
role definition:

{

 name: roleNameA ;

 description: "textual description of roleNameA …" ;

 services:

 (

  IPPacketModificationService ;

 description: "informal details of this service" ;

 invocation: void setIPHeaderValues(byte[]) ;

 service requirements:

 {

   int[] IPDecode(byte[]): "a service to perform IP
                           packet decoding" ;

   void IPCode(byte[]): "a service which encodes IP
                        packets" ;

 };

 );

 other services within this role definition

};
```

Role definitions have both an informal textual description and a formal definition in terms of provided services and required services. Each service is named and has a textual description, as well as being formally specified in terms of an interface signature and required method signatures.

5.2   Component Parameters

Component template definitions first relate product features derived from the feature model, to sub-component architecture, and then relate sub-component contents to supported roles (i.e. to interfaces). Clearly most component instances can be expected to take parameters. Moreover the parameters required by a component instance will include any parameters required by its nested sub-components. However, the sub-component architecture is not fixed and consequently the parameter requirements are not fixed either. For example, the parameter group required by an optional sub-component will be required only if the sub-component is included.

In the textual definition of a component template, parameters required by an outer component are detailed individually. Parameters required by a sub-component are represented by an identifier. The fragment below illustrates the structure that a parameter definition section might take for the component illustrated in figure 2. If the sub-component is optional, its parameter identifier will be preceded by a question mark, e.g. *paramsSc_2*. When there are alternative sub-components, the related parameter identifiers are bracketed as illustrated.

```
parameters:

{individual parameters for the outer component,

 paramsSc_1, ?paramsSc_2, [ paramsSc_3|paramsSc_4 ] };
```

5.3 Components as Collections of Relations

Component template definitions establish three relationships. The first is the relationship between product features and sub-component architecture. The next is the relationship between sub-component architecture and supported interfaces, expressed in terms of roles. The final relationship established is that between sub-component architecture and required parameters. A component template can therefore be considered to define a collection of relationships, each of which may be expressed as a 4-tuple of the form:

$$<F, S, R, P>$$

where F is feature set, S is a set of sub-components, R is a set of roles and P is a set of required parameters. Each 4-tuple represents one possible component instance configuration. The number of possible 4-tuples depends on the number of optional and alternative features associated with the component template. If we know what features a component instance must support in a particular product, that fixes the sub-component architecture, which in turn fixes the set of roles (i.e. the interface) and the required parameters. If we make feature names unique within the complete feature model for the family, then the feature set for a specific product is all we need to identify the configuration of all the components required within that product's architecture. Let F_P be the complete feature set for product P and F_C the *characteristic feature set* for component C, (i.e. the set of *all* features related to component template C). The set intersection of F_P and F_C gives us F_{CI}; the feature set which must be supported by the instance of C, needed within this product. F_{CI} selects the appropriate 4-tuple, i.e. it fixes the required sub-component architecture, the supported roles (interface) and the required parameters. Of course the sub-components within C may themselves be derived from component templates. Let S_C be a component template from which a sub-component within C is derived and let F_{SC} be its characteristic feature set. Then the intersection of F_{CI} and F_{SC} identifies the feature set F_{SCI} that the sub-component instance must support. That in turn enables the detailed architecture of the sub-component instance S_{CI}, to be identified. Thus the detailed architecture of component instances and their sub-component instances can be identified by a process of recursively taking the intersection of feature sets, starting from the complete feature model for a particular product.

In a parallel stream of research we are engaged in developing programming techniques for *adaptable* software components in both the C++ [6] and Java languages. This work is still ongoing, but the techniques currently available allow component template definitions to be directly mapped into adaptable software components. As described in [6] adaptable components use their parameter lists to determine their internal architecture and interfaces, as well as to customize their method functionalities. The relationship between ADLARS architectural component templates and software adaptable components is illustrated fully in figure 3. We can program an adaptable software component that matches, in software, a component template definition. We can create, at the architectural level, a component instance from a component template, once we have identified the feature set *F*, which the component instance must support.

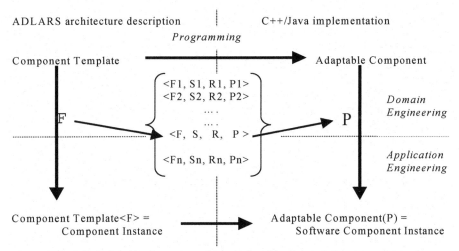

Fig. 3. Relationships between architectural and implementation components.

The feature set F selects the appropriate 4-tuple from this set. This both fixes the internal architecture and interfaces (roles) of the required component instance, and identifies the parameter set, *P*, needed to customize the matching adaptable component implementation.

6 Task Templates

Task template definitions have many similarities with component template definitions. Interaction themes, responsibilities and features supported are specified in a similar way. Like component templates, a task template has an associated *characteristic feature set*. Likewise the definition of the internal component contents has the same form as that of the sub-component contents section within a component template definition. Task template definitions differ in having a major section concerned with the definition of the task's event alphabet. This is the repertoire of event messages that the task expects to receive and is prepared to handle. The event alphabet definition section comprises sub-sections defining the task template's input alphabet and its output alphabet. Input events may be pre-qualified by a set of components, to indicate that task instances can only handle these events when the specified components are present. In the definition below, *c3* is an optional component that must be included within a task instance required to accept the event *evName1*. Each input event has an associated *event category*. Event categories are described in the system dictionary section of the architecture definition.

```
input alphabet:
{
  ({c3}::evName1: eventCategoryName ;
  implications: "text description" ;
   data:
     {
     byte[2] dataName1 ;
     byte[2 - 50] dataName2 ;
     } ;
  occurrence: {random | periodic(100) | timed} ;
  deadline: 20 millisecs ;
  response:
  {
    c1.serviceName >> {any secondary events } ;
  };
 );    // end of evName1
( other events )
};
```

Events often carry data and an important aspect of the definition of an input event is the decomposition of its data. Since it is common, in real-time applications, to pack information into the minimum space required, individual bits may be significant and we allow data fields to be described in terms of groups of bits. Variable length fields are also allowed. Also included is a definition of the expected pattern of occurrence of events: random, periodic, or at specific regular times. Events may have associated deadlines and this information is also stored. Finally we provide a linkage between arriving events and the internal software within the task, by defining the services invoked from internal components in order to handle the event. Execution of event handling functionality may cause secondary events to be generated and the names of these events are also indicated. More detailed information about secondary events is then provided in an output alphabet definition section.

6.1 Relational Model for Task Templates

Task template definitions have an associated relational model. A task template definition embeds the relationships between product features and the task's internal components and their required parameters. It also embeds the relationships between the
internal components and the event alphabet that the task supports. Thus each task
template definition gives rise to an implied set of 4-tuples of the form

$$<F, C, A, P>$$

where F is a supported feature set, C is a set of included components, A is the supported event alphabet, and P is the parameter set needed by the task's internal components. To create a task instance from a task template, we begin with the feature model
F_p for the target product. The intersection of F_p with the task template's characteristic
feature set F_T gives the feature set F_{TI} associated with the required task instance. That
in turn selects the appropriate 4-tuple defining the task's component architecture and
event alphabet. The components of course will be derived from component templates.
For any contained component we can take the intersection of its characteristic feature
set with F_{TI}, to obtain its instance feature set, as described in section 4.3. Thus once
the feature set for a required product is known, the detailed architecture of task instances and their contained component instances can be derived by a process that is
essentially seamless.

7 The System Description Layer

A system description layer forms the top level in an ADLARS architecture description. A system description contains a definition of all the tasks in the system, along
with any customizing feature sets that they require. It will also contain a listing of
connections and the event names that pass along those connections.

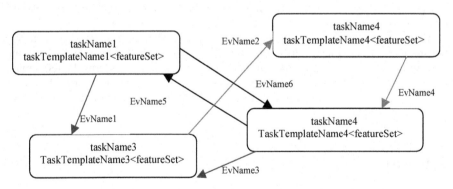

Fig. 4. System Representation in terms of Interacting tasks.

There may be multiple task instances derived from the same task template, and multiple event communications between any two tasks. Colour coding is used to identify
event categories.

8 Discussion

ADLARS is a work in progress rather than a finished product and this paper has provided just an outline of the language, with many points of detail omitted. Its intended application is the definition of flexible architectures for families of software systems. It is an intermediate design notation, for use along with feature-oriented domain modeling. Compared to other notations, its main innovation is the emphasis on capturing the relationships between features and architecture. At its core is the relational model which links features with architectural structure, interfaces or event alphabets, and customizing parameters. Task or component template definitions embody a set of such relationships, each expressible in terms of a 4-tuple.

It is worth considering how the language may be used within a product-line engineering process. It is envisaged that an ADLARS reference architecture for an intended product family would be designed and specified as part of the domain engineering process. This would come after domain modeling so that the complete feature model would be available. Task and component templates would be defined at this stage, complete with feature dependencies. At the application engineering phase, creating instances from templates requires only the appropriate feature set, which may be obtained as a simple set intersection operation using the specific feature set for the intended product. Thus capturing feature relationships in the reference architecture description, as ADLARS does, makes the task of deriving product-specific architectures, entirely straightforward.

As discussed above, a related, but separate stream of research is focussed on techniques and issues related to the implementation of adaptable software [6]. This work clearly addresses a different aspect of the problem of implementing families of systems. ADLARS component and task templates provide design level support for the implementation of the kind of adaptable component described in [6]. In more recent work, reported in a companion paper [8], transformational code generation techniques have been developed which automate the software customization process. These techniques require an XML based descriptor that could readily be derived from ADLARS component or task instance definitions. Thus the two research streams complement one another while not being strictly dependent.

Much work remains to refine aspects of the ADLARS language and provide supporting tools. In the longer term, it is intended to extend the language to provide support for the use of generic architectural entities such as design patterns. Patterns play a major role in framework architectures, which must be regarded as a form of product-line architecture. However work in this area is at an early stage and is outside the scope of this paper.

References

1. K. C. Kang, S. G. Cohen, J. A. Hess, W. E. Novak and A. S. Patterson, "Feature Oriented Domain Analysis (FODA) feasibility study". Technical Report CMU/SEI-90-TR-21, available from the Software Engineering Institute, Carnegie-Mellon University 1990.
2. "A Framework for Software Product Line Practice – version 2", P. Clements and L.M. Northrop, Software Engineering Institute, Carnegie-Mellon University, 1999.

3. K. Lee, K. C. Kang, W. Chae, and B. B. Choi, "Feature-based approach to object-oriented engineering of applications for reuse", Software Practice and Experience, Vol. 30, pp. 1025 - 1046, 2000.
4. K. C. Kang, S. Kim, J. Lee and K. Lee, "Feature-Oriented Engineering of PBX Software for Adaptability and Reusability", Software Practice and Experience, vol. 29(10), pp. 875 - 896, 1999.
5. D. Fey, R. Fajta and A. Boros, "Feature Modeling: A Meta-model to Enhance Usability and Usefulness", Proceedings of the 2nd International Conference on Software Product lines (SPLC2), August 2002, ed. Gary Chastek, published by Springer-Verlag LNCS no. 2379, pp. 198 – 216, 2002.
6. T. J. Brown, I. Spence and P. Kilpatrick, "Adaptable Components for Software Product-line Engineering", Proceedings of the Second International Conference on Software Product lines (SPLC2) August 2002, ed. Gary Chastek, published by Springer-Verlag LNCS no. 2379, pp. 154 – 175, 2002.
7. Rob van Ommering, Frank van der Linden, Jeff Kramer and Jeff Magee, "The Koala Component Model for Consumer Electronics Software", IEEE Computer, pp. 78-85, March 2000.
8. I. McRitchie, T. J. Brown and I. Spence, "Managing Component.Variability within Embedded Software Product Lines via Transformational Code Generation", Proceedings of the 5th International Workshop on Product Family Engineering (PFE-5), November 2003, Sienna, Italy.
9. N. Medvidovic, "A classification and Comparison Framework for Software Architecture Description Languages", Technical Report UCI-ICS-97-02, University of California, Irvine CA.

Planning and Managing Product Line Evolution

Louis J.M. Taborda

Macquarie Graduate School of Management
Macquarie University, NSW 2109, Australia
ltaborda@procentric.com

Abstract. This paper addresses the management and evolution of products that comprise a configuration of reusable components. Software product lines provide an example, as their development requires the cooperation of multiple product teams that utilize common domain components. The different perspectives of the product and component teams in such environments are reviewed and contrasted, since the concerns of each have to be managed and balanced as the product line evolves. A matrix representation is used to depict the dependencies, recording both the individual agreements made between stakeholders and the aggregated plan. Matrices are shown to succinctly describe the marketplace or enterprise view capturing the two complementary but orthogonal perspectives of component producers and consumers. The Release Matrix is introduced as the multi-dimensional form of a traditional release plan and is related to formal Configuration Management principles as they apply to complex environments.

1 Introduction

The vision of reusable software components has resulted in increased architectural abstraction that allows developers to mimic the practices of hardware engineering disciplines. This has culminated in the realization of product lines in a software context [1] that aims to move the software industry from traditional one-at-a-time system development towards systematic large-scale reuse. The relative newness of Product Line Architectures (PLAs) and Component Based Development (CBD) techniques is evidenced by the fact that much of the industry's attention focuses on the enabling technologies, architectures and frameworks that are instrumental in the creation of such applications [2, 3]. As the underlying technologies mature and these architectures become increasingly common, there is a corresponding need to construct models and methods to manage their development and evolution.

It has been observed [4, 5] that traditional approaches to managing development projects, while adequate for the creation of standalone software systems, is less suitable for complex CBD environments. The large-scale reuse necessary to support the PLAs' multiple product variants is difficult to manage as development groups suffer from conflicting priorities that can threaten the viability of such programs [6]. The result is that the management challenge increases in these complex environments that

F. van der Linden (Ed.): PFE 2003, LNCS 3014, pp. 296–309, 2004.

are characterized by significant reuse and multiple streams of product development, as indicated by the highlighted quadrant in Figure 1. While practitioners grapple with these concerns on a daily basis, there is little in the way of methods and tools to guide their endeavors.

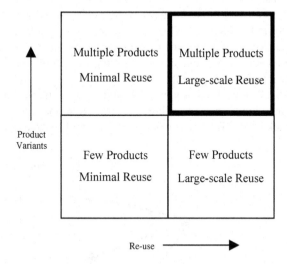

Fig. 1. PLAs typify systematic reuse across multiple products.

Development of the individual products[1] in a product line is just one aspect of the challenge. They, and the underlying domain architecture, have to evolve reliably over time to ensure the reuse framework achieves longevity and provides a return on the initial investment. Traditional development models need to be supplemented by new management paradigms or PLA programs will struggle even as the necessary technological infrastructure is put in place.

This paper explores the familiar relationship between products and their underlying domain architecture and applies it as an organizing principle to support the planning and management of evolving PLAs. A concise representation of the different dependencies and stakeholder priorities is proposed that indicates the important role that configuration (CM) principles play in addressing these challenges. The remainder of this paper is organized as follows. Section 2 discusses the different viewpoints that can be considered a management pattern in the evolution of product lines. Section 3 reviews the orthogonality of products and their architectural components, introducing a matrix notation to represent the relationship. Section 4 discusses the potential application of the representation and sketches its use in release planning, team communication, and the management of the competing concerns inherent in complex, reusable infrastructures.

---

[1] The term product is used throughout this paper although application or system can be equally valid in certain contexts. Similarly services may be substituted for components.

2 Management Patterns

While there are significant benefits provided by component architectures that localize and insulate changes, the trade-off is that their development also presents new management problems. The challenge shifts from classic, one-off development to the management of a configuration of inter-dependent components that have to be integrated into one or more products. While these conditions arise in many environments, the dependencies are most pronounced (and recognized) in PLAs, which are characterized by parallel streams of development that impact a common or shared configuration of largely reusable components.

The CM problem in such environments is significantly increased, and it is recognized [7, 8] that common CM techniques are often inadequate or have to be "stretched" to tackle the different levels at which the problem manifests itself.

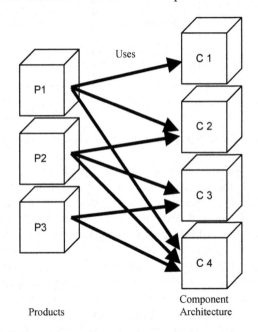

Fig. 2. Product utilization and reuse of system components.

The inter-relationships between products and components that are exemplified by PLAs are simplistically illustrated in Figure 2. Each product in the diagram uses or relies upon the capabilities of several components, which are themselves reused across different products. These interdependencies illustrate that a higher, system or enterprise level context exists that has to be managed, and this higher-order configuration also requires the application of CM to identify and control the whole environment as it evolves.

The multi-dimensional role that CM is required to play needs further investigation to identify management methods that can address this new layer of complexity.

Krueger [9] demonstrates how CM can differ for product lines and includes the mechanisms for introducing product variability into a PLA. Further, the increasing interconnectedness of software components has been recognized [10] with the suggestion that these dependencies be considered a distinct problem. A complicating factor in managing these environments is that each element in Figure 2 can also have associated activities, and so must also address their individual CM and release planning issues. The product-specific architectural elements that are not amenable to reuse may be considered as an extension of the reusable domain infrastructure (as in the case of C1 in Figure 2). The end products can therefore be considered a purely business or marketing entity that is based upon a configuration of product-specific and reusable domain components that comprise a PLA.

2.1 Different Viewpoints

In attempting to understand the challenges of evolving software architecture, the motivations of the different stakeholders involved have to be considered. The separate views of component producers and the product managers that utilize (or consume) these components have to be understood, together with the management and coordination required to balance them [11].

2.1.1 Component Perspective

While the organizational structures adopted can vary [12], specialized domain teams are commonly responsible for the development and maintenance of the core software assets, or platform capabilities, of the PLA. These teams are the "component producers" and are often charged with decoupling the domain capabilities from originally product-specific features and evolving them as independent, reused components. They then have to protect the coherence of these components against the natural tendency for divergence that occurs during product line evolution.

Producers focus on delivering the services or capabilities provided by their component; and like vendors of Commercial-off-the-Shelf (COTS) software – which some components may indeed be - they have to satisfy the demands of the different products that utilize their component. They must balance these demands against the quality and reliability of the component, ensuring it adheres to published interfaces and performance characteristics. For each new component release, there is a need to prioritize or negotiate the competing, potentially conflicting, requirements across the user-base and package the selected ones into the component's release plan.

From a CM perspective, each component producer also needs to be aware of the products that utilize its capabilities and manage the so-called "where-used" problem to minimize the impact of component changes on a product. The consequences of poor change management and design abstraction can result in consumers switching to a different component supplier or, in the case of in-house producers, losing the benefits of reuse.

2.1.2 Product Perspective

The products are the marketed applications or systems that are the result of integrating or gluing together components (both domain and product-specific). As such, product related activities are more visible, business-level efforts that rely on existing components to improve time-to-market and reduce total lifecycle costs.

While product managers stand to gain from cost-effective, reusable components, these benefits come at the cost of reduced influence and control over the evolution of the component's capabilities. Where new product features rely on underlying changes to one or more reused components, product schedules have to rely on and work-around the separate (sub) releases of the component producers.

As such, product managers may need to adjust their (product) release plans to accommodate the relevant component releases as described in the scenario below. This can give rise to tensions as product schedules make demands on component producers who must be responsive to these demands while maintaining the integrity and reusability of their component. These stresses have to be managed and an agreeable resolution negotiated or the effectiveness of the reuse program can be undermined.

Product groups need to perform CM functions that include identification of the versions of the components that are utilized in the integrated end product. This ensures that each product release can be reliably recreated and its dependencies controlled.

2.1.3 Management Perspective

While understanding the different viewpoints of component producers and product managers can be valuable, the ultimate goal is to have the different stakeholders collaborate effectively to ensure the PLA is to be sustainable. In large-scale component reuse programs exemplified by PLAs, the entire management context comprises multiple products or product variants and numerous component producers, each with their associated development activities and release plans.

The complex inter-dependencies between these stakeholders may be viewed as a complex ecosystem [13] that has to be managed in its entirety to maintain the balance between their different interests. The multiplicity of co-dependent participants in a PLA program can be seen as a generalization of the two-party, supplier-customer relationship that is at the heart of most software industry standards and best practices. In such circumstances all stakeholders have to manage their own development activities and releases, while also being aware and responsive, not simply to a single customer, but through a web of inter-dependencies, to other parties in the product line environment.

2.2 Release Planning Scenario

As a real-world example of the inter-dependencies that have to be addressed, consider this simple scenario. A Billing System product line has a high-priority requirement to support a more elaborate bill-print format that displays a variable customer greeting. Achieving this capability might require coordinated changes to (say) the display, storage and print-management components. Changing just one component alone is inadequate since all three capabilities (and so components) have to be released together to achieve the desired business result.

Add to this scenario the fact that the print-management component is reused by another product that has a low priority request to support a new output device. It becomes evident that anytime there is reuse there arises the possibility of conflicting priorities that have to be managed. With limited resource, which requirement should the print-manager component team work on first? Irrespective of the apparent urgency, it may be that longer timescales for changing the display and storage components make it pointless for the print-manager component team to schedule the corresponding formatting changes with the same priority. In that case the smarter thing for the team to do would be to work on support of the new output device first. After that task is completed, then the formatting changes can be implemented, still allowing the synchronized release of the new bill-print format at the earliest possible time.

Juggling the priorities and balancing the competing concerns across products and components is what release planning in a product line environment is primarily about. To manage limited resources optimally requires us to be able to easily recognize and adjust for the inter-dependencies between the change activities and the components that they affect.

3   Representing the Product Line Ecosystem

In order to grasp the product line management context at the highest-level we need to find a simple means to represent and view all the inter-relationships between component producers and consumers. At the enterprise level, we need to identify all the reused components that participate in the PLA, and clearly indicate the products that are reliant on these components.

In this section, the separation between component and product perspective is clarified and extended by focusing on the dependencies between the products and their constituent software assets.

3.1   The Marketplace Pattern

Resolving the separate producer and consumer perspectives and their priorities necessitates increased collaboration between PLA stakeholders. Separating the concerns of product managers from those of the component teams suggests they be represented orthogonally. A table can capture the numerous individual plans and competing commitments that bind a PLA ecosystem together, with each column representing the perspective of a component producer while each row denotes a particular product's scope or viewpoint.

We term this recognizable relationship the Marketplace Pattern in recognition of the fact that not all elements or stakeholders need reside within the one organization, and there are business imperatives at the heart of the relationship. For most PLAs the relationship is more likely to represent the enterprise view however it can easily be extended to arbitrarily large architectures and product lines. As an illustration we apply the viewpoint to the previous example comprising three products and four components to arrive at the table shown in Figure 3.

In practice the table would be populated with pertinent management information described in Section 4, however by way of example a Boolean is used to denote the presence of a usage relationship between a product and component. The shaded column represents the perspective of the team responsible for Component 3 that needs to balance the demands of products P2 and P3. The shaded row corresponds to the reliance Product 2 has on three components, C2, C3 and C4, that may need to have coordinated releases to effect a business change.

	C1	C2	C3	C4
P1	1	1	0	1
P2	0	1	1	1
P3	0	0	1	1

Fig. 3. The Marketplace Pattern showing product-component dependencies.

The intersection of these two perspectives indicates the need to establish a specific plan or contract between the P2 and C3 teams. Similar plans will have to be negotiated for all non-null cells as they represent the coordination the different stakeholder teams have to undertake to support the architecture. In general, Figure 3 shows that each component producer must weigh and prioritize the demands of its customers shown in that column, while each product must coordinate the components it utilizes across the row. These orthogonal perspectives represent the different tensions that have to be balanced in a product line environment. The PuLSE Methodology [14] addresses similar relationships with its Product Map taking a finer grained approach that considers the characteristics of the components that can be included in an evolving product line. The Marketplace Pattern differs somewhat in its elevation of the fundamental relationship between architectural components and the products, both of which can drive the evolution of the PLA [15].

The Marketplace Pattern adopts the principle of separation of concerns to isolate the product and component perspectives, applying it as a template to capture pertinent characteristics of the environment. Each cell in the simple tabular notation can record a variety of management and technical information necessary to coordinate different activities around the PLA, including:

- Allocated requirements that new product features place on each component.
- Implementation tasks to be conducted by each component team.
- Schedule and planning information relating to these tasks.
- Status and progress of the development, test and integration activities.

3.2 Matrix Notation

The Marketplace Pattern captures an essential aspect of a product line and its utility is in the scoping of each stakeholder's responsibility. Echoing the organizational structures widely adopted by business, matrices provide a convenient means of capturing the inter-relationships between the product line stakeholders.

A matrix notation highlights the separation between the product and component perspectives, reinforcing their orthogonal nature and helping to identify the span of traditional management practices; as well as identifying the tuning and clarification needed when applying them to PLAs.

3.2.1 The Configuration Vector

We can define a PLA as comprising a configuration of (n) related architectural components that we will denote as a vector. The configuration (or C) vector can therefore be represented as follows:

$$C = (c_1, c_2, c_3, \ldots\ldots c_n)$$

The C-vector can be seen as signifying the high-level elements of the system architecture and fulfils the classic identification process required by formal or system-level CM [16]. Each element, c_i, can be considered an architectural Configuration Item (CI) that is part of the product line. The selection of these CIs is a result of applying CM identification practices that have to balance granularity and architectural detail against management attention and visibility. If the number of components were too numerous, then experience [17] and CM principles would guide us to consolidate these components into a manageable number of high-level CIs. Therefore the C-vector itself may change as the domain architecture is refactored and the high-level identification of reusable and product-specific CI's are refined over time.

The management goal is clearly to select only the most appropriate, high-level component CI's and hide the remaining details in the lower levels of the design. While this is not always achieved in practice and architectures can be notoriously intermeshed, from a management viewpoint if not from a design one, each CI can be decomposed into the more detailed component implementations. The recursive application of the Marketplace Pattern described can be shown to represent this management decomposition.

3.2.2 The Product Vector

The products are built by combining and integrating the component CIs together and can be denoted by a vector of (m) products. The product (or P) vector can be represented as follows:

$$P = (p_1, p_2, p_3, \ldots\ldots p_m)$$

Each p_j can be considered as representing a particular product's perspective, while the P-vector embodies the entire product line that is based on the shared component architecture. As new opportunities are identified the product line's expansion can be represented by an extension of the P-vector's dimension.

Since the products are the entities that have customers to satisfy, they have business significance and separate product managers to guide the evolution of each product. New product features give rise to distinct requirements that impact the shared architecture, necessitating careful design and coordinated implementation. These may require new components to be developed or necessitate the modification of existing component capabilities. In any event, the relationship between the product and configuration vectors needs to be recorded and managed as the PLA evolves.

3.2.3 The Marketplace Matrix

To capture the dependencies between the products represented by the P-vector and the high-level, system components (or CIs) represented by the C-vector, we introduce the marketplace (or M) matrix. The M-matrix can be defined with reference to the previously described vectors as corresponding to the matrix product, $P \approx M\,C$, where each element m_{ij} relates a specific product and component as follows:

$$p_j \approx \Sigma m_{ij}\, c_i$$

The above notation is not intended to be mathematically rigorous and so, with license, an $n \times m$ matrix will be used to generally represent the Marketplace Pattern, irrespective of the contents of its cells. The matrix representation for a configuration of four components ($n=4$) and three products ($m=3$) described in the prior example is illustrated in Figure 4.

$$\begin{pmatrix} p_1 \\ p_2 \\ p_3 \end{pmatrix} \approx \begin{pmatrix} 1 & 1 & 0 & 1 \\ 0 & 1 & 1 & 1 \\ 0 & 0 & 1 & 1 \end{pmatrix} \times \begin{pmatrix} c_1 \\ c_2 \\ c_3 \\ c_4 \end{pmatrix}$$

Fig. 4. Matrix representation of the Marketplace Pattern.

The decoupling of the C and P-vectors is enabled by the introduction of the M-matrix that records the inter-dependencies, with each cell, m_{ij}, being used to describe the relationship between the product p_i and the component c_j. The succinct format of the M-matrix indicates the possibility of extending the notation to better present and understand a product line ecosystem.

The family of M-matrices captures each component's "where used" information as well as each product's reliance on the components. As a function of time they can track the evolution of a product line and its dependencies. At given points in the PLA's lifecycle an M-matrix can be used to provide a baseline of the architecture and the products that are built upon it. The M-matrix serves as a template where each cell can record the component versions that a product utilizes and, as a whole, represents the product line configuration at an enterprise level.

4 Applications of the Notation

This paper is only able to offer a brief overview of applications that are the subject of further research investigations. The potential richness and utility of the matrix notation can be illustrated by the following early examples.

4.1 Organization and Communication

At the simplest level, the separation of concerns supported by the Marketplace Pattern provides an organizing principle and a convenient means of recording and communicating the interrelated commitments or agreements that underlie complex technology ecosystems.

Determining the form of an M-matrix itself is an important and non-trivial activity that scopes the PLA and establishes its boundaries. It can be helpful in the early stages of PLA adoption [18], assisting in the identification of stakeholders and provides a format to present the players and their roles in terms of the products and components.

Each M-matrix provides an enterprise view of the PLA that can aid team communications by establishing appropriate lines of responsibility and corresponding organizational structures. The impact of any changes can be easily identified due to the explicit identification of the dependencies in the M-matrix. Even with its Boolean entries, the relationships shown in Figure 4 visibly indicates the potential impact of changes to either product or component, so they can be anticipated early in the planning. As such it identifies the players that should have a role in guiding the evolution of the PLA and might formally be termed Configuration Control Boards (CCBs).

4.2 Development Artifacts

The family of matrices that reflect the Marketplace Pattern are based on relationships that fundamentally define the PLA and so can act as a template to record and maintain management and development information. They can capture and categorize critical aspects of the environment, offering a framework that ensures stakeholder inter-dependencies are visible and specifically addressed.

An M-matrix offers both a detailed perspective of each stakeholder's commitments, as well as an aggregated or enterprise view of the PLA context that assists in the impact assessment of any proposed changes. Each cell records the agreements made between a pair (i, j) of stakeholders, capturing the interaction between the consumer and producer of each component.

The conciseness of the matrix representation and its encapsulation of the orthogonal relationship between products and components can have application in formatting the PLA's development artifacts. The contents of the matrices will vary dependent upon the information being presented but the pattern it captures can be used as a template for documentation across the lifecycle.

Using M-matrices to record requirements is a potentially fruitful utilization of the pattern. When an M-matrix is baselined it can be viewed as being a configuration of (requirements or design) specifications, each cell holding the set specific to that product-component pair. Each product (or marketing) requirement can be considered individually and, in line with Requirements Engineering practices, allocated to impacted components as part of the high-level design process. At this fine-grained level, each product requirement therefore fills the cells in a row with derived requirements that the affected components have to incorporate into their release plans – along with any domain related component requirements.

4.3 The Release Matrix

Whereas a PLA's baseline configuration can be represented by an M-matrix, the planned changes can be represented in what we term the Release Matrix. This matrix has the same dimensions as the M-matrix but captures the changes that drive product line evolution. Each cell r_{ij} of the Release Matrix can be viewed as the collection of requirements that establish the scope for the next iteration of the PLA.

The multiplicity of releases that are a feature of product line environments could benefit from the clarification offered by such a matrix or tabular representation (Figure 5). Each column in the Release Matrix represents a component release plan defined as the sum of the requirements it is to implement in the that release. A row represents a product's release plan that must be compatible with the component releases that the product is reliant upon. As a whole, the Release Matrix represents a master release plan that consolidates and synchronizes the individual release plans of the modified products and components.

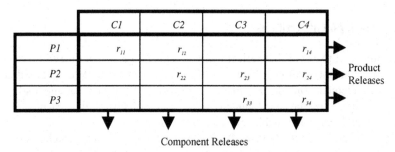

Component Releases

Fig. 5. Orthogonal, inter-dependent product and component releases.

The potential dependency of a product feature on multiple component releases, as illustrated by the Billing System scenario previously described, means that if any component's release plan is incompatible with the product schedule, i.e. it cannot deliver the required capabilities when needed, then the entire product feature's release may need to be rescheduled till another compatible set of synchronized component releases can be organized.

The Release Matrix can therefore be considered as a necessary generalization of the concept of an individual product release, as it relates to the multi-dimensional, product line ecosystem. It is a manifestation of the Marketplace Pattern and captures the complexity and dynamism that is the evolution of a PLA, where an adjustment to any element of the plan can have multiple impacts requiring intense communication and collaboration in order to achieve a stable and agreed master plan.

4.4 Reporting Status

Gauging the status of development in a product line environment can be problematic due to the inter-dependencies between the component and product development streams. The matrix notation has the potential to be used in tracking the status of product line activities and determining the impact of any adjustments to the master-release plan.

The Release Matrix could be used to provide an overview of the progress of the requirements as they are implemented. The status of each component's development can be presented in a similarly formatted reporting matrix that indicates when a product's allocated requirements have been met and the integration and test of the product can proceed.

The representation could also indicate the parties that may be affected by a component's schedule slip and provides the means of communicating the impact. Applying the Release Matrix could therefore be a means to preempt problems and renegotiate commitments, reducing the risk of unexpected and uncontrolled impacts rippling through the PLA program.

4.5 Supporting Technology[2]

The availability of tools that provide appropriate management support for product line environments is naturally limited while the understanding of underlying issues remains inadequate. The representations described in this paper can benefit from technology support that offered the ability to manipulate (slice and dice or drill-down) the information as desired. Particular views could support the different perspectives with consistency checking algorithms ensuring the integrity and reliability of the release plans.

Agreement on a master plan would be greatly assisted by collaborative features that supported the difficult tasks of negotiating, achieving and maintaining a self-consistent Release Matrix. This could be achieved "one cell at a time" if the dependencies and potential conflicts were flagged by a tool as they occurred. Stakeholders could subscribe for changes or issues concerning possible impacts to their work, reducing the risk of any unpleasant surprises.

While the tabular or matrix presentation offers increased management clarity, there is potential for more sophisticated technology support. The notation suggests the

---

[2] Technology support for the representations described in this paper is the subject of patent applications to protect the commercialization of these concepts.

possibility of matrix operations that can manipulate management information and provide new insights into the state of the product line environment. The release planning scenario previously described anticipates a future of rigorous operations and algorithms that may be applied to optimize the use of resources across the enterprise.

5   Conclusion

The development and evolution of PLAs represents a significant management challenge. It has been shown that traditional management disciplines do not satisfactorily address the complexity associated with systematic reuse across multiple system components.

This paper has identified and applied a simple, yet key, management pattern that is present in all product line environments. Instead of the two-party, customer-supplier paradigm that is the basis of traditional management disciplines, a product line environment is better described as a marketplace where numerous component producers negotiate individual contracts with multiple product managers. The inter-dependence of these entities gives rise to the need for a higher-order of management and coordination that must ensure the consistent and synchronized evolution of the PLA and its constituent components. The Marketplace Pattern can be represented in a tabular or matrix notation that clearly identifies the interactions and concerns of each stakeholder while maintaining the "big-picture" context. This compact means of recording management information highlights the orthogonal and potentially conflicting perspectives of the component producers and consumers that have to be balanced to achieve stable evolution of the PLA.

The introduction of the Release Matrix offers a useful technique to develop a master plan for the product line that can help consolidate and align the individual release schedules of the different products and components. The Release Matrix offers a means to coordinate and record each incremental step in the PLA's evolution, and is presented as a generalization of release planning in complex reuse contexts.

The proposed applications suggest that the pattern introduced in this paper can provide a basis for clearer communication of the issues that have to be juggled in evolving product lines. Further research and investigation is required to expand these concepts into a model that provides guidance on how to orient and align practitioners throughout the PLA's lifecycle.

References

1. Meyer, M. H., Seliger, R.: Product Platforms in Software Development. Sloan Management Review, Cambridge (1998).
2. Lowy, J.: Programming .NET Components. O'Reilly & Associates (2003).
3. Halloway, S. D.: Component Development for the Java Platform. Addison-Wesley (2001).
4. Bosch, J.: Product-Line Architectures in Industry: A Case Study. Proceeding of ICSE (1999).

5. Crnkovic, I. and Larsson, M.: Challenges of component-based development. Journal of Systems and Software (2002).
6. Fichman, R.G., Kemerer, C. F.: Incentive Compatibility and Systematic Software Reuse. Journal of Systems and Software, Vol. 57, No. 1 (2001).
7. A Framework for Software Product Line Practice, Version 4.1, Software Engineering Institute, http://www.sei.cmu.edu/plp/framework.html.
8. Sowrirajan, S., Van der Hoek, A.: Managing the Evolution of Distributed and Inter-related Components. Proceedings of the 11th International Workshop on Software Configuration Management (2003).
9. Krueger, C.: Variation Management for Software Production Lines. Proceedings of the 2nd International Software Product Line Conference (2002).
10. Dellarocas, C.: Software Component Interconnection Should be Treated as a Distinct Design Problem. Proceedings of the 8th Annual Workshop on Software Reuse (1997).
11. Toft, P., Coleman, D., Ohta, J.: A Cooperative Model for Cross-Divisional Product Development for a Software Product Line. Proceedings of the 1st Software Product Line Conference (2000).
12. Bosch, J.: Software Product Lines: Organizational Alternatives. Proceedings of the 23rd International Conference on Software Engineering (2001).
13. Highsmith, J.: Agile Software Development Ecosystems. Addison-Wesley, Boston (2002).
14. Bayer, J., Flege, O., Knauber, P. et. al.: PuLSE: A Methodology to Develop Software Product Lines. Proceedings of the Symposium on Software Reusability (1999).
15. Kellomäki, P., Mikkonen T.: Separating Product Variance and Domain Concepts in the Specification of Software Product Lines. ECOOP Workshop on Aspects and Dimensions of Concerns (2000).
16. ANSI/EIA-649-1998EIA, National Consensus Standard for Configuration Management (1998).
17. Sullivan, K.J., and Knight, J.C.: Experience Assessing an Architectural Approach to Large-Scale Systematic Reuse. Proceedings of ICSE (1996).
18. Böckle, G., Muñoz, J.B., Knauber, P. et. al.: Adopting and Institutionalizing a Product Line Culture. Proceedings of the 2nd International Software Product Line Conference (2002).

A Cost Model for Software Product Lines

Günter Böckle[1], Paul Clements[2], John D. McGregor[3], Dirk Muthig[4],
and Klaus Schmid[4]

[1] Siemens
guenter.boeckle@siemens.com
[2] Software Engineering Institute
clements@sei.cmu.edu
[3] Clemson University
johnmc@cs.clemson.edu
[4] Fraunhofer Institute for Experimental Software Engineering
{muthig,Klaus.Schmid}@iese.fhg.de

Abstract. In this paper we present a first-order cost model that describes the costs associated with developing products in a product line organization. The model addresses a number of issues that we present as a set of scenarios. The goal of this work is to develop models of varying granularity that support a manager's decision-making needs at a variety of levels. The basis of these models is the relationships among the artifacts of the product line.

Introduction

Software product lines have been touted as a preferred software development paradigm because of the large (in some cases, order-of-magnitude) economic improvements they bring compared to one-at-a-time software system development. However, this economic argument has to date been based on singular data points derived from case studies [1], convincing arguments based on reasonableness and simplistic cost curves such as the one in [9].

We believe the time has come to do better. At the recent Dagstuhl seminar on product family development [2], the authors of this paper constituted a working group that began to form an economic model for product lines that will help a manager answer questions such as:

- Should I develop our next product as a member of an existing product line, or by itself? What are the costs and benefits of each approach?
- Will it pay to merge two product lines together, or will we be better off by keeping them separate? If we merge, what will it cost?
- Which product in our planned product line would be most cost-effective to build first?

The contribution of this work is to build on previous work [4,8] to produce a model that can have immediate practical application.

The product line approach to software development seeks to provide benefit by achieving strategic levels of software reuse. Much work has been done in the area of

F. van der Linden (Ed.): PFE 2003, LNCS 3014, pp. 310–316, 2004.

software reuse economics [2,5,6,7,9]. This work has provided a valuable starting point for our model; however, the benefits of a product line stem from more than the reuse of software. The long-term goal of our work is to build a comprehensive model that fully represents the relationships among the artifacts of a product line organization and the contribution of those artifacts to the costs and benefits of the product line.

Economic Models and Cost Models

An economic model of a system presents all of the variables, such as costs and benefits, which are needed to explain how changes in a cost affect an anticipated benefit. While a full-fledged economic model for product line development is certainly needed, it is a long way off. Such a model would let a manager predict return on investment in a product line initiative in all of its various forms: new market share, staffing needs, productivity, time to market, and cost. For the time being, however, we limit ourselves to a first-order model of the cost aspect: What will be the development cost of starting, running, adding to, merging, splitting, or retiring a product line?

Of course, even the most sophisticated economic model might not replace a manager's experience or instincts. The best economic model probably won't take into account intangibles such as customer loyalty, organizational culture, political influences, or personality factors. It will, however, constitute an important tool in a savvy manager's decision-making tool kit.

Requirements for a Cost Model

Two levels of cost models are needed. A first-order model is needed for quick, gross estimates and a more detailed model is needed for detailed planning. Our work currently focuses on the first-order model. We feel that the first-order cost model should have the following qualities:

- It should provide gross estimates quickly and easily
- It should apply to most, if not all, of the scenarios with which a product line manager is faced (more on these in the next section);
- It should, where possible, make use of cost models that already exist for software development and not re-invent them.
- It should provide guidance and insight into commonly occurring product line situations and answer commonly asked cost-based questions.

To address the last requirement, we make use of product line scenarios.

Product Line Scenarios

To begin work on a cost model, it is useful to think of a set of common situations that occur in product line practice for which cost information would be helpful, such as the scenarios given in Table 1.

Table 1. Scenario descriptions.

Scenario #	Description
1	An organization has a set of products in the marketplace that were developed more or less independently. It wishes to explore the possibility of converting them to a software product line, built from a common set of core assets.
2	An organization has a set of products that it plans to bring to the marketplace, but which are not yet under development. It wishes to explore the possibility of building them as a software product line on top of a common set of core assets.
3	An organization has a set of products that it plans to bring to the market, and is planning to build them as a software product line. It wishes to explore building a core asset base to support a larger set of the products than the ones currently planned. This scenario is similar to #2 except that here the organization intends to perform the product line analysis without knowing all of the products that will be in the product line.
4	An organization has two or more software product lines that appear to have some overlap with each other. It wishes to know if it would be economical to merge them – that is, to merge the core assets bases and to build the affected products from the new combined platform.
5	An organization is planning to bring a new product to market, and wishes to know what the cost implications are of developing this product under the auspices of an already-existing product line, or building it in a stand-alone fashion.
6	An organization wishes to start a new software product line on the basis of already existing ones. It wishes to know the best strategy from a cost perspective: Should it build a new asset base? Should it reuse one of the asset bases and extend it as needed? Should it "scavenge" one or more of the asset bases to produce the new one? And should it keep or abandon the old asset bases once the new product line is deployed?
7	An organization currently has at least one product line. Due to changing marketing conditions, the organization is considering dropping a product that was previously planned as part of the product line but has not been built yet. The manager would like to know the cost benefit of dropping the product.

Examining these and other scenarios reveals a pattern that can be exploited to our benefit. Each can be seen as a special case of a general product line scenario, see Fig. 1, which can be described as follows:

We have n product lines, each comprising a set of products, and we have s1 stand-alone products. We wish to transition to the state in which we have m product lines, each comprising a (perhaps different) set of products, and we have s2 stand-alone products. Along the way, we add k products or delete d products.

By judiciously setting the general scenario's parameters, we are able to express each of the seven scenarios above, as shown in Table 2. Note that this simple model does not distinguish between scenarios two and three. In a more comprehensive model, the information for the additional products would be tagged with a higher risk level than the products in scenario two.

As a next step, the long-term evolution of an organization, its products, and its product lines can be viewed as a series of these basic scenarios. To illustrate this view, we compare proactive and reactive adoption strategies for the same green field situation aiming at a single product line covering n products: the reactive adoption strategy corresponds to n applications of Scenario #5 (i.e., each application adds a single product to the product line). The proactive strategy corresponds to a single application of Scenario #2 with $k=n$.

Table 2. Scenario summary.

Scenario #	N	S1	k	d	m	S2
#1	0	S1 >0	0	0	1	0
#2	0	0	k>0	0	1	0
#3	0	0	k>0	0	1	0
#4	P1>=2	0	0	0	P2<P1	0
#5	1	0	1	0	1	0 or 1
#6	P1>=1	0	k>0	0	P2 > P1	0
#7	P1>=1	0	0	1	P2=P1	0

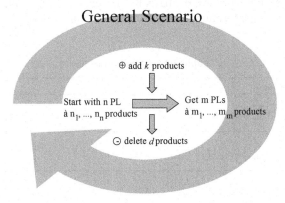

Fig. 1. General Scenario.

Components of the Cost Model

In keeping with the requirement to provide a first-order estimate quickly and easily, we introduce a cost model based on three *cost functions*:

- $C_{unique}()$ is a function that, given the relevant parameters, returns the development cost to develop unique software that itself is not based on a product line platform. The result might be a complete product, or it might be the unique part of a product whose remainder is built atop a product line core asset base.
- $C_{cab}()$ is a function that, given the relevant parameters, returns the development cost to develop a core asset base suited to satisfy a particular scope. C_{cab} differs from C_{unique} in that it must take into account the cost of performing a commonal-

ity/variability analysis, the cost of designing and then evaluating a generic (as opposed to one-off) software architecture, and the cost of developing the software so designed. C_{cab} may be invoked to tell us the cost of developing a core asset base where none currently exists, or it may be invoked to tell us the cost of deriving a desired core asset base from one or more already in place.

- $C_{reuse}()$ is a function that, given the relevant parameters, returns the development cost to reuse core assets in a core asset base. C_{reuse} includes the cost of locating and checking out a core asset, tailoring it for use in the intended application, and performing the extra integration tests associated with reusing core assets.

These cost functions represent a divide-and-conquer approach to the question of how much software product line development costs. Each of these functions represents a separate idea and can be implemented through a variety of approaches including existing measures in some cases. The estimated cost of developing the product line will only be as accurate as the measures used to implement each of the cost functions. With these cost functions in hand, however implemented, we can now observe that the cost of developing a software product line can be expressed as

$$C_{unique} + C_{cab} + C_{reuse}.$$

This simple expression will form the basis for prosecuting each of the scenarios listed above. Table 3 gives the formulation for each scenario in terms of the cost model.

Table 3. Scenario Formulae.

Scenario #	Formula
1	$C_{cab} + \sum_{i=1}^{s1} C_{unique}(p_i) + \sum_{i=1}^{s1} C_{reuse}(p_i)$
2	$C_{cab} + \sum_{i=1}^{k} C_{unique}(p_i) + \sum_{i=1}^{k} C_{reuse}(p_i)$
3	$C_{cab} + \sum_{i=1}^{k} C_{unique}(p_i) + \sum_{i=1}^{k} C_{reuse}(p_i)$
4	$C_{cab} + \sum_{i=1}^{n_1+n_2} C_{unique}(p_i) + \sum_{i=1}^{n_1+n_2} C_{reuse}(p_i)$
5	$C_{cab} + C_{unique}(p) + C_{reuse}(p)$
6	$C_{cab} + \sum_{i=1}^{n_i} C_{unique}(p_i) + \sum_{i=1}^{n_i} C_{reuse}(p_i)$
7	$(C_{cab} + \sum_{i=1}^{sum} C_{unique}(p_i) + \sum_{i=1}^{sum} C_{reuse}(p_i)) - (C_{cab} + \sum_{i=1}^{sum-1} C_{unique}(p_i) + \sum_{i=1}^{sum-1} C_{reuse}(p_i))$ $\because sum = \sum_{i=0}^{s1} n_i$

Example

To see how this model might be applied in practice, let us consider a small but reasonable example. A company has three stovepipe products in the market, and is planning to market another three products soon. Management wishes to know whether it should move to a product line approach or stay with the one-at-a-time development paradigm.

The cost to build the three new systems (sys4, sys5, and sys6) in a stovepipe fashion can be estimated by using past experience (if, for instance, they resemble the three existing products in complexity), or by traditional software development prediction methods:

$$\sum_{i=4,5,6} Cost(Sys_i) \tag{1}$$

The cost on the other hand of migrating to a product line approach is calculated by applying a series of scenarios that leads to the desired result. One way of describing the migration process in the example is the application of the sequence of scenarios: #1, #3, and #5. The migration cost thus involves the cost for transforming the three existing products (sys1, sys2, and sys3) into a software product line (as in Scenario #1) while building a core asset base general enough to handle all six products (as in Scenario #3), plus the cost of developing sys4-sys6 as part of that product line as in Scenario #5, (except that C_{cab} is now equal to 0):

$$C_{cab} + \sum_{i=1,2,3} C_{unique}(p_i) + \sum_{i=1,2,3} C_{reuse}(p_i) + \sum_{i=4,5,6} C_{unique}(p_i) + \sum_{i=4,5,6} C_{reuse}(p_i) \tag{2}$$

Comparing these two sums, equations 1 and 2, indicates which is the better strategy, based on development cost. Factoring in maintenance would involve hypothesizing a series of specific maintenance upgrades and comparing the cost under both circumstances, modeling each change as discussed previously.

Conclusions

The introduction of product line development today is based on the personal conviction of people, usually strong individuals, who have a strong belief in the merits of product line development and drive the whole development towards a product line approach.

This is of course not a mature engineering approach. In a mature engineering field, it is possible to explicitly analyze the potential of different alternatives. While people still play a strong role, they are supported by strong methods. Due to the shortcomings of our existing models for the merits of product line development, at this point we have not yet reached this stage. However, we regard the economic model we are about to develop as a key step towards sound engineering for product line development.

References

1. P. C. Clements and L. M. Northrop. *Salion, Inc.: A Software Product Line Case Study*, CMU/SEI-2002-TR-038, 2002.
2. Dagstuhl Seminar No. 03151, 2003.
3. John M. Favaro. *A comparison of approaches to reuse investment analysis*. In Proceedings of the Fourth International Conference on Software Reuse, pages 136–145, 1996.
4. Peter Knauber, Jesus Bermejo, Günter Böckle, Julio Cesar Sampaio de Prado Leite , Frank van der Linden, Linda Northrop, Michael Stark, David M. Weiss. *Quantifying Product Line Benefit*. In Proceedings of the Fourth International Workshop on Product Family Engineering, 2001.
5. Wayne C. Lim. *Reuse economics: A comparison of seventeen models and directions for future research*. In Proceedings of the Fourth International Conference on Software Reuse, pages 41–50, 1996.
6. A. Mili, S. Fowler Chmiel, R. Gottumukkala, and L. Zhang. *An integrated cost model for software reuse*. In Proceedings of the 22nd International Conference on Software Engineering, 2000.
7. Jeffrey S. Poulin. *Measuring Software Reuse*. Addison–Wesley, 1997.
8. Klaus Schmid. An Initial Model of Product Line Economics. In Proceedings of the Fourth International Workshop on Product Family Engineering, pp. 38-50, LNCS 2290, Springer, 2001.
9. David M. Weiss and Chi Tau Robert Lai. *Software Product-Line Engineering*. Reading, MA: Addison Wesley, 1999.
10. Ed Wiles, Economic models of software reuse: a comparison and validation, Ph.D. Thesis, University of Wales. 2002.

Salion's Experience
with a *Reactive* Software Product Line Approach

Ross Buhrdorf, Dale Churchett, and Charles W. Krueger

Salion, Inc., 720 Brazos St., Ste. 700
Austin TX 78701 USA
{ross.buhrdorf,dale.churchett}@salion.com
BigLever Software, Inc., 10500 Laurel Hill Cove
Austin TX 78730 USA
ckrueger@biglever.com

Abstract. Using a *reactive* software product line approach, Salion made the transition to software product lines with 2 person-months of effort, the equivalent of 1% of the effort required to build its baseline enterprise software product. This is two orders-of-magnitude less than the effort typically reported with *proactive* software product line transition efforts. Since the transition, Salion has achieved 90-day time-to-market intervals for seven new commercial products in its software product line, with each new product deployment requiring only 10% of the effort required to build its baseline enterprise software product. This report summarizes Salion's experience with a reactive software product line approach, some of the unique contributions of the experience, and generalizations that characterize how other organizations may benefit from reactive product line techniques.

1 Introduction

The Salion product line story offers insights into the opportunities and benefits of the *reactive* approach to software product lines as well as to the conditions under which a reactive approach is suitable. In this report, we first discuss the specifics of the Salion experience along a timeline: (1) the *start-state* prior to adopting a software product line approach, (2) the *transition* to a reactive software product line approach, and (3) the *steady-state* where products are deployed and maintained using a reactive software product line approach. Subsequently we draw generalizations from the experience to characterize ways in which other organizations might benefit from reactive software product line techniques. Additional details on the Salion product line experience can be found in an SEI case study[3].

The distinction between a *reactive* approach and a *proactive* approach to software product lines is in how the scope of the product line implementation is managed. In a proactive approach, all product line variations on the foreseeable horizon are implemented, in advance of when they may actually be needed in a deployed product instance. In a reactive approach, only those product line variations needed in current products are implemented[1][2].

F. van der Linden (Ed.): PFE 2003, LNCS 3014, pp. 317–322, 2004.

2 Start State

Salion is a software startup, creating a new product for a new market[4]. As such, there was no prior experience building commercial systems in the domain.

The marketing and engineering teams started by analyzing, designing and implementing a generic baseline system intended to serve the target customer base. Software engineering techniques such as use case analysis, architectural focus, and modular design and implementation were utilized, though initially no software product line techniques were employed.

As Salion approached the market with the new product concept and baseline product, the need for a product line – as opposed to a single general purpose product – became clear. The need was identified for two binding times of variation, product build time (referred to as product *customization*) and product startup/runtime (referred to as product *configuration*).

3 Transition

Being a startup, Salion could not afford the upfront time, cost, and effort typically associated with adopting a proactive software product line approach. The baseline product required 190 engineer-months over the course of 12 months. If we extrapolate using the typical effort data described in the side bar *It Takes Two* on page 226 in [3], a traditional proactive transition would have taken Salion 2 to 3 times the effort of the baseline product, or 380-570 engineer-months over 24-36 months. This time and effort would have doomed the company.

Two key decisions characterize Salion's transition to a reactive product line approach:

- The unmodified architecture, design, and source modules from the baseline product served as the core assets for the product line. Initially, no variations were introduced into the core assets.
- Tools and techniques to support product variation were put in place in order to efficiently react to new requirements for product variants. BigLever Software GEARS, an off-the-shelf software product line technology, was utilized to extend Salion's existing configuration management and build system to allow multiple product variations to be created from its core assets[5]. Details of the product line approach adopted by Salion can be found in [8] and [3].

By utilizing the existing baseline product for core assets and off-the-shelf technology for software product line management and automation, Salion made the transition to a software product line approach in 2 person-months of planning and implementation effort.

4 Steady State

In the steady state, the Salion core asset base undergoes constant evolution in rapid reaction to new requirements. Requirements for change come from two sources: (1)

requirements from new customers that cannot be satisfied from the existing product line, and (2) new internal marketing requirements to extend or refine existing capabilities of the product line.

Using this reactive approach, Salion has maintained 90-day time-to-market deployments for new customers. The total effort to implement these new product variants ranges from 5% to 10% of the effort required for the baseline product (i.e., factor of 10 to 20 productivity improvement)[9].

In order to maintain high levels of efficiency, Salion utilizes a GEARS *software mass customization production line* to generate all products from the core assets. All products in the product line can always be automatically "manufactured", or generated, from the evolving core asset base. Products are never directly modified after being generated by the production line, so there is never any wasted effort on divergence, duplication, merge forward, or merge backward (see pages 41-43 in [8]).

Over time, Salion has gained experience on optimizing the balance between "thinking ahead, but not too far ahead" in its reactive approach. Being excessively proactive has proved to be wasteful due to inaccurate guesses about what customers might want. In contrast, much less time is spent reengineering when specific variants are implemented reactively when they are needed and when abstractions are refactored as they emerge from the evolving product line. An unexpected result is that the total source code line count of the core asset base continues to shrink even as new products, features, and variants are added to the product line[6][7].

The following two subsections describe two reactive scenarios, the first for new customer requirements and the second for new internal marketing requirements.

4.1   Reacting to New Customer Requirements

The security system in place at Salion is divided into two subsystems: Authentication and Authorization. The authentication subsystem is a common component and therefore is out of scope of any customization requirements. The authorization system is also a common component, but the rules that dictate who can do what in the system is configurable; the rules of which reside in an XML document.

Due to the complicated nature of the authorization rules, and the inherent cost of testing every permutation of user roles in the system, it was decided not to customize this area of the product.

After two years of using a stable and understood set of authorization rules, a new customer required a complex modification involving field-level security on the input screens and the addition of a group permissions mechanism. The latter requirement seemed reusable across all product instances, and was easily turned into a common feature. The daunting task of customizing the authorization rules remained.

Using a reactive approach and GEARS, the file containing the authorization rules was converted into a variation point, allowing the previously existing rules to be used by previously existing product instances, while the new rules were implemented and applied only for the new customer. The effort required to define the new rules was minimal and no common code was touched because (1) the framework mechanism was well-designed (it did not know or care about the rules contained in the XML definition file) and (2) the framework simply expected the file to exist (no coding tricks were required in order to ensure the correct XML definition file was loaded per customer).

A combination of the component based architecture, smart deployment strategy and early plans to mitigate such risks by installing GEARS allowed Salion to react quickly to a customer request that might have otherwise stressed the product line architecture.

4.2   Reacting to Internal Marketing Requirements

Salion's *Supplier Customer Relationship Management Solutions*™, an enterprise software system for companies whose revenue stream starts by receiving and bidding on *requests for quotes* (RFQs), consist of three modules: Opportunity Manager, Proposal Manager and Knowledge Manager. Opportunity Manager deals with the pre-quote sales and sales process management activities. Proposal Manager deals with the process and collaboration around the generation of the quote. Knowledge Manager deals with the analysis of the data that is gathered in the course of using the product suite.

In the initial design and development of the Knowledge Manager module, Salion knew there would be a need for summary "reports". The challenge with creating a new product category is to focus on the vision of the critical parts of your solution and not spend too much time on solutions for the many non-critical parts. Reports were one of these non-critical areas that needed a good answer on a partially flushed out concept.

The initial attempt at defining the reports system proved to be too proactive, attempting to define in great detail all possible requirements that might be reasonable for the target customers. After 4 months of specification, analysis, and preliminary design on a reporting toolkit, it became clear that there was considerable effort, uncertainty, and risk associated with implementing the reports feature. At this point, we stopped and asked, "Is this where we should be spending so much of our time at this stage of the product?"

It was this uncertainty and the necessity to use resources wisely that led us back to a more reactive product line approach. Simply put, given that we were unsure about the long-term vision for reports, we chose to implement only the reports required to support the current customers, developing each customer-specific report as a product line variant. After implementing the reports for a few customers, abstractions have begun to emerge that can be refactored into the common core assets of the product line. This was the first of many areas where we utilized the reactive approach to put off the long-term definition efforts until experience with customers gave us accurate requirements.

Having the ability to focus on the critical functional design points and not on the non-critical areas has been a great benefit for the product and the customer. No time is wasted on proactive product definition in non-critical areas for which there are no clear customer requirements. Being reactive, we get it right the first time with each customer until we discover the right combination of features and functions for a given product area. The efficiency and effectiveness of our reactive product line approach gives us a competitive advantage over other enterprise class software companies.

5   Generalizing Lessons Learned for Reactive Approach

We believe that many of the lessons learned in the Salion experience with a reactive software product line approach can be generalized and broadly applied to other product line initiatives. In the following paragraphs we group the generalized lessons learned according to the timeline used earlier in this report (start state, transition, steady state).

Generalizations for the start state:

- If the proactive approach represents an adoption barrier due to the associated risks and investments in time and effort, then a reactive approach offers a lower risk and lower cost alternative.

Generalizations for the transition:

- If one or several existing systems have a good representative architecture, design, and implementation, then they can be used with almost no effort to create the baseline of the core assets for the product line (and the initial product), even if they were not created with product lines in mind.
- Off-the-shelf software product line tools and technology reduce the upfront time and transition effort.

Generalizations for the steady state:

- If at all possible, avoid divergence and duplication among products and core assets by engineering and generating every product build from the core asset base. Avoid further development on products generated from the core assets.
- If you can accomplish the previous bullet, then don't make a hard distinction between domain engineering and application engineering. Everyone should be working on the core assets and the production line that generates all products.
- Use customization and refactoring to find emerging abstractions in order to avoid inaccurate and over-generalized proactive design efforts.
- Initially use reactive customization for features that are not fully understood or that are low priority. A more proactive design and implementation can be effectively deferred until sufficient domain knowledge and time is available.

6   Conclusions

By broadly applying reactive techniques, we believe that software product line initiatives can be easier to launch, offer greater benefit, are more accurate, more agile, and more efficient, plus introduce less risk.

References

1. Krueger, C. *Easing the Transition to Software Mass Customization* . Proceedings of the 4th International Workshop on Product Family Engineering. October 2001. Bilbao, Spain. Springer-Verlag, New York, NY.
2. Clements, P. and Krueger, C., *Being Proactive Pays Off / Eliminating the Adoption Barrier.* IEEE Software, Special Issue of Software Product Lines. July/August 2002, pages 28-31.

3. Clements, P. and Northrop, L., *Salion, Inc.: A Software Product Line Case Study* , Software Engineering Institute (SEI) Technical Report CMU/SEI-2002-TR-038, Carnegie Mellon University, Pittsburgh, PA, November 2002.
4. Salion, Inc. Austin, TX. www.salion.com.
5. BigLever Software, Inc. Austin, TX. www.biglever.com.
6. Krueger, C. and Churchett, D., *Eliciting Abstractions from a Software Product Line* , in Proceedings of the OOPSLA 2002 PLEES International Workshop on Product Line Engineering. Seattle, Washington. November 2002, pages 43-48.
7. Buhrdorf, R. and Churchett, D., *The Salion Development Approach: Post Iteration Inspections for Refactoring (PIIR)* , Rational Edge, www.therationaledge.com/content/mar_02/ m_salionDevelopment_rb.jsp, March 2002.
8. Krueger, C., *Variation Management for Software Product Lines* , in Proceedings of Second International Conference, SPLC 2, San Diego, CA, August 2002, pages 257-271.
9. Krueger, C. *Data from Salion's Software Product Line Initiative* , Technical Report 2002-07-08-1, BigLever Software, Austin, TX, July 2002, available as http://www.biglever.com/papers/SalionData.pdf.

Towards a Taxonomy for Software Product Lines

Charles W. Krueger

BigLever Software, Inc., 10500 Laurel Hill Cove
Austin TX 78730 USA
ckrueger@biglever.com

Abstract. Drawing from the growing number of software product line experiences and case studies, this report describes a taxonomy for characterizing different software product line approaches. The taxonomy helps to illuminate the general principles of software product line engineering and the effectiveness of different software product line solutions in different situations.

1 Introduction

Software product line case studies have reported some of the greatest improvements in software engineering productivity, cost, and quality since high-level languages were introduced in the late 1950's[1]. One would expect a rush by the software industry to exploit the competitive advantages offered by software product lines. However, our experience in marketing commercial software product line technology and services at BigLever Software is that most of the software industry is either unaware of the emerging field of software product lines, or if an organization is aware they don't understand how software product lines might be applied in their situation[2][3].

Part of the problem is that case studies and descriptions of product line approaches often take a narrow view of a specific solution without the perspective of a point solution in a broader solution space[4]. Uninitiated readers have reported difficulty to us in making the leap from these point solutions to both the general and specific principles that might apply to their particular situation.

What is missing is a clear and concise taxonomy describing the space of software product line problems and associated solutions. There is sufficient research and experience in the field to start drawing generalizations and identifying how specific solutions and case studies lay as point solutions within a generalized taxonomy.

2 What Should a Taxonomy Illustrate?

The objective of a software product line is to optimize software engineering effectiveness and efficiency by capitalizing on the commonality and managing the variation that exists within a product line of similar software systems. As such, a taxonomy for software product lines should illuminate how well an approach capitalizes on commonality and manages variation.

F. van der Linden (Ed.): PFE 2003, LNCS 3014, pp. 323–331, 2004.

In order to *capitalize on commonality*, duplication and divergence must be avoided for software artifacts in a software product line. Common artifacts should be consolidated and maintained in a single source. Similar artifacts should be consolidated and maintained in a single source along with the variations explicitly represented.

In order to effectively and efficiently *manage variation*, the complexity and combinatorics associated with software variation must be constrained. Variations should be explicitly and formally represented so that they can be easily viewed, reasoned about, and mechanized.

Therefore, in the taxonomy proposed here, the primary focus is on how a software product line approach avoids duplication and divergence, consolidates commonality, controls complexity and combinatorics, and formally represents and mechanizes variation.

3 Building Blocks of the Taxonomy

The primary distinction between software product line engineering and conventional software engineering is the presence of *variation* in some of the software artifacts. In the early stages of software product line engineering, software artifacts contain variations that represent unbound choices about how a final software product will behave. At some point during the engineering process, decisions are bound for the variations, after which the behavior of the final software product is full specified. This is illustrated in Figure 1.

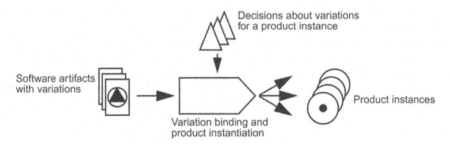

Fig. 1. Binding Decisions about Variation.

It is possible to have multiple binding times for variation in a single software product line approach. In this case, some decisions are bound earlier in the process while some decisions are deferred until later in the process. Examples of different binding times and mechanisms include:

- Source reuse time. Specialization, glue, frameworks, binary components.
- Development time. Clone-and-own, independent development, design/architecture
- Static code instantiation time. CM branches & labels, directory naming, GEARS.
- Build time. Preprocessors, script variants, application generators, templates, aspects.
- Package time. Assembling collections of binaries/executables/resources, GEARS.
- Customer customizations. Code modifications, glue code, frameworks.

- <u>Install time</u>. Install config file. Wizard choices, licensing.
- <u>Startup time</u>. Config files, database settings, licensing.
- <u>Runtime</u>. Dynamic settings, user preferences.

The representation of multiple binding times in the taxonomy is illustrated in Figure 2.

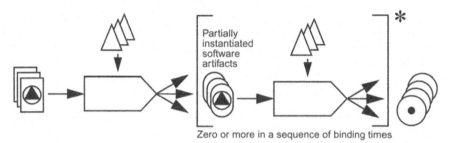

Fig. 2. Multiple Binding Times.

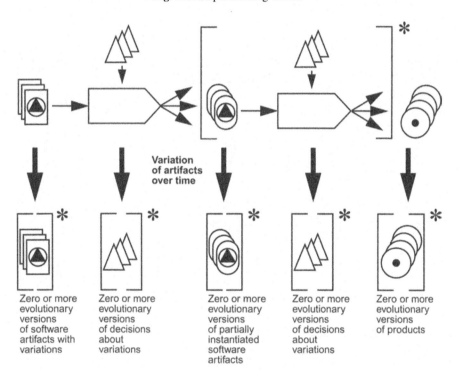

Fig. 3. Evolution of Software Artifacts over Time.

As with conventional software engineering, the software artifacts in a software product line are subject to maintenance and evolution. The variation of software artifacts over time – as well as the variation within the space of the product line – is an important factor in the software product line taxonomy[5]. The taxonomy's representation of variation over time for software product line artifacts is illustrated in Fig. 3.

Evolutionary changes to an artifact or decision may require that those changes be propagated to the upstream or downstream artifacts in the product line workflow. The possible dependencies that need to be considered include:

- Update paths. A change made to an upstream artifact may need to be reflected in all existing downstream artifacts previously derived from the original artifact.
- Feedback paths. If downstream artifacts can be manually modified, then a change made to a downstream artifact may need to be fed back to the original artifact or artifacts from which the original downstream artifact was derived. When upstream artifacts are modified, update paths may need to be recursively applied (as described in the previous bullet).
- Cross-merge paths. If downstream artifacts can be manually modified, then a change made to a downstream artifact may also need to be reflected in its peers.

Figure 4 illustrates the potential upgrade, feedback, and cross-merge paths in the taxonomy.

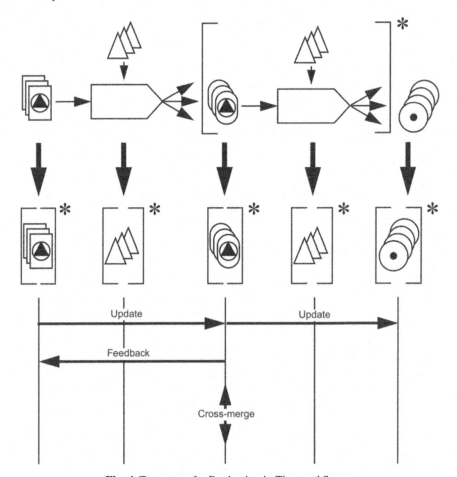

Fig. 4. Taxonomy for Production in Time and Space.

3.1 Production

A binding time in the taxonomy represents a step in a software engineering process where fully or partially instantiated products are created from software artifacts that contain variation. This *production* step is a key discriminator between different software product line approaches, so the taxonomy represents information useful in distinguishing among the approaches. Refer to Figure 5 for the following descriptions of information characterizing the production step.

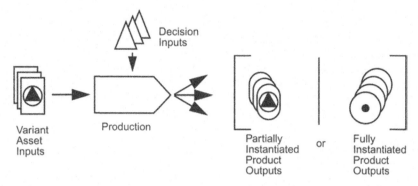

Fig. 5. Production for a Single Binding Time.

Production Activity

- Automated versus manual production. The production activity can be fully automated, completely manual, or somewhere in between. Examples of fully automated approaches include application generators, where high level decisions are sufficient to generate product outputs. Examples of completely manual approaches include the textual *production plan*, where software engineers interpret and follow directives in the plan and the decision inputs to tailor, integrate, and provide "glue code" around reusable core variant assets to create product outputs.
- Production roles. Some product line approaches define a separate role for the production activity called *product engineering* (or *application engineering*), distinct from the *domain engineering* role responsible for engineering the variant asset inputs. Other approaches do not distinguish between these two roles. Separate roles are common in approaches with manual production while a single role is more common in approaches with fully automated production.
- Periodic production. As with conventional software engineering, the production step in software product line engineering is typically not a one-shot activity. Products may need to be periodically reproduced to reflect enhancements to the variant asset inputs, decision inputs, and production techniques. The frequency of periodic production may be measured in terms of hours in agile approaches with high degrees of production automation or in terms of year in sequential and highly manual production approaches.

Decision Inputs
- Decision representation. Different formats are utilized to represent decision inputs, ranging from informal language descriptions to formal machine-interpreted languages.
- Decision guidance. Different types of decision making guidance can be provided during the decision process for a particular product, ranging from written heuristics to constraint checking to full-blown expert system guidance. The size and complexity of decision set and the degree of automation desired influence the level of decision guidance.
- Decision role. The decision making role for a particular product may be separate from other engineering roles (e.g., a product marketing role) or it may simply be part of the application engineering or overall production engineering role.
- Replayable decisions. For periodic production of products, the previously made decisions for each product may need to be "replayed" rather than rederived from first principles. Persistent representations and replay mechanisms for decisions vary based on the need for automation and the frequency of periodic production.

Variable Asset Inputs
- Representation. The variable asset inputs (also referred to as *core assets* for the first stage in a multiple binding time sequence) can come in different formats, such as binary executable representations, formats requiring further automated instantiation or translation, or mutable reusable source code that is manually instantiated, modified, tailored, or extended as needed during production.
- Variation mechanisms. Different variation mechanisms are utilized in support of different production approaches. During production, the decision inputs are utilized to instantiate the asset inputs using the variation mechanisms in the assets inputs. A variation mechanism can be as simple as an empty block in source code that an application developer must fill in, or as complex as a translation system that generates source code from high-level requirement specifications.

Product Outputs
- Representation. Similar to the asset inputs, the product outputs from production can take on many different formats: binary or source, mutable or immutable, partially or fully instantiated.
- Partial instantiation. If the product outputs are partially instantiated in one stage of variation binding, the unbound variations become the variable asset inputs for the next stage and can be characterized accordingly.

3.2 Product Line Evolution

The taxonomy characterizes how a product line approach avoids duplication and divergence, consolidates commonality, and controls complexity and combinatorics during the evolution of a product line. This information is illuminated by the character and number of update, feedback, and cross-merge paths required during evolution. Refer to Figure 6 for the following descriptions of information used in the taxonomy to characterize product line evolution.

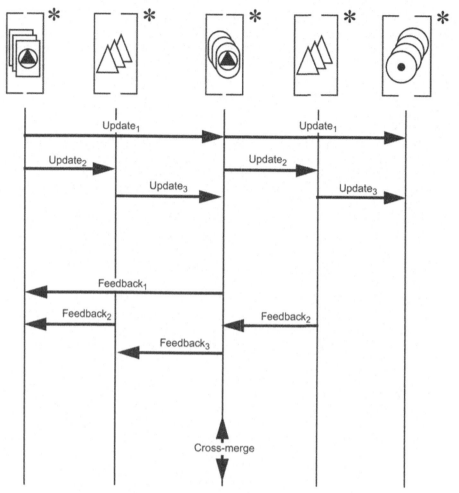

Fig. 6. Update, Feedback and Cross-merge During Evolution.

Updates

- <u>Asset-to-product updates</u> (see Update$_1$ arrows in Figure 6). Updates to products may be required whenever a new version of an asset is created. For every product produced from the original asset, an update operation is required. If the software assets are mutable during production, then the update operation may require a manual merge for each product. If multiple binding times are utilized, updates may need to be applied recursively. If decisions cannot be replayed automatically, decisions and production may have to be manually replayed for each product.

- <u>Asset-to-decision updates</u> (see Update$_2$ arrows in Figure 6). If modifications to asset inputs result in new or different ways of making decisions, then updates may be required for the decision model, decision mechanisms, and replayable decisions. Some or all products may need to be recursively updated to reflect updates to the decisions.

- Decision-to-product updates (see Update₃ arrows in Figure 6). Any changes to the decisions for a particular product may require an update for the product. Changes to the way that decisions are mapped to products may require all downstream products be updated. If the production process is manual or if manual modifications have been applied to the downstream products, then manual production and merging may be required for each product.

Feedback

- Product-to-asset feedback (see Feedback₁ arrows in Figure 6). If asset inputs are mutable during production, then evolutionary changes to a product may need to be fed back to the originating assets. Resulting changes to asset inputs may require that updates be recursively applied to all other products created from the asset, as described in the previous section.
- Decision-to-asset feedback (see Feedback₂ arrows in Figure 6). Changes to the decision model or mechanism may require feedback to upstream asset inputs to make them consistent with the decisions, usually affecting the variabilities in the asset inputs. This must be done prior to updating the downstream products with the modifications to the decision inputs.
- Product-to-decision feedback (see Feedback₃ arrow in Figure 6). If asset inputs are mutable during production, then evolutionary changes to a product may need to be reflected in the decision model, decision mechanisms, and replayable decisions. Some or all products may need to be recursively updated to reflect updates to the decisions.

Cross-Merge

- If asset inputs are mutable during production, then changes to a product may need to also be cross-merged to some or all peer products. This may be an interim solution while a longer term feedback and updates are performed, as described in the previous sections.

4 Scope Management

The taxonomy distinguishes between two methods for managing the scope of a software product line, *proactive* and *reactive* [2][6]. In the case of a pure proactive approach, all of the products needed on the foreseeable horizon are supported by the product line. In the case of a pure reactive approach, only the products needed in the immediate term are supported by the product line. There is, of course, a continuum between the two.

The reactive approach typically requires less upfront effort than the proactive approach since the initial scope coverage is smaller. To implement the same scope coverage, the reactive approach incrementally defers the cost and effort over longer period of time compared to the proactive approach.

It is possible for upstream artifacts in a software product line (e.g., the architecture) to have a more proactive scope than downstream artifacts (e.g., the source code). However, the overall scope of the product line is defined by the scope of final product set that can be produced, tested, and deployed.

5 Transition

There are a variety of approaches for transitioning to, or adopting, a new software product line approach. The taxonomy distinguishes among the following characteristics:

- Source of core asset inputs. The primary distinction is between the *green field* versus *extractive* approach[2]. With the green field approach, the core assets are coded from scratch (i.e., reusing no existing products). With the extractive approach, existing software artifacts from one or more existing products are extracted and reengineered to serve as the core asset inputs for the product line. An interesting special case of the extractive approach is where a single product serves as the core asset baseline, followed by a reactive approach to incrementally extend the scope to include additional products.

- New versus enhancement. Another distinguishing characteristic for the transition to a software product line approach is whether or not a product line already exists. If a product line exists, then the taxonomy described in this document can be used to characterize both the *initial state* of the product line and the *target state* of the product line. The transition can then be characterized in terms of how to move from the initial state characterization to the target state characterization. Note that if the initial state has multiple products managed using even the most primitive, ad hoc, conventional techniques such as clone-and-own or IFDEFs, it is still a product line that can be characterized using the taxonomy.

6 Conclusions

This software product line taxonomy helps to both (1) characterize the space of possible approaches to engineering a software product line and (2) provide a framework for comparing and contrasting different point solutions and the associated trade-offs among them. Ideally this will provide a means to educate novices to the field of software product lines and help identify optimal choices when defining a product line approach.

References

1. Clements, P. and Northrop, L., Software Product Lines: Practices and Patterns, Addison-Wesley, 2000.
2. Krueger, C. Easing the Transition to Software Mass Customization . Proceedings of the 4th International Workshop on Product Family Engineering. October 2001. Bilbao, Spain. Springer-Verlag, New York, NY.
3. BigLever Software, Inc. Austin, TX. www.biglever.com
4. Bosch, J., Maturity and Evolution in Software Product Lines: Approaches, Artefacts and Organization , in Proceedings of Second International Conference, SPLC 2, San Diego, CA, August 2002, pages 257-271
5. Krueger, C., Variation Management for Software Product Lines, in Proceedings of Second International Conference, SPLC 2, San Diego, CA, August 2002, pages 257-271
6. Clements, P. and Krueger, C., Being Proactive Pays Off / Eliminating the Adoption Barrier . IEEE Software, Special Issue of Software Product Lines. July/August 2002, pages 28-31.

Architecture Recovery for Product Families

Martin Pinzger[1], Harald Gall[1], Jean-Francois Girard[2], Jens Knodel[2],
Claudio Riva[3], Wim Pasman[4], Chris Broerse[4], and Jan Gerben Wijnstra[5]

[1] Distributed Systems Group, Vienna University of Technology, Vienna, Austria
{pinzger,gall}@infosys.tuwien.ac.at
[2] Institute for Experimental Software Engineering, Fraunhofer, Kaiserslautern, Germany
{girard,knodel}@iese.fhg.de
[3] Software Architecture Group, Nokia Research Center, Helsinki, Finland
claudio.riva@nokia.at
[4] Philips Medical Systems, Eindhoven, The Netherlands
{wim.pasman,chris.broerse}@philips.com
[5] Philips Research Laboratories, Eindhoven, The Netherlands
jangerben.wijnstra@philips.com

Abstract. Software product families are rarely created right away but they emerge when a domain becomes mature enough to sustain their long-term investments. The typical pattern is to start with a small set of products to quickly enter a new market. As soon as the business proves to be successful new investments are directed to consolidating the software assets. The various products are migrated towards a flexible platform where the assets are shared and new products can be derived from. In order to create and maintain the platform, the organization needs to carry out several activities such as recovering the architectures of single products and product families, designing the reference architecture, isolating the variable parts, and generalizing software components. In this paper, we introduce a product family construction process that exploits related systems and product families, and we describe methods and tools used. We also present an approach for classifying platforms according to platform coverage and variation and describe three techniques to handle variability across single products and whole product families.

1 Introduction

Software product families aim at sharing more than the design effort (i.e. code, designs, requirements, and test cases) to reduce development costs and increase the number of product introduction. Typically, families are built on top of existing, related software systems whereas the common artifacts among these systems are integrated to a common asset base. In terms of software architecture these common assets are architectural artifacts used to design the reference architecture of resulting product families. We refer to reference architecture as core architecture for subsequent product families (and products) independently of implementation. A product family architecture follows a reference architecture and is the basis for single products with respect to achieving maximum sharing of parts in the implementation [8].

Constructing a reference architecture out of related products and existing product families basically is a non-trivial task, because knowledge and experiences from previous architectural designs cannot be transferred explicitly. Additionally, architecture

F. van der Linden (Ed.): PFE 2003, LNCS 3014, pp. 332–351, 2004.

descriptions are often not available or insufficient and diverge from implemented concrete architectures. And there is a lack of commonality analysis methodologies to determine the common architectural artifacts that are mandatory for the construction of the reference architecture. As a consequence the amount of manual work is high and the costs of introducing a product family approach increase.

In the context of the European project CAFÉ (from Concepts to Application in system-Family Engineering) [5] we concentrated on these research issues along constructing reference architectures and product family architectures. In this paper we briefly describe our easy-to-use, yet flexible process for reference architecture construction and point out new techniques that aid architects in this context. Our construction process combines techniques and tools that are used to analyze related systems, determine common assets, and integrate these assets along with new ones into the design of a reference architecture.

Variability is a key issue in designing the reference architecture and building the platform. We address these issues and describe an approach for classifying platforms according to two properties: (1) coverage of the platform as indicator of how much additional work is needed to make a specific family member based on the assets in the platform; (2) type of variation mechanism as indicator of how easy it is to produce/develop a specific family member and what might be the impact of unforeseen requirements that must be supported. The outcome of our classification is a guideline that can be used to select the proper variation mechanism for a product family platform. Further, we report on experiences we gained through an investigation of a number of existing product families and in particular describe three approaches to handle changes to platforms.

The remainder of this paper is organized as follows: Section 2 introduces our reference architecture construction process and describes each phase in detail. In Section 3 we describe our approach for classifying platforms according platform coverage and variation. Section 4 shows three approaches to handle changes to platforms and how to adapt the reference architecture. Results are presented in Section 5 and Section 6 draws the conclusions and indicates future work.

2 Reference Architecture Construction by Exploiting Related Prior Systems

Product families are rarely developed on a green meadow; on the contrary, they are most often based on pre-existing systems. An integral part of every product family is the reference architecture that specifies the fundamental architectural concepts in a domain to which resulting product families and products have to conform to [4, 8].

We have developed a reference architecture construction approach that exploits related existing systems and takes into account knowledge gained out of the individual systems and experiences made with already field-tested solutions and reference architecture fragments obtained in prior systems. Figure 1 depicts our construction process. Four major steps are performed:

- Determine architectural views and concepts
- Architecture recovery
- Analysis of recovered architecture
- Design of a reference architecture

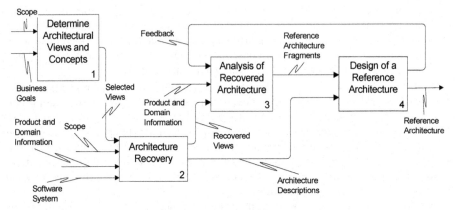

Fig. 1. Reference architecture construction process.

In the following sections we describe each process step in more detail and point out techniques and tools we used (the subsection numbers correspond to the steps in Figure 1).

2.1 Determine Architectural Views and Concepts

For the recovery of the architecture of each individual system, engineers have to agree upon the architectural aspects to be extracted and upon which architectural description language to use for representing them. Basically, the description language should be the same among all individual systems to ease and facilitate the application of commonality analysis (tools).

In the context of our architecture recovery approach we refer to architectural aspects as *architectural concepts* and *architectural views*. Regarding architectural concepts we particularly concentrate on the architectural style by which a software system is built. The style defines the types of building blocks that can be used to compose the system (e.g. components, classes, applications) and the communication infrastructure that enables the components to interact at runtime (e.g. software busses, remote procedure calls, function calls) [12]. Such concepts represent the way developers think of a system, and they are first class entities the terminology of the reconstruction process.

Architectural views such as described by Hofmeister et al. [5] and Kruchten [10] are abstractions of underlying entities (e.g. source model entities) and each view focuses on certain properties of the software architecture such as, for example, structure, control, or communication.

In order to select the proper architectural concepts the business goals and the scope of the emerging reference architecture of planned product families are taken into account. In terms of our architecture recovery approach we focus on the extraction of the following set of architectural views:

- *Component view* to show the high-level dependencies among the logical packages (groups of components).
- *Development view* to show the source code organization and include dependencies.

- *Task view* to show the grouping of components in different OS tasks and the inter-task communication due to the exchange of messages.
- *Management view* to show the organization of the component factories and their dependencies (caused by component usage among different factories).
- *Organizational view* to show the geographical distribution of the components in the development sites.
- *Feature view* to show the implementation of a set of features at the component level.

The decision, which views should be selected for reconstruction, is important to the next steps of our approach, since the selected views form the foundation of the following activities.

2.2 Architecture Recovery

The architecture of each related prior individual software system has to be recovered next. The architecture will be documented in terms of the selected architectural views and elicited concepts. The architecture recovery step is strongly influenced by product and domain information (e.g. domain expert input, requirements specification, user manuals, (mostly outdated) design documentation, etc).

Figure 2 depicts the process we use for the extraction of architectural concepts and views. It consist of four major phases whereas we start with the definition of architectural concepts based on existing design documentation and expert knowledge from designers and developers of the system.

The second step is concerned with creating a raw model of the system containing the basic facts about the system at a low level of abstraction. The facts can be extracted with a variety of methods: lexical or parser-based tools for analyzing the

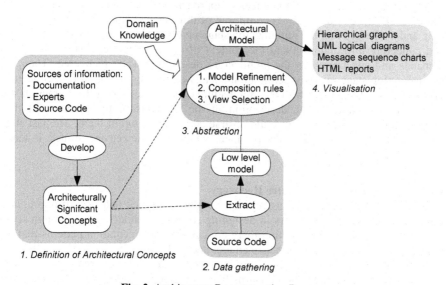

Fig. 2. Architecture Reconstruction Process.

source code, profiling tools for the dynamic information, manual analysis of design documents, and interviews with the developers. The raw model is typically a large and unstructured data set.

In the third step we enrich the model by classifying and structuring the model elements in hierarchies and by removing architecturally irrelevant information. This task requires the human input of the domain experts and combines the raw facts with the domain-specific knowledge of the system. The result is the selected set of architectural views that describe specific concerns of the architecture.

The fourth step is about visualization of the results. Basically, we rely on three visualization formats: *hierarchical relational graphs* for navigating and manipulating the graphs; *hyperlinked web documents* for publishing the architectural models on the web; and *UML* diagrams that can be imported in traditional CASE tools (e.g. Rational Rose or Together).

Apparently, the process step of abstracting meaningful higher-level views from the low-level model or source code is the most complex task. A lack of appropriate (semi)automatic tools increases manual work. To reduce this manual effort we have developed techniques along with tools that were integrated into our reconstruction process. In following paragraphs we briefly describe three techniques addressing the abstraction issue and point out reference architecture construction relevance. For a detailed description we refer the reader to related publications [2, 16, 17].

Semi-automatic Component Recovery

Software components represent basic building blocks (i.e. assets) of software systems that can be reused in single products and products of product families. For the construction of a common asset base, the product family architecture, and the more abstract reference architecture knowledge about components realized by each product family candidate system is mandatory. A first step towards this is the extraction of potential software components and the relationships between them.

We developed a semi-automatically approach that extracts components from source code [2]. Our approach is composed of three stages: initialization, reconstruction, and analysis. First, the initialization stage involves identifying the desired results and collecting information about the context of the architecture. The context poses demands and constraints on the architecture description to be recovered. Then, the reconstruction stage involves semi-automatically extracting one or more architectural views and reviewing them with the architecture expert. The goal of the extraction step is to obtain an as accurate description of the elements of the system and their interrelations as needed, and to build abstracted views on top of them. The last stage involves analyzing the results. The produced views are reviewed and refined, if necessary, with a group of experts.

Pattern-Supported Architecture Recovery

Architectural styles and patterns represent widely observed and occurring architectural concepts that aid engineers in designing software architectures. Although styles do not imply their implementation there are certain implementation patterns that are typically used by engineers to realize an architectural style.

In our pattern-supported architecture recovery approach we concentrate on the extraction of such implementation patterns from source code and related files (e.g. meta data information, configuration files) and the lower-level model. Often important architecture related information about the realization of a particular style is specified in configuration files such as, for example, the configuration of which and how components communicate with each other.

Concerning textual data files we apply extended string pattern matching as described in [16, 17] and demonstrated in [9, 15]. Our lexical analysis tool facilitates the specification of simple and complex pattern definitions and allows for the generation of user-defined output formats. Extracted information about matched pattern instances result in "pattern views" that indicate the use of a particular architectural style. Further, the extracted information complements lower-level source models extracted by parsers [9].

For the investigation of lower-level models we use relational algebra tools such as Grok [7]. Based on domain and expert knowledge engineers specify new or load existing pattern definitions from a pattern repository. Similar to the lexical analysis technique described before matched pattern instances are indicators for certain architectural styles.

Combining the results of both analysis techniques, engineers gain information about the architecture and implementation of each product family candidate system that is mandatory for the integration and the construction of a reference architecture.

2.3 Analysis of Recovered Architecture

This task aims at producing useful information for the design of the reference architecture by detailed analysis and comparison of the prior software systems. A comparison of multiple systems is possible and reasonable, because all prior systems are related to each other:

- They implement similar features to a certain degree.
- They operate in the same set of domains.
- They provide similar functionality.
- They were developed within the same organization (most of the time).

In the following two sections we describe the basics and the process of our analysis approach that compares and assesses the software architectures of product family candidate systems.

Principles and Goals of Architecture Comparison

The comparison is based on the architectural descriptions of the individual systems (or partial descriptions containing most relevant information). The goal is to learn about different solutions applied in the same domain, to identify advantages and drawbacks of the solutions, and to rate the solutions with respect to requirements of the product family. By achieving these goals, architecture comparisons contribute to the fulfillment of the given quality goals in the design process of reference architectures.

Product and domain information is used to answer questions when comparing the architecture of different systems and extracting plausible rationales. Existing architecture descriptions are rarely up-to-date or rarely contain all the needed views. However, they offer an anchor point from which the reverse architect produces a description close to the expert mental model of the system. Explicitly recording the concepts,

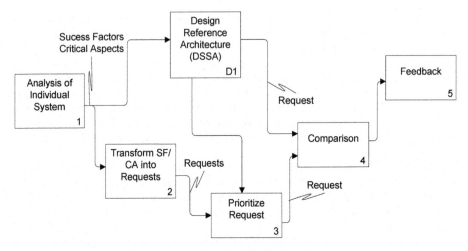

Fig. 3. The Architecture Comparison Process.

features and functionality expected in the system can guide the reverse architect and help the production of a description expressed in the terms used by experts.

The experts then annotate the architecture descriptions with rationales. When comparing the prior systems' architecture, more detailed information about concepts, solutions or additional views may be needed. This has to be fulfilled by another iteration of architecture recovery. The architecture descriptions are then completed by the newly gained information (e.g., trade-offs involved in the choices of multiple system, integration strategies).

The infrastructure and the architecture style present in the individual systems constitute key inputs to the design of the reference architecture. In addition they offer a good point to anchor initial comparisons. Analyzing the recovered architectures of different systems has the goal to find out how and why they address the requirements in the way they do. It also documents the implementation strategies employed by each system to address a given concern and evaluates their success in their respective context and compares the strategies with respect to criteria relevant to the product family. It captures the conjectured rationales and trade-offs involved in selecting the strategies used in a system (similar to Parnas' idea of a "rational development process and why we should fake it" [12]).

Architecture Comparison Process

According to the principles and goals described in the previous section we developed an iterative architecture comparison process as depicted in Figure 3. The process consists of five major steps:

1. Analysis of Individual Systems:
   The process starts with an analysis of all given individual systems (the later phase of architecture recovery). The architecture of each system is recovered with the help of the techniques mentioned above. The goal of this step is to learn about the essential characteristics of each software system. There are two main categories: Success factors (SF) report about means, patterns, and strategies that worked well,

i.e. with the help of these factors advantages were gained. Success factors of different solutions provide essential input to the design process of the reference architecture. The software architect can learn about what worked out well, and why it was a success. Critical aspects (CA) are circumstances (e.g., a pattern, or infrastructure) that leaded to negative, sensitive consequences. For the design process of the reference architecture, it is necessary to handle those aspects with caution (or to avoid them at all if possible).

2. Transform Success Factors and Critical Aspects into Requests:
In the second step, the success factors and the critical aspects are transformed into scenarios, if possible. These scenarios extend the scenario list built when designing a reference architecture. A scenario captures functional and quality requirements of the product family the architecture is designed for.

3. Prioritize Requests:
This optional step orders the scenarios with regard to their PuLSE.DSSA priorities (see Section 2.4), so that potentially important ones are processed first. As the order in which scenarios are addressed is very important, those scenarios that are considered to have the highest significance for the architecture should be selected first.

4. Comparison of Different Systems:
For a comparison, three activities have to be performed one after the other:
a. *Select Systems:*
   To start, the software systems to be compared against each other have to be selected. The elicitation of these comparison candidates is an activity, which has to be performed carefully for two reasons. On the one hand, the effort for comparing a sound set of comparison candidates is significantly lower than comparing all systems. On the other hand, choosing too few systems leads to more or less useful results in the context of a product family
b. *Detailed Analysis:*
   In the second activity, the selected systems underlie a detailed analysis focusing on issues concerning the requests. For each system, it will be analyzed how it addresses the requirements reflected in the request. Several questions will be answered after this activity: why was it done this way, what were the trade-offs, and how does the solution fulfill the requirements.
c. *Conditioning:*
   Each system will contribute to the concluding results, but the more systems are compared, the more data about these systems is produced. To reduce the amount of information, the results are conditioned so that the most important data and the essential gains in experience are returned.

5. Feedback:
In the final step, feedback is integrated into the process. A new iteration may be started because of the feedback. Or the information gained in several feedbacks may lead to new insights about the product family context, so that more information about some solutions is required. Due to the learning effects during the detailed analysis, new scenarios refine the design process of the reference architecture.

The resulting reference architecture should be of a higher quality when using recovered information gained from prior systems than when designing a new one from scratch. Exploiting the pre-existing, individual software systems is worthwhile, since it helps to understand success factors and critical aspects of applied solutions in individual systems. Furthermore, it can avoid bottlenecks by already knowing about consequences, and it promotes the learning about applied solutions. The detailed analysis of recovered architectural descriptions and the comparison of different but related systems are crucial in order to benefit from the existing systems by reusing implemented knowledge, as well as field-tested architectural means (e.g., patterns, strategies and infrastructure, etc.). Hence, we are able to draw conclusions about the applied solutions of the individual systems within their specific context and we learn about the consequences of specific solutions, and therefore this step contributes substantially to the design process of the reference architecture.

2.4 Design of Reference Architecture

PuLSE-DSSA [1] is an iterative and scenario-based method for the design of reference architectures. The basic ideas of PuLSE-DSSA are to develop a reference architecture incrementally by applying scenarios in decreasing order of architectural significance and to integrate evaluation into architecture creation. The quality of the architecture is monitored and assured in each development iteration. Figure 4 shows the main inputs to the PuLSE-DSSA method. In order to design a reference architecture the architect has to consider information obtained through architecture recovery as well as a prioritized list of business goals, given functional and quality requirements, and architectural means and patterns. The inputs are used to produce a reference architecture that satisfies the given goals and requirements of the product family and that is documented using a number of previously selected or defined architectural views. The PuLSE-DSSA method guides software architects in systematically making design decisions based on identified and documented business and quality goals and in assessing whether the architecture under design really satisfies the requirements. The design process might request to deepen the analysis and comparison of the architecture of prior systems, to refine views, or to produce other specialized views.

The following architecture recovery information is gained during the analysis of recovered architectures and fed into the design process of the reference architecture:

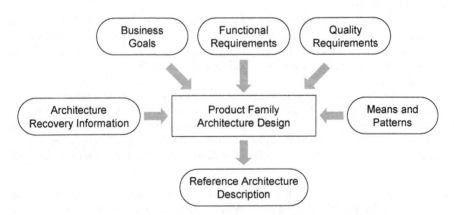

Fig. 4. Inputs and Outputs of the Reference Architecture Design Process.

- **Rationales:**
  Solutions in individual systems have been applied in certain contexts to fulfill requirements. Learning about the rationales behind these solutions can help when facing similar or the same requirements for the whole product family.
- **Means and Patterns:**
  Architectural means and patterns used in existing systems and identified in architecture recovery can extend the collection from which the architect can choose in the design process of the reference architecture. The catalogue of means and patterns is expected to come from three different information sources, collected from literature, gathered from other architecture design projects, or recovered from existing systems.
- **Consequences and Pattern Instantiations:**
  Similar to the previous step, information about patterns and their instantiation obtained during architecture analysis of recovered systems can be used as an input when designing reference architectures. Consequences resulting from the instantiation of a specific pattern should be considered when designing the reference architecture. A consequence of a pattern instantiation for instance may be an impact on a quality goal.
- **Evaluation of the Architecture:**
  The evaluation of the reference architecture with respect to functional and quality requirements and the achievement of business goals can benefit from existing individual systems, since the decision whether or not a requirement or goal is fulfilled can not always be answered on the architectural level but by experimentation with a prior system that fulfills the goal with the same underlying concept.
- **Documentation:**
  To document the reference architecture of a product family, recovered architecture descriptions of individual systems can be reused, when the reference architecture and the individual systems have an architectural fragment in common (e.g., when one of the prior systems forms the basis for the product family, or when distinguishable fragments of a single system contribute to the product family).

The knowledge gained in the analysis of the recovered architectures is integrated into the design process of the reference architecture. The construction of the reference architecture provides feedback on what is important for the design process, and which views should be presented in more details.

3 Reference Architecture and the Platform Type

Based on the reference architecture the platform with reusable assets for the product family will be built. The definition of the reference architecture and the platform is an iterative process. The reference architecture can be considered as a high-level description, whereas the platform contains the actual building blocks from which members of the product family can be constructed.

Every product family will have its own unique context, for example a specific business strategy and a specific application domain. As a consequence, each product family approach has its own specific characteristics that fit in such a context. This means again that the type of platform that is used for a product family must also be tuned to this context. This leads to a vast range of platform types. In order to get a grip on this range, we have analyzed a number of product families and their platforms. This analysis led to two dimensions for classifying platforms, namely:

- coverage of the platform
- type of variation mechanism

These dimensions will aid the classification of product family approaches and will both facilitate the selection of a new platform approach for a particular context and support the evaluation of existing approaches. When considering the four steps for the construction of a reference architecture as discussed above, these dimensions can be used at several places. For example in the fourth step where the reference architecture is designed, the two dimensions provide guidelines on which variation mechanisms to use and which platform coverage to apply. Both dimensions also support the evaluation of a reference architecture. Both dimensions are explained below; more on this topic can be found in [24].

3.1 Platform Coverage

Roughly speaking, the coverage indicates the relation between the size of the platform and the additional artifacts that are required to make a complete product within the family. The decision about the coverage of the platform is influenced by several factors including non-technical ones related to business, process and organization (see also [23]).

To explain the platform coverage in some more detail, the concept of subdomains within an architecture is important. By subdomain we mean a sub area within a system that requires some specific knowledge, for example the image processing subdomain or the image acquisition subdomain in a medical imaging system. These subdomains may deal with application knowledge relating to the end user, or with technical knowledge relating to the peripheral hardware or computing infrastructure knowledge. In the context of design and realization, such a subdomain usually results in one (or a few) modules/components with a well-defined interface. In Figure 5, a schematic reference architecture is shown with different coverages for the subsystems. The two leftmost subsystems are completely covered, indicated by the gray color. The

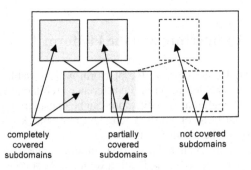

Fig. 5. Reference Architecture and Coverage of Subdomains.

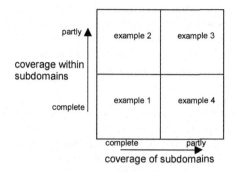

Fig. 6. Classification of Platform Coverage.

two subsystems next to them are partly covered, so that specific functionality has to be added to make a concrete product. The two rightmost subsystems have dotted lines, meaning the no generic functionality is provided for them, but additional subsystems can be added to make concrete product.

Based on the subdomains we can now express the coverage of a platform. In our study we had one product family that was set up in such a way that each delivered family member contained the same software. As a consequence, the platform contained all subsystems of the family, and each of these subsystems was covered completely, resulting in a complete coverage. Another example was a platform that contained all subsystems, but allowed the product development group to add specific functionality to the subsystems. So all subsystems are covered, but the subsystems are internally partially covered. Here, about 75% of the functionality was handled by the platform, leaving 25% to be added by the product groups. A third example was a platform that only dealt with a subset of the subdomains, and these subdomains were only partly covered. A fourth situation is where a part of the subdomains are dealt with, but these subdomains are completely covered. This leads to four areas in which platform coverage can be classified, see Figure 6. It depends on the actual platform, how much of the functionality is already realized inside the platform and how much work still needs to be done by the product groups to make the specific products.

3.2 Variation Mechanisms

In the context of designing reference architectures variability is a key issue. The used variability mechanisms influence the flexibility of the platform, the way specific products can be made with it, the effort needed to make a product, etc. In our investigation we encountered various types of variation mechanisms and classified them in a two-dimensional space. This classification is made from an architectural point-of-view:

- *below architectural level*
  When an architect is defining an architecture, he/she amongst others defines the main components from which the system will be built. These components have interfaces via which they will interact. When the variation of the system stays within the components and does not impact the architecture, we classify the mechanism

as being below architectural level. Examples of mechanisms in this category are configurable components, component frameworks with plug-in components, or even components for which only the interface is defined. The architect must be aware of the variation that can be realized within such components and provides rules and guidelines on how to do so. But, the variation is realized by the developers of the components.

- *at architectural level*
  At the architectural level, components and interfaces are important entities, along with rules and guidelines. The product family architect can identify the components from which the system should be built. If the members of the product family cannot be built from such a fixed set of components, another possibility is to define a basic platform to which the development groups can add their own specific components, preferably via predefined interfaces. A third possibility is to capture important architectural concepts in interfaces. The interfaces should then allow new components to work with each other, even if they were not identified from the beginning. This allows addition of new components to the system.

More information on this classification and the variation mechanisms can be found in [24].

4   Component Generalization in Product Families

Technology for platforms is changing rapidly and requires adaptation of reference architectures to make them resilient to these changes. The solution can be found by making the whole or certain areas of the architecture of the product families more explicit and especially pay attention to the variation mechanisms. Summarized, in CAFÉ we considered the following approaches:

- Trace features to components to support migrating shareable features to the platforms.
- Add a technology abstraction layer in the platform.
- Compare similar products families, to identify commonalities and extend the framework of a product family to serve different families.

4.1   Feature-Oriented Reverse Engineering

The definition of the term "feature" is often domain dependent and in the literature there are several interpretations. We reference to the work of Tuner et al. [25] for an extensive discussion of this definition. In this article, we use the term "feature" to mean a "coherent and identifiable bundle of system functionality" that is visible to the user via the user interface.

We distinguish between the *problem domain* and the *solution domain*. The problem domain focuses on the user's perspective of the system and describes the requirements (functional and non-functional) that the system has to satisfy. The solution domain is centered on the developer's perspective and concerns with the implementation of the system. The problem domain specifies *what* the system is supposed to do.

The solution domain specifies *how* the system achieves what is promised. The features represent the contact point between the problem and the solution domain. At this level, marketing people and developers can speak a common language and they can understand each other.

Features (typically used to advertise the product) are implemented by particular architectural elements (such as components, classes, functions). They also represent the highest elements of abstraction we can decompose a system in the solution domain. This leads to the concept of *"feature oriented reverse engineering"* proposed by Turner et al. [25]. From a *feature engineering* perspective, the goal of reverse engineering is to discover how the features have been implemented, what are they interactions, or what are the necessary components for their execution. In the mobile phone example, reverse engineering could be used to identify how the feature *"make call"* has been implemented in a GSM and a 3G phone, or to discover how the feature "receive call" interferes with game playing, or to recover the procedure that has been used to set up a WAP connection with GPRS.

Understanding the implementation of the features is a crucial activity in the context of a product family. Features represent reusable assets that are available in the platform and are shared among different products. Each product development project can select the platform features, configure them and integrate them in the products. Features are combined together to create a particular product and they are presented in the user interface (UI) in a simple and coherent way. This approach puts a strong pressure on the integration phase and in the design of the UI. In particular, the problems of feature interaction (functional or logical dependency between features) are often unavoidable and difficult to control.

To avoid costly delays in the integration phase, we require

- to identify and specify the possible feature interactions as early as possible during the design phase and
- to analyze the implementation of the features (and their interaction) during the development of the product.

To tackle the first point Lorentsen et al. [11] have proposed a method for modeling the feature interactions in mobile phones with explicit behavioral models of the features. The approach is based on the Colored Petri Nets and allows the UI designers to simulate particular features and analyze their behavior with automatically generated Message Sequence Charts (MSC).

To support the second point, our reverse engineering technique is based on the extraction of static and dynamic information from the implementation of the system. The static information is extracted from the source code following the process described in Section 2.2. The dynamic information is extracted by instrumenting the system and tracing the execution of the features. The result is combined in the *feature view* that describes the implementation of a set of features at the architectural level. Our approach emphasizes the correct choice of architecturally significant concepts as described in Section 2.1, the abstraction as the key activity for creating high-level sequence diagrams, and relies on combining static and dynamic information in the same architectural views [21].

Our method is based on the following steps:

1. Create a use case that covers the set of features under analysis.
2. Execute the use case on the instrumented system and trace all the relevant information (such as function calls, messages, inter task communication, memory accesses).
3. Create the feature view by combining the extracted traces with a high level static view (typically, the component view or the task view).
4. Abstract the feature view by detecting interaction patterns to reduce its size.
5. Navigate the feature view by expanding/collapsing the participants and messages of the MSC, by filtering un-relevant information and by slicing the static views with particular dynamic scenarios.

This method allows us to derive insights about the implementation of the features and to navigate them in a high level abstracted form.

4.2   Adding Abstractions

An Operating System (OS) offers functionality towards all important system resources such as memory, timers, synchronization and communication mechanisms, I/O and underlying hardware, etc. Typically applications depend on this functionality and build upon it. In small systems not many applications use the offered functionality of the OS and if they do, designers and architects focus on a dependency that is as small and thin as possible.

In larger systems however more applications depend on the OS functionality. This increases the use of the OS and calls for a well-defined use of the offered functionality. Systems may even grow to a point where more than one computer is used and maybe even more than one OS. Rather than having software engineers to cope with the differences between OS's, an Operating System Abstraction Layer (OSAL) offers standardized functionality to all software engineers running on different OS platforms.

Thus an OSAL helps in standardizing usage of OS functionality, one can focus on solving domain problems rather then having to dig in OS differences. It even helps when changing from one OS to another (although this a job you do not want to do often). If an OSAL is build upon two different OS's, one will certainly run into compromises. Compromises will most certainly be found in the following fields: processes and threads, support for asynchronicity and real time behavior.

The easiest way to start an OSAL is to look at functionality widely used by all applications in the entire system. OS functionality that meets this requirement is usually: file I/O, memory management, synchronization principles, serial I/O and sockets. By focusing on these aspects, one has a quick win: in a short period of time, a large amount of functionality is abstracted which helps a lot of software engineers.

4.3   Generalization of a Framework

A product family is usually based on a platform, a set of common components and interfaces to be shared amongst the various members of the product line. At the beginning each of these components fits perfectly within the architecture of the product line, adhering to its set of architectural rules and designed according to its architectural paradigm(s). A common reuse problem occurs however when either the scope of the product line (and with that its architecture) is significantly changed (usually extended) or a component from it is extracted to be reused in the scope of another (possibly also a product line) architecture. Now probably there will appear architectural mismatches between the component and its new environment(s), which can range from differences in architectural styles, interface mechanisms, technology, etc. The component probably has to be redesigned to deal with two different environments, a process in which also the evolution of the existing architectures and possible compatibility issues play an important role. In this section we describe a case from the medical imaging domain at Philips Medical Systems in which a component developed in the context of single product family architecture is reused in a much wider scope. It addresses both the architectural changes involved in this generalization as well as aspects concerning backward compatibility.

Within the hospitals, more and more different imaging modalities with new application areas are used. Examples of such modalities are X-ray, Computed Tomography, Magnetic Resonance Imaging, and Ultra Sound. Furthermore, to give the best treatment to the patient, it is important that the various modalities are integrated in the hospital. This also poses more requirements on the servicing of this equipment.

The component for remote access as described in this section was originally developed within the context of the product family architecture for a single modality. This component provides important field service functionality to improve customer support (shorten reaction times) and lower overall service costs. It has been realized as a component framework with plug-ins, allowing field service procedures for specific hardware to be supported by specific plug-ins. After introduction of this component it appeared very attractive to enlarge the scope of it to multiple modalities, which needed the same type of functionality. However all of these modalities have of course their own (product family) architectures.

A product family architecture effort was already under way aiming at the definition of components for very generic (and non modality specific) functionality, see [22]. The main requirement for this architecture is that its components can be reused over multiple modalities that each maintains their own private architectures. It was therefore decided to lift the remote access level component to this level.

Moving the remote access component from its dedicated modality restricted product family architecture to a broader scope introduced four main groups of problems, which are discussed below.

- *requirements matching*
  Historically, there exists a plethora of detailed differences between the field service requirements for the different modalities, although the global service requirements are of course very similar over all medical imaging equipment. Fortunately the original set-up of the remote access component with its plug-ins already allows a great differentiation since all the actual hardware related tests are implemented in the plug-ins.
- *compatibility requirements*
  The remote access component was already deployed in its original product family architecture before it was elected for promotion to a much broader scope. Furthermore extensive investments were made in the development of the remote access plug-in components for this system. It is clear that the generalization of the remote access component was not allowed to nullify these investments.

- *architectural mismatches*
  The architectural differences between the various modalities are quite large. De-composition, interfacing, general mechanisms, but also low level issues like data-base access are very different from modality to modality. It is clear that the intro-duction of a generic remote access component is only feasible when it does not enforce a major turnover of the systems that want to incorporate it. Another issue encountered in the analysis of differences is a large number of more or less hidden dependencies of the framework on the original product family it was designed for. The main dependencies are on the operating system, the database, and mecha-nisms such as installation, registration and licensing.
- *technological differences*
  Several major technological differences exist between the various product lines in which the remote access component is deployed. The most important differences are in technologies such as operating systems, languages and middleware that must be supported by the remote access component.

So, there are many aspects to be taken into account in the migration of the remote access component to a wider scope. This is probably quite usual for this kind of mi-gration. Below, some choices to deal with these aspects are discussed.

- *operating system, middleware and language*
  For the time being the generalized component will be realized on the Windows platform, since this platform was used in most products. For the remote access component, also the COM/.NET framework is used. It must be noted here that this lock-in is circumvented for some of the generic components deployed in medical systems. Any explicit reference to a single middleware model (such as COM) in the core components is avoided. Separate wrapper layers are developed to map the components to a certain required interface mechanism like COM.
- *dependencies to infrastructure mechanisms*
  The remote access framework was dependent on the infrastructure of the original product family it was developed for, e.g. for installation. To break this link a pragmatic solution has been chosen: the relevant parts of the infrastructure have been copied to the context of the remote access component and are maintained separately from the original product line they were developed for initially.
- *component interfacing*
  For the generic components that are reused within several modalities within medi-cal systems, a set of generic interfaces and so-called information models have been defined. For example, interfaces exist for accessing patient or image data, to using logging of configuration data. Also, an interface is defined for the execution of a "job". The interfaces themselves are small and limited with all further infor-mation stored in data structures. The interface of a component in this case consists of its methods and a detailed description of the data model (called the information model) that goes with it. These principles are described in more detail in [22].

What are now the consequences of this approach for the remote access component? The original remote access component uses a strongly typed interface style with a extensive set of interfaces and interface methods for all the different stages in a field service procedure. This enforces a fixed order of activities, which is not desirable for all modalities. Furthermore these broad interfaces impose a certain maintenance risk.

Finally they restrict the flexibility for other modalities to build user interfaces and procedures according to their specification. Therefore a transfer to the much more generic interface and information models described above is made.

When considering the four steps as discussed in Section 2, the focus has been on the third and fourth step: the analysis of the different product families in which the generalized component will be used and the design that has to make the reuse of this component across multiple modalities possible. When considering the classifications as mentioned in Section 3, the modality from which the remote access component was taken has a high coverage. It uses amongst others component frameworks and plug-ins to realize variation (just as for the remote access component). The product family to which the remote access component has been transferred has a much broader scope. As a consequence, the platform coverage is much lower, relatively speaking. In this product family, generic interfaces are an important means for realizing variation across the different modalities. But also the component framework mechanism is still used for the remote access component. More on this generalization work can be found in [18].

5   Results

In the CAFÉ project we developed methods, techniques and tools for architecture recovery, product family and reference architecture construction, and component generalization in the context of product families. In particular, we:

- introduced a reference architecture construction process (Section 2);
- extended and devised architecture recovery methods and techniques (Section 2.2);
- described platform classification mechanisms and created guidelines that aid in platform selection (Section 3);
- described methods for handling platform variation and adaptation of reference architecture (Section 4).

To evaluate our methods, techniques and tools, we carried out a number of case studies with mobile phone systems, medical systems and a stock market system. More details about our achievements can be found in our common task deliverable (to be published), as well as in referenced publications or the CAFÉ website [5].

6   Conclusions

In this paper we focused on product family engineering and in particular concentrated on reference architecture construction by exploiting related pre-existing systems and on handling variability across single products and product families. The main contribution of our paper is a reference architecture construction process that integrates architecture recovery, architecture analysis and comparison, and the reference architecture design process. For each process step we pointed out key activities and described new, revised and extended techniques used.

Further, we addressed the handling of variability in platforms and the reference architecture that is a major issue of product family engineering. Particularly, we described two techniques for classifying platforms with respect to platform coverage and variation. The outcome of our classification is a guideline that aids engineers in selecting the proper variation mechanism for the product family platform. In addition to our classification techniques we presented three approaches to handle variability across single products and whole product families. These techniques base on the concept of making the whole or certain areas of the architecture of product families more explicit. Concerning these areas we took into account features, technology abstraction layers, and framework extension by commonalities identified across similar product families.

Future work will be focused on two issues that are concerned with the improvement of presented techniques and tools, as well as the integration of these techniques and tools into a workbench. Consequently, we have to devise a common data format for the data extracted and generated by our tools. We also plan to perform additional case studies to further evaluate and improve our reference architecture construction process and platform classification methods.

Acknowledgments

We are grateful to the national ministries of Austria, Germany, Finland, and The Netherlands for funding our work under EUREKA 2023/ITEA-ip00004 'from Concepts to Application in system-Family Engineering (CAFÉ)'. We further thank our industrial partners Philips, Nokia, and MarketMaker for providing the case studies. Finally, we would like to thank the anonymous reviewers for their feedback.

References

1. Anastasopoulos, M., Bayer, J., Flege, O., Gacek, C.: A Process for Product Line Architecture Creation and Evaluation – PuLSE-DSSA Version 2.0. Technical Report, No. 038.00/E, Fraunhofer IESE. (2000).
2. Bayer, J., Girard, J. F., Schmid, K.: Architecture Recovery of Existing Systems for Product Families. Technical Report, Fraunhofer IESE. (2002).
3. Bayer, J., Ganesan, D., Girard, J. F., Knodel, J., Kolb, R., Schmid, K.: Definition of Reference Architecture Based on Existing Architectures. Technical Report. (2003).
4. Bosch, j.: Design and Use of Software Architectures: Adopting and evolving a product line approach. Addison Wesley, Mass. and London. (2000).
5. CAFÉ (from Concepts to Application in system-Family Engineering): (http://www.esi.es/en/Projects/Cafe/cafe.html).
6. Hofmeiser, C., Nord, R., Soni, D.: Applied Software Architecture. Addison-Wesley, Reading, Mass. and London. (2000).
7. Holt, R. C.: Software Architecture Abstraction and Aggregation as Algebraic Manipulations. In: Proceedings of the 1999 conference of the Centre for Advanced Studies on Collaborative research (CASCON), Toronto, Canada. (1999).
8. Jazayeri, M., Ran, A., van der Linden, F.: Software Architecture for Product Families: Principles and Practice. Addison-Wesley, Mass. and London. (2000).
9. Knodel, J., Pinzger, M.: Improving Fact Extraction of Framework-Based Software Systems. In: Proceedings of the 10th Working Conference on Reverse Engineering (WCRE). (2003) to appear.

10. Kruchten, P. B.: The 4+1 View Model of architecture. IEEE Software, Vol. 12 Issue 6. (1995) 42-50.
11. Lorentsen L., Tuovinen A-P., Xu J.: Modelling Feature Interaction Patterns in Nokia Mobile Phones using Coloured Petri Nets and Design/CPN. In: Proceedings of the 7th Symposium on Programming Languages and Software Tools, Szeged, Hungary. (2001) 15-16.
12. Mehta, N. R., Medvidovic, N., Phadke, S.: Towards a taxonomy of software connectors. In: Proceedings of the 22nd International Conference on Software Engineering (ICSE), Limerick, Ireland. (2000) 178 – 187.
13. Parnas, D.L., Clements, P. C.. A Rational Design Process: How and Why to Fake It. IEEE Transactions on Software Engineering, Vol. 19, Issue 2. (1993) 251-257.
14. Pasman, W.: Platform Coverage and Variation in Product Family Approaches. Technical Report, Philips.
15. Pinzger, M., Gall, H., Jazayeri, M., Riva, C.: Extracting Architectural Views from Large Telecommunications Software: A Case Study. Technical Report TUV-1841-2002-50, Vienna University of Technology. (2002).
16. Pinzger, M., Fischer, M., Gall, H., Jazayeri, M.: Revealer: A Lexical Pattern Matcher for Architecture Recovery, In: Proceedings of the 9th Working Conference on Reverse Engineering (WCRE). (2002) 170-178.
17. Pinzger, M., Gall, H.: Pattern-Supported Architecture Recovery. In: Proceedings of the 10th International Workshop on Program Comprehension (IWPC). (2002) 53-61.
18. Pronk, B. J.: Component generalization in a multi product family context. Technical Report CAFÉ consortium-wide. (2002).
19. Riva, C.: Architecture Reconstruction in Practice. In: Proceedings of the 3rd Working IEEE/IFIP Conference on Software Architecture (WICSA). (2002).
20. Riva, C., Yang, Y.: Generation of Architectural Documentation using XML. In: Proceedings of the 9th Working Conference on Reverse Engineering (WCRE). (2002) 161-169.
21. Riva, C., Rodriguez, J. V.: Combining Static and Dynamic Views for Architecture Reconstruction. In: Proceedings of the 6th European Conference on Software Maintenance and Reengineering (CSMR). (2002) 47-55.
22. Wijnstra, J.G.: Components, Interfaces and Information Models within a Platform Architecture. In: Proceedings of the 3rd International Conference on Generative and Component-Based Software Engineering, Erfurt, Springer Verlag LNCS 2186. (2001) 25-35.
23. Wijnstra, J.G.: Critical Factors for a Successful Platform-based Product Family Approach. In: Proceedings of the 2nd Software Product Line Conference, San Diego, Springer Verlag LNCS 2379. (2002) 68-89.
24. Wijnstra, J.G.: Classifying Product Family Approaches using Platform Coverage and Variation. submitted for publication to Software: Practice and Experience.
25. Turner C. R., Fuggetta A., Lavazza L., Wolf A. L.: A conceptual basis for feature engineering. The Journal of Systems and Software, Vol. 49, Elsevier. (1999).

Software Product Family Evaluation

Frank van der Linden[1], Jan Bosch[2], Erik Kamsties[3],
Kari Känsälä[4], Lech Krzanik[5], and Henk Obbink[6]

[1] Philips Medical Systems
frank.van.der.linden@philips.com
[2] University of Groningen
Jan.Bosch@cs.rug.nl
[3] University of Duisburg-Essen
kamsties@sse.uni-essen.de
[4] Nokia Research Center
Kari.Kansala@nokia.com
[5] University of Oulu
lech.krzanik@oulu.fi
[6] Philips Research Laboratories
henk.obbink@philips.com

Abstract. This paper proposes a 4-dimensional software product family engineering evaluation model. The 4 dimensions relate to the software engineering concerns of business, architecture, organisation and process. The evaluation model is meant to be used within organisations to determine the status of their own software family engineering. Evaluation results may be used for benchmarking or improvement plans.

Introduction

The main arguments for introducing product families in industrial companies are to increase productivity, to decrease for time to market, and to increase of quality (dependability). To improve the family capability, Philips Medical Systems and Nokia are involved partners in a series of ITEA projects, ip99005 ESAPS (1999-2001), if00004 CAFÉ (2001-2003) and if02009 FAMILIES (2003-2005) [10]. A *software product family evaluation model* was prepared during CAFÉ. In this paper a first draft version of that model is presented. Within the FAMILIES project improved and more refined versions will be produced.

Since the late 80ies, a number of capability evaluation models have been developed for various fields of software development assessments with a focus towards process improvement. The proposed evaluation model takes into account, in addition to the process, other software engineering concerns. It collects and structures characteristics of a software production unit, division, or company, which are proven by experience to be effective. The purpose of the model is to:

- Serve as benchmark for effective software product family development
- Support assessments of software product family development for capability evaluations of software production units, divisions, or companies
- Support software product family development improvement, which involves performing assessments and creating improvement plans

F. van der Linden (Ed.): PFE 2003, LNCS 3014, pp. 352–369, 2004.
© Springer-Verlag Berlin Heidelberg 2004

The benchmark function helps in determining why and how to do family development, and in comparing and classifying existing cases of family development. Capability evaluations (internal or independent, e.g., competition analysis) may in principle be used for checking whether a software production unit, division, or a company satisfies the required family development capability conditions. The improvement function tells whether the improvement is necessary and what and how to improve.

We have identified 4 interdependent software development concerns according to the BAPO approach [1]:

- Business, how to make profit from your products
- Architecture, technical means to build the software
- Process, roles, responsibilities and relationships within software development
- Organisation, actual mapping of roles and responsibilities to organisational structures.

We will use this separation of concerns to provide 4 dimensions of the family evaluation framework. An organisation may have separate evaluation levels for each of these concerns. The fact that the BAPO concerns are interdependent materialises itself in the fact that actions that change one of them will have consequences for the others. In fact, improving the evaluation for one concern may introduce a lower level of evaluation for the others.

Background

Since the late 80ies, a number of capabilities evaluation models have been developed for various fields of assessment including systems engineering, software engineering, software acquisition, workforce management and development, and integrated product and process development. The overall idea is to compare a process carried out by an organisation to an ideal that is presented by a capability evaluation model. Process improvement is the elimination of differences between the current and the ideal process. This approach can be characterised as top-down. The assumption behind this approach is that improved processes led themselves to improved products.

The most prominent process improvement framework is the Capability Maturity Model (CMM), which was developed by the Software Engineering Institute (SEI) and published in 1993 [12] in the USA. The international counterpart of the CMM is the ISO/IEC 15504 Standard for Software Process Assessments (commonly called SPICE). For systems engineering, the SE-CMM and later EIA/IS 731 were developed. The CMMI (CMM Integrated) has been created recently by the SEI to integrate the SEI's Capability Evaluation Model for Software (SW-CMM), EIA/IS 731, and the Integrated Product Development Capability Evaluation Model (IPD-CMM) into a single coherent process improvement framework [6], [7]. Some of the developments resulting in the CMMI are shown in Fig. 1.

Bottom-up approaches to software process improvement take into account the individual goals of an organisation. Process improvement is driven by the characteristics of local environment. The assumption is here that an organisation must first completely understand its process, products, software characteristics, and goals before it can select a set of changes to improve its process. Software is not all the same and necessary process improvement actions differ as to whether an organisation aims at high quality or market-driven software [13]. The bottom-up approach is implemented

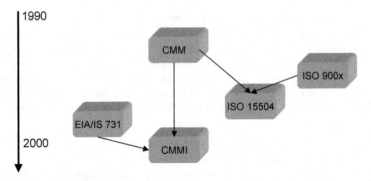

Fig. 1. History of Process Improvement Frameworks.

for example by Vic Basili's Experience Factory approach, which was introduced to institutionalise the collective learning of an organisation, which in turn is at the root of continual improvement and competitive advantage [2], [3].

Both the SEI and the European CAFÉ project are working on maturity frameworks for software product family development. SEI's Product Line Technical Probe (PLTP) allows examining an organisation's readiness to adopt or its ability to succeed with a software product family approach. The PLTP is based on the SEI's Framework for Software Product Line Practice[SM] (version 4.0 was published in [4]) as a reference model in collection and in analysis of data about an organisation. The results of applying the PLTP include a set of findings, which characterise an organisation's strengths and challenges relative to its product family effort, and a set of recommendations.

The Framework for Software Product Line Practice[SM] distinguishes 29 practice areas, which are divided loosely into three categories. *Software engineering* practice areas are necessary to apply the appropriate technology to create and evolve both core assets and products. *Technical management* practice areas are those management practices necessary to engineer the creation and evolution of the core assets and the products. *Organisational management* practice areas are necessary for the synchronization of the entire software product family activities [8].

The Information Technology for European Advancement (ITEA) project CAFÉ (From Concepts to Application in System-Family Engineering) has developed a reference framework for product family practices (CAFÉ-RF) [8]. The CAFÉ-RF consists of several models: a reference IT life-cycle for system families (identifies the major phases in an IT organisation when carrying out a system family effort), a process reference model (CAFÉ-PRM, represents major engineering activities operating on the core assets) shown in Fig. 2, and an asset reference model (CAFÉ-ARM, represents the major assets of interest).

BAPO

Within The ITEA project CAFÉ (From Concepts to Application in System-Family Engineering) we have identified 4 interdependent software development concerns, BAPO[1] [1]:

---

[1] The term BAPO originates from Henk Obbink, Philips Research.

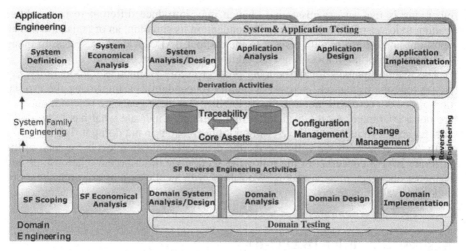

Fig. 2. CAFE Process Reference Model.

- **B**usiness, how to make profit from your products
- **A**rchitecture, technical means to build the software
- **P**rocess, roles, responsibilities and relationships within software development
- **O**rganisation, actual mapping of roles and responsibilities to organisational structures.

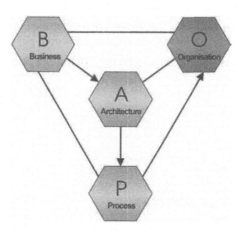

Fig. 3. The BAPO concerns.

We will use this separation of concerns to provide 4 dimensions of the family evaluation framework. An organisation may have separate evaluation levels for each of these concerns. The fact that the BAPO concerns are interdependent materialises itself in the fact that actions that change one of them will have consequences for the others. In fact, improving the evaluation for one concern may introduce a lower level of evaluation for the others. A simple connection is the fact that an improvement programme will cost money and resources, reducing the profit (Business concern). Another one is that an organisational change may introduce different responsibilities leading to lower process evaluation. Dependent on its situation, an organisation has an optimum level (profile) with respect to the distinct BAPO evaluation scales. In many situations the optimum level is not the highest level for each of them.

The main arguments for introducing product family are increase productivity, decrease for time to market, increase of quality (dependability). Improving the evaluation of one concern will increase the probability that these goals are reached, but they are not a guarantee. As the evaluation models mainly indicate what has to be done, and not how it should done, there is still a lot of freedom in not doing it right.

In the next sections we will describe the different evaluation levels for each of the different BAPO concerns. In the following section we describe the relationships and influences between these concerns. We follow with a collection of example situations and their evaluation levels.

Business Dimension (BAPO-B)

The business evaluation dimension deals with the way the organisation is able to manage and predict and steer the cost and the profit of the development. Four aspects can be identified which influence the evaluation in the business dimension:

- **Identity** – how well has the organisation formulated an identity relating to the family products it offers
- **Vision** – how well does the organisation aims for a future where the family products fit
- **Objectives** – how well does the organisation determine its future goals
- **Strategic planning** – how well does the organisation plan the family

We have defined the following level structure. Below we discuss them in more detail:

1. **Reactive**
2. **Extrapolate**
3. **Proactive**

Level 1, Reactive

- **Identity:** implicit
- **Vision:** short term (just cash flow)
- **Objectives:** missing
- **Strategic planning:** missing

This is the basic level for the business dimension. There is no vision, objectives and a business planning process to support the product family development. The available product family assets are reused in product development for opportunistic reasons. Decisions whether to make family assets, or buy, mine, or commission them are only taken for opportunistic reasons. There is no separate strategy to align marketing to product family development. Products from the family are marketed just as any other product.

Forces. In a very dynamic market this may be the only level obtainable. Marketing and business decisions have to be taken upon very short notice, resulting in strategic planning and long-term vision to be rather useless. However, if the market is more stable, moving towards the next level may be advantageous.

Relation to architecture, process and organisation. As there is no vision and real objectives, it cannot be expected that the architecture reflects them. Family requirements are only based upon the best guess of the architects. This may result in many ad hoc decisions in the architecture design. The process and the organisation will probably reflect the lack of business objectives and vision, in such a way that there are no targets for them, and it may be very difficult to adapt them to product family development.

Level 2, Extrapolate

- **Identity:** identified
- **Vision:** medium term
- **Objectives:** qualitative
- **Strategic planning:** ad hoc process

In this level planning for the product family is available. Scoping is performed to determine the borders of the family and roadmaps are used to plan the development of the family and to decide upon make family assets, or buy, mine, or commission them. Often the roadmaps are based upon business and technological scenarios. On a regular basis the roadmaps and scopes are updated.

There is an ad hoc strategy to align marketing to product family development. Products from the family are mainly marketed just as any other product. However, the marketing long-term vision is taken into account in scoping and the family planning.

Forces. Again, the domain is an important force. If the domain does not allow long term planning, this may be the best level obtainable. In mature or established markets a move towards the next level may be appropriate.

Relation to architecture, process and organisation. The architecture should be able reflect the business vision and the objectives. Moreover, the architecture will provide feedback towards the strategic planning process. Family requirements can be based upon the strategic plan and the marketing inputs. The process and the organisation will take into account the structure and roles related to this business level.

Level 3, Proactive

- **Identity:** managed
- **Vision:** long term
- **Objectives:** quantitative
- **Strategic planning:** institutionalised process

At this level decisions are based on quantitative cost models. Scoping is based upon expectations on the return of investment of the product family development effort. Roadmaps will be based upon intra-company agreements, time-to-market estimations and on profit expectations. Scoping and roadmaps are aligned between the different units within a single company. Resource availability, key and core technology for the company, time-to-market expectations, and profit and cost models influence decisions upon make family assets, or buy, mine, or commission them.

Marketing is aligned to product family development. The family will be marketed as a whole, and the position of the product in the family is part of the marketing strategy. Products involving cheap developments are pushed. Those that involve expensive developments are to be avoided.

Forces. The business aspects need maintenance. Moreover they should be in line with each other. Without this they will not be valid after some time, moving the evaluation in this dimension towards the previous level.

Relation to architecture, process and organisation. The business aspects give direction to the architecture planning. They are necessary inputs to enable the definition of the process and the organisation. Business activities have to be implemented by the process and the organisation.

Architecture Dimension (BAPO-A)

The technological approach taken to the development of software products varies substantially between different organisations. From our experience, these approaches can be categorised in five levels, where the first level exhibits no sharing of software artefacts and the highest level requires no product specific software development. The preferred approach for an organisation depends on the business goals that the organisation aims to achieve with the product family as well as the application domain of the software products and the maturity of the organisation in the process and organisation dimensions.

In our experience, one can identify four aspects that define the five approaches to the technology of the software product family. Below these aspects are discussed in more detail:

- **Product family architecture:** The product family architecture (PFA) can exist at several levels. The PFA may only distinguish between infrastructural and internal components, partially specify the software architecture in terms of components and their relations, fully specify the architecture or, finally, enforce the software architecture.
- **Product quality:** The quality of the products resulting from the family is, at lower levels, typically accidental as all attention is towards providing the right functionality. At higher levels, quality is managed more and more explicitly.
- **Reuse levels:** The reuse level indicates the amount of relative effort is spent on domain engineering when compared to application or product engineering.
- **Domain:** The final aspect that we discuss here is the domain of the products. Domains may be emerging, maturing or established. An emerging domain evolves rapidly and unpredictable, whereas a maturing domain still evolves rapidly, but more predictably. An established domain has a highly predictable and slower evolution path. Although the domain is of great importance to the success of the product family, it is an external factor that cannot be changed by the organisation.

We have defined the following level structure [4]. Below we discuss them in more detail:

1. **Independent Product Development**
2. **Standardised Infrastructure**
3. **Software Platform**
4. **Software Product Family**
5. **Configurable Product Base**

Level 1, Independent Product Development

- **Product family architecture:** not established
- **Product quality:** ignored or managed in an ad-hoc fashion
- **Reuse level:** Although ad-hoc reuse may occur, there is no institutionalised reuse
- **Domain:** emerging
- **Software variability management:** absent

An organisation developing products independently has no sharing of external or internal software artefacts. The commonality between products is not exploited.

Forces. For any software product family, there has to be a business case in terms of the family contributing to the business goals. Obviously, if there is no commonality to be exploited, this approach is the preferred one. However, if there is commonality, the organisation should consider evolving to one of the next levels.

Relation to organisation, process and business. Although it is not necessary, in most product development organisations, often product responsibility is assigned to different business units. Typically, each business unit is an independent profit and loss centre. There is no sharing, so neither the processes nor the business aspects require any integration.

Level 2, Standardised Infrastructure

- **Product family architecture:** specified external components
- **Product quality:** infrastructure supports certain qualities, for the remaining qualities an over-engineering approach is used
- **Reuse level:** only external components
- **Domain:** later phases of emerging or the early phases of maturing domain
- **Software variability management:** limited variation points from the infrastructure components

The first step that an organisation typically takes when evolving towards exploiting commonality in its products is to standardise the infrastructure based on which the products are developed. This infrastructure typically consists of the operating system and the typical commercial components on top of it such as a database management system and a graphical user interface. In addition, the organisation may acquire some domain-specific components from external sources. These components are typically integrated through some proprietary glue code.

Forces. This model allows for effective sharing of infrastructure knowledge between units, which is valuable as good understanding of the infrastructure reduces the amount of effort spent on rework in response to interface or behavioural mismatches or not fulfilled quality requirements.

Relation to organisation, process and business. The processes and business inter-ests of the business units are still unrelated, but at the organisational level there is a need to define the infrastructure and to harmonise its evolution.

Level 3, Software Platform

- **Product family architecture:** only the features common to all products are cap-tured
- **Product quality:** inherited from the platform
- **Reuse level:** reuse of internal platform components
- **Domain:** mature
- **Software variability management:** managed at platform level

As a first step in achieving *intra-organisational* reuse of software artefacts the organi-sation may develop, maintain and evolve a platform based on which the products or applications are created. A platform typically includes a standardised infrastructure as a basis, as discussed in the previous section that typically contains generic functional-ity. On top of that, the platform captures domain functionality that is common to all products or applications. The common functionality that is not provided by the infra-structure is implemented by the organisation itself, but typically the application de-velopment treats the platform as if it was an externally bought infrastructure.
Forces. This model reduces double work in the organisation, since core software is produced only once.
Relation to organisation, process and business. Larger parts of the organisation become involved in the development because they all use the same platform. The process should reflect the distinction between platform and product development, and the business should determine a means to determine the profit of the platform devel-opment.

Level 4, Software Product Family

- **Product family architecture:** fully specified
- **Product quality:** a key priority for development
- **Reuse level:** managed
- **Domain:** late stages of maturing or the early stages of the established phase
- **Software variability management:** many variation points and dependencies between them

Once the benefits of exploiting the commonalities between the products become more accepted within the organisation, a consequent development may be to increase the amount of functionality in the platform to the level where functionality common to several but not all products becomes part of the shared artefacts. Now we have reached the stage of a software product family. Functionality specific to one or a few products is still developed as part of the product derivation. Functionality shared by a sufficient number of products is part of the shared product family artefacts, with the consequence that individual products may sacrifice resource efficiency or develop-ment effort for being part of the product family.

Forces. The freedom of development teams is reduced, since they have to stick to the defined product family architecture. However this means also that they have less work in the definition of the architecture and the determination of the consequences of design choices.

Relation to organisation, process and business. Organisations will be committed to a very large extent, since only then they are able to use the family architecture. The process should take into account the wishes from the stakeholders present in the involved organisations.

Level 5, Configurable Product Base

- **Product family architecture:** enforced
- **Product quality:** quality attributes are implemented as variation points in the architecture and components
- **Reuse level:** automatic generation of product family members
- **Domain:** established
- **Software variability management:** automated selection and verification of variants at variation points has been optimised

Especially if the organisation develops products in relatively stable domains and derives many product instances, there is a tendency to further develop the support for product derivation. The consequence is that the organisation, rather than developing a number of different products, moves towards developing only one configurable product base that, either at the organisation or at the customer site, is configured into the product bought by the customer. Some companies use, for instance, license key driven configuration, shipping the same code base to each and every customer. The code base configures itself based on the provided license key, allowing access to certain parts of the functionality while blocking others.

Forces. It becomes very difficult to change the architecture, Therefore, It has to be stable for a very long time. Adaptations have to be planned for the long term, and executed only after drawbacks and profits are considered well enough.

Relation to organisation, process and business. The complete organisation has to support the enforced family architecture. The process and the business should reflect the interdependencies of the different departments involved in the development, giving rise to many interdependent processes, and accounting measures.

Process Dimension (BAPO-P)

The process dimension emphasises both the process, roles, work products, and corresponding responsibilities and relationships within software development. Because the CMM (for Software) and its current successor CMMI [6], [7] is the de-facto standard in assessing and evaluating software processes, then CMMI is the most natural choice to be basis for the software product family evaluation approach in the BAPO-P dimension. The levels of CMMI (Staged Representation) [7] are briefly introduced in the following by utilising the following aspects to depict their differences:

- **Predictability** – how predictable is software development at each level
- **Repeatability** – how repeatable is the development process at each level
- **Quantifiability** – how quantifiable is software development

The staged representation of the CMMI [7] offers its maturity levels to be used also in the software product family context:

1. **Initial**
2. **Managed**
3. **Defined**
4. **Quantitatively managed**
5. **Optimising**

Level 1: Initial

- **Predictability:** unpredictable
- **Repeatability:** not repeatable at all, i.e. there is no related learning in the organisation.
- **Quantifiability:** no data available about past projects.

As described in the CMMI [7]: "Processes are usually ad hoc and chaotic. The organisation usually does not provide a stable environment. Success in these organisations depends on the competence and heroics of the people in the organisation and not on the use of proven processes. In spite of this ad hoc, chaotic environment, maturity level 1 organisations often produce products and services that work; however, they frequently exceed the budget and schedule of their projects. Maturity level 1 organisations are characterised by a tendency to over commit, abandon processes in the time of crisis, and not be able to repeat their past successes."

Level 2: Managed

- **Predictability:** tolerably predictable
- **Repeatability:** good practices can be applied and bad practices can be avoided
- **Quantifiability:** data available on past projects

"The organisation has achieved all the specific and generic goals of the maturity level 2 process areas. In other words, the projects of the organisation have ensured that requirements are managed and that processes are planned, performed, measured, and controlled. The process discipline reflected by maturity level 2 helps to ensure that existing practices are retained during times of stress. When these practices are in place, projects are performed and managed according to their documented plans. At maturity level 2, requirements, processes, work products, and services are managed. The status of the work products and the delivery of services are visible to management at defined points (for example, at major milestones and at the completion of major tasks). Commitments are established among relevant stakeholders and are revised as needed. Work products are reviewed with stakeholders and are controlled. The work products and services satisfy their specified requirements, standards, and objectives."

Level 3: Defined

- **Predictability:** satisfactorily predictable
- **Repeatability:** process is tailored from the organisational software process
- **Quantifiability:** data available on past projects, and data has been analysed and summarised to be more effectively utilised by next projects

"The organisation has achieved all the specific and generic goals of the process areas assigned to maturity levels 2 and 3. At maturity level 3, processes are well characterised and understood, and are described in standards, procedures, tools, and methods. The organisation's set of standard processes, which is the basis for maturity level 3, is established and improved over time. These standard processes are used to establish consistency across the organisation. Projects establish their defined processes by tailoring the organisation's set of standard processes according to tailoring guidelines. The organisation's management establishes process objectives based on the organisation's set of standard processes and ensures that these objectives are appropriately addressed."

Level 4: Quantitatively Managed

- **Predictability:** very predictable
- **Repeatability:** process is tailored from the organisational software process with corresponding quantifiable data
- **Quantifiability:** software development data from past projects have been packaged into quantified models to be used to estimate and predict next projects

"The organisation has achieved all the specific goals of the process areas assigned to maturity levels 2, 3, and 4 and the generic goals assigned to maturity levels 2 and 3. Sub-processes are selected that significantly contribute to overall process performance. These selected sub-processes are controlled using statistical and other quantitative techniques. Quantitative objectives for quality and process performance are established and used as criteria in managing processes. Quantitative objectives are based on the needs of the customer, end users, organisation, and process implementers. Quality and process performance are understood in statistical terms and are managed throughout the life of the processes. For these processes, detailed measures of process performance are collected and statistically analysed. Special causes of process variation are identified and, where appropriate, the sources of special causes are corrected to prevent future occurrences. Quality and process performance measures are incorporated into the organisation's measurement repository to support fact-based decision making in the future."

Level 5: Optimising

- **Predictability:** extremely predictable
- **Repeatability:** fully repeatable given the commonalities and variabilities between past and new projects
- **Quantifiability:** process of new projects can be optimised based on data and corresponding analysis on past projects

"The organisation has achieved all the specific goals of the process areas assigned to maturity levels 2, 3, 4, and 5 and the generic goals assigned to maturity levels 2 and 3. Processes are continually improved based on a quantitative understanding of the common causes of variation inherent in processes. Maturity level 5 focuses on continually improving process performance through both incremental and innovative technological improvements. Quantitative process-improvement objectives for the organisation are established, continually revised to reflect changing business objectives, and used as criteria in managing process improvement. The effects of deployed process improvements are measured and evaluated against the quantitative process-improvement objectives. Both the defined processes and the organisation's set of standard processes are targets of measurable improvement activities."

Case: Nokia

In 1996 the Nokia-wide software metrics program (Nokia Software Process Initiative) was launched, including the CMM (for Software) as the key metric for assessing the evaluation of software engineering in Nokia. Since then CMM became the key basis for software process improvement in Nokia, and later Nokia decided to move to the CMMI, which happened in 2002 [8]. It became, however, evident that to be able effectively assess the evaluation of system family engineering (SFE) in software related product families, the scope of CMMI has to be expanded to measure the evaluation of SFE either by applying an existing SFE-related assessment framework in conjunction with the CMMI or by expanding the scope of the CMMI towards product families. The latter alternative was chosen, because the CMM(I) was already "business-as-usual" in Nokia, and thus there was no need for marketing new assessment approaches.

In summer 2001 Nokia Research Center (NRC) started working in the European CAFÉ project, dealing with the challenges of SFE. As a part of that project a tentative assessment model for software product families was created using the approach described above, focusing especially on integration and testing within software product families, i.e. on related CMMI process areas Verification (VER) and Validation (VAL) [9]. The pilot model was reviewed using two real R&D settings in two different Nokia business units, and the model was finalised in summer 2003. According to the current plan the same approach will be applied when developing the BAPO-P dimension in the FAMILIES project.

Organisational Dimension (BAPO-O)

The Organisational dimension deals with the way the organisation is able to deal with complex relationships and many responsibilities. Three aspects can be identified which influence the evaluation in the organisational dimension:

- **Structure:** how complex is the organisation: Projects, Departments, Hierarchy vs. Network (flat), business lines
- **Culture:** what are the shared values: internally or cooperative focussed, individual- or central-valued, conservative vs. innovative, product vs. process focussed

- **Roles & Responsibilities:** how well does the organisation manage the distinct responsibilities and relationships: undifferentiated vs. specialised roles for. product family development

We have defined the following level structure. Below we discuss them in more detail:

1. **Unit oriented**
2. **Business lines oriented**
3. **Business group/division**
4. **Inter-division/companies**
5. **Open business**

Level 1, Unit Oriented

- **Structure:** projects
- **Culture:** internally focussed
- **Roles & Responsibilities:** product family undifferentiated

At this level the family development is concentrated within single development units. People working close to each other perform the development. Therefore no complex organisational structures and differentiated roles are necessary to keep the process manageable. The internally focussed culture supports the trust and respects that people have for each other, leading to ease in the distribution of work, and taking over work from each other.

Forces. As soon as the complexity family grows, no one is able to have a complete overview of the development. In addition, the unit may not be able to deal with the complete development itself. This may lead to co-operations over unit borders, and the next level may be more appropriate.

Relation to Business, architecture and process. There is no strong need to have a high level of business, architecture and process. Communication lines are short, and everybody is aware about almost everything within the organisation. Implicit knowledge is shared easily because of this.

Level 2, Business Lines Oriented

- **Structure:** separate one domain and multiple application engineering unit
- **Culture:** cooperative within business line
- **Roles & Responsibilities:** product family roles and asset roles

At this level the family development takes place in a single business line involving several development units. A specific development unit is assigned the responsibility for producing the domain assets, which are to be reused by the application units that make products out of them. People are relatively close to each other, but the number of developers within the family is large, and therefore specialisation is necessary. In particular the roles for family development and application development are recognised and distributed. People are assigned to be responsible for the maintenance of certain family assets, such as components, or the architecture.

Forces. Neighbouring business lines may express a need for co-operation. Initially they start to reuse domain assets. Then a growth towards the next level may be appropriate.

Relation to Business, architecture and process. This level requires that the common family architecture have to be shared, and processes have to be defined to ensure co-operation between the domain and the application departments.

Level 3, Business Group/Division

- **Structure:** multiple domain engineering
- **Culture:** cooperative across business lines
- **Roles & Responsibilities:** coordinated roles across business lines

At this level the family development takes place over different business lines within a single business group or division. There is a structure of co-operating domain engineering units over the business lines. Each of them has the responsibility of part of the domain development. For instance they may be organised in a hierarchy. A central domain-engineering unit provide basic assets to all business lines. Each business line itself has its own domain-engineering unit that builds upon this to provide assets, used internally.

Forces. There may become a need for outsourcing certain parts of the family development. This may be a drive to move to the next level. Competition between business lines may break up the structure, enforcing the organisation to move to the previous level.

Relation to Business, architecture and process. It has to be ensured that each business line is able to stay alive. That means that the business-related decisions of the different business lines have to be aligned and money flows between them have to be agreed upon. The architecture should be able to take into account the needs of the different business lines. Processes should be defined to enable negotiations over business lines borders.

Level 4, Inter-division/companies

- **Structure:** consortium-based cooperation
- **Culture:** externally focussed
- **Roles & Responsibilities:** liaison roles (between companies)

At this level the development is spread over several co-operating companies. Some of them will act as subcontractor of others.

Forces. As the consortium grows there may become a time that it is difficult to get a clear consortium overview. Alternatively more and more partners in the consortium may make their own business based upon the common assets. This may be a reason to move to the next level.

Relation to Business, architecture and process. Each involved partner in the consortium has to be able to make its own business. It should be clear what are the responsibilities of the different consortium members.

Level 5, Open Business

- **Structure:** industry-wide cooperation
- **Culture:** extremely cooperative, competitive
- **Roles & Responsibilities:** lobbying, marketing, standardization bodies

At this level there is an open standard for the product family. Several companies improve the family through additions adhering to the standard. Often, but not necessarily (see open source), there is a single company that is strong enough to set the standard.

Forces. Not enough other parties are willing to contribute. This may enforce that the standard may become obsolete, and e step towards the previous level may be necessary.

Relation to Business, architecture and process. The sole fact that others are able to contribute additions to the family improves the business value of the standard. Therefore the owner(s) the standard will need to use this in their business models. The cost models should take this into account

Profiles

An evaluation profile is the representation of software product family evaluation for an organisation, using the evaluation model with four separate evaluation scales for Business, Architecture, Process, and Organisation evaluation. Depending on the purpose of the use of this evaluation model, benchmark, evaluation profiles or target profiles types may be involved.

A separate procedure sets details of creating an evaluation profile (beyond the scope of this paper) taking into account the specifics of individual evaluation dimensions. The resulting evaluation profile generally depends on the company input profile including domain type and business strategy.

Domain evaluation can be roughly classified as emerging, maturing, and established. Business strategy can be classified as shaper, or follower. Thus six general benchmark profile types can be distinguished.

Setting the target evaluation profiles for improvement of software product family development has to include the consideration of possible dependencies and tradeoffs between the evaluation dimensions. The dependencies associate selected levels of different evaluation dimensions. The overall BAPO model determines them. The tradeoffs are the effect of the multi-criteria evaluation optimisation subject to implementation and adoption constraints such as limited resources. Typical optimisation goals refer to productivity, time to market, dependability, return on investment, etc. For the same reasons, and depending on the input profiles, the optimisation task may indicate an optimal solution that is different than the uppermost level for each evaluation dimension. A complete dynamic optimisation should provide a transition path from the identified current evaluation profile to the target evaluation profile. Due to the complexity of such a task, special attention is given to sub-optimal, e.g., incremental improvement policies. An example of an incremental policy is to change one selected dimension within certain limits while keeping all other dimensions at their current evaluation levels.

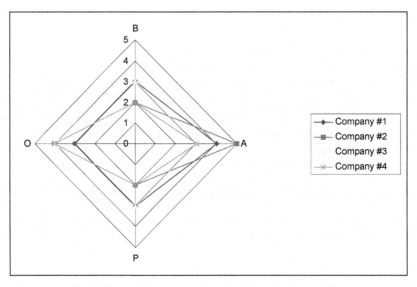

Fig. 4. Sample software product family evaluation profiles.

Summary and Future Actions

This document proposes an evaluation framework for family development. The framework serves for benchmarking the organisation against others, enable assessments for single organisations and provide directions for improvement. As there are 4 groups of development concerns (BAPO) we have identified 4 distinct evaluation scales. Evaluation of an organisation will lead to a profile with separate values for each of the 4 scales. Dependent on the organisation context there will be an optimum profile for that organisation. The organisation may use the framework to find whether it has the optimum profile, or if not which actions should be done in order to reach the optimum. Care should be taken that improvement actions for one of the profile scales may lead to reduction of the values for the other scales.

We plan to improve the present evaluation framework by providing more details, taking into account the practices in present industrial software family development. This improvement will mainly performed in the FAMILIES project.

References

1. Pierre America, Henk Obbink, Rob van Ommering, Frank van der Linden, CoPAM: A Component-Oriented Platform Architecting Method Family for Product family Engineering, Proceedings SPLC-1 pp. 167-180.
2. Victor Basili, Gianluigi Caldiera, Frank McGarry, Rose Pajersky, Gerald Page, and Sharon Waligora. The Software Engineering Laboratory – an operational Software Experience Factory. In Proceedings of the 14th International Conference on Software Engineering, pages 370–381, May 1992.

3. Victor R. Basili, Gianluigi Caldiera, and H. Dieter Rombach. Experience Factory. In John J. Marciniak, editor, Encyclopedia of Software Engineering, volume 1, pages 469–476. John Wiley & Sons, 1994.
4. Jan Bosch, Maturity and Evolution in Software Product Lines: Approaches, Artefacts and Organization, Proceedings of the Second International Conference on Software Product Lines (SPLC 2), Springer LNCS 2379 pp. 257-271, August 2002.
5. Clements, Paul; Northrop, Linda; Software Product Lines – Practices and Patterns, Addison Wesley, 2001.
6. CMMISM for Systems Engineering/Software Engineering/Integrated Product and Process Development/Supplier Sourcing, Version 1.1, Continuous Representation (CMMI-SE/SW/IPPD/SS, V1.1, Continuous), *Technical Report* CMU/SEI-2002-TR-011, Carnegie Mellon University, Pittsburgh, 2002.
7. CMMISM for Systems Engineering/Software Engineering/Integrated Product and Process Development/Supplier Sourcing, Version 1.1, Staged Representation (CMMI-SE/SW/IPPD/SS, V1.1, Staged), *Technical Report* CMU/SEI-2002-TR-012, Carnegie Mellon University, Pittsburgh, 2002.
8. Kari Känsälä and Petri Voltti. How Nokia moved from SW-CMM to CMMI in a year. European SEPG Conference. June 16-19, 2003, London, UK.
9. Kari Känsälä. Assessing the maturity of Nokia's SW product lines. Dagstuhl Seminar 03151 on Product family Development. April 7-10, 2003, Dagstuhl, Germany.
10. Frank van der Linden, Software Product families in Europe: The Esaps and Café Projects, IEEE Software, July/August 2002, pp. 41-49.
11. Northrop, et al. A Framework for Software Product Line Practice Version 4.1. http://www.sei.cmu.edu/plp/framework.html.
12. M. Paulk et al. Capability Maturity Model of Software, Version 1.1. Tech Report CMU/SEI-93-TR24, Carnegie Mellon University, Pittsburgh, 1993.
13. Martyn Thomas and Frank McGarry. Top-Down vs. Bottom-Up Process Improvement. IEEE Software, 12-13, July 1994.

Design for Quality

Joachim Bayer

Fraunhofer Institute for Experimental Software Engineering (IESE)
Sauerwiesen 6, 67661 Kaiserslautern, Germany
bayer@iese.fraunhofer.de

Abstract. This paper summarizes the work and achievements of the CAFÉ Task 2.3 "Design for Quality"[1]. A number of partners collaborated for two years in the context of the European CAFÉ project to jointly research how quality can be built into product family architectures and how the quality of product family architectures can be assessed. The main achievement of the collaboration is a common general process for design for quality accompanied by a metamodel that both have been instantiated by the different partners for their respective organizational context and projects. This paper briefly introduces this general process and metamodel.

1 Introduction

Quality is of great importance for most of today's software systems. This is especially true for software product families that are the basis for a number of related products. The quality requirements that must be fulfilled by a product family are determined by business considerations and vary depending on the actual project context. During the last decade, software architecture has been increasingly recognized as critical for fulfilling the quality requirements of software system and product families. Capturing the earliest, most fundamental design decisions, the software architecture largely determines the quality attributes of the resulting software systems and serves as the first opportunity for realizing the quality requirements of the systems. Although quality goals are realized by architecture and architectural decisions mostly have a great impact on the consequent quality of software systems, quality goals are currently not being made explicit throughout the life cycle. Experience shows that during architectural design, analysis, and maintenance, quality goals are generally addressed by a rather informal process. This approach has a number of consequences.

First of all, the creation of an architecture for a software system that fulfills specified quality requirements largely depends on the knowledge of the architects and their experience with similar systems. In addition, it is generally not clear how to achieve the quality goals, whether and when to stop, and how to analyze an architecture in order to predict the quality attributes of the final system. Finally, it is easy to corrupt or destroy the quality during the maintenance of an architecture if the maintainer does not know where it is realized. To improve this situation, the goal of the CAFÉ task 2.3

---

[1] This work has been partially funded by Eureka Σ! 2023 Programme, ITEA project ip00004, CAFÉ.

F. van der Linden (Ed.): PFE 2003, LNCS 3014, pp. 370–380, 2004.

"Design for Quality" was to provide quality-centric approaches to the analysis and the design of product family architectures.

The remainder of this paper presents the main results of the collaboration.

2 Collaboration

The different partners that agreed on jointly working in the field of design for quality brought different research questions and approaches addressing these questions into the project, one being the very basic question of what product family specific quality characteristics are. The different partners introduced their experience to understand if there are quality characteristics that are unique or important to software product families.

To use quality characteristics as major driver for developing and maintaining a product family architecture, the characteristics and their impact on the product family architecture have to be modeled explicitly. We agreed to do this using quality models that capture quality attributes and the influence they have on each other. The influence of quality attributes on a product family architecture can be documented in the architecture description using architectural views that show how the quality requirements are realized in the architecture.

Once the quality requirements are known and documented, they can be used to drive the design and can serve as a basis for analyzing the resulting product family architectures. Existing approaches to the design of product family architectures have been extended using the results gained in the CAFÉ project. Also static, dynamic, and context-dependent architecture analysis methods were defined or existing ones were extended. The integration of the analysis of product family architectures into their design in order to analyze whether the design is on the right track and to conduct corrective measures if this is not the case was another important topic.

For product family architectures the question of derivation is crucial. Family members should be produced cost-effectively and the recognized quality characteristics should be taken into account by developers at the product design phase. Domain-specific modeling languages and generators are promising a way to enable a higher degree of automation and de facto use of quality attributes in family member production.

Product families are often developed in a context where a number of successful systems already exist. To exploit the knowledge embedded in such legacy systems, recovery approaches can be used to extract information that can be used as a basis for a product family architecture. This information extraction is especially interesting for the ways that have been used in the legacy systems to achieve certain quality characteristics. Architecture recovery can be extended to extract architecture properties from different architectures and combine them in a reference architecture.

As the range of questions and approaches just presented suggests, quality is pervasive throughout the complete life cycle of a product family architecture. We, therefore, developed a common process that encompasses the complete life cycle of a product family architecture. The process is shown in Figure 1. It is a generic process that describes how quality can be achieved in a product family architecture. It is accompanied by a metamodel that defines the products used in the process. The meta-

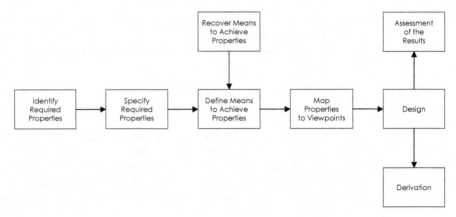

Fig. 1. Design for Quality Process.

model defines the different concepts that are related to quality in product family architectures and the means to achieve it.

The process steps are described in more detail in the following subsections.

2.1 Identify Required Properties

The required properties and characteristics a product family include the functional and quality requirements on the product family. To understand these requirements, we start with eliciting the business goals of an organization that have a strong impact on the required properties. Later in the process the quality attributes that address these business goals are captured in quality models.

Even though every organization has a business strategy, they are often not documented in a way that enables their exploitation for developing software. Often, the only documented aspects of the business strategy that can be used for the architecture are the functional characteristics of the products to be built. In order to develop software that provides not only a technical, but also economically optimal solution, however, it is essential to take other, non-technical aspects into account as well when dealing with product family architectures. The business strategy has impact on the complete life cycle of the products and often spans the life cycle of more than one product generation. However, business strategies are not cast in iron and change over time in order, for example, to adapt to changing environments or extend to new market segments. To use these important architectural drivers throughout the life cycle of an architecture, they have to be documented properly.

The explicit documentation of the business goals of the organization building a product family is the first step we take to elicit the quality requirements on the product family. The goal is to document the business goals of an organization in a form so that they can be used to determine the planned products, the concrete requirements on these products, and a schedule for developing these products as a product family. Optionally, constraints are captured together with business goals, because they are often at the same level of granularity. The documentation of constraints is, however, continued throughout later activities.

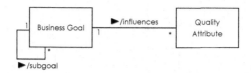

Fig. 2. Metamodel for Expressing Business Goals.

We capture business goals based on a simple metamodel as informal, hierarchically organized goals. The metamodel for business goals is shown in Figure 2. In addition to the name of the business goal and the influenced quality attribute, we optionally capture the time frame for satisfying the respective business goal and its relative importance.

Business goals are elicited during brainstorming sessions and later consolidated and documented. We propose to distinguish between internal business goals (i.e., goals of the organization developing the product family) and external business goals (i.e., goals of the customers) to provide information on the criticality and importance of the different goals. The classification into internal and external goals provides initial information on the criticality and importance of the different goals.

Constraints are captured informally in lists. For better readability and easier reference, we usually group them. Example groups are "Resource", "Organization", or "Functional".

2.2 Specify Required Properties

In the CAFÉ task "Design for Quality", the quality model is the central artifact. It contains and relates the quality attributes that are important to a product family. Quality models are used to understand and document the impact of design decisions on the quality of a product family architecture, to support the design of high quality product family architectures, and to assess the quality of a given product family architecture.

This section introduces the metamodel that provides the basis for codifying and packaging information that is used for the quality-centered design, analysis, and maintenance of software architectures. The metamodel defines the language for expressing quality, as well as the different concepts that are related to quality and architectures. We developed the metamodel based on established standards, like the IEEE Standard for a Software Quality Metrics Methodology [7] and the ISO/IEC 9126 standard for quality characteristics and guidelines for their use [9], and on approaches for evaluating software architectures, like the Software Architecture Analysis Method (SAAM) [10] and the Architecture Trade-Off Analysis Method (ATAM) [11].

The result is the metamodel shown in Figure 3. It contains the definition of quality attributes and of how they are related to yield a quality model. As depicted in the figure, a quality model consists of a number of quality attributes.

A quality attribute is a non-functional characteristic of a software product or process such as maintainability, reusability, or reliability. Quality attributes can be refined, meaning that they have one or more sub-characteristics. The quality attribute "Reliability", for example, can be refined into "Fault Tolerance" and "Recoverability". As described above, the presence and importance of quality attributes is determined by business goals. The positive or negative influence between quality attributes is captured by documenting the pair-wise influence relationships between two quality at-

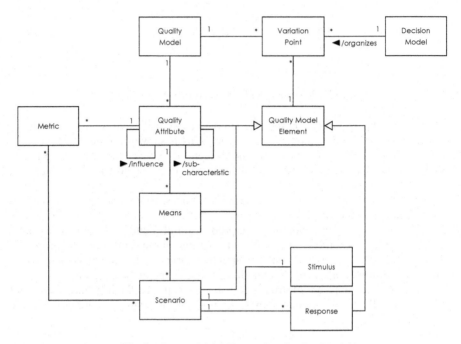

Fig. 3. Metamodel for Expressing Quality Models.

attributes. Each quality attribute can be associated with a number of metrics that can be used to measure the degree to which an architecture or the resulting system satisfies a particular quality requirement for the quality attribute. A quality requirement is an actual requirement on a software architecture derived from a certain quality attribute. For the quality attribute "Fault Tolerance", for instance, a quality requirement might be "The system shall be able to provide its services in the case of a hardware fault". Quality requirements are documented using scenarios. Scenarios are given by stimulus/response pairs and can be associated to a number of metrics. A stimulus is an event that causes an architecture to respond or change, whereas the response is the activity undertaken or the property observable after the arrival of the stimulus. Each scenario has exactly one stimulus and can have one or more responses. The scenario for the requirement stated above has the stimulus "Hardware Fault" and the response "Availability" and reads "High availability in the presence of hardware faults". A possible metric for this scenario is "Mean Time to Failure".

Certain elements of the metamodel can be variable to cope with the fact that quality models for product families are documented. This is achieved by introducing variation points that are organized using a decision model.

The quality model was used by the different partners in the task. Fraunhofer IESE collected product family specific quality attributes and documented the product family specific quality attributes using the common metamodel [2]. Thales extended the common metamodel to capture quality of service profiles for the UML. This extension has been submitted to the OMG for inclusion in the UML.

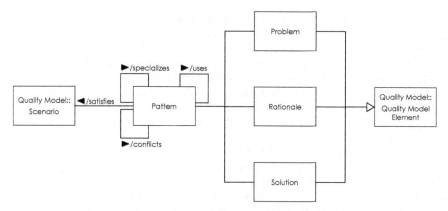

Fig. 4. Metamodel for Expressing Patterns.

2.3 Define Means to Achieve Properties

A promising approach to systematic, quality-centric product family architecture creation is to base design, analysis, and maintenance of product family architectures on
reusable design knowledge such as codified in patterns and styles and to make use of
models that relate quality attributes of systems to observable properties of product
family architectures that can be influenced by appropriate design decisions. Architectural styles and patterns capture existing, well-proven solutions to recurring problems
and hence serve as building blocks for architecture design.

We developed a metamodel for patterns and related it to the quality model metamodel to enable the documentation of the influence a pattern has on the achievement
of certain quality requirements. The metamodel is shown in Figure 4. As defined in
the metamodel, scenarios are satisfied by patterns. A pattern is a generic, pre-defined,
and documented solution for a recurring problem in the design of product family
architectures. Patterns have proven to be beneficial in certain situations and as they
have been applied repeatedly, their impact on an architecture is known.

A pattern can use another pattern or can be refined through specializations. For example, the pattern "layered architecture" can be specialized into "strictly layered
architecture" and "loosely layered architecture". Furthermore, two patterns can be in
conflict, meaning that they cannot be applied at the same time. Patterns are given by a
problem addressed, a rationale justifying why the pattern solves the problem, and a
description of the actual solution. The justification given in the rationale addresses
known effects on quality attributes imposed on the software system in which the pattern is applied.

The relation between quality attributes or quality requirements and patterns is established via the scenarios in the metamodel. Scenarios describe the anticipated behavior that is assured by a pattern. In general, however, a number of patterns can be
selected to achieve a certain quality requirement. Therefore, so-called means have
been introduced as an intermediate step. Means are principles, techniques, or mechanisms that facilitate the achievement of certain qualities in an architecture. Similar to
patterns, means capture a way to achieve a certain quality requirement, but are not
concrete enough to be used directly and hence have to be instantiated as patterns.
Examples of means for the quality attribute "reliability" are redundancy and excep-

tions. In case of redundancy, possible instantiations are the patterns "Homogenous Redundancy" and "Diverse Redundancy". Usually, means are taken from the experience of the organization developing a software system. When designing an architecture, first the means most appropriate for the quality requirements of the system are selected by comparing the scenarios associated with the means with the requirements. In a later stage, only the patterns related to the selected means have to be considered when deciding which patterns are to be used in the architecture. The detailed process for selecting means and patterns during the design of software architectures is described in Section 3.4.2.

The pattern metamodel was adapted and used by the different partners in the task. One application is described by Fraunhofer IESE in [3], where patterns and their relationships to quality attributes have been used to support architectural design decisions in the design of a product family architecture. Another application was the creation of a pattern catalogue for product family specific quality attributes by ICT Norway [4].

2.4 Map Properties to Viewpoints

Software architectures are usually described by means of a number of architectural views. Each of these views highlights certain aspects of the architecture. Quality attributes can be the basis for defining additional views that highlight how quality requirements are satisfied in the architecture.

The goal is to define an optimal set of architectural views that are used to document the architectures of the planned products based on the required properties. There are cases in which an existing view set can be used without adaptation. However, often the proposed views are not sufficient to describe all relevant architectural aspects. Then, a new view set must be defined. This can be done based on one of the view sets found in literature or from scratch. We use the IEEE Recommended Standard 1471 for Architecture Description as a basis for doing that [8]. It defines a metamodel for view-based architecture descriptions. However, it does not provide concrete views or any process support for defining, creating, and using view-based software architectures.

The view sets found in literature (e.g., in [5], [6], and [14]) have in common that their focus is on the description of functional aspects of a software architecture. Quality attributes can be the basis for defining additional views that highlight how quality requirements are satisfied in the architecture. The use of quality attributes as a basis for additional views on software architectures has a number of effects. Views for certain quality attributes enable a clear separation of concerns during architecture development. The architects can concentrate on one important aspect of the software architecture at a time. The concentration on one aspect per view increases the comprehensibility of the software architecture description. The effect is that the quality of the documentation, that is, of the architecture description, is increased. This, in turn, supports the creation, as well as the maintenance and evolution of the architecture description. However, there are also challenges that have to be mastered when using views for quality attributes, the first being to select the views to be used so that they form an optimal set that is neither too big nor too small. Once the views have been selected, the consistency among them must be ensured and they must be maintained properly.

2.5 Design

The design of product family architectures takes as input the requirements on a product family and results in a product family architecture description. The goal of the task work with respect to design was to integrate quality aspects in the creation of product family architectures. The results of the steps described above, that is the quality models, the patterns, and the architectural views, are, therefore, used to integrate the notion of quality in the design of product family architectures in an explicit way. The quality models make the requirements on the respective product family architecture explicit, the patterns document the means that are present in the architecture to achieve the quality requirements, and the views describe the important aspects of the product family architecture.

The different partners proposed different approaches to design for quality. Nokia developed a general framework for architecture design along with a general process that integrates the common metamodel for quality aspects described above in a metamodel for architectural design. The metamodel for architectural design is decomposed into the subject areas requirements, architecture design, architecture assessment, reference architecture, and architecture description and is accompanied by a general process covering these areas [19].

ICT Norway developed an approach for designing domain-specific reference architectures and guidelines for developing concrete software architectures for products in the respective domain based on the reference architecture [4]. The approach is supported by establishing the relationships between architectural patterns and quality in a way that is suited for supporting architectural design decisions. The approach is to use architecturally significant scenarios, as known from scenario based architecture evaluation methods, as a way to exemplify concrete quality requirements and to serve as a link between quality attributes and architectural patterns.

Fraunhofer IESE used the common work on design for quality to extend an existing method for the design, evaluation, and maintenance of product family architectures, the PuLSE-DSSA method [1]. The work on design for quality was used to integrate business goals as the source and driver for quality requirements into the PuLSE-DSSA method. Additionally, the relationship between quality requirements and patterns is used in the improved version of PuLSE-DSSA to support the designers in their work by providing experience in terms of working solutions for given problems.

All of these approaches have in common that the design of a product family architecture is an iterative process that incrementally develops and documents architectural views to capture a solution for the different product family members.

Another approach that was also followed is the application of domain-specific modeling that captures product family concepts and rules (and related quality characteristics) in a design language. Here, the metamodel is directly instantiated as the variant definition language. This makes the product family explicit in the development organization and can guarantee that variants specified follow the product family. Dedicated languages provide also means to increase the productivity as they allow automating family member production (as discussed in section 2.7).

2.6 Assessment of the Results

There are a number of approaches to assess the quality of software architectures. One of these, the Architecture Tradeoff Analysis Method (ATAM) [11], has been adapted by ICT Norway towards product families and integrating analysis with design. This was done to assess the suitability of existing and emerging product family architectures for their intended use, as well as to validate the relationships between quality attributes and patterns claimed by the reference architecture they developed. The resulting approaches to assessing product family architectures have been applied in several architecture evaluations [4].

2.7 Derivation

The derivation of product family members from a product family infrastructure is an essential task in product family engineering. To support this task, domain-specific languages can be used to express the characteristics of the different product family members. Domain-specific languages promises fast variant development, support the introduction of product family engineering into organizations, and leverage domain expertise among the people and teams in an organization. The domain-specific method proposed by MetaCase is a method for the production of product family members [18] [20]. First, a variant design and specification language is defined based on the characteristics of the product family (compare Section 2.5). Second, code generators are defined to fit to the requirements of product family derivation. Application engineers then find the solution only once by visually modeling using familiar domain concepts. The final products are automatically generated from these high-level specifications. There is no longer any need to make error-prone mappings from domain concepts to design concepts and on to programming language concepts. This enables fast and highly automated variant production. A third part of a complete domain-specific modeling environment is a domain framework with an interface for the target platform and programming language that provides primitives, components, as well as platform services that are called by the generated code. Such a domain-specific modeling environment enables generators to automatically derive product family members from the infrastructure. Noteworthy, the quality attributes instantiated at design models can be applied to guide generators that support automated product derivation.

A number of case studies investigating domain-specific modeling languages and associated generators have been conducted by MetaCase in the context of the CAFÉ project [12] [15] [18].

2.8 Recover Means to Achieve Properties

The architecture of a software system has a major impact on its quality attributes. Architectural styles and patterns are part of software architectures. In this context, architecture recovery can be used to verify the realization and use of certain architectural styles and patterns by a software system and in this way associates corresponding quality attributes to it.

The TU Vienna worked on a pattern-based approach to use architecture recovery to support the design of product family architectures [16]. The approach aims at extracting properties of existing architectures as patterns and visualizing them to use them to understand common and variable properties of different architectures. This information can then be used to develop a reference architecture for a complete product family. An iterative and interactive process has been developed that is partially supported by tools. This approach has been evaluated in a number of case studies in the context of the CAFÉ project [13] [17].

3 Conclusions

The work in the CAFÉ task "Design for Quality" brought together a number of organizations that were working on different aspects of quality for product family architectures and that also had different ideas to solve the problems they were facing. In a number of discussions, a common understanding of the issues and problems in product family architectures and the ways to address and solve these problems was developed. This common understanding resulted in the common general process and metamodel that was briefly introduced in this paper.

The common approach was an invaluable base for discussions and meetings. It was also adapted by the different partners to their respective contexts and used in a number of projects and case studies.

Acknowledgements

The work described in this paper was a joint effort of all the partners collaborating in the CAFÉ task 2.3 "Design for Quality". I lead this task; the enthusiasm and commitment of the task members made this an interesting and fruitful experience. Therefore, I want to thank all the members of the CAFÉ task 2.3 "Design for Quality": Guido W. Schmitt and Martin Verlage (MARKET MAKER), Janne Luoma and Juha-Pekka Tolvanen (MetaCase), Juha Savolainen (Nokia), Rene Krikhaar (Philips), Svein Hallsteinsen, Tor Erlend Fægri, and Dag Helge Lorås, (Sintef), Laurent Rioux (Thales), Martin Pinzger (TU Vienna), as well as Michalis Anastasopoulos and Ronny Kolb (Fraunhofer IESE).

References

1. M. Anastasopoulos, J. Bayer, O. Flege, and C. Gacek. A Process for Product Line Architecture Creation and Evaluation: PuLSE-DSSA Version 2.0, Technical Report, No. 038.00/E, Fraunhofer IESE, June 2000.
2. M. Anastasopoulos and J. Bayer. Product Family Specific Quality Attributes, Technical Report, No. 042.02/E, Fraunhofer IESE, June 2002.
3. J. Bayer and R. Kolb. Architecture Patterns for Product Families. Technical Report, No. 085.02/E, Fraunhofer IESE, September 2002.
4. DAIM Software Engineering Handbook. IKT-Norge, 2002.

5. Davis, M. J., and Williams, R. B. Software Architecture Characterization. Proceedings of the 1997 Symposium on Software Reusability (SSR'97). Boston, Massachusetts, USA, 1997.
6. C. Hofmeister, R. Nord, and D. Soni. Applied Software Architecture. Addison-Wesley, 1999.
7. IEEE Computer Society, IEEE Standard for a Software Quality Metrics Methodology, IEEE Standard 1061-1998, 1998.
8. IEEE Computer Society, IEEE Recommended Practice for Architectural Descriptions of Software-Intensive Systems, IEEE Std-1471-2000, 2000.
9. International Organization for Standardization, ISO/IEC Standard 9126 – Quality Characteristics and Guidelines for their Use, 1992.
10. R. Kazman, L. Bass, G. Abowd, and M. Webb. SAAM: A Method for Analyzing the Properties of Software Architectures, In Proceedings of the 16th International Conference on Software Engineering (ICSE), 1994, pp. 81–90.
11. R. Kazman, M. Klein, M. Barbacci, T. Longstaff, H. Lipson, and S. J. Carriere. The Architecture Tradeoff Analysis Method, Software Engineering Institute, Technical Report CMU/SEI-98-TR-008, 1998.
12. S. Kelly, Tolvanen, J.-P. Visual domain-specific modeling: Benefits and experience with metaCase Tools International workshop on Model Engineering, ECOOP 2000, (eds. Bezivin), 2000.
13. Jens Knodel and Martin Pinzger. Improving Fact Extraction of Framework-Based Software Systems. In Proceedings of the 10th Working Conference on Reverse Engineering (WCRE), IEEE Computer Society Press, Victoria, British Columbia, Canada, November 2003.
14. P. Kruchten. The 4+1 View Model of Architecture. IEEE Software, November 1995 12(6):42–50.
15. MetaCase, Automated Product Family Development: Nokia Tetra Terminals. 2003 (http://www.metacase.com/papers/MetaEdit_in_Nokia_Tetra.pdf).
16. Martin Pinzger and Harald Gall. Pattern-Supported Architecture Recovery. In 10th International Workshop on Program Comprehension (IWPC), pages 53-61, IEEE Computer Society Press, Paris, France, June 2002.
17. Martin Pinzger, Harald Gall, Mehdi Jazayeri, and Claudio Riva. Extracting Architectural Views from Large Telecommunications Software: A Case Study. Technical Report TUV-1841-2002-50 Vienna University of Technology, October 2002.
18. R. Pohjonen, J.-P. Tolvanen. Automated Production of Family Members: Lessons Learned. Proceedings of International workshop of Product Line Engineering, Fraunhofer IESE Technical Report IESE-Report 056.02/E (eds. K. Schmid, B. Geppert) 2002.
19. Savolainen, Juha., Kuusela, Juha., Framework for Goal Driven System Design, In the Proceedings of the Twenty-Sixth Annual International Computer Software & Applications Conference (COMPSAC02), pp.749-756, Oxford, England, August 2002.
20. J.-P. Tolvanen. Keeping it in the family, Application Development Advisor, July-August 2002.

Economics of Software Product Lines

Dale R. Peterson

Convergys Corporation
Cincinnati, OH 45202 USA
dale.peterson@convergys.com

Abstract. Software Product Lines (SPL) offer tremendous potential to improve a company's competitive position and responsiveness to changing market needs. However, unless the full benefits and costs are well understood by executive-level stakeholders, the probability of success will be low. An SPL economic analysis framework is presented that is based on the author's experience with SPL adoption at Convergys. While derived from the Convergys experience, it is hoped that this framework will be of value to other companies contemplating a transition to an SPL.

1 Introduction

The transition from traditional software development where products are developed independently from one another to an approach that is based on multiple development groups working in a collaborative fashion to deliver products to market requires a massive change in how things are done. The investment costs and risks, as well as the downstream benefits can be significant. Gaining executive stakeholder buy-in to making the investment requires a business case that translates the qualitative benefits so often cited for software product lines into concrete business benefits. The business case process can be an effective decision making tool for not only deciding *whether* an organization should transition to an SPL, but also *how* best to make the transition a success. An understanding of the size and timing of the cash flows will enable the organization to assess its transition strategy, and determine the degree to which it should adopt an incremental and iterative approach. This paper describes the approach that was used at Convergys[1] to assess the financial impact associated with its transition to an SPL. While it is based on the Convergys experience, it is hoped that it will be of value to others considering a similar transition.

This paper is organized as follows. Section 2 provides the context behind the Convergys initiative. This context should enable others to determine its potential applicability outside of the original setting. Section 3 contains a high level description of an heuristic model for quantifying the economic benefits. Section 4 provides a qualitative discussion of the major cost elements, and time and cost drivers associated with the transition project. Section 5 contains an example economic analysis that is based on a simple transition project scenario. Section 6 describes a set of metrics that could be used to

---

[1] Convergys (R) is a registered trademark of Convergys Corporation or its wholly owned subsidiaries.

F. van der Linden (Ed.): PFE 2003, LNCS 3014, pp. 381–402, 2004.
© Springer-Verlag Berlin Heidelberg 2004

track business case results against the economic model predictions. Section 7 contains a summary and set of conclusions. The Appendix contains a more detailed derivation of the benefits model.

2   Context

The scenario that this framework is based on is as follows.

Existing Product Family. There is a family of products already in existence. While there may be an opportunity to deliver new products in the future, the focus is on improving the way existing products are developed and delivered.

Independent Product Development. The starting point for the transition is a set of products that are independently developed by different organizations that utilize a diverse set of platforms, technologies, development processes, and product architectures.

Large, Complex, Mission-Critical Systems. The products are large, complex systems with footprints that span multiple application domains. The systems must meet stringent requirements for performance, scalability, availability, and operational cost.

Preserve Existing Software Assets. There continues to be a significant investment in the existing products. The time and cost to build a product line based on new components is prohibitive and/or the risks are too high. Therefore, the decision is made to mine the existing asset base, possibly with new development in selected (and small) domains.

Component-Based Product Line Architecture. The strategy is to adopt a component-based product line architecture, consisting of a common set of platform technologies, middleware components/frameworks, and business-level application components.

Very Large-Grained Components. Because the strategy is to mine existing assets, the approach is to start with very large-grained components, and to subsequently break down the large components into smaller components.

Component Factory. The vision for the software factory is a set of component groups that act as suppliers to the product groups.

Figure 1 shows a conceptual model of the envisioned software factory. Individual products serve specific vertical markets. The market needs are translated into requirements against the various products, and new features are allocated by a common architecture group to the different components (in general, a given feature will span multiple components). The common component groups deliver new releases to the product groups, which then extend, adapt, configure, and integrate the components to deliver new product releases.

3   Financial Flexibility

The benefits that motivated the SPL approach at Convergys are:

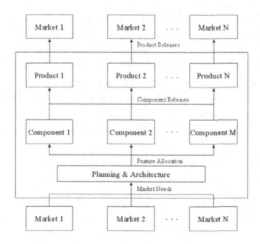

Fig. 1. Conceptual model of the component-based software factory.

R&D Investment. The ability to leverage the R&D investment across the product family by reusing a common set of components.

Subject Matter Expertise. The ability to leverage subject matter experts across the product family by concentrating domain subject matter experts with similar skills and knowledge into centralized groups that serve all products.

Productivity and Quality. Improving productivity and quality by breaking large, monolithic applications into smaller, more manageable projects, and by utilizing components that encapsulate their functionality.

Time to Market. Increasing the rate of delivery of new capabilities to market and enabling new products to be delivered faster by reusing well established components.

People Mobility. Provide employees with more career development opportunities by standardizing on the development environment and processes, thereby reducing the learning curve associated with a move to a new project.

Supplier Relationships. Standardizing on the platforms and development environment enables a more effective leverage of supplier relationships.

Geographic Flexibility. Standardizing on component-based development facilitates the distribution of development responsibilities across locations.

Sourcing Flexibility. A modular architecture enables greater flexibility to build, license, or acquire software.

Product Refresh. A modular architecture facilitates the process of refreshing the product family as new technologies and/or software components become available.

Given the anticipated size of the investment, it was necessary to go beyond the qualitative arguments listed above, and to develop a quantitative statement of the benefits. The approach taken was to focus on the benefits associated with productivity improvement and leverage associated with establishing a common set of components upon which members of the product family would be based. Over the years, numerous software reuse economic models have been developed (cf. [1–3]). Most of the models focus on the benefits associated with cost reduction or cost avoidance. Others have taken a more strategic view of product line economics in the context of a company's overall business strategy and market goals[4]. The motivation for developing yet another model was the desire to relate the concepts of commonality and variability, which are fundamental to software product lines, more directly to the economic benefits.

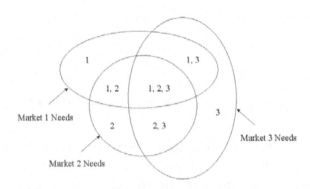

Fig. 2. A Venn diagram illustrating market needs overlap for a family of three products.

To motivate the benefits model, consider Fig. 2 below. It depicts the set of needs for three distinct markets. In general, there will be needs that are unique to each market. However, there will also be an overlap between those needs. Some needs will be common to two of the three markets, while other needs will be common to all three markets. The question then becomes, is there an architecture that enables common components to be built that incorporate the common needs, but also allow for variations and extensions to accommodate the unique needs? Based on an understanding of the requirements commonalties and variabilities, as well as on the component architecture, it should be possible to quantify how much of the development work will be performed by the component groups versus the product groups.

The Appendix describes a model that quantifies the benefits associated with improved productivity and the use of common components, based on the concept of overlapping market needs. The first version of the model considers the people savings associated with eliminating redundant software development and increasing productivity. The result is (for a single component):

$$\Delta S = \left[1 - \frac{1}{(1 + \delta p)(1 + (N\lambda - 1)\omega)}\right] \tilde{S} \qquad \text{(Reduce Cost Version)} \qquad (1)$$

The notation is as follows. First, $\tilde{S}$ stands for the number of developers required in the case of independent development (no reuse, no productivity gain). Next, N stands for the number of products using the common component. The parameter δp stands for the *relative* change (positive or negative) in productivity (for example a value of zero means no improvement, while a value of $1/4$ means a 25% increase). The parameter ω quantifies the *commonality* among the product requirements. In terms of Fig. 2, a commonality of one would mean a totally overlapping set of requirements, while a commonality of zero would mean the set of requirements for the different markets would be completely disjoint from one another. Finally, the parameter λ is a measure of the *leverage* that the product groups gain from the work performed by the component groups. The reason for this parameter entering the model is that not all features developed by the component groups will benefit all of the product groups.

Note that the cost to reuse a component is not explicit in the above equation. The cost of reuse in this model enters in two ways. First, the productivity change, δp may be negative. This would be the case if the productivity improvement associated with the component approach is offset by the resulting overhead due to the component groups building for reuse rather than a single product, as well as the management, governance, and coordination overhead that accompanies the collaborative development paradigm. Second, the costs associated with establishing a common set of reusable components enters by way of the investment needed to reengineer the existing product family, which is the subject of the transition cost model.

This version of the model corresponds to the "decrease the development effort per product" hypothesis discussed in [5].

We note that for the special case where $\delta p = 0$, $\omega = \lambda = 1$, this equation reverts to the simple form:

$$\Delta S = \frac{(N-1)}{N} \tilde{S} \tag{2}$$

The second version of the model looks at the benefits associated with increasing the throughput of the software factory (i.e. by doing more work with the same number of people):

$$\Delta \tilde{S} = [(1 + \delta p)(1 + (N\lambda - 1)\omega) - 1]\tilde{S} \qquad \text{(Increase Throughput Version)} \tag{3}$$

This expression is derived by allocating the staff savings from equation (1) back to the component and product groups, and comparing the resulting throughput with the baseline (independent development) case. The expression above then is a statement of how many additional people would be needed in the baseline case to obtain the equivalent level of throughput as is realized by the new software factory. The figure below illustrates the relative benefits associated with the two versions of the model. Intuitively, increasing throughput should result in a more competitive set of products, which in turn should drive revenue growth and market share. However, we have taken the more conservative approach to quantifying the benefits. This version of the model corresponds to the "develop more features with a given amount of money" hypothesis discussed in [5]. In general, the savings associated with increasing throughput are greater than the savings associated with staff reductions.

To summarize, the model suggests that the adoption of a common set of components provides *financial flexibility*[2], i.e. the ability to reduce investment while maintaining the

---

[2] See reference [6] for another view of flexibility.

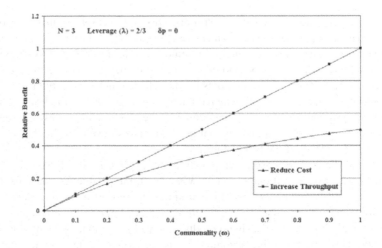

Fig. 3. Graph showing relative cost avoidance benefit for selected parameters.

same rate of delivery of new capabilities to market; or the ability to increase that rate of delivery without increasing investment levels. Combinations of the two approaches are also possible.

4   Transition Time and Cost

For many organizations, transitioning to an SPL is a complex and investment-intensive undertaking (cf. [7–13]). The complexity derives from the many, simultaneous changes that must occur to the organization, processes, architecture, and software assets associated with the product family. These changes must be coordinated in such a way as to minimize the disruption to ongoing product development projects.

This section contains a qualitative discussion of the types of costs that the Convergys business case had to account for, along with a discussion of the major factors that we have seen drive the size of the effort, and their *duration*. Time is important because the business case in general will be sensitive to the relative timing of the costs and benefits. We begin with a high-level description of the major cost elements. Next, we outline some of the key factors that have driven the transition cost level and time duration. Finally, we show the mapping between the cost elements and the drivers.

4.1   Cost Elements

The cost elements are grouped into four categories: architecture, process, organization, and implementation.

Architecture. This category covers all costs associated with establishing a target product line architecture, technology standards, and an architectural evolution strategy and plan.

Domain Analysis. Domain analysis is concerned with understanding and documenting the requirements commonalties and variabilities. This is a key input to defining the target architecture.

Target Architecture. The target architecture specifies the common component boundaries, scope, interfaces, and variation points.

Technology Standards. A common set of technology standards must be agreed on that deal with operating systems, programming languages, data base management systems, graphical user interface technologies and user interface look and feel standards.

Current Architecture. In order to establish realistic architecture migration plans, an understanding of the current architectures employed across the product family are needed.

Migration Strategy and Plan. The architecture migration strategy and plan is the roadmap for evolving the existing product family to the target architecture. It addresses how and when architectural modifications will occur across all products and domains.

Process. This category covers all costs associated with establishing a target process architecture and set of process standards, as well as establishing a process migration strategy and plan.

Target Process. The transition may require a major overhaul to existing processes. Critical areas to examine include the software release planning, specification, and commitments process (a given product group will depend on the timely delivery of new component releases from multiple components groups, and the component groups will find themselves having to meet the needs of multiple product groups); capacity planning and management (allocating staff between the product groups and component groups is a complex production scheduling problem); software support (defining the technical support tiers and support service level agreements between component and product groups); and technology coordination (coordinating the upgrade to third party software, such as operating system upgrades, new releases of data base management systems, etc.).

Current Process. An understanding of the suite of existing processes across the organization is needed to develop realistic process migration strategies and plans.

Process Standards. Standards that must be agreed to by the various component and product groups to ensure the smooth operation of the software factory (for example, component documentation and packaging standards, establishment of a common set of artifacts, especially artifacts that cross component-product boundaries, such as requirements specifications, and project status tracking and reporting).

Tools Standards. Establishment of development environment standards, such as requirements and design documentation, testing, and configuration management.

Metrics. Establishment of a common set of process metrics.

Technical Governance. The establishment of a set of processes and infrastructure to ensure conformance to the architecture, technology, and process standards.

Migration Strategy and Plan. Establishment of a process migration strategy and plan that addresses how and when the new processes will be deployed within the organization.

Organization. This category covers all costs associated with organizational architecture, training, change management, and overall transition planning and management.

Strategic Planning. Development, communication, and enrollment in the SPL vision and umbrella transition strategy.

Program Management. Managing the inter-organizational and inter-project dependencies during the transitioning effort, communicating status, progress and jeopardies to the major stakeholders.

Change Management. Focused on enrolling the organization in the need for change, fostering awareness, communicating success, and working organizational change management issues throughout the transition.

Training Curriculum. Curriculum development that addresses critical skills gaps within the organization, such as domain analysis, component-based development methods, and process design, as well as curriculum development associated with the new software development processes and process standards.

Organizational Design. Mapping the target process architecture into an organizational structure.

Migration Strategy and Plan. Developing the overall organization migration strategy and plan.

Implementation. This category covers all costs associated with implementing the strategies and plans for transforming the organization, process, and software assets to conform to the target architecture.

Components. Instantiation of the components defined in the target component architecture through a combination of reengineering, mining, new development, and licensing/acquisition.

Products. Instantiation of members of the product line based on the target architecture and common components. This work involves some combination of reengineering existing products to use the common components, and/or retiring existing products and building new ones from the common components.

Process. Implementing the new processes, conducting process pilots, training the organization on the new processes, process standards, and tools.

Organization. Restructuring the organization to operationalize the new software factory.

4.2   Cost Drivers

The factors that we have seen influence costs are as follows.

NP - Number of Products. The number of products within the existing family will have an impact on all four of the cost categories.

NC - Number of Components. The number of components that are within the scope of the product line have an impact on the architecture and implementation categories.

PC - Number of Product-Component Combinations. There are some elements that are sensitive to the number of product-component combinations.

AQ - Architectural Quality. Adherence of the existing software assets to such architectural qualities as modularity, maintainability, etc. can have a major impact on the architecture and implementation efforts.

TS - Technology Standardization Level. The level of technology standardization across the existing products (the number and variety of platforms, programming languages, use of third party software, adherence to industry standards, etc.) can have a major impact on the architecture and implementation costs.

PS - Process Standardization Level. The level of software process standardization will impact process and implementation costs.

OS - Organizational Size. The size of the development organization will impact the process, organization, and implementation costs.

DP - Software Development Practice. There are a number of software development practice areas that can have a major impact on the effort to architect the product line. In particular, the existence of good requirements and architecture documentation practices will greatly facilitate the domain analysis, current architecture, and architecture migration planning efforts. Lack of good practice in these areas may require that these artifacts be re-constructed as a precursor to making forward progress.

4.3   Time Drivers

In general, the cost drivers discussed above also have a direct impact on the time its takes to transition to an SPL. In addition to these drivers, there are drivers that, while not having a major impact on the cost, nevertheless can have a dramatic impact on the time it takes to effect the transition. Since the business case depends critically on the timing of the cash flows, these drivers should be factored into the SPL timeline as much as possible. The factors that we have seen influence the transition timeline are as follows:

SM - Subject Matter Expertise. Availability of subject matter experts (people with specific skills, such as architects, or people with specific domain knowledge) is a major factor across all categories. It is insufficient to have the investment dollars. Subject matter experts will be needed in the architecture, process, organizational, and implementation areas. However, subject matter experts are typically a scarce resource that are needed to support the existing product development projects. The inability to assign these resources to the SPL transition can have a negative impact on the rate of progress.

RD - R&D Constraints. The company will have to decide between the level of investment in the SPL versus investing in its existing business. This issue tends to surface when the transitioning effort becomes investment intensive, i.e., during the middle phases of the project.

CL - Culture. The SPL approach requires the organization to establish a common set of cultural values and a common way of doing things. Organizations that have a tradition of independence can find it difficult to let go of the established norms, and resist change on any kind. Thus, lack of a culture that is conducive to the SPL paradigm will have a major impact across all categories.

LE - Lexicon. Organizations that have worked independently from one another tend to establish their own terminology to describe concepts relevant to their application. Thus different terms are used by different groups to describe the same concept. When these groups attempt to work together to conduct, for example, a domain analysis, a communications barrier may exist due to a single term having multiple conflicting interpretations, or due to multiple terms that refer to the same concept.

GE - Geography. A highly distributed development organization presents a number of challenges that are not unique to SPL, yet need to be factored into the transition timeline. In particular, communications and coordination can be a major challenge if the organization is highly distributed.

LC - Learning Curve. The SPL approach requires a new set of skills not typically found in the development community, such as domain oriented software engineering, component-based development, and formal architecture methods and practices. The lack of experience in these areas can have a major impact on the architecture and implementation timelines.

4.4   Element to Driver Mapping

The table below summarizes the mapping between the various cost elements and time and cost drivers.

Weighting factors have not been applied in the table above, therefore not all "x's" are of equal importance. The major cost drivers are architectural quality, technology standardization level, organization size, and the number of components. As can be seen from the table, availability of Subject Matter Experts (SME's) is a major driver of transition time. An important benefit of the SPL approach is that it alleviates the problem associated with a limited supply of SME's, however, during the transition period, the transition project actually worsens the problem since it results in an additional drain on these limited resources. In addition, R&D constraints have a major impact during the implementation phase, since the investment requirements become most intensive during this period. As with subject matter experts, the SPL goal is to lessen the R&D burden, however, the investment requirement during the implementation phase has the opposite effect.

5   Economic Analysis

The derivation of economic measures such as Net Present Value, Internal Rate of Return, and Payback Period involves modeling the cash flows associated with the investment[1].

The cash flows are based on the benefits as discussed in Section 3, while the costs are those discussed in Section 4. In this section, we present a simple transition scenario in order to illustrate the application of the benefits model. While simplistic and idealized, it nevertheless provides insight into the types of issues that the business case must address.

Cost Element → Mapping														
Category/Element	NP	NC	PC	AQ	TS	PS	OS	DP	SM	RD	CL	LE	GE	LC
Architecture														
Domain Analysis		x						x	x		x	x		x
Current Architecture	x	x	x	x	x			x	x				x	
Target Architecture	x	x	x	x	x				x		x	x	x	x
Technology Standards					x				x	x				
Migration Plan	x	x	x	x	x				x					
Process														
Current Process	x					x		x	x			x		
Target Process	x					x			x		x	x	x	x
Process Standards						x			x	x	x			
Tools Standards									x	x	x			
Metrics									x	x				
Technical Governance				x	x	x			x		x			
Migration Plan	x					x	x		x			x		
Organization														
Strategic Planning	x	x	x		x	x	x		x				x	
Program Management	x	x	x				x		x				x	
Change Management	x	x	x	x	x	x	x	x	x				x	
Training Curriculum					x	x	x		x				x	x
Organizational Design	x	x					x		x		x		x	x
Migration Plan	x	x					x		x		x		x	
Implementation														
Components		x		x	x				x	x			x	x
Products	x			x	x				x	x		x		x
Process	x					x	x		x	x			x	x
Organization	x	x					x		x	x			x	x

We start with some assumptions that simplify the analysis. First, we assume that the number of products is constant over the planning period. Further, we assume that the loaded cost per person per year is fixed. Finally, we assume that the investment is additive to the existing investment, and that people with the necessary skills can be added to work the transition without impacting the existing product development efforts. In what follows, we will use the more conservative approach to quantifying benefits (constant throughput, cost avoidance in terms of staff reductions).

We divide the business case planning period into four sequential phases. The first phase ("Ramp") involves a linear ramp up of staff to work the SPL transition. This phase is all costs - there are no benefits. The duration of this phase will depend on how quickly people with the right skill set can be added to the project. The next phase ("Engineering") is where most of the transition effort occurs. We assume a constant staffing level during this phase. No benefits accrue during this phase - only costs. The third phase ("Deployment") involves the successive introduction of the reusable components into the product line, and the completion of the SPL transition. During this phase, costs

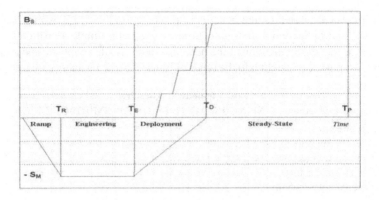

Fig. 4. Planning timeline and milestones.

decrease from their maximum run rate at the beginning of the phase to zero at the end. On the other hand, the benefit run rate progressively increases from zero at the beginning of the phase to its maximum value at the end. The last phase ("Steady-State") begins with the completion of the SPL transition and runs until the end of the planning period. During this phase, there are no transition costs, and the benefit run rate is constant. Figure 2 shows the different phases along the planning timeline. We assume a five year planning horizon. We consider the scenario summarized in the table below.

Model Example - Baseline Parameters		
Parameter	**Value**	**Units**
Number of Products	4	-
Total Independent Staff Level	100	People
Loaded Cost	10,000	$ Per Person-Month
Planning Horizon	60	Months
Total Transition Effort	600	Person-Months
Maximum Transition Staff	25	People
Ramp-Up Time	6	Months
Component Deployment Interval	3	Months Per Product
Cost of Capital	12%	Per Year
Commonality	2/3	-
Leverage	3/4	-
Productivity Improvement	1/4	-
Independent Investment	12	($1,000,000) Per Year
Total Transition Cost	6	($1,000,000)
Engineering Complete (T_E)	21	Months
Deployment Complete (T_D)	33	Months

The economic measures are summarized below.

Model Example - Baseline Measures		
Measure	**Value**	**Units**
Net Present Value	7.7	($1,000,000)
Internal Rate of Return	64	% Per Year
Payback Period	41	Months

The Net Present Value and Internal Rate of Return are satisfactory. However, the Payback Period of 41 months suggests a high risk associated with the investment.

We next consider the sensitivity of the results to variations in the key input parameters. The table below summarizes the sensitivities for selected variations. The parameter being changed, along with its new value are shown in the first two columns. The remaining columns show the new values of the measures as well as their change from the baseline case. The top half of the table shows downside scenarios (more pessimistic assumptions), while the bottom half shows the upside scenarios (more optimistic assumptions).

Model Example - Sensitivity Analysis							
Parameter	Value	NPV	ΔNPV	i_{IROR}	Δi_{IROR}	T_{PB}	ΔT_{PB}
Total Effort	750	3.7	-4.0	34.8	-29.0	51	10
Maximum Staff	20	5.0	-2.7	47.3	-16.6	48	7
Ramp-Up Time	12	6.4	-1.3	59.2	-4.6	45	4
Commonality	1/2	6.5	-1.2	59.8	-7.1	43	2
Leverage	1/2	4.1	-3.6	40.9	-22.9	47	6
Productivity Improvement	0	5.8	-1.9	52.5	-11.3	44	3
Total Effort	450	12.0	4.3	110.0	46.1	32	-9
Maximum Staff	30	9.7	1.9	76.1	12.3	37	-4
Ramp-Up Time	3	8.2	0.4	63.8	0	41	0
Commonality	3/4	8.2	.0.5	66.7	2.9	41	0
Leverage	7/8	8.9	1.2	70.8	6.9	40	-1
Productivity Improvement	1/2	8.5	0.8	68.0	4.2	41	0

Not surprisingly, the results are highly sensitive to the total transition effort. An increase of 25% in the total effort yields marginal results with a very long (four year) payback period. Note that, even with a 25% reduction in the total effort, the payback period is still 32 months. Changes to the staffing level also result in significant changes to the results. The baseline scenario assumed a staffing level equal to 25% of the total size of the development organization (a rather optimistic assumption). A decrease of 25% in the maximum transition staffing level versus a 25% increase results in a swing of almost $5,000,000 in the net present value, and an eleven month swing in the payback period. This result must be kept in mind in the business case process, since diversion of skilled and knowledgeable developers from existing product development efforts to the transitioning effort is problematic at best - the transition projects are best carried out by people who have an in-depth understanding of the existing code base. Unfortunately, these are also the same people who are in greatest demand to support existing projects. The results are also sensitive to the productivity improvement, commonality, and leverage parameters. Since the entire business case rests on a reasonably accurate estimate of these parameters, the impact of over estimating them should be closely examined to determine how robust the business case is against estimation error.

In addition to examining the effects of changing a single parameter, we have developed a practice of defining "scenarios" by which groups of parameters are changed simultaneously to see their combined impact on the measures.

In summary, the results indicate a long pay-back period, even though the net present value and internal rate of return are reasonable in the baseline scenario. Of course, the major drivers behind the pay-back period are the total transition effort and staffing profile.

In order to mitigate the risks associated with the investment, a different strategy may be in order. The transition strategy that this example is based on can be characterized as the "big bang" approach, since all of the costs are incurred up front, with the benefits following during the later phases. This suggests the need to look for alternative strategies that spread the costs out over time, and that deliver smaller, more incremental benefits earlier. This type of strategy will result in a much lowered investment risk, which will facilitate gaining stakeholder buy-in to the project. On the down side, an incremental approach could result in a very long investment cycle, along with compromises to the product line architecture and associated software assets. Further, the incremental approach can be more costly in the long term, since multiple iterations are needed, with each iteration requiring re-integration and certification of the deliverables. There is no clear-cut strategy that is optimal in all cases. However, the above example does stress the need to carefully examine the effect that the strategy will have on the cash flows and end results.

6   Metrics

Critical to success is a set of metrics that allow the organization to track progress against the predictions documented in the business case. By providing a feedback mechanism, the business case can be updated based on positive and negative variances from the anticipated results. The benefits model is based on the concept of "cost avoidance." Unfortunately, it is not feasible to directly measure whether or not costs were avoided without conducting some sort of experiment with a control group that continues to develop the old way, and comparing the control group results with the SPL results. Furthermore, business conditions are constantly changing, R&D investment levels fluctuate from year to year, and new products are brought to market while others retire, etc. Finally, the company may have other initiatives underway that target areas that overlap with the transition, such as quality and productivity improvement projects. However, there are some metrics that follow directly from the economic model that allow for an indirect measure of the economic impact. The metrics are summarized in the table below. In addition to these metrics, standard quality metrics such as defect density and defect removal effectiveness are essential, however, since these metrics are not unique to the our approach, they are not considered here.

Recommended SPL Economic Metrics		
Metric	Units	Scope
Staff	-	Product-Component
Throughput	FP/Year	Product
Throughput	FP/Year	Component
Productivity	FP/Person-Year	Product
Productivity	FP/Person-Year	Component
Commonality	Percentage	Component
Commonality	Percentage	Product-Component
Leverage	Percentage	Component
Leverage	Percentage	Product-Component

The implementation of the commonality and leverage metrics requires a measurement program that properly accounts for the demand across all product - component combinations. In particular, the front end of the development process will need to be modified to include a categorization of new enhancement requests according to which products and components are impacted. Function point counts need to be tracked for component-product pair. The Convergys approach is centered on large-scale components, therefore, the number of component-product combinations is manageable.

7   Conclusions

The stakes associated with a transition to an SPL are high - the investment requirements and risks, as well as the downstream benefits can be significant. Therefore it is essential that a business case be developed that properly accounts for the costs, benefits, and risks. A good understanding of the size and timing of the cash flows will enable the organization to assess its transition strategy, and determine the degree to which it should adopt an incremental and iterative approach. An understanding of the cost elements, and the cost and time drivers is an important input to this process. During the early phases, the business case will by necessity be at a high level. As the transition progresses, the strategies, plans, costs, and benefits will become more specific and accurate. Therefore, the business case should be updated on a regular basis to incorporate new information and feedback in terms of actual versus predicted results. A good set of metrics and associated measurement program will be needed to implement the feedback loop. In summary, the business case can be an effective tool for not only helping an organization decide *whether* to transition to an SPL, but also *how* to make the transition in such a way as to maximize return and minimize risk.

Going forward, the SPL benefits model requires validation. Additional work is needed in defining a standard measurement process for the metrics that have been recommended.

In closing, it should be stressed that there are additional considerations beyond pure economics that must be taken into account before the decision is made to transition to an SPL. The most important consideration is that the SPL approach requires *massive change* to the organization. In particular, the culture typified by the Independent scenario, where each development organization controls all of the resources, and is used to making decisions totally optimized for their particular product, is not conducive to an approach where development groups must depend on one another for their success. Organizations usually resist change of any significance. An effective awareness and enrollment program is needed to address stakeholder concerns, and to articulate why the change is needed. A clear vision and practical implementation strategy for achieving the vision are essential to addressing the SPL skeptics. Therefore, effective change management, organizational leadership, and *persistence* are critical to success.

References

1. J. Poulin. Measuring Software Reuse: Principles, Practices, and Economic Models. Addison-Wesley, 1997.
2. J. Gaffney and R. Cruickshank. A General Economics Model of Software Reuse. Proceedings of the International Conference on Software Engineering, Melbourne Australia. ACM, 1992.
3. R. Malan and K. Wentzel. Economics of Software Reuse Revisited. Hewlett-Packard Technical Report HPL-93-31, 1993.

4. K. Schmid. Integrated Cost- and Investmentmodels for Product Family Development. IESE-Report No. 067.03/E Version 1.0, 2003.
5. P. Knauber, J. Bermejo, G. Böckle, J. Sampaio do Prado Leite, F. Van der Linden, L. Northrop, M. Stark, and D. Weiss. Quantifying Product Line Benefits. Software Product-Family Engineering, 4th International Workshop, PFE 2001, Bilbao Spain, October, 2001.
6. J. Favaro, K. Favaro, P. Favaro. Value Based Software Reuse Investment. Annals of Software Engineering 5, 1998.
7. P. Clemens and L. Northrop. Software Product Lines: Practices and Patterns, Addison-Wesley, 2001.
8. I. Jacobson, M. Griss, and P. Jonsson. Software Reuse: Architecture, Process and Organization for Business Success, ACM Press, 1997.
9. G. Böckle, J. Muñoz, P. Knauber, C. Krueger, J. Sampaio do Prado Leite, F. van der Linden, L. Northrop, M. Stark, and D. Weiss. Adopting and Institutionalizing a Product Line Culture. Software Product Lines: Second International Conference, SPLC 2, San Diego, CA, USA, August 2002 Proceedings. Springer-Verlag, 2002.
10. D. Fafchamps. Organizational factors and reuse. IEEE Software, September, 1994.
11. J. Sametinger. Software Engineering with Reusable Components. Springer-Verlag, 1997.
12. T. Jolley, D. Kasik, and C. Kimball. Governance Polarities of Internal Product Lines. Software Product Lines: Second International Conference, SPLC 2, San Diego, CA, USA, August 2002 Proceedings. Springer-Verlag, 2002.
13. J. Bosch. Maturity and Evolution in Software Product Lines: Approaches, Artefacts and Organization. Software Product Lines: Second International Conference, SPLC 2, San Diego, CA, USA, August 2002 Proceedings. Springer-Verlag, 2002.

A   Model Concepts

The economic model is based on the comparison of software product development costs in two scenarios. The first scenario ("Independent") is based on a family of products developed independently from one another. In this scenario, each product has its own dedicated funding source and development organization. This scenario represents the baseline "business as usual" case for economic comparison purposes. The second scenario ("SPL") assumes that assets common to multiple products are developed and supported by a "component factory," which delivers new component[3] releases to the product groups. The product groups are responsible for integrating the common components, and adapting/extending the common component functionality to deliver new products/product releases that meet the needs of specific vertical markets.

A.1   Requirements Demand

We begin by considering the requirements (both functional and technical) placed on a family of products. Let N denote the number of products in the product family. For now, we confine ourselves to a single application "domain." The extension of the model to

---

[3] We use the term "component" to mean a set of software programs that encapsualtes it's functionality, and has well-defined and documented interfaces that define services provided and services expected. There is no implicit assumption regarding component size. Components can be small-grained, or very large-grained. Further, there is no assumption regarding how components are implemented.

multiple domains will be discussed below. We confine ourselves to some planning period of length T_P. In what follows, the index k will label products (k = 1, 2, ..., N). Let $\mathfrak{R}_k$ represent the set of requirements associated with product k. The set of requirements for the entire product family is the union of the requirements for the individual products:

$$\mathfrak{R} = \bigcup_k \mathfrak{R}_k \qquad (1)$$

We partition the set $\mathfrak{R}$ into disjoint subsets in such a way that all requirements in a given subset apply to the same set of products. Let $\{\pi\}$ denote the set of N - dimensional vectors that satisfy: $|\pi| > 0$; $\pi_k = 0$ or 1. Then a partition, $\mathfrak{R}_\pi \subseteq \mathfrak{R}$, is defined as:

$$\mathfrak{R}_\pi \equiv \left(\bigcap_{\{k|\pi_k=1\}} \mathfrak{R}_k \right) \cap \left(\bigcup_{\{k|\pi_k=0\}} \mathfrak{R}_k \right)^C \qquad (2)$$

where the complement is defined relative to $\mathfrak{R}$. In general, there will be $2^N - 1$ such partitions. Fig. 1 below illustrates the case for $N = 3$. In this example, $\mathfrak{R}_{100}$ represents the requirements unique to the first product, whereas $\mathfrak{R}_{110}$ represents the set of requirements shared by products 1 and 2, but not shared by product 3. In general, a "1" appearing in the kth position means the kth product is a member of the partition, whereas a value of "0" indicates the product is not a member of the partition.

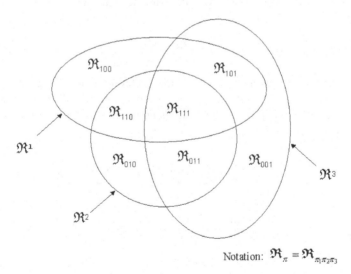

Notation: $\mathfrak{R}_\pi \equiv \mathfrak{R}_{\pi_1\pi_2\pi_3}$

Fig. 5. A Venn diagram illustrating requirements partitions for a family of three products. There are three partitions ($\mathfrak{R}_{100}$, $\mathfrak{R}_{010}$, $\mathfrak{R}_{001}$) that contain requirements unique to a single product, three partitions ($\mathfrak{R}_{110}$, $\mathfrak{R}_{101}$, $\mathfrak{R}_{011}$) that contain requirements common to two of the products, and a single partition ($\mathfrak{R}_{111}$) that contains requirements common to all products.

We define the partition "weight" as the number of products that are members of the partition: $n(\boldsymbol{\pi}) \equiv \sum_k \pi_k$. Thus, in Fig. 1, the partitions $(\mathfrak{R}_{100}, \mathfrak{R}_{010}, \mathfrak{R}_{001})$ have weight $n(\boldsymbol{\pi}) = 1$, $(\mathfrak{R}_{110}, \mathfrak{R}_{101}, \mathfrak{R}_{011})$ have weight $n(\boldsymbol{\pi}) = 2$, and the partition $(\mathfrak{R}_{111})$ possesses a weight of $n(\boldsymbol{\pi}) = 3$. For a given N, the number of partitions with a given weight, n, is given by the binomial coefficient, $\binom{N}{n}$. Application domains for which there is significant overlap in requirements are good candidates for the SPL approach. However, in order to take advantage of these overlapping requirements, an architecture is needed that capitalizes on the commonalties, accomodates the variabilities, *and* still provides sufficient system scalability, performance, and operational cost-effectiveness. Accordingly, we define a mapping which associates a number for each partition:

$$M_\pi = \mathcal{M}\left(\mathfrak{R}_\pi\right) \tag{3}$$

It is understood in the above equation that architectural/design constraints may limit the size of M_π. The units that we shall adopt for M_π are function points (FP).

The *demand function* is then defined as the average rate of new requirements that are placed on the product family during the planning period:

$$D_\pi \equiv \frac{1}{T_P} M_\pi \tag{4}$$

The demand function has units of function points per unit time (e.g. FP/Year).

In the Independent scenrio, each product group must develop, enhance, and maintain its own code base to meet the set of requirements, even though other products may share many of those requirements. For a given domain, the demand placed on a given product is given by:

$$D_k = \sum_{\{\pi\}} \hat{k} \cdot \boldsymbol{\pi} \, D_\pi \tag{5}$$

where the factor $\hat{k} \cdot \boldsymbol{\pi}$ ensures that only demand relevant to the kth product is included in the sum. Here, $\hat{k}$ is the unit vector whose components are all 0 except for the kth component which is equal to 1. The total *effective demand* across all products in the Independent scenario is then:

$$\tilde{D} = \sum_{k=1}^{N} D_k = \sum_{k=1}^{N} \sum_{\{\pi\}} \hat{k} \cdot \boldsymbol{\pi} D_\pi = \sum_{\{\pi\}} n(\boldsymbol{\pi}) D_\pi \tag{6}$$

By contrast, in the SPL scenario, functionality for a given partition is implemented once. The total demand in the SPL case is then:

$$D = \sum_{\{\pi\}} D_\pi \tag{7}$$

The Independent demand function carries a weighting factor equal to $n(\boldsymbol{\pi})$. This weighting is a measure of the demand redundancy inherit in the Independent scenario. In order to quantify this redundancy, we introduce the concepts of "commonality" and "leverage."

A.2   Commonality and Leverage

We start by assuming that, in the SPL scenario, functionality common to two or more products is developed by the common component factory, while functionality specific to a vertical market is implemented by the product group responsible for that vertical. Let $\{\pi\}^c$ represent the set of partitions which apply to two or more products, and let $\{\pi\}^v$ represent the set of partitions that are unique to a single vertical market product. Then $\{\pi\} = \{\pi\}^c \bigcup \{\pi\}^v$. Next, we define the common demand and vertical demand functions as:

$$\tilde{D}^C \equiv \sum_{\{\pi\}^c} n(\pi) D_\pi; \qquad \tilde{D}^V \equiv \sum_{\{\pi\}^v} D_\pi \tag{8}$$

$$D_k^C \equiv \sum_{\{\pi\}^c} \hat{k} \cdot \pi D_\pi; \qquad D_k^V \equiv \sum_{\{\pi\}^v} \hat{k} \cdot \pi D_\pi = D_{\hat{k}} \tag{9}$$

$$D^C \equiv \sum_{\{\pi\}^c} D_\pi; \qquad D^V \equiv \sum_{\{\pi\}^v} D_\pi = \tilde{D}^V \tag{10}$$

Then:

$$D = D^C + D^V; \qquad \tilde{D} = \tilde{D}^C + D^V \tag{11}$$

Here, D_k^C is the size of demand on the kth product that is served by the common component group, while D_k^V is the size of the demand on the kth product that is met by the product group itself. D^C is the total demand that is common to two or more products, while D^V is the total demand unique to the various products. Similarly, $\tilde{D}^C$ is the size of the demand that is common across the product family, weighted by the redundancy factors, while $\tilde{D}^V$ is the size of the total demand unique to the various products. The redundancy weighting factor for the vertical market partitions is one, therefore $\tilde{D}^V = D^V$.

Next, we introduce the *commonality* parameters:

$$\omega_k \equiv \frac{D_k^C}{D_k}; \qquad \omega \equiv \frac{D^C}{D}; \qquad \tilde{\omega} \equiv \frac{\tilde{D}^C}{\tilde{D}} \tag{12}$$

The interpretation of these quantities is as follows. ω_k is that fraction of demand placed on the kth product that is shared by other products in the product family. ω is that fraction of demand that is shared by two or more products - it represents the total demand placed on the component factory in the SPL scenario. Finally, $\tilde{\omega}$ represents the fraction of demand in the Independent case that is shared by multiple products, properly weighted by the redundancy factors.

Next, we introduce the notion of *leverage*:

$$\lambda_k \equiv \frac{D_k^C}{D^C}; \qquad \lambda \equiv \frac{1}{N} \sum_k \lambda_k \tag{13}$$

The parameter λ_k represents the fraction of new capabilities produced by the component factory that benefit the kth product, hence the term "leverage." λ is just the numerical average of the leverage factors across all products.

We are now ready to quantify the demand redundancy in the Independent scenario. Based on the above definitions, we have:

$$D^V = \tilde{D} - \tilde{D}^C = (1 - \tilde{\omega}) \tilde{D} = D - D^C = (1 - \omega) D \Rightarrow \frac{\tilde{D}}{D} = \frac{(1 - \omega)}{(1 - \tilde{\omega})} \qquad (14)$$

Also:

$$\lambda = \frac{1}{N} \sum_k \lambda_k = \frac{1}{N} \sum_k \frac{D_k^C}{D^C} = \frac{1}{N \omega D} \sum_k \omega_k D_k = \frac{\tilde{D}\tilde{\omega}}{N \omega D} \Rightarrow \frac{\tilde{D}}{D} = \frac{N \lambda \omega}{\tilde{\omega}} \qquad (15)$$

Hence:

$$\frac{\tilde{D}}{D} = 1 + (N\lambda - 1)\,\omega \qquad (16)$$

Note that the redunancy increases as the number of products, commonality, and leverage increase.

A.3   Productivity and Throughput

Software development organizations respond to market demand by delivering new releases of their product that enhance its value to potential customers. Let ΔF_k represent the average size of new product releases (in function points) over the planning period, T_P, for product k. Also, let $\tilde{S}_k$, S_k, represent the average staffing level associated with product k in the Independent and SPL scenarios, respectively. The *productivity* is then defined as:

$$\tilde{p}_k \equiv \tfrac{\Delta F_k}{\tilde{S}_k} \text{ Independent Case}$$

$$p_k \equiv \tfrac{\Delta F_k}{S_k} \text{ SPL Case} \qquad (17)$$

The *throughput* (Independent scenario) is defined as:

$$\tilde{T}_k \equiv \tilde{p}_k \tilde{S}_k \qquad (18)$$

Throughput has the same units as demand: function points per unit time.

B   SPL Benefits

B.1   Relationship between Independent and SPL Staffing Levels

Having introduced the basic concepts, we now quantify the SPL benefits. In the SPL case, the development staff is allocated between the common component factory and the individual product groups. Let S and p represent the total staff and average productivity, respectively for the SPL scenario. Let S^C denote the common component staff, and let S^V denote the product (vertical market) staff. The allocation of the two will be in accordance with the relative demand:

$$S^C = \omega S; \qquad S^V = (1 - \omega) S \qquad (19)$$

In addition, S^V will be split between the various products as:

$$S_k^V = \frac{D_{\hat{k}}}{D^V} S^V \tag{20}$$

To determine S, we require that the SPL scenario provide the same level of throughput as the Independent scenario:

$$T_k = \tilde{T}_k \tag{21}$$

The SPL throughput is:

$$T_k = p\left(\lambda_k S^C + S_k^V\right) = p\left(\lambda_k \omega + \frac{D_k}{D^V}(1-\omega)\right) S \tag{22}$$

In the above, the leverage factor, λ_k accounts for the fact that not all of the component factory output benefits the product in question. Setting the SPL throughput equal to the Independent throughput, and summing over all products, we obtain:

$$p\left(1 + (N\lambda - 1)\omega\right) S = \tilde{p}\tilde{S} \tag{23}$$

Hence:

$$\frac{S}{\tilde{S}} = \frac{\tilde{p}}{p}\frac{D}{\tilde{D}} \tag{24}$$

Thus we see that the SPL staffing is reduced due to the elimination of redundant demand (assuming $N\lambda > 1$), and due to an increase in productivity (assuming $p > \tilde{p}$). Letting $r \equiv \tilde{p}/p$, and using the result from equation (25), we obtain:

$$S = r\left[1 + (N\lambda - 1)\omega\right]^{-1}\tilde{S} \tag{25}$$

Equation (34) suggests that we can lower staffing levels and still maintain throughput equivalent to the Independent case. Expressing p as $p \equiv \tilde{p}(1 + \delta p)$, and letting $\Lambda \equiv (N\lambda - 1)\omega$ we obtain the following expressions for the staff savings:

$$\Delta S \equiv \tilde{S} - S = \left[1 - \frac{1}{r(N\lambda - 1)\omega}\right]\tilde{S} = \left[1 - \frac{1}{(1 + \delta p)(1 + \Lambda)}\right]\tilde{S} \tag{26}$$

The break-even condition is obtained as follows.

$$\Delta S \geqslant 0 \Rightarrow (1 + \delta p)(1 + \Lambda) \geqslant 0 \tag{27}$$

B.2   Financial Flexibility

The SPL approach has a lower staffing requirement than the Independent approach. Let L represent the fully loaded cost per person per year. The annual investment requirements are:

$$\tilde{I} = L\tilde{S} \text{ Independent;} \qquad I \equiv LS \text{ SPL} \tag{28}$$

Therefore, the cost avoidance per annum due to improved productivity and the elimination of redundant development is:

$$\Delta I \equiv \tilde{I} - I = L\Delta S = \left[1 - \frac{1}{(1 + \delta p)(1 + \Lambda)}\right]\tilde{I} \tag{29}$$

Thus, the obvious way to quantify the benefit is in terms of the cost avoidance implied by equations (39) and (40).

However, there is another way to look at equation (35). Instead of reducing the staffing levels, the staff can be re-allocated back to the component groups and product groups in order to *increase throughput*. Assuming that the staff is allocated in the same way as in equation (28), we obtain a higher throughput level:

$$T \longrightarrow T + \Delta T = (1 + \delta p)(1 + \Lambda)\tilde{T} \tag{30}$$

To achieve this higher throughput level in the Independent scenario, we would have to add staff (and increase the investment level) by:

$$\Delta \tilde{S} = \frac{\Delta T}{\tilde{p}} = [(1 + \delta p)(1 + \Lambda) - 1]\tilde{S} \Rightarrow \Delta \tilde{I} = [(1 + \delta p)(1 + \Lambda) - 1]\tilde{I} \tag{31}$$

Comparing equations (39) and (42), we see that:

$$\frac{\Delta \tilde{I}}{\Delta I} = (1 + \delta p)(1 + \Lambda) > 1 \tag{32}$$

B.3 Time Dependence of the Benefits

During the period when the component is being deployed to the various products, the benefits will have a dependence on the number of products using that component. Let $n(t)$ represent the number of products using the component at time t. Then we have:

$$\Delta I(t) = \left[1 - \frac{1}{(1 + \delta p(t))(1 + \Lambda(t))}\right]\tilde{I}(t)$$
$$\Delta \tilde{I}(t) = [(1 + \delta p(t))(1 + \Lambda(t)) - 1]\tilde{I}(t) \tag{33}$$

where:

$$\delta p(t) = \frac{n(t)\delta p}{N}; \qquad \Lambda(t) = [1 + (n(t)\lambda - 1)\omega]; \qquad \tilde{I}(t) = \frac{n(t)}{N}\tilde{I} \tag{34}$$

B.4 Multiple Components

For the case of multiple components, we attached a component subscript (α) to all parameters, where $\alpha = 1, 2, \ldots$ Number of Components).

$$\Delta I_\alpha(t) = \left[1 - \frac{1}{(1 + \delta p_\alpha(t))(1 + \Lambda_\alpha(t))}\right]\tilde{I}_\alpha(t)$$
$$\Delta \tilde{I}_\alpha(t) = [(1 + \delta p_\alpha(t))(1 + \Lambda_\alpha(t)) - 1]\tilde{I}_\alpha(t) \tag{35}$$

Then the total benefits are given by:

$$\Delta I(t) = \sum_\alpha \Delta I_\alpha(t); \qquad \Delta \tilde{I}(t) = \sum_\alpha \Delta \tilde{I}_\alpha(t) \tag{36}$$

A Case Study
of Two Configurable Software Product Families

Mikko Raatikainen, Timo Soininen, Tomi Männistö, and Antti Mattila

Software Business and Engineering Institute (SoberIT)
Helsinki University of Technology
P.O. Box 9600, FIN-02015 HUT, Finland
{Mikko.Raatikainen,Timo.Soininen,
Tomi.Mannisto,Antti.Mattila}@hut.fi

Abstract. A configurable software product family allows the deployment of individual products without customer-specific design or programming effort. Despite the fact that such software product families have recently gained research interest, there are only few empirical studies on them. This paper presents some results of a descriptive case study undertaken in two companies that develop and deploy configurable software product families. The similarities found in comparisons between characteristics of the configurable software product families were remarkable, although the companies, products, and application domains were different. The study shows that the configurable software product family approach is already applied in the industry. Furthermore, the approach seems to be a feasible and even efficient way to systematically develop a family of products and manage the variability within it.

1 Introduction

The *software product family* approach aims at producing a set of products that are developed on a basis of a common *software product family architecture* and a set of *shared assets* [1]. The shared assets and the software product family architecture are developed for reuse in a *development process* and reused to build products in a prescribed way in a *deployment process* [2], [3]. One class of such software product families is the configurable product base [4], for which we use the term *configurable software product family* (CSPF), meaning that at least a significant part of deployment is performed by *configuring*, for example, by setting parameter values or by selecting components or modules without programming.

The CSPF approach is considered in [4] the most systematic software product family approach and is appealing because it seems to promise an efficient and systematic deployment of products. However, there are only a few reported empirical research results on the nature and benefits of the CSPF approach, the established methods and practices for such an approach, and the problems encountered when applying the approach.

We have carried out a descriptive case study in five Finnish companies in order to characterize the state of the software product family approach in practice [5]. In the study, we found two companies that apply the CSPF approach. In this paper, we describe how the two companies apply the CSPF approach from the points of view of

F. van der Linden (Ed.): PFE 2003, LNCS 3014, pp. 403–421, 2004.
© Springer-Verlag Berlin Heidelberg 2004

the characteristics of, the adoption of, the variability within, the deployment process of, and the configuration-tool support for a CSPF, as well as the after-sales and maintenance of products deployed from the CSPF. The results indicate that the CSPF approach is applicable in the industry. There were remarkable similarities between the companies, although the CSPFs were developed independently from each other, and for different application domains.

The rest of the paper is organized as follows. In Section 2, we present the research method. In Section 3, the characteristics of the companies and their CSPFs are described, while in Section 4, they are compared with each other. In Section 5, the results are discussed particularly in the light of the characteristics of the CSPF approach and the factors influencing its feasibility. Section 6 provides a comparison of the results to related work, while, in Section 7, the validity and reliability of the results are discussed. Finally, Section 8 draws conclusions and presents some ideas for future work

2   Research Method

The research design was a descriptive case study [5] undertaken in a number of companies. The objectives of the study were to characterize the state of the software product family approach in Finnish industry in practice. For the study, we looked for companies that potentially had a software product family.

To form an initial theory for the study, i.e., to gain a preliminary understanding of the software product family approach, we conducted a literature study of previous research results. Before starting the interviews, we developed a set of mostly open-ended and qualitative interview questions. The structure of the interviews was broken down into business, artifact, process, and organizational (BAPO) concerns, similar to the one described in [6], but we replaced the word 'architecture' with the word 'artifact' in order to emphasize that the term referred to several kinds of assets in addition to only software architecture. The BAPO analysis framework was used for triangulation purposes in order to find out different points of views on the software product family approach.

Data was collected in an interview and additional documentation analysis in each company at the turn of the year 2002, in a validation session a few months later, and through enabling the responders to read and comment on the reports we had written, including this paper.

In Company A, we interviewed a product manager, who was present when interviewing on business and process issues for about two hours, the manager of the deployment process, who was present for about half an hour when interviewing on deployment process issues, and a software engineer responsible for developing the CSPF, who was present for about two hours during the interview on artifact-specific issues. In addition, the chief architect was present all the time.

In Company B, we conducted the interview in two sessions. In the first session, we interviewed the architect about the business issues for a half an hour, the quality manager about the primary development process and organizational issues for one hour, and finally the architect, again together with a software engineer, about artifact-specific issues for two and a half hours. In the second session, we interviewed a business area manager about business issues and the deployment process for two hours.

In the interviews, we skipped some questions that seemed unimportant for the particular company, changed wordings and the order of the questions, and asked additional clarificatory questions, questions that deepened the topic under discussion and summarized comments into question format to generalize responses and enable the responders to correct our misinterpretations and misunderstandings. We tape-recorded the interviews and took notes, and later transcribed the interviews.

A few months later, we held an about 3-hour validation session in each company. In these sessions, we presented our findings to the company and asked questions to clarify issues that had remained unclear. We tape-recorded validation sessions.

We analyzed data from each company, first separately, and then across cases [7]. The analysis was based on a discussion of the impressions of researchers who were present at the interviews, as well as on the recordings, received documentation, written notes and transcripts of the interviews. The notes from the validation session were added afterwards. In the analysis, we used ATLAS.ti [8], which is an application designed for qualitative data analysis. The results of the analysis were validated in the validation sessions and by enabling the responders to read this report. For further details on the research method, see [9].

3   Companies

In this section, the characteristics of the companies are described first in Section 3.1 and their CSPF are illustrated in more depth in terms of the characteristics of the CSPF - variability, deployment, configurator, and after-sales and maintenance - in the following two sections.

3.1   The Companies

In Table 1, the major characteristics of each company and its products are given. The application domain refers to the application domain for which the CSPF is developed. In fact, Company A also operates and develops products for other closely related domains, although the focus is on the CSPF, whereas Company B operates only in the medical information management domain and does not develop products other than the CSPF. The number of employees and software engineers is the total number of people working within the companies. In Company A, several of the employees also work with other products, but most of the time they work with the CSPF studied; this is especially true of the software engineers. The type of CSPF refers to the kind of product the CSPF is. The operating environment of the CSPF is the software platform that a delivered product based on the CSPF installs and operates when in use. Total size of code in the CSPF means the total number of lines of code that is associated with shared assets in the CSPF; each delivery contains all or part of the assets and, in addition, a possible small amount of product specific code. The programming language refers to the programming languages that the companies have used in developing the CSPF.

Table 1. Characteristics of the companies.

	Company A	Company B
Application domain	Factory automation	Medical information management
Employees	200	130
Software engineers	25	35
Type of CSPF	Software augments electronics and mechanics	Software product
Operating environment	PC, MS Windows	PC, MS Windows
Total size of code	0.5 MLOC	Over 1 MLOC
Programming language	Visual basic, C++	C++

3.2   Company A

General Characteristics. Company A produces factory automation *products*. The company delivers about 50 products a year and assumes the number of annual deliveries stays relatively stable in the long term. The product is an investment good that is used for years or even decades. The company has decades of experience in the application domain as it has developed products for the same domain.

Before the CSPF approach, similar products were delivered in projects for each customer separately and each project used the source code and other deliverables of earlier projects non-systematically copy-pasting as a basis for a new delivery. In the mid 1990's, Company A realized the opportunity to improve the effectiveness of the deliveries by systemizing the reuse of common parts between the projects; following this through, they ended up developing the CSPF. Another objective during the initiation of the CSPF approach was to systemize variability to a generic configurable product that enabled efficient deployment. At the time of the initiation, Company A had some experience of developing a software product family because a similar approach had been applied to other products in the application domain as well.

A delivered product based on the CSPF is integrated to work with existing systems in the customer-environment, intermediating between, managing, and cooperating with the systems. Depending on the customer's order, a product includes a varying amount of features so that some tasks in the factory can be performed automatically using the system. A delivery includes mechanical and electronic systems that are controlled by software derived from the CSPF. The application domain of the CSPF is well understood and relatively stable. The interfaces in the application domain are relatively stable and to some extent standardized.

The employees in the software development department (Figure 1) have roles according to the domain engineering model [1] in which the work is divided between those developing the software product family and those doing the deployment projects. According to the responders, a few employees work in both roles. Both developers and deployers are all located close to each other in the same office premises.

The responders estimated that Company A has been able to double the number of product deliveries in a year with roughly the same number of employees as a result of adopting the CSPF approach. Furthermore, the CSPF approach was seen as the only

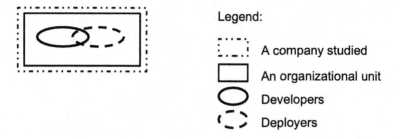

Legend:

A company studied
An organizational unit
Developers
Deployers

Fig. 1. Software development organization in Company A.

reasonable way to develop products. They even went as far as to state that the CSPF approach is the only reasonable way to do the business, despite the initial investment that was needed for building the CPSF. However, the company had not done a more precise analysis of, for example, the return on the investment of the CSPF.

Variability. Variability in the CSPF is achieved by *configuring* and *tailoring*. For Company A, configuring means setting parameter values without developing or modifying the source code. Tailoring, on the other hand, involves modifications that require developing new source code or modifying the existing source code.

The company divided configurable variability into *vertical* and *horizontal* variability. Vertical variability concerns the existence of *major functions*, which are large entities adding significant functionality to a product. In total, a product can contain about a dozen major functions that can enable some tasks in the factory to be performed automatically using the system. Horizontal variability typically involves adapting products to the customer-environment and preferences ranging from system-level features, such as the type of alarm when something goes wrong in the factory, to detailed issues, such as the numeric values specifying the length and width dimensions of the physical environment.

Vertical variability (Figure 2) is organized into five stacks, each containing a few major functions and a *base* that contains major functions common to all products. A customer can select the major functions needed for her purposes from the stack, while the base is included in all products. The order of the major functions in the stacks specifies how a selection can be done: The functions are selected such that all functions from the lowest to the desired level in the same stack have to be selected, although there may not be holes in the stack, resulting in one function not being selected, while a function above it is selected.

Tailoring typically involves introducing new interfaces to exchange data with, or report data to, another system; it rarely adds new features or modifies the existing features. Typically, tailoring is accomplished by adding new modules to the CSPF. Therefore, even if a product is tailored, the product is, and has to be, configured, as the configuring affects the parts of the product that are not changed in tailoring.

All deployed products are, in practice, based on the same source code. Parameter values specify what parts of the code are executed and which of the major functions or features are enabled.

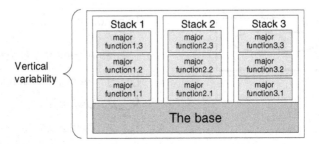

Fig. 2. The vertical variability stacks in Company A. The actual number of major functions is not exactly the same in the figure as in the CSPF studied.

The responders pointed out that there is a risk that customers might require more tailoring, beyond the scope achievable by configuring, and that this might lead to large scale changes to the CSPF that may, in turn, lead to further problems in the maintenance of the CSPF. However, such a problem had not occurred so far.

Deployment. In a deployment process (Figure 3), a product is first tailored if necessary, after that, auxiliary software and the product are installed on a PC. After the product is installed, it is configured by changing parameter values using a specific configuration tool. The product is tested with its mechanical and electronic systems integrated in order to ensure that it works as required; finally, it is shipped to the customer.

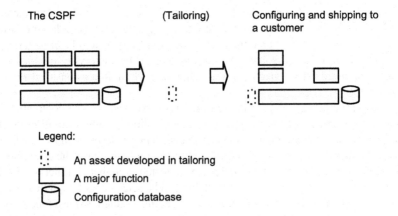

Fig. 3. Deployment process in Company A. The number of major functions in the figure is not exactly the same as in the actual CSPF.

The parameter values are initially set to default values. The responders estimated that the number of parameter values set in a deployment is typically about 200, although, as a minimum, the number may be closer to 100. A checklist that contains guidelines as to which parameter values have to be checked in configuring is used to ensure that all necessary parameter values are checked and set.

Tailoring is performed in addition to configuring in the case of only approximately 30% of the delivered products. Tailoring is usually very simple and routine and takes from a few days to a few weeks for two software engineers.

The responders stated that an employee who has experience on deploying products based on the CSPF sets most parameter values correctly in deployment and the dependencies between parameter values, for example, are clear to her from the context. Configuring needs primarily deep application domain knowledge, but hardly any software engineering knowledge. In fact, the employees who deploy products have their background in automation, not in software engineering. The responders estimated that a new employee needs at least three months of experience in the application domain and with the CSPF before she has a good enough understanding to be able to configure the system correctly by herself.

Deployment takes roughly one person-day, half of which is spent on configuring. Even with tailoring, the software part of the delivery typically takes such a short time that software development is not a bottleneck in the total process, which also includes mechanical and electronic manufacturing processes. The total process takes from weeks to a few months.

Configurator. The *configurator* is a software application that Company A has developed for configuring. The configurator is used to resolve horizontal and vertical variability by setting and storing the parameter values in a configuration database. The configurator has a graphical user interface.

The configurator is developed for a particular CSPF and is not usable in any other CSPF without reprogramming; this is because it includes parts that were specific to the CSPF such a configuration database scheme and checks to ensure that parameter values were set correctly according to rules that were embedded into the configurator. The configurator checked the correctness of some parameter values and their combinations but only for a small subset. Thus, the checks that the configurator carries out do cover the correctness of some, but not all, parameter values and therefore it is possible to specify a non-working product using the configurator. A configuration explanation, which is a textual description in natural language, is attached to each parameter to describe, for example, what kind of effect the parameter has on the product, what the possible parameter values are and what the parameter values mean. The user interface for setting parameter values is developed using typical graphical user interface components such as text fields, combo-boxes and radio buttons.

Configuring in the configurator is done by setting optional values, selecting alternatives from a set of alternatives, or specifying numeric values. To enable an optional parameter value means that, for example, some feature exists in a product. For alternative parameter values, there are typically about five possible values; selecting an alternative means, for example, selecting one of a set of similar features for use. For numbers, there is a field where a value, such as an integer, has to be entered and an allowed range for the number. A numeric parameter can, for example, specify the physical length and width dimensions of the physical environment of the facility where the product is located.

After-sales and Maintenance. The typical customer buys a product and then uses it without changes for years. Updates to newer main versions of the CSPF are made in some cases, but it is relatively rare. In fact, Company A does not see selling new features to old customers as a viable business model. A more typical product update for customers is made if a serious bug is noticed in the CSPF and the update includes a fix for the bug. Updating, either to a newer version or as a bug fix, is easy if a product is not tailored, because in that case all customers have the same code. Company A does not guarantee that it is possible to update a tailored product, at least not with as low a price as non-tailored ones. However, tailoring typically does not change a product to such an extent that it could not be easily updated if necessary. Nevertheless, by requiring tailoring, a customer may complicate updating her software.

A product can also be *reconfigured* later. Reconfiguring means that a parameter value is set to a different value, when, for example, something in the customer-environment changes. However, reconfiguring is only rarely carried out. Customers could, in principle, reconfigure the product by themselves, but the configurator is password-protected. Company A, does not give access to the customer, probably for both business and technical reasons, such as wishing to earn money from reconfiguring and wishing to prevent customers configuring a product improperly.

3.3   Company B

General Characteristics. A *system* delivered by Company B consists of several *products* for the medical domain. Dozens of systems are sold each year and each customer is typically sold several similar systems. The customers use the systems for years. Company B was founded in the early 1990's for emerging markets, and expects these markets to continue to grow.

The CSPF was developed from scratch when the company was founded in the early 1990's. From the very beginning, Company B had as an objective the development of a generic configurable system that is deployable efficiently and without source-code modification. Since its initial development, the CSPF has been further developed and new features have been added.

A delivered system based on the CSPF presents, monitors, produces, analyzes, and stores data regarding customer business processes that are safety-critical. The functionality of each product that consists of a system is different and focuses on different aspects of the application domain. The products complement each other such that one, for example, performs analysis for data, one combines data from multiple sources, and one stores data. The products in a system share data, data models, architectural principles, and some other minor assets. The system has interfaces to other systems in the customer-environment, enabling it to exchange data with them. It is also possible to customize the kind of data handled and how is it presented in the system. The application domain is relatively young, but nonetheless quite stable, standardized, and even governmentally regulated.

The organizational structure in Company B (Figure 4) follows the domain engineering model [1]. The CSPF is developed in a development organizational unit, while separate deployment organizational units and partner companies deploy systems. Furthermore, the CSPF development organization is in a single location, whereas the de-

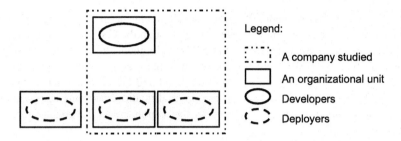

Fig. 4. Software development organization in Company B.

ployment organizations are located in several locations and countries and separated geographically from each other and from the development unit.

Company B has never applied another approach to develop software, and therefore there is no analysis of, for example, the benefits of the CSPF approach compared with some other software development approach. Nevertheless, the responders reported that they saw the CSPF approach as the best way to develop the products in Company B.

Variability. A system delivered on the basis of the CSPF is only varied by *configuring*, that is, without developing or modifying the source code. The configurable variability in the CSPF can be broken down into *high-level* and *low-level* variability. In addition, separate products or components that complement the system, but which are separate and not included in the system, might be developed by a deployment organization in a deployment project.

At the high level, variability pertains to selecting a particular set of products for a system. In principle, a customer can select any subset of about ten products, but, in practice, combinations are not arbitrary because one of the products forms a basis for the others and is always included in a system. Only the selected products of a system are delivered and installed for a customer.

At the low level, variability pertains to adapting a system to the customer-environment by configuring. Configuring sets parameter values that influence, for example, the kind of external devices a system interacts with, as well as the kind of data and the form in which the data is presented.

The source code in the CSPF is practically never changed for a single customer. If assets in the CSPF have to be changed in such a way that the source code is modified according to a single customer's requirements, then the modifications are immediately put into use for all other customers, as well as for part of the CSPF. Thus there is no customer-specific code, but the CSPF may be further developed to meet customer requirements. However, deployment organizations may develop additional components or products on their own to complement the CSPF. The degree of separation between the development and deployment organizations is such that the development organization does not even necessarily know about the additional components or products implemented by the deployment organization and the deployment organization does not have access to the source code. These components or products, for example, export data, perform some special data handling or wrap an interface in order to be compatible with the existing customer-environment. Therefore, development that resembles tailoring takes place occasionally in deployment projects, even though the CSPF itself is not tailored.

The responders estimated that 30% of CSPF development effort is put into developing configurability. If the CSPF were not to meet customer requirements, the possible effort wasted on developing configurability and the fixed and laboriously changeable scope of the CSPF due to not allowing source code modification, and thus being inflexible compared to competitors, were perceived by the responders as the greatest threats for the success of the CSPF.

Deployment. Deployment (Figure 5) begins with selecting a set of products for a system. Then the system is shipped to a customer and installed with auxiliary software. Finally, the system is configured using a configurator tool. A deployment project typically deploys several similar systems for the same customer.

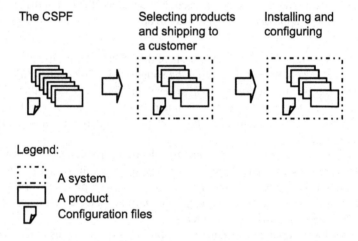

Fig. 5. Deployment process in Company B. The number of products in the figure does not correspond to the actual CSPF.

The company has developed a default configuration in which the parameter values are set to default values in order to avoid the need to set all parameter values from scratch. Despite the default configuration, in order to specify the correct configuration for each customer, hundreds or even thousands parameter values still need to be set.

Developing additional components or products in a way that resembles tailoring as noted earlier is not, strictly speaking, included in the deployment project, but they are developed in a separate project.

Finding a correct configuration relies on application domain knowledge and testing the configuration. Deployment projects include application domain experts and experts with computers, such as system administrators, but not necessarily software engineers who develop software.

A deployment project takes from a few days to a few weeks for two experts and often includes not only installing and configuring a system but also setting up, or at least making modifications to, customer infrastructure, including, for example, PCs and network. Deployment is completed at the customer site. System deployment is straightforward, whereas finding out the customer requirements takes more time. In fact, finding out customer requirements, specifying the environment, and training users may extend the total project duration, including deployment, by up to several months.

Configurator. One of the products in the CSPF is an in-house developed *configurator* that is a tool with a graphical user interface developed for configuring a system. The configurator is used to configure the low-level variability by setting and storing the parameter values in configuration files.

There are a few checks to ensure that parameter values are set correctly, but the configurator does not check that all parameter values are set correctly. The configurator is not usable without modifications in other CSPFs because it is developed for a particular CSPF, including its CSPF-specific configuration checks, for example. A more in-depth configurator is described in a manual of over 300 pages.

After-sales and Maintenance. Company B considers updates as a business opportunity and, in practice, requires a maintenance contract from every customer. Whenever a new version of the CSPF is released, it is delivered to customers who have the update contract. Because the CSPF itself is never tailored, the customers have the same source code, so updating is relatively easy.

A system can be reconfigured, which means setting parameter values to different values in order to readapt a system to a changed environment, for example. The set of products included in the system cannot be changed by reconfiguring. Reconfiguring primarily requires an understanding of the application domain and of how the system works, not software engineering skills. Even end users can use the configurator to reconfigure the system; reconfiguring is therefore common.

4   Comparison

In this section, we compare the characteristics of the CSPFs studied. A summary of the comparison is presented in Table 2.

4.1   Similarities

Similarities between the CSPF approaches studied were striking, despite the differences between the companies, products, and application domains. Both companies saw that their business was to deliver adaptable software rapidly to their customers, and according to customer requirements.

Both companies have applied the CSPF approach for about a decade and the success of the CSPF approach have forced them to make compromises that were also perceived as threats; these included, for example, fixing the scope of the CSPF, relaxing the demand

Table 2. Comparison of the characteristics of the CSPFs.

	Company A	Company B
Adopting CSPF	Evolutionary, old products	Revolutionary, new SPF
Organization	Roles according to domain engineering model in the same premises	Units according to domain engineering model and separated geographically
Deliveries	50	Dozens
Deployment process	Tailoring, installing, configuring, shipping	Selecting products, shipping, installing, configuring
Configuring	About 10 major functions, hundreds parameter values in adapting to environment	About 10 products, thousands parameter values in adapting to environment
Tailoring	30% of deployments	Not allowed, additional products
Delivered code	Everything	Only code for the selected products
Configurator	In-house developed, GUI, modify parameter values, not general purpose. Configuration rules embedded in the configurator, don't check entire validity of a configuration	In-house developed, GUI, modify parameter values, not general purpose. Configuration rules embedded in the configurator, don't check entire validity of a configuration
Parameter values	In a database	In configuration files
Configuring	Company A itself	Deployment organizations of Company B, partners, customers
Knowledge needed for configuring	Application domain knowledge, no software engineering skills required	Application domain knowledge, no software engineering skills needed
Reconfiguring	Rare, Company A reconfigures	Typical, customers can reconfigure
Updates	Rare	Update contract for new versions nearly always

for new features and fulfilling every customer-specific requirement that needs code modifications. However, the responders in both companies saw that the conscious decision to develop a CSPF was advantageous, despite this meaning that some of the flexibility in satisfying customer requirements compared with modifying the source code would be lost. Nevertheless, neither of the companies had any quantitative data to support the benefits of the CSPF approach.

Both companies were roughly the same size and had a similar organizational structure, which followed the domain engineering model. The operating environments of both the CSPFs were PCs running the Microsoft Windows operating system. The number of annual deliveries was roughly the same, i.e., a few dozens.

The application domain and interfaces with the environment were relatively stable in both CSPFs. Fundamental properties of the products did not change rapidly and application domain experts employed with the companies were able to predict variability reasonably well and communicate it to software engineers.

The deployment project in both companies took a relatively short time for the software, when considering the size of the delivered code and the fact that it always included as an essential part the configuring that was carried out without modifying the existing source code, or developing a new one. In fact, the time taken by configuring was quite short compared with, for example, hardware manufacturing, training, the sales process, and requirements specification.

Deployment was conducted in both companies by first selecting about ten large functional entities: In Company A, the entities were the configurable major functions in the stacks for a product, and in Company B, the entities were the products for a system. Second, in both companies, a product was configured to adapt to the customer-environment by setting numerous parameters using a configurator. The parameter values were separated from the source code and were initially set to default values in both CSPFs.

Neither of the companies typically changed the source code during deployment, for example, in programming, compiling or linking time, but configuring was performed on the executable code by setting parameter values.

For configuring, both companies had, in principle, a very similar configurator. The configurators were developed in-house and had a graphical user interface. The configurators were developed for the particular CSPF and could not be used in any other CSPF without modifications.

The configurators were easy to use and provided guidance for the user, who primarily needed an understanding of the target environment and application domain, but no more than basic software engineering skills. In configuring, the configurators modified the parameter values, but did not guarantee that all parameter values were set correctly; configuration rules to check the correctness of parameter values were embedded in the configurators in both CSPFs.

In both companies, their use of the configurators during deployment relied heavily on the user's experience in the application domain and on testing the configuration, as it was possible that parameter values were set incorrectly.

Finally, in both companies, deployed products or systems could be reconfigured in the customer's environment using the configurator.

4.2 Differences

The main differences between the CSPFs studied seemed in many cases to lie in the different decisions made with regard to equally feasible choices. In fact, when we explicitly asked about these differences, the responders told us that they could have decided in a way similar to the other company.

The CSPF adoption strategy was probably the most notable difference. Company A followed the evolutionary strategy for old products [1], whereas Company B followed the revolutionary strategy for a new product family [1].

Company A expected its markets to be relatively stable, whereas Company B expected the markets to have a large growth potential.

Although the organization model in both companies was similar, in Company A, deployers and developers were separated by role level, whereas, in Company B, they were separated into different organizational units and geographically.

Company A had explicitly defined how major functions for a product can be selected. Company B allowed, in principle, an arbitrary selection of products for a system, but, in practice, one of the products was always selected in a way similar to the base in

Company A. In Company A, all customers received all the code of the CSPF, while the parameter values determined whether a piece of code was to be executed, whereas, in Company B, only the code of the installed products was shipped to a customer.

In Company A, a database was used, while, in Company B, configuration files were used to store the parameter values.

Unlike Company B, Company A allowed tailoring. However, even in the case of Company A, tailoring took place typically on the interfaces, while the basic functionality of a product remained untouched. Furthermore, most deployment projects in Company A were completed without tailoring. In the case of Company B, new products or components, in addition to a deployed system, could be developed in addition to the system. However, in fact, customers typically got the same code and parameter values specified by the configuration in both cases.

Configuring in Company A took only half a day, whereas in Company B it typically took from a few days to a few weeks longer. Nevertheless, in both companies, understanding the application domain and the customer-environment was more challenging than configuring.

Company A configured the products itself, whereas Company B or its partners did an initial configuration and customers were able to reconfigure systems later. The reason for this difference was a business decision based on the characteristics of the application domain and business model, not on technical grounds. For similar practical reasons, Company A configured the products at its own facilities, whereas, in Company B, systems were configured at the customer's site.

After-sales and maintenance strategies were completely different. Company A did not allow a customer to reconfigure a product and did not see updates or reconfiguring as a core business. Company B allowed reconfiguring and saw updating and maintaining the systems as a business strategy.

5   Discussion

5.1   Characteristics of the CSPF Approach

The results in this study show that the CSPF approach is, in practice, applied in the industry. To the best of our knowledge, the companies had developed their CSPFs independently of each other. Since the companies operate in very different application domains, their successful use of the CSPF approach is probably not tied to a specific application domain but a similar approach can be applied in other application domains as well.

The responders in both companies indicated that the CSPF approach provided a competitive advantage compared with competitors who modify and develop the source code in deployment projects. For both companies, the CSPF approach seemed an efficient way to systemize the software development and enable an efficient control of versions and variants in a set of systems. They even went as far as to state that the CSPF approach is the only reasonable way to do business, regardless of the initial investment needed to build the CPSF. However, neither of the companies had estimates of investment payback times or other economic justifications when compared with, for example, project-based software development.

An intuitively appealing opportunity in the CSPF approach is the kind of reconfiguring that allows variability-binding operation time, in which binding is not fixed in the sense that the selected parameter value can be changed, as is noted to be a tendency in [10]. The CSPF approach enabled the companies to delay variability binding to installation and even operation time. Nevertheless, reconfiguring was effectively taken advantage of only in Company B.

What clearly differentiated the CSPF approach from the other software product family approaches in the three other companies in the case study was that the configurators were one of the key enablers for very efficient deployment. The fact that two companies had developed a tool for configuration on their own exemplifies the feasibility of developing and using configurators. Furthermore, in the companies, configurators seemed to be essential enablers for a large number of different parameters values that customize software for customers. These parameter values were set correctly even though the configurators did not check all aspects of the correctness of configuration, because the people using them were experts in the application domain and tested the system after configuring. In fact, by using the configurators, the companies were able to deploy products in such a way that, in practice, there is no software engineering knowledge needed.

Both companies had parameterized variability and separated parameter values from the source code to the configuration files in Company A and to the configuration database in Company B. Another approach could be to change the source code, for example, or compile time parameters, but if configuring is performed to non-executable code it would, in fact, probably not allow reconfiguration as flexibly as in the case of Company B. Furthermore, in both companies, because separate storage for parameter values is used, configuration is independent from implementation in the sense that software can be changed to another improved version, which does not include many new features, and the configuration and software remain operational even after the change.

5.2   Applicability of the CSPF Approach

In the two companies studied, there seemed to be several factors that had a positive influence on the success of the CSPF approach. However, due to the relatively small sample size and lack of more detailed data obtained by, for example, observing the operations in the companies in more depth, rigorous analysis of the influence they had is not possible. The following discussion should therefore be treated as speculative in nature and the issues therein as hypotheses to be tested.

The number of deliveries that was large enough to make the CSPF approach feasible for these companies in these application domains is probably a necessary but not sufficient prerequisite for the CSPF approach to be economically feasible; this is because of the investment required for developing the configurator and configurability.

Application domain understanding was emphasized often in both companies: Developing configurability and configuring seem to be especially reliant on knowledge of the application domain.

It also seems that the application domain and interfaces to the environment should be as near stable as possible so there are no frequent changes to the fundamentals and so the new variability can be predicted reasonably well.

A clear separation of development and deployment organizationally, at least in roles, seemed to be beneficial, even in small organizations. In both companies, parameter values separated from the source code seemed to be a feasible way to achieve variability.

We did not find any special relationship between special software engineering skills, such as those specific to product family development and very advanced process models, methods, modelling and implementation tools, the CSPF approach adopting strategy, or application domain or company maturity at the time of the initiation of the CSPF approach and the success of the CSPF approach. In fact, it seemed that most of the software developers had their work and educational background in the application domain rather than in software engineering. Neither of the companies had developed a large repository or library of assets from which an applicable asset could be selected, but all assets that existed were included in the CSPF, and parameters were used to achieve variability. To develop the CSPFs, the companies did not use any special product family oriented tools or methods but, rather, state-of-the-practice tools and methods that probably could be found in any other company such as Microsoft Visio, Word, and IDE, and UML for modeling.

The possible drawbacks of the CSPF approach seemed to pertain mainly to the evolution of the CSPF. Evolution was seen as especially unpromising as far as the ability to meet customer requirements by configuring was concerned. If the configuring was not enough to meet customer requirements, the need for tailoring would increase. Alternatively, in the worst case, the scope of the CSPF would not be right and configuring would be useless, meaning that the considerable effort put into developing the CSPF would be wasted. The respondents felt that evolving software seems to be hard to manage and that keeping software configurable even increased the burden.

6   Related Work

There are some empirical studies on companies that exhibit a great deal of variability and are at least on the threshold of developing a CSPF, for example, CelsiusTech [11] and MarketMaker [3]. These companies have not systemized their SPF approach or developed configurators to the extent that the companies in this study have. However, because changing dozens of lines in configuration files is "burdensome, error-prone, and annoying", a need for a tool that sets parameter values was identified in MarketMaker. Apparently, a similar configurator as that developed by the companies in this study would be the kind of tool MarketMaker is hoping to have, although does not necessarily need. In addition, Securitas had developed a configuration tool Win512 [1], but there are not enough details available for detailed comparison.

Component-based software engineering [12] focuses on components, their composition and integration, while in the generative approach [13], products are constructed automatically on the basis of a precise specification; both these approaches are comparable to the CSPF approach. In fact, it seems both these could be used to develop a CSPF. However, the companies studied used neither the component based nor generative approach. When comparing the approaches, a drawback of the generative approach may be that it does not allow as much flexibly as the reconfiguring in the companies studied; this is because it requires the generation of the code again, and updating software, because not all customers have the same code. In the case of the component-based approach, it seems that components need to be parameterized in order to achieve similar customization, as in the companies studied in setting parameter values; the result of this might be a need for a configurator similar to that used in the companies in this study.

Linux Familiar, which is a Linux distribution for PDA devices, has been successfully modeled using a logic-based product configurator [14]. Futhermore, configuring in Linux is based on selecting components, while the companies in this study used almost only parameter values for this purpose.

BigLever [15] uses an approach that is similar to the CSPF approach and has developed a tool for deploying products. However, the lack of details of the aspects described in this paper makes detailed comparison difficult.

Configurable product families, or configurable products have also been studied in the field of mechanical and electronic products [16] and there are some initiatives to combine the results with software engineering [17], [18], [19].

7   Validity and Reliability

Case study as a qualitative method forces us to delve into the complexity of the problem as a whole, rather than to abstract it away [7]. Therefore, the quality of qualitative research pertains to how well the phenomenon under study has been understood. [20]. However, Yin [5] suggests the use of *construct*, *internal* and *external validity* and *reliability* to judge the quality of a case study.

Construct validity pertains to establishing measures correct for the concept being studied. To ensure construct validity, we based our initial understanding of the software product family approach on the results presented in the literature, used multiple responders in the interviews and documentation, carefully stored and used as much original data, such as transcripts, as possible, held validation sessions in the companies and allowed the companies to see and comment on the report before publishing. However, a possible weakness in the construct validity is that the study lasted a relatively short time, did not include observing the operations in the companies in more depth, and therefore could not cover all the details, and because a part of the data was based on only one source, our triangulation did not cover everything. However, we felt that the atmosphere in the interviews was open and trustworthy, while responders did not hesitate to answer our questions honestly.

The internal validity relates to causal relationships. We do not consider these relevant to this study because we have concentrated on describing the CSPF approach and tried not to make claims for causal relationships.

External validity means establishing the correct domain to which results can be generalized. Since only five software product families not randomly chosen were studied, two of these being CSPFs, we cannot make statistical generalizations as to the commonality of the CSPF approach in the industry. However, we believe that some of the commonalities found between the two CSPFs described are generalizable and would be found in other possible CSPFs as well.

Reliability means that operations of the study can be repeated with similar results. In order to ensure reliability, we used tools designed for qualitative data analysis and developed rigorous procedures, including interview questions, analysis framework, and data storage that could be followed to conduct similar research again.

8   Conclusions and Future Work

We described some results of a descriptive case study of the configurable software product family approach in two companies that had developed the approach independently. The study shows that the configurable software product family approach can be a feasible and even efficient way to systematically develop a family of products and to manage the variability within it. When compared, the characteristics of the configurable software product families turned out to be strikingly similar. The application domain and interfaces with the environment were relatively stable and the fundamentals of the product did not change; variability could be predicted reasonably well by application domain experts and could be bound by configuring.

Similarities were also found in the deployment and variability of the software product family, and in organizing software development. An application domain expert carried out deployment using a configurator tool. Variability included selecting a set of about ten major functional entities and adapting according to hundreds of parameter values. Organizationally, developers and deployers were clearly separated.

The clearest differences between the companies were to be found in the product family adoption approach and the after-sales strategy. The first company, which used the evolutionary approach to replace existing products, did not consider after-sales as a business strategy, and did not allow reconfiguring. The second company, which used the revolutionary approach for new products, allowed reconfiguring, and wanted customers to buy after-sales services.

On the basis of the results in this study, it is suggested that the configurable software product family approach may well be an important phenomenon for further study. A more detailed study and comparison of the similarities and differences between companies that have, and do not have, a configurable software product family should be carried out to elicit more indications of the potential applicability, success factors, and benefits of the configurable software product family approach. In addition, in both configurable software product families, there were hundreds of parameters with many possible values; the two companies studied had developed in-house configurators to assist in setting the parameter values and to do some error-checking of them. Despite the fact that the two companies had developed their configurators by themselves, it would seem to be advantageous to develop generic variability management and configuration methods and tools to model the variability evidenced by the parameters, and to assist in setting them correctly in deployment, in order to help companies that aim at developing a configurable software product family.

Acknowledgments

We gratefully acknowledge the financial support of Technology Development Centre of Finland and Academy of Finland (grant number 51394).

References

1. Bosch, J.: Design and Use of Software Architecture. Addison-Wesley (2000)
2. Weiss, D., Lai, C.T.R.: Software product-line engineering: a family based software development process. Addison Wesley (1999)
3. Clements, P., Northrop, L.M.: Software Product Lines: Practices and Patterns. Addison-Wesley (2001)
4. Bosch, J.: Maturity and evolution in software product line: Approaches, artefacts and organization. Lecture Notes in Computer Science (SPLC2) **2379** (2002) 257–271
5. Yin, R.K.: Case study Research. 2nd edn. Sage (1994)
6. van der Linden, F.: Software product families in europe: The esaps and cafe projects. IEEE Software **19** (2002) 41–49
7. Seaman, C.B.: Qualitative methods in empirical studies of software engineering. IEEE Transactions on software engineering **25** (1999) 557–572
8. Scientific Software Development, ATLAS.ti User's Manual and Reference, version 4., http://www.atlasti.de/.
9. Raatikainen, M.: A research instrument for an empirical study of software product families. Master's thesis, Helsinki University of Technology (2003)
10. van Ommering, R., Bosch, J.: Widening the scope of software product lines - from variation to composition. Lecture Notes in Computer Science (SPLC2) **2379** (2002) 328–346
11. Bass, L., Clements, P., Klein, D.V.: Software architecture in practice. Addison-Wesley (1998)
12. Szyperski, C.: Component Software. ACM Press (1999)
13. Czarnecki, K., Eisenecker, U.W.: Generative Programming. Addison-Wesley (2000)
14. Kojo, T., Soininen, T., Männistö, T.: Towards intelligent support for managing evolution of configurable software product families. Lecture Notes in Computer Science (SCM-11) **2649** (2003) 86–101
15. Biglever Software inc, http://www.biglever.com.
16. Faltings, B., Freuder, E.C.: Special issue on configuration. IEEE intelligent systems & their applications (1998) 29–85
17. Männistö, T., Soininen, T., Sulonen, R.: Product configuration view to software product families. In: Proceedings of Software Configuration Management Workshop (SCM-10) of ICSE01. (2001)
18. Hein, A., MacGregor, J.: Managing variability with configuration techniques. In: International Conference on Software Engineering, International Workshop on Software Variability Management. (2003)
19. Hotz, L., Krebs, T.: Supporting the product derivation process with a knowledge-based approach. In: International Conference on Software Engineering, International Workshop on Software Variability Management. (2003)
20. Maxwell, J.A.: Understanding and validity in qualitative research. Harvard Educational Review **62** (1992) 279–300

Software Architecture Helpdesk

Anssi Karhinen, Juha Kuusela, and Marco Sandrini

Leegur Oy, Tallberginkatu 2
FIN-00180 Helsinki, Finland
{Anssi.Karhinen,Juha.Kuusela,Marco.Sandrini}@leegur.com

Abstract. Software architecture has been identified as a main tool for high quality system development. Software architecture provides the basis for the reuse in a software product line. Unfortunately the potential benefits of a well designed software architecture can be lost if the software architecture is not followed in the design of the products. We suggest that a software architecture help desk could play an important role in enabling the dissemination of software architecture and in improving the communication between designers and architects.

1 Introduction

The product line approach benefits from using a common design for all family members. Software architecture defines the quality attributes that the system or family of systems possesses. The architecture should have properties that satisfy all major requirements of the members of the product line. That is, the architecture reflects the common characteristics of the product line while allowing specialization of products in detailed market segments.

Architecting process relies on a correct understanding of the wanted features and the non-functional requirements. In the case of product lines, developers must understand common requirements of multiple products.

Successful product families can have over one hundred products. The combined development effort can amount to several thousand man years. Most of this development is not done by the software architecture team. This creates a need to efficiently communicate the software architecture to those who develop products based on it.

Software architectures are not static. They go through a complex and fairly long lifecycle. New products are added to the family, integration needs evolve and underlying platforms change. Also the developer community evolves. New employees are recruited, old ones change position, and new subcontractors are contracted. The needs for communication evolve with the architecture.

In this paper we suggest that organizations should set up a Software Architecture Help Desk. That would work as the focal point of software architecture communication within the development organization.

The paper is organized as follows: Chapter two introduces architectural design cycle that forms the basis of our approach. In the chapter three, we describe the essential difference between requirements and design. We also show how the definition hierarchy approach can solve many of the common system development problems. Design model is described in the chapter four.

F. van der Linden (Ed.): PFE 2003, LNCS 3014, pp. 422–428, 2004.

2 Architectural Design Cycle

There are different needs to propagate architectural information in different phases of the life cycle of a SW product or family.

2.1 Phase I: Initial Development

Software architecture is usually developed by a small architect team working together. Internal communication is informal. External interaction is frequent with marketing, business development and sometimes with potential customers to understand the needs and requirements of the new product family. There is no need for explicit software architecture communication systems.

However, the planning and building of architecture helpdesk must begin in this stage. A lot of material is needed. Architecture documents (like development guidelines, work distribution and estimates, component definitions, interface descriptions, platform choices, data base schemas, communication patterns etc) have to be developed and structured into a document repository.

2.2 Phase II: Ramp-up of the Organization

Once the architecture has been accepted it is possible to rapidly increase the size of the development organization. The needs to disseminate software architecture information peak in this ramp-up phase.

New developers, who do not have expertise in the new product and posibly in many technologies used, start developing new products based on the architecture.

They probably have different backgrounds which makes the design of a training path very difficult. The contact networks have not yet emerged which makes it hard for new developers to find experts with correct answers. Geographical distribution of development sites and/or the use of several subcontractors make things even harder.

System architects get no feedback because new programmers easily assume that architecture is "ready". If the architecture does not seem to support the needs of a programmer he assumes that the architecture cannot be improved and just tries to work around it. The architecture for him becomes more of an obstacle that the supporting structure that it is intended to be. This can lead to early decay of the SW product family architecture.

Lack of knowledge or the feeling that the architecture is inadequate to the needs makes it easy for developers to bypass the architecture. Examples of often bypassed architecture level mechanisms are the error handling or resource allocation conventions. These omissions cause system to loose its intended properties and lead into hard to find errors.

Heterogeneity is not limited to developers and their organizations. Different configurations in workstations and test machines lead to same problems being solved several times, often in several different ways.

2.3 Phase III: Evolution and Maintenance

When the architecture enters evolution and maintenance phase changes in the organization and in the architecture become less frequent. This does not diminish the role of the help desk. Since introductory courses are now very infrequent new developers don't necessarily find contact points and informationthey require. There is a tangible risk that they get stuck. They may also be afraid to bother architects who seem to be far away and already working with something else.

Local developer communities are of course able to support new developers much better. Unfortunately this is the time when different dialects and variants of the architecture emerge at different sites, organizational units or products. The increase in variation slowly kills the product family framework if it is not controlled. Architectural help desk is needed to keep everything in sync.

Although architectural evolution has slowed down it has not stopped. Now and then new architectural assets are deployed. The communication of these changes is a big challenge. Since developers already know the "correct" approach to all their tasks it is difficult to motivate them to change. A change may also require quite a large amount of rework to update the existing products. It is crucial that help desk has a reliable contact list of the architects and the key developers so that the changes and the reasoning behind them can be communicated and product updates planned properly.

3 Software Archiecture Help Desk

The structure of software architecture help desk is described in ramp up phase because we think it is the most intensive period regarding the helpdesk load. Structural requirements (responsibility in parenthesis)

1. There must be a personal contact for the help desk with phone number (help desk)
2. There must be well organized and version controlled document repository that contains:
   - Official, up to date, credible specifications (architects)
   - Descriptions of standard ways to solve common development issues in this architecture (architects)
   - Contact information ("who is who") (help desk)
   - Mailing lists, special interest groups (help desk)
   - FAQs (help desk)
   - Known open problems lists (help desk, architects)
   - Open change proposals (help desk, architects)
   - Latest changes lists (help desk, architects)
   - Calendar of upcoming training sessions
3. There must be at least one architect contact for each technical area or technology. These architects own the official documents.
4. There must be a fulltime (at least half-time if the other half is also connected to the project, being an architect for example) responsible/contact person for the architecture.
5. Structured contact and feedback mechanism based on email, news, telephone, public web access & search has to be developed.

The main task of software architecture help desk in the ramp-up phase is to help new software developers to become productive and at the same time maintain architectural consistency.

If the help desk is successful it will also slow the inception of architectural subcultures within the development organization.

During ramp-up phase architects get the first real feed-back regarding the correctness of the design choices they have made. Software architecture help desk can improve the quality of this feedback by providing a channel for developers to directly discuss with the architects.

4 Functional Description

The functionality of an architectural help desk is best described by a set of representative use-cases. We assume that these use-cases take place in the context of a ramp-up phase.

Typical use case for SW designer:
1. I'm stuck with a design problem and the architecture doesn't seem to provide solution.
2. I contact the help desk and describe my situation.
3. Help desk can pull the answer from his hat or
   - help desk knows which document to look at or
   - help desk checks the FAQs or
   - help desk asks the responsible architect
4. The help desk determines if FAQs require updating.
5. The help desk can suggest updating the official docs.
6. The help desk and architect can propose an architectural change.

Developing contacts use case:
1. I'm doing some database related application and want to know who are doing related stuff in order to arrange a sauna party for data base developers.
2. I contact helpdesk stating my problem
3. The help desk provides info and possibly updates contact information.

A designer reporting a bug in a document:
1. I'm doing something according to the architecture docs but it doesn't seem to make sense or looks outdated or inconsistent with latest training.
2. I alarm the helpdesk about the state of this document
3. The help desk asks the responsible architect if this is a known problem.
4. Action by the help desk after consulting the responsible architect
   - Update the list of open problems and/or
   - Propose updating the document

Maintenance use cases by an architect:
1. He updates a document owned by him
2. He inform the help desk about recent changes
3. He updates the latest common lists of known problems, standard solutions, etc.

As these use cases show help desk is mostly a tool to ease communication, help the creation of communication networks and to improve that quality of software architecture documentation. Help desk is an administrative tool.

5 Roles and Responsibilities

In essence help desk is a middle man connecting the sources of software architecture information (architects) with the consumers of it (developers). In reality the roles and responsibilities of these parties are much more complex.

First of all architects are also consumers of architectural information produced by other architects. Once the team has dissolved many of the original architects have only sporadic exposure to the evolution of the system. When they have to answer a question that relates to their special area of expertise they often have to consult architectural documentation and other architects to understand how the system has evolved.

Software developers are also sources of architectural information. As the system evolves the developers are often better aware of the needs to change the architecture than the architects. Some times the developers can also suggest a good solution to a problem they have found.

Also the contact needs vary and developers often need contacts to other developers.

However, the basic responsibilities stay the same.

Software architects are responsible of the software architecture, its documentation, and the validity of the standard ways to solve common problems. During the evolution architects take care that enough education is available, that all the pressing problems are resolved and that the architecture is not allowed to drift so far that the system level properties are compromised.

Designers' responsibility is to be aware of all the relevant software architecture documents and to follow all the guidelines. It is their responsibility to report all inconsistencies and difficulties that they find in designing new products.

Software Architecture Help Desk is mainly responsible for the availability and consistency of the contact details and software architecture documentation. Help Desk keeps lists of requests, events and changes. They support delayed queries and inform different stakeholders about relevant changes.

Software Architecture Help Desk functions if all the parties respect their responsibilities. If the documentation is allowed to become irrelevant and contact information bogus, designers will start to ignore the architecture and the architects. As a result software architecture help desk can become just another addition to software process bureaucracy.

6 Experiences

We tried software architecture help desk for the first time with our former employee. We developed the architecture for a fairly large telecommunication component. This architecture was based on a platform that was new for most of the developers. The development organization was distributed to five sites in two countries and had over 100 designers.

The need for software architecture help desk was clear. To give an example at ramp-up phase an organizational restructuring forced over twenty designers to suddenly start work on the system with no previous experience of the platform. Earlier some developers also had to start application development even before the platform was ready.

We made quite a few mistakes in setting up the help desk. We found out the need for it too late when turning from phase I to phase II and therefore many documents needed were missing during the early months of the operation of the help desk.

Also the management challenge was quite evident. Three types of courses (architecture, technology, how to develop applications) where given regularly in different sites when ever new groups of programmers started. As documents where not ready early enough a lot of notifications had to be distributed to reflect the evolution of documentation.

Despite of implementation shortcomings, overall the architecture help desk proved to be highly successful and helped a lot in completing the products.

We are now trying our software architecture help desk in a smaller case.

At Leegur we are still working in Phase 1. This time we want to have the assets needed for the architectural helpdesk prepared in time. The members of the initial architecture development team have been assigned clear responsibilites in technologies, functional area and platform components. Architectural documentation with rationales behind the solutions is being developed and stored in a structured shared repository. Code level frameworks to use the architecture in practical problem solving have been developed and tested by the original team. Communication channels between the architects and developers have been established and maintained on regular basis. The goal is to have the infrastructure described in this paper ready for the second phase: production ramp-up.

7 Related Work

In essence software architecture help desk is an organisatorial structure built to ensure proper communication.

Dikel and colleagues [1] have promoted organizational patterns to address common problems in managing software architecture based development. In particular they promote reciprocity as a solution to promote the use of the software architecture within its designed constraints. Our approach is aligned to the basic principles of their approach. The use of architecture help desk promotes the architecture to the development organization.

The efficient interaction with the architecture and the detailed design is inevitable and necessary. The improved understanding of the properties of the architecture and its limitations force close iterations during the evolutions of the software intensive system. This process relies that the rationale of the architectural choices is communicated to the development teams. Putman [2] calls this the patterns of reasoning that needs to be shared with the whole development organization. However, this is typically hard to achieve in a way that a written document could guarantee compliancy to the architecture rules. We have found that given close support using the architecture help desk concept can improve the conformance of the software design to the architecture.

Philippe Kruchten [3] has identified common problems in software architecting. Among these problems are the lack of interaction between the software architects and the developers. The architects may appear as working in an 'ivory tower' or acting as a committee. The appearance of the software architecture team may be improved by promoting help desk type of approach where the interaction between the software architecture team and the development organization can be extended to cover the actual problems that the developers are facing.

References

1. David M. Dikel, David Kane, and James R. Wilson. Software Architecture - Organizational Principles and Patterns, Prentice Hall, 2001.
2. Janis R. Putman. Architecting with RM-ODP, Prentice Hall, 2001.
3. Philippe Kruchten, The Software Architect, in Software Architecture, Patrick Donohoe (eds.), Kluwer Academic Publishers, 1999.

Different Aspects of Product Family Adoption

Parastoo Mohagheghi[1,2,3] and Reidar Conradi[2,3]

[1] Ericsson Norway-Grimstad, Postuttak, NO-4898 Grimstad, Norway
parastoo.mohagheghi@ericsson.com
[2] Department of Computer and Information Science, NTNU, NO-7491 Trondheim, Norway
conradi@idi.ntnu.no
[3] Simula Research Laboratory, P.O.BOX 134, NO-1325 Lysaker, Norway

Abstract. Ericsson has successfully developed two large-scale telecommunication systems based on reusing the same software architecture, software process, and many other core assets. The approach to initiating a product family has been a lightweight approach, and many artifacts are evolved during product family adoption, although not to the same degree. The software architecture has evolved to support reuse and handling of variations, while the software process model is not updated for product family engineering and reuse. We discuss what works and doesn't work in the current process model, and why it is important to synchronize it with the practice of software development. Product family adoption has raised challenges in many aspects of software development such as requirement management, and measurement. These processes should also be evolved to fit the software development approach.

1 Introduction

Many organizations are using a product family engineering approach for software development by exploiting commonalities between software systems, reusing software architecture, and a set of core assets. The approach to start a product family and evolve it varies, depending on the context, and the term *product family* is used for a wide range of approaches to develop software with reuse. For example, the degree to which some reusable assets are identified before the first product is used to distinguish between heavyweight, and lightweight approaches to initiate a product family.

Ericsson has developed two large-scale telecommunication systems that share software architecture, software process model, and other core assets using a lightweight approach. The software architecture has evolved to an architecture that promotes reuse, and product family engineering. Although the software process model is evolved in parallel with product family adoption, it has not been adapted for this aspect of development, and lacks explicit guidelines for domain engineering and reuse. I.e. there is a gap between the software process model, the adapted Rational Unified Process (RUP), and the actual process (the practice of software development). The internally developed guidelines, existing knowledge, and expertise compensate to some degree for shortcomings in the process model. Adopting product family engineering has impact on many aspects of software development. If these

F. van der Linden (Ed.): PFE 2003, LNCS 3014, pp. 429–434, 2004.

aspects are not evolved harmoniously, conflicts may appear in areas such as requirement engineering where a product family approach is more feature-oriented, while RUP is use-case driven. Resolving these conflicts is part of the adoption process, and analyzing experiences is important for learning feedbacks.

The remainder of the paper is structured as follows. Section 2 describes some state-of-the-art. Section 3 describes the Ericsson context, and section 4 discusses the strengths, and weaknesses of the current process model. The paper is concluded in section 5.

2   A Brief State-of-the-Art

Parnas wrote the first paper on development of systems with common properties in 1976. He wrote: "We consider a set of programs to constitute a *family*, whenever it is worthwhile to study programs from the set by *first* studying the common properties of the set, and *then* determining the special properties of the individual family members" [14]. He called these systems *program families*, while other terms are *system families*, *product lines,* or, as we prefer to call it-*product families*. Product families are built around *reuse*: reuse of requirements, software architecture and design, and implementation. Bosch writes, "the software product line approach can be considered to be the first intra-organizational software reuse approach that has proven successful" [3].

Several software development processes support product family engineering, see for example [1, 2, 5, 7, 8]. The Software Engineering Institute (SEI) defines three essential product family activities [13]:

1. D*omain engineering* for developing the architecture and the reusable assets (or development *for* reuse as called in [8]).
2. *Application engineering* to build the individual products (or development *with* reuse as called in [8]).
3. *Management* at the technical and organizational level.

In [10] approaches for introducing a product family are divided into *heavyweight,* and *lightweight*. In the heavyweight approach, commonalities are identified *first* by domain engineering, and product variations are foreseen. In the lightweight approach, a first product is developed, and the organization then uses mining efforts to extract commonalities. The choice of approach also affects cost and the organization structure. Krueger claims that the lightweight approach can reduce the adoption barrier to large-scale reuse, as it is a low-risk strategy with lower upfront cost [9]. Johnson and Foote write in [6] that useful abstractions are usually designed from the bottom up; i.e. they are discovered not invented.

If the approach to initiate a product family is a lightweight approach, the shared artifacts such as the software process should evolve in order to be reusable. By a *software process* we mean all activities, roles and artifacts that produce a software product, and a s*oftware process model* is a representation of it. These artifacts are not always evolved harmoniously and synchronously, and some of them are more critical for the success of the product family. The process of change is a composition of organizational, business, and technical factors.

3 An Industrial Example of Product Family Adoption

The General Packet Radio Service (GPRS) system provides a solution to send packet data over the cellular networks. GPRS was first developed to provide packet data capability to the GSM (Global System for Mobile communication) cellular network. A later recognition of common requirements with the forthcoming WCDMA system (Wide-band Code Division Multiple Access) lead to reverse engineering of the developed architecture to identify reusable parts across applications, and to evolve the software architecture to an architecture that can support both products. This was a joint development effort across organisations for almost one year, with negotiations and renegotiations.

The initial software architecture is shown in the left part of Figure 1. Components are tightly coupled, and all use services of the platform (WPP), and a component that provides additional middleware functionality. Evolution of the software architecture was mainly done in two steps:

- Extracting the reusable components, and evolving the architecture into the one shown in the right part of Figure 1. Old components are inserted in the layers based on their reuse potential, and some are split into several new components in different layers.
- Removing coupling between components that break down the layered architecture. These removed couplings are shown with red dashed arrows in the left part of Figure 1. Components in the lower layers should be independent of components in the higher layers.

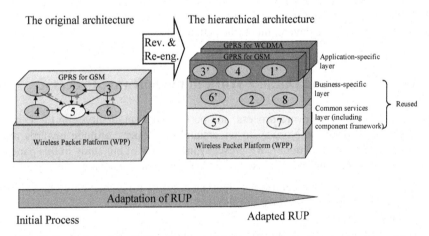

Fig. 1. Evolution of the GSN software architecture and the software process model.

The reused components in the business-specific layer (that offers services for the packet switching networks), and the common services layer (includes a customized component framework for building robust real-time applications, and other services) stand for 60% of the code in an application, where an application in this context consists of components in the three upper layers. The size of each application is over 1000 NKLOC (Non-Commented Kilo Lines Of Code measured in equivalent C code).

The approach to product line adoption has been a *lightweight* approach. The first product was initially developed and released, and the commonalities between it, and the requirements for the new product lead to the decision on reuse. The products are developed incrementally, and new features are added to each release of the products. Several Ericsson organizations have been involved in development and testing.

The software process has been developed in parallel with the products. The first release of the GPRS for GSM product used a simple, internally developed software process, describing the main phases of the lifecycle and the related roles and artifacts. After the first release, the organization decided to adapt the Rational Unified Process (RUP) [15]. The adaptation is done by adding, removing or modifying phases, activities, roles, and artifacts in the standard RUP process. RUP is an *architecture-centric* process, which is an advantage when dealing with products using the same reference architecture. But RUP in its original form is not a process for product families, and we argue that it has not been adapted for this aspect of development:

- The main workflows (requirement, analysis and design, implementation and testing) are described as if there is a single product development, while configuration management activities handle several versions and several products.
- There is no framework engineering in the adapted RUP, and developing framework components (or in general reusable components) is an indistinguishable part of application engineering.

To provide the information needed for software developers, artifacts such as internally developed modeling guidelines, and design rules are linked to the workflows in RUP. We mean that there is a gap between the process model (the adapted RUP), and the practice of software development (the actual process).

4   What Works and Doesn't Work in the Software Process?

We have studied the software process, and performed a small survey in the Ericsson organization in Grimstad-Norway to understand developers' attitude towards reuse, and the software process model. We present some results of our study in this paper.

The adapted RUP has been in use for almost four years, and have some benefits:

1) RUP is architecture-centric, as mentioned. Software architecture plays the key role in engineering product families.
2) RUP is adaptable.
3) Rational delivers RUP together with a whole range of other tools for requirement management, configuration management etc.
4) The developed web pages for RUP are understandable.

We asked whether the lack of explicit reuse-related activities in the process model affects the reuse practice. The survey results indicate such impact. For example, developers mean that the reused components are not sufficiently documented, and assessing components for reuse is not easy.

Some suggestions for improving the process model for reuse are given in [12], and [16]. Some of the suggestions are easier to introduce than others. Example is adding the activity *Record reuse experience* to the *Conclusion Phase* (Ericsson has added the Conclusion Phase to the adapted RUP as the last phase of a project). On the other hand, distinguishing domain, and application engineering has impact on several workflows, and is more difficult to carry out.

Product family adoption has impact on all aspects of the software process and raises challenges that should be solved. Some of our observations are:

1) Requirement management for reusable components is difficult. The attempts to specify requirements in terms of use cases that should be included or extended in the application use cases (as proposed in [5]) was not successful as complexity grows, and dependencies become unmanageable. Use cases were therefore dropped for reusable parts, and replaced by textual documents that describe functionality and variation points.

2) There is a measurement program in the organization, but specific metrics for reuse, and product family engineering should be more stressed.

3) Requirements to each release of the systems are defined in terms of features, and it is features that distinguish releases, and products from each other, while RUP is use-case driven. Tracing from features to use cases, and later design, and deliveries is difficult.

We have started working on some of these issues like metrics. We have collected trouble reports and requirement changes from several releases, and defined hypotheses that can be verified based on the available data. Results of this study can be used to assess the development approach, and to improve the measurement program, as described in [11].

5   Conclusions

We described an industrial example of product family adoption, where the products have a high degree of reuse, and share a common software architecture and software process. The lightweight approach to adoption has been successful in achieving shorter time-to-market and lower development costs. The role of the software architecture in product family adoption has been critical. The software architecture distinguishes reusable components from application-specific components, and promotes reuse. The software process model has not evolved to the same degree, and does not reflect the practice. As the software is developed incrementally, and the development projects have been running for 5 years, the existing knowledge, and the internally developed guidelines compensate to some degree for shortcomings in the process model. We discussed strengths and shortcomings in the adapted RUP, and described some aspects of software development that are affected in adopting product family engineering. The inadequate adoption of the software process model has impact on the reuse practice (such as insufficient documentation of reusable parts, and lack of metrics to evaluate reuse gains), and we think that the organization can benefit through more adopting it to product family engineering.

Acknowledgements

The work is done in the context of the INCO project (INcremental and COmponent-based Software Development [4]), a Norwegian R&D project in 2001-2004, and as part of the first author's PhD study. The survey on developers' attitude to reuse, and some improvement suggestions regarding reuse are part of two MSc diploma theses [12, 16]. We thank Ericsson in Grimstad for the opportunity to perform the studies.

References

1. Atkinson, C, Bayer, J., Bunse, C., Kamsties, E., Laitenberger, O., Laqua, R., Muthig, D., Paech, B., Wüst, J., Zettel, J.: Component-based Product Line Engineering with UML. Addison-Wesley (2002).
2. Bosch, J.: Design and Use of Software Architecture: Adpoting and Evolving a Product-Line Approach. Addison-Wesley (2000).
3. Bosch, J.: Maturity and Evolution in Software Product Lines: Approaches, Artifacts and Organization. In Proc. of the Second Software Product Line Conference- SPLC2 (2002). Available at http://www.cs.rug.nl/~bosch/.
4. INCO project: http://www.ifi.uio.no/~isu/INCO/.
5. Jacobson, I., Griss, M., Jonsson, P.: Software Reuse: Architecture, Process and Organization for Business Success. ACM Press (1997).
6. Johnson, R.E., Foote, B.: Designing Reusable Classes. Journal of Object-Oriented Programming, 1(3): 26-49 (1998).
7. Kang, K., Cohen, S., Hess, J., Novak, W., Peterson, A.: Feature-Oriented Domain Analysis (FODA) Feasibility Study. Software Engineering Institute Technical Report CMU/SEI-90-TR-21, ADA 235785 (1990).
8. Karlsson, E.A. (Ed.): Software Reuse, a Holistic Approach. John Wiley & Sons (1995).
9. Krueger, C.: Eliminating the Adoption Barrier. IEEE Software, 19(4): 29-31 (2002).
10. McGregor, J.D., Northrop, L.M., Jarred, S., Pohl, K.: Initiating Software Product Lines. IEEE Software, 19(4): 24-27 (2002).
11. Mohagheghi, P., Conradi, R.: Using Empirical Studies to Assess Software Develoment Approaches and Measurement Programs. Forthcoming at the 2nd Workshop in Workshop Series on Empirical Software Engineering (WSESE'03), Rome-Italy (2003).
12. Naalsund, E., Walseth, O.A.: Decision Making in Component-Based Development. NTNU diploma thesis, 92 p. (2002) www.idi.ntnu.no/grupper/su/su-diploma-2002/naalsund_-_CBD_(GSN_Public_Version).pdf.
13. Northrop, L.M.: SEI's Software Product Line Tenets. IEEE Software, 19(4):32-40 (2002).
14. Parnas, D.L.: On the Design and Development of Program Families. IEEE Trans. Software Eng., SE-2(1):1-9 (1976).
15. Rational Unified Process, www.rational.com.
16. Schwarz, H., Killi, O.M., Skånhaug, S.R.: Study of Industrial Component-Based Development. NTNU pre-diploma thesis, 105 p. (2002) http://www.idi.ntnu.no/grupper/su/sif8094-reports/2002/p2.pdf.

Dynamic Software Reconfiguration
in Software Product Families

Hassan Gomaa and Mohamed Hussein

Department of Information and Software Engineering
George Mason University
Fairfax, VA 22030, USA
{hgomaa,mhussein}@gmu.edu

Abstract. This paper describes an approach for the dynamic reconfiguration of software product families. A software reconfiguration pattern is a solution to a problem in a software product family where the configuration needs to be updated while the system is operational. It defines how a set of components participating in a software pattern cooperate to change the configuration of a system from one configuration of the product family to another. An approach for the design of reconfiguration patterns and a change management model for software product families are also described. The paper concludes with a description of case studies and a proof-of-concept prototype.

1 Introduction

Many software product families can be specified and designed as a software architecture representing a family of software systems characterized by the similarities and variations among the members of the product family. Software configuration is the process of adapting the architecture of the software product family to create an architecture for a specific product family member. Many approaches to software product families address the configuration of a family member prior to system operation. A more difficult problem is how to change the configuration of a product family member after it has started operation. This paper addresses the problem of dynamic system reconfiguration by changing the configuration of the running system from one member of the product family to another. Static configuration of family members from the product family architecture is addressed by current approaches. The challenge therefore is to perform the dynamic reconfiguration.

Dynamic software reconfiguration is concerned with changing the application configuration at runtime after it has been deployed. Three important requirements in a dynamic reconfiguration process are: (i) Non interference with those parts of the application that are not impacted by the reconfiguration. (ii) During reconfiguration, impacted components must complete their current computational activity before they can be reconfigured. (iii) Reconfiguration concerns must be separated from application concerns [10]. These requirements make dynamic software reconfiguration difficult. Dynamic software reconfiguration is useful for many purposes: A system needs to evolve after it has been deployed and the configuration is required to be updated dynamically. Other systems need to handle changing external and internal conditions

F. van der Linden (Ed.): PFE 2003, LNCS 3014, pp. 435–444, 2004.
© Springer-Verlag Berlin Heidelberg 2004

dynamically. Architecture-based evolution [11] can greatly benefit from dynamic reconfiguration. Current approaches address the design of the dynamic reconfiguration of distributed software architectures in an ad hoc manner. There is a need for an approach that systematically models possible configurations of an application as a product family capable of automatically reconfiguring from one configuration of the family to another. This paper describes an approach for dynamic software reconfiguration in software product families based on software reconfiguration patterns. With the execution of the possible dynamic reconfiguration scenarios in a product family, the solution presented in this paper allows for the automatic management of the evolution of the product family.

2   Reconfigurable Evolutionary Product Family Life Cycle

Three research areas related to dynamic reconfiguration provided for methods, techniques, protocols, and software engineering environments applicable in the design of dynamically reconfigurable software systems: a) Research into dynamic reconfiguration environments and consistency [10, 13, 14] provided for a dynamic reconfiguration model, a change management protocol and techniques for software architecture design and description. This research did not, however, provide for a systematic design method for reconfigurable product family architectures. b) Research into design, architecture, and product family specific architecture patterns [5, 6, 3] provided for systematic reuse concepts and guidelines for the design of applications, but did not address systematic reuse concepts for application reconfiguration. c) Research into reusable and configurable product family architectures [1, 2, 4, 12, 6, 8] provided for product family engineering and product family architecture configuration design methods, tools, and software engineering environments, but did not address dynamic software reconfiguration. The research described in this paper, while building on these three bodies of research, aims to provide for an integration of the approaches taken in the three research areas with the advancement of the concept of reconfiguration patterns for dynamically reconfigurable software product family architectures.

In order to support dynamic software reconfiguration in software product families, the Reconfigurable Evolutionary Product Family Life Cycle (REPFLC) is a new life cycle which builds on previous research into software product families [6, 8] and extends it significantly to support dynamic reconfiguration. Figure 1 shows the REPFLC. In addition, a proof-of-concept prototype, the Reconfigurable Product Line UML Based Software Engineering Environment (RPLUSEE), has been developed to automate the REPFLC. RPLUSEE builds on earlier research [8].

The REPFLC method and the RPLUSEE automated tool support consist of three major activities: a) Product Family Engineering. b) Target System Configuration. c) Target System Reconfiguration. During Product Family Engineering, similarities and variations among the members of the product family are established through modeling and analysis of the product family requirements. By considering appropriate software patterns in the product family, members of the product family are designed to be reconfigurable using the configuration change management modeling method. The product family architecture is designed in terms of components and their interconnections. As described in a previous paper [15], the software architecture of a product family is based on software architecture patterns, some of which are product family

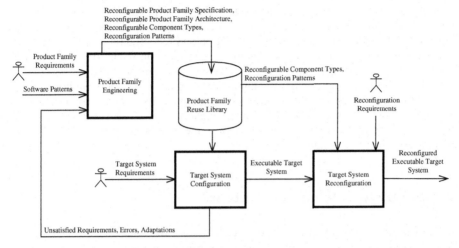

Fig. 1. Reconfigurable Evolutionary Product Family Life Cycle (REPFLC).

specific. During Target System Configuration, specific target systems (i.e., family members) are configured on the basis of user-required features. During Target System Reconfiguration, users can specify runtime configuration changes so that an executable system is dynamically changed from the old configuration to the new configuration.

3 Dynamic Software Reconfiguration

In order to address the systematic design of the dynamic reconfiguration of product families, the following general approach is taken. By considering component functionality and application characteristics, each component is designed to be capable of transitioning to a state where it can be reconfigured. Although this approach could be used on an application-by-application basis, it benefits greatly if reuse concepts are applied. The approach used in this paper is to provide software reconfiguration patterns [9] for dynamic software reconfiguration in software product families. Software reconfiguration patterns provide a solution to a recurring dynamic reconfiguration problem.

The approach is to develop the software product line architecture by reusing appropriate software architecture and design patterns and then designing corresponding software reconfiguration patterns. The resulting reconfiguration patterns may then be reused in other product family architectures that require dynamic reconfiguration capabilities. Reconfiguration Patterns address smaller sections of large dynamically reconfigurable software architectures and are therefore more manageable. The approach also incorporates a systematic design method that models possible configurations of an application as a product family capable of automatically reconfiguring from one configuration of the family to another. The solution takes the following approach: (a) Design intended reconfiguration behavior needed for a given architecture or design pattern. (b) Reuse resulting reconfiguration patterns in the design of product family architectures.

A Reconfiguration Pattern requires state- and scenario-based reconfiguration behavioral models to provide for a systematic design approach. These models are captured in UML with reconfiguration collaboration and reconfiguration statechart models. A Reconfiguration Pattern also requires reconfiguration scenarios to address different reconfiguration requirements and a change management model to describe the sequence of transitioning impacted components to states where they can be reconfigured and, where necessary, the cooperation of components to allow reconfiguration. Reconfiguration Scenarios describe different situations where the configuration of an application is changed from one product family member to another, based on the architecture of the product family.

4 Software Reconfiguration Patterns

A Software Reconfiguration Pattern defines how a set of components that make up a design, an architecture or a product family specific architecture pattern dynamically cooperate to change the configuration of the pattern to a new configuration under a set of reconfiguration commands. Reconfiguration Statecharts are the main approach used for the description of Reconfiguration Patterns.

A reconfiguration statechart defines the sequence of states a component goes through during reconfiguration and may consist of one or more statecharts that are orthogonal to each other. An Operating Statechart defines operational transactions of components participating in a software pattern. A transaction is defined as the sequence of one or more messages exchanged between two or more components. In a Reconfiguration Pattern, each component participating in the software pattern executes one or more of the following orthogonal statecharts:

1. A Main Reconfiguration Statechart is designed to handle reconfiguration-related events using generalized reconfiguration states. In a Main Reconfiguration Statechart a component is either in the Active, Passive, or Quiescent state [10]. A component is in the Active state when it is engaged in its operational computations. Components that are in the process of being reconfigured transition through Passivating, Passive, Waiting For Acknowledgement, and Quiescent states. The actual states and transitions are pattern dependent, as described for the example in Section 5.

2. One or more Operating with Reconfiguration Statechart(s) may also be designed to handle some reconfiguration-related events in a component's Operating Statechart. An Operating with Reconfiguration Statechart is modeled with the same states the component uses in its Operating Statechart. However, the statechart also handles reconfiguration-related events and actions.

3. One or more Neighbor Component State Tracking Statechart(s) may also be designed for components to track the states of interconnected components during reconfiguration. These statecharts are reconfiguration pattern-dependent..

The Main, Operating with Reconfiguration, and Neighbor Component State Tracking statecharts of components participating in the software pattern collectively define a Reconfiguration Pattern for the group of components. Embedded in the Reconfiguration Pattern is how components of the software pattern cooperatively contribute to the dynamic reconfiguration of the product family from one configuration to another configuration of the product family. Several Reconfiguration Patterns have been developed and are described below:

1. In a Master-Slave Reconfiguration Pattern, which is based on a Master-Slave pattern [3], a Master component can be removed or replaced after the responses from all slave components are received. Slave components can be removed or replaced after Master is quiescent. The Master-Slave Reconfiguration Pattern is used in a reconfigurable factory automation product family.

2. In a Centralized Control System Reconfiguration Pattern, which is based on a Centralized Control System pattern, and is widely used in real-time control applications [7], the removal or replacement of any component in the system requires the Central Controller to be quiescent. The Centralized Control System Reconfiguration Pattern is used in a reconfigurable cruise control product family.

3. In a Client / Server Reconfiguration Pattern, which is based on the Client / Server pattern, clients can be added or removed after completing a transaction they initiated. Servers can be removed or replaced after completing the current transaction. The Client / Server Reconfiguration Pattern is used in a reconfigurable factory automation product family.

4. In a Decentralized Control System Reconfiguration Pattern, which is based on a Decentralized Control System pattern, and is widely used in distributed control applications [7], control components notify each other if going quiescent. A control component in this Reconfiguration Pattern can cease to communicate with its neighboring component, but can continue with other processing. The Decentralized Control System Reconfiguration Pattern is used in a reconfigurable factory automation product family.

5   Reconfiguration Statechart

For each pattern, there are one or more reconfiguration statecharts that define the different states of the components in the pattern. For example, the Main Reconfiguration statechart shown in Figure 2 is one of the statecharts that define the Decentralized Control System Reconfiguration Pattern. An operational component is in the Active state. As defined by Kramer et. al. [10], a component is in the Passive state when it is not currently engaged in a transaction it initiated, and will not initiate new transactions. A component transitions to the Quiescent state if it is Passive, is not currently engaged in servicing a transaction, and no transactions have been or will be initiated by other components which require service from this component. In this research this state model is extended for reconfiguration patterns so that a component can also be in the Passivating and Waiting For Acknowledgement states. A component is in the Passivating state when it is disengaging itself from any transactions it has been participating and those it has been initiating. A component is in the Waiting For Acknowledgement state if it has sent notification message(s) to interconnected components to inform them of its need to go passive and is waiting for positive acknowledgements.

In this pattern, a control component communicates with its two neighboring control components. In the statechart shown in Fig. 2, if a passivate command arrives while

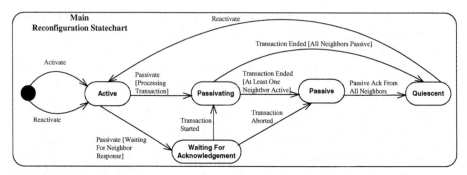

Fig. 2. Main Reconfiguration Statechart For Decentralized Control System Reconfiguration Pattern.

the component is processing a transaction, it transitions to Passivating state. When the transaction ends, it either transitions to Passive state, because one of its neighbors is still active, or it transitions directly to Quiescent state if all neighbors are passive. If the control component receives a passivate command after it has requested its neighbor to start a transaction but before it has received a response (i.e., while the condition Waiting For Neighbor Response is true), then it sends a notification to its neighbor component informing it that it wishes to cancel the outstanding request. It then transitions to the Waiting For Acknowledgement state. If the neighbor responds that the transaction has started, the component transitions to the Passivating state. Otherwise, if the neighbor responds that the transaction was aborted, the component transitions to the Passive state. The reason for the Waiting for Acknowledgement state is to prevent a race condition. In this pattern, a Neighbor Component State Tracking Statechart is also modeled with states representing whether or not the neighboring component is active or passive.

6   Change Management Model

A Change Management Model is used to establish a region of quiescence so that Reconfiguration Scenarios may be executed. The change management model, which is an extension of the change management protocol in [10], consists of:

a. Extended Change Rules which describe rules for component removal, component interconnection linking and unlinking, and component creation. In the prior work [10], a component's interconnections could only be unlinked and the component removed when it was Quiescent. In this research, a component can be allocated extra interconnections if it is Quiescent. Moreover, some of the interconnections of a component may be unlinked if the component is Quiescent with respect to such interconnections because a component can be designed so that it can be partially quiescent, i.e., quiescent with respect to some interconnections but not others.

b. Change Transaction Model which describes reconfiguration actions required to reconfigure applications. The Change transaction model consists of two parts:

1. Impacted Sets: The Impacted sets are sets of components that are affected by the reconfiguration process and must be driven to the Quiescent state so that they can be reconfigured. Impacted sets are of four types: Behavioral, Topological, Inter-component Behavioral, and Reconfiguration Pattern Impacted. The order of the construction of the sets is important because the model relies on the orderly placement of components into the sets.
2. Reconfiguration Commands: Reconfiguration commands describe reconfiguration actions associated with user required changes, or reconfiguration scenarios. The reconfiguration commands are passivate, checkpoint, unlink, remove, create, link, activate, restore, and reactivate. The passivate command may take zero or more interconnection names as parameters. A component that receives a passivate command with no parameters must eventually transition to the Quiescent state. If the command has parameters, the component must go partially quiescent, i.e., be inactive along the interconnections named as parameters.

Existing methods address dynamic reconfiguration by dynamically replacing one component at a time [10, 13, 14]. For product family architectures, four types of reconfiguration scenarios are possible: Product Configuration for initial runtime product configuration, Product Reconfiguration for reconfiguration of a running product into another product, Feature Reconfiguration for the dynamic addition, removal, or replacement of a feature (and the components the feature depends on), and Component Reconfiguration for the addition, removal or replacement of a component at runtime. The interactions of the components that support a feature are considered a product family specific pattern.

The contents of the Change Transaction Model are summarized in a Change Transaction as follows:

a. A passivate command with no parameters is sent to components in the current configuration that need to be driven to the quiescent state. A passivate command with parameters is sent to components that are required to be partially quiescent with respect to one or more of their interconnections.
b. A checkpoint command is sent to components that have to store their state information before they can be reconfigured.
c. An unlink command is used to unlink one or more of the interconnections of components in the current configuration.
d. A remove command is used to remove components that will no longer be part of the new configuration.
e. A create command is used to create components that support the new configuration.
f. A link command is used to link components that are required to support the new configuration.
g. A reactivate command is sent to a new or an existing component and causes it to initialize or to reawaken after it has been in the quiescent state.
h. A restore command is sent to components that replace others that have been removed and need to restore state information that has been checkpointed by the removed component in the previous configuration.
i. An activate command is sent to new components that support the new configuration, but do not receive a reactivate command.

7 Case Studies and Validation

Two product families were modeled using the REPFLC development method:

1. A reconfigurable automobile cruise control product family was designed. This case study uses the Centralized Control System Reconfiguration Pattern.
2. A reconfigurable factory automation product family architecture was designed and implemented. This case study uses the Master-slave, Client / Server, & Decentralized Control System Reconfiguration Patterns.

The RPLUSEE prototype uses the commercial Rational Rose Real Time (Rose RT). Components are mapped to Rose RT capsules. In Rose RT, capsules execute Rose RT statecharts which represent transitions as events guarded by conditions. Actions are implemented with Rose RT functions and C++ code. Capsules communicate through exchange of messages sent and received through ports. As part of the validation process, three techniques, provided by the model execution capability of Rose RT, were employed: execution control, visual component instance monitoring, and analysis of message trace outputs. The validation process confirmed that reconfiguration scenario change transactions executed correctly and that component reconfigurations took place as planned.

One of the reconfiguration scenarios in the reconfigurable factory automation product family architecture involves the dynamic reconfiguration of a High Volume Manufacturing Product, which uses the Decentralized Control System Reconfiguration Pattern. Figure 3 shows the current configuration and the new configuration of this scenario, which involves deleting a component from the Product. Assume Line Workstation Controller M is to be deleted from the current configuration, where Line Workstation Controller M is interconnected to Line Workstation Controller M - 1 and Line Workstation Controller M + 1.

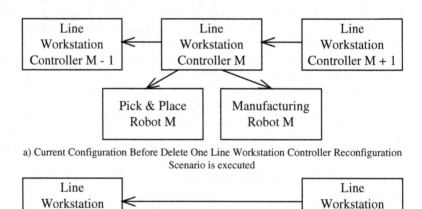

a) Current Configuration Before Delete One Line Workstation Controller Reconfiguration
Scenario is executed

b) New Configuration After Delete One Line Workstation Controller Reconfiguration
Scenario is executed

Fig. 3. Delete Line Workstation Controller M Reconfiguration Scenario: Current and New Configurations.

In this reconfiguration scenario, first, Line Workstation Controller M component is passivated, which means that the component must be driven into the quiescent state in Fig. 2. Then, Line Workstation M component is unlinked from Line Workstation Controller M – 1, Pick & Place Robot M, Manufacturing Robot M, and Line Workstation Controller M + 1 components. Next, Line Workstation Controller M, Pick & Place Robot M, and Manufacturing Robot M components are removed from the current configuration. Then, Line Workstation Controller M - 1 and Line Workstation Controller M + 1 components are linked. Finally, Line Workstation Controller M + 1 is reactivated.

8   Conclusions

This paper has described a novel approach to dynamic software reconfiguration in software product families. The paper described an approach that systematically models possible configurations of an application as a product family capable of automatically reconfiguring from one configuration of the family to another. The four reconfiguration scenarios of Product Configuration, Product Reconfiguration, Feature Reconfiguration, and Component Reconfiguration described in the paper allow for the automatic management of the evolution of a product family. The strength of the approach is demonstrated by the reusable reconfiguration Patterns, which provide a foundation for the design of reconfigurable component-based product family architectures.

Acknowledgements

This research was supported in part by the National Science Foundation.

References

1. Colin Atkinson et al, Component-Based Product Line Engineering with UML, Addison-Wesley, 2001.
2. Bayer, J. et al, PuLSE: A Methodology to Develop Software Product Lines, Proc Fifth Symposium on Software Reusability, 1999.
3. Frank Buschmann et al, Pattern-Oriented Software Architecture: System Of Patterns, John Wiley & Sons, 1996.
4. Paul Clements and Linda Northrop, Software Product Lines: Practice and Patterns, Addison Wesley, 2002.
5. Erich Gamma et al, Design Patterns: Elements of Reusable Object-Oriented Software, Addison-Wesley, 1995.
6. H. Gomaa and G.A. Farrukh, Methods and Tools for the Automated Configuration of Distributed Applications from Reusable Software Architectures and Components, IEE Proc - Software, Vol. 146, No. 6, December 1999.
7. H. Gomaa, Designing Concurrent, Distributed, and Real-Time Applications with UML, Addison-Wesley, 2000.

8. H. Gomaa and M.E. Shin, Multiple-View Meta-Modeling of Software Product Lines, Proceedings of the IEEE International Conference on the Engineering of Complex Computer Systems, Greenbelt, MD, December 2002.
9. Mohamed Hussein, A Software Architecture-based Method and Framework for the Design of Dynamically Reconfigurable Product Line Software Architectures, Ph.D. Dissertation, George Mason University, May 2003.
10. Jeff Kramer and Jeff Magee, The Evolving Philosophers Problem: Dynamic Change Management, IEEE Transactions on Software Engineering, Vol. 16, No. 11, November 1990.
11. Nenad Medvidovic, David S. Rosenblum, and Richard N. Taylor, A Language And Environment For Architecture-based Software Development And Evolution, Proc. Intl. Conf. Software Engineering, May 1999.
12. D. M Weiss and CTR Lai, Software Product-Line Engineering, Addison Wesley, 1999.
13. Lucent Technologies Inc., Uniform Configuration Controller For Replicated Component Systems, United States Patent 6,591,373, Ardis , et al. July 8, 2003.
14. Lucent Technologies Inc., Graphical User Interface For Providing Component Relational Information For A Uniform Configuration Controller For Replicated Component Systems, United States Patent 6,580,439, Ardis et. al, June 17, 2003.
15. H. Gomaa and G. Farrukh, Composition of Software Architectures from Reusable Architecture Patterns, Proc. IEEE International Workshop on Software Architectures, Orlando, Florida, November 1998.

Architecture True Prototyping of Product Lines Using Personal Computer Networks

Fons de Lange and Jeffrey Kang

Philips Research Laboratories, Prof. Holstlaan 4
5656AA Eindhoven, The Netherlands
Fons.de.Lange@philips.com

Abstract. A big problem in the consumer electronics industry of to-day is the growing gap between research and development. There is no lack of ideas for new products and new product features. On the contrary, Philips Research is generating and prototyping so many new ideas that product divisions are incapable of absorbing or even assessing a significant part of them. One of the major problems is "architecture mismatch". I.e., it is very hard to fit a feature – proto-typed on a powerful computer – into an existing product line, be-cause of incompatible interfaces and interactions between new fea-tures and existing ones. This paper proposes a prototyping approach that – although based on PCs and networking – strongly reduces the "architecture mismatch" problem and creates "product-line aware-ness" among researchers working on future Consumer Electronics applications. A PC based "architecture prototyping" platform should be a prominent part of a product-line.

1 Introduction

Product lines are continuously being extended with new products, usually having more and more features. At the same high pace, cheaper and more powerful chips are replacing outdated hardware. Furthermore, there is a growing part of "standard" soft-ware, e.g. networking or database software, typically supplied by third parties, which is continuously being upgraded and modified. These three factors are not independent from one another, especially when advanced new media processing features[1] are in-troduced that rely on new hardware, new software as well as on external standards, e.g. HTTP and UPnP [1].

The research branch of consumer electronics R&D focuses on the exploration and prototyping of advanced new features. Since these features are often highly advanced, they cannot be prototyped on a realistic consumer electronics platform. Instead, typi-cally a PC is used to show the functional behavior of a specific set of features. This clearly has great advantages, like a wealth of development and debugging tools, an

---

[1] An example of an advanced feature in a DVD+RW Recorder is "automatic chapter genera-tion through real-time audio/video content analysis". This is used to enable enhanced naviga-tion [2] through recorded content on disc.

F. van der Linden (Ed.): PFE 2003, LNCS 3014, pp. 445–453, 2004.
© Springer-Verlag Berlin Heidelberg 2004

adequate choice of powerful operating systems and no time consuming code downloading to a target consumer platform. However, a big drawback of PC based "functional" prototyping is that it that it does not address "architecture". As a consequence, new features will not "fit" in the architecture of existing product lines. Features that rely on new hardware are even more difficult to map to a consumer platform, since the PC hardware architecture differs considerably from embedded hardware.

In this paper, a different approach is presented that tackles the problems described above. Like functional prototyping, it enables fast prototyping of complex systems by means of standard personal computers (PCs), standard development tools, standard networking (TCP/IP) and off-the-shelf PCI plug-in cards. However, the approach considerably differs from functional prototyping in that it explicitly addresses system architecture in such a way that mapping to a consumer electronics product line is straightforward. This PC based way of "architecture prototyping" should be part of the development process of a product-line to support the rapid development and integration of features into this product-line.

Architecture-true prototyping is possible by making a well-defined separation between platform independent and platform dependent components. I.e., if the implementation of a component will be different in a consumer system than it is on the PC prototype, than this component should be treated as a black box, only accessible through well-defined interfaces that are invariant across all platforms. The same holds for the interconnection technology, available on different platforms that enable components to interact and exchange data or media streams on a local system or across a network. On a PC this can be TCP/IP and UPnP [1], while on a (stand-alone) consumer system no networking and only local control is possible. If on a PC advanced networking technologies are used for prototyping, it must still be easy to map these to simple protocols on stand-alone consumer systems according to the architecture rules imposed by the product line. The next section describes this in more detail. It introduces the STAGE[2] approach for prototyping the architecture of embedded systems according to product-line rules. Section 3 presents some results obtained with the STAGE approach, while section 4 summarizes the approach and gives the main conclusions.

2   Overview of the Prototyping Approach

While PCs offer the required performance, flexibility and off-the-shelf media processing components (PCI plug-in boards) for fast prototyping, it may not be so clear to what extent a PC based prototype can serve as a realistic model of a resource constrained consumer system. In the approach described here however, the focus is on component/interconnection architecture, i.e. the subdivision of the total system in hardware and software components and their interconnections/ interactions. At the highest level of abstraction, the architecture model on PCs should be exactly the same as on a resource constrained consumer system. At the very low levels of abstraction this evidently cannot be true, but adequate partitioning should enable a straightforward mapping.

---

[2] STAGE is the name of the prototyping approach and platform that is the subject of this paper.

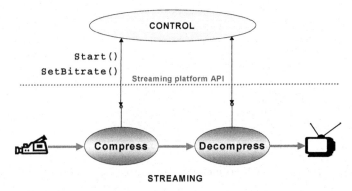

Fig. 1. Simplified system representation of an advanced digital video bit-rate converter.

As an example, consider the following simplified system consisting of an advanced digital-video bit-rate converter, consisting of an encoder and a decoder, see Figure 1.

The horizontal arrows indicate signal flow (streaming), while the vertical arrows indicate control. As an example of typical control functions for the compression logical component, two functions are shown: `Start()` and `SetBitRate()`, for starting the encoding and choosing a specific bit-rate for the conversion. The encoding and decoding functionality is modeled by two components with well-defined interfaces for streaming and control. The control interfaces are such that implementation of control software is the same for all members of a product family, irrespective of the underlying streaming platform implementing encoding and decoding functionality.

In a consumer system, the functionality of Figure 1 is typically implemented on a single chip including a CPU, memories (both on-chip and off-chip), slave processors and dedicated hardware. Such a simple hardware set-up is shown in Figure 2.

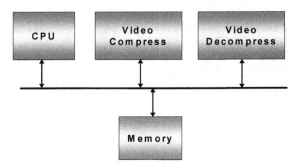

Fig. 2. Typical single chip hardware for system of Figure 1.

Note that for more complex systems additional dedicated hardware blocks and signal processors will be present, which all connect to a central bus.

In an embedded consumer system of a particular product line, the software has similar modularity, see Figure 3.

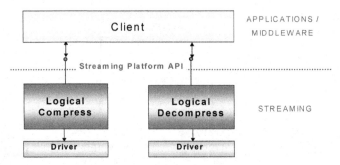

Fig. 3. Typical embedded (simplified) software architecture for system of Figure 1.

Shown here is *client* software, expecting the mandatory control interface of the streaming subsystem of the product line. Hardware dependent *drivers* control the compression and decompression hardware blocks of Figure 2. Important to notice are the *logical compress* and *decompress* software components that implement the required interfaces for higher-level client-software according to internal architecture standards imposed by the product line.

This hardware/software setup can be prototyped on PC and PC networks, while sticking to the interconnection architecture of the product line. This is shown in Figure 4.

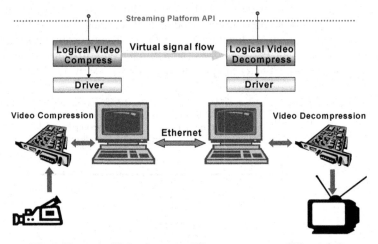

Fig. 4. Networked PC prototype of bit-rate converter of Figure 1–3.

Here, two PCs are used, where one PC implements the compression functionality and another PC implements the decompression functionality, while both use additional hardware (plug-in cards) to realize the advanced functionality and performance. Also here, software implements a compression *logical component* and a decompression *logical component*, exporting the mandatory logical control interfaces for encoding and decoding according to product line rules. Separate software modules, called *physical components*, typically do the actual implementation of this functionality.

This is shown in Figure 5. Signal flow (streaming) between the video compression and video decompression components is done via Ethernet. To this purpose, the video compression and decompression logical components use a "virtual" streaming channel that exports interfaces for reading and writing data packets see Figure 5. The stream buffer associated with a channel is typically mapped to a shared memory. To facilitate the mapping of a PC prototype to an embedded system, the concept of shared memory is modeled as a separate memory server running on some PC in the network.

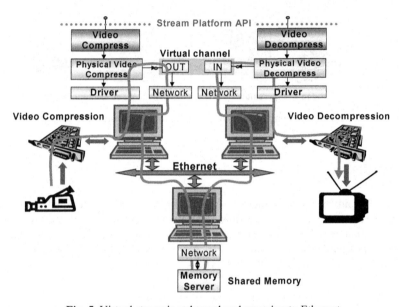

Fig. 5. Virtual streaming channel and mapping to Ethernet.

The virtual channel "component" implements streaming using standard TCP/IP over sockets. In an embedded system this is evidently replaced by embedded software/hardware protocols – according to product line rules – while the streaming interface, exported by the virtual channel, remain the same between PC network and embedded product implementation.

Figure 6 shows how control interfaces are implemented on the PC network. The client is unaware of the location of the video compression and video decompression logical components. A logical component proxy is present on the client machine, which routes the control via the network to the decompression PC. A decompression stub takes care of calling the functions of the local video decompression logical component.

In this set-up, logical components and the underlying implementation technology can be moved between any PC in the network. The only limitation is available bandwidth, which is no issue in most system set-ups.

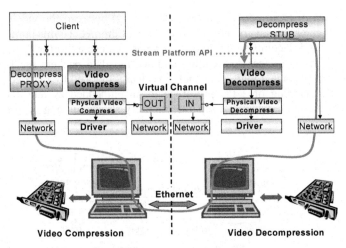

Fig. 6. Mapping of control interfaces to the network PC prototype.

3 Results

A number of advanced consumer storage systems have been prototyped. This includes a multi-stream audio/video hard-disk (HDD) recorder/player, a DVD+RW – HDD combi-appliance and systems with advanced, real-time audio/video content analysis, content management and navigation [2]. As an example, Figure 7 shows four views on the DVD+RW – HDD combi prototype.

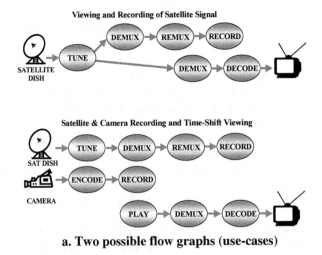

a. Two possible flow graphs (use-cases)

Fig. 7. Four views on the DVD+RW – HDD combi prototype.

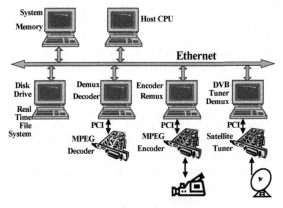

b. PC – network

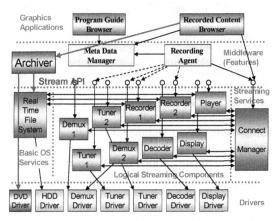

c. Software architecture view

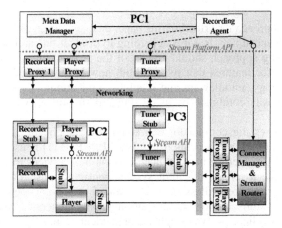

d. Part of software architecture: network view

Fig. 7. (Cont).

This system implements two "use cases", see Figure 7a, involving different stream-ing components. This functionality is prototyped on 5 PCs connected to Ethernet, see Figure 7b. One PC runs a real-time file system [4], the DVD+RW driver and a com-ponent making archives on DVD (*Archiver*). Figure 7c shows the software architec-ture. Shown are graphics applications for recording content and for browsing through recorded content. Middleware components such as a meta-data manager separate the applications from the underlying streaming platform. The streaming-layer contains several "logical " components, representing streaming functionality. They rely on drivers and on a *Connection Manager*. Finally, the *recorder* and *player* components rely on a *Real-Time File System*. Considering the hardware partitioning of Figure 7b, different components run on different PCs. Figure 7d shows the associated "net-worked" software architecture for a number of logical components. *Proxy* and *Stub* components hide all networking from clients using the streaming components.

Streaming bandwidth is measured by using a dedicated PC that emulates system memory; see Figure 7b, while the CPU performance requirements of individual com-ponents, e.g. the "Recorder" in Figure 7c is measured by annotating its code with "operation counters".

The goal of this prototyping-effort is 4-fold.

1. Show advanced new consumer-storage features in a realistic system context,
2. Define, implement and test streaming platform APIs according to architecture rules set by Philips Semiconductors [3].
3. Investigate the integration of new middleware components into the architecture of future consumer systems, e.g. audio/video databases.
4. Assess other important system architecture issues, such as system partitioning options, component interconnections and interactions, memory-bandwidth re-quirements for streaming, streaming-latency, performance requirements for in-dividual features and the hardware-software partitioning of such features.

4   Conclusions

The prototyping approach described in this paper enables fast architecture true system prototyping of advanced new features according to product line architecture rules. As such the prototyping approach should be part of the product line. Architecture proto-typing is possible for features that require both new hardware and software. Media processing technology, middleware and graphics applications – developed by differ-ent parties – are easily combined by using standard streaming protocols and control APIs.

Each media-processing component is a stand-alone application, which is able to communicate with other components using TCP/IP. UPnP [1] is used to enable each such a component to advertise its presence, location and services to the system. As a result, it is possible to create different system configurations/ interconnections on request of an application regardless of the location of each component. For each com-ponent, proxy and stub components are automatically generated, making both the components and the client software highly independent of any changes in networking technology and easing the substitution of PC networking by embedded / local imple-mentations.

It is relatively easy to convert both hardware and software models – as prototyped on a PC – to a real HW/SW architecture on a consumer system, while sticking to product line architecture rules. With respect to software, this is achieved by simply removing the proxy and stub components and the networking libraries and making a direct connection between middleware/applications and component control interfaces. If there are multiple processors in an embedded system, proxies and stubs only need to be re-generated for the current target. With respect to hardware, A PC with plug-in board – implementing a logical component – can be replaced by an equivalent hardware block on an IC.

Using the approach, system partitioning options and complexity can be assessed at an early stage of predevelopment. For example one can identify building blocks, define interfaces and study interactions. All these remain the same both on PC prototype as on the actual product of the product line. Performance analysis is more limited. However, one can determine the memory bandwidth and communication bandwidth, as well as the number of operations per second for tasks and components in the system. A major advantage of the approach proposed in this paper, is that by sticking to strict streaming platform independent API standards, all middleware can be developed and tested before the actual embedded system hardware is available from the IC manufacturer.

References

1. UPnP, *The Univeral Plug and Play Forum*, http://www.upnp.org.
2. Real time music-image-speech-image-video content analysis for content management, *Jan Nesvadba et.al .*, Several publications, see http://www.extra.research.philips.com/cassandra.
3. Philips Semiconductor's Nexperia platform, http://www.semiconductors.philips.com/products/nexperia/.
4. O. Mesut, N. Lambert, *HDD Characterization for A/V Streaming Applications*, IEEE transactions on consumer electronics, volume 48, August 2002.

Making Variability Decisions during Architecture Design

Len Bass, Felix Bachmann, and Mark Klein

Software Engineering Institute
Carnegie Mellon University
Pittsburgh, PA USA 15213
{ljb,fb,mk}@sei.cmu.edu

Abstract. Two different models for variability are used to enable selections among various architectural choices to achieve variability. A cost model is used to justify and rationalize choices among architectural mechanisms intended to defer the binding time. A dependency model is used to justify and rationalize architectural choices intended to keep a variability from affecting more than the necessary number of modules.

Introduction

You are a designer who has been given the task of designing a product line that will support a variety of different sensors. You have a number of design options including:

- do nothing special originally and modify the system as needed when a new sensor must be incorporated
- define a virtual sensor layer to support all possible sensors, and
- construct a plug-in framework within which it is the responsibility of the sensor vendor to provide software that interfaces the sensor to your framework.

Those options have all their advantages and disadvantages in terms of:

- how much it cost to include a specific variability mechanism when developing the software,
- how much it cost to use the variability mechanism to support a new sensor, and
- who is actually paying for the creation (e.g. your organization) and use (e.g. vendor) of the variability mechanism.

Exploring what is known and what is unknown about this problem is the topic of this paper.

There is general agreement that managing variability is an important aspect of developing a product line. The treatment of variability has focused on recognizing it and representing it [5, 7], Limited attention, however, has been paid to the subject of justifying architectural decisions for variability [3, 4, 9].

From the perspective of a designer who is incorporating variability into a system, a list of architectural mechanisms to achieve variability is available but little guidance exists as to how to choose among the options. We use cost modeling and dependency modeling to discuss how to guide the designer through the available choices. We also highlight open issues in terms of these models.

F. van der Linden (Ed.): PFE 2003, LNCS 3014, pp. 454–465, 2004.

We begin by discussing existing work. We then discuss some of the possible architectural decisions in light of a cost model. Next we discuss other architectural decisions in terms of a dependency model. Finally, we discuss open issues with respect to making design decisions to support variability.

Prior Work

Prior work exists in three areas relevant to this paper – cost modeling, mechanisms for achieving variability, and characterizing the points in the development cycle at which variability can be achieved. Some of the ideas in this paper have appeared in preliminary form in two SEI technical reports [1, 2].

Cost Modeling

The creation of a product line is primarily a business decision. Weiss [12] is the best known reference with respect to the cost and benefits of creating a product line. A recent Dagstuhl workshop on product lines is producing an issue paper [6] about the economic considerations associated with product line production but this work is all oriented toward the manager. Its goal is to enable a manager to make decisions about the scope and extent of variability to include in products. These considerations manifest themselves as requirements to the designer – e.g. support a variety of products that have different feature sets.

Our concerns in this paper are the business considerations from the point of view of the designer. For example, what is the cost of introducing a virtual machine to support a variety of different sensors versus the cost of supporting the different sensors through plug-ins. Both architectural options support the same requirement (supporting variability of sensors) but existing cost models do not support decision making by the designer. The most current work in this area can be found in [8].

Reducing time to market is another major driver for product lines. Architectural decisions will either support or hinder the achievement of this requirement. Again, to our knowledge, there is no scheduling model that enables a designer to understand the time differences in particular architectural decisions. We do not discuss scheduling in this paper but believe that the cost discussion applies equally well to scheduling.

Mechanisms for Achieving Variability

Bosch [4] gives five mechanisms for achieving variability – inheritance, extensions, configuration, template instantiation, and generation. We have enumerated a list of "architectural tactics" for achieving variability (modifiability) [3]. Our list of tactics subsumes the Bosch list and so we focus our discussion of variability mechanisms around architectural tactics. Our list is grouped into three major categories – localize changes, prevent the ripple effect, and defer binding time.

Both of these lists are descriptive – they present the technique. Neither gives any guidance to the designer as to rationale for choosing one tactic over another. Also, neither list presents any surprises to a designer. Their purpose rather is to provide a checklist for designers to consider when attempting to achieve various forms of variability. In this paper, we begin to rationalize the choice of one tactic in place of another.

Development Cycle

Jaring and Bosch [9] identify eight different phases during the development cycle when a variability can be introduced and subsequently realized. These phases are requirements, architecture, design, implementation, compile, link, installation, and run time. A variability is introduced (once) at one of these phases and realized (multiple times) at a subsequent phase. Since we are concerned with the perspective of the software designer, the phases that we consider do not include the requirements phase. That is, as a designer, a requirement for a variability is handed to us from one of the stakeholders of the system (maybe ourselves). The introduction from our perspective, then, can only happen at architecture design time or later.

We will use the seven remaining phases as a setting both for discussing cost models and for discussing variability tactics in the remainder of this paper.

Business Considerations in Architecture Design

First observe that the software designer needs to consider the possibility of not introducing any tactic to support variability. This is the nominal case. The cost for making N realizations in that case is:

   1) N * (cost of a single realization).
In the case where a variability tactic is introduced, the cost is:

   2) Cost of introducing the tactic + N * (cost of exercising the tactic at architectural design time
      + cost of exercising the tactic at detailed design time
      + cost of exercising the tactic at implementation time
      + cost of exercising the tactic at compile time
      + cost of exercising the tactic at link time
      + cost of exercising the tactic at installation time
      + cost of exercising the tactic at run time)

Note that the cost of exercising the tactic includes costs for every phase subsequent to the realization phase as well as the realization phase. Depending on the tactic used, some of the costs do not exist. For example, if the variability is supported by setting a compiler switch, then there will be no link time costs, installation time cost, etc.

To illustrate the influence of tactics on the cost for an organization to fulfill requirements we assume that a designer has been given the task of designing a product line that will support a variety of different sensors. Figure 1 shows three possible designs that would fulfill this requirement:

- do nothing special originally and modify the system as needed when a new sensor must be incorporated
- define a virtual sensor layer to support all possible sensors, and
- construct a plug-in framework within which it is the responsibility of the sensor vendor to provide software that interfaces the sensor to your framework.

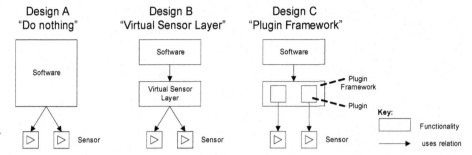

Fig. 1. Possible choices to support different sensors.

The presented designs very much differ in the cost for introducing a variability tactic and exercising the tactic to support a different sensor. To show the effect of the different designs on the cost for supporting different sensors we create a fictional cost model. Tables 1 to 3 show the assumed cost in terms of person effort in days. We also assume that the organization estimated that over the next five years 20 new sensors have to be supported (N = 20).

Table 1. Cost for supporting 20 sensors in case of design A.

Design A (numbers are effort in days)	Introducing the variability tactic	exercising the variability tactic (N times)	
		Adding new functionality to control the new sensor	Adaptation of the existing software to use new sensor
cost of exercising the tactic at architectural design time	0	0	0
cost of exercising the tactic at detailed design time	0	1	1
cost of exercising the tactic at implementation time	0	5	8
cost of exercising the tactic at compile time	0	0	1
cost of exercising the tactic at link time	0	0	0
cost of exercising the tactic at installation time	0	0	0
cost of exercising the tactic at run time	0	0	0
Sum	0	6	10
Cost for introducing the variability tactic	0		
Cost for exercising the variability tactic one time		16	
Complete cost to support 20 sensors	20 * 16 = 320		
Part for development org.	320		
Part for sensor vendor	0		

Table 2. Cost for supporting 20 sensors in case of design B.

Design B (numbers are effort in days)	Introducing the variability tactic	exercising the variability tactic (N times)	
		Adding new functionality to control the new sensor	Adaptation of the existing software to use new sensor
cost of exercising the tactic at architectural design time	5	0	0
cost of exercising the tactic at detailed design time	10	1	0
cost of exercising the tactic at implementation time	25	5	0
cost of exercising the tactic at compile time	2	0	0
cost of exercising the tactic at link time	0	0	0
cost of exercising the tactic at installation time	0	0	0
cost of exercising the tactic at run time	0	0	0
Sum	42	6	0
Cost for introducing the variability tactic	42		
Cost for exercising the variability tactic one time		6	
Complete cost to support 20 sensors	20 * 6 + 42 = 162		
Part for development org.	162		
Part for sensor vendor	0		

The tables show that if the product line would not have to support more than approximately four new sensors, design A (not applying any variability tactic) would be the most cost efficient solution. They also show that design C, although the most complicated solution, would be the most desirable for the development organization, if it is possible that the sensor vendors are responsible for the plug-in development cost.

The choices a designer makes would have a better basis if cost models like this would exist. Although the numbers must be estimated, they still would show tendencies of effect of different designs.

Formula 2) also provides a means for discriminating among the architectural tactics in the category "Defer Binding Time". These tactics are: runtime registration, configuration files, polymorphism, component replacement, adherence to defined protocols [3]. One could expect to see higher cost for introducing a tactic at later phases, such as downloading new software, while the cost for exercising are lowered. This helps deciding on binding time tactics dependent on the expected number of changes.

Table 3. Cost for supporting 20 sensors in case of design C.

Design C (numbers are effort in days)	Introducing the variability tactic	exercising the variability tactic (N times)	
		Adding new functionality to control the new sensor	Adaptation of the existing software to use new sensor
cost of exercising the tactic at architectural design time	8	0	0
cost of exercising the tactic at detailed design time	15	1	0
cost of exercising the tactic at implementation time	30	8	0
cost of exercising the tactic at compile time	2	0	0
cost of exercising the tactic at link time	0	0	0
cost of exercising the tactic at installation time	0	0	1(install plug-in)
cost of exercising the tactic at run time	0	0	0
Sum	55	9	1
Cost for introducing the variability tactic	55		
Cost for exercising the variability tactic one time		10	
Complete cost to support 20 sensors	20 * 10 + 55 = 255		
Part for development org.	55 + 20 * 1 = 75 (plug-in framework + installation of plug-ins)		
Part for sensor vendor	20 * 9 = 180 (plug-in development)		

A tactic that we have placed in the "localize changes" category can also be rationalized by the direct use of the cost model. This tactic is "Limit options". The limit option tactic is intended to reduce the scope of the variation. This manifests itself in a reduction of the cost of introducing the tactic. An example of "limit option" might be in a case where a tactic is introduced to prepare for processor variation. If the set of possible processors is restricted to processors in the same family, for example, then the cost of introducing the variation will be reduced.

A large deficiency in this use of cost models to assist in decisions among architectural tactics is that such cost models are not documented. The cost to implement configuration files, for example, is not something that can be found in a reference volume. This lack, however, does not keep experienced software designers from making reasonably good estimates. Paulish [10] points out that cost estimates are more accurate when they are made on the basis of a detailed design and made by the people responsible for the implementation. Software designers have the intuition and the knowledge to make comparative estimates that suffice for the purposes we have described above.

We discuss cost in this section but the same discussion also applies to schedule. We are also making simplifying assumptions during this discussion such as assuming the cost for all realizations is the same. Since no such cost models yet exist, these simplifying assumptions will not affect our discussion to any large extent.

Dependency Model

The costs shown in Table 1 to 3 are a little bit too optimistic. The assumption was that introducing a tactic like "virtual sensor layer" would make the software completely independent from changes on the sensor level. The column "Adaptation of the existing software to use new sensor" in the tables reflects this. Unfortunately, in a realistic product line this will not always be the case. Dependent on how well the designers did their work some percentage of changes for introducing new sensors will have an effect on the remaining software. For example, a new sensor provides new features the designers did not think of. This requires changing the interface of the virtual sensor layer, which may require a change in the software that uses this interface.

From this follows that there exists a dependency between the layer and the other software, which with some probability leads to additional costs for supporting a new sensor. For that reason, the realization of a variability extends beyond one module if there is a dependency of the responsibilities in the second module on the responsibilities in the first. In [3], we identified eight different types of dependencies that might cause propagation of a variability beyond a single responsibility.

The packaging of responsibilities into modules also affects the cost of both implementing and realizing a variability. We take it as an article of faith among designers that there will be side effects within a module when realizing a variability. A side effect is an impact on a responsibility within the module that is not directly involved in realizing the variability.

These then are the two measurement criteria we use when discussing the various architectural tactics for variability:

- the number of responsibilities affected by the exercise of a variability and
- the probability of side effects on responsibilities not involved in the variability itself.

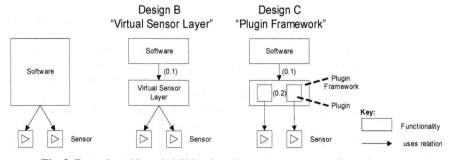

Fig. 2. Examples with probabilities that changes propagate to other software parts.

Back to our example. As with the cost models, we are really considering two different cases of a design: the case of realizing a variability when no provision has been made for its realization and the case of realizing the variability when provision has been made. In Figure 2 we added probabilities that a change in a location prepared for certain variability might propagate to places not prepared for this variability. Those probabilities are added along the uses relations, because this type of relation introduces dependencies between modules.

Design A is not affected because we did not do anything to support variability. In design B we assume that support for every 10th new sensor will affect not only affect the virtual sensor layer, but also will require adaptations in the other software. This leads to a probability of 0.1 between the layer and the software.

In design C we assume that there exist a 0.2 chance that adding a new plug-in will require adaptations of the plug-in framework, which then with a 0.1 chance will require an adaptation of the other software. This adds additional costs to those presented in Table 2 and Table 3. In design B we have to add:

(cost of changing the remaining software) * 0.1 * N, with N = 20

while for design C we have to add:

((cost for changing the plug-in framework * 0.2) +

(cost of changing the remaining software * 0.1 * 0.2)) * N, with N = 20

We view a system as a collection of responsibilities partitioned into modules. The extent of the realization of a variability depends on the number of modules affected by that realization and the modules which are dependent on the module being varied. Thus, as shown in Figure 3, we model a design for a system as a directed graph with the nodes being modules containing responsibilities with a "cost of change" property assigned, and the arcs being dependencies among the modules [11] with probabilities assigned. We then discuss our architectural tactics for variability as a means of transforming one directed graph into another. The measures of the effectiveness of the transformation are the two mentioned above: the extent of a variability realization in terms of modules affected by the realization and side effects within a module of realizing a variability.

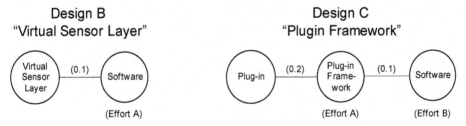

Fig. 3. Dependency graph of modules for design B and C.

Furthermore, we have two different cases that might be used when measuring the effectiveness of a transformation. A worst case analysis is the assumption that any variation will propagate to dependent modules depending upon the type of dependency. An expected case analysis introduces a probability of propagation to the type of dependency.

As we mentioned above, we have categorized the architectural tactics to support variability into "localize changes", "prevent the ripple effect", and "defer binding time". We have rationalized the "defer binding time" tactics in terms of a cost model based on the phases of realizing a variability. We now rationalize the "localize changes" and "prevent the ripple effect" tactics.

Localize Changes

The goal of the tactics in the Localize Changes category is to reduce the extent and the possibility of side effects when a variability is realized. Some tactics do this by collecting responsibilities that are related to each other in some fashion into a module. The intention behind these collections of responsibilities is that the cost of implementing a variation will likely be reduced if the responsibilities associated with that variation are together in a module and that module is distinct from other collections of responsibilities.

The two tactics that use this strategy are "Isolate the Expected Changes" and "Maintain Semantic Coherence". These are forms of improving cohesion.

Other tactics reduce the possibility of side effects by being more general in their approach. By being more general, different realizations will already be included in implementation and will both take less effort to realize a variation and will reduce the possibility of side effects from that realization. The two tactics that use this strategy are "Abstract Common Services" and "Raise the Abstraction Level".

Prevent the Ripple Effect

The goal of the tactics in the Prevent the Ripple Effect category is to keep realizations from affecting more than the modules that contain the responsibilities implementing the realization. Some do this by restricting the visibility of responsibilities. These tactics are Hide information, Maintain Existing Interfaces, Limit Communication Paths and Separate the Interface from the Implementation. All of these tactics are intended to keep reduce the set of dependencies that exist across modules, which in fact reduces the probability that a ripple effect occurs along the dependencies.

Other tactics are intended to break dependencies that do cross modules. These tactics include Use an Intermediary such as a name server, publish subscribe, or virtual machine. There is a different type of intermediary (with a different name) for different types of dependencies. Making the Data Self-identifying, for example, will break a dependency on the syntax of either the data or sequence of a protocol. A name server breaks a run time location dependency, and so on.

Tactics with Multiple Rationales

We have presented a rationale for each tactic in terms either of a cost model or a dependency model. The output of the dependency model (number of modules or responsibilities impacted by realization of a variability – possibly with an associated probability) is intended to provide input into a cost model. Some tactics, however, can be justified both in terms of the dependency model and directly from the cost model.

Consider a Use an Intermediary tactic such as publish/subscribe. This not only replaces the syntactic dependency between the publisher and the subscriber with syntactic dependencies of the publisher and the subscriber on an intermediary but also allows for the deferring of the binding time from architectural design time to either link time or run time (depending on the exact form of the intermediary). Thus, an analysis of the impact of this tactic would require both the dependency analysis to determine the extent of the variation and the cost analysis to determine the savings caused by deferring the binding time.

Summary

We have presented a rationalization for different tactics to implement and realize variability. Our rationales are summarized in Table 4. There are two major open issues: 1) the availability and utility of cost models based on other than experience and intuition, and 2) determining the types of dependencies among modules and the probabilities of propagation when realizing the variability.

Since variability is intimately concerned with reducing costs of realizations, the designer when choosing a tactic to achieve variability must consider the consequences of the choices. In some cases, the cost models themselves can be used to understand the consequences, in other cases, a dependency model provides the rationale, and in some cases, both models are relevant. Consideration of other factors such as performance and reliability will also enter into design choices but being able to understand the benefits of design choices with respect to variability provides the designer with an important tool.

Table 4. Tactics for achieving variability.

Tactics	Tactic definition	Rationale
Limit options	Limiting the set of possible modifications will reduce the scope of the variation	Reduce the cost of introducing the tactic for a variation
Isolate the expected changes	Separating the responsibilities that are *likely* to change from those that are *unlikely* to change separates an architecture into fixed and variant parts	Reduce number of modules dependent on a variation
Raise the abstraction level	Raising the abstraction level, and thus making a module more general, allows that module to calculate a broader range of functions based on input.	Reduces the probability that a change becomes visible outside the module boundary.
Limit options	Limiting the set of possible modifications will reduce the variations that need to be considered in the design and simplify constructing a system suitable for modification	Reduces the number of changes the architecture has to care about

Table 4. (Cont).

Tactics	Tactic definition	Rationale
Maintain semantic coherence	Grouping responsibilities that have similar semantic meaning increases probability that a particular change will be localized to those responsibilities	Reduce number of modules dependent on a variation
Abstract common services	Localize services that are used by a variety of consumers	Reduce responsibilities necessary in customer modules so that scope of a variation is reduced.
Hide information	Make as many responsibilities as possible invisible to external modules	Reduces dependencies by making fewer external modules dependent on a given module.
Maintain existing interfaces	Keep interfaces constant through the implementation of a variability	Reduces ripple effect since no syntactic change to an interface is allowed.
Separate the interface from the implementation	Realize the implementation of a module later in the development process than its specification	Reduces costs since defers binding until implementation.
Use an intermediary	Break a dependency chain by inserting a module whose responsibilities are to manage a particular type of dependency.	Reduces ripple effect of a change by breaking dependencies.
Limit communication paths	Restricting the modules with which a given module will communicate ensures that no dependency exists between the two modules.	Reduces scope of implementing a variation.

References

1. Bachmann, F., Bass, L., Klein, M. Illuminating the Fundamental Contributors to Software Architecture Quality, CMU/SEI-2002-TR-025.
2. Bachmann, F.; Bass, L.; Klein, M., Deriving Architectural Tactics: A Step Toward Methodical Architectural Design, CMU/SEI-2003-TR-004.
3. Bass, L, Clements, P, Kazman, R. Software Architecture in Practice, 2nd edition, Addison Wesley, 2003.
4. Bosch, J. Design & Use of Software Architectures, Addison Wesley, 2000.

5. Chastek, G., Donohoe, P., Kang, K., and Thiel, S. Product Line Analysis: A practical Introduction. CMU/SEI-2001-TR-001, June, 2001.
6. Dagstuhl workshop report on economics of product lines, 2003.
7. Dagstuhl workshop report on managing variability, 2003.
8. EDSER-5, Proceedings Economics-Driven Software Engineering Research (EDSER-5), International Conference on Software Engineering Workshop, 2003.
9. Jaring, M., and Bosch, J. Representing Variability in Software Product Lines: A Case Study, in Software Product Lines, Chastek (ed), 2002, Springer, LNCS 2379.
10. Paulish, D. Architecture-Centric Software Project Management, Addison-Wesley, 2002.
11. Stafford, J., Richardson, D. and Wolf, A. Chaining: A Software Architecture Dependence Analysis Technique Technical Report CU-CS-845-97, University of Colorado. 1997.
12. Weiss, D. Lai, C, Software Product Line Engineering: A Family-Based Software Development Process, Addison-Wesley, 2000.

Decision Model and Flexible Component Definition Based on XML Technology

Jason Xabier Mansell and David Sellier

European Software Institute, Parque Technológico #204
E-48170 Zamudio, Bizkaia, Spain
{Jason.Mansell,David.Sellier}@esi.es

Abstract. Currently the software development industries have to face strict time to market and quality requirements in order to be competitive. As a result, companies are forced to considerably improve their processes for developing applications faster while maintaining a high level of quality. This paper introduces the concept of XML flexible component which is used for implementing an automatic derivation process within a system family approach; as well as, a XML solution to formally define the decision model and open decisions

Introduction

Currently the software development industries have to face strict time to market and quality requirements in order to be competitive. As a result, companies are forced to considerably improve their processes for developing applications faster while maintaining a high level of quality. In this context, system families are considered one of the most adapted solutions for quickly tailoring applications according to market requirements, particularly, when system family engineering techniques are strengthened by an automatic derivation process.

Implementing the automation of the derivation process implies that the derivation process supports variability handling management with the concept of Flexible Components (FC). Basically, FC is a piece of program, which is capable of tailoring product assets according to defined requirements (open decisions). Although, applying FC as an automatic derivation process requires that open decisions be used by the derivation process which should be well-formatted and structured in order to allow the FC to easily interpret their value for deriving product assets.

This paper is structured in three parts. The first section explains the method to formally define open decisions within the Decision Model (DM). This section clarifies the different steps used to define the meta-model characteristics, the decision model and open decisions. The second section introduces the concept of FC. This part develops the FC concept by defining the structure of the FC as well as the notion of variability handling. The last section explains how XML technology has been used for mapping all artefacts of the system family engineering process in order to support the automation of the derivation process.

F. van der Linden (Ed.): PFE 2003, LNCS 3014, pp. 466–472, 2004.
© Springer-Verlag Berlin Heidelberg 2004

Decision Modelling

The variability modelling within the system family approach follows two analytic steps. The first analysis defines the structure and the elements making up the decision model. Whereas, the second part specifies the decision characteristics, which are the essential parts of the variability modelling.

Decision Model Analysis

The decision model is *the document defining the decisions that must be made to specify a member of a domain* [WEI 1999]. It is the first step to implement a new process in order to produce family members.

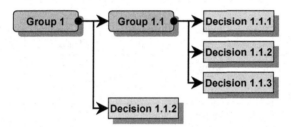

Fig. 1. Decision Information.

Within the decision model, decisions can be grouped as a set of decisions in order to organise the decisions within the decision model. An easy way to represent the decisions is to use the tree representation.

Each decision presented within the decision model is defined with a set containing the following information:

- A *name* identifying the decision with a unique identifier within the decision model
- A *description* giving the necessary information to support the decision making
- The *type* expressing the possible values supporting by the decision
- The *default value* indicating the value automatically affecting the decision if the decision is not taken explicitly
- The *validity* indicating the criteria to make or not to make the decision
- The *dependencies* which explicitly allow the specification of the relationships between different decisions

Decision Analysis

Basically, the decision analysis determines the type of decisions found within the decision model. The different decision types can be specified using an XML schema and can be treated using the XML Stylesheet document. There are two kinds of decisions: the *unrestricted decisions* and the *restricted decisions*. Most of the time, these types of decisions can be grouped into the same entity, since these are decisions that must be taken once. Although, there are some cases in which a decision must be made several times. This structure is called *collection* (or collection of decisions) and can be seen as a repetitive way for asking the same question or set of questions. Matrixes, tables, arrays are collections of decisions.

Unrestricted Decisions: The Unrestricted Decisions (see Decision01 and decision02 within the table) are decisions that do not support constraints other than their data type restrictions. The Unrestricted Decisions are decisions supporting the:

- String value
- Numeric value such as integer, float, unsigned integer...
- Other type of value such as time, date and so on

Restricted Decisions: The Restricted Decisions are decisions, which have other restriction specifications making their specification and their implementation within the XML documents more complex. The following table gives some example of Restricted Decisions.

Decision Name	Desc	Type	Restriction	Default Value	Validity	Dependencies
Decision01: Machine Acronym	...	String	None	Mac	...	...
Decision02: Number of Machines	...	Integer	None	10	...	...
Decision03: Machine Initial Speed	...	Integer	[0..200]	100	...	...
Decision04: Speed Number	...	Unsigned long	{1	2}	1	...	...
Decision05: Selected Machine	...	String	{Machine 1 ; Machine 2 ; Machine 3 }	Machine1; Machine2	...	...
Decision06: Selected Jog	...	String	{Jog 1	Jog 2	Jog 3 }	Jog 1	...	...

The restriction types are:

- Minimum value and Maximum value specification (Decision03)
- List of value specification, which can accept a single choice (Decision04 and Decision06)
- Or support multi-choice (Decision05)

Collection of Decisions: Collections of decisions are the repetition of a decision (Unrestricted or restricted decision) or a set of decisions. The number of instances can be specified as a collection restriction. The following table shows an example of a collection of decisions.

Decision Name	Desc	Type	Restriction	Default Value	Validity	Dependencies
Collection01: Machine List	...	-	Min occurrence = 1 Max occurrence = 10			
Decision01: Machine Name	...	String	None	Machine 1	...	...
Decision02: Engine Break	...	String	{yes | no}	Yes	...	...
Decision03: Jog Number	...	Unsigned long	[1..10]	1	...	...

The collection characteristics are: a name, a description, and some restrictions concerning the minimum and the maximum number of instances that can support the collection. The collections do not have a default value and have a range specification because collections are not decisions to make, but an entity grouping set of decisions which can be made several times.

Meta-model of the Decision Model

From the analysis of the DM and the decisions, a meta-model can be defined. The DM Meta-model is represented in UML and explains elements that form a DM, the overall relationships between the different elements, and restrictions that apply to a decision.

Flexible Component and Variability Handling

A FC is a special kind of component that is able to modify its behaviour based on a set of predetermined parameterisation parameters. The FC appears to be a necessity in order to reduce the number of reusable components that a programmer should know in order to develop a new application [FER 2000]. So, instead of having to know about 10000 components, the programmer will only have to know about 20 components.

- A FC is the representation of a set of components that support a certain degree of evolution, and that are usable several times (both within the same domain and among different domains).
- A FC may be adapted to different contexts.

Mainly, FC implements application functionalities that depend on the variability-commonality within the domain. The core of the FC implements both the common and variable portion of the domain.

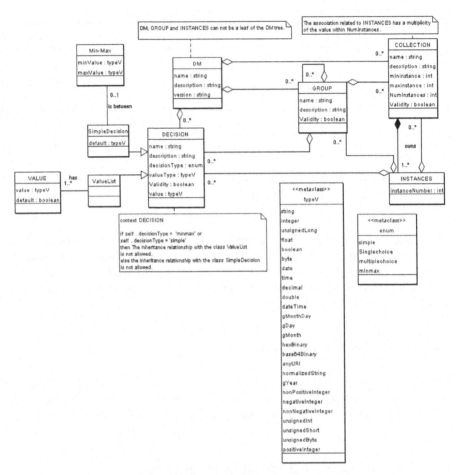

Fig. 2. Meta-Model to Specify a Decision Model.

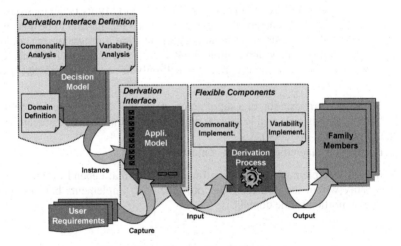

Fig. 3. FC and System Family Engineering.

The variability within FC consists of a set of variation points in which values determine the tailoring required to form parameterisation/instantiation. These are the characteristics that a FC should have:

- A FC must be flexible and adaptable to different specific contexts
- Derivation interface, which is the way the FC offers to be instantiated in one of the multiple instances it was built for.
- The body is in charge to manage the commonality and the variability of the product assets. The variable portion mainly consists of the implementation of the variation points of the system within the common portion of the specification of the asset. Variation points represent the tailoring implementation of the asset according to the value specified within the derivation interface.

The variability points are part of the assets that should be modified according to the open decision values. Basically there are three types of variation points:

- *Hiding or Showing Information:* a part of the asset should be hidden or shown according to decision values. These kinds of variation points are managed using the if-statement instruction.
- *Data Insertion:* Some data from the Application Model should be included directly within the asset. These kinds of variation points are managed using the instructions for getting information from the Application Model.
- *Cycles:* A part of the Application Model data should be treated with a repetitive method applying a treatment to some identical decisions with a repetitive method, can be made using loop statements such as while-statement or for-statement.

System Family Engineering and XML Technology

The whole approach implies that the open decision specification can be defined using formal languages to allow the FC to interpret the input (open decisions) in order to tailor the product assets. As the open decision specification, the variation point implementation also requires its own language.

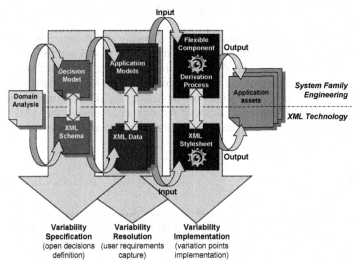

Fig. 4. System Family Approach and XML Technology.

The choice of XML technology is based on a reasoned analysis:

- On the one hand, XML allows the definition of all the existing types of decisions which allows structuring decisions in a decision model and provides the programmatic functionality to implement dependency.
- On the other hand, the variation points associated to each decision can be implemented in the derivation process using the XML Stylesheet notation. This provides a powerful mechanism to automate the generation/instantiation of a product from the user requirements (open decisions).

The whole system family process can be specified, represented, and implemented with the three XML technology elements. The mapping of the different artefacts between both technologies will be made using:

- The XML Schema to specify and define the decision model
- The XML Data to represent the application model and to bind the open decision required for the instantiation of the product assets
- The XML Stylesheet to implement the derivation process

Conclusion

System family engineering is one of the most efficient solutions for developing faster new applications according to market requirements. System family approach is becoming much more useful when the derivation is implemented in such a way that it supports the automatic generation of the product assets.

One of the solutions for implementing the automation of the derivation is introduced with the concept of FC. FC is a structured piece of code capable of tailoring the product assets according to the open decisions. Basically, the core of the FC consists of the variation point handling within the common portion of the product asset. The open decisions are specified and captured using the interface of derivation of the FC. By automating the derivation of the system family obliges it to define the open decisions in such way that the FC will easily interpret these inputs and will adapt the product asset as a result.

This approach requires a formal language allowing at the same time: the specification of the open decisions within a structured decision model and the implementation of FC with the implementation of the variation point. The XML technology presents significant advantages used in the mapping of the system family artefacts. First, XML schema document offers possibilities for modelling the decision model. Second, the XML Data is used for capturing the user requirements. Finally the XML Stylesheet document completely supports the implementation of the architecture of FC.

References

[WEI 1999]   David M. Weiss, Chi Tau Robert Lai. "Software Product Line Engineering, A Family-Based Software Development Process", Addison-Wesley, 1999.

[FER 2000]   Pablo Ferrer, Jason Xabier Mansell, "Techniques to build flexible components", ESI, May 2001, www.esi.es.

A Product Derivation Framework
for Software Product Families

Sybren Deelstra, Marco Sinnema, and Jan Bosch

Department of Mathematics and Computer Science, University of Groningen
PO Box 800, 9700 AV Groningen, The Netherlands
{s.deelstra,m.sinnema,j.bosch}@cs.rug.nl
http://www.rug.nl/informatica/search

Abstract. From our experience with several organizations that employ software product families, we have learned that deriving individual products from shared software artifacts is a time-consuming and expensive activity. In the research community, product derivation methodologies are rather scarce, however. By studying product derivation, we believe we will be better able to provide and validate industrially practicable solutions for application engineering. In this paper, we present a framework of terminology and concepts regarding product derivation that serves as basis for further discussion. We exemplify this framework with two industrial case studies, i.e. Thales Nederland B.V. and Robert Bosch GmbH.

1 Introduction

Since the 1960s, reuse has been the long-standing notion to solve the cost, quality and time-to-market issues associated with development of software applications. A major addition to existing reuse approaches since the 1990s are software product families [Bosch 2000][Clements 2001][Weiss 1999]. The basic reuse philosophy of software product families is intra-organizational reuse through the explicitly planned exploitation of similarities between related products. This philosophy has been adopted by a wide variety of organizations and has proved to substantially decrease costs and time-to-market, and increase the quality of their software products.

In a software product family context, software products are developed in a two-stage process [Linden 2002], i.e. a domain engineering stage and a concurrently running application engineering stage. Domain engineering involves, amongst others, identifying commonalities and differences between product family members and implementing a set of shared software artifacts in such a way that the commonalities can be exploited economically, while at the same time the ability to vary the products is preserved. During application engineering individual products are derived from the product family, viz. constructed using a subset of the shared software artifacts.

Over the past few years, domain engineering has received substantial attention from the software engineering community. Most of those research efforts are focused on methodological support for designing and implementing shared software artifacts in such a way that application engineers should be able to derive applications more easily. Most of the approaches, however, fail to provide substantial supportive evidence. The result is a lack of methodological support for application engineering and, consequently, organizations fail to exploit the full benefits of software product families.

F. van der Linden (Ed.): PFE 2003, LNCS 3014, pp. 473–484, 2004.
© Springer-Verlag Berlin Heidelberg 2004

Rather than adopting the same top-down approach, where solutions that are focused on methodological support for domain engineering imply benefits during application engineering, we adopt a bottom-up approach in our research. By studying product derivation, we believe we will be better able to provide and validate industrially practicable solutions for application engineering.

The main contribution of this paper is that we provide a framework of concepts regarding product derivation that serves as basis for further discussion. This framework is based on our experience with organizations that employ software product families. The framework is exemplified with two industrial case studies, i.e. Robert Bosch GmbH and Thales Nederland B.V. The case study was part of the first phase of ConIPF (Configuration of Industrial Product Families), a research project sponsored by the IST-programme [ConIPF 2003]. Robert Bosch GmbH and Thales Nederland B.V. are industrial partners in this project. Both companies are large and mature industrial organizations that mark two ends of a spectrum of product derivation; Robert Bosch produces thousands of medium-sized products per year, while Thales Nederland produces a small number of very large products.

The remainder of this article is organized as follows. In the next section, we describe our product derivation framework. In section 3, we exemplify the framework with the industrial case studies. Related work is presented in section 4, and the paper is concluded in section 5.

2   Product Derivation Framework

In this section, we present a product derivation framework that is based on the results of case studies of the aforementioned and other organizations. This framework consists of a two-dimensional classification for product families, as well as a generic software derivation process. We discuss both in the next two subsections.

2.1   Product Family Classification

As illustrated in the introduction, product families are a successful form of intra-organizational reuse that is based on exploiting common characteristics of related products. Most of the product families we encountered in practice can be classified according to two dimensions of scope, i.e. scope of reuse and domain scope.

The first dimension, *scope of reuse*, denotes to which extent the commonalities between related products are exploited. We identify four levels of scope of reuse, ranging from reusing the way products are built (standardized infrastructure), to capturing most common functionality (platform), to exploiting both common functionality and functionality that is shared by a sufficiently large subset of family members (software product line), to capturing almost all common and different characteristics of the product family members (configurable product family).

In addition to the scope of reuse dimension, we identify a second dimension, *domain scope*. The domain scope denotes the extent of the domain or domains in which the product family is applied, and consists of four levels of scope, i.e. single product family, programme of product families, hierarchical product families [Bosch 2000] and product population [Ommering 2002]. Due to limited space, we leave a detailed discussion on both classification dimensions beyond the scope of this paper. In the following sections, we focus on product derivation in a single product family, i.e. the scope where a single product family is used to derive several related products.

2.2   A Generic Product Derivation Process

We have generalized the derivation processes we encountered in single product families to a generic process as illustrated in Figure 1. The generic product derivation process consists of two phases, i.e. the initial and the iteration phase. In the initial phase, a first configuration is created from the product family assets. In the iteration phase, the initial configuration is modified in a number of subsequent iterations until the product sufficiently implements the imposed requirements.

In addition to the phased selection activities described above, typically some code development is required during product derivation. This adaptation aspect can occur in both the iteration phase and the initial phase. Below, we provide a more detailed description of both phases, as well as a separate description of the adaptation aspect.

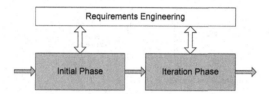

Fig. 1. The generic product derivation process. *The shaded boxes denote the two phases. Requirements engineering manages the requirements throughout the entire process of product derivation.*

2.2.1 Initial Phase
The input to the initial phase is a (sub)set of the requirements that are managed throughout the entire process of product derivation (see Figure 1). These requirements originate from, among others, the customers, legislation, the hardware and the product family organization. In the initial phase, two different approaches towards deriving the initial product configuration exist, i.e. assembly and configuration selection (see also Figure 2). Both approaches conclude with the initial validation step.

Assembly: The first approach to initial derivation involves the assembly of a subset of the shared product family assets to the initial software product configuration. We identify three types of assembly approaches.

- In the *construction* approach the initial configuration is constructed from the product family architecture and shared components. The first step in the construction process, as far as necessary or allowed, is to derive the product architecture from the product family architecture. The next step is, for each architectural component, to select the closest matching component implementation from the component base. Finally, the parameters for each component are set.

- In case of *generation*, shared artifacts are modeled in a modeling language rather then implemented in source code. From these modeled artifacts, a subset is selected to construct an overall model. From this overall model an initial implementation is generated.
- The *composition* type is a composite of the types described above, where the initial configuration consists of both generated and implemented components, as well as components that are partially generated from the model and extended with source code. This type is not represented in Figure 2.

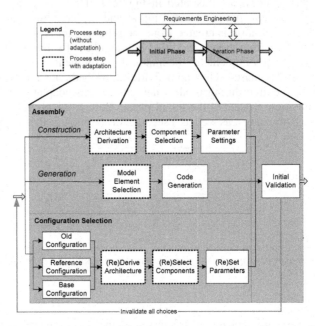

Fig. 2. The initial phase. *During the initial phase, products are derived by assembly or configuration selection.*

Configuration Selection: The second approach to initial derivation involves selecting a closest matching existing configuration. An existing configuration is a consistent set of components, viz. an arrangement of components that, provided with the right options and settings, are able to function together.

- An *old configuration* is a complete product implementation that is the result from a previous project. Often, the selected old configuration is the product developed during the latest project as it contains the most recent bug-fixes and functionality.
- A *reference configuration* is (a subset of) an old configuration that is explicitly designated as basis for the development of new products. A reference configuration may be a partial configuration, for example if almost all product specific parameter settings are excluded, or a complete configuration, i.e. the old configuration including all parameter settings.
- A *base configuration* is a partial configuration that forms the core of a certain group of products. A base configuration is not necessarily a result from a previous product. In general, a base configuration is not an executable application as many

options and settings on all levels of abstraction (e.g. architecture or component level) are left open. In contrast to a reference and old configuration, where the focus during product derivation is on reselecting components, the focus of product derivation with a base configuration is on adding components to the set of components in the base configuration.

The selected configurations are subsequently modified by rederiving the product architecture, adding, re- and deselecting components and (re)setting parameters.

The effectiveness of configuration selection in comparison to assembly is a function of the benefits in terms of effort saved in selection and testing, and the costs in terms of effort required for changing invalidated choices as a result of new requirements. Configuration selection is especially viable in case a large system is developed for repeat customers, i.e. customers who have purchased a similar type of system before. Typically, repeat customers desire new functionality on top of the functionality they ordered for a previous product. In that respect, configuration selection is basically reuse of choices.

Initial Validation: The initial validation step is the first step that is concerned with determining to what extent the initial configuration adheres to the requirements. In the rare case that the initially assembled or selected configuration does not provide a sufficient basis for further development, all choices are invalidated and the process goes back to start all over again. In case the initial configuration sufficiently adheres to the requirements, the product is finished. Otherwise, the product derivation process enters the iteration phase.

2.2.2 Iteration Phase

The initial validation step marks the entrance of the iteration phase (illustrated in Figure 3). In some cases, an initial configuration sufficiently implements the desired product. In most cases, however, one or more cycles through the iteration phase are required, for a number of reasons.

First, the requirements set may change or expand during product derivation, for example, if the organization uses a subset of the collected requirements to derive the initial configuration, or if the customer has new wishes for the product. Second, the configuration may not completely provide the required functionality, or some of the selected components simply do not work together at all. This particularly applies to embedded systems, where the initial configuration is often a first 'guess'. This is mainly because the exact physics of the controlled mechanics is not always fully known at the start of the project, and because the software performs differently on different hardware, e.g. due to production tolerances and approximated polynomial relationships. Finally, the product family assets used to derive the configuration may have changed during product derivation, for example, due to bug fixes.

During the iteration phase, the product configuration is therefore modified and validated until the product is deemed ready.

Modification: A configuration can be modified on three levels of abstraction, i.e. architecture, component and parameter level. Modification is accomplished by selecting different architectural component variants, selecting different component implementation variants or changing the parameter settings, respectively.

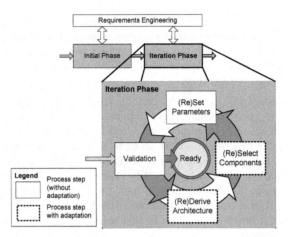

Fig. 3. The iteration phase. *The product configuration is modified in a number of iterations, until the product is deemed ready by the validation step.*

Validation: The validation step in this phase concerns validating the system with respect to adherence to requirements and checking the consistency and correctness of the component configuration.

2.2.3 Adaptation

Requirements that are not accounted for in the shared product family artifacts can only be accommodated by adaptation (denoted by the dashed boxes in Figure 2 and Figure 3). Adaptation involves adapting the product (family) architecture and adapting or creating component implementations. We identify three levels of artifact adaptation, i.e. product specific adaptation, reactive evolution and proactive evolution.

Product Specific Adaptation: The first level of evolution is where, during product derivation, new functionality is implemented in product specific artifacts (e.g. product architecture and product specific component implementations). To this purpose, application engineers can use the shared artifacts as basis for further development, or develop new artifacts from scratch. As functionality implemented through product specific adaptation is not incorporated in the shared artifacts, it cannot be reused in subsequent products unless an old configuration is selected for those products.

Reactive Evolution: Reactive evolution involves adapting shared artifacts in such a way that they are able to handle the requirements that emerge during product derivation, and can also be shared with other product family members. As reactively evolving shared artifacts has consequences with respect to the other family members, those effects have to be analyzed prior to making any changes.

Proactive Evolution: The third level, proactive evolution, is actually not a product derivation activity, but a domain engineering activity. It involves adapting the shared artifacts in such a way that the product family is capable of accommodating the needs of the various family members in the future as opposed to evolution as a reaction to requirements that emerge during product derivation. Proactive evolution requires both analysis of the effects with respect to current product family members, as well as analysis of the predicted future of the domain and the product family scope. Domain and scope prediction is accomplished in combination with technology roadmapping [Kostoff 2001].

Independent of the level of evolution, the scope of adjustment required on architecture or component level varies in four different ways.

Add Variation Points: A new variation point has to be constructed if functionality needs to be implemented as variant or optional behavior, and no suitable variation point is available. To this purpose, an interface has to be defined between the variable behavior and the rest of the system. Furthermore, an appropriate mechanism and associated binding time have to be selected and the mechanisms and variant functionality have to be implemented. In addition, in the situation where existing stable functionality is involved, the functionality has to be clearly separated from the rest of the system and re-implemented as a variant that adheres to the variation point interface. In case the binding time is in the post-deployment stage, software for managing the variants and binding needs to be constructed.

Change the Realization of Existing Variation Points: Adjustment to a variation point may be required for a number of reasons. Changes to a variation point interface, for example, may be required to access additional variable behavior. Furthermore, mechanism changes may be required to move the point at which the variant set is closed to a later stage, while a change to the binding time may be required to increase flexibility or decrease resource consumption. In addition, variation point dependencies and constraints may need to be alleviated. In any case, changes to a variation point may affect all existing variants of the variant set in the sense that they have to be changed accordingly in order to be accessible.

Add or Change Variant: When the functionality fits within the existing set of variation points, it means that the functionality at a point of variation can be incorporated by adding a variant to the variant set. This can be achieved by extending or changing an existing variant, or developing a new variant from scratch. These new or changed variants have to adhere to the variation point interface, as well as existing dependencies and constraints.

Remove a Variant or Variation Point: A typical trend in software systems is that functionality specific to some products becomes part of the core functionality of all product family members, e.g. due to market dominance, or that functionality becomes obsolete. The need to support different alternatives, and therefore variation points and variants for this functionality, may disappear. As a response, all but one variant can be removed from the asset base, or the variation point can be removed entirely. If in the latter case one variant is still needed, it has to be re-implemented as stable behavior.

3   Case Description

In the previous section, we have established a framework of concepts regarding product derivation. In this section, we present the case studies we performed at Thales

Nederland B.V. and Robert Bosch GmbH. The business units we interviewed for this case study apply a single product family domain scope to derive their software products. We present a brief description of the companies and their product families, in which we show how the derivation processes instantiate the generic process discussed in section 2.

3.1 Thales Naval Netherlands

Thales Nederland B.V., the Netherlands, is a subsidiary of Thales S.A. in France and mainly develops Ground Based and Naval Systems in the defense area. Thales Naval Netherlands (TNNL), the Dutch division of the business group Naval, is organized in four Business Units, i.e. Radars & Sensors, Combat Systems, Integration & Logistic Support, and Operations. Our case study focused on software parts of the TACTICOS naval combat systems family produced by the Business Unit Combat Systems, more specifically, the Combat Management Systems.

A Combat Management System (CMS) is the prime subsystem of a TACTICOS (TACTical Information and COmmand System) Naval Combat System. Its main purpose is to integrate all weapons and sensors on naval vessels that range from fast patrol boats to frigates. The Combat Management System provides Command and Control and Combat Execution capabilities in the real world, as well as training in simulated worlds.

The asset base used to derive combat management systems is also referred to as the infrastructure. It contains both in-house developed and COTS (Commercial-Off-The Shelf) components, and captures functionality common to all combat management systems. The Tacticos product family is therefore classified as a family with a platform as the scope of reuse.

Derivation Process at Business Unit Combat Systems

Initial Phase. Combat Systems uses configuration selection to derive the initial product configurations. To this purpose, the collected requirements are mapped onto an old configuration, whose characteristics best resemble the requirements at hand. When in subsequent steps all components and parameters are selected, adapted and set, the system is packaged and installed in a complete environment for the initial validation. If the configuration does not pass the initial validation, the derivation process enters the iteration phase.

Iteration Phase. The initial configuration is modified in a number of iterations by re- and de-selecting components, adapting components and changing existing parameter settings, until the product sufficiently adheres to the requirements.

Adaptation. Combat Systems applies both reactive evolution and product specific changes when components need to be adapted (see section 2.2.3). Components are also adapted through proactive evolution during domain engineering. Whether requirements are handled by reactive evolution or product specific adaptation, is determined by several Change Control Boards, i.e. groups of experts (such as architects) that synchronize change requests within and between different projects.

3.2 Robert Bosch GmbH

Robert Bosch GmbH, Germany, was founded in 1886 in Stuttgart. Currently, it is a worldwide operating company that is active in the Automotive, Industrial, Consumer Electronics and Building Technology areas. Our case study focused on two business units, which for reasons of confidentiality, we refer to as business unit A and B, respectively. The systems produced by both business units consist of both hardware, i.e. the sensors and actuators, and software.

The product family assets of business unit A capture both common and variable functionality. Family A is therefore classified as a family with a software product line as scope of reuse. The product family assets of business unit B provide functionality that is common to many products in the family. Therefore, product family B is classified as a product family with a platform as scope of reuse.

Derivation Process at Business Unit A

Initial Phase. Starting from requirements engineering, business unit A uses two approaches in deriving an initial configuration of the product: one for lead products and one for secondary products. For lead products, the initial configuration is constructed using the assembly approach. For secondary products, i.e. in the case a similar product has been built before, reference configurations are used to derive an initial configuration. Where necessary, components from the reference configuration are replaced with ones that are more appropriate.

Iteration Phase. In the iteration phase, the initial configuration is modified in a number of iterations by reselecting components, adapting components, or changing parameters.

Adaptation. If the inconsistencies or new requirements cannot be solved by selecting a different component implementation, a new component implementation is developed through reactive evolution, by copying and adapting an existing implementation, or developing one from scratch.

Derivation Process at Business Unit B

Initial Phase. Each time a product needs to be derived from the platform of business unit B, a project team is formed. This project team derives the product by assembly. It copies the latest version of the platform and selects the appropriate components from this copy. Finally, all parameters of the components are set to their initial values.

Iteration Phase. When the set of requirements changes, or when inconsistencies arise during the validation process, components and parameters are reselected and changed until the product is deemed finished.

Adaptation. When during the initial and iteration phase the requirements for a product configuration cannot be handled by the existing product family assets, copies of the selected components are adapted by product specific adaptation.

4   Related Work

After being introduced in [Parnas 1976], the notion of software product families have received substantial attention in the research community since the 1990s. The adoption of product families has resulted in a number books, amongst others [Bosch 2000] [Clements 2001] [Jacobson 1997] [Weiss 1999], workshops (PFE 1-4), conferences (SPLC 1 and 2), and several large European projects (ARES, PRAISE, ESAPS and CAFÉ).

Several articles that were published through these channels are related to this paper. The notion of a variation point was introduced in [Jacobson 1997]. The notion of variability is further discussed in, amongst others, [Gurp 2001] and [Bachmann 2001]. [Geyer 2002] and [Salicki 2001] present the influence of expressing variability on the product derivation process. They assume a more naïve unidirectional process flow, however, rather then a phased process model with iterations for reevaluating the choice for variants. Well-known process models that resemble the ideas of the phased product derivation model are the Rational Unified Process [Kruchten 2000] and Boehm's spiral model [Boehm 1988].

The 2-dimensional maturity classification of product families briefly discussed in this paper is an extension and refinement of the 1-dimensional maturity classification presented in [Bosch 2002].

5   Conclusions

Software product families have received wide adoption in industry. Most product families we encountered can be classified according to two dimensions of scope, i.e. scope of reuse and domain scope. In this paper, we focused on the scope of reuse dimension in a single product family domain scope, i.e. the dimension that denotes to which extent commonalities between related products are exploited in a single product family. The levels of scope in this dimension are standardized infrastructure, platform, software product line, and configurable product family.

The work presented in this paper is motivated by the impression that despite the substantial attention in the software product family research community to designing reusable software assets, deriving individual products from shared software assets is a rather time-consuming and expensive for a large number of organizations. In this paper, we have presented a product derivation framework as basis for further discussion. This framework consists of the product family classification mentioned above and a software derivation process that we generalized from practice.

The generic derivation process consists of two main phases, i.e. the initial and the iteration phase. In the initial phase, a first configuration is created from the product family assets by assembling a subset of shared artifact or by selecting a closest matching existing configuration. The initial configuration is then validated to determine to what extent the configuration adheres to the requirements imposed by, amongst others, the customer and organization. If the configuration is not deemed finished, the derivation process enters the iteration phase. In the iteration phase, the initial configuration is modified in a number of subsequent iterations until the product sufficiently implements the imposed requirements.

Requirements not accounted for in the shared artifacts are handled by adapting those artifacts. We have identified three levels of adaptation, i.e. *product specific adaptation, reactive evolution,* and *proactive evolution.* Proactive evolution is actually not a product derivation activity, but a domain engineering activity that we added for completeness sake.

The main distinct characteristics of the product families from our case study are summarized in the table below. As shown, the derivation processes at both organizations represent a subset of the generic process we discussed above.

Table 1. The main characteristics of the product families at the business unit Combat Systems at Thales Netherlands B.V., and two business units of Robert Bosch GmbH (A and B).

Product Family	Scope of reuse	Initial derivation phase	Adaptation
Combat Systems	Platform	Old configuration	Reactive & product specific
Bosch A	Product line	Reference configuration & assembly	Reactive
Bosch B	Platform	Assembly	Product specific

In [Deelstra 2003], we discuss several challenges that the industrial partners of the ConIPF project face during product derivation in terms of the framework presented in this paper. Future work of the ConIPF project aims to define and validate methodologies that are practicable in industrial application and that address those product derivation problems.

Acknowledgements

This research has been sponsored by ConIPF (Configuration in Industrial Product Families), under contract no. IST-2001-34438. We would like to thank the business unit Combat Systems at Thales Nederland B.V., as well as two business units at Robert Bosch GmbH, for their valuable input. In particular, we would like to thank Paul Burghardt (Thales), as well as John MacGregor and Andreas Hein (Bosch).

References

[Bachman 2001] F. Bachmann, L. Bass, Managing Variability in Software Architecture, In Proceedings of the ACM SIGSOFT Symposium on Software Reusability (SSR'01), pp. 126–132, 2001.
[Boehm 1988] B. W. Boehm, 1988. A spiral model of software development and enhancement, IEEE Computer, Vol. 21, No. 5, pp. 61–72, 1998.
[Bosch 2000] J. Bosch, Design and Use of Software Architectures: Adopting and Evolving a Product Line Approach, Pearson Education (Addison-Wesley & ACM Press), ISBN 0-201-67494-7, 2000.
[Bosch 2002] J. Bosch, Maturity and Evolution in Software Product Lines; Approaches, Artefacts and Organization, Proceedings of the Second Software Product Line Conference, pp. 257-271, 2002.

[Clements 2001] P. Clements, L. Northrop, Software Product Lines: Practices and Patterns. SEI Series in Software Engineering. Addison-Wesley, ISBN: 0-201-70332-7, 2001.

Addison-Wesley, ISBN: 0-201-70332-7.

[ConIPF 2003] The ConIPF project (Configuration of Industrial Product Families), http://www.rug.nl/informatica/onderzoek/programmas/softwareengineering/conipf

[Deelstra 2003] S. Deelstra, M. Sinnema, J. Bosch, Experiences in Software Product Families: Problems and Issues during Product Derivation, submitted for publication, 2003.

[Jacobson 1997] I. Jacobson, M. Griss, P. Jonsson, Software Reuse. Architecture, Process and Organization for Business Success. Addison-Wesley, ISBN: 0-201-92476-5, 1997.

[Geyer 2002] L. Geyer, M. Becker, On the Influence of Variabilities on the Application Engineering Process of a Product Family, Proceedings of the Second Software Product Line Conference, pp. 1–14, 2002.

[Gurp 2001] J. van Gurp, J. Bosch, M. Svahnberg, On the notion of Variability in Software Product Lines, Proceedings of The Working IEEE/IFIP Conference on Software Architecture, pp. 45-55, 2001.

[Kostoff 2001] R. N. Kostoff, R. R. Schaller, Science and Technology Roadmaps, IEEE Transactions on Engineering Management, Vol. 48, no. 2, pp. 132-143, 2001.

[Kruchten 2000] P. Kruchten. The Rational Unified Process: An Introduction (2nd Edition), ISBN 0-201-707101, 2000.

[Linden 2002] F. v.d. Linden. Software Product Families in Europe: The Esaps & Café Projects, IEEE Software, Vol. 19, No. 4, pp. 41-49, 2002.

[Macala 1996] R. Macala, L. Stuckey, D. Gross. Managing Domain-Specific, Product-Line Development. IEEE Software, pages 57–67, 1996.

[Ommering 2002] R. van Ommering, Building Product Populations with Software Components, Proceedings of the International Conference on Software Engineering 2002, 2002.

[Parnas 1976] D. Parnas, On the Design and Development of Program Families, IEEE Transactions on Software Engineering, SE-2(1):1–9, 1976.

[Salicki 2001] S. Salicki, N. Farcet, Expression and Usage of the Variability in the Software Product Lines, Proceedings of the Fourth International Workshop on Product Family Engineering (PFE-4), pp. 287–297, 2001.

[Svahnberg 1999] M. Svahnberg, J. Bosch, Evolution in Software Product Lines, Journal of Software Maintenance – Research and Practice, Vol. 11, No. 6, pp. 391-422, 1999.

[Weiss 1999] D. M. Weiss, C.T.R. Lai, Software Product-Line Engineering: A Family Based Software Development Process, Addison - Wesley, ISBN 0-201-694387, 1999.

Author Index

Lecture Notes in Computer Science

For information about Vols. 1–2956

please contact your bookseller or Springer-Verlag

Vol. 3008: S. Heuel, Uncertain Projective Geometry. XVII, 205 pages. 2004.

Vol. 3007: J.X. Yu, X. Lin, H. Lu, Y. Zhang (Eds.), Advanced Web Technologies and Applications. XXII, 936 pages. 2004.

Vol. 3006: M. Matsui, R. Zuccherato (Eds.), Selected Areas in Cryptography. XI, 361 pages. 2004.

Vol. 3005: G.R. Raidl, S. Cagnoni, J. Branke, D.W. Corne, R. Drechsler, Y. Jin, C.G. Johnson, P. Machado, E. Marchiori, F. Rothlauf, G.D. Smith, G. Squillero (Eds.), Applications of Evolutionary Computing. XVII, 562 pages. 2004.

Vol. 3004: J. Gottlieb, G.R. Raidl (Eds.), Evolutionary Computation in Combinatorial Optimization. X, 241 pages. 2004.

Vol. 3003: M. Keijzer, U.-M. O'Reilly, S.M. Lucas, E. Costa, T. Soule (Eds.), Genetic Programming. XI, 410 pages. 2004.

Vol. 3002: D.L. Hicks (Ed.), Metainformatics. X, 213 pages. 2004.

Vol. 3001: A. Ferscha, F. Mattern (Eds.), Pervasive Computing. XVII, 358 pages. 2004.

Vol. 2999: E.A. Boiten, J. Derrick, G. Smith (Eds.), Integrated Formal Methods. XI, 541 pages. 2004.

Vol. 2998: Y. Kameyama, P.J. Stuckey (Eds.), Functional and Logic Programming. X, 307 pages. 2004.

Vol. 2997: S. McDonald, J. Tait (Eds.), Advances in Information Retrieval. XIII, 427 pages. 2004.

Vol. 2996: V. Diekert, M. Habib (Eds.), STACS 2004. XVI, 658 pages. 2004.

Vol. 2995: C. Jensen, S. Poslad, T. Dimitrakos (Eds.), Trust Management. XIII, 377 pages. 2004.

Vol. 2994: E. Rahm (Ed.), Data Integration in the Life Sciences. X, 221 pages. 2004. (Subseries LNBI).

Vol. 2993: R. Alur, G.J. Pappas (Eds.), Hybrid Systems: Computation and Control. XII, 674 pages. 2004.

Vol. 2992: E. Bertino, S. Christodoulakis, D. Plexousakis, V. Christophides, M. Koubarakis, K. Böhm, E. Ferrari (Eds.), Advances in Database Technology - EDBT 2004. XVIII, 877 pages. 2004.

Vol. 2991: R. Alt, A. Frommer, R.B. Kearfott, W. Luther (Eds.), Numerical Software with Result Verification. X, 315 pages. 2004.

Vol. 2989: S. Graf, L. Mounier (Eds.), Model Checking Software. X, 309 pages. 2004.

Vol. 2988: K. Jensen, A. Podelski (Eds.), Tools and Algorithms for the Construction and Analysis of Systems. XIV, 608 pages. 2004.

Vol. 2987: I. Walukiewicz (Ed.), Foundations of Software Science and Computation Structures. XIII, 529 pages. 2004.

Vol. 2986: D. Schmidt (Ed.), Programming Languages and Systems. XII, 417 pages. 2004.

Vol. 2985: E. Duesterwald (Ed.), Compiler Construction. X, 313 pages. 2004.

Vol. 2984: M. Wermelinger, T. Margaria-Steffen (Eds.), Fundamental Approaches to Software Engineering. XII, 389 pages. 2004.

Vol. 2983: S. Istrail, M.S. Waterman, A. Clark (Eds.), Computational Methods for SNPs and Haplotype Inference. IX, 153 pages. 2004. (Subseries LNBI).

Vol. 2982: N. Wakamiya, M. Solarski, J. Sterbenz (Eds.), Active Networks. XI, 308 pages. 2004.

Vol. 2981: C. Müller-Schloer, T. Ungerer, B. Bauer (Eds.), Organic and Pervasive Computing – ARCS 2004. XI, 339 pages. 2004.

Vol. 2980: A. Blackwell, K. Marriott, A. Shimojima (Eds.), Diagrammatic Representation and Inference. XV, 448 pages. 2004. (Subseries LNAI).

Vol. 2979: I. Stoica, Stateless Core: A Scalable Approach for Quality of Service in the Internet. XVI, 219 pages. 2004.

Vol. 2978: R. Groz, R.M. Hierons (Eds.), Testing of Communicating Systems. XII, 225 pages. 2004.

Vol. 2977: G. Di Marzo Serugendo, A. Karageorgos, O.F. Rana, F. Zambonelli (Eds.), Engineering Self-Organising Systems. X, 299 pages. 2004. (Subseries LNAI).

Vol. 2976: M. Farach-Colton (Ed.), LATIN 2004: Theoretical Informatics. XV, 626 pages. 2004.

Vol. 2973: Y. Lee, J. Li, K.-Y. Whang, D. Lee (Eds.), Database Systems for Advanced Applications. XXIV, 925 pages. 2004.

Vol. 2972: R. Monroy, G. Arroyo-Figueroa, L.E. Sucar, H. Sossa (Eds.), MICAI 2004: Advances in Artificial Intelligence. XVII, 923 pages. 2004. (Subseries LNAI).

Vol. 2971: J.I. Lim, D.H. Lee (Eds.), Information Security and Cryptology -ICISC 2003. XI, 458 pages. 2004.

Vol. 2970: F. Fernández Rivera, M. Bubak, A. Gómez Tato, R. Doallo (Eds.), Grid Computing. XI, 328 pages. 2004.

Vol. 2968: J. Chen, S. Hong (Eds.), Real-Time and Embedded Computing Systems and Applications. XIV, 620 pages. 2004.

Vol. 2967: S. Melnik, Generic Model Management. XX, 238 pages. 2004.

Vol. 2966: F.B. Sachse, Computational Cardiology. XVIII, 322 pages. 2004.

Vol. 2965: M.C. Calzarossa, E. Gelenbe, Performance Tools and Applications to Networked Systems. VIII, 385 pages. 2004.

Vol. 2964: T. Okamoto (Ed.), Topics in Cryptology – CT-RSA 2004. XI, 387 pages. 2004.

Vol. 2963: R. Sharp, Higher Level Hardware Synthesis. XVI, 195 pages. 2004.

Vol. 2962: S. Bistarelli, Semirings for Soft Constraint Solving and Programming. XII, 279 pages. 2004.

Vol. 2961: P. Eklund (Ed.), Concept Lattices. IX, 411 pages. 2004. (Subseries LNAI).

Vol. 2960: P.D. Mosses (Ed.), CASL Reference Manual. XVII, 528 pages. 2004.

Vol. 2959: R. Kazman, D. Port (Eds.), COTS-Based Software Systems. XIV, 219 pages. 2004.

Vol. 2958: L. Rauchwerger (Ed.), Languages and Compilers for Parallel Computing. XI, 556 pages. 2004.

Vol. 2957: P. Langendoerfer, M. Liu, I. Matta, V. Tsaoussidis (Eds.), Wired/Wireless Internet Communications. XI, 307 pages. 2004.